W9-CLF-156

System Programming

Vol. II

Revised Edition

Jin-Jwei Chen

Chen Publishing LLC

System Programming

June 2024 – Revised edition (240606)

December 2020 – First printing

ISBN: 978-1-7361930-1-3

Dedication

To my loving parents, SoonDer Chen and BauUyi Gor Chen, my grandpa, JonSern Chen, and my grandpa-in-law, WounSwu Gor, for their loves, sacrifices and encouragements. To my very handsome and wonderful twin sons, Stephen and Jason, and my beautiful granddaughter Olivia for the joy they bring. To my ex-wife, JinRwei Lai, for her support.

Preface

This book is meant to be a first course in system programming for students of computer science or engineering major at undergraduate or graduate level (either a one-year System Programming course or a one-semester System Programming followed by another semester of Network Programming). It is also meant to be a reference or self-study guide for computer professionals already working in the computer software industry.

This book aims at providing a systematic education to readers in cross-platforms software development at the system level using POSIX APIs. It covers fundamental concepts, knowledge, issues, technologies, techniques, skills and solutions in system programming space. It discusses basic operating system APIs required in developing various system software products including database systems, networking and distributed systems, operating systems and tools, cluster systems, client-server applications and many others.

APIs from the POSIX Standard (2018 edition) are used whenever applicable. Example programs included in the book are meant to be portable across most, if not all, platforms. Almost all example programs are tested in RedHat Linux, IBM AIX, Oracle/Sun Solaris, HP HP-UX, and Apple Darwin except those in the network security (OpenSSL) chapter which are tested in Linux and Apple Darwin only. The networking programs are also tested in Windows platform as well so long as Windows support is available.

POSIX APIs introduced in the book include file operations, signals, process management, interprocess communications, multithreading, concurrency control, shared memory, network socket programming, socket options and performance tuning of network applications.

For extremely high-performance concurrency control, designing and implementing your own locking routines in assembly language is introduced. Performance gains of up to 80+% are observed. Program examples in Intel x86, IBM Power PC, Oracle/Sun SPARC, HP PARISC, and HP/DEC Alpha processors are provided.

Advanced security using OpenSSL is also discussed. Example programs doing message digest, HMAC, encryption, decryption, PKI, digital signature and SSL/TLS are presented. How to create self-signed X.509 certificates, how to create, use and verify certificate chains in doing SSL/TLS, and how to require client authentication in SSL/TLS are also covered.

Many common real-world problems in system software, distributed systems and cross-platform development are presented and very simple, elegant, and once-for-all solutions are provided. Update loss, cross-endian, alignment, versioning, backward compatibility, reentrance, mutual exclusion, performance comparisons of various mutual exclusion technologies, producer-consumer problem, thread-local storage, fixing dangling mutex, avoiding deadlocks, asynchronous connect, automatic reconnect, multicast, using fixed or dynamic ports, shared memory, system tuning, and design of error codes and error handling, just to name a few. These examples illustrate programming is an art of knowing how to do the minimum and achieve the maximum.

In addition, software design principles and programming tips for developing first-class computer software are discussed.

System Programming

Why do I write this book?

Working in the computer software industry in the U.S. for over three decades, I have had the opportunities and privileges to work on a very wide range of system software products, including development of AT&T UNIX System V Release 3 and 4 for multiprocessor computers, development of multiple database systems, clustered systems, network management, Web Server, Web services and application server products. I have learned a lot from these experiences. I have seen excellent quality system software like AT&T Unix System V R3 and R4. Yet I have also worked on the worst system software products I have ever seen.

Throughout my career, my frustrations built up over the years after seeing countless unnecessary complexities in the software products that I had to work on during the late stage of my career. I have seen enormous unnecessary complexities in some of the world-famous system software products used around the world. The extraordinary inefficiencies and problems within the products, the excessive time and resources wasted in supporting, maintaining and improving the products, and the so many unpleasant disruptions to the customers' operations are just unimaginable!

I saw so many problems that can be solved in much simpler ways with very substantially less lines of code having top-notch quality. So many things can be simplified by 50 to 100 times. It made me feel so strongly that I need to share what I learned and know.

There are just too many very basic problems that did not get solved the right way which creates incredible amount of completely unnecessary complexities and work, resulting in way too many bugs, lowering product quality, wasting too much time and resources, unnecessarily reducing the productivity and customer satisfaction, and very significantly increasing the product development and maintenance costs.

I saw too many software engineers working in the computer software industry today are so inadequately educated and trained that many of the basics are not even done right or practiced. Yes, thanks to the fast expansions of computer applications and creation of so many jobs. But the computer software industry as a whole can be and needs to be a lot more efficient and productive. Many software products need to be much leaner, simpler, less buggy, easier to use, and less costly to maintain and support. The developers need to be better trained and more knowledgeable, the software products need to be much better designed and have much higher quality, and the end users deserve a much more productive and pleasant experience.

Besides, I see a software quality crisis from two other places. First, from the poor quality of many world-famous system software products produced by world-leading companies and the huge blunders these companies made in recent years in immediately cancelling new releases whose mistakes are so obvious to me. I see a lack of expert software engineers, architects and managers. Second, going through the computer courses taught at hundreds of top universities, I see lots of more colleges are teaching object-oriented programming in Java/C++ than system programming in C while we all know that although object-oriented paradigm is conceptually very neat, its hierarchical nature just does not model most real-world problems very well except a very small number of high-level applications. A huge number of objected-oriented database systems were born in 1980s and all of them faded away is just an example of object-orientation is not really a best choice for system software.

This is why I decided to write this book. I hope through reading a book like this, computer software engineers all become very well prepared for their jobs, knowing what technologies, basic building blocks and tools are available and how to solve many of the basic problems the right way, build extremely lean and solid foundations and robust infrastructures at the core of every software product they develop.

Most importantly, after reading this book, I believe readers will not stray into a wrong direction while trying to figure out how to solve a problem in the very first place, which is where all of the unnecessary complexities start. Readers will know enough to not go into a wrong direction in formulating the solution to a problem and avoid all the unnecessary complexities.

I also hope that when people read the software code you develop, they will say, "Wow, this was developed by some real expert!", "It's very easy to read and understand this code. It's a real treat!", "This software is very easy to maintain because it simply has no bugs."

I have always believed that the purpose of a person's life is to provide a better environment for the future generations. And part of that is to pass on what our generation has learned as a payback to what our ancestors have passed on to us so that we could build upon. This is my intended paying back. Writing this book is my way of fulfilling that responsibility.

Finishing this book completes the biggest dream of my life; I have always had the dream of wanting to help out others and the young. Hopefully, this book will make a tiny contribution to the world's computer education, computer software industry, and to better the quality of software products developed around the world. I'll be very happy if it does.

English is my third language. I really wish my English is better than this. However, I have tried my best. So if you find any errors, mistakes or imperfectness, please pardon me. Thank you very much for your support. I hope you will find what I share here useful. Happy reading!

Sincerely,

Jin-Jwei Chen

Table of Contents

System Programming i

Dedication iii

Preface v

Volume I

1 Basic Computer Concepts 1

1-1 Two Necessary Parts -- Hardware and Software 1

1-2 Overview of Computer Hardware 2

    1-2-1 Functions of Various Computer Hardware Components 2

        1-2-1-1 Processor 2

        1-2-1-2 Memory (ROM and RAM) 9

        1-2-1-3 Bus 10

        1-2-1-4 Input/Output Controllers 12

        1-2-1-5 DMA Controllers 13

        1-2-1-6 Basic Input/Output Devices 13

        1-2-1-7 Storage Devices 13

        1-2-1-8 Network Adapters 14

1-3 Basic Operations of a Computer 15

1-4 Computer Software 16

    1-4-1 Programming Languages at Different Levels 17

1-5 Operating System 19

    1-5-1 Time-sharing and Multitasking 20

    1-5-2 Functional Components of the Operating System 21

    1-5-3 Two Spaces of the Operating System 22

    1-5-4 APIs of the Operating System 24

    1-5-5 Two Modes of a Process 25

    1-5-6 Program to Standard OS APIs -- the POSIX Standard 26

        1-5-6-1 POSIX Standards (and Their Names) 27

1-6 Program, Process and Thread 29

1-7 Layers in Computer 30

1-7-1 Layers in Computer Hardware 30

1-7-2 Layers in Computer Software 31

Exercises 35

Projects 36

2 Software Development and Engineering Processes 37

2-1 Software Development Process 37

2-1-1 A Word on Code Review Comments 40

2-2 Source Control System and Process 41

2-3 Software Release Process 44

2-4 Building the Product in Different Modes 45

2-5 Project Building Tools 47

2-5-1 Make 47

2-5-2 Makefile 49

2-5-2-1 The Name of Makefile 50

2-5-2-2 Typical Makefile Targets 51

2-5-3 Makefile Macros 51

2-5-4 Some Special Characters for Commands 53

2-5-5 Makefile Implicit Rules 54

2-5-6 Makefile Examples 55

2-5-7 Makefile Directives 58

2-5-7-1 The include Directive 58

2-5-7-2 The ifdef and ifndef Directives 59

2-5-7-3 The ifeq and ifneq Directives 59

2-5-8 Some Useful Make Command Switches 60

2-5-9 Example of Building a Small Project Using Make 61

2-6 Regression Suites 65

2-7 Compiled versus Interpretative Languages 66

2-7-1 Types of Program Languages and Execution 66

2-7-2 Process of Program Compilation 67

2-8 Choosing Programming Languages 69

Exercises 70

   References 71

3 Building Programs and Libraries 73

   3-1 What Is a Library? 73

      3-1-1 Always Re-use Code 74

   3-2 Archive Library and Shared Library 76

   3-3 Two Phases of Building a Program or Library 77

   3-4 Static Linking versus Dynamic Linking -- Two Ways of Building a Program 79

   3-5 How Does the Linker Find the Static and Dynamic Libraries 82

      3-5-1 The ldd Command 83

      3-5-2 How to Make the Linker Find the Libraries 83

   3-6 How Does an Application Find Shared Libraries at Run Time 85

   3-7 Dynamic Loading -- No Linking 86

      3-7-1 How to Program Dynamic Loading 87

   3-8 Compile Time, Load Time and Run Time 88

   3-9 Mixed Mode Linking 89

   3-10 Example of Building and Using Your Own Library 90

      3-10-1 Build Your Own Static Library (libtst1.a/libtst1.lib) 92

      3-10-2 Build Your Own Dynamic Library (libtst1.so/libtst1.dll) 93

      3-10-3 Develop an Application Using Your Own Library 94

      3-10-4 Build an Application That Links with Your Own Static Library 95

      3-10-5 Build an Application That Links with Your Own Dynamic Library 97

      3-10-6 Develop and Build an Application That Dynamically Loads Your Own Library 98

   3-11 Quick Reference of the Commands 103

   Exercises 108

   Projects 109

4 File I/O 111

   4-1 Structure of a Disk 111

      4-1-1 Physical Structure of a Disk 111

      4-1-2 Partitions and File Systems 113

   4-2 Some Concepts About Files 115

      4-2-1 Two Different Views of a File 115

4-2-2 Steps to Manipulate a File...115

4-2-3 The Current File Offset..116

4-3 Two Programming Interfaces 117

4-4 File Descriptor and Associated Kernel Data Structures 120

4-4-1 Inodes...120

4-4-2 Inode Table...121

4-4-3 System Open File Table...121

4-4-4 User File Descriptor Table...121

4-5 Opening and Creating a File 123

4-6 Writing a File 126

4-7 Write Robust Software Doing I/O...129

4-8 Reading a File 129

4-9 Sequential I/O...131

4-10 Sharing a File Between Concurrent Processes 134

4-11 Random I/O 137

4-12 Vectored I/O 142

4-12-1 What Is Vectored I/O?...142

4-12-2 How to Do Vectored I/O..143

4-13 Asynchronous I/O 147

4-13-1 What Is Asynchronous I/O?...147

4-13-2 How to do Asynchronous I/O 148

4-13-3 Different Programming Paradigm 155

4-13-4 Synchronous or Asynchronous I/O?...155

4-14 Direct I/O 156

4-14-1 What Is Direct I/O?...156

4-14-2 How to Do Direct I/O?..157

4-14-3 Notes on Direct I/O 162

4-15 I/O Buffering..162

4-15-1 The sync(), fsync() and fdatasync() Functions 163

4-16 Notes on Concurrent Updates of Files 165

Questions...165

Programming Assignments..166

References 167

5 Files and Directories **169**

5-1 File Types and Permissions 169

   5-1-1 Types of Files 169

   5-1-2 Permissions of Files 171

5-2 Create and Remove a Directory 173

   5-2-1 The mkdir() and mkdirat() Functions..173

   5-2-2 The rmdir() Function 173

5-3 Create Links 174

   5-3-1 What Is a Link? 174

   5-3-2 The link() and linkat() Functions...174

5-4 Create Symbolic Links...178

   5-4-1 What Is a Symbolic Link 178

   5-4-2 The symlink() and symlinkat() Functions 178

5-5 Remove and Rename a File or Directory 180

   5-5-1 The unlink() and unlinkat() Functions..180

   5-5-2 The remove() Function 181

   5-5-3 The rename() and renameat() Functions 182

5-6 Get Values of Configurable Parameters 184

   5-6-1 The pathconf() and fpathconf() Functions...184

5-7 Get and Change Current Working Directory 186

   5-7-1 The getcwd() Function...186

   5-7-2 The chdir() and fchdir() Functions 187

5-8 Get Status and Information of a Directory Entry..188

   5-8-1 The stat(), fstat() and lstat() Functions...189

5-9 Open and Read a Directory 193

   5-9-1 The opendir(), fdopendir() and closedir() Functions 193

   5-9-2 The readdir() and readdir_r() Functions 193

5-10 Change Permission 198

   5-10-1 The chmod(), fchmod() and fchmodat() Functions 198

5-11 Change Owner 200

5-11-1 The chown(), fchown(), fchownat() and lchown() Functions 200

5-12 Duplicate a File Descriptor 203

5-12-1 The dup() and dup2() Functions 203

5-13 The fcntl() Function 206

5-13-1 File Locking Using fcntl() 208

5-13-2 Other Examples 212

5-14 The ioctl() Function 215

5-15 File and Directory Permission Mask 220

5-15-1 Permission Mask Environment Variable 220

5-15-2 The umask() Function 221

5-16 Set-User-ID, Set-Group-ID and Sticky Bits 223

5-17 The access() and faccessat() Functions 224

5-18 Change Access and Modification Times 226

5-18-1 The utime() function 226

Further Readings 229

Questions 229

Exercises 229

References 230

6 Signals 231

6-1 Introduction to Signals 231

6-1-1 Different Types of Signals 231

6-1-2 What Are the Signals 232

6-1-3 Job Control 235

6-1-3-1 Basics of Job Control 235

6-1-3-2 Job Control Signals 236

6-1-4 How to Send Signals 240

6-2 Signal Actions 241

6-2-1 Default Action 242

6-2-2 Ignore Action 243

6-2-3 Catching a Signal 244

6-2-4 Calling Functions from a Signal Handler Function 244

6-2-5 Set a Signal Action Using sigaction() 245

6-2-6 Determine If an Optional Signal Is Supported 251

6-2-7 Summary on Signal Actions 251

6-3 Sending a Signal Using kill() 251

6-3-1 Killing Self 254

6-3-2 Signal Impacts on Other Functions 254

6-4 Signal Masks -- Blocked Signals 255

6-4-1 Signal Set Functions 255

6-4-2 Alter Signal Mask Using the sigprocmask() Function 258

6-4-3 Ignoring Signals 262

6-4-4 Behavior of Blocking SIGILL, SIGSEGV and SIGFPE Signals 263

6-5 Receive Pending Blocked Signals 263

6-5-1 The sigpending() Function 263

6-5-2 The sigsuspend() Function 265

6-5-3 The sigwait() Function 268

6-5-4 The sigtimedwait() and sigwaitinfo() Functions 271

6-6 Signals Reserved for Applications 272

6-7 Optional Signals Defined by Implementations 275

6-8 Impacts of Signals on the sleep() Function 275

6-9 Caveats of Signals 278

6-10 Summary on Signals 278

6-11 Other Signal Functions 279

Review Questions 279

Exercises 281

References 282

7 Processes **283**

7-1 Some Concepts and Functions Related to Process 283

7-1-1 What Is a Process? 283

7-1-2 The getpid() and getppid() Functions 286

7-1-3 The getuid() and geteuid() Functions 286

7-1-4 The getgid() and getegid() Functions 287

7-1-5 The setuid() and setgid() Functions 287

7-1-6 Process Groups and Sessions 288

7-1-7 The getpgid(), setpgid(), getpgrp() and setpgrp() Functions 289

7-1-8 The setsid() Function 290

7-2 Create a New Process with fork() 291

7-2-1 After the fork() Function 293

7-3 Parent Waits for Child 293

7-3-1 The waitpid() Function 296

7-4 Create a New Process to Run a Different Program 299

7-4-1 The exec() Functions 299

7-4-2 The execl() Function 301

7-4-3 The execlp() Function 303

7-4-4 The execv() and execvp() Functions 305

7-4-5 The execle() and execve() Functions 306

7-4-6 After the exec() Functions 307

7-5 Communications Between Parent and Child Processes 308

7-5-1 What Is a Pipe? 308

7-5-2 Creating and Using a Pipe 309

7-6 Orphaned and Zombie Processes 314

7-7 Process Termination 315

7-7-1 The exit() Function 315

7-7-2 The _exit() and _Exit() Functions 316

7-7-3 The atexit() Function 317

7-7-4 The abort() Function 319

7-7-5 The assert() Function 320

7-8 The getenv() and sysconf() Functions 321

7-8-1 The getenv() Function 321

7-8-2 The sysconf() Function 322

7-9 The system() Function 325

7-10 Process Resource Limits 326

7-10-1 Getting Limits of Process Resources 327

7-10-2 Setting Limits of Process Resources 331

7-11 Other User and Group Related Functions 334

   7-11-1 The getlogin() Function 334

   7-11-2 The getpwnam(), getpwuid() and getpwent() Functions 337

   7-11-3 The getgrnam() and getgrgid() Functions 341

   7-11-4 The getgroups() Function 343

   7-11-5 The getgid() and getegid() Functions 344

Questions 344

Exercises 345

References 347

8 Pthreads Programming **349**

8-1 Why Multithreaded Programming? 349

   8-1-1 Paradigm of Modern Server Programs 349

   8-1-2 Processes Versus Threads 350

   8-1-3 What Is Thread? 352

8-2 Pthreads Basics 353

   8-2-1 How to Create and Join a Thread 353

   8-2-2 How to Pass Arguments to a Thread 355

   8-2-3 How to Return Values from a Thread 358

8-3 Pthreads Attributes 361

   8-3-1 Detached Thread 368

8-4 Types of Problems in Concurrency Control 370

   8-4-1 Update Loss Problem 370

   8-4-2 Producer-consumer Problem 371

8-5 Mutex 373

   8-5-1 What Is Mutex? 373

   8-5-2 Initialize a Mutex 373

   8-5-3 Mutex Attributes 375

   8-5-4 Destroy a Mutex 381

   8-5-5 Lock and Unlock a Mutex 381

      8-5-5-1 Lock Recursively or Wrongly Unlock 386

      8-5-5-2 Fix a Dangling Mutex – Robust Mutex 390

8-5-6 Avoiding Deadlock 398

8-5-7 Performance Considerations in Mutex Implementation 398

8-6 Condition Variables 399

8-6-1 What Is a Condition Variable? 399

8-6-2 Condition Variable Attributes 400

8-6-3 Initializing and Destroying a Condition Variable 401

8-6-4 How Condition Variables Work? 402

8-6-5 Major Functions on Condition Variable 404

8-6-5-1 Condition Wait 404

8-6-5-2 Condition Signal 405

8-6-6 Solving Producer-Consumer Problem 406

8-7 Read-Write Locks 415

8-8 Thread-Specific Data 425

8-8-1 What Is Thread-Specific Data 425

8-8-2 Examples of Using Thread-Specific Data 426

8-8-3 Destructor Function of Thread-Specific Data Key 440

8-9 Pthreads Cancellation 444

8-9-1 Pthreads Cancellation Attributes 445

8-9-2 Thread Cancellation Points 450

8-9-3 Cancel-safe 452

8-10 Signal Handling with Threads 452

8-10-1 pthread_sigmask() and pthread_kill() Functions 453

8-10-2 Using a Signal Handling Thread 454

8-11 Further Readings 459

8-12 List of Pthreads APIs 459

8-13 Functions with Cancellation Points 462

Review Questions 467

Programming Assignments 468

References 469

9 Concurrency Control and Locking 471

9-1 Introduction to Concurrency Control 471

9-1-1 The Update Loss Problem 472

9-1-2 Solve Concurrency Problems via Locking 473

9-1-3 Terms 474

9-1-4 Three Required Elements 475

9-1-5 Many Concurrency Control Facilities Are Available 475

9-2 Introduction to System V IPC Resources 476

9-2-1 Identifier of a System V IPC Resource 477

9-2-2 Access to System V IPC Resources 478

9-2-3 Useful Commands Related to System V IPC 479

9-3 System V Semaphore 480

9-3-1 What Is a Semaphore? 480

9-3-2 Binary Semaphore and Counting Semaphore 481

9-3-3 Create a Semaphore Set 482

9-3-4 Remove a Semaphore Set 484

9-3-5 How to Use a Semaphore 488

9-3-6 Perform Various Operations on Semaphores 492

9-3-7 A Concurrent Update Example 500

9-4 Different Types of Locks 514

9-4-1 Exclusive (Writer) Lock Versus Shared (Reader) Lock 514

9-4-2 Trylock, Spinlock and Timeoutlock 515

9-5 Design and Implement Your Own Locking Routines 517

9-5-1 Designing Your Own Locking Routines 518

9-5-1-1 What Is Required? 520

9-5-1-2 Don't Implement the Locking Routine in High Level Language 521

9-5-2 Implement Your Own Locking Routines 521

9-5-2-1 Intel x86 Architecture (Linux and Unix) 522

9-5-2-2 Apple Mac Pro on Intel x86 (Darwin) 530

9-5-2-3 IBM PowerPC Architecture (AIX) 531

9-5-2-4 Oracle Sun SPARC Architecture (Solaris) 533

9-5-2-5 HP PARISC Architecture (HP-UX) 536

9-5-2-6 HP/DEC Alpha Architecture (Tru64 Unix or Digital Unix) 538

9-5-2-7 Concurrent Updates Using Our Own Lock 540

9-5-2-8 Performance Comparison of Semaphore and Our Own Lock 550

9-6 POSIX Semaphore 554

9-6-1 Unnamed POSIX Semaphores 555

9-6-2 Named POSIX Semaphores 562

9-6-3 Comparison of System V and POSIX Semaphores 568

9-7 Comparison of Mutual Exclusion Technologies 568

9-8 Semaphores and Mutexes in Windows 569

9-8-1 Mutexes in Windows 569

9-8-2 Semaphores in Windows 571

9-9 Deadlock 572

9-9-1 What Is Deadlock? 572

9-9-2 Necessary Conditions for Deadlocks 573

9-9-3 Three Approaches to Deadlocks 573

9-9-4 Deadlock Detection and Recovery 574

9-9-5 Deadlock Prevention 575

9-9-5-1 Request All Needed Resources at Once 575

9-9-5-2 Ordering All Resources 575

9-9-5-3 Preemption 576

9-9-6 Livelock 577

9-9-7 Starvation 577

9-9-8 Preventing Deadlock in Reentrant Situation 577

9-10 System Tuning Parameters Related to System V Semaphore 587

9-10-1 Querying Kernel Parameters 588

9-10-2 Changing Kernel Parameters 591

9-11 Summary of Concurrency Problems and Solutions 592

9-11-1 Locking Facilities 592

9-11-1-1 Update Loss Problem 592

9-11-2 A Quick Recap 593

Questions 594

Exercises 595

Projects 595

References 596

10 Shared Memory 597

10-1 Introduction to Shared Memory 597

10-2 System V Shared Memory APIs 602

  10-2-1 How to Use System V Shared Memory 603

  10-2-2 Creating Shared Memory -- shmget() 603

    10-2-2-1 Key and Id of System V IPC Resources 604

    10-2-2-2 Converting Shared Memory Key to Shared Memory Id 606

    10-2-2-3 Special Shared Memory Key IPC_PRIVATE 607

    10-2-2-4 Example Program 607

  10-2-3 Attaching to Shared Memory -- shmat() 617

  10-2-4 Detaching from Shared Memory -- shmdt() 619

  10-2-5 Controlling Shared Memory -- shmctl() 619

  10-2-6 Changing the Ownership and Permission of a Shared Memory Segment 621

  10-2-7 Operating System Tunable Parameters 623

10-3 Shared Memory Examples 624

  10-3-1 Design of Shared Memory Contents 624

  10-3-2 Read Shared Memory 625

  10-3-3 Update Shared Memory 628

  10-3-4 Summary 635

Review Questions 636

Exercises 637

Programming Assignments 637

References 638

11 More on Interprocess Communication Mechanisms 639

11-1 Overview of IPC Mechanisms 639

  11-1-1 Signals 639

  11-1-2 Semaphores 640

  11-1-3 Shared Memory 641

  11-1-4 Socket 642

  11-1-5 Pipes 642

11-1-6 Named Pipes 642

11-1-7 Message Queues 643

11-1-8 Memory-mapped Files 643

11-1-9 Summary 643

11-2 Named Pipes (FIFOs) 644

11-2-1 The mkfifo() Function 644

11-2-2 The mkfifoat() Function 649

11-3 System V Message Queues 649

11-3-1 Create a Message Queue -- msgget() 649

11-3-2 Send and Receive Messages -- msgsnd() and msgrcv() 651

11-3-3 Perform Control Commands on Message Queue -- msgctl() 656

11-3-4 Remove a Message Queue 659

11-4 Memory-mapped Files 660

11-4-1 The mmap() and munmap() Functions 660

11-4-2 Pros and Cons of Using Memory-mapped Files 667

11-4-3 Memory-mapped File Is Not Shared Memory 667

Questions 668

Exercises 668

References 669

Volume II

12 Socket Programming 671

12-1 Some Basic Network Concepts 672

12-1-1 The Seven-Layer Model 672

12-1-2 Layer Positions of Most Popular Network Protocols 677

12-1-3 IPv4 and IPv6 678

12-1-4 RFC 679

12-2 What Is Socket? 680

12-2-1 Different Types of Sockets 681

12-2-2 The socket() Function 682

12-2-3 Socket Types 687

12-2-4 Socket Addresses and Structures 689

12-2-5 IP Address Within Socket Address 691

12-2-6 The Include File for Socket 692

12-3 Styles of Computer Network Communication 693

12-4 Connectionless Communication Using Datagram Sockets 695

12-4-1 Sending and Receiving Datagram Messages 695

12-4-1-1 The sendto() Function 695

12-4-1-2 The recvfrom() Function 696

12-4-2 A Datagram Server 697

12-4-2-1 The bind() Function 698

12-4-2-2 Cross Platform Support 704

12-4-3 Using connect() Call on Datagram Sockets 709

12-5 Wildcard Server Address and Endian 713

12-5-1 Wildcard Server Address 713

12-5-2 Endianness and Byte Order Conversion 714

12-6 Connection-Oriented Communication Using Stream Sockets 716

12-6-1 Creating a Connection-Oriented Socket 717

12-6-2 Server Advertises Itself -- The bind() Function 717

12-6-3 Server Accepts a Connection Request -- The accept() Function 719

12-6-4 Server Sets Its Listener Queue Length -- The listen() Function 720

12-6-5 Client Initiates a Connection Request -- The connect() Function 721

12-6-6 Data Exchange -- The send() and recv() Functions 724

12-6-7 The read() and write() Functions 725

12-6-8 Skeleton of Connection-Oriented Client and Server 725

12-7 Socket Options 732

12-7-1 The getsockopt() and setsockopt() Functions 737

12-8 Support for Multiple Platforms 738

12-8-1 Linux and Unix 738

12-8-2 Windows 739

12-8-3 Example Programs 742

12-9 Look Up a Host's IP Address Using Hostname 751

12-9-1 Host Name Translation 751

12-9-2 The getaddrinfo() Function 753

12-9-3 The getnameinfo() Function..754

12-9-4 Errors from getaddrinfo() and getnameinfo()...754

12-10 Support for IPv4 and IPv6..755

12-10-1 Migrate Your Networking Code from IPv4 to IPv6...756

12-11 Get a Peer's Address and Port Number...757

12-12 IP Agnostic Programs..767

12-12-1 Use getaddrinfo() on Client and IPv6 Socket on Server................................767

12-13 Common Socket Errors and Their Resolutions..777

12-14 Local Communication -- Unix Domain Sockets...780

12-15 Asynchronous Socket Operations..787

12-15-1 Asynchronous Socket I/O...787

12-15-1-1 Using select() Function..788

12-15-1-2 The pselect() Function...799

12-15-1-3 Pitfalls of the select() Function 800

12-15-2 Asynchronous Socket Connect..801

12-16 Detecting Peer Termination and Auto-reconnect..809

12-17 Multicasting..823

12-17-1 Forming a Multicast Group 823

12-17-2 How to Program Multicasting?..824

12-17-3 Multiple Multicast Receivers on Same Host...833

12-17-4 Multicasting on Windows..834

12-18 Multitasking Server 835

12-18-1 Single-threaded Server..835

12-18-2 Concurrent or Parallel Processing 835

12-18-3 Multiprocess Server 836

12-18-4 Multithreaded Server..840

12-18-5 Potential Socket Resource Issue..846

12-19 Port Numbers -- Reserve it or not 847

12-19-1 Introduction to Port Numbers..847

12-19-2 Privileged Port Numbers 848

12-19-3 Look Up Server's Port Number Dynamically -- Service Registration Database 848

12-19-4 Use Fixed Port or Dynamic Port? 854

12-19-5 Quick Recap 856

12-20 Summary 856

Questions..857

Programming Assignments..859

References 860

13 Socket Performance Tuning and Socket Options 861

13-1 Tuning Basics 861

13-2 How to Tune Kernel Parameters in Various Operating Systems 862

13-2-1 How to Tune Kernel Parameters in Linux..862

13-2-2 How to Tune Kernel Parameters in AIX...864

13-2-3 How to Tune Kernel Parameters in Solaris..864

13-2-4 How to Tune Kernel Parameters in HPUX 864

13-2-5 How to Tune Kernel Parameters in Apple Darwin and FreeBSD 865

13-2-6 How to Tune Kernel Parameters in Windows 865

13-3 Tuning Socket Buffer Sizes...866

13-3-1 Socket Send and Receive Buffers 866

13-3-2 Tuning Socket Buffer Sizes 867

13-3-3 Tuning Socket Buffer Sizes at Application Level 868

13-3-4 Tuning Socket Buffer Sizes at Operating System Kernel Level 879

13-3-4-1 Linux...879

13-3-4-2 AIX 883

13-3-4-3 Solaris...884

13-3-4-4 HP-UX 886

13-3-4-5 Apple Darwin...887

13-3-4-6 FreeBSD 888

13-3-4-7 Windows 889

13-3-5 Summary of Socket Options on Send/Receive Buffer Sizes 890

13-4 The SO_KEEPALIVE Socket Option..891

13-4-1 What Is SO_KEEPALIVE Socket Option? 892

13-4-2 Parameters Implementing the SO_KEEPALIVE Option 893

13-4-3 Changing Keepalive Tunable Parameters...896

13-4-3-1 Change TCP Keepalive Parameters at Application Level 896

  13-4-3-1-1 Linux and AIX 897

  13-4-3-1-2 Solaris 905

  13-4-3-1-3 HP-UX 914

  13-4-3-1-4 Apple Darwin and FreeBSD Unix 916

  13-4-3-1-5 Windows 917

13-4-3-2 Change TCP Keepalive Parameters at Operating System Kernel Level 917

  13-4-3-2-1 Linux 917

  13-4-3-2-2 AIX 918

  13-4-3-2-3 Solaris 919

  13-4-3-2-4 HP-UX 920

  13-4-3-2-5 Apple Darwin and FreeBSD Unix 922

  13-4-3-2-6 Windows 923

13-4-3-3 Summary of SO_KEEPALIVE Socket Option 924

13-5 The SO_LINGER Socket Option 926

13-6 What Happens at Closing a TCP Socket Connection 937

13-6-1 TCP TIME_WAIT state 939

13-7 The SO_REUSEADDR and SO_REUSEPORT Socket Options 940

13-7-1 The SO_REUSEADDR Socket Option 940

13-7-2 Testing the SO_REUSEADDR Option 949

13-7-3 The SO_REUSEADDR and SO_EXCLUSIVEADDRUSE Socket Options in Windows 951

13-7-4 The SO_EXCLBIND Socket Option in Solaris 957

13-7-5 The SO_REUSEPORT Socket Option 958

13-7-6 Tuning the SO_REUSEADDR Option 964

13-7-7 Summary 968

13-8 The SO_RCVTIMEO and SO_SNDTIMEO options 968

13-9 The SO_RCVLOWAT and SO_SNDLOWAT options 977

Review Questions/Exercises 978

Programming Assignments/Projects 979

References 980

14 Design of Distributed Software **983**

14-1 Endian 983

14-1-1 What Is Endian? 983

14-1-2 Why Endianness Matters? 984

14-1-3 When Endianness Matters? 985

14-1-4 How to Determine the Endianness of a Computer 986

14-1-5 Different Ways to Solve the Cross-Endian Problem 987

14-1-6 Writing/Reading Binary Files Portable Across Different Endian Formats 988

14-1-7 How to Do Endian Conversion -- The Endian Utility Functions 1001

14-1-8 Summary 1004

14-2 Design of Distributed Applications 1005

14-2-1 Design of General Communication Protocol 1005

14-2-1-1 Initial Connection Packet 1005

14-2-1-2 Dealing with Denial of Service (DOS) Attacks 1006

14-2-1-3 Data Header 1006

14-2-1-4 Avoid Alignment Snag 1009

14-2-1-5 Guidelines for Header Structure Definition 1010

14-2-2 Versioning, Backward Compatibility and Interoperability 1011

14-2-2-1 Version Numbers 1012

14-2-2-2 Changes Between Versions 1013

14-2-2-3 Actual Code Changes 1014

14-2-2-4 Making the Server Program Robust 1057

14-2-2-5 Sample output 1057

14-3 Summary 1060

Review Questions 1061

Programming Assignments 1061

15 Computer Network Security 1063

15-1 OpenSSL 1063

15-1-1 What Is OpenSSL? 1064

15-1-2 Download and Build OpenSSL Software 1065

15-1-3 Building and Running SSL/TLS Applications Using OpenSSL 1068

15-2 Aspects in Computer Network Security 1069

15-3 Message Integrity 1071

15-3-1 Checksum 1071

15-3-2 Message Digest Algorithms (Hash Functions) 1072

15-3-2-1 MD Family of Message Digest Algorithms 1074

15-3-2-2 SHA Family of Message Digest Algorithms...1075

15-3-2-3 RIPEMD-160 1078

15-3-2-4 Programming Examples 1078

15-4 Message Secrecy -- Encryption and Decryption 1083

15-4-1 What Is Encryption? 1083

15-4-2 Symmetric and Asymmetric Cryptography 1084

15-4-2-1 How Symmetric and Asymmetric Cryptography works 1084

15-4-2-2 Strength of Encryption Algorithms...1086

15-4-2-3 Performance and Use of Encryption Algorithms..1086

15-4-3 Symmetric Encryption (Secret Key Cryptographic) Algorithms 1086

15-4-3-1 Key, Block, IV and Padding...1086

15-4-3-2 Stream Ciphers and Block Ciphers 1089

15-4-3-3 Modes of Block Cipher Operation 1092

15-4-3-4 Block and Key Sizes of Encryption/Decryption Algorithms 1097

15-4-4 Asymmetric Encryption (Public Key Cryptographic) Algorithms 1097

15-4-4-1 Diffie-Hellman 1097

15-4-4-2 RSA 1099

15-4-5 Programming Examples..1100

15-4-5-1 Encryption and Decryption using OpenSSL 1100

15-4-5-1-1 Using Different APIs for Encryption and Decryption................................1101

15-4-5-1-2 Using Same APIs for Encryption and Decryption 1116

15-4-5-1-3 Summary 1119

15-4-5-2 Encrypting Client-Server Communications 1119

15-5 Message Authentication...1133

15-5-1 Message Authentication Code (MAC) 1133

15-5-2 Keyed-Hash Message Authentication Code (HMAC)...1134

15-5-3 Programming Examples...1136

15-5-3-1 Encrypted communication with Message Integrity and Authentication 1141

15-6 Sender Authentication -- Digital Signatures 1149

15-6-1 How Digital Signature Works 1149

15-6-2 Different Digital Signature Algorithms 1151

15-6-2-1 RSA 1151

15-6-2-2 DSA/DSS 1152

15-6-2-3 Differences Between RSA and DSA Signatures 1154

15-6-2-4 Caveats of Digital Signatures 1154

15-6-2-5 Applications of Digital Signatures 1155

15-6-2-6 MAC/HMAC Versus Digital Signatures 1155

15-6-3 Programming Examples 1156

15-6-3-1 Shared Functions 1157

15-6-3-1-1 Signature Signing -- get_signature() 1157

15-6-3-1-2 Signature Verifying -- verify_signature() 1159

15-6-3-2 Standalone Signature Signing and Verifying 1161

15-6-3-2-1 RSA 1162

15-6-3-2-2 DSA 1163

15-6-3-3 Using Digital Signature in Client-server Applications 1169

15-6-3-3-1 RSA 1169

15-6-3-3-2 DSA 1180

15-7 Public Key Infrastructure (PKI) 1190

15-7-1 Applications of Public Key Cryptography 1191

15-8 X.509 Certificates 1191

15-8-1 What Is a Certificate? 1192

15-8-2 Structure of X.509 Certificates 1192

15-8-3 Formats of Certificate Files 1194

15-8-3-1 PEM format 1194

15-8-3-2 DER Format 1195

15-8-3-3 PKCS #12 1195

15-8-4 Certificate Authority (CA) 1196

15-8-5 Certificate Chain 1196

15-8-6 Certificate Verification 1197

15-8-7 Certificate Revocation List 1198

15-9 Create X.509 Certificates 1199

15-9-1 Create a Self-Signed Server Certificate 1200

15-9-1-1 Generate a Private Key 1201

15-9-1-2 Create a Certificate Signing Request and Sign It 1201

15-9-2 Create a Chain of Certificates...1203

15-9-2-1 Create a Self-Signed Root Certificate 1204

15-9-2-2 Create a Certificate for an Intermediate CA...1205

15-9-2-3 Bundle All CAs' Certificates into a Single File 1208

15-9-2-4 Create Server and Client Certificates Signed by the Intermediate CA 1209

15-9-3 Verifying Certificates 1211

15-9-4 Converting Between Different Certificate Formats...1213

15-10 SSL and TLS 1214

15-10-1 What Is SSL/TLS? 1214

15-10-2 SSL/TLS History..1215

15-10-3 SSL/TLS Features 1216

15-10-4 SSL 1216

15-10-5 Key Establishment/Exchange 1220

15-10-5-1 Why Key Establishment/Exchange? 1221

15-10-5-2 Key Establishment/Exchange Algorithms..1221

15-10-5-2-1 Diffie-Hellman (DH)..1221

15-10-5-2-2 RSA 1224

15-10-5-2-3 TLS Support 1224

15-10-5-2-4 Key Establishment/Exchange Message 1224

15-10-6 Makeup of SSL/TLS Cipher Suites 1225

15-10-7 Considerations in Using SSL/TLS...1226

15-11 SSL/TLS Programming..1228

15-11-1 Basic TLS/SSL Client-Server 1228

15-11-1-1 SSL/TLS Client...1237

15-11-1-2 SSL/TLS Server...1239

15-11-2 Loading Certificates and Private Keys 1240

15-11-2-1 Loading Certificates..1240

15-11-2-2 Loading Private Keys 1242

15-11-2-3 Verify Private Keys 1243

15-11-3 Verifying a Self-Signed Server Certificate...1243

15-11-3-1 How to verify a certificate..1243

15-11-4 Verifying a Server Certificate Signed by a Chain of CAs 1254

15-11-4-1 Loading Certificate Chains 1263

15-11-4-2 Verify a Certificate Chain Using openssl Command 1263

15-11-5 Doing Client Authentication 1264

15-11-5-1 Client-side Code 1264

15-11-5-2 Server-side Code 1264

15-11-5-3 Possible Errors 1266

15-11-5-4 Program Examples 1267

15-11-5-5 Verifying Certificates Signed by Multiple CA Chains 1282

15-11-6 Setting Cipher Suite 1293

15-12 Error Handling in OpenSSL 1294

15-12-1 Printing Errors 1294

15-12-2 Clear Error Queue 1295

15-12-3 Getting Error Code 1295

15-12-4 Translate Error Code into Error String 1297

15-13 Source Code of Library Functions 1298

Questions 1338

Exercises 1339

References 1340

16 Software Design Principles and Programming Tips 1343

16-1 Art, Science and Engineering of Programming 1343

16-2 Designing and Developing First-class Software 1344

16-3 Software Design Principles -- Tips at Design Level 1344

16-3-1 Robustness and No Single Point of Failure 1345

16-3-2 Always Store Data in a Single Place 1346

16-3-3 Always Ensure Integrity of Shared Data 1346

16-3-4 Always Have Necessary Synchronization 1347

16-3-5 Simplicity - Always Make Things Simple 1348

16-3-6 Ease of Use and User-friendly 1349

16-3-6-1 Try Not to Change User Interface 1349

16-3-6-2 Make It Self-Configured, Self-Tuned or Dynamically Reconfigurable 1350

16-3-7 Always Share Code -- Build and Use Subroutines and Library Functions 1351

16-3-8 Maintain Backward Compatibility 1352

16-3-9 Always Design Security In 1354

16-3-10 Make It Very High-performance 1354

16-3-11 Make It Scalable 1355

16-3-12 Error Code Design and Error Handling 1356

16-3-12-1 Design the Error Codes Right 1356

16-3-12-2 Handle Every Error Correctly 1358

16-3-13 Make It Generic 1359

16-3-14 Make It Agnostic 1359

16-3-15 Make It Idempotent When It Makes Sense 1360

16-3-16 Don't Introduce Regression 1360

16-3-17 Don't Break Upgrade or Downgrade 1361

16-3-18 Do It Right the First Time and Do It Once for All 1361

16-4 Programming Tips 1363

16-4-1 Always Initialize a Variable 1363

16-4-1-1 Basics of Initializing a Variable 1364

16-4-2 Always Check a Pointer Before Using It 1365

16-4-3 Always Check Every Input Function Argument Before Using Them 1365

16-4-4 A Function Should Always Return Status 1365

16-4-5 Ensure No Memory Leak 1366

16-4-6 Keep the Logging and Tracing Simple 1367

Appendix A   List of Example Programs 1371

INDEX 1377

12 Socket Programming

This chapter discusses socket programming. It introduces the basic, fundamental APIs for network and distributed programming which is at the core of so many networking, distributed and web applications or even database systems today.

Many engineers and programmers are building networking, distributed, or even web applications these days, socket APIs are the lowest level and most fundamental APIs that one can use for building these applications.

The socket APIs we introduce in this chapter are part of the POSIX standard. Thus, socket programs presented in this chapter work across all operating systems supporting the POSIX standard. They have been tested in platforms such as Linux, Unix (including Oracle/Sun Solaris, IBM AIX, and HP HPUX), Apple Darwin and most have also been tested in Windows as well.

There are many different ways of doing network and distributed programming using different APIs at different levels. Different engineers develop different networking software using different APIs at different levels. But the most fundamental and common one is to use the **socket APIs** at the bottom level of operating system interfaces. Since this book is all about system programming, socket APIs are discussed.

One layer above the socket interface, there is the **RPC** (Remote Procedure Call) programming interface, which is available in C language as well. RPC calls are essentially wrapper C functions of socket APIs we will discuss. It's one layer above the socket APIs.

And then there are even higher layer of APIs such as the HTTP/HTTPS, SOAP, REST, etc. which very often use socket and/or RPC APIs beneath.

Socket APIs are at the level of application programming interfaces closest to an operating system. These APIs use services at the transport and network layers of the operating system, and other layers below. They are typically implemented by and within an operating system kernel. **They provide the programming interfaces for any two programs to communicate with each other across the network, or even within the same computer host/system. It's what has made Internet possible on the software side.** Its significance and the value it has provided are just beyond people's realization and imagination. It' the most important infrastructure component that makes so many distributed and web applications (for instance, those on smart phones and the Internet Browser) possible and work today.

Today, Internet is almost everywhere and almost everyone has some experience of using it. From a computer software engineer's point of view, using

Internet essentially involves running two programs on two computers, which might be physically far apart on two different continents, connected with each other via the Internet (i.e. TCP/IP) network. The two programs are using socket to communicate with each other where socket is just an API into the TCP/UDP and IP network protocols implemented inside each operating system.

Although a typical user uses and sees only one of the two programs, i.e. the client which is the web browser, it is the other program -- the server which is identified by the URL the user enters into his/her browser -- that is collaborating to retrieve and send all the information and data that the user sees in his or her browser. Hence, at the core it's two (sometimes more than two) socket programs working together to deliver all the wonderful Internet experiences so many people have. You get the sense of how important socket programming is for people around the world using Internet.

Socket programming is really the foundation of most networking software products, distributed systems, and high-level protocols used to build so many wonderful Internet applications. Therefore, knowing it would be very helpful for any and all software engineers in understanding how existing software applications and distributed systems work, in maintaining them, as well as in designing and building new ones.

This chapter introduces the socket APIs, discusses how socket works, and how to develop networking, distributed and web applications using socket APIs. Readers will learn how to write socket programs using TCP, UDP and Unix Domain sockets, doing synchronous or asynchronous connect, multicasting, multithreaded servers, looking up port number dynamically, and more.

After reading this chapter, readers will be able to program distributed systems using the lowest level and most efficient socket APIs.

12-1 Some Basic Network Concepts

12-1-1 The Seven-Layer Model

```
---------------------
| Application Layer  |  e.g. HTTP, HTTPS, SMTP, ftp, telnet, REST API
|--------------------|
| Presentation Layer |
|--------------------|
| Session Layer      |  e.g. SSL, TLS, sockets APIs
|--------------------|
| Transport Layer    |  e.g. TCP, UDP
|--------------------|
| Network Layer      |  e.g. IPv4, IPv6, IPsec
|--------------------|
| Data Link Layer    |  e.g. Ethernet
|--------------------|
| Physical Layer     |
---------------------
```

Figure 12-1 The OSI model of network architecture

When dealing with network or distributed applications, because it's very complicated and there are so many different components and pieces working together, it's always very helpful to have in mind the abstract seven-layer model of networking software and systems. It helps one understand, organize and troubleshoot. **Please don't get scared away by so many terminologies in this section. No worry at all if you don't understand them.**

The seven-layer model of computer network architecture we present here is the OSI (Open Systems Interconnection) model, as shown in Figure 12-1.

The Physical Layer

At the bottom layer is the physical layer which is the network cable that physically connects the computers on a network in the case of a wired network, or the air media in the case of a wireless network. This layer concerns with actual transmission of the data or digital signals, a series of 0s and 1s. It deals with electronic issues like voltage and noises.

The physical wiring depends on the type of networks: wired or wireless, LAN (Local Area Network), MAN (Metropolitan Area Network) or WAN (Wide Area Network), and what topology and technology.

Note that everything above the physical layer is software.

The Data Link Layer

The data link layer deals with access of the physical network media, network topology, error detection and correction, packet damage, packet loss, packet duplication, authentication, and speed discrepancy between the sending and receiving devices.

In order to accomplish its tasks, data link layer breaks data byte streams into data frames.

The data link layer has to perform some **flow control**.
Reasons include data frames may get lost or mangled during transmission, or the speed of the transmitter and receiver may vary a lot.
The sender may have to buffer outgoing frames either because the receiver is much slower than the sender or because some of the frames may have to be retransmitted due to packet loss or damage. A sliding window algorithm or something similar is normally used for flow control.

The data link layer is divided into two sublayers: the higher sublayer is called **Logical Link Control (LLC)** and the lower sublayer is called the **Medium Access Control (MAC)**. For example, IEEE 802 is a very famous family of standards for local area networks (LANs). It defines 802.1 (Higher Layer LAN Protocols, e.g. bridging), an LLC (802.2) and several MAC protocols including 802.3(Ethernet), 802.4(Token Bus), 802.5(Token Ring) and 802.11 (Wireless LAN Network Standards, including 802.11a, 802.11b, 802.11g and 802.11n).
The IEEE 802.11 standards are for wireless local area networking, which is the Wi-Fi technology many people are familiar with and use at home, airports, shopping malls and various stores like bookstores and coffee shops. These are different technologies/protocols in the Data Link Layer.

Different network topologies or physical media access protocols are

also implemented at the data link layer.
Some of the popular data link layer protocols include the following:
  LAN: Ethernet (CSMA/CD), Token Ring, FDDI
  WAN: Frame Relay, ATM, X.25
  Wireless: CSMA/CA
  Point-to-point Link: SLIP (Serial Line IP), PPP (Point-to-Point protocol),
    HDLC (High-Level Data link)

The software implementing the data link layer is sometimes called the
network driver.

The Network Layer

The network layer deals with connectivity between the two entities
communicating with each other. It is the lowest layer dealing with
end-to-end transmission. The main task of the network layer is to route
network packets from the source to its destination based on the source and
destination IP addresses of the packets or connection.

In addition, the network layer also provides congestion control.

When the number of data packets existing in a subnet approaching or
exceeding the maximum capacity of the subnet, performance degrades.
That's a congestion. While the data link and transport layers do flow
control, the network layer performs congestion control to keep the network
performance under control. There are different strategies for congestion
control, some involve using flow control. However, flow control cannot
really solve congestion problems because computer network traffic tends
to be bursting.

In short, the network layer provides **routing of packets** and **congestion
control**.

In the case of local area network (LAN), the network layer is the IP layer.
It is the layer that actually implements the IP protocols: **IPv4, IPv6,**
and the secure **IPsec.** Therefore, the IP layer uses the IP addresses.
Of course, there are other protocols in this layer and other layers
that we don't mention because they are not of interest here.

The Transport Layer

The transport layer provides services for end-to-end communication.
It takes messages handed down from the upper session layer, breaks it down
to smaller units called **transport protocol data units** (**TPDU**) if necessary,
and hands it down to the network layer.

To serve different needs from the upper layers, the transport layer
provides two types of services: a reliable, connection-oriented service
and a connectionless datagram service.

In providing the connection-oriented service, the transport layer handles
creation and deletion of connections between the two endpoints of
a communication.

The **connection-oriented service** provides a **virtual circuit (VC)** type of
service where a connection between two endpoints of the communication is

established before data exchange starts and torn down at end.
This means resources are reserved from the source host, through all the
intermediate routers and devices, to the destination host during the
lifetime of the connection. It effectively establishes a virtual circuit
between the two communicating programs or entities which can physically be
thousands of miles apart located in two different continents. This allows
the programs to reliably stream large amount of data through the connection.
Once a connection is established, reliable delivery of the messages is
guaranteed unless the hardware really breaks down. In order to achieve this
goal, the transport layer detects and handles message loss and damages.
Almost all Internet traffic uses this connection-oriented type of service.
Needless to say, all data packets travel through exactly the same route
during a connection.

The **connectionless service** does not establish (at start) and thus release
(at end) a virtual circuit or connection. It provides a message-by-message
best-effort delivery service. Since no connection or virtual circuit is
established, resources are not pre-allocated or reserved. As a result,
messages can get lost when a host, router or device along the way
runs out of resources. It's up to the upper layers to detect message loss
and damage and deal with it.

Apparently, data packets may travel through different routes during the
data exchange session between the two communication endpoints in a
connectionless service.

The connection-oriented transport service is provided by the **TCP** protocol
whereas the connectionless service is provided by the **UDP** protocol in this
layer. TCP (Transmission Control Protocol) provides **reliable** end-to-end
data transfer while UDP (User Datagram Protocol) offers fast, no-guarantee,
best-effort datagram delivery service. Data packets could get lost with the
UDP protocol. Its service is not guaranteed to be always reliable.

The transport layer provides an application interface which is truly
independent of the underlying network(s), whether it is LAN or WAN.
It adds another layer of error handling to improve the quality of
services provided to upper layers in face of lower layer errors.

The transport layer is a layer that also provides some **quality of service**
(QOS). One of the tasks of the transport layer is to enhance the quality
of service provided by the network layer and the layers below.
Ideally, regardless of the types of physical networks and services provided
at lower layers, transport layer should make it transparent to the users
and provide a consistent service and behavior. This means if the underlying
physical network is one not as reliable or one with much lower speed,
the transport layer should try to bridge the gap as much as it can
to meet user's expectation.

Many quality-of-service parameters are supported at the transport layer.
They include throughput, transit delay, priority, connection establishment
and release delays, error rate and others.

Just like the data link layer, the transport layer also needs to do **flow
control** as well to prevent a fast sender from overrunning a slow receiver.
It may need to buffer outgoing data packets in case they need to be
retransmitted because of packet loss or damage. Typically, a sliding

window algorithm or something similar is used.

The TCP/IP protocol suite, with TCP protocol at the transport layer and the IP protocol at the network layer, is what the Internet uses.

The Session Layer

The layers above the transport layer sometimes are not as clear-cut as other lower layers in some applications. Some applications may even mix these layers together or not have some of them. These layers provide some common functionalities that various applications need and users desire.

Initially when the ARPANET was designed, there were no session or presentation layer. It's the OSI model that emerged later added these. (ARPANET was the first wide-area packet-switching network established by the Advanced Research Projects Agency (ARPA) of the US Department of Defense. It's one of the first networks to implement the TCP/IP protocol suite which is at the core of the Internet today.)

The session layer allows applications or users to establish sessions between them. Each session is a series of message exchanges or a dialogue. One key property of a session is whether traffic is allowed in both directions at the same time (full duplex) or it can go only in one direction at a time. The session layer manages that.

The session layer also provides failure or crash management, trying to minimize the impact in case the underlying hardware fails or crashes.

Some **security features** are implemented in session layer. Authentication and encryption/decryption are among the examples.

Examples of session layer protocols include the Remote Procedure Call (RPC) protocol, Layer 2 Tunneling (L2TP) protocol, Session Initiation Protocol (SIP), Network File System (NFS) protocol, Server Message Block (SMB) protocol, the name resolution and file sharing protocol NetBIOS in Windows, and others. **Socket APIs** are located in session layer, too.

Internet security protocols such as Secure Sockets Layer (**SSL**) and Transport Layer Security (**TLS**) are mainly session layer protocols. They implement encryption, hash and other security features over the reliable TCP protocol to ensure communication sessions between the two end points are secure.

Remote login protocol SSH (Secure Shell) can be considered an example of session layer protocol as well, although it may be viewed as an application protocol, too.

The Presentation Layer

The presentation layer deals with issues like **data representation**, data encoding, and meaning of data. It makes sure data is represented and presented in a machine-independent way.

For numeric binary data, **endianness** is handled and data is converted if necessary to ensure little endian computers can communicate with big endian computers, and vice versa, without any problem.

For text data, appropriate data encoding schemes (e.g. ASCII, EBCDIC, UTF-8) are chosen and data is converted when necessary. Nowadays some form of **Unicode** (e.g. UTF-8, UTF-16, UTF-32) is commonly employed to support multi-byte characters for internationalization. Many countries (e.g. Japan, China and others) use languages consisting of thousands or even tens of thousands of characters and thus it requires multiple bytes of data to represent each character. That's when Unicode is used.

The Application Layer

The application layer implements the application logic to accomplish what the application promises to do using services provided by the presentation layer and layers below. Some common applications include electronic mail using the application layer protocol SMTP, file transfer using ftp or tftp application protocol, remote login using the telnet, rlogin or SSH protocols, web browsing using the HTTP/HTTPS protocols, Internet telephony such as Skype which uses a proprietary protocol over TCP and UDP, and many others.

Figure 12-2 lists some of the popular application layer protocols

Application	Application/Session layer protocol	Underlying Transport protocol
Web browsing	HTTP/HTTPS	TCP
File transfer	FTP	TCP
Email	SMTP	TCP
Remote Procedure Call	RPC	TCP and UDP
Network file system	NFS	UDP initially, now TCP
Remote terminal access	Telnet	TCP
Network management	SNMP	UDP
Server Message Block	SMB	TCP and UDP
File sharing on Windows	NetBIOS	TCP and UDP
Session Initiation Protocol	SIP	TCP or UDP
Layer 2 Tunneling Protocol	L2TP	UDP
Point-to-Point Tunneling	PPTP	TCP
Internet telephony (Skype)	SIP, RTP	Mostly UDP
Streaming multimedia	HTTP, RTP	TCP or UDP

Figure 12-2 Sample Application Protocols

12-1-2 Layer Positions of Most Popular Network Protocols

There are so many different protocols in the computer network space. They sometimes are very confusing to many people. It helps to know where they locate in the network architecture hierarchy.

They are a lot of protocols in the application/presentation/session layers. Figure 12-3 shows only a very small fraction of them.

There are only two most popular protocols at the transport layer: TCP and UDP.

Some application layer protocols use only TCP in the transport layer. Some use only UDP. But some could use either. Examples of protocols that could use either TCP or UDP include, but not limited to, Remote Procedure Call (RPC), Domain Name Service (DNS), Session Initiation Protocol (SIP), and NetBIOS.

There are three popular protocols in the network layer: IPv4, IPv6 and IPsec.

There are many network topologies and technologies in the data link and physical layers. We have mentioned some of them in the preceding section.

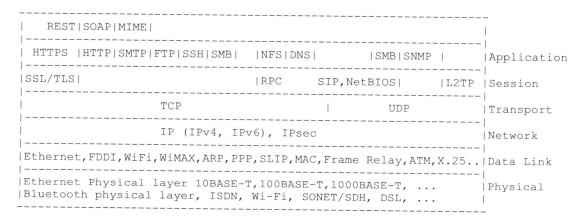

```
-------------------------------------------------------------------
|   REST|SOAP|MIME|                                               |
|-----------------------------------------------------------------|
| HTTPS  |HTTP|SMTP|FTP|SSH|SMB|  |NFS|DNS|        |SMB|SNMP  |    |Application
|-----------------------------------------------------------------|
|SSL/TLS|                       |RPC       SIP,NetBIOS|  |L2TP |Session
|-----------------------------------------------------------------|
|               TCP                     |        UDP           |Transport
|-----------------------------------------------------------------|
|               IP (IPv4, IPv6), IPsec                       |Network
|-----------------------------------------------------------------|
|Ethernet,FDDI,WiFi,WiMAX,ARP,PPP,SLIP,MAC,Frame Relay,ATM,X.25..|Data Link
|-----------------------------------------------------------------|
|Ethernet Physical layer 10BASE-T,100BASE-T,1000BASE-T, ...     |Physical
|Bluetooth physical layer, ISDN, Wi-Fi, SONET/SDH, DSL, ...     |
-------------------------------------------------------------------
```

Figure 12-3 Layer Positions of Common Network Protocols

12-1-3 IPv4 and IPv6

Just as each house on a street has a unique address, each computer or device connected to a network or the Internet needs a unique IP address to identify itself.

When Internet (the massive global network speaking the TCP/IP protocol) was first developed decades ago, each computer on the Internet was identified by a unique IP address of four bytes (32 bits) long, for instance, 11.150.212.102. This type of IP address is called the **IPv4 address.** At that time and some decades after, essentially only "big" computers are connected to computer networks. There were not as many computers on networks and hence a 32-bit IPv4 address suffices.

As laptop computers and mobile devices proliferate and their users want Internet access, the computer community realized that a 32-bit IP address may no longer be sufficient to uniquely identify all of the devices wanting to connect to the Internet. Thus, the Internet Engineering Task Force (IETF) initiated the design and development of the newer IPv6 protocol in 1994 and an **IPv6 address** becomes 128-bit long, which should be sufficient for a long time to come.

Today, we are still living in a world where most network devices are still using IPv4 addresses while some of them have started to use IPv6 addresses. As a result, most software applications are supporting both IPv4 and

IPv6 protocols.

Almost all computer operating systems support both IPv4 and IPv6 protocols now. The two protocols can co-exist and operate side-by-side. Indeed, it's entirely possible that on a single system program A is communicating with a program on another computer using the IPv4 protocol while program B (or even the program A itself) on the same computer is communicating with a program in another computer using the IPv6 protocol. As a matter of fact, author has written many server programs at different companies that can talk to both IPv4 and IPv6 clients at the same time, dating back to 2005. Yes, computer network devices using IPv4 addresses can communicate with those using IPv6 addresses without problems.

Different nations are moving toward IPv6 at different paces, with many Asian countries having adopted IPv6 as the standard in government organizations. It is fair to say that IPv6 has been coming, but at a slow speed. In the foreseeable future, IPv4 and IPv6 will continue to co-exist for quite some time to come.

IP Addresses

In a C-language program, an IPv4 address is represented by the **in_addr_t** data type, which is **'struct in_addr'**. It's 4 bytes, or 32 bits, long. For example, 192.168.1.10 is an IPv4 address. An IPv6 address is represented by **'struct in6_addr'**. It's 16 bytes, or 128 bits, long. For example, FE80::3054:1B1E:F0DD:401B is an IPv6 address.

Both 'struct in_addr' and 'struct in6_addr' are defined in the header file in.h. To get these data types, your program needs to include the following line:

```
#include <netinet/in.h>
```

A short-hand notation in_addr_t is defined for 'struct in_addr'. However, there is no in6_addr_t defined for 'struct in6_addr'. It's a little odd.

12-1-4 RFC

As we said it before, there are so many different networking protocols defined and implemented so far. They spread over different layers of the network architecture. They are also defined, approved and documented in different ways. Some of the protocols are very formally defined and adopted as IEEE standards. Examples include the IEEE 802 standards. Others are not.

These days many network protocols are defined or specified as RFCs (Request For Comments).

A **Request for Comments** (**RFC**) is a type of document or publication from the Internet Engineering Task Force (IETF), the Internet Architecture Board (IAB), and the Internet Society (ISOC). It has become the official publication channel for the Internet research and development community.

An RFC is typically authored by engineers and computer scientists who did the research or drafted by a committee working on a standard. It is then submitted for peer or public review. The IETF adopts some of the proposals published as RFCs as Internet Standards. Some RFCs are just informational.

Once an RFC becomes an Internet standard, no further comments or changes are permitted. Changes to it can only be made through a subsequent RFC that supersedes the previous RFC or elaborates on all or parts of it.

Here are some examples of networking protocols specified as RFCs:

The most common version of HTTP that has been in use is HTTP/1.1. It was defined in RFC 2068 in 1997. Subsequently, it was obsoleted by RFC 2616 in 1999 and then again by RFC 7230 and family in 2014. HTTP/2 was standardized in 2015 and published in RFC 7540.

HTTPS (HTTP Secure or HTTP over SSL) is documented in RFC 2818.

The TLS protocol version 1.0 is defined in RFC 2246.

The Simple Mail Transfer Protocol (SMTP) is described in RFC 821.

The SSH-2 protocol is defined in a set of RFCs: RFC 4251 to RFC 4256.

As an engineer, you will find that you often need to read RFC documents to dig out details about some network protocols.

12-2 What Is Socket?

The concept of (computer network) socket originated in ARPANET in 1970s.

Socket is an abstraction through which programs can send and receive data. A socket represents a communication endpoint in a program. A socket is a software representation of a communication point in a computer. It has the capability to send data to and receive data from another socket.

The socket facility and feature are available to software programs through a set of software subroutines named **socket APIs**. The socket APIs allow software programs to access the transport layer and network layer protocols implemented inside the operating system kernel and to communicate with other programs across a computer network.

Socket APIs are implemented in an operating system as a session layer service. They are right above the transport layer. They are also immediately above the operating system kernel.

The very first socket APIs were developed at University of California at Berkeley in BSD Unix operating system version 4.2 in 1983. It was called the BSD socket API, or Berkeley sockets.

For a program P1 running in computer A to communicate with another program P2 running in computer B, a communication endpoint is needed in computer A for program P1 and another communication endpoint is needed in computer B for program P2. Each communication endpoint is a network socket, or simply a socket, if the two programs are using socket API to communicate with each other, which is true in almost all cases. In abstract, a communication end point is just some facility that allows a program to send and/or receive data.

For software programs to communicate with each other across computer networks using network sockets, there is a set of functions for programs to use. Collectively, this set of socket functions or subroutines is called the 'socket API'. The socket API is part of the POSIX.1 standard. This is what this chapter will introduce to readers.

Note that the socket API, although it is mostly used in inter-computer communications between two software programs, it works for communications between two programs running on the same computer as well. Because of this and because an application can send almost anything through a socket, socket has become one of the most important, popular and powerful interprocess communication (IPC) mechanisms.

Sockets is a software feature that enables programs running on different computers connected via a computer network or the Internet to communicate and exchange data with one other.

12-2-1 Different Types of Sockets

There are different types of sockets, based on the underlying protocols used and the quality and characteristics of the sockets.

First, there are **Internet sockets** and **Unix domain sockets**.
Internet sockets are mainly designed for use in inter-process communications between software programs running on different computers across a network, although they also work equally well for communications between programs running on the same computer too. Internet sockets use an Internet protocol suite such as TCP/IP or UDP/IP, which is the foundation of all Internet activities.

In contrast, Unix domain sockets are designed for inter-process communications between programs running on the same computer system only. In one sense, Unix Domain sockets are very similar to other inter-process communication mechanisms we talked about in the early chapters, such as System V IPC, because it's for processes running on the same system. In another it is also different from some of the other IPC schemes in that the two processes communicating using a Unix Domain socket do not have to have any relationship, for example, the parent-child relationship.

Second, within the Internet sockets, depending on the network protocol suite used, there are three different types of sockets: Stream, Datagram and Raw.

We briefly introduce these different types of sockets below.

1. **Stream sockets.** Stream sockets are connection-oriented sockets because the underlying protocol used in the transport layer is the connection-oriented Transmission Control Protocol (TCP). The TCP protocol allocates and reserves the network resources required for the duration of a connection when the connection is established. Because of that, reliability is guaranteed. It essentially provides a 'virtual circuit' service for the connection.

When reliability is a requirement, Stream sockets is the choice.

2. **Datagram sockets**. Datagram sockets are connection-less sockets because the underlying protocol used in the transport layer is User Datagram Protocol (UDP), which is connectionless in its nature, meaning no virtual circuit is established and not all required network resources are pre-allocated and reserved. As a result, reliability is not guaranteed in using the UDP protocol and thus the Datagram sockets. Network packets can be lost using Datagram sockets.

   However, Datagram sockets are easier to set up and use. It's simpler. It also consumes less resources than Stream sockets.

3. **Raw sockets**. Raw sockets are also known as Raw IP sockets. They are typically used in network equipment such as routers. The transport layer is bypassed here and the packet headers are made accessible to the application.

   Note that the Raw sockets functionality is optional in POSIX standard.

The three types of sockets above are Internet sockets.

4. **Unix domain sockets**. Unix domain sockets are sometimes called IPC sockets. They are designed for inter-process communication between processes running on the same system (i.e. a single computer). Because of this, Unix domain sockets are uniquely identified by file system entries instead of network IP addresses with ports.

   The good thing about Unix domain sockets is from a programming standpoint its use is almost identical to Internet sockets. The only difference is when the socket is created you need to specify a different socket type and a server socket needs to be bound to a pathname instead of an IP address. It makes life much easier because the same set of APIs are used.

```
                                --- Stream socket
              -- Internet socket --|-- Datagram socket
              |                     --- Raw socket
socket -|
              -- Unix Domain socket (for within same computer only)
```

Figure 12-4 Different types of sockets

12-2-2 The socket() Function

As mentioned earlier, the first thing that is needed for a program to be able to communicate with another program, in either another computer via a network or even within the same computer, is a network socket. A network socket is a communication endpoint. As depicted in Figure 12-5, two programs can communicate with each other with each using a communication endpoint -- a socket. This section discusses how to create a socket.

The socket() function creates a network socket used in interprocess communication. It creates an endpoint for communication. The socket() function returns a file descriptor representing the opened socket. In POSIX

-compliant systems, many things are treated as a file. That includes
network sockets. The socket() function has the following specification:

```
#include <sys/types.h>
#include <sys/socket.h>

int socket(int domain, int type, int protocol);
```

The first parameter of the socket() call specifies a domain, which is also
referred to as **'Address Family' (AF)** or **'Protocol Family (PF)'**.
The three major domains supported by the POSIX standard are defined as
symbolic constants in the <sys/socket.h> header file and they are as follows:

```
AF_INET  (PF_INET) - Internet domain sockets for use with IPv4 addresses.
AF_INET6 (PF_INET6) - Internet domain sockets for use with IPv6 addresses.
AF_UNIX  (PF_UNIX) - UNIX domain sockets.
```

To avoid confusion, we will call these Internet sockets and UNIX domain
sockets, respectively.

```
      Process 1                        Process 2

   -----------------              -----------------
   |               |              |               |
   |   --------    | communication|   --------    |  communication
   |   |socket|    |<- endpoint   |   |socket|    | <- endpoint
   | ------------  |              | ------------  |
   | | TCP / UDP | |              | | TCP / UDP | |
   | |-----------| |              | |-----------| |
   | | IPv4/IPv6 | |              | | IPv4/IPv6 | |
   | |-----------| |              | |-----------| |
   | |    :      | |              | |    :      | |
   |               |              |               |
   -----------------              -----------------
           ^                              ^
           |      computer network        |
   --------------------------------------------
```

Figure 12-5 Network communication via Internet sockets

Note that AF_INET is the same as PF_INET, AF_INET6 is same as PF_INET6,
and AF_UNIX is same as PF_UNIX. In fact, below is what you will see in
/usr/include/sys/socket.h on a Unix system:

```
#define AF_UNIX      1          /* local to host (pipes, portals) */
#define AF_INET      2          /* internetwork: UDP, TCP, etc. */
#define AF_INET6     26         /* Internet Protocol, Version 6 */

#define PF_UNIX      AF_UNIX
#define PF_INET      AF_INET
#define PF_INET6     AF_INET6
```

And below is what you will see in /usr/include/bits/socket.h on a
Linux system:

```
#define PF_LOCAL     1          /* Local to host (pipes and file-domain). */
```

```
#define PF_UNIX        PF_LOCAL  /* POSIX name for PF_LOCAL.  */
#define PF_INET        2         /* IP protocol family.  */
#define PF_INET6       10        /* IP version 6.  */

#define AF_UNIX        PF_UNIX
#define AF_INET        PF_INET
#define AF_INET6       PF_INET6
```

Notice the constant defined for AF_INET6/PF_INET6 is different between
Unix and Linux. It's all right because that value gets to be used within
a system itself only; it does not get sent across network.

Passing in the value AF_UNIX if you are creating a Unix domain socket.
Passing in the value AF_INET or AF_INET6 if you are creating an Internet
socket and using an IPv4 or IPv6 address, respectively.

Unix domain sockets are used for interprocess communication between processes
running on the same computer. Internet sockets are used for interprocess
communication between processes running on different computers connected
via a computer network or the Internet. Note that Internet sockets work
perfectly fine even if the two end points are on the same computer.
This makes it simple because programmers do not need to know or worry about
if the two entities communicating with each other will be on the same
computer or not. You just program it exactly the same way!

The second parameter of the socket() call specifies a socket type.
The socket types supported by the POSIX standard are defined as
symbolic constants in the <sys/socket.h> header file and they are as follows:

   SOCK_STREAM - Byte-stream socket.
   SOCK_DGRAM - Datagram socket.
   SOCK_RAW - Raw Protocol Interface. This functionality is optional.
   SOCK_SEQPACKET - Sequenced-packet socket.

Passing in SOCK_STREAM in the type argument if you intend to create a
reliable connection-oriented socket. Use SOCK_DGRAM for a connectionless
socket connection. Passing in SOCK_RAW for creating raw network protocol
sockets, which normally requires the call to have a super user privilege.
SOCK_SEQPACKET type of sockets provide a sequenced, reliable, two-way
connection-based data communication path for datagrams of fixed maximum
length. The receiver is required to read an entire packet with each read.

Note that not all socket types are implemented by each protocol family.
For instance, SOCK_SEQPACKET is not implemented for AF_INET protocol family.
Therefore, if you specify AF_INET as the domain, you cannot pass in
SOCK_SEQPACKET as the type. But it is supported in AF_UNIX domain.

The third parameter of the socket() function specifies a protocol.
The protocol parameter specifies a particular protocol to be used with the
socket. Most of the time only a single protocol exists to support a
particular socket type within a given protocol family, in which case
protocol can be specified as 0. However, sometimes multiple protocols may
exist. In that case, a particular protocol must be specified.

Figure 12-6 lists a program that demonstrates the use of socket() function.
It tests what combinations of protocol family, socket type and network

protocol are supported on a system.

Note that as we mentioned above, using the SOCK_RAW type of sockets requires super user privilege. Hence, if you run the program as a non-root user, trying to create a raw socket will get error EPERM (1) -- permission denied.

Figure 12-6 Finding what types of sockets are supported (socket.c)

```
/*
 * socket()
 * Different combinations of socket types and protocols that are supported.
 * Authored by Mr. Jin-Jwei Chen.
 * Copyright (c) 1993-2016, Mr. Jin-Jwei Chen. All rights reserved.
 */

#include <stdio.h>
#include <errno.h>
#include <sys/types.h>
#include <sys/socket.h>
#include <netinet/in.h>      /* protocols such as IPPROTO_TCP, ... */
#include <unistd.h>

int main(int argc, char *argv[])
{
  int     sockfd;

  sockfd = socket(AF_INET, SOCK_STREAM, 0);
  if (sockfd == -1)
    fprintf(stderr, "socket(AF_INET, SOCK_STREAM, 0) failed, errno=%d\n", errno);
  else
  {
    fprintf(stdout, "socket(AF_INET, SOCK_STREAM, 0) is supported\n");
    close(sockfd);
  }

  sockfd = socket(AF_INET, SOCK_DGRAM, 0);
  if (sockfd == -1)
    fprintf(stderr, "socket(AF_INET, SOCK_DGRAM, 0) failed, errno=%d\n", errno);
  else
  {
    fprintf(stdout, "socket(AF_INET, SOCK_DGRAM, 0) is supported\n");
    close(sockfd);
  }

  sockfd = socket(AF_INET, SOCK_STREAM, IPPROTO_TCP);
  if (sockfd == -1)
    fprintf(stderr, "socket(AF_INET, SOCK_STREAM, IPPROTO_TCP) failed, errno=%d\n",
errno);
  else
  {
    fprintf(stdout, "socket(AF_INET, SOCK_STREAM, IPPROTO_TCP) is supported\n");
    close(sockfd);
  }

  sockfd = socket(AF_INET, SOCK_DGRAM, IPPROTO_UDP);
  if (sockfd == -1)
```

```
      fprintf(stderr, "socket(AF_INET, SOCK_DGRAM, IPPROTO_UDP) failed, errno=%d\n",
errno);
  else
  {
    fprintf(stdout, "socket(AF_INET, SOCK_DGRAM, IPPROTO_UDP) is supported\n");
    close(sockfd);
  }

  sockfd = socket(AF_UNIX, SOCK_STREAM, 0);
  if (sockfd == -1)
    fprintf(stderr, "socket(AF_UNIX, SOCK_STREAM, 0) failed, errno=%d\n", errno);
  else
  {
    fprintf(stdout, "socket(AF_UNIX, SOCK_STREAM, 0) is supported\n");
    close(sockfd);
  }

  sockfd = socket(AF_UNIX, SOCK_DGRAM, 0);
  if (sockfd == -1)
    fprintf(stderr, "socket(AF_UNIX, SOCK_DGRAM, 0) failed, errno=%d\n", errno);
  else
  {
    fprintf(stdout, "socket(AF_UNIX, SOCK_DGRAM, 0) is supported\n");
    close(sockfd);
  }

  sockfd = socket(AF_UNIX, SOCK_SEQPACKET, 0);
  if (sockfd == -1)
    fprintf(stderr, "socket(AF_UNIX, SOCK_SEQPACKET, 0) failed, errno=%d\n", errno);
  else
  {
    fprintf(stdout, "socket(AF_UNIX, SOCK_SEQPACKET, 0) is supported\n");
    close(sockfd);
  }

  sockfd = socket(AF_INET, SOCK_RAW, IPPROTO_RAW);
  if (sockfd == -1)
    fprintf(stderr, "socket(AF_INET, SOCK_RAW, IPPROTO_RAW) failed, errno=%d\n",
errno);
  else
  {
    fprintf(stdout, "socket(AF_INET, SOCK_RAW, IPPROTO_RAW) is supported\n");
    close(sockfd);
  }

  sockfd = socket(AF_INET, SOCK_RAW, IPPROTO_ICMP);
  if (sockfd == -1)
    fprintf(stderr, "socket(AF_INET, SOCK_RAW, IPPROTO_ICMP) failed, errno=%d\n",
errno);
  else
  {
    fprintf(stdout, "socket(AF_INET, SOCK_RAW, IPPROTO_ICMP) is supported\n");
    close(sockfd);
  }

  sockfd = socket(AF_INET, SOCK_RAW, IPPROTO_EGP);
```

```
if (sockfd == -1)
    fprintf(stderr, "socket(AF_INET, SOCK_RAW, IPPROTO_EGP) failed, errno=%d\n",
errno);
else
{
    fprintf(stdout, "socket(AF_INET, SOCK_RAW, IPPROTO_EGP) is supported\n");
    close(sockfd);
}

sockfd = socket(AF_INET, SOCK_RAW, IPPROTO_RSVP);
if (sockfd == -1)
    fprintf(stderr, "socket(AF_INET, SOCK_RAW, IPPROTO_RSVP) failed, errno=%d\n",
errno);
else
{
    fprintf(stdout, "socket(AF_INET, SOCK_RAW, IPPROTO_RSVP) is supported\n");
    close(sockfd);
}

return(0);
}
```

From running the example program named socket, you can find the following combinations of socket types and protocols are normally supported.

```
socket(AF_INET, SOCK_STREAM, 0)
socket(AF_INET, SOCK_DGRAM, 0)
socket(AF_INET, SOCK_STREAM, IPPROTO_TCP)
socket(AF_INET, SOCK_DGRAM, IPPROTO_UDP)
socket(AF_UNIX, SOCK_STREAM, 0)
socket(AF_UNIX, SOCK_DGRAM, 0)
socket(AF_INET, SOCK_RAW, IPPROTO_RAW)
socket(AF_INET, SOCK_RAW, IPPROTO_ICMP)
socket(AF_INET, SOCK_RAW, IPPROTO_EGP)
socket(AF_INET, SOCK_RAW, IPPROTO_RSVP)
```

Be aware that the last four combinations above require super user (root user) privilege.

12-2-3 Socket Types

A network socket is created with a specific type. Different socket types use different network communication protocols and have different communication semantics and behavior. As we have mentioned, four socket types are defined: SOCK_STREAM, SOCK_DGRAM, SOCK_RAW and SOCK_SEQPACKET. The first two types are the most frequently used and they are what this chapter will focus on.

The SOCK_STREAM Socket

The SOCK_STREAM socket type provides reliable, sequenced, full-duplex, two-way byte streams between the socket and a peer to which the socket is connected. A socket of type SOCK_STREAM must be in a connected state before any data can be sent or received. Record boundary is not maintained. The data sent by the sender forms a stream of bytes at the receiving end.

The sender and receiver can use different sizes of buffers to send or receive data. SOCK_STREAM sockets are normally implemented using the TCP and IP (IPv4 or IPv6) protocols at layer 4 and 3, respectively. We will call sockets of SOCK_STREAM type **Stream sockets** or TCP sockets.

Once a Stream socket is created and a connection is made, an application can simply send as much data as it wants before stop. That is essentially streaming data. That's why it is called stream socket.

Note that the TCP protocol forms a virtual circuit between the two communication endpoints by pre-allocating resources required for the communication. It also does error checking to ensure no packet loss or packet duplication as well as ensuring packets are delivered to the receiver in correct sequence. Flow control may also be done. All of these are done to achieve reliability.

Data may be buffered. A successful return from an output function does not imply that the data has been delivered to the peer or even transmitted from the local system.

If data cannot be successfully transmitted within a given amount of time, the connection is considered broken and subsequent operations will fail. A SIGPIPE signal is raised if a thread or process attempts to send data on a broken stream socket, except that the signal is suppressed if the MSG_NOSIGNAL flag is used in calls to send(), sendto(), and sendmsg() functions. Support for out-of-band data transmission is protocol-specific.

The SOCK_DGRAM Socket

The SOCK_DGRAM socket type supports connectionless data transfer in which reliability is not guaranteed. SOCK_DGRAM sockets are usually implemented using the UDP and IP protocols at layer 4 and 3, respectively. Therefore, they are sometimes called **Datagram sockets** or UDP sockets.

Note that the SOCK_DGRAM socket provides a datagram service in which a best effort is made in delivery and reliability is not guaranteed. Data packets can potentially be lost for different reasons including system running out of resources. It's the responsibility of the application to ensure all data is delivered.

A datagram or message must be sent in a single output operation and must be received in a single input operation. The maximum size of a datagram is protocol-specific. Output datagrams may be buffered within the system; thus, a successful return from an output function does not guarantee that the data is actually sent or received. However, the implementation is expected to try to detect and report any errors before the output function returns.

Datagrams may be sent to the address specified (possibly multicast or broadcast) in each output operation, and incoming datagrams may be received from multiple sources. The source address of each datagram is available for the receiving application at receiving time. An application may also pre-specify a peer address, in which case calls to output functions that do not specify a peer address shall send to the pre-specified address. If a peer address has been specified, then only datagrams from that address will be received.

The SOCK_RAW Socket

The SOCK_RAW socket type is similar to the SOCK_DGRAM type.
It differs in that it is normally used with communication providers that underlie those used for the other socket types. For this reason, the creation of a socket with type SOCK_RAW normally requires super user privilege. The format of datagrams sent and received with this socket type generally includes specific protocol headers, and the formats are protocol-specific and implementation-specific.

The SOCK_SEQPACKET Socket

The SOCK_SEQPACKET socket type is similar to the SOCK_STREAM type. It is also connection-oriented. The only difference between these two types is that record boundaries are maintained using the SOCK_SEQPACKET type. A record can be sent using one or more output operations and received using one or more input operations, but a single operation never transfers amount of more than one record. Record boundaries are visible to the receiver via the MSG_EOR flag in the received message flags returned by the recvmsg() function. It is protocol-specific whether a maximum record size is imposed.

12-2-4 Socket Addresses and Structures

Remember we said that each computer has a unique IP address to identify itself. We also said that a socket represents a communication endpoint on a computer. Each socket has a unique socket address for identification as well. Since a computer can have many sockets created and being used at the same time, a socket address encompasses an IP address.
To distinguish one socket from another, each network socket is given a number. This number is called a **port number**. Its size is 16 bits. Hence, to uniquely identify a socket, one needs an IP address to first uniquely identify the computer or device the socket is on. In addition, you also need the port number the socket is associated with to uniquely identify the socket on that computer. As a result, a socket address essentially is an IP address plus a port number.

    socket address = IP address + port number

But this is not all. A further subtle detail is that as we said earlier, today's Internet is using the TCP/UDP-IP protocol suite. That means there are two protocols, TCP and UDP, existing in the transport layer.
Since a communication endpoint is using either TCP or UDP protocol, but not both, at a time in the transport layer, depending on whether it is a STREAM or DATAGRAM socket type, transport protocol plays a role in uniquely identifying a socket as well. This means a computer can have two sockets using the same port number at the same time, as long as one is using the TCP transport protocol and the other using UDP. Therefore, a complete socket address includes at least the following three components:

socket address = IP address + port number + transport protocol (TCP or UDP)

This understanding is very important. If you look at the /etc/services file on a Linux/Unix system, which reserves port numbers for many services, you will find entries like these:

```
ftp              21/tcp
ftp              21/udp              fsp fspd
```

In other words, port numbers are qualified with a transport protocol. This is exactly what we just explained.

The data structures holding socket addresses need some explanation.

Doing network socket programming involves using multiple socket address structures. The rest of this section gives a brief introduction of these structures.

First, there is a generic socket address structure, 'struct sockaddr'. It's used in function parameters to receive either type of socket address. It is 16 bytes long, with a 2-byte sa_family followed by a 14-byte data.

```
struct sockaddr
{
  sa_family_t sa_family;
  char sa_data[14];
};
```

Many socket APIs, such as connect() and bind(), which support both IPv4 and IPv6 protocols, use this generic socket address so that these functions can take in either an IPv4 or IPv6 socket address.

Second, there is the IPv4 socket address represented by 'struct sockaddr_in', which contains an IPv4 host IP address in it. It contains a 2-byte sin_family, a 2-byte port number, a 4-byte IPv4 address (struct in_addr), followed by a padding of 8 bytes, totaling 16 bytes long. Note that it is usually a good practice to fill the padding portion with zero.

```
struct sockaddr_in
{
  sa_family_t sin_family;
  in_port_t sin_port;
  struct in_addr sin_addr;
  unsigned char sin_zero[sizeof (struct sockaddr) -
    (sizeof (unsigned short int)) -
    sizeof (in_port_t) -
    sizeof (struct in_addr)];
};
```

Third, an IPv6 socket address, struct sockaddr_in6, is a socket address with an IPv6 host IP address in it. It contains a 2-byte sin_family, a 2-byte port number, a 4-byte flow information, a 16-byte IPv6 address (struct in6_addr), and a 4-byte scope_id, totaling 28 bytes long.

```
struct sockaddr_in6
{
  sa_family_t sin6_family;
  in_port_t sin6_port;
  uint32_t sin6_flowinfo;
  struct in6_addr sin6_addr;
```

```
    uint32_t sin6_scope_id;
};
```

Lastly, there is the 'struct sockaddr_storage' used to store either type of socket address so that it can be passed around. Since 'struct sockaddr' is not big enough to hold an IPv6 socket address, 'struct sockaddr_storage' is designed so that it can accommodate either. A program can use a 'struct sockaddr_storage' to hold either a 'struct sockaddr_in' or a 'struct sockaddr_in6', pass it around, and then typecast it back later.

The 'struct sockaddr_storage' is 128 bytes long, beginning with a 2-byte ss_famliy, followed by a 8-byte alignment and a padding of 112 bytes. Because of the enforcing 8-byte alignment padding, it forces the second field, __ss_align, to start at byte offset 8 and the third field, __ss_padding, to start at byte offset 16. Thus the __ss_padding is 128-(2 * 8)=112 bytes.

struct sockaddr_storage

```
{
   sa_family_t ss_family;
   __uint64_t __ss_align;
   char __ss_padding[(128 - (2 * sizeof (__uint64_t)))];
};
```

Note that these socket address structures may look a bit confusing, at least it could be so for beginners. But at a conceptual level, the address of a socket essentially consists of the following three components:

- a protocol family (e.g. Internet or Unix Domain socket)
- an IP address
- a port number

The protocol family specifies whether the socket is an Internet socket essentially for inter-computer communication or Unix domain socket for intra-computer communication.

The IP address uniquely identifies a computer host or system on the network or the Internet. A port number, combined with the socket type (that is, the transport protocol) specified in the second argument of the socket() call, uniquely identifies a program or process running within that computer system. In other words, only one process on a particular system can be using a socket with a particular port number (say, 3456), with TCP protocol. Though another process could be using that same port number with the UDP protocol. Together, these four pieces of information items (the three listed above plus the transport protocol) uniquely identify the socket used by a particular process running on a particular computer host on the Internet around the globe.

12-2-5 IP Address Within Socket Address

Notice that among other things such as a port number, a socket address consists of an Internet IP address in it.

That is, a 'struct sockaddr_in' contains a 'struct in_addr' in it which is an IPv4 address stored in binary form. It's a 32-bit binary value.

A string format IP address must be converted into the binary form before it can be assigned to this field. Most Linux and Unix systems define in_addr_t to be uint32_t and define 'struct in_addr' to be in_addr_t. Hence, these three data types are often used interchangeably.

```
struct sockaddr_in  /* IPv4 socket address */
{
    :
  struct in_addr sin_addr;  /* host IPv4 address in binary format */
    :
};
```

Similarly, a 'struct sockaddr_in6', which is an IPv6 socket address, contains a 'struct in6_addr' in it, which is an IPv6 address. 'struct in6_addr' is 128-bit (i.e. 16 bytes) long.

```
struct sockaddr_in6  /* IPv6 socket address */
{
    :
  struct in6_addr sin6_addr;  /* host IPv6 address in binary format */
    :
};
```

When programs communicate with each other via socket, they can find out what its peer's socket address is and from the socket address it knows what the peer's IP address and port number are. This is sometimes useful for identification purpose.

12-2-6 The Include File for Socket

The POSIX standard says that socket related APIs and constants shall be defined in <sys/socket.h>. In fact, to use network sockets in your C program, the first include statement your C program needs to add is the following:

```
#include <sys/socket.h>
```

In many operating systems, the socket related APIs and constants are defined in the include file <sys/socket.h>. However, some operating systems split the information into multiple files. For instance, in Linux, the <sys/socket.h> header file defines the socket APIs, including the following:

```
socket(), listen(), accept(), connect(), send(), recv(), sendto(),
recvfrom(), sendmsg(), recvmsg(), getsockopt(), setsockopt(), ...
```

The socket related constants such as the types of sockets (SOCK_*), the protocol families (PF_*), the address families (AF_*), the bits in the flags argument in send()/recv() calls (MSG_*), and the socket options (SO_*) are defined in <bits/socket.h>.

```
Types of sockets: SOCK_STREAM, SOCK_DGRAM, SOCK_RAW, ...
Protocol families: PF_INET, PF_UNIX, PF_INET6, ...
Address families: AF_INET, AF_UNIX, AF_INET6, ...
Flags in send/recv calls: MSG_PEEK, MSG_OOB, MSG_DONTWAIT, MSG_EOR, ...
```

The socket options are defined in <asm-generic/socket.h> in Linux.

In other words, in Linux the socket related APIs and constants are defined in at least four or five different header files: <sys/socket.h>, <bits/socket.h>, and <asm-generic/socket.h>.
However, your program only needs to include <sys/socket.h> to get all of them. This is because <sys/socket.h> includes <bits/socket.h> and <bits/socket2.h>. Then <bits/socket.h> in turn includes <bits/sockaddr.h> and <asm/socket.h> and <asm/socket.h> then includes <asm-generic/socket.h>. Below is the include hierarchy (the indentations show who include who):

```
#include <sys/socket.h> /* This is the header file your program includes. */
    /* It in fact includes the following in Linux. */
    #include <bits/socket.h>
        #include <bits/sockaddr.h>
        #include <asm/socket.h>
            #include <asm-generic/socket.h>
    # include <bits/socket2.h>
```

Be aware that for your socket programs to work or even compile, you usually need to include multiple header files. Using a function usually requires some specific header file(s). To get the header file(s) required, just run the man (man page) command on the API you are trying to use. For instance, in Linux/Unix the command below tells you what header files are needed by socket():

```
$ man socket
```

Or search socket on the MSDN if you are using Windows.

12-3 Styles of Computer Network Communication

Before we dive into talking about how to write programs communicating with each other across network, let us give a brief quick overview of the typical styles of network communication between programs.

When two programs are communicating with each other, there are usually three types of setup in terms of the role each plays.

1. Client-Server model.

   A client-server model is the most common in network communication. In this model, a server sits in a loop and listens for requests from clients. It services the client's request and returns the result. In a client-server model, it's always the client that initiates a communication.

```
    ----------    1. request     ----------
    |        |--------------->|          |
    | client |                |  Server  |
    |        |<---------------|          |
    ----------    2. response    ----------
```

   Figure 12-7a Client-server model

Web applications that use the HTTP/HTTPS protocol at the application layer, file transfer applications that use the ftp protocol at the application layer, and network file systems that use the NFS protocol are just some very popular examples of client-server communication.

2. Peer-to-Peer model.

In a peer-to-peer model, the two communicating parties play an equal or similar role. Either one can initiate a communication.

```
 ---------       message       ---------
|         |--------------->|          |
|  Peer   |                |  Peer   |
|         |<---------------|          |
 ---------       message       ---------
```

Figure 12-7b Peer-to-peer model

One example is in a clustered system, cluster nodes often need to exchange heartbeat messages to let the other nodes know that I'm still alive. Often this is done by a daemon program. The relationship between these daemon programs exchanging heartbeat messages with one another is neither client-server, nor master-slave. They are just peers to one another.

3. Master-Slave or Manager-Worker model.

In the master-slave model, there are usually one master process communicating with multiple slave or worker processes. Typically, the master process initiates a communication by sending work or order to a slave. The slave process does the work or executes the order and then gets back to the master.

The master is sometimes called the manager and the slave called worker.

There are a number of possible variations of the master-slave model. In first dimension, the slaves/workers can be either processes or threads. Second, the worker/slave processes or threads can be pre-created and managed as a pool or they can be created and destroyed on demand. Third, the number of total slaves/workers can be fixed or variable. Sometimes system configuration parameters may need to be tuned if this number hits certain limit.

Often the master-slave model is used to implement a multitasking server program on a single system, although in rare cases the slaves may be spread across multiple systems forming a distributed computing job.

```
 --------------------          --------------------
|      Master       |        |      Manager      |
 --------------------          --------------------
  | ^             | ^          | ^             | ^
  v |    ...      v |          v |    ...      v |
 -------        -------        --------        --------
|Slave|        |Slave|        |Worker|        |Worker|
 -------        -------        --------        --------
```

Figure 12-7c Master-slave model

Usually this model is used to implement a very busy server where a server needs to serve a large number of clients and a single-threaded server wouldn't be able to meet the quick response time requirement. A Web server is a very typical example.

As we just said, there are many variations in implementing such a server. And some of them may not use socket as the communication channel because they are other alternatives or options.

12-4 Connectionless Communication Using Datagram Sockets

As a first example of writing programs communicating with each other, in this section we show you how to write a pair of client and server programs using the connectionless Datagram sockets.

Note that typically the two endpoints in a communication use the same type of sockets; it's either both use Stream sockets or both use Datagram ones.

12-4-1 Sending and Receiving Datagram Messages

Once you know how to create a network socket, the easiest way to establish a communication with another process is to use the Datagram socket because it requires no establishment of a connection. All you need to do is to know the socket address of your partner. As long as you have that, you can just send a message to that address. That's it! It's very much like the postal mail. If you know someone's name and mailing address, you can send him/her a postal mail at any time you want. It's that simple. But if he/she has moved, he/she may never receive whatever you send. Or if he/she is out of town for some time, he/she may not receive it after some time has gone by. Of course, there is also a very slight chance that the mail could get lost.

Sending messages over a Datagram socket has very similar characteristics. The messages sent can be lost or arrive out of order. And there is no guarantee in delivery. However, it is simple, flexible and has minimum overhead. And it normally works just fine unless there is some hardware problem or the system(s) is extremely busy and runs out of resources.

12-4-1-1 The sendto() Function

To send a message via a Datagram or unconnected socket, a program invokes the sendto() function.

```
#include <sys/socket.h>

ssize_t sendto(int sockfd, const void *msgbuf, size_t bufsz,
    int flags, const struct sockaddr *dest_addr,
    socklen_t dest_len);
```

The sockfd argument gives the open file descriptor of the socket to be used to send the message. It should be the value returned by a successful socket() function call.

The msgbuf argument is a pointer to the output buffer containing the message to be sent. The bufsz argument specifies the size in bytes of the message to be sent.

The dest_addr argument specifies the socket address of the intended receiver of the message. It should be a pointer to a sockaddr structure containing the destination address. The actual format and length of destination address depend on the address family of the socket. The dest_len argument specifies the length (size in bytes) of destination address (i.e. the sockaddr structure).

The fourth argument is flags. This argument can take the logical OR'ing of zero or more of the following values:

   MSG_OOB - Sends out-of-band data on sockets that support out-of-band data. The significance and semantics of out-of-band data are protocol-specific.

   MSG_NOSIGNAL - Requests not to send the SIGPIPE signal if an attempt to send is made on a stream-oriented socket that is no longer connected. The [EPIPE] error shall still be returned.

   MSG_EOR - Terminates a record (if supported by the protocol).

Note that a successful completion of calling the sendto() function does not guarantee delivery of the message. For instance, the system where the receiver program is running may run out of resources and the message could be dropped on the floor even if it reaches there.

Upon successful completion, sendto() returns the number of bytes sent by the sending system. If an error was detected locally at the sending host, sendto() returns -1 and errno is set to indicate the error.

One can also use the sendto() function to send datagrams over a socket of SOCK_RAW type as well.

12-4-1-2 The recvfrom() Function

Receiving a message from a Datagram or unconnected socket is similar to sending except that the recvfrom() function is used instead. This function has the following specification:

```
#include <sys/types.h>
#include <sys/socket.h>

ssize_t recvfrom(int sockfd, void *msgbuf, size_t bufsz, int flags,
                 struct sockaddr *from_addr, socklen_t *from_len);
```

The sockfd argument provides the file descriptor of the socket being used to receive the message. Again, it must be a value returned from a successful socket() call.

The msgbuf argument gives the starting address of the input buffer used to receive the message. The bufsz argument specifies the size in bytes of the input buffer.

The flags argument specifies a set of flags. Its value can be a
logically OR'ing of zero or more of the following values:

MSG_PEEK
    Peeks at an incoming message. The data is treated as unread and the
    next recvfrom() or similar function shall still return this data.

MSG_OOB
    Requests out-of-band data. The significance and semantics of out-of-band
    data are protocol-specific.

MSG_WAITALL
    On SOCK_STREAM sockets this flag requests that the function blocks until
    the full amount of data can be returned. The function may return a
    smaller amount of data if the socket is a message-based socket,
    if a signal is caught, if the connection is terminated, if MSG_PEEK was
    specified, or if an error is pending for the socket.

If a non-NULL pointer is provided, when the function returns, the from_addr
argument will return the address of the sender of the message.
The from_len argument specifies the size of the socket structure given in
the from_addr argument. If the calling process does not need to
know or get the sender's address, a NULL pointer should be provided for
both of the from_addr and from_len arguments.

As you can see, the recvfrom() function returns the next datagram along with
the address of its sender.

The recvfrom() function returns the number of bytes that were actually
received. If an error occurred, recvfrom() returns -1 and errno is set
to indicate the error.

12-4-2 A Datagram Server

The most typical network or distributed applications are client-server
applications in which a server program services requests from many different
client programs. In this type of application, the server program starts
first and runs at a particular port number over a particular protocol on a
particular system. The server program makes its "address" known by the
clients.

The address of a server program essentially is the address of the server
socket that the server program is using which, as we said it before,
consists of an IP address, a port number and a protocol. The IP address
uniquely identifies a computer host or system on the network.
The combination of port number and protocol further uniquely identifies a
process inside that server host. This is how clients and servers on the
Internet around the globe find each other and never mess up.

So, remember this! Every server program must have and use a unique combination
of an IP address and a port number. It must also bind the server socket to
that address so that clients can find it. This is always true, be it a web
server, a ftp server, or any other type of server.

A server program can choose to use either a Stream socket (TCP protocol) or Datagram socket (UDP protocol). Again, the difference is **reliability**. A Stream socket using the TCP protocol guarantees messages are always delivered in order and no loss of packets while a Datagram socket does not.

In this section we explain how to create a Datagram Server -- a server program using a Datagram socket. We will talk about how to create a server using a Stream socket in a later section.

12-4-2-1 The bind() Function

The key thing in a server program is that it must bind itself to a socket address. Binding a server socket to a known address is common between Stream sockets and Datagram sockets. The reason is that way clients will know what server address to connect themselves to. Binding a server socket to a known address is done by invoking the bind() function.

```
#include <sys/types.h>
#include <sys/socket.h>

int  bind(int sockfd, const struct sockaddr *srvaddr, socklen_t addrlen);
```

As shown above, the bind() function takes three input arguments.

The first argument is the open file descriptor of the socket, which should be the return value of a successful call to the socket() function. The second argument specifies the address that the socket wants to bind to. The third argument is the size (in bytes) of the socket address structure given in the second argument.

For example, below is an example of binding a socket to an IPv4 address. Because it is using IPv4 protocol, the socket address is stored in a 'struct sockaddr_in' structure. The first step zeros out the entire socket address buffer. This is always a very good practice. Then it sets the protocol family to AF_INET, indicating we are creating an Internet socket for cross-system network communication.

```
struct sockaddr_in    srvaddr;  /* server's socket address */
socklen_t             srvaddrsz = sizeof(struct sockaddr_in);
in_port_t             portnum = 2345; /* server's port number */
int                   sfd, ret;

sfd = socket(AF_INET, SOCK_DGRAM, 0);

memset((void *)&srvaddr, 0, (size_t)srvaddrsz); /* clear address buffer */
srvaddr.sin_family = AF_INET;        /* Internet socket with IPv4 address  */
srvaddr.sin_addr.s_addr = htonl(INADDR_ANY); /* bind to wildcard address */
srvaddr.sin_port = htons(portnum);     /* server's port number */

if ((ret = bind(sfd, (struct sockaddr *)&srvaddr, srvaddrsz)) != 0) {
  fprintf(stderr, "error: bind() failed, errno=%d\n",  errno);
  exit(-1);
}
```

The step after sets the IP address of the socket to be htonl(INADDR_ANY). IP address **INADDR_ANY** is a **wildcard**; it has a value of zero. Note that this is very standard. For a server socket, typically you want to bind it to the wildcard IP address 0, meaning **any incoming client requests arriving at any network interfaces on this host will be accepted.**

The wild card IP address makes it very simple and very convenient for engineers. Without it, each server program would have to take an IP address as input before it can start because the IP address of each computer is different and is not known in advance when engineers are developing the software. This makes it easy to develop server programs that can run on any computer without knowing its IP address in advance.

Notice that while a server program can use the wildcard address as its own IP address for binding, a client program cannot specify the wildcard address as the server's IP address unless the server program it is talking to is running on the same computer. In other words, if the client and server programs are running on two different computers, the client must know and use a specific server IP address in the server's socket address in order to reach it. If a client knows only the host name of the server, it can convert the hostname into an IP address using the getaddrinfo() function, which we will introduce in a later section.

Applying the htonl() function to a network address is also very standard practice too. It takes care of the endianness discrepancy between the computers communicating with each other -- the byte order issue. We will further discuss this in the next section.

The fourth step sets the port number of the server socket. Ideally, this port number should be one reserved specifically for this application in the system's /etc/services file. If not, it should be a number that is known between the server and its clients and it is not being used by any other applications.

These four steps of setting a server socket's address are very standard.

Please notice that only a server program must bind its socket. A client program never needs to bind its socket.

Figures 12-8a and 12-8b list a pair of client and server programs that exchange messages using Datagram sockets.

Figure 12-8 A pair of client-server programs using Datagram sockets

(a) A server program using Datagram sockets (udpsrv.c)

```
/*
 * A connectionless server program using Datagram socket.
 * Usage: udpsrv [port#]
 * Authored by Mr. Jin-Jwei Chen.
 * Copyright (c) 1993-2018, 2020 Mr. Jin-Jwei Chen. All rights reserved.
 */

#include <stdio.h>
#include <errno.h>
#include <sys/types.h>
#include <sys/socket.h>
#include <netinet/in.h>      /* protocols such as IPPROTO_TCP, ... */
```

```c
#include <string.h>          /* memset() */
#include <stdlib.h>          /* atoi() */
#include <unistd.h>          /* close() */

#define  BUFLEN      1024    /* size of message buffer */
#define  DEFSRVPORT  2345    /* default server port number */

int main(int argc, char *argv[])
{
  int    ret, portnum_in=0;
  int    sfd;                          /* file descriptor of the socket */
  struct sockaddr_in    srvaddr;    /* socket structure */
  int    srvaddrsz=sizeof(struct sockaddr_in);
  struct sockaddr_in    clntaddr;   /* socket structure */
  socklen_t    clntaddrsz=sizeof(struct sockaddr_in);
  in_port_t    portnum=DEFSRVPORT; /* port number */
  char   inbuf[BUFLEN];               /* input message buffer */
  char   outbuf[BUFLEN];              /* output message buffer */
  size_t    msglen;                   /* length of reply message */

  fprintf(stdout, "Connectionless server program ...\n");

  /* Get the port number from user, if any. */
  if (argc > 1)
    portnum_in = atoi(argv[1]);
  if (portnum_in <= 0)
  {
    fprintf(stderr, "Port number %d invalid, set to default value %u\n",
      portnum_in, DEFSRVPORT);
    portnum = DEFSRVPORT;
  }
  else
    portnum = portnum_in;

  /* Create the Datagram server socket. */
  if ((sfd = socket(AF_INET, SOCK_DGRAM, 0)) < 0)
  {
    fprintf(stderr, "Error: socket() failed, errno=%d, %s\n", errno,
      strerror(errno));
    return(-1);
  }

  /* Fill in the server socket address. */
  memset((void *)&srvaddr, 0, (size_t)srvaddrsz); /* clear the address buffer */
  srvaddr.sin_family = AF_INET;                    /* Internet socket */
  srvaddr.sin_addr.s_addr = htonl(INADDR_ANY);    /* server's IP address */
  srvaddr.sin_port = htons(portnum);              /* server's port number */

  /* Bind the server socket to its address. */
  if ((ret = bind(sfd, (struct sockaddr *)&srvaddr, srvaddrsz)) != 0)
  {
    fprintf(stderr, "Error: bind() failed, errno=%d, %s\n", errno,
      strerror(errno));
    close(sfd);
    return(-2);
  }
```

```
/* Set the reply message */
sprintf(outbuf, "%s", "This is a reply from the server program.");
msglen = strlen(outbuf);

fprintf(stdout, "Listening at port number %u ...\n", portnum);

/* Receive and service requests from clients. */
while (1)
{
  /* Receive a request from a client. */
  errno = 0;
  inbuf[0] = '\0';
  ret = recvfrom(sfd, inbuf, BUFLEN, 0, (struct sockaddr *)&clntaddr,
         &clntaddrsz);
  if (ret > 0)
  {
    /* Process the request. We simply print the request message here. */
    inbuf[ret] = '\0';
    fprintf(stdout, "\nReceived the following request from client:\n%s\n",
      inbuf);

    /* Send a reply. */
    errno = 0;
    ret = sendto(sfd, outbuf, msglen, 0, (struct sockaddr *)&clntaddr,
      clntaddrsz);
    if (ret == -1)
      fprintf(stderr, "Error: sendto() failed, errno=%d, %s\n", errno,
        strerror(errno));
    else
      fprintf(stdout, "%u of %lu bytes of the reply was sent.\n", ret, msglen);
  }
  else if (ret < 0)
    fprintf(stderr, "Error: recvfrom() failed, errno=%d, %s\n", errno,
      strerror(errno));
  else
    fprintf(stdout, "The client may have disconnected.\n");
}  /* while */
}
```

(b) A client program using Datagram sockets (udpclnt.c)

```
/*
 * A connectionless client program using Datagram socket.
 * Usage: udpclnt [srvport# [server-ipaddress]]
 * Authored by Mr. Jin-Jwei Chen.
 * Copyright (c) 1993-2018, 2020 Mr. Jin-Jwei Chen. All rights reserved.
 */

#include <stdio.h>
#include <errno.h>
#include <sys/types.h>
#include <sys/socket.h>
#include <netinet/in.h>     /* protocols such as IPPROTO_TCP, ... */
#include <arpa/inet.h>      /* inet_pton() */
#include <string.h>         /* memset() */
```

```
#include <stdlib.h>          /* atoi() */
#include <unistd.h>          /* close(), sleep() */

#define  BUFLEN         1024    /* size of input message buffer */
#define  DEFSRVPORT     2345    /* default server port number */
#define  MAXMSGS        3       /* Maximum number of messages to send */
#define  IPV4LOCALADDR "127.0.0.1"  /* IPv4 address for local host */

int main(int argc, char *argv[])
{
  int    ret, portnum_in=0;
  int    sfd;                          /* file descriptor of the socket */
  struct sockaddr_in    srvaddr;       /* socket structure */
  int    srvaddrsz=sizeof(struct sockaddr_in);
  struct sockaddr_in    fromaddr;      /* socket structure */
  socklen_t fromaddrsz=sizeof(struct sockaddr_in);
  in_port_t portnum=DEFSRVPORT;        /* port number */
  char     inbuf[BUFLEN];              /* input message buffer */
  char     outbuf[BUFLEN];             /* output message buffer */
  size_t   msglen;                     /* length of reply message */
  size_t   msgnum=0;                   /* count of request message */
  char *ipaddrstr = IPV4LOCALADDR;     /* IP address in string format */
  in_addr_t ipaddrbin;                 /* IP address in binary format */

  fprintf(stdout, "Connectionless client program ...\n");

  /* Get the port number from user, if any. */
  if (argc > 1)
  {
    portnum_in = atoi(argv[1]);
    if (portnum_in <= 0)
    {
      fprintf(stderr, "Port number %d invalid, set to default value %u\n",
        portnum_in, DEFSRVPORT);
      portnum = DEFSRVPORT;
    }
    else
      portnum = (in_port_t)portnum_in;
  }

  /* Get the server's or peer's IP address from user, if any. */
  if (argc > 2)
    ipaddrstr = argv[2];

  /* Convert the server/peer IP address from string format to binary */
  ret = inet_pton(AF_INET, ipaddrstr, &ipaddrbin);
  if (ret == 0)
  {
    fprintf(stderr, "%s is not a valid IP address.\n", ipaddrstr);
    return(-1);
  }

  /* Create the client socket. */
  if ((sfd = socket(AF_INET, SOCK_DGRAM, 0)) < 0)
  {
    fprintf(stderr, "Error: socket() failed, errno=%d, %s\n", errno,
```

```
      strerror(errno));
   return(-2);
}

/* Fill in the server's address. */
memset((void *)&srvaddr, 0, (size_t)srvaddrsz); /* clear the address buffer */
srvaddr.sin_family = AF_INET;                    /* Internet socket */
if (ipaddrstr)
   srvaddr.sin_addr.s_addr = ipaddrbin;          /* server/peer is remote */
else
   srvaddr.sin_addr.s_addr = htonl(INADDR_ANY);  /* server/peer is local */
srvaddr.sin_port = htons(portnum);               /* server's port number */

fprintf(stdout, "Send request messages to server(%s) at port %d\n",
   ipaddrstr, portnum);

/* Send request messages to the server and process the reply messages */
while (msgnum < MAXMSGS)
{
   /* Send a request message to the server. */
   sprintf(outbuf, "%s%4lu%s", "This is request message ", ++msgnum,
      " from the client program.");
   msglen = strlen(outbuf);
   errno = 0;

   ret = sendto(sfd, outbuf, msglen, 0, (struct sockaddr *)&srvaddr, srvaddrsz);
   if (ret >= 0)
   {
      /* Print a warning if not entire message was sent. */
      if (ret == msglen)
        fprintf(stdout, "\n%lu bytes of message were successfully sent.\n",
          msglen);
      else if (ret < msglen)
        fprintf(stderr, "Warning: only %u of %lu bytes were sent.\n",
          ret, msglen);

      if (ret > 0)
      {
         /* Receive a reply from the server. */
         errno = 0;
         inbuf[0] = '\0';
         ret = recvfrom(sfd, inbuf, BUFLEN, 0, (struct sockaddr *)&fromaddr,
              &fromaddrsz);

         if (ret > 0)
         {
            /* Process the reply. */
            inbuf[ret] = '\0';
            fprintf(stdout, "Received the following reply from server:\n%s\n",
               inbuf);
         }
         else if (ret == 0)
            fprintf(stdout, "Warning: Zero bytes were received.\n");
         else
            fprintf(stderr, "Error: recvfrom() failed, errno=%d, %s\n", errno,
              strerror(errno));
```

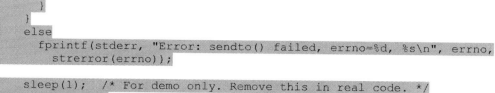

```
        }
    }
    else
        fprintf(stderr, "Error: sendto() failed, errno=%d, %s\n", errno,
            strerror(errno));

    sleep(1);  /* For demo only. Remove this in real code. */
}  /* while */

close(sfd);
return(0);
}
```

As you can see, writing a pair of client and server programs to exchange messages isn't really that hard.

For applications that need to be simple, flexible, low overhead, and 100% reliability is not required, Datagram sockets are very good candidates. For example, the standard network management protocol SNMP (Simple Network Management Protocol) is all based on UDP datagrams. Some applications use Datagram sockets to send heartbeat messages between collaborating systems as well to let other systems know that I'm still alive, although others use Stream sockets to do this. The famous Network File System (NFS) developed at Sun Microsystems started out with using Datagram sockets too.

Since connectionless communication is message oriented and no connection is established, if one side crashes or dies, all is needed is to reboot and re-start it. When it comes back up online, business resumes as normal. The other side may not even notice its peer has disappeared and come back. Nor does it need to restart. In other words, crashes on one side usually doesn't affect the other side. It won't be this clean and easy in recovering if it is a connection-oriented communication.

12-4-2-2 Cross Platform Support

Socket programs normally are pretty portable across all flavors of Linux and Unix platforms at the socket API level (thanks to the POSIX Standard), although you will find they sometimes still differ a little bit between these platforms in behavior and parameter types of some API as well as support of some socket options.

Windows has some more differences than these platforms, particularly in setup and closing down as well as include files. We will discuss these differences in a later section.

For readers using the Windows platform, Figure 12-8c-d is a version of udpclnt.c and udpsrv.c that works on multiple platforms including Windows.

Figure 12-8c, 12-8d Datagram client-server application supporting multiple platforms -- udpsrv_all.c and udpclnt_all.c

(c) udpsrv_all.c

```
/*
```

```c
 * A connectionless server program using Datagram socket.
 * Usage: udpsrv_all [port#]
 * Authored by Mr. Jin-Jwei Chen.
 * Copyright (c) 1993-2020, Mr. Jin-Jwei Chen. All rights reserved.
 */

#include "mysocket.h"

int main(int argc, char *argv[])
{
  int     ret, portnum_in=0;
  int     sfd;                        /* file descriptor of the socket */
  struct sockaddr_in    srvaddr;      /* socket structure */
  int     srvaddrsz=sizeof(struct sockaddr_in);
  struct sockaddr_in    clntaddr;     /* socket structure */
  socklen_t    clntaddrsz=sizeof(struct sockaddr_in);
  in_port_t    portnum=DEFSRVPORT;    /* port number */
  char    inbuf[BUFLEN];              /* input message buffer */
  char    outbuf[BUFLEN];             /* output message buffer */
  size_t    msglen;                   /* length of reply message */
#if WINDOWS
  WSADATA wsaData;                    /* Winsock data */
  char* GetErrorMsg(int ErrorCode);   /* print error string in Windows */
#endif

  fprintf(stdout, "Connectionless server program ...\n");

  /* Get the port number from user, if any. */
  if (argc > 1)
    portnum_in = atoi(argv[1]);
  if (portnum_in <= 0)
  {
    fprintf(stderr, "Port number %d invalid, set to default value %u\n",
      portnum_in, DEFSRVPORT);
    portnum = DEFSRVPORT;
  }
  else
    portnum = portnum_in;

#if WINDOWS
  /* Initiate use of the Winsock DLL. Ask for Winsock version 2.2 at least. */
  if ((ret = WSAStartup(MAKEWORD(2, 2), &wsaData)) != 0)
  {
    fprintf(stderr, "Error: WSAStartup() failed with error %d: %s\n",
      ret, GetErrorMsg(ret));
    return (-1);
  }
#endif

  /* Create the Datagram server socket. */
  if ((sfd = socket(AF_INET, SOCK_DGRAM, 0)) < 0)
  {
    fprintf(stderr, "Error: socket() failed, errno=%d, %s\n", ERRNO,
      ERRNOSTR);
#if WINDOWS
    WSACleanup();
```

```
#endif
    return(-2);
  }

  /* Fill in the server socket address. */
  memset((void *)&srvaddr, 0, (size_t)srvaddrsz); /* clear the address buffer */
  srvaddr.sin_family = AF_INET;                    /* Internet socket */
  srvaddr.sin_addr.s_addr = htonl(INADDR_ANY);     /* server's IP address */
  srvaddr.sin_port = htons(portnum);               /* server's port number */

  /* Bind the server socket to its address. */
  if ((ret = bind(sfd, (struct sockaddr *)&srvaddr, srvaddrsz)) != 0)
  {
    fprintf(stderr, "Error: bind() failed, errno=%d, %s\n", ERRNO,
      ERRNOSTR);
    CLOSE(sfd);
    return(-3);
  }

  /* Set the reply message */
  sprintf(outbuf, "%s", "This is a reply from the server program.");
  msglen = strlen(outbuf);

  fprintf(stdout, "Listening at port number %u ...\n", portnum);

  /* Receive and service requests from clients. */
  while (1)
  {
    /* Receive a request from a client. */
    errno = 0;
    inbuf[0] = '\0';
    ret = recvfrom(sfd, inbuf, BUFLEN, 0, (struct sockaddr *)&clntaddr,
          &clntaddrsz);
    if (ret > 0)
    {
      /* Process the request. We simply print the request message here. */
      inbuf[ret] = '\0';
      fprintf(stdout, "\nReceived the following request from client:\n%s\n",
        inbuf);

      /* Send a reply. */
      errno = 0;
      ret = sendto(sfd, outbuf, msglen, 0, (struct sockaddr *)&clntaddr,
        clntaddrsz);
      if (ret == -1)
        fprintf(stderr, "Error: sendto() failed, errno=%d, %s\n", ERRNO,
          ERRNOSTR);
      else
        fprintf(stdout, "%u of %lu bytes of the reply was sent.\n", ret, msglen);
    }
    else if (ret < 0)
      fprintf(stderr, "Error: recvfrom() failed, errno=%d, %s\n", ERRNO,
        ERRNOSTR);
    else
      fprintf(stdout, "The client may have disconnected.\n");
  }  /* while */
```

```
}

    (d) udpclnt_all.c

/*
 * A connectionless client program using Datagram socket.
 * Usage: udpclnt_all [srvport# [server-ipaddress]]
 * Authored by Mr. Jin-Jwei Chen.
 * Copyright (c) 1993-2019, 2020 Mr. Jin-Jwei Chen. All rights reserved.
 */

#include "mysocket.h"

int main(int argc, char *argv[])
{
  int     ret, portnum_in=0;
  int     sfd;                        /* file descriptor of the socket */
  struct sockaddr_in    srvaddr;      /* socket structure */
  int     srvaddrsz=sizeof(struct sockaddr_in);
  struct sockaddr_in    fromaddr;     /* socket structure */
  socklen_t fromaddrsz=sizeof(struct sockaddr_in);
  in_port_t portnum=DEFSRVPORT;       /* port number */
  char      inbuf[BUFLEN];            /* input message buffer */
  char      outbuf[BUFLEN];           /* output message buffer */
  size_t    msglen;                   /* length of reply message */
  size_t    msgnum=0;                 /* count of request message */
  char *ipaddrstr = IPV4LOCALADDR;    /* IP address in string format */
  in_addr_t ipaddrbin;                /* IP address in binary format */
#if WINDOWS
  WSADATA wsaData;                    /* Winsock data */
  char* GetErrorMsg(int ErrorCode);   /* print error string in Windows */
#endif

  fprintf(stdout, "Connectionless client program ...\n");

  /* Get the port number from user, if any. */
  if (argc > 1)
  {
    portnum_in = atoi(argv[1]);
    if (portnum_in <= 0)
    {
      fprintf(stderr, "Port number %d invalid, set to default value %u\n",
        portnum_in, DEFSRVPORT);
      portnum = DEFSRVPORT;
    }
    else
      portnum = (in_port_t)portnum_in;
  }

  /* Get the server's or peer's IP address from user, if any. */
  if (argc > 2)
    ipaddrstr = argv[2];

#if WINDOWS
  /* Initiate use of the Winsock DLL. Ask for Winsock version 2.2 at least. */
  if ((ret = WSAStartup(MAKEWORD(2, 2), &wsaData)) != 0)
```

707

```
  {
    fprintf(stderr, "Error: WSAStartup() failed with error %d: %s\n",
      ret, GetErrorMsg(ret));
    return (-1);
  }
#endif

  /* Convert the server/peer IP address from string format to binary */
  ret = inet_pton(AF_INET, ipaddrstr, &ipaddrbin);
  if (ret == 0)
  {
    fprintf(stderr, "%s is not a valid IP address.\n", ipaddrstr);
#if WINDOWS
    WSACleanup();
#endif
    return(-2);
  }

  /* Create the client socket. */
  if ((sfd = socket(AF_INET, SOCK_DGRAM, 0)) < 0)
  {
    fprintf(stderr, "Error: socket() failed, errno=%d, %s\n", ERRNO, ERRNOSTR);
#if WINDOWS
    WSACleanup();
#endif
    return(-3);
  }

  /* Fill in the server's address. */
  memset((void *)&srvaddr, 0, (size_t)srvaddrsz); /* clear the address buffer */
  srvaddr.sin_family = AF_INET;                   /* Internet socket */
  if (ipaddrstr)
    srvaddr.sin_addr.s_addr = ipaddrbin;          /* server/peer is remote */
  else
    srvaddr.sin_addr.s_addr = htonl(INADDR_ANY);  /* server/peer is local */
  srvaddr.sin_port = htons(portnum);              /* server's port number */

  fprintf(stdout, "Send request messages to server(%s) at port %d\n",
    ipaddrstr, portnum);

  /* Send request messages to the server and process the reply messages */
  while (msgnum < MAXMSGS)
  {
    /* Send a request message to the server. */
    sprintf(outbuf, "%s%4lu%s", "This is request message ", ++msgnum,
      " from the client program.");
    msglen = strlen(outbuf);
    errno = 0;

    ret = sendto(sfd, outbuf, msglen, 0, (struct sockaddr *)&srvaddr, srvaddrsz);
    if (ret >= 0)
    {
      /* Print a warning if not entire message was sent. */
      if (ret == msglen)
        fprintf(stdout, "\n%lu bytes of message were successfully sent.\n",
          msglen);
```

```
    else if (ret < msglen)
        fprintf(stderr, "Warning: only %u of %lu bytes were sent.\n",
            ret, msglen);

    if (ret > 0)
    {
        /* Receive a reply from the server. */
        errno = 0;
        inbuf[0] = '\0';
        ret = recvfrom(sfd, inbuf, BUFLEN, 0, (struct sockaddr *)&fromaddr,
            &fromaddrsz);

        if (ret > 0)
        {
            /* Process the reply. */
            inbuf[ret] = '\0';
            fprintf(stdout, "Received the following reply from server:\n%s\n",
                inbuf);
        }
        else if (ret == 0)
            fprintf(stdout, "Warning: Zero bytes were received.\n");
        else
            fprintf(stderr, "Error: recvfrom() failed, errno=%d, %s\n", ERRNO,
                ERRNOSTR);
    }
    else
        fprintf(stderr, "Error: sendto() failed, errno=%d, %s\n", ERRNO,
            ERRNOSTR);

#if WINDOWS
    Sleep(1000); /* Unit is ms. For demo only. Remove this in real code. */
#else
    sleep(1);    /* For demo only. Remove this in real code. */
#endif
  } /* while */

  CLOSE(sfd);
  return(0);
}
```

12-4-3 Using connect() Call on Datagram Sockets

As we have said and demonstrated above, to exchange messages between two communication endpoints using Datagram sockets, there is no connection established or needed. This means neither side ever needs to invoke the connect() function, which is mainly used in the connection-oriented communication to be discussed in the next section.

Nonetheless, it is legitimate to use the connect() function with a Datagram socket.

Earlier we said a program uses the sendto() function to send a message from a Datagram socket. Each sendto() call specifies a destination socket address which says where the current message is going to. This means a program can use the same Datagram socket to send messages to different recipients at different socket addresses. Very flexible, isn't it?

If a program using a Datagram socket always communicates with the same target/peer, then it may invoke the connect() function to specify and fix the destination address once for all instead of having to specify it every single time in the sendto() function.

When used with a Datagram socket, the connect() call associates a socket with a specific target or peer address. The socket address specified in the connect() call will be the default target address that every message sent through the current socket is addressed to and the only source address that this socket will receive messages from.

In other words, calling the connect() function once before using a Datagram socket waives the caller from having to specify the target address in each sendto() call.

It's worth pointing out that a program can call the connect() function more than once to switch to a different target/peer after it is done communicating with the current one.

In addition, invoking the connect() function on a Datagram socket transforms the socket into a connected state. And that makes it legitimate for the program to use the send(), recv(), read() and write() functions to send and receive messages on the Datagram socket, as opposed to using sendto() and recvfrom().

Figure 12-9 displays an example of using connect() with a Datagram socket. This program is a slight change from the udpclnt_all.c shown above. It can be tested with the udpsrv_all.c.

You can see that with the addition of a connect() call before sendto(), now the sendto() does not need to specify a target socket address anymore.

Figure 12-9 Use connect() on a Datagram socket (udpclnt_conn_all.c)

```
/*
 * A connectionless client program using connect() with Datagram socket.
 * Usage: udpclnt_conn_all [srvport# [server-ipaddress]]
 * Authored by Mr. Jin-Jwei Chen.
 * Copyright (c) 1993-2019, 2020 Mr. Jin-Jwei Chen. All rights reserved.
 */

#include "mysocket.h"

int main(int argc, char *argv[])
{
    int     ret, portnum_in=0;
    int     sfd;                        /* file descriptor of the socket */
    struct sockaddr_in    srvaddr;      /* socket structure */
    int     srvaddrsz=sizeof(struct sockaddr_in);
    struct sockaddr_in    fromaddr;     /* socket structure */
    socklen_t fromaddrsz=sizeof(struct sockaddr_in);
    in_port_t portnum=DEFSRVPORT;       /* port number */
    char      inbuf[BUFLEN];            /* input message buffer */
```

```
  char        outbuf[BUFLEN];              /* output message buffer */
  size_t      msglen;                      /* length of reply message */
  size_t      msgnum=0;                    /* count of request message */
  char *ipaddrstr = IPV4LOCALADDR;         /* IP address in string format */
  in_addr_t ipaddrbin;                     /* IP address in binary format */
#if WINDOWS
  WSADATA wsaData;                         /* Winsock data */
  char* GetErrorMsg(int ErrorCode);        /* print error string in Windows */
#endif

  fprintf(stdout, "Connectionless client program ...\n");

  /* Get the port number from user, if any. */
  if (argc > 1)
  {
    portnum_in = atoi(argv[1]);
    if (portnum_in <= 0)
    {
      fprintf(stderr, "Port number %d invalid, set to default value %u\n",
        portnum_in, DEFSRVPORT);
      portnum = DEFSRVPORT;
    }
    else
      portnum = (in_port_t)portnum_in;
  }

  /* Get the server's or peer's IP address from user, if any. */
  if (argc > 2)
    ipaddrstr = argv[2];

#if WINDOWS
  /* Initiate use of the Winsock DLL. Ask for Winsock version 2.2 at least. */
  if ((ret = WSAStartup(MAKEWORD(2, 2), &wsaData)) != 0)
  {
    fprintf(stderr, "Error: WSAStartup() failed with error %d: %s\n",
      ret, GetErrorMsg(ret));
    return (-1);
  }
#endif

  /* Convert the server/peer IP address from string format to binary */
  ret = inet_pton(AF_INET, ipaddrstr, &ipaddrbin);
  if (ret == 0)
  {
    fprintf(stderr, "%s is not a valid IP address.\n", ipaddrstr);
#if WINDOWS
    WSACleanup();
#endif
    return(-2);
  }

  /* Create the client socket. */
  if ((sfd = socket(AF_INET, SOCK_DGRAM, 0)) < 0)
  {
    fprintf(stderr, "Error: socket() failed, errno=%d, %s\n", ERRNO, ERRNOSTR);
#if WINDOWS
```

```
    WSACleanup();
#endif
    return(-3);
  }

  /* Fill in the server's address. */
  memset((void *)&srvaddr, 0, (size_t)srvaddrsz); /* clear the address buffer */
  srvaddr.sin_family = AF_INET;                    /* Internet socket */
  if (ipaddrstr)
    srvaddr.sin_addr.s_addr = ipaddrbin;           /* server/peer is remote */
  else
    srvaddr.sin_addr.s_addr = htonl(INADDR_ANY);  /* server/peer is local */
  srvaddr.sin_port = htons(portnum);               /* server's port number */

  /* Fix our target/peer address */
  ret = connect(sfd, (struct sockaddr *)&srvaddr, srvaddrsz);
  if (ret != 0)
  {
    fprintf(stderr, "Error: connect() failed, errno=%d, %s\n", ERRNO, ERRNOSTR);
    CLOSE(sfd);
    return(-4);
  }

  fprintf(stdout, "Send request messages to server(%s) at port %d\n",
    ipaddrstr, portnum);

  /* Send request messages to the server and process the reply messages */
  while (msgnum < MAXMSGS)
  {
    /* Send a request message to the server. */
    sprintf(outbuf, "%s%4lu%s", "This is request message ", ++msgnum,
      " from the client program.");
    msglen = strlen(outbuf);
    errno = 0;

    ret = sendto(sfd, outbuf, msglen, 0, (struct sockaddr *)NULL, 0);
    if (ret >= 0)
    {
      /* Print a warning if not entire message was sent. */
      if (ret == msglen)
        fprintf(stdout, "\n%lu bytes of message were successfully sent.\n",
          msglen);
      else if (ret < msglen)
        fprintf(stderr, "Warning: only %u of %lu bytes were sent.\n",
          ret, msglen);

      if (ret > 0)
      {
        /* Receive a reply from the server. */
        errno = 0;
        inbuf[0] = '\0';
        ret = recvfrom(sfd, inbuf, BUFLEN, 0, (struct sockaddr *)&fromaddr,
          &fromaddrsz);

        if (ret > 0)
        {
```

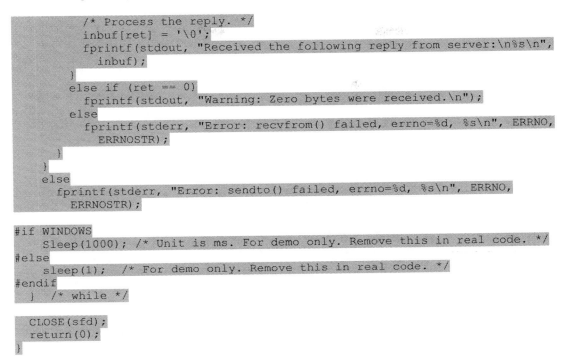

```
        /* Process the reply. */
        inbuf[ret] = '\0';
        fprintf(stdout, "Received the following reply from server:\n%s\n",
            inbuf);
      }
      else if (ret == 0)
        fprintf(stdout, "Warning: Zero bytes were received.\n");
      else
        fprintf(stderr, "Error: recvfrom() failed, errno=%d, %s\n", ERRNO,
            ERRNOSTR);
    }
  }
  else
    fprintf(stderr, "Error: sendto() failed, errno=%d, %s\n", ERRNO,
        ERRNOSTR);

#if WINDOWS
    Sleep(1000); /* Unit is ms. For demo only. Remove this in real code. */
#else
    sleep(1);   /* For demo only. Remove this in real code. */
#endif
  } /* while */

  CLOSE(sfd);
  return(0);
}
```

12-5 Wildcard Server Address and Endian

Knowing how to develop a socket-based client-server application,
let us next discuss the wildcard server IP address and the byte order
a bit further. These issues are common to all types of communications.

12-5-1 Wildcard Server Address

We just said in the last section that binding a server program to the wild
card IP address is a very standard practice.

Note that this is very different from binding the server socket to the
loopback local host address "127.0.0.1". Therefore, don't mix up the two.

To re-emphasize, binding a server socket to the wildcard IP address allows
client connect requests arriving at any network interfaces available on
the computer to get to the server program.

This is very useful and convenient because many computers often have multiple
network adapters and interfaces and thus have multiple IP addresses for
clients to get to. Having a way for the server program to specify "any"
comes very handy.

Indeed, there are "two" wildcard IP addresses, one for IPv4 and the other
for IPv6. The wildcard IP address is **INADDR_ANY** for IPv4 and **in6addr_any**
for IPv6. Remember that this value is different between IPv4 and IPv6.
INADDR_ANY is a 4-byte value of zero. in6addr_any is a constant of type

'struct in6_addr'. Its value is 16 bytes of zero.

As a result, below is how one would set a server socket's IP address
to the wildcard IP address before invoking the bind() function:

```
/* bind to an IPv4 wildcard address - four bytes of zero */
serveraddr.sin_addr.s_addr = htonl(INADDR_ANY);

/* bind to an IPv6 wildcard address - 16 bytes of zero */
serveraddr.sin6_addr   = in6addr_any;
```

Binding a server socket to the wildcard server address or a well-known
server address is common to both connectionless and connection-oriented
network communications. It applies to server programs using Datagram
or Stream sockets. It is independent of socket types.

12-5-2 Endianness and Byte Order Conversion

Please be reminded that this topic discussed here applies to both
connectionless and connection-oriented network communications, too.

What Is Endian?

Computer processors (CPUs) in the world have two major flavors in terms of
how they store a multi-byte integer in memory, the so-called **endianness**
or **byte-ordering**.

The big-endian processors store the most significant byte first in the
lowest memory byte address while the little-endian processors do exactly
the opposite, storing the least significant byte first -- in the lowest
memory byte address.

Examples of big-endian processors include IBM Power and PowerPC processors,
Oracle/Sun SPARC processors, and HP PARISC processors.
Examples of little-endian processors include Intel x86 and HP/DEC Alpha
processors.

Why Is Endianness Important?

Endianness, or byte-ordering, is very important in distributed computing.
When two computers communicate and exchange information, one computer can be
big-endian and the other little-endian. Because they store and thus interpret
integers stored in binary form differently, unless conversion is done,
an integer of a certain value can be interpreted as a completely
different value when it is sent across network from one computer to another.
For example, the integer value 2345 sent from a big-endian computer will be
interpreted as integer 10505 if it is received on a little-endian computer
and no byte-order conversion is done.

To solve this problem, the design of Internet uses a convention that all
binary integers should travel in a single known endian format when they are
sent across the network to ensure correct interpretation of the data at the
receiving end. This means all **multi-byte binary integers** must be converted
to the **network byte order**, which is indeed the **big-endian** byte order, before
they are sent across the network. And the receiver program must then

convert the binary integers it receives from the network byte order to its local, native host byte order. This way, sending integer values across network is guaranteed to work correctly even if the sending computer has a different endian format than the receiving one.

Remember that the Internet uses the network byte order which is really the big-endian byte order in all implementations.

To address the endian issue, the following functions are designed for performing host and network byte order conversions. The letter 'h' in the function names stands for 'host' or 'host byte order' and the letter 'n' stands for 'network' or 'network byte order'. In other words, hton stands for 'from host format to network format' and ntoh stands for 'from network format to host format'.

```
#include <arpa/inet.h>

uint16_t htons(uint16_t hostshort);

uint32_t htonl(uint32_t hostlong);

uint16_t ntohs(uint16_t netshort);

uint32_t ntohl(uint32_t netlong);
```

The htons() and htonl() functions convert a 2-byte and 4-byte integer from the local host byte order to the network byte order, respectively. They are typically used in programs sending integer data over network. Conversely, the ntohs() and ntohl() functions convert a 2-byte and 4-byte integer from the network byte order back to the local host's byte order, respectively. They are typically used by programs receiving binary integer data from network.

Since one never knows whether the integer data a program sends is going to be received by another computer with the same endianness or not, and a program receiving an integer data does not know whether the data originates from a computer with the same endianness or not, the only way to guarantee that it will always work is to always invoke the htons() or htonl() on the integer data being sent and always invoke the ntohs() or ntohl() on the received integer data to retrieve it.

That said, it is very important that you always remember to do the endian conversions when you write programs to send or receive binary integer data that is longer than one byte. A single-byte integer value needs no byte order conversion at all because it's just one byte long and hence there is no byte ordering or swapping involved. In addition, string data requires no byte order conversions either because string data is usually encoded in a byte-oriented encoding scheme such as ASCII or UTF-8. Therefore, it is not subject to the endian issue. The endian issue applies only to sending (or writing) and receiving (or reading) **multiple-byte integer data stored in binary format.** This is why we use htons(portnumber) and htonl(INADDR_ANY) in our program examples.

What data items need to be converted? In computer communication using sockets, the data an application program sends across the wire needs to be converted if it contains multi-byte binary integer data. In addition, at the socket level, the socket structure containing the IP address and port number that identifies the communicating entity is sent across network, too. Since the IP address itself and the port number are both integers stored in binary form, they are endian specific and must be endian converted, too. This is because the computer receiving the entire structure could be one that has a completely different endianness. Therefore, in order for the receiving computer to be able to interpret the IP address and the port number correctly, these values must be sent in network byte order format. Using the htonl() function around the IP address and htons() function on the port number does just that.

Note that using the htonl() function on INADDR_ANY is a bit redundant because its value is 0. A value of zero is byte order neutral because its value remains 0 no matter how you swap its bytes. In other words, a value of 0 is always interpreted as 0 in both big-endian and little-endian processors. However, in case the IP address is not zero, using the htonl() function is necessary.

There is no byte-order conversion function defined for in6addr_any because it is 16-byte long and is defined as a structure rather than an integer. Plus, you don't really need one because a value with every byte zero is byte-order neutral, no matter how long it is. So, you really don't need to do byte-order conversion on in6addr_any.

Note that this byte order or endianness conversion does not happen automatically anywhere. It is the **responsibility of every programmer** to be aware of the endianness issue in sending integer values across the network and to always make sure multi-byte binary integer data are converted whenever needed such that they can be correctly interpreted by the receiver of the data in every data exchange and communication.

Also remember that the byte order conversion discussed here in this section apply to both Datagram and Stream sockets. It is independent of the type of the socket. It is related to the byte order formats of the computer processors executing the program code at both ends of a communication or data transfer.

12-6 Connection-Oriented Communication Using Stream Sockets

As we mentioned before, connectionless network communication using Datagram sockets, which uses the underlying UDP transport protocol, is flexible and easy to set up and use. However, it may not be 100% reliable. Because of that, most distributed applications tend to use connection-oriented communication based on the TCP transport protocol. The web protocols HTTP and HTTPS and the file transfer protocol ftp are among the most typical examples of connection-oriented network communication.

Compared to connectionless communication, connection-oriented communication requires a connection between the two communicating parties being set up. It is a bit more complicated, is slightly harder to set up, and still occupies the reserved system resources until the connection is closed even when there is no actual data exchanges going on. But it is reliable. Applications don't need to worry about issues like packets being lost, damaged, duplicated or delivered out of order.

Below is an outline of connection-oriented communication:

- Both parties must use a Stream socket.
- The server still needs to bind its socket to a known address.
- The server program must set itself up to be in the listening mode.
- The client must make a connection request to the server in an attempt to establish a connection.
- The server must accept the client's connection request to establish a connection.
- Data exchanges can then begin once a connection is established.
- send() and recv() functions are used to send and receive messages, respectively. Though write() and read() can be used as well.

We will explain each of these steps in the following sections.

12-6-1 Creating a Connection-Oriented Socket

In a connection-oriented communication using the TCP transport, both parties, whether it's a client-server, peer-to-peer, or master-slave relationship, must create a Stream socket for use in the communication. This is done by the following statement:

```
int sfd = socket(AF_INET, SOCK_STREAM, 0);
```

The first argument, AF_INET, says the caller wants an Internet socket with the IPv4 protocol at the network layer. This value would be AF_INET6 instead if the caller wants to use the IPv6 protocol.
As we stated before, using PF_INET and PF_INET6 is the same as using AF_INET and AF_INET6, respectively.

The second argument, SOCK_STREAM, denotes the caller wants to create a Stream socket. This essentially selects the TCP protocol in the transport layer.

The third argument to the socket() call specifies a particular network protocol to be used with the socket. Normally only a single protocol exists to support a particular socket type within a given protocol family, in which case protocol can be specified as 0. However, it is possible that multiple protocols could exist. In that case, this argument must specify the protocol to be used.

On success, the socket() call returns a file descriptor for the new socket just created. On error, -1 is returned and the global variable errno is set to indicate the reason for failure.

Creating a Stream socket is very similar to creating a Datagram socket. The only thing different is the type of socket you specify in the second argument of the socket() function must be SOCK_STREAM.

12-6-2 Server Advertises Itself -- The bind() Function

As we said it in the connectionless communication section above, a server program must bind its socket to a wildcard or known server address such that clients can connect to it. This is also always true for a server program in a connection-oriented communication.

The syntax of the bind() function is the same as what was introduced in the previous section.

Note that the bind() call is invoked by a server program only; never a client has to make the bind() call.

Typically, a server binds its socket to the wildcard address so that all client requests arriving at any network interfaces on the host computer can be accepted. The wildcard server address is INADDR_ANY in IPv4 and in6addr_any in IPv6. Yes, one is in upper case and the other lower.

Alternatively, a specific IP address can be used too in the bind() call. But this approach has two disadvantages. First, it "hardwires" the server program to a particular computer with that specific IP address. Consequently, the program won't be able to run on any other computers. Second, if that computer has multiple network interface cards, this may limit the server program to use only one interface card.

In addition to binding to an IP address, a server program must bind its socket to a specific port number, too. This port number further helps identify the server program within the computer.

Below is **how a server program binds its server socket to a wildcard address:**

IPv4:

```
struct sockaddr_in    serveraddr;   /* socket structure */

/* Fill in the server socket address. */
memset((void *)&serveraddr, 0, (size_t)sizeof(serveraddr)); /* clear the address
buffer */
serveraddr.sin_family = AF_INET;                /* Internet socket IPv4 */
serveraddr.sin_addr.s_addr = htonl(INADDR_ANY); /* server's IP address */
serveraddr.sin_port = htons(srvport);           /* server's port number */

/* Bind the server socket to its address. */
ret = bind(sfd, (struct sockaddr *)&serveraddr, sizeof(serveraddr));
```

IPv6:

```
struct sockaddr_in6    serveraddr;   /* socket structure */

/* Fill in the server socket address. */
memset((void *)&serveraddr, 0, (size_t)sizeof(serveraddr)); /* clear the address
buffer */
serveraddr.sin6_family = AF_INET6;         /* Internet socket IPv6 */
serveraddr.sin6_addr  = in6addr_any;       /* server's IP address */
serveraddr.sin6_port  = htons(srvport);    /* server's port number */

ret = bind(sd, (struct sockaddr *)&serveraddr, sizeof(serveraddr));
```

Unlike the connectionless communication in which a server program uses only one socket, a server program in a connection-oriented communication

typically uses multiple sockets: one listener socket for listening incoming client requests for connections and another for forming an actual connection with a client and exchanging data with that client.
If the server is having communications with multiple clients at the same time, there will be multiple client data sockets, one for each client.

When we talk about a server binding its socket with a wildcard or known address in a connection-oriented communication using Stream socket, we are actually referring to the listener socket of the server.

In a connection-oriented client-server communication, it is always the server binds its listener socket to a certain address and the client calls the connect() function to establish a connection with the server's client socket. Then messages are exchanged; that is, the client sends requests and the server replies with results. Of course, the server has to be started already when the client tries to connect, or the connect request will fail.

12-6-3 Server Accepts a Connection Request -- The accept() Function

The code of a typical server program in a connection-oriented communication has the server sitting in a loop in which it listens for incoming client connection requests, accepts a connection request, creates a thread or forks another process to service that client, and then loops again to listen for the next client connect request.

A server in a connection-oriented communication uses the accept() call to accept a client's connect request. The accept() function has the following synopsis:

```
#include <sys/types.h>
#include <sys/socket.h>

int accept(int sockfd, struct sockaddr *addr, socklen_t *addrlen);
```

Note that the accept() call is blocking. The caller is blocked by this call until a client's connect request arrives. In accepting a client connect request, the accept() call will create a new connected socket and return the file descriptor of the newly created socket. Note that the newly created socket is just a plain socket; it is not in the listening state.
Rather it is connected to the client's socket.

The first argument to the accept() call provides the file descriptor of the server's listener socket. This socket must have been bound to a local address via the bind() call.

The second argument is a pointer to a sockaddr structure.
If provided (i.e. this pointer is not null), on return this argument will contain the peer's socket address. Its actual format depends on which protocol family is being used. This socket address tells what entity the server is talking to -- at what IP address and what port number.
This saves the server program from making another call to get the peer's address.

Figure 12-10 depicts what happens when a network connection is being established. It starts from a client taking an initiative and making the connect() call in an attempt to create a connection. That request arrives at the server, picked up by the accept() call. In accepting the connect request, the accept() call creates a new socket which is connected to the client's socket and returns the file descriptor of this new socket. This allows the server to use this new socket to service the client by further receiving the client's data exchange requests and sending responses. The details about the new socket is in a connected state and who it is currently connected to are remembered in the operating system's kernel. Notice that three sockets are actually involved.

```
      client                            server
   ----------                       ------------------

   socket *                         listener socket **

   connect() ------------------> accept()
            connection request       |
      |                               v
      v                           a new socket is created ***
            <------------------->
        connection established for
        data exchanges between client
        socket and server's data socket
```

Figure 12-10 Establishing a network connection -- 3 sockets involved

12-6-4 Server Sets Its Listener Queue Length -- The listen() Function

The first socket a server program creates in a connection-oriented communication is typically the listener socket. After creating the listener socket and before entering the loop of listening for client connect requests, a server typically invokes the listen() call once to set the length of its listening queue.

In other words, below is a **typical sequence of steps of a server**:

IPv4:

```
#define BACKLOG_LEN  200
struct sockaddr_in   serveraddr;
int                  sfd, sfd2, ret;

sfd = socket(AF_INET, SOCK_STREAM, 0);
/* fill in the fields in serveraddr here ... */
ret = bind(sfd, (struct sockaddr *)&serveraddr, sizeof(serveraddr));
ret = listen(sfd, BACKLOG_LEN);
sfd2 = accept(sfd, NULL, NULL);
```

IPv6:

```
#define BACKLOG_LEN  200
struct sockaddr_in6  serveraddr;
int                  sfd, sfd2, ret;

sfd = socket(AF_INET6, SOCK_STREAM, 0);
```

```
/* fill in the fields in serveraddr here ... */
ret = bind(sfd, (struct sockaddr *)&serveraddr, sizeof(serveraddr));
ret = listen(sfd, BACKLOG_LEN);
sfd2 = accept(sfd, NULL, NULL);
```

Invoking the **listen() function** to **set the listener socket's queue length**
is important because in a real server application, very often during the
time period that a server is handling a client connect request there could
be multiple other new client connect requests arriving already.
Since the server is not ready to take these requests yet, they need to be
buffered or they will get lost. How big this buffer is **has an impact on
the server's throughput** and performance. It is one of the factors that
determine whether the server will drop incoming connect requests on the
floor or not.

The listen() function used by a server to set the length or depth of its
listener socket's buffer or queue has the following format:

```
#include <sys/socket.h>

int listen(int sockfd, int backlog);
```

The first parameter specifies the file descriptor of the server's listener
socket. The second parameter, backlog, specifies the maximum number of
incoming requests that can be buffered at the server at any time.

Apparently, a server with heavy load needs to set this queue length bigger.
Sometimes, this number can go up to thousands.

Normally two factors determine the maximum throughput of a server:
the size of this listener queue and the time it takes to service each
client. The latter is affected by the performance of the computer processor
and the amount of work that needs to be done to service each client.
Sometimes it may also be bounded by the maximum number of processes or
threads that a user is allowed to have by the operating system.
Consequently, tuning some or all of these may be necessary.

The listen() call applies only to sockets of type SOCK_STREAM or
SOCK_SEQPACKET. Both of these are connection-oriented socket types.

12-6-5 Client Initiates a Connection Request -- The connect() Function

Before messages can be exchanged, a connection between the two communication
endpoints must be established in a connection-oriented communication.
Whoever starts this process is usually called the client. The communication
starts with the client making the connect() function call to request a
connection being established with the server. The address of the server is
specified in the call.

The synopsis of the connect() function is shown below:

```
#include <sys/types.h>
#include <sys/socket.h>

int  connect(int sockfd, const struct sockaddr *srvaddr, socklen_t
```

```
                    addrlen);
```

When a program (e.g. a client) wants to establish a network connection with
another (e.g. a server) via the socket it has, it invokes the connect() call.
When used with a Stream socket, the connect() function tries to establish
a network connection between the socket, as specified in the first argument,
of the calling process and another socket to be created in the server
process whose address is specified in the second argument, srvaddr.
The size of the srvaddr (the second argument) is given in the third argument.
This size is different depending on whether an IPv4 or IPv6 socket address
is provided in the second argument.

The length and format of the address given in the srvaddr argument
depend on the address family of the socket.

Upon successful return from the connect() function, the caller has a network
connection between the specified socket and another socket at the address
identified by the srvaddr argument. Data exchanges can then begin.

If the connection request succeeds, connect() returns zero.
On error, connect() returns -1 and errno is set to indicate the error.

Below is the **first part of a client program** in a connection-oriented
communication (IPv4 version):

```
  struct sockaddr_in   server;      /* socket structure */
  in_port_t            portnum = DEFAULT_SRV_PORT; /* server's port number */
  int                  sfd, ret;

  char  *ipaddrstr = "127.0.0.1";  /* server's IP address in string format */
  in_addr_t ipaddrbin;             /* server's IP address in binary format */

  /* Create a Stream socket for the client */
  sfd = socket(AF_INET, SOCK_STREAM, 0);

  /* Fill in the server's address */
  ret = inet_aton(ipaddrstr, &ipaddrbin);
  memset((void *)&server, 0, (size_t)sizeof(server)); /* clear addr buffer */
  server.sin_family = AF_INET;                    /* Internet socket */
  if (ipaddrstr)
    server.sin_addr.s_addr = ipaddrbin;           /* server address is known */
  else
    server.sin_addr.s_addr = htonl(INADDR_ANY); /* assume server is local */
  server.sin_port = htons(portnum);             /* server's port number */

  /* Connect to the server. */
  ret = connect(sfd, (struct sockaddr *)&server, sizeof(server));
```

As you can see from the code here, a client invokes the connect() function
to connect to a server. In order to be able to connect to a server program
running on some host, a client program must know either the hostname or
IP address of the host that the server program runs on, as well as a port
number that the server program uses. The client needs to fill in these
pieces of information into the server's socket address structure before
it can use that server socket address to connect to the server.

The server's IP address uniquely identifies the computer or device in the
world that the server program runs on. And the port number uniquely
identifies the server process on that particular computer or device.

Now we understand that for one program to communicate with another using
socket, it needs to know and construct the socket address of its server
or peer socket. The socket address must contain the IP address (in binary
format) of the computer host where the server or peer socket locates as
well as a port number in order to uniquely identify that socket on the
target host.

For simplicity and just to illustrate the connect() call, here we hardwire
the server's IP address to be "127.0.0.1" which means the local computer.
In real applications, you don't want to hardwire it like this. Rather, you
want to take the hostname or IP address of the server from user or caller.

Below is some more details about the connect() call.

If the socket specified in the call has not already been bound to a local
address, connect() will bind it to an unused local address, unless the
socket's address family is AF_UNIX.

If the initiating socket is connection-mode (e.g. a Stream socket),
then connect() shall attempt to establish a connection to the address
specified by the server argument.

If the connection cannot be established immediately and O_NONBLOCK is
not set for the socket file descriptor, connect() will block for up
to a certain timeout interval until the connection is established.
If the timeout interval expires before the connection is established,
connect() shall fail and the connection attempt will be aborted.
If connect() is interrupted by a signal that is caught while blocked
waiting to establish a connection, connect() shall fail and set errno to
[EINTR], but the connection request shall not be aborted, and the connection
shall be established asynchronously.

If the connection cannot be established immediately and O_NONBLOCK is set
for the file descriptor for the socket, connect() shall fail and set errno
to [EINPROGRESS], but the connection request shall not be aborted,
and the connection shall be established asynchronously. Subsequent calls
to connect() for the same socket, before the connection is established,
shall fail and set errno to [EALREADY].

Notice that the connect() call can also be invoked on a non-connection-mode
socket, such as a Datagram socket as well.
If the initiating socket is not connection-mode, then connect() shall set
the socket's peer address, and no connection is made. For SOCK_DGRAM sockets,
the peer address identifies where all datagrams are sent to on subsequent
send() functions, and limits the remote sender for subsequent recv()
functions. If the sa_family member of address is AF_UNSPEC, the socket's
peer address shall be reset. Note that for a non-connection-mode socket,
the term "connected" is used to describe a connectionless-mode socket
for which a peer address has been set. No actual connection is made.

When the connection has been established asynchronously, pselect(), select(),
and poll() shall indicate that the file descriptor for the socket is ready

for writing.

12-6-6 Data Exchange -- The send() and recv() Functions

In contrast to sendto() and recvfrom() are used to send and receive messages to and from an unconnected Datagram socket, send() and recv() functions are used for a connected socket. Please notice the differences in names.

On a connected socket, the client and the server use the send() function to send a message to its communication partner.

The send() function is similar to but simpler than sendto(); it does not need the dest_addr and dest_len arguments at end because the sockets are already connected.

```
#include <sys/types.h>
#include <sys/socket.h>

ssize_t send(int s, const void *buf, size_t len, int flags);
```

Upon successful completion, send() returns the number of bytes sent. Otherwise, -1 is returned and errno is set.

Successful completion of a send() call does not guarantee delivery of the message. A return value of -1 indicates only locally-detected errors.

Similarly, the recv() function is used to receive a message from a connected socket. The recv() function is similar to but simpler than recvfrom(); it does not need the from_addr and from_len arguments at end because the partner is already connected.

```
#include <sys/types.h>
#include <sys/socket.h>

ssize_t recv(int s, void *buf, size_t len, int flags);
```

The recv() call returns the number of bytes received. It returns 0 if the peer has shut down. The function returns -1 if an error occurred.

Remember that a recv() call can return any number of bytes, up to the size of the buffer passed in to the call. There is no guarantee that it will return a message completely fills the input buffer.

Let Client Close the Connection

A very typical session between a client and a server is that the client sends a request and then the server does some computation to service the request. An easy novice mistake to make is one may close the socket connection from the server side as soon as the server has sent a reply. Please be aware that this is a bug. This is because although the server has sent the reply, the client may not receive it yet. And if the server closes the socket connection right after it sends the reply, the client who has not got the reply yet may never get it. Hence, it is very important to always let the client close the connection. And as we will talk about later, this practice also has another benefit.

12-6-7 The read() and write() Functions

In POSIX systems, many things are viewed as files. A socket is a file from
what I/O is concerned. This is why a socket is represented by a file
descriptor in a C program. Linux is the same. Because of this, instead of
using the send() and recv() functions, a program can alternatively invoke
the file I/O functions, that is, the write() and read() system calls,
to send and receive messages over a network connection as well.
When using read() and write() to receive and to send a message through
a socket, the flags argument is usually not needed.

12-6-8 Skeleton of Connection-Oriented Client and Server

Connectionless client-server applications are easy to write.
For a connectionless server, it simply creates a Datagram socket, binds
it to the server address, and then sits in a loop of doing recvfrom().
That's it! For a connectionless client, it just creates a Datagram socket,
fills in the server's address in a socket address structure, and then
invokes sendto() to send the message to the server's address. That's all.
It's very straight-forward.

```
          client                           server
------------------------------   ------------------------------------------------
socket() create client socket    socket() - create server listener socket
                                  bind() - bind server socket to its address
                                  listen() - set queue length of listener socket
                                  Loop

   connect()   ---->              new_sock_fd = accept() <- a new socket created
                                  start servicing the client

   conversations begin
     client socket      <---->    new data socket on the server
        :                            :
     send()          ----------->  recv()
                 client's request
                                     : server processing

   recv()         <-----------    send()
                 server's response
------------------------------------------------------------------------------------
```

Figure 12-11 Outline of connection-oriented client-server communication

A connection-oriented client-server application gives you the benefits of
messages are guaranteed to be delivered in order and to be not lost.
At the same time, it is a bit more complicated to write. More steps are
required. First, a client needs to connect to the server first, before it
can send messages, by invoking the connect() function. The server, since it
needs to handle multiple connections at the same time, requires at least two
extra steps. As Figure 12-11 shows, first, it must invoke the listen() call
to set a request queue length. Second, it must sit in a loop of calling the
accept() function to listen for and then accept incoming connection requests
from the clients.

Since each client is going to have its own separate connection with the
server to carry on its conversations, each time when the accept() call
accepts a new client connection request, it will create a new socket on
the server side for communicating with that client. This socket is for
carrying out data communication with a client. It's different and separate
from the socket that the server initially creates and listens on for
incoming connection requests.

Skeleton of a connection-oriented client

```
/* Step 1: Create a Stream socket. */
sfd = socket(AF_INET, SOCK_STREAM, 0);

/* Step 2: Fill in the server's address. */
    : (see below)

/* Step 3: Establish a connection to the server. */
ret = connect(sfd, (struct sockaddr *)&srvaddr, srvaddrsz);

/* Step 4: Send a request. */
ret = send(sfd, outbuf, msglen, 0);

/* Step 5: Receive the response. */
ret = recv(sfd, inbuf, BUFLEN, 0);
```

Skeleton of a connection-oriented server

```
/* Step 1: Create a Stream socket. */
sfd = socket(AF_INET, SOCK_STREAM, 0);

/* Step 2: Fill in the server's address. */
    : (see below)       .

/* Step 3: Bind the server socket to its address. */
ret = bind(sfd, (struct sockaddr *)&srvaddr, srvaddrsz);

/* Step 4: Set maximum connection request queue length. */
ret = listen(sfd, BACKLOG);

/* Step 5: Listen for and accept incoming client connection requests. */
newsock = accept(sfd, (struct sockaddr *)&clntaddr, &clntaddrsz);

/* Step 6: Receive a request from a client. */
ret = recv(newsock, inbuf, BUFLEN, 0);

/* Step 7: Send a reply. */
ret = send(newsock, outbuf, msglen, 0);
```

How to fill in the server's address

```
/* Fill in the server socket address. */
memset((void *)&srvaddr, 0, (size_t)sizeof(srvaddr)); /* clear address buffer */
srvaddr.sin_family = AF_INET;                      /* Internet socket */
srvaddr.sin_addr.s_addr = htonl(INADDR_ANY);   /* server's IP address */
srvaddr.sin_port = htons(portnum);             /* server's port number */
```

Above shows skeletons of connection-oriented client and server (IPv4 version).
Note that in filling in the server's address a client must replace the wildcard
address with server's real IP address if the server is on another computer.

Figure 12-12 lists a pair of connection-oriented client and server programs.

Figure 12-12a Connection-oriented server program (tcpsrv1.c)

```c
/*
 * A connection-oriented server program using Stream socket.
 * Single-threaded server.
 * Usage: tcpsrv1 [port#]
 * Authored by Mr. Jin-Jwei Chen.
 * Copyright (c) 1993-2018, 2020 Mr. Jin-Jwei Chen. All rights reserved.
 */

#include <stdio.h>
#include <errno.h>
#include <sys/types.h>
#include <sys/socket.h>
#include <netinet/in.h>     /* protocols such as IPPROTO_TCP, ... */
#include <string.h>         /* memset() */
#include <stdlib.h>         /* atoi() */
#include <unistd.h>         /* close() */

#define   BUFLEN       1024    /* size of message buffer */
#define   DEFSRVPORT   2345    /* default server port number */
#define   BACKLOG        50    /* length of listener queue */

int main(int argc, char *argv[])
{
  int     ret, portnum_in=0;
  int     sfd;                         /* file descriptor of the listener socket */
  int     newsock;                     /* file descriptor of client data socket */
  struct sockaddr_in    srvaddr;       /* socket structure */
  int     srvaddrsz=sizeof(struct sockaddr_in);
  struct sockaddr_in    clntaddr;      /* socket structure */
  socklen_t    clntaddrsz=sizeof(struct sockaddr_in);
  in_port_t    portnum=DEFSRVPORT;     /* port number */
  char    inbuf[BUFLEN];               /* input message buffer */
  char    outbuf[BUFLEN];              /* output message buffer */
  size_t  msglen;                      /* length of reply message */
  unsigned int  msgcnt;                /* message count */

  fprintf(stdout, "Connection-oriented server program ...\n");

  /* Get the port number from user, if any. */
  if (argc > 1)
  {
    portnum_in = atoi(argv[1]);
    if (portnum_in <= 0)
    {
      fprintf(stderr, "Port number %d invalid, set to default value %u\n",
        portnum_in, DEFSRVPORT);
      portnum = DEFSRVPORT;
```

```c
    }
    else
      portnum = (in_port_t)portnum_in;
  }

  /* Create the Stream server socket. */
  if ((sfd = socket(AF_INET, SOCK_STREAM, 0)) < 0)
  {
    fprintf(stderr, "Error: socket() failed, errno=%d, %s\n", errno,
      strerror(errno));
    return(-1);
  }

  /* Fill in the server socket address. */
  memset((void *)&srvaddr, 0, (size_t)srvaddrsz); /* clear the address buffer */
  srvaddr.sin_family = AF_INET;                  /* Internet socket */
  srvaddr.sin_addr.s_addr = htonl(INADDR_ANY);   /* server's IP address */
  srvaddr.sin_port = htons(portnum);             /* server's port number */

  /* Bind the server socket to its address. */
  if ((ret = bind(sfd, (struct sockaddr *)&srvaddr, srvaddrsz)) != 0)
  {
    fprintf(stderr, "Error: bind() failed, errno=%d, %s\n", errno,
      strerror(errno));
    return(-2);
  }

  /* Set maximum connection request queue length that we can fall behind. */
  if (listen(sfd, BACKLOG) == -1) {
    fprintf(stderr, "Error: listen() failed, errno=%d, %s\n", errno,
      strerror(errno));
    close(sfd);
    return(-3);
  }

  /* Wait for incoming connection requests from clients and service them. */
  while (1) {

    fprintf(stdout, "\nListening at port number %u ...\n", portnum);
    newsock = accept(sfd, (struct sockaddr *)&clntaddr, &clntaddrsz);
    if (newsock < 0)
    {
      fprintf(stderr, "Error: accept() failed, errno=%d, %s\n", errno,
        strerror(errno));
      close(sfd);
      return(-4);
    }

    fprintf(stdout, "Client Connected.\n");

    msgcnt = 1;
    /* Receive and service requests from the current client. */
    while (1)
    {
      /* Receive a request from a client. */
      errno = 0;
```

```
    inbuf[0] = '\0';
    ret = recv(newsock, inbuf, BUFLEN, 0);
    if (ret > 0)
    {
      /* Process the request. We simply print the request message here. */
      inbuf[ret] = '\0';
      fprintf(stdout, "\nReceived the following request from client:\n%s\n",
        inbuf);

      /* Construct a reply */
      sprintf(outbuf, "This is reply #%3u from the server program.", msgcnt++);
      msglen = strlen(outbuf);

      /* Send a reply. */
      errno = 0;
      ret = send(newsock, outbuf, msglen, 0);
      if (ret == -1)
        fprintf(stderr, "Error: send() failed, errno=%d, %s\n", errno,
          strerror(errno));
      else
        fprintf(stdout, "%u of %lu bytes of the reply was sent.\n", ret, msglen);
    }
    else if (ret < 0)
    {
      fprintf(stderr, "Error: recv() failed, errno=%d, %s\n", errno,
        strerror(errno));
      break;
    }
    else
    {
      /* The client may have disconnected. */
      fprintf(stdout, "The client may have disconnected.\n");
      break;
    }
  } /* while - inner */
  close(newsock);

  } /* while - outer */
}
```

Figure 12-12b Connection-oriented client program (tcpclnt1.c)

```
/*
 * A connection-oriented client program using Stream socket.
 * Connecting to server on the same (local) host or a different remote host.
 * Usage: tcpclnt1 [srvport# [server-ipaddress]]
 * Authored by Mr. Jin-Jwei Chen.
 * Copyright (c) 1993-2018, 2020 Mr. Jin-Jwei Chen. All rights reserved.
 */

#include <stdio.h>
#include <errno.h>
#include <sys/types.h>
#include <sys/socket.h>
#include <netinet/in.h>      /* protocols such as IPPROTO_TCP, ... */
#include <arpa/inet.h>       /* inet_pton(), inet_ntoa() */
```

729

```c
#include <string.h>          /* memset() */
#include <stdlib.h>          /* atoi() */
#include <unistd.h>          /* close(), sleep() */

#define   BUFLEN        1024    /* size of input message buffer */
#define   DEFSRVPORT    2345    /* default server port number */
#define   MAXMSGS          3    /* Maximum number of messages to send */
#define   IPV4LOCALADDR "127.0.0.1"  /* IPv4 address for local host */

int main(int argc, char *argv[])
{
  int     ret, portnum_in=0;
  int     sfd;                       /* file descriptor of the socket */
  struct sockaddr_in     server;     /* socket structure */
  int     srvaddrsz=sizeof(struct sockaddr_in);
  struct sockaddr_in     fromaddr;   /* socket structure */
  socklen_t     fromaddrsz=sizeof(struct sockaddr_in);
  in_port_t     portnum=DEFSRVPORT;  /* port number */
  char    inbuf[BUFLEN];             /* input message buffer */
  char    outbuf[BUFLEN];            /* output message buffer */
  size_t     msglen;                 /* length of reply message */
  size_t     msgnum=0;               /* count of request message */
  char *ipaddrstr = IPV4LOCALADDR;   /* server's IP address in string format */
  in_addr_t ipaddrbin;               /* server's IP address in binary format */

  fprintf(stdout, "Connection-oriented client program ...\n");

  /* Get the port number from user, if any. */
  if (argc > 1)
  {
    portnum_in = atoi(argv[1]);
    if (portnum_in <= 0)
    {
      fprintf(stderr, "Port number %d invalid, set to default value %u\n",
        portnum_in, DEFSRVPORT);
      portnum = DEFSRVPORT;
    }
    else
      portnum = (in_port_t)portnum_in;
  }

  /* Get the server's IP address from user, if any. */
  if (argc > 2)
    ipaddrstr = argv[2];

  /* Convert the server's IP address from string format to binary */
  ret = inet_pton(AF_INET, ipaddrstr, &ipaddrbin);
  if (ret == 0)
  {
    fprintf(stderr, "%s is not a valid IPv4 address.\n", ipaddrstr);
    return(-1);
  }

  /* Create the client socket. */
  if ((sfd = socket(AF_INET, SOCK_STREAM, 0)) < 0)
  {
```

```
      fprintf(stderr, "Error: socket() failed, errno=%d, %s\n", errno,
        strerror(errno));
      return(-2);
   }

   /* Fill in the server's address. */
   memset((void *)&server, 0, (size_t)srvaddrsz); /* clear the address buffer */
   server.sin_family = AF_INET;                    /* Internet socket */
   if (strcmp(ipaddrstr, IPV4LOCALADDR))
      server.sin_addr.s_addr = ipaddrbin;
   else
      server.sin_addr.s_addr = htonl(INADDR_ANY);  /* server's IP address */
   server.sin_port = htons(portnum);               /* server's port number */

   /* Connect to the server. */
   ret = connect(sfd, (struct sockaddr *)&server, srvaddrsz);
   if (ret == -1)
   {
      fprintf(stderr, "Error: connect() failed, errno=%d, %s\n", errno,
        strerror(errno));
      close(sfd);
      return(-3);
   }

   fprintf(stdout, "Send request messages to server(%s) at port %d\n",
     ipaddrstr, portnum);

   /* Send request messages to the server and process the reply messages. */
   while (msgnum < MAXMSGS)
   {
      /* Send a request message to the server. */
      sprintf(outbuf, "%s%4lu%s", "This is request message ", ++msgnum,
        " from the client program.");
      msglen = strlen(outbuf);
      errno = 0;

      ret = send(sfd, outbuf, msglen, 0);
      if (ret >= 0)
      {
         /* Print a warning if not entire message was sent. */
         if (ret == msglen)
           fprintf(stdout, "\n%lu bytes of message were successfully sent.\n",
             msglen);
         else if (ret < msglen)
           fprintf(stderr, "Warning: only %u of %lu bytes were sent.\n",
             ret, msglen);

      if (ret > 0)
      {
         /* Receive a reply from the server. */
         errno = 0;
         inbuf[0] = '\0';
         ret = recv(sfd, inbuf, BUFLEN, 0);

         if (ret > 0)
         {
```

731

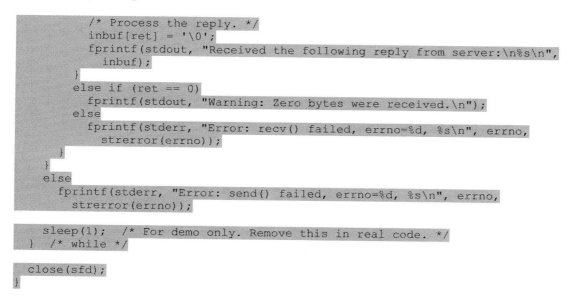

```
        /* Process the reply. */
        inbuf[ret] = '\0';
        fprintf(stdout, "Received the following reply from server:\n%s\n",
            inbuf);
    }
    else if (ret == 0)
        fprintf(stdout, "Warning: Zero bytes were received.\n");
    else
        fprintf(stderr, "Error: recv() failed, errno=%d, %s\n", errno,
            strerror(errno));
    }
}
    else
        fprintf(stderr, "Error: send() failed, errno=%d, %s\n", errno,
            strerror(errno));

    sleep(1);    /* For demo only. Remove this in real code. */
}  /* while */

close(sfd);
}
```

12-7 Socket Options

When you write your own programs using socket, there are a number of things
that you want to be aware of and perhaps do something about it.
Specifically, there are a number of socket options available that allow
you to change or control the behavior of a socket, which you may find
very useful later when some day you find your socket programs no longer
behave to your satisfaction. These socket options include changing socket
buffer size, controlling timeouts, gracefully closing a connection, enabling
socket data broadcasts, detecting lost connection earlier, and many others.

Table 12-1 below shows the socket options as defined by the POSIX standard.

It's worth noting that you may be able to completely ignore the socket
options and not touch any of them and your applications still work.
But they may not work in the best way or conditions if you just
take and use all of the defaults for these options. Or they may work just
fine for a while and later you find when they hit certain conditions the
behavior is not that satisfactory anymore.

We will use some of the socket options in this chapter and more in the
next chapter when we talk about tuning socket programs.

Table 12-1: Socket-Level Options

Option	Data Type	Meaning
SO_ACCEPTCONN	int	A non-zero value means the socket listening is enabled -- the socket is accepting connections.
SO_BROADCAST	int	A non-zero value requests transmission of broadcast messages being supported.

```
                              This is for SOCK_DGRAM sockets only.

   SO_DEBUG        int       A non-zero value requests debugging information
                              being recorded.

   SO_DONTROUTE    int       A non-zero value requests bypass of normal routing
                              and to route based on destination address only.

   SO_ERROR        int       Requests and clears pending error information on
                              the socket (getsockopt() only).

   SO_KEEPALIVE    int       A non-zero value requests periodic transmission of
                              keepalive messages. Behavior is protocol-specific.

   SO_LINGER   struct linger Socket lingers on close.
                              Specify actions to be taken for queued, unsent
                              data on close() call. Two attributes to set are
                              linger on/off and linger time in seconds.

   SO_OOBINLINE    int       A non-zero value requests that out-of-band data
                              be transmitted in line, that is, be placed
                              into normal data input queue as received.

   SO_RCVBUF       int       Size of receive buffer (in bytes).

   SO_RCVLOWAT     int       Low water mark for a receive operation.
                              Minimum amount of data to return to application
                              for a receive operations (in bytes).

   SO_RCVTIMEO  struct timeval  Timeout value for a receive operation.

   SO_REUSEADDR    int       A non-zero value requests reuse of local addresses
                              in bind() (protocol-specific).

   SO_SNDBUF       int       Size of send buffer (in bytes).

   SO_SNDLOWAT     int       Low water mark for a send operation.
                              The minimum amount of data to send for send
                              operations (in bytes).

   SO_SNDTIMEO struct timeval  Timeout value for a send operation.

   SO_TYPE         int       Socket type (getsockopt() only).
-----------------------------------------------------------------------
```

Figure 12-13 shows a program that does a getsockopt() call on every
socket option at the socket level as defined in the POSIX Standard.

   Figure 12-13 All socket level socket options (get_all_sockopt.c)

```
/*
 * Get all socket options at the socket level (SOL_SOCKET).
 * Authored by Mr. Jin-Jwei Chen.
 * Copyright (c) 1993-2016, 2018-2020 Mr. Jin-Jwei Chen. All rights reserved.
 */
```

```c
#include <stdio.h>
#include <errno.h>
#include <sys/types.h>
#include <sys/socket.h>
#include <netinet/in.h>      /* protocols such as IPPROTO_TCP, ... */
#include <unistd.h>          /* close() */
#include <netinet/tcp.h>
#include <string.h>          /* memset() */
#include <sys/time.h>        /* struct timeval */

int main(int argc, char *argv[])
{
  int    ret;
  int    sfd;                          /* file descriptor of the socket */
  int         option;                  /* option value */
  socklen_t optlen;                    /* length of option value */
  struct linger  linger;               /* linger on/off & time */
  struct timeval  tmout;               /* send/receive timeout */

  /* Create a Stream socket. */
  if ((sfd = socket(AF_INET, SOCK_STREAM, 0)) < 0)
  {
    fprintf(stderr, "Error: socket() failed, errno=%d\n", errno);
    return(-1);
  }

  /* Get the SO_ACCEPTCONN socket option. */
  option = 0;
  optlen = sizeof(option);
  ret = getsockopt(sfd, SOL_SOCKET, SO_ACCEPTCONN, &option, &optlen);
  if (ret < 0)
    fprintf(stderr, "Error: getsockopt(SO_ACCEPTCONN) failed, errno=%d\n", errno);
  else
    fprintf(stdout, "SO_ACCEPTCONN's current setting is %d\n", option);

  /* Get the SO_BROADCAST socket option. */
  option = 0;
  optlen = sizeof(option);
  ret = getsockopt(sfd, SOL_SOCKET, SO_BROADCAST, &option, &optlen);
  if (ret < 0)
    fprintf(stderr, "Error: getsockopt(SO_BROADCAST) failed, errno=%d\n", errno);
  else
    fprintf(stdout, "SO_BROADCAST's current setting is %d\n", option);

  /* Get the SO_DEBUG socket option. */
  option = 0;
  optlen = sizeof(option);
  ret = getsockopt(sfd, SOL_SOCKET, SO_DEBUG, &option, &optlen);
  if (ret < 0)
    fprintf(stderr, "Error: getsockopt(SO_DEBUG) failed, errno=%d\n", errno);
  else
    fprintf(stdout, "SO_DEBUG's current setting is %d\n", option);

  /* Get the SO_DONTROUTE socket option. */
  option = 0;
  optlen = sizeof(option);
```

```c
ret = getsockopt(sfd, SOL_SOCKET, SO_DONTROUTE, &option, &optlen);
if (ret < 0)
  fprintf(stderr, "Error: getsockopt(SO_DONTROUTE) failed, errno=%d\n", errno);
else
  fprintf(stdout, "SO_DONTROUTE's current setting is %d\n", option);

/* Get the SO_ERROR socket option. */
option = 0;
optlen = sizeof(option);
ret = getsockopt(sfd, SOL_SOCKET, SO_ERROR, &option, &optlen);
if (ret < 0)
  fprintf(stderr, "Error: getsockopt(SO_ERROR) failed, errno=%d\n", errno);
else
  fprintf(stdout, "SO_ERROR's current setting is %d\n", option);

/* Get the SO_KEEPALIVE socket option. */
option = 0;
optlen = sizeof(option);
ret = getsockopt(sfd, SOL_SOCKET, SO_KEEPALIVE, &option, &optlen);
if (ret < 0)
  fprintf(stderr, "Error: getsockopt(SO_KEEPALIVE) failed, errno=%d\n", errno);
else
  fprintf(stdout, "SO_KEEPALIVE's current setting is %d\n", option);

/* Get the SO_LINGER socket option. */
optlen = sizeof(struct linger);
memset((void *)&linger, 0, optlen);
ret = getsockopt(sfd, SOL_SOCKET, SO_LINGER, &linger, &optlen);
if (ret < 0)
  fprintf(stderr, "Error: getsockopt(SO_LINGER) failed, errno=%d\n", errno);
else
  fprintf(stdout, "SO_LINGER's current setting is onoff=%u linger_time=%u\n",
    linger.l_onoff, linger.l_linger);

/* Get the SO_OOBINLINE socket option. */
option = 0;
optlen = sizeof(option);
ret = getsockopt(sfd, SOL_SOCKET, SO_OOBINLINE, &option, &optlen);
if (ret < 0)
  fprintf(stderr, "Error: getsockopt(SO_OOBINLINE) failed, errno=%d\n", errno);
else
  fprintf(stdout, "SO_OOBINLINE's current setting is %d\n", option);

/* Get the SO_RCVBUF socket option. */
option = 0;
optlen = sizeof(option);
ret = getsockopt(sfd, SOL_SOCKET, SO_RCVBUF, &option, &optlen);
if (ret < 0)
  fprintf(stderr, "Error: getsockopt(SO_RCVBUF) failed, errno=%d\n", errno);
else
  fprintf(stdout, "SO_RCVBUF's current setting is %d\n", option);

/* Get the SO_RCVLOWAT socket option. */
option = 0;
optlen = sizeof(option);
ret = getsockopt(sfd, SOL_SOCKET, SO_RCVLOWAT, &option, &optlen);
```

```
  if (ret < 0)
    fprintf(stderr, "Error: getsockopt(SO_RCVLOWAT) failed, errno=%d\n", errno);
  else
    fprintf(stdout, "SO_RCVLOWAT's current setting is %d\n", option);

  /* Get the SO_RCVTIMEO socket option. */
  optlen = sizeof(struct timeval);
  memset((void *)&tmout, 0, optlen);
  ret = getsockopt(sfd, SOL_SOCKET, SO_RCVTIMEO, &tmout, &optlen);
  if (ret < 0)
    fprintf(stderr, "Error: getsockopt(SO_RCVTIMEO) failed, errno=%d\n", errno);
  else
    fprintf(stdout, "SO_RCVTIMEO's current setting is %lu:%u\n",
      tmout.tv_sec, tmout.tv_usec);

  /* Get the SO_REUSEADDR socket option. */
  option = 0;
  optlen = sizeof(option);
  ret = getsockopt(sfd, SOL_SOCKET, SO_REUSEADDR, &option, &optlen);
  if (ret < 0)
    fprintf(stderr, "Error: getsockopt(SO_REUSEADDR) failed, errno=%d\n", errno);
  else
    fprintf(stdout, "SO_REUSEADDR's current setting is %d\n", option);

  /* Get the SO_REUSEPORT socket option. */
  option = 0;
  optlen = sizeof(option);
  ret = getsockopt(sfd, SOL_SOCKET, SO_REUSEPORT, &option, &optlen);
  if (ret < 0)
    fprintf(stderr, "Error: getsockopt(SO_REUSEPORT) failed, errno=%d\n", errno);
  else
    fprintf(stdout, "SO_REUSEPORT's current setting is %d\n", option);

  /* Get the SO_SNDBUF socket option. */
  option = 0;
  optlen = sizeof(option);
  ret = getsockopt(sfd, SOL_SOCKET, SO_SNDBUF, &option, &optlen);
  if (ret < 0)
    fprintf(stderr, "Error: getsockopt(SO_SNDBUF) failed, errno=%d\n", errno);
  else
    fprintf(stdout, "SO_SNDBUF's current setting is %d\n", option);

  /* Get the SO_SNDLOWAT socket option. */
  option = 0;
  optlen = sizeof(option);
  ret = getsockopt(sfd, SOL_SOCKET, SO_SNDLOWAT, &option, &optlen);
  if (ret < 0)
    fprintf(stderr, "Error: getsockopt(SO_SNDLOWAT) failed, errno=%d\n", errno);
  else
    fprintf(stdout, "SO_SNDLOWAT's current setting is %d\n", option);

  /* Get the SO_SNDTIMEO socket option. */
  optlen = sizeof(struct timeval);
  memset((void *)&tmout, 0, optlen);
  ret = getsockopt(sfd, SOL_SOCKET, SO_SNDTIMEO, &tmout, &optlen);
  if (ret < 0)
```

```
      fprintf(stderr, "Error: getsockopt(SO_SNDTIMEO) failed, errno=%d\n", errno);
else
      fprintf(stdout, "SO_SNDTIMEO's current setting is %lu:%u\n",
        tmout.tv_sec, tmout.tv_usec);

/* Get the SO_TYPE socket option. */
option = 0;
optlen = sizeof(option);
ret = getsockopt(sfd, SOL_SOCKET, SO_TYPE, &option, &optlen);
if (ret < 0)
      fprintf(stderr, "Error: getsockopt(SO_TYPE) failed, errno=%d\n", errno);
else
      fprintf(stdout, "SO_TYPE's current setting is %d\n", option);

  close(sfd);
}
```

Most of the socket options are very useful. People with experience
developing and troubleshooting network and distributed applications are
probably familiar with some of the frequently encountered issues in
these applications. They include, but not limited to, the following:

  - Performance is slow.
  - There is occasional data loss.
  - Restarting a server program sometimes gets error.
  - Application seems to be hung.

In the following sections, we will touch upon some of the most common issues
and introduce the socket options that can be used to address those issues.
But we will discuss most of these socket options in the next chapter.

12-7-1 The getsockopt() and setsockopt() Functions

The POSIX standard includes two functions that allow applications to get
and set the values of the defined socket options. The getsockopt() function
performs the get operation while the setsockopt() does the set.

```
#include <sys/socket.h>

int getsockopt(int sock, int level, int optname, void *optval, socklen_t
    *optlen);

int setsockopt(int sock, int level, int optname, const void *optval,
    socklen_t optlen);
```

The get and set functions have the same set of parameters.
The only difference is that the last parameter, optlen, is input only for
the setsockopt() while it is both input and output in getsockopt().
Be aware that the getsockopt() requires a pointer (address) of it.

The first parameter provides the open file descriptor of the socket being
manipulated. It identifies the socket whose option value is being read or set.

The second parameter specifies the protocol level at which the option resides.
To access options at the socket level, SOL_SOCKET should be used.

To access options at other levels, supply the appropriate level identifier for the protocol controlling the option. For example, to get or set an option controlled at the TCP protocol level, use IPPROTO_TCP, which is defined in the header file <netinet/in.h>.

The third parameter, optnam, specifies the option being get or set. For socket level options, use one of the options listed in table 12-1 above.

The fourth parameter, optval, returns or provides the value of the option. As shown in table 12-1, almost all socket options have a value of int type. The exceptions are: the SO_LINGER option requires a value of 'struct linger' type and the SO_SNDTIMEO and SO_RCVTIMEO options have a value of 'struct timeval' type. If the option is about enabling or disabling a feature, then usually a value 0 means disabling and 1 or non-zero means enabling.

The last parameter, optlen, is the size in bytes of the fourth parameter, optval. For setsockopt(), this is provided by the calling program. It is usually sizeof(optval) -- the size of the option value. For getsockopt(), if the actual size of the option value being returned is greater than what the optlen parameter says, the value returned in the optval parameter will be silently truncated. Otherwise, the value of this parameter will be modified to indicate the actual length of the value of the option being returned.

Note that appropriate privileges may be required to get or set some of the options.

Upon successful completion, getsockopt() and setsockopt() return 0; otherwise, -1 is returned and errno is set to indicate the error.

We will have example programs using these functions later in this and next chapters.

12-8 Support for Multiple Platforms

This section discusses general issues in developing socket applications across multiple operating systems.

For the cross-platform example socket programs in this chapter, we name them as xxx_all.c where _all in the names means it works in Windows too.

12-8-1 Linux and Unix

Since the socket API functions are included in the POSIX standard, a socket program generally works across platforms with just a recompilation. This is especially true among the different Unix and Linux implementations. However, you may still run into subtle implementation differences going from one such operating system to another, which will occasionally require minor source code modifications. We will point them out whenever these cases arise. But in general this is rare.

12-8-2 Windows

For readers not using the Windows platform, this section can be skipped.

Windows is an exception. There are at least a number of major differences in socket programming between Windows and other platforms.

First, in Windows a socket program must explicitly start up Windows Socket in the beginning and shut it down at end. And every successful invocation of the Windows Socket startup must be matched by a shutdown.
The startup and shutdown of Windows Socket are performed by the WSAStartup() and WSACleanup() functions, respectively. This means if a program calls WSAStartup() five times, it must call WSACleanup() five times, too.

The WSAStartup() function initiates use of the Winsock DLL by a process. A program must successfully invoke the WSAStartup() function BEFORE it can execute any socket-related functions. As shown below, the function allows you to specify which version of Windows Socket you like to use. For modern Windows versions, you want a Windows Socket of at least version 2.2 or above.

```
#if WINDOWS
  /* Start up Windows Socket. */
  /* Ask for Winsock version 2.2 at least. */
  if ((ret = WSAStartup(MAKEWORD(2, 2), &wsaData)) != 0)
  {
    fprintf(stderr, "WSAStartup() failed with error %d: %s\n",
      ret, PrintError(ret));
    return (-1);
  }
#endif

    :

#if WINDOWS
  /* Shut down Windows Socket. */
  WSACleanup();
#endif
```

In other words, in Windows platform, just as a program or DLL must perform a successful WSAStartup() call before it can use Windows Sockets services, after it has completed using Windows Sockets, the application or DLL must call WSACleanup() to deregister itself from Windows Sockets and free all resources allocated for it by the Windows Sockets implementation.

Notice that the WSAStartup() function must execute successfully first before any other socket-related functions can work. Therefore, one usually places it at the very beginning of an application.
Besides, once a program successfully executes the WSACleanup() function, no more socket related function can be executed after unless another WSAStartup() is called. Hence, the function is typically executed at the very end of a socket program, after all other socket functions.

Second, closing a socket in Windows is different, too.
In Unix and Linux, many things are viewed and implemented as a file.
This includes socket. Therefore, it's very easy to close a socket. One just

calls the close() function and passes in the socket file descriptor.
That's it!

```
close(sfd);   /* sfd is socket file descriptor */
```

In Windows, it takes two steps to close a socket as shown below.
One needs to shut down a socket first to stop the socket from sending,
receiving, or both, before closing it. The shutdown() function takes two
arguments. The first argument is the socket file descriptor to be shut
down. The second argument is SD_SEND, SD_RECEIVE, or SD_BOTH, indicating
whether you like to disable transmission, reception, or both, respectively.
Notice that the name of the close() function in Windows is different too.

```
shutdown(sfd, SD_BOTH);
closesocket(sfd);
```

Third, handling of socket errors is different in Windows.

In Unix and Linux, the common practice is a system call returns 0 to
indicate success and -1 for error. And in case of error, the global
variable errno is set to return the error code/number.
Of course, this requires your program includes the header file <errno.h>.
The beauty is that in these operating systems all the socket APIs are
implemented as or like system calls and follow the same convention.
Therefore, programmers don't need to do anything differently or special
in handling errors from socket operations.

Nonetheless, in Windows, even if your program includes the header file
<errno.h>, at end of the socket calls, the error number is not returned
in the errno global variable. Instead, a program needs to invoke the
WSAGetLastError() to get it. The WSAGetLastError() function in Windows
returns the error number for the last Windows Sockets operation that failed.

Besides, in Linux and Unix a program can easily print the error message
string using the strerror(errno) call. However, in Windows,
if you feed the socket error code returned by WSAGetLastError()
to the strerror() function like below:

```
fprintf(stderr, "Error: socket() failed, errno=%d, %s\n",
  WSAGetLastError(), strerror(WSAGetLastError()));
```

Unfortunately, strerror() in Windows will return "Unknown error":

```
Error: socket() failed, errno=10047, Unknown error
```

Hence, we use the GetErrorMsg() function, as shown in Figure 12-14c,
to obtain socket error string in Windows.

In order to simplify the error handling code for cross platform applications
so that we can use a single printf() statement for all platforms,
we define the following two macros:

```
#if WINDOWS
#define ERRNO WSAGetLastError()
#define ERRNOSTR GetErrorMsg(WSAGetLastError())
#else
```

```
#define ERRNO errno
#define ERRNOSTR strerror(errno)
#endif
```

and use them like below for all platforms:

```
fprintf(stderr, "Error: socket() failed, errno=%d, %s\n",
  ERRNO, ERRNOSTR);
```

Fortunately, in Windows, almost all socket functions return 0 on success and either SOCKET_ERROR or INVALID_SOCKET (both of these are -1) on error. This makes checking the function return value and success or failure of an operation a bit easier because it is consistent with Linux and Unix platforms. It's just the way of getting the actual error code and error string is different between Windows and the Linux/Unix world.

Fourth, definitions of some data types are different.
For instance, the Internet socket port number type in_port_t is defined in <netinet/in.h> in Unix and Linux but is not defined in Windows.
That's why we add this declaration in Windows:

```
typedef unsigned short in_port_t;
```

Fifth, some function calls are different. For instance, the function call to set a socket blocking or non-blocking is different between Windows and Linux/Unix. One calls **fcntl**() in Linux/Unix whereas **ioctlsocket**() is called in Windows. In addition, the bit flags used have different names as well as shown below:

```
#if WINDOWS
   if (ioctlsocket(sfd, FIONBIO, &opt) != 0) /* make socket non-blocking */
#else
   if (fcntl(sfd, F_SETFL, fcntl(sfd, F_GETFL, 0) | O_NONBLOCK) != 0)
#endif
```

Sixth, the default behavior of an IPv6 server socket is different in Windows.

In Unix and Linux, if you create an IPv6 server socket, by default, it can accept connection requests from both IPv6 and IPv4 clients. However, **in Windows, if you create an IPv6 server socket, by default, it is IPv6 only**. In order for an IPv6 server socket to be able to also accept connection requests from IPv4 clients in Windows, **you must explicitly turn off the IPV6_V6ONLY socket option** by calling a setsockopt() function. You don't need to do so in Unix or Linux because that is the default behavior.

Lastly, I'm sure there might be some other discrepancies too beyond what we mention here.

To compile the example programs in this chapter for Windows platform, you must define the macro WINDOWS. For instance, you can run the following command-line commands to compile tcpclnt_all.c and tcpsrv_all.c:

```
cl -DWINDOWS tcpclnt_all.c ws2_32.lib kernel32.lib
cl -DWINDOWS tcpsrv_all.c ws2_32.lib
```

Note that to do console mode development outside Microsoft Visual Studio, you may have to run a setup script named vsvars32.bat from your command line prompt first.

```
C:\myprog>vsvars32.bat
Setting environment for using Microsoft Visual Studio 2010 x86 tools.
```

Microsoft does a good job documenting all of the socket APIs in Windows. Please visit Microsoft MSDN web site for detailed descriptions of Windows socket APIs.

```
https://msdn.microsoft.com
```

12-8-3 Example Programs

Figure 12-14a shows a connection-oriented server program that works on Unix, Linux, Apple Darwin and Windows platforms.

Figure 12-14b lists a version of the connection-oriented client program that works on all of these platforms, too. Figure 12-14c shows mysocket.h.

Figure 12-14a Connection-oriented server with multiple platforms support (tcpsrv_all.c)

```c
/*
 * A connection-oriented server program using Stream socket.
 * Support for IPv4 and IPv6. Default to IPV6. Compile with -DIPV4 to get IPV4.
 * Support for multiple platforms including Linux, Windows, Solaris, AIX, HPUX
 * and Apple Darwin.
 * Usage: tcpsrv_all [port#]
 * Authored by Mr. Jin-Jwei Chen.
 * Copyright (c) 1993-2018, 2020 Mr. Jin-Jwei Chen. All rights reserved.
 */

#include "mysocket.h"

int main(int argc, char *argv[])
{
  int     ret;                    /* return code */
  int     sfd;                    /* file descriptor of the listener socket */
  int     newsock;                /* file descriptor of client data socket */
#if IPV4
  struct sockaddr_in     srvaddr;    /* socket structure */
  int     srvaddrsz=sizeof(struct sockaddr_in);
  struct sockaddr_in     clntaddr;   /* socket structure */
  socklen_t     clntaddrsz=sizeof(struct sockaddr_in);
#else
  struct sockaddr_in6    srvaddr;    /* socket structure */
  int     srvaddrsz=sizeof(struct sockaddr_in6);
  struct sockaddr_in6    clntaddr;   /* socket structure */
  socklen_t     clntaddrsz=sizeof(struct sockaddr_in6);
  int     v6only = 0;             /* IPV6_V6ONLY socket option off */
#endif
  in_port_t     portnum=DEFSRVPORT;  /* port number */
  int     portnum_in = 0;         /* port number entered by user */
  char    inbuf[BUFLEN];          /* input message buffer */
```

```c
  char    outbuf[BUFLEN];                  /* output message buffer */
  size_t msglen;                           /* length of reply message */
  unsigned int  msgcnt;                    /* message count */

#if WINDOWS
  WSADATA wsaData;                         /* Winsock data */
  char* GetErrorMsg(int ErrorCode); /* print error string in Windows */
#endif

  fprintf(stdout, "Connection-oriented server program ...\n");

  /* Get the port number from user, if any. */
  if (argc > 1)
  {
    portnum_in = atoi(argv[1]);
    if (portnum_in <= 0)
    {
      fprintf(stderr, "Port number %d invalid, set to default value %u\n",
        portnum_in, DEFSRVPORT);
      portnum = DEFSRVPORT;
    }
    else
      portnum = (in_port_t)portnum_in;
  }

#if WINDOWS
  /* Initiate use of the Winsock DLL. Ask for Winsock version 2.2 at least. */
  if ((ret = WSAStartup(MAKEWORD(2, 2), &wsaData)) != 0)
  {
    fprintf(stderr, "WSAStartup() failed with error %d: %s\n",
      ret, GetErrorMsg(ret));
    return (-1);
  }
#endif

  /* Create the Stream server socket. */
  if ((sfd = socket(ADDR_FAMILY, SOCK_STREAM, 0)) < 0)
  {
    fprintf(stderr, "Error: socket() failed, errno=%d, %s\n", ERRNO, ERRNOSTR);
#if WINDOWS
    WSACleanup();
#endif
    return(-2);
  }

  /* Fill in the server socket address. */
  memset((void *)&srvaddr, 0, (size_t)srvaddrsz); /* clear the address buffer */
#if IPV4
  srvaddr.sin_family = ADDR_FAMILY;              /* Internet socket */
  srvaddr.sin_addr.s_addr = htonl(INADDR_ANY);   /* server's IP address */
  srvaddr.sin_port = htons(portnum);             /* server's port number */
#else
  srvaddr.sin6_family = ADDR_FAMILY;             /* Internet socket */
  srvaddr.sin6_addr = in6addr_any;               /* server's IP address */
  srvaddr.sin6_port = htons(portnum);            /* server's port number */
#endif
```

```
    /* If IPv6, turn off IPV6_V6ONLY socket option. Default is on in Windows. */
#if !IPV4
   if (setsockopt(sfd, IPPROTO_IPV6, IPV6_V6ONLY, (char*)&v6only,
     sizeof(v6only)) != 0)
   {
     fprintf(stderr, "Error: setsockopt(IPV6_V6ONLY) failed, errno=%d, %s\n",
       ERRNO, ERRNOSTR);
     CLOSE(sfd);
     return(-3);
   }
#endif

   /* Bind the server socket to its address. */
   if ((ret = bind(sfd, (struct sockaddr *)&srvaddr, srvaddrsz)) != 0)
   {
     fprintf(stderr, "Error: bind() failed, errno=%d, %s\n", ERRNO, ERRNOSTR);
     CLOSE(sfd);
     return(-4);
   }

   /* Set maximum connection request queue length that we can fall behind. */
   if (listen(sfd, BACKLOG) == -1) {
     fprintf(stderr, "Error: listen() failed, errno=%d, %s\n", ERRNO, ERRNOSTR);
     CLOSE(sfd);
     return(-5);
   }

   /* Wait for incoming connection requests from clients and service them. */
   while (1) {

     fprintf(stdout, "\nListening at port number %u ...\n", portnum);
     newsock = accept(sfd, (struct sockaddr *)&clntaddr, &clntaddrsz);
     if (newsock < 0)
     {
       fprintf(stderr, "Error: accept() failed, errno=%d, %s\n", ERRNO, ERRNOSTR);
       CLOSE(sfd);
       return(-6);
     }

     fprintf(stdout, "Client Connected.\n");

     msgcnt = 1;
     /* Receive and service requests from the current client. */
     while (1)
     {
       /* Receive a request from a client. */
       errno = 0;
       inbuf[0] = '\0';
       ret = recv(newsock, inbuf, BUFLEN, 0);
       if (ret > 0)
       {
         /* Process the request. We simply print the request message here. */
         inbuf[ret] = '\0';
         fprintf(stdout, "\nReceived the following request from client:\n%s\n",
           inbuf);
```

```
    /* Construct a reply */
    sprintf(outbuf, "This is reply #%3u from the server program.", msgcnt++);
    msglen = strlen(outbuf);

    /* Send a reply. */
    errno = 0;
    ret = send(newsock, outbuf, msglen, 0);
    if (ret == -1)
      fprintf(stderr, "Error: send() failed, errno=%d, %s\n", ERRNO,
        ERRNOSTR);
    else
      fprintf(stdout, "%u of %lu bytes of the reply was sent.\n", ret, msglen);
    }
    else if (ret < 0)
    {
      fprintf(stderr, "Error: recv() failed, errno=%d, %s\n", ERRNO,
        ERRNOSTR);
      break;
    }
    else
    {
      /* The client may have disconnected. */
      fprintf(stdout, "The client may have disconnected.\n");
      break;
    }
  } /* while - inner */
  CLOSE1(newsock);
} /* while - outer */

CLOSE(sfd);
return(0);
}
```

Figure 12-14b Connection-oriented client with multiple platforms support (tcpclnt_all.c)

```
/*
 * A connection-oriented client program using Stream socket.
 * Connecting to a server program on any host using a hostname or IP address.
 * Support for IPv4 and IPv6 and multiple platforms including
 * Linux, Windows, Solaris, AIX, HPUX and Apple Darwin.
 * Usage: tcpclnt_all [srvport# [server-hostname | server-ipaddress]]
 * Authored by Mr. Jin-Jwei Chen.
 * Copyright (c) 1993-2018, 2020 Mr. Jin-Jwei Chen. All rights reserved.
 */

#include "mysocket.h"

int main(int argc, char *argv[])
{
  int     ret;
  int     sfd;                        /* socket file descriptor */
  in_port_t portnum=DEFSRVPORT;       /* port number */
  int     portnum_in = 0;             /* port number user provides */
  char    *portnumstr = DEFSRVPORTSTR; /* port number in string format */
```

```c
  char    inbuf[BUFLEN];                    /* input message buffer */
  char    outbuf[BUFLEN];                   /* output message buffer */
  size_t  msglen;                           /* length of reply message */
  size_t  msgnum=0;                         /* count of request message */
  size_t  len;
  char    server_name[NAMELEN+1] = SERVER_NAME;
  struct  addrinfo hints, *res=NULL;  /* address info */

#if WINDOWS
  WSADATA wsaData;                          /* Winsock data */
  char* GetErrorMsg(int ErrorCode);    /* print error string in Windows */
#endif

  fprintf(stdout, "Connection-oriented client program ...\n");

  /* Get the server's port number from command line. */
  if (argc > 1)
  {
    portnum_in = atoi(argv[1]);
    if (portnum_in <= 0)
    {
      fprintf(stderr, "Port number %d invalid, set to default value %u\n",
        portnum_in, DEFSRVPORT);
      portnum = DEFSRVPORT;
      portnumstr = DEFSRVPORTSTR;
    }
    else
    {
      portnum = (in_port_t)portnum_in;
      portnumstr = argv[1];
    }
  }

  /* Get the server's host name or IP address from command line. */
  if (argc > 2)
  {
    len = strlen(argv[2]);
    if (len > NAMELEN)
      len = NAMELEN;
    strncpy(server_name, argv[2], len);
    server_name[len] = '\0';
  }

#if WINDOWS
  /* Initiate use of the Winsock DLL. Ask for Winsock version 2.2 at least. */
  if ((ret = WSAStartup(MAKEWORD(2, 2), &wsaData)) != 0)
  {
    fprintf(stderr, "Error: WSAStartup() failed with error %d: %s\n",
      ret, GetErrorMsg(ret));
    return (-1);
  }
#endif

  /* Translate the server's host name or IP address into socket address.
   * Fill in the hints information.
   */
```

```
  memset(&hints, 0x00, sizeof(hints));
    /* This works on AIX but not on Solaris, nor on Windows. */
    /* hints.ai_flags    = AI_NUMERICSERV; */
  hints.ai_family   = AF_UNSPEC;
  hints.ai_socktype = SOCK_STREAM;
  hints.ai_protocol = IPPROTO_TCP;

  /* Get the address information of the server using getaddrinfo().
   * This function returns errors directly or 0 for success. On success,
   * argument res contains a linked list of addrinfo structures.
   */
  ret = getaddrinfo(server_name, portnumstr, &hints, &res);
  if (ret != 0)
  {
    fprintf(stderr, "Error: getaddrinfo() failed, error %d, %s\n", ret,
      gai_strerror(ret));
#if !WINDOWS
    if (ret == EAI_SYSTEM)
      fprintf(stderr,"System error: errno=%d, %s\n", errno, strerror(errno));
#else
    WSACleanup();
#endif
    return(-2);
  }

  /* Create a socket. */
  sfd = socket(res->ai_family, res->ai_socktype, res->ai_protocol);
  if (sfd < 0)
  {
    fprintf(stderr,"Error: socket() failed, errno=%d, %s\n", ERRNO, ERRNOSTR);
#if WINDOWS
    WSACleanup();
#endif
    return (-3);
  }

  /* Connect to the server. */
  ret = connect(sfd, res->ai_addr, res->ai_addrlen);
  if (ret == -1)
  {
    fprintf(stderr, "Error: connect() failed, errno=%d, %s\n", ERRNO, ERRNOSTR);
    CLOSE(sfd);
    return(-4);
  }

  fprintf(stdout, "Send request messages to server(%s) at port %d\n",
    server_name, portnum);

  /* Send request messages to the server and process the reply messages. */
  while (msgnum < MAXMSGS)
  {
    /* Send a request message to the server. */
    sprintf(outbuf, "%s%4lu%s", "This is request message ", ++msgnum,
      " from the client program.");
    msglen = strlen(outbuf);
    errno = 0;
```

```
    ret = send(sfd, outbuf, msglen, 0);
    if (ret >= 0)
    {
      /* Print a warning if not entire message was sent. */
      if (ret == msglen)
        fprintf(stdout, "\n%lu bytes of message were successfully sent.\n",
          msglen);
      else if (ret < msglen)
        fprintf(stderr, "Warning: only %u of %lu bytes were sent.\n",
          ret, msglen);

      if (ret > 0)
      {
        /* Receive a reply from the server. */
        errno = 0;
        inbuf[0] = '\0';
        ret = recv(sfd, inbuf, BUFLEN, 0);

        if (ret > 0)
        {
          /* Process the reply. */
          inbuf[ret] = '\0';
          fprintf(stdout, "Received the following reply from server:\n%s\n",
            inbuf);
        }
        else if (ret == 0)
          fprintf(stdout, "Warning: Zero bytes were received.\n");
        else
          fprintf(stderr, "Error: recv() failed, errno=%d, %s\n", ERRNO,
            ERRNOSTR);
      }
    }
    else
      fprintf(stderr, "Error: send() failed, errno=%d, %s\n", ERRNO, ERRNOSTR);

    /* Sleep a second. For demo only. Remove this in real code. */
#if WINDOWS
    Sleep(1000); /* Unit is ms. For demo only. Remove this in real code. */
#else
    sleep(1);   /* For demo only. Remove this in real code. */
#endif
  }  /* while */

  /* Free the memory allocated by getaddrinfo() */
  freeaddrinfo(res);
  CLOSE(sfd);
  return(0);
}
```

Figure 12-14c Header file for cross-platform example socket programs
mysocket.h

```
/*
 * Include file for cross-platform socket applications.
 * Supported operating systems: Linux, Unix (AIX, Solaris, HP-UX), Windows.
```

```
/*
 * Standard include files for socket applications
 */

#include <stdio.h>
#include <errno.h>
#include <string.h>            /* memset(), strerror() */
#include <stdlib.h>            /* atoi() */
#include <ctype.h>             /* isalpha() */

#ifdef WINDOWS

#define WIN32_LEAN_AND_MEAN
#include <Winsock2.h>
#include <ws2tcpip.h>
#include <mstcpip.h>
#include <Windows.h>           /* Sleep() - link Kernel32.lib */

/* Needed for the Windows 2000 IPv6 Tech Preview. */
#if (_WIN32_WINNT == 0x0500)
#include <tpipv6.h>
#endif

#define STRICMP  _stricmp
typedef unsigned short in_port_t;
typedef unsigned int in_addr_t;

#else  /* ! WINDOWS */

/* Unix and Linux */
#include <sys/types.h>
#include <sys/socket.h>
#include <netinet/in.h>        /* protocols such as IPPROTO_TCP, ... */
#include <arpa/inet.h>         /* inet_pton(), inet_ntoa() */
#include <netdb.h>             /* struct hostent, gethostbyaddr() */
#include <time.h>              /* nanosleep() */
/* The next four are for async I/O. */
#include <unistd.h>
#include <fcntl.h>
#include <sys/time.h>
#include <sys/select.h>
/* Below is for Unix Domain socket */
#include <sys/un.h>

#endif

/*
 * Some constants: port number, buffer length, etc.
 */
#define  BUFLEN           1024    /* size of I/O buffer */
#define  BUFLEN1           128    /* size of small I/O buffer */
#define  DEFSRVPORT       2345    /* default server port number */
#define  DEFSRVPORTSTR   "2345"   /* default server port number string */
```

```
#define   NAMELEN              63      /* max. length of names */
#define   MAXMSGS              2       /* maximum number of messages to exchange */
#define   BACKLOG              50      /* length of listener queue */
#define   IPADDRSZ             128     /* size of buffer for IP address */
#define   MAXSOURCES           5       /* Maximum number of message sources */
#define   SLEEPS               3       /* number of seconds to sleep */
#define   SLEEPMS              10      /* number of milliseconds to sleep & wait */
#define   PEERADDRLEN          64      /* length of buffer for peer address */
#define   SRVIPLEN             64      /* max. length of IP address */
#define   MAXCONNTRYCNT        5       /* Maximum connect try count */
#define   FALSE                0
#define   NETDB_MAX_HOST_NAME_LENGTH  256    /* max. length of a host name */
#define   SERVER_NAME          "localhost"   /* default server's host name */
#define   NOHOST               ""
#define   IPV6LOCALADDR     "::1"    /* IPv6 address for local host */
/* These are for Unix domain socket. */
#define   SERVER_PATH    ".udssrv_name"   /* file pathname of the server */
#define   CLIENT_PATH    ".udsclnt_name"  /* file pathname of the client */
/* These are for getservbyname() call. */
#define   SVCNAME             "dbm"     /* default service name */
#define   PROTOCOLNAME        "tcp"     /* default protocol name */
#define   IPV4LOCALADDR "127.0.0.1"        /* IPv4 address for local host */
/* These below are for multicasting. */
#define   MULTICASTGROUP   "224.0.0.251"   /* address of the multicast group */
#define   MULTICASTGROUP2 "224.1.1.1"    /* address of the multicast group */
#define   LOCALINTFIPADDR "127.0.0.1"    /* address of local interface */
#define   MCASTPORT            3456       /* multicast group port number */

/*
 * Macros for printing and handling socket errors
 */

#if WINDOWS
#define ERRNO WSAGetLastError()
#define ERRNOSTR GetErrorMsg(WSAGetLastError())
#define CLOSE(sfd)  shutdown(sfd, SD_BOTH); closesocket(sfd); WSACleanup();
#define CLOSE1(sfd) shutdown(sfd, SD_BOTH); closesocket(sfd);
#else
#define ERRNO errno
#define ERRNOSTR strerror(errno)
#define CLOSE(sfd) close(sfd)
#define CLOSE1(sfd) close(sfd)
#endif

/* IP address family */
#if IPV4
#define   ADDR_FAMILY AF_INET          /* IPv4 */
#else
#define   ADDR_FAMILY AF_INET6         /* IPv6 */
#endif

/*
 * Function to get error message in Windows
 */

#if WINDOWS
```

```
#define ERRBUFLEN1 512
char* GetErrorMsg(int ErrorCode)
{
    static char ErrorMsg[ERRBUFLEN1];

    /* For multi-threaded applications, use FORMAT_MESSAGE_ALLOCATE_BUFFER
     * or malloc-ed buffer here instead of a static buffer.
     */
    FormatMessage(FORMAT_MESSAGE_FROM_SYSTEM | FORMAT_MESSAGE_IGNORE_INSERTS |
                  FORMAT_MESSAGE_MAX_WIDTH_MASK,
                  NULL, ErrorCode, MAKELANGID(LANG_NEUTRAL, SUBLANG_DEFAULT),
                  (LPSTR) ErrorMsg, ERRBUFLEN1, NULL);
    return (ErrorMsg);
}
#endif
```

12-9 Look Up a Host's IP Address Using Hostname

The example programs given so far work just fine if you run both the client and server programs on the same host or if you provide the server's IP address to the client. In a real application, the client and the server programs often run on different hosts. In that case, a client can no longer use INADDR_ANY as the server's IP address. That is, the following line of code will no longer work for the client:

```
srvaddr.sin_addr.s_addr = htonl(INADDR_ANY);   /* server's IP address */
```

In addition, in most cases, the client may be given the hostname instead of IP address of the server.

When a client program runs on a different host than the server program and if it is given the hostname of the server, it will have to translate the hostname into an IP address in order to fill in the server's address before calling the connect() function. This is because only an IP address in binary format, not a host name, can be used to form a socket address.

12-9-1 Host Name Translation

When writing a networking program, you want it to work on any computer. Hence, you don't want to hardwire any IP address in your program. Because of this, as all of our example programs have demonstrated so far, you bind the listening socket of your server program to the wild card address INADDR_ANY (IPv4) or in6addr_any (IPv6), rather than a specific IPv4 (e.g. 10.120.135.46) or IPv6 (e.g. 1:0:1:1000:ff3f:7408:ff3f:7594 or fd00:18d:808f:1::30) address. This is how you write a server program. It uses the generic wild card address so that it can run on any computer without changes. In addition, using the wild card address also allows the server program to accept client connect requests coming in from any network interfaces (IP addresses) on the computer.

A client program is a little different. When a client program wants to connect to a server program, it must know and specify the server's IP address as the destination address.

You don't want to hardwire the server's IP address in the client program either. So, the typical practice is to write a client program with the target server's hostname as input. This enables the same client program to be able to talk to any server that you or the user specify.
Since the socket API functions use IP address instead of hostnames, the work to do then is to convert the hostname into an IP address.

Converting or translating a symbolic host name such as myserver.xyz.com into an IP address is done by an operating system service generally called the **Domain Name Service**. It is provided by a system daemon program named Domain Name Service Daemon (DNSD). As a software engineer, you invoke an API to use this service.

In the old days, before IPv6 came along, a program invokes the gethostbyname() or gethostbyaddr() function to convert a hostname or string IP address, respectively, into a 'struct hostent' structure and uses that to fill in a server's address:

```
char    server_name[NAMELEN+1] = "localhost";
struct sockaddr_in server;
struct hostent *hp;
hp = gethostbyname(server_name);
memcpy(&(server.sin_addr), hp->h_addr, hp->h_length);
server.sin_family = hp->h_addrtype;
```

or

```
char    server_ip_dot_addr[NAMELEN+1] = "127.0.0.1";
struct sockaddr_in server;
struct hostent *hp;
unsigned int addr;

addr = inet_addr(server_ip_dot_addr);
hp = gethostbyaddr((char *)&addr, sizeof(addr), AF_INET);
memcpy(&(server.sin_addr), hp->h_addr, hp->h_length);
server.sin_family = hp->h_addrtype;
```

These functions return pointers to static data which may be overwritten by later calls and thus are not thread-safe. In addition, they do not support IPv6. For these reasons, POSIX.1-2001 Standard has declared them obsolete. The POSIX.1-2004 Standard, which is equivalent to the IEEE Std 1003.1, 2004 Edition, still lists them but marks them as obsolete. The 2008 and later versions no longer list them.

The only reason these still exist is for backward compatibility, that is, for old applications to continue to run without any change. Developers should stop using them.

The **getaddrinfo() function** is what programs should instead use now. The getaddrinfo() function works for IPv4 and IPv6 host names and IPv4 and IPv6 IP addresses. **It is thread-safe** because it returns results in dynamically allocated memory, instead of static memory. **It supports both IPv4 and IPv6. And it takes both hostname and IP address as input.**

So the getaddrinfo() function is the API to use now for translating a hostname or IP address in string form into a socket address in binary form that is ready to be used in other socket functions such as connect(). The getnameinfo() function is the inverse of getaddrinfo(), translating an IP address into a symbolic host name. We introduce these new APIs in the sections below.

Note that in a client-server communication model, usually it's the client program that needs to use the getaddrinfo() function but not the server. This is because a server program usually binds its server listener socket to the wildcard IP address so that it can listen to all client connection requests coming in from all network interfaces on the system. Therefore, it does not need to go through this host name to IP address conversion step.

12-9-2 The getaddrinfo() Function

Below is the synopsis of the getaddrinfo() function:

```
#include <sys/types.h>
#include <sys/socket.h>
#include <netdb.h>

int getaddrinfo(const char *host, const char *service,
            const struct addrinfo *hints,
            struct addrinfo **res);
```

The getaddrinfo() function combines the functionalities provided by the gethostbyname() and getservbyname() functions into a single API.

The getaddrinfo() function creates and returns one or more socket address structures associated with the given host specified in the first parameter. The result is returned in the last argument, res. The first three arguments of the call are input and provided by the caller. The first argument host provides the host name or IP address of the host. The second argument specifies a service name or port number. The third argument provides some hints, done via a number of fields and a set of flags. The fields can specify information such as protocol family and type of socket.

If success, the getaddrinfo() function will return a linked list of addrinfo structures in the 'res' argument. The link list contains all of the IP addresses corresponding to the input host name.

The address(es) returned by getaddrinfo() is usually used in a connect() call in a client program or in a bind() call in a server program.

The memory holding the returned result is dynamically allocated by the getaddrinfo() function. This memory must be freed by the caller after use to not cause memory leak. The caller must call the following function to free that memory:

```
void freeaddrinfo(struct addrinfo *res);
```

Just a side note here. Note that although the getaddrinfo() function is defined by the POSIX standard, I found it does not always behave exactly the same way across all operating systems. Some of the details differ. For instance, I noticed some minor discrepancies on Windows and AIX as compared to Linux and Solaris in support of flags of the hints and in the addresses returned. Some of them may also have to do with actual network configurations.

Note that getaddrinfo() function can potentially return more than one IP address for a given hostname. In that case, it will return a linked list of addrinfo structures linked by the ai_next member. In this case, the order of the addresses may vary between different operating systems.

Be aware that in Windows the WSAStartup() call must execute successfully before getaddrinfo() can be called.

12-9-3 The getnameinfo() Function

The getnameinfo() function does the opposite of getaddrinfo(). It translates a socket address in binary form into a hostname and a service name. It combines the functionalities of gethostbyaddr() and getservbyport(). Its synopsis is shown below:

```
#include <sys/socket.h>
#include <netdb.h>

int getnameinfo(const struct sockaddr *restrict sa, socklen_t salen,
     char *restrict node, socklen_t nodelen, char *restrict service,
     socklen_t servicelen, int flags);
```

The first argument sa is a pointer to a generic socket address which contains an IP address and a port number. The second argument salen specifies the size of the sa argument in bytes.

The translated hostname will be returned in the third argument 'node' whose size is specified in the fourth argument 'nodelen'. Similarly, the translated service will be returned in the fifth argument, 'service', whose size is specified in the 'servicelen' argument.

The flag argument modifies the behavior of getnameinfo().

12-9-4 Errors from getaddrinfo() and getnameinfo()

Note that, contrary to ordinary socket functions, the getaddrinfo() does not return -1 (or SOCKET_ERROR, which is -1, in Windows) on failure. Therefore, you should never check if its return value equals to -1. It returns 0 on success and a non-zero value (typically, a negative value) indicating the real error. The error is directly returned from the function, not via the errno variable! To translate the error code returned by getaddrinfo() into an error message, you must call a special function named gai_strerror().

In addition, in Linux/Unix, getaddrinfo() could return EAI_SYSTEM which indicates other system error. In that case, the real error will be available in the errno variable.

Note that the way getnameinfo() returns its result and errors is similar to getaddrinfo(). The errors they return are similar too. Thus, the two can be handled in the same way.

Figure 12-14b shows a connection-oriented client program which uses the getaddrinfo() function, takes the server's hostname or IP address from command-line as input, and connects and communicates with the server. The server's hostname or IP address can be IPv4 or IPv6. If the host name and port number are omitted from the command line, localhost and the default port number are used respectively. If you need to specify a hostname then it requires you to specify a port number as well. It is so arranged because presumably "tcpclnt_all port_num" would be what most people do to test these programs on the same host.

The syntax of using this program is as follows:

```
    $ tcpclnt_all  [server_port_number [server_host_name]]
 or
    $ tcpclnt_all  [server_port_number [server_ip_address]]
```

The command-line arguments enclosed in brackets are optional and can be omitted. This means, you could omit the hostname or IP address (in that case, the default will be "localhost") or you could omit both arguments (in that case, the default port number will be used).

Note that for simplicity, in this example program we do not bother checking if multiple IP addresses are returned by getaddrinfo(). We simply take the first one returned and use it.

12-10 Support for IPv4 and IPv6

When TCP/IP was designed in the 1960s and 1970s as a research project by the DARPA (The Defense Advanced Research Projects Agency) sponsored by the U.S. Department of Defense, there were not that many network devices. Hence, a 32-bit IP address was used and it has been working just fine for decades. However, after the Internet boom in the 1990s, with the proliferation of laptop computers, smart phones and intelligent home appliances, the world was running out of 32-bit IP addresses. That's why there is IPv6, which uses 128-bit IP addresses.

In terms of the adoption of IPv6, some nations are moving faster than others. As a result, we have been and are still living in a world where both IPv4 and IPv6 devices co-exist. And this will continue for quite some time ahead. Because of that, for software engineers, it has been a reality that one has to deal with both types of communications. Therefore, writing software programs that work with both IPv4 and IPv6 has been a must.

Because of the mixed world, the best strategy to write a server program is to **use an IPv6 server listener socket and bind it to IPv6 wildcard address in6addr_any** because that allows the server to be able to accept client connection requests from both IPv6 and IPv4 clients.

A reality you also observe from playing with these programs is that
an IPv6 client can never connect to an IPv4 server. In other words,
it is backward compatible but not forward compatible. That is, an IPv6 server
socket is backward compatible and it can be used to communicate with
partners of both IPv4 and IPv6. But an IPv4 server socket just does not
know how to handle an IPv6 client or partner at all which came after IPv4.

Therefore, the bottom line is that the best strategy is to run an IPv6 server
because it will be able to accept connection requests from clients of both
IPv6 and IPv4. Because of this, our example program tcpsrv_all.c does
exactly that. The program uses an IPv6 server listener socket by default.
To compile it into an IPv4 program, you have to pass in the -DIPV4 compiler
flag to the C compiler command.

Figure 12-14a is a connection-oriented server program using an IPv6 listener
socket such that it can accept requests from both IPv6 and IPv4 clients.

12-10-1 Migrate Your Networking Code from IPv4 to IPv6

If you are maintaining some existing networking code, it's very likely
that it was written for IPv4. In that case, you might want to start
migrating it to IPv6 or IPv4 and IPv6, if that hasn't already been done.

To convert an existing socket program using IPv4 to one using the newer
IPv6, you could follow the following steps:

1. Familiarize yourself with the data structures

   A socket address contains information about IP address, port number,
   address family (IPv4, IPv6, etc.) and others.
   The traditional IPv4 socket address structure is 'struct sockaddr_in'
   and the new IPv6 socket address structure .is 'struct sockaddr_in6'.

   In addition, on the server side, the "any" address that a server program
   is typically bound to is different between IPv4 and IPv6.
   This address is INADDR_ANY for IPv4 and in6addr_any for IPv6.

2. The next step is to simply change 'struct sockaddr_in' in an IPv4 program
   to 'struct sockaddr_in6' and see what happens. This means
   everything in the contents of the structure remains IPv4, just the
   structure is changed to IPv6 version. You will notice it does
   not break anything. The IPv4 program continues to work.
   This indicates the design of the IPv6 socket address structure is
   backward compatible.

3. To actually migrate from IPv4 to IPv6, you really need to change the
   contents of the socket address structure from IPv4 to IPv6.
   This includes changing the following fields:

   ```
   'struct sockaddr_in'      ->   'struct sockaddr_in6'
   --------------------           -------------------------
   sin_family (AF_INET)     ->     sin6_family (AF_INET6)
   sin_addr (INADDR_ANY)    ->     sin6_addr (in6addr_any)
   sin_port                 ->     sin6_port
   ----------------------------------------------------------
   ```

12-11 Get a Peer's Address and Port Number

In a networking program, at times it is necessary or useful to find out
and know whom the application is talking to at the other end. That is,
you might want to find out the IP address and port number of the program
that your program is communicating with. This is completely do-able in
both connection-oriented socket connections using the TCP protocol and
connectionless socket connections using the UDP protocol.
This section tells you how.

Please notice that in this context, when we say peer, it generically means
the communication partner at the other end of the communication channel.
The role of that partner could be a client or server as in a client-server
communication or a peer as in a peer-to-peer configuration. As far as
finding out who the communication partner is, the role does not really
matter or make any difference.

TCP

Once a TCP connection is established, a program can always invoke the
getpeername() POSIX function to get the IP address and port number of a peer.
This means a server can get the IP address and port number of a client
it is communicating with. And a client can get the IP address and port number
of a server it is talking to, although a client usually already knows the
server's address and port number because that's what it connects to.
This function works in a peer-to-peer setting too.

The getpeername() function is as follows:

```
#include <sys/socket.h>

int getpeername(int socket, struct sockaddr *restrict address,
    socklen_t *restrict address_len);
```

The first argument is the socket being used for the connection.
The second argument is a pointer to a 'struct sockaddr' which is to hold
the peer socket address returned by the function. The third argument is
a pointer to a buffer which contains the size in bytes of the buffer in the
second argument.

The getpeername() function returns 0 on success. It returns -1 on error and
errno is set to indicate the error. If success, on return the third argument
contains the actual size in bytes of the socket structure returned,
from which the caller can tell whether an IPv4 or IPv6 socket address is
being returned by checking if the returned size is equal to sizeof(struct
sockaddr_in) or sizeof(struct sockaddr_in6).

Below is the code to **get and print a peer's IP address and port number**:

```
struct sockaddr_in6   peeraddr6;  /* IPV6 socket structure */
struct sockaddr_in    *peeraddr4p; /* IPV4 socket structure */
socklen_t    peeraddr6sz=sizeof(struct sockaddr_in6);
char    peeraddrstr[PEERADDRLEN]; /* IP address of peer socket, string form */
```

```
/* Get and print peer's IP address and port number */
memset((void *)&peeraddr6, 0, (size_t)peeraddr6sz);
memset(peeraddrstr, 0, PEERADDRLEN);
errno = 0;
ret = getpeername(sfd, (struct sockaddr *) &peeraddr6, &peeraddr6sz);
if (ret == 0)
{
  /* The return structure size indicates IPv4 or IPv6. */
  if (peeraddr6sz > sizeof(struct sockaddr_in))
  {
    inet_ntop(AF_INET6, &(peeraddr6.sin6_addr), peeraddrstr, PEERADDRLEN);
    fprintf(stdout, "Server's IP address from getpeername(): %s port=%u\n",
      peeraddrstr, ntohs(peeraddr6.sin6_port));
  } else {
    peeraddr4p = (struct sockaddr_in *)&peeraddr6;
    inet_ntop(AF_INET, &(peeraddr4p->sin_addr.s_addr), peeraddrstr, PEERADDRLEN);
    fprintf(stdout, "Server's IP address from getpeername(): %s port=%u\n",
      peeraddrstr, ntohs(peeraddr4p->sin_port));
  }
}
else
  fprintf(stderr, "Error: getpeername() failed, errno=%d\n", errno);
```

After invoking the getpeername() function to get the peer's socket address, we then use the **inet_ntop**() function to convert the peer's IP address from binary to string format for printing. The peer's port number is also converted from network byte order to the local host's byte order by the **ntohs**() function before it's printed.

Please be aware that when using the inet_ntop() or inet_ntoa() function to convert an Internet host address from binary format to its string format, your C program must include all of the following three header files:

```
#include <sys/socket.h>
#include <netinet/in.h>
#include <arpa/inet.h>
```

If you forget to include the third one, #include <arpa/inet.h>, then you will find the call to the function inet_ntop() or inet_ntoa() may get a "Segmentation fault" error and cause your program to die.

Also notice that inet_ntoa() function is the old version of the conversion function to use because it works for IPv4 only. The new function to use is inet_ntop() which works for both IPV4 and IPv6. That is, inet_ntop() supports multiple address families. It is an extension of inet_ntoa().

In reverse, to convert a character string IP address (IPv4 or IPv6) into binary format, use the **inet_pton**() function.

Notice that in a TCP server program, you don't really have to use the getpeername() function. This is because a TCP server calls the accept() function to accept a client's connection. When the accept() function returns successfully, it returns the client's address in the second argument. This means **a TCP server has two ways to get a client's address: accept() and getpeername**().

Figure 12-15 is a pair of client and server programs that display the peer's IPv6 address and port number. This pair of programs were tested in Linux, AIX, Solaris, HP-UX, Apple Darwin and Windows 7. They ran successfully using all of the following three types of IPv6 addresses:

```
::1
fe80::dce3:7621:7024:4467%11
2001:0:9d38:6ab8:189d:1d52:e7dd:d627
```

Figure 12-15 Get peer's IP address -- tcpsrv_peeraddr_all.c, tcpclnt_peeraddr_all.c
  (a) tcpsrv_peeraddr_all.c

```c
/*
 * A connection-oriented server program using Stream socket.
 * Support for IPv4 and IPv6. Default to IPV6. Compile with -DIPV4 to get IPV4.
 * Support for multiple platforms including Linux, Windows, Solaris, AIX, HPUX
 * and Apple Darwin.
 * Usage: tcpsrv_peeraddr_all [port#]
 * Authored by Mr. Jin-Jwei Chen.
 * Copyright (c) 1993-2018, 2020 Mr. Jin-Jwei Chen. All rights reserved.
 */

#include "mysocket.h"

int main(int argc, char *argv[])
{
  int     ret;                        /* return code */
  int     sfd;                        /* file descriptor of the listener socket */
  int     newsock;                    /* file descriptor of client data socket */
#if IPV4
  struct sockaddr_in    srvaddr;      /* socket structure */
  int     srvaddrsz=sizeof(struct sockaddr_in);
  struct sockaddr_in    clntaddr;     /* socket structure */
  socklen_t    clntaddrsz=sizeof(struct sockaddr_in);
#else
  struct sockaddr_in6   srvaddr;      /* socket structure */
  int     srvaddrsz=sizeof(struct sockaddr_in6);
  struct sockaddr_in6   clntaddr;     /* socket structure */
  socklen_t    clntaddrsz=sizeof(struct sockaddr_in6);
  int     v6only = 0;                 /* IPV6_V6ONLY socket option off */
#endif
  in_port_t    portnum=DEFSRVPORT;    /* port number */
  int     portnum_in = 0;             /* port number entered by user */
  char    inbuf[BUFLEN];              /* input message buffer */
  char    outbuf[BUFLEN];             /* output message buffer */
  size_t msglen;                      /* length of reply message */
  unsigned int  msgcnt;               /* message count */
  struct sockaddr_in6   peeraddr6;    /* IP address of peer socket */
  socklen_t    peeraddr6sz=sizeof(struct sockaddr_in6);
  char    peeraddrstr[PEERADDRLEN];   /* IP address of peer socket, string form */

#if WINDOWS
  WSADATA wsaData;                    /* Winsock data */
  char* GetErrorMsg(int ErrorCode);   /* print error string in Windows */
```

```c
#endif

    fprintf(stdout, "Connection-oriented server program ...\n");

    /* Get the port number from user, if any. */
    if (argc > 1)
    {
      portnum_in = atoi(argv[1]);
      if (portnum_in <= 0)
      {
        fprintf(stderr, "Port number %d invalid, set to default value %u\n",
          portnum_in, DEFSRVPORT);
        portnum = DEFSRVPORT;
      }
      else
        portnum = (in_port_t)portnum_in;
    }

#if WINDOWS
    /* Initiate use of the Winsock DLL. Ask for Winsock version 2.2 at least. */
    if ((ret = WSAStartup(MAKEWORD(2, 2), &wsaData)) != 0)
    {
      fprintf(stderr, "WSAStartup() failed with error %d: %s\n",
        ret, GetErrorMsg(ret));
      return (-1);
    }
#endif

    /* Create the Stream server socket. */
    if ((sfd = socket(ADDR_FAMILY, SOCK_STREAM, 0)) < 0)
    {
      fprintf(stderr, "Error: socket() failed, errno=%d, %s\n", ERRNO, ERRNOSTR);
#if WINDOWS
      WSACleanup();
#endif
      return(-2);
    }

    /* Fill in the server socket address. */
    memset((void *)&srvaddr, 0, (size_t)srvaddrsz); /* clear the address buffer */
#if IPV4
    srvaddr.sin_family = ADDR_FAMILY;               /* Internet socket */
    srvaddr.sin_addr.s_addr = htonl(INADDR_ANY);    /* server's IP address */
    srvaddr.sin_port = htons(portnum);              /* server's port number */
#else
    srvaddr.sin6_family = ADDR_FAMILY;              /* Internet socket */
    srvaddr.sin6_addr = in6addr_any;                /* server's IP address */
    srvaddr.sin6_port = htons(portnum);             /* server's port number */
#endif

    /* If IPv6, turn off IPV6_V6ONLY socket option. Default is on in Windows. */
#if !IPV4
    if (setsockopt(sfd, IPPROTO_IPV6, IPV6_V6ONLY, (char*)&v6only,
      sizeof(v6only)) != 0)
    {
      fprintf(stderr, "Error: setsockopt(IPV6_V6ONLY) failed, errno=%d, %s\n",
```

```
      ERRNO, ERRNOSTR);
   CLOSE(sfd);
   return(-3);
  }
#endif

  /* Bind the server socket to its address. */
  if ((ret = bind(sfd, (struct sockaddr *)&srvaddr, srvaddrsz)) != 0)
  {
    fprintf(stderr, "Error: bind() failed, errno=%d, %s\n", ERRNO, ERRNOSTR);
    CLOSE(sfd);
    return(-4);
  }

  /* Set maximum connection request queue length that we can fall behind. */
  if (listen(sfd, BACKLOG) == -1) {
    fprintf(stderr, "Error: listen() failed, errno=%d, %s\n", ERRNO, ERRNOSTR);
    CLOSE(sfd);
    return(-5);
  }

  /* Wait for incoming connection requests from clients and service them. */
  while (1) {

    fprintf(stdout, "\nListening at port number %u ...\n", portnum);
    newsock = accept(sfd, (struct sockaddr *)&clntaddr, &clntaddrsz);
    if (newsock < 0)
    {
      fprintf(stderr, "Error: accept() failed, errno=%d, %s\n", ERRNO, ERRNOSTR);
      CLOSE(sfd);
      return(-6);
    }

    fprintf(stdout, "Client Connected.\n");

    /* Print the peer's IP address & port# returned from accept() */
    memset(peeraddrstr, 0, PEERADDRLEN);
    inet_ntop(AF_INET6, &(clntaddr.sin6_addr), peeraddrstr, PEERADDRLEN);
    fprintf(stdout, "Client's IP address from accept(): %s port=%u\n",
      peeraddrstr, ntohs(clntaddr.sin6_port));

    /* Get and print peer's IP address & port# returned from getpeername() */
    memset(&peeraddr6, 0, peeraddr6sz);
    memset(peeraddrstr, 0, PEERADDRLEN);
    errno = 0;
    ret = getpeername(newsock, (struct sockaddr *)&peeraddr6, &peeraddr6sz);
    if (ret == 0)
    {
      inet_ntop(AF_INET6, &(peeraddr6.sin6_addr), peeraddrstr, PEERADDRLEN);
      fprintf(stdout, "Client's IP address from getpeername(): %s port=%u\n",
        peeraddrstr, ntohs(peeraddr6.sin6_port));
    }
    else
      fprintf(stderr, "Error: getpeername() failed, errno=%d, %s\n", ERRNO,
        ERRNOSTR);
```

```
    msgcnt = 1;
    /* Receive and service requests from the current client. */
    while (1)
    {
      /* Receive a request from a client. */
      errno = 0;
      inbuf[0] = '\0';
      ret = recv(newsock, inbuf, BUFLEN, 0);
      if (ret > 0)
      {
        /* Process the request. We simply print the request message here. */
        inbuf[ret] = '\0';
        fprintf(stdout, "\nReceived the following request from client:\n%s\n",
          inbuf);

        /* Construct a reply */
        sprintf(outbuf, "This is reply #%3u from the server program.", msgcnt++);
        msglen = strlen(outbuf);

        /* Send a reply. */
        errno = 0;
        ret = send(newsock, outbuf, msglen, 0);
        if (ret == -1)
          fprintf(stderr, "Error: send() failed, errno=%d, %s\n", ERRNO,
            ERRNOSTR);
        else
          fprintf(stdout, "%u of %lu bytes of the reply was sent.\n", ret, msglen);
      }
      else if (ret < 0)
      {
        fprintf(stderr, "Error: recv() failed, errno=%d, %s\n", ERRNO,
          ERRNOSTR);
        break;
      }
      else
      {
        /* The client may have disconnected. */
        fprintf(stdout, "The client may have disconnected.\n");
        break;
      }
    } /* while - inner */
    CLOSE1(newsock);
  } /* while - outer */

  CLOSE(sfd);
  return(0);
}
```

(b) tcpclnt_peeraddr_all.c

```
/*
 * A connection-oriented client program using Stream socket.
 * Connecting to a server program on any host using a hostname or IP address.
 * Support for IPv4 and IPv6 and multiple platforms including
 * Linux, Windows, Solaris, AIX, HPUX and Apple Darwin.
 * Usage: tcpclnt_peeraddr_all [srvport# [server-hostname | server-ipaddress]]
```

```
 * Authored by Mr. Jin-Jwei Chen.
 * Copyright (c) 1993-2018, 2020 Mr. Jin-Jwei Chen. All rights reserved.
 */

#include "mysocket.h"

#undef   MAXMSGS
#define  MAXMSGS                1    /* Maximum number of messages to send */

int main(int argc, char *argv[])
{
  int     ret;
  int     sfd;                       /* socket file descriptor */
  in_port_t  portnum=DEFSRVPORT;     /* port number */
  char    *portnumstr = DEFSRVPORTSTR; /* port number in string format */
  int     portnum_in = 0;            /* port number provided by user */
  char    inbuf[BUFLEN];             /* input message buffer */
  char    outbuf[BUFLEN];            /* output message buffer */
  size_t  msglen;                    /* length of reply message */
  size_t  msgnum=0;                  /* count of request message */
  size_t  len;
  char    server_name[NAMELEN+1] = "localhost";
  struct addrinfo hints, *res=NULL;  /* address info */
  char *ipaddrstr = IPV6LOCALADDR;   /* server's IP address in string format */
  struct in6_addr  ipaddrbin;        /* server's IP address in binary format */
  struct sockaddr_in6    peeraddr6;  /* IPV6 socket structure */
  struct sockaddr_in    *peeraddr4p; /* IPV4 socket structure */
  socklen_t    peeraddr6sz=sizeof(struct sockaddr_in6);
  char    peeraddrstr[PEERADDRLEN];  /* IP address of peer socket, string form */

#if WINDOWS
  WSADATA wsaData;                        /* Winsock data */
  int winerror;                           /* error in Windows */
  char* GetErrorMsg(int ErrorCode);       /* print error string in Windows */
#endif

  fprintf(stdout, "Connection-oriented client program ...\n");

  /* Get the server's port number from command line. */
  if (argc > 1)
  {
    portnum_in = atoi(argv[1]);
    if (portnum_in <= 0)
    {
      fprintf(stderr, "Port number %d invalid, set to default value %u\n",
        portnum_in, DEFSRVPORT);
      portnum = DEFSRVPORT;
      portnumstr = DEFSRVPORTSTR;
    }
    else
    {
      portnum = (in_port_t)portnum_in;
      portnumstr = argv[1];
    }
  }
```

```c
  /* Get the server's host name or IP address from command line. */
  if (argc > 2)
  {
    len = strlen(argv[2]);
    if (len > NAMELEN)
      len = NAMELEN;
    strncpy(server_name, argv[2], len);
    server_name[len] = '\0';
  }

#if WINDOWS
  /* Ask for Winsock version 2.2 at least. */
  if ((ret = WSAStartup(MAKEWORD(2, 2), &wsaData)) != 0)
  {
    fprintf(stderr, "Error: WSAStartup() failed with error %d: %s\n",
      ret, GetErrorMsg(ret));
    return (-1);
  }
#endif

  /* Translate the server's host name or IP address into socket address.
   * Fill in the hints information.
   */
  memset(&hints, 0x00, sizeof(hints));
    /* This works on AIX but not on Solaris, nor on Windows. */
    /* hints.ai_flags     = AI_NUMERICSERV; */
  hints.ai_family   = AF_UNSPEC;
  hints.ai_socktype = SOCK_STREAM;

  /* Get the address information of the server using getaddrinfo(). */
  ret = getaddrinfo(server_name, portnumstr, &hints, &res);
  if (ret != 0)
  {
    fprintf(stderr, "Error: getaddrinfo() failed. Host %s not found.\n",
      gai_strerror(ret));
#if WINDOWS
    /* Windows supports EAI_AGAIN, EAI_BADFLAGS, EAI_FAIL, EAI_FAMILY,
       EAI_MEMORY, EAI_NONAME, EAI_SERVICE, EAI_SOCKTYPE, but no EAI_SYSTEM */
    fprintf(stderr, "getaddrinfo() failed with error %d: %s\n",
        WSAGetLastError(), GetErrorMsg(WSAGetLastError()));
    WSACleanup();
#else
    if (ret == EAI_SYSTEM)
      perror("getaddrinfo() failed");
#endif
    return (-2);
  }

  /* Create a socket. */
  sfd = socket(res->ai_family, res->ai_socktype, res->ai_protocol);
  if (sfd < 0)
  {
    fprintf(stderr,"Error: socket() failed, errno=%d, %s\n", ERRNO,
      ERRNOSTR);
#if WINDOWS
    WSACleanup();
```

```
#endif
    return (-3);
  }

  /* Connect to the server. */
  ret = connect(sfd, res->ai_addr, res->ai_addrlen);
  if (ret == -1)
  {
    fprintf(stderr, "Error: connect() failed, errno=%d, %s\n", ERRNO,
      ERRNOSTR);
    CLOSE(sfd);
    return(-4);
  }

  /* Get and print peer's IP address and port number */
  memset((void *)&peeraddr6, 0, (size_t)peeraddr6sz);
  memset(peeraddrstr, 0, PEERADDRLEN);
  errno = 0;
  ret = getpeername(sfd, (struct sockaddr *) &peeraddr6, &peeraddr6sz);
  if (ret == 0)
  {
    /* The return structure size indicates IPv4 or IPv6. */
    if (peeraddr6sz > sizeof(struct sockaddr_in))
    {
      inet_ntop(AF_INET6, &(peeraddr6.sin6_addr), peeraddrstr, PEERADDRLEN);
      fprintf(stdout, "Server's IP address from getpeername(): %s port=%u\n",
        peeraddrstr, ntohs(peeraddr6.sin6_port));
    } else {
      peeraddr4p = (struct sockaddr_in *)&peeraddr6;
      inet_ntop(AF_INET, &(peeraddr4p->sin_addr.s_addr), peeraddrstr, PEERADDRLEN);
      fprintf(stdout, "Server's IP address from getpeername(): %s port=%u\n",
        peeraddrstr, ntohs(peeraddr4p->sin_port));
    }
  }
  else
    fprintf(stderr, "Error: getpeername() failed, errno=%d, %s\n", ERRNO,
      ERRNOSTR);

  fprintf(stdout, "Send request messages to server(%s) at port %d\n",
    server_name, portnum);

  /* Send request messages to the server and process the reply messages. */
  while (msgnum < MAXMSGS)
  {
    /* Send a request message to the server. */
    sprintf(outbuf, "%s%4lu%s", "This is request message ", ++msgnum,
      " from the client program.");
    msglen = strlen(outbuf);
    errno = 0;

    ret = send(sfd, outbuf, msglen, 0);
    if (ret >= 0)
    {
      /* Print a warning if not entire message was sent. */
      if (ret == msglen)
        fprintf(stdout, "\n%lu bytes of message were successfully sent.\n",
```

```
        msglen);
    else if (ret < msglen)
      fprintf(stderr, "Warning: only %u of %lu bytes were sent.\n",
        ret, msglen);

    if (ret > 0)
    {
      /* Receive a reply from the server. */
      errno = 0;
      inbuf[0] = '\0';
      ret = recv(sfd, inbuf, BUFLEN, 0);

      if (ret > 0)
      {
        /* Process the reply. */
        inbuf[ret] = '\0';
        fprintf(stdout, "Received the following reply from server:\n%s\n",
          inbuf);
      }
      else if (ret == 0)
        fprintf(stdout, "Warning: Zero bytes were received.\n");
      else
        fprintf(stderr, "Error: recv() failed, errno=%d, %s\n", ERRNO,
          ERRNOSTR);
    }
    else
      fprintf(stderr, "Error: send() failed, errno=%d, %s\n", ERRNO,
        ERRNOSTR);

#if WINDOWS
    Sleep(1000); /* Unit is ms. For demo only. Remove this in real code. */
#else
    sleep(1);  /* For demo only. Remove this in real code. */
#endif
  }  /* while */

  /* Free the memory allocated by getaddrinfo() */
  freeaddrinfo(res);
  CLOSE(sfd);
  return(0);
}
```

UDP

With Datagram sockets, there is no need to call a separate function to obtain a peer's IP address and port number. When a program invokes the recvfrom() function to receive a message on a Datagram socket, that function returns the socket address of the peer that has just sent the message. The peer's IP address and port number are contained in the 'struct sockaddr' returned via the fifth argument of the recvfrom() function. One can extract and print them the same way as we did above in a TCP connection. A such usage is shown below:

```
struct sockaddr_in    fromaddr;  /* socket structure */
socklen_t    fromaddrsz=sizeof(struct sockaddr_in);
```

```
ret = recvfrom(sfd, inbuf, BUFLEN, 0, (struct sockaddr *)&fromaddr,
        &fromaddrsz);
```

12-12 IP Agnostic Programs

As we mentioned it earlier, in the foreseeable future, it's going to be a world of mixing IPv4 and IPv6 as IPv6 is gradually ushered in and IPv4 gradually bowing out over time. As software engineers developing distributed applications, this means it would be best and necessary to develop software working with both IPv4 and IPv6 at the same time.

This section presents a pair of client and server socket applications that can do just that. The same set of programs work without modification regardless if you use an IPv4, IPv6, or mixed network.

12-12-1 Use getaddrinfo() on Client and IPv6 Socket on Server

The key to writing IP-agnostic client-server programs is to use the set of newer socket and networking APIs and features that support both IPv4 and IPv6 protocols. Among them the following two things stand out.

1. On the **client** side, use the **getaddrinfo**() function to translate hostnames into IP addresses. This function supports both IPv4 and IPv6 and is thread-safe. It also takes hostnames or IP addresses as input.

2. On the **server** side, always create and use an **IPv6 server socket** so that it accepts both IPv6 and IPv4 incoming client connection requests. Remember that on most platforms, by default, an IPv6 socket supports both IPv6 and IPv4. But on a very small number of platforms (for instance, Windows), by default an IPv6 socket supports IPv6 only and you have to explicitly turn off the IPV6_V6ONLY option to support IPv4.

Figure 12-16 shows a pair of IP-agnostic client-server programs.

Figure 12-16 IP-agnostic client-server programs: ip_ag_srv_all.c, ip_ag_clnt_all.c
    (a) ip_ag_srv_all.c

```
/*
 * A cross-platform IP-agnostic TCP Server program.
 * This is a very flexible IP-agnostic TCP server program.
 * It supports IPv4 and IPv6 at the same time.
 * This program allows users to easily test IPv4 and IPv6 combinations.
 * If the user does not specify a host name argument, this program
 *    determines if IPv6 is supported in the localhost. If yes, it starts an
 *    IPv6 listener server socket and accepts both IPv4/IPv6 client connections.
 *    If IPv6 is not supported, it starts an IPv4 server.
 * If the user specifies a hostname, this program creates a server socket
 *    matching the IP type of that hostname so the user has control over
 *    which IP to use.
 *    Should the host be dual-IP with a single name, whichever IP address type
 *    returned first by getaddrinfo() will be used.
 *    Note that this approach of using hostname to control the IPv4 vs. IPv6
```

```
 *    type of socket seems to work well on Solaris and Linux. But it might not
 *    work on some Windows Server 2003 where using an IPv4 hostname may lead to
 *    a Link Local IPv6 address (that begins with fe80) in some environment and
 *    an IPv6 server socket was used. Specifying the IPv4 address in place of
 *    the IPv4 hostname works around the problem.
 * This program also prints the communication partner's IP address.
 * Support for multiple platforms including Linux, Windows, Solaris, AIX, HPUX
 *    and Apple Darwin.
 * Usage: ip_ag_srv_all [port_num [hostname_or_IPaddr]]
 * By default, if user specifies nothing, an IPv6 server socket is used.
 * The user can specify an IP address or hostname as the second command-line
 * argument, after the port number, to select an IP type he/she prefers.
 *
 * Authored by Jin-Jwei Chen.
 * Copyright (c) 2005-2018, 2020 Mr. Jin-Jwei Chen. All rights reserved.
 */

#include "mysocket.h"

void  printSockType(int);

int main(int argc, char **argv)
{
  /* Variable and structure definitions */
  int lsnr=-1, clntsk=-1;                /* socket file descriptors */
  int on=1, datasz=BUFLEN;               /* value of socket option */
  char buf[BUFLEN];                      /* input & output buffer */
  /*struct sockaddr_in6 serveraddr, clientaddr;*/
  struct sockaddr_storage clntaddr;   /* client's address */
  struct sockaddr_in    srvaddr4;     /* server's IPv4 address */
  struct sockaddr_in6   srvaddr6;     /* server's IPv6 address */
  /* unsigned long addrlen = sizeof(clntaddr); */ /* AIX*/
  socklen_t addrlen = sizeof(clntaddr); /* Solaris, Linux, HPUX, Windows */
  short srvport = DEFSRVPORT;            /* port number server listens on */
  char  *srvhost = NOHOST;               /* name of the server host */
  char  hostaddr[IPADDRSZ];              /* buffer for host's string IP address */
  char  straddr[INET6_ADDRSTRLEN+1];  /* IP address in string format */
  int   v6only = 0;                      /* IPV6_V6ONLY socket option off */
  struct addrinfo hints, *res=NULL, *aip;
  int   ret=0, success=0;

  /* On AIX getaddrinfo() always fails with EAI_NONAME if service="" */
#if AIX
  char *service = NULL;   /* e.g. set to "ftp" works */
#else
  char *service = "";
#endif
  int  niflags = (NI_NUMERICHOST|NI_NUMERICSERV); /* getnameinfo() flags */
  char clntipaddr[NI_MAXHOST];          /* client's string IP address */
#if WINDOWS
  short       addrFam;                   /* protocol family (IPv4 or IPv6) */
#else
  sa_family_t addrFam;                   /* protocol family (IPv4 or IPv6) */
#endif
#if WINDOWS
  WSADATA wsaData;                       /* Winsock data */
```

```
  int winerror;                            /* error in Windows */
  char* GetErrorMsg(int ErrorCode);    /* print error string in Windows */
#endif

  /* Get server's port number and hostname or IP address provided by user */
  if (argc > 1)
    srvport = atoi(argv[1]);
  if (argc > 2)
    srvhost = argv[2];

  fprintf(stdout, "srvhost=%s  port_num=%d\n", srvhost, srvport);

#if WINDOWS
  /* Use at least Winsock version 2.2 */
  if ((ret = WSAStartup(MAKEWORD(2, 2), &wsaData)) != 0)
  {
    fprintf(stderr, "WSAStartup failed with error %d: %s\n",
      ret, GetErrorMsg(ret));
    return (-1);
  }
#endif

  /* Server's service loop */
  do
  {
    if ( !strcmp(srvhost, NOHOST) )
    {
      /* No host name or IP address is given. Use Ipv6 over Ipv4 if it works. */
      addrFam = AF_INET6;
      if ((lsnr = socket(addrFam, SOCK_STREAM, 0)) < 0)
      {
        fprintf(stdout, "IPv6 does not seem to be supported. Try IPv4.\n");
        addrFam = AF_INET;
        if ((lsnr = socket(addrFam, SOCK_STREAM, 0)) < 0)
        {
          fprintf(stdout, "IPv4 does not seem to be supported, either.\n");
          fprintf(stderr, "socket() failed, errno=%d, %s\n", ERRNO, ERRNOSTR);
          ret = (-2);
          break;
        }
      }

      /* A server socket was successfully created. */
      printSockType(addrFam);

    } else {

      /* A server host name or IP address is given by the user. Do lookup and
         use that IP type. */

      /* Set up the hints for lookup */
      memset(&hints, 0, sizeof(hints));
      hints.ai_flags = AI_PASSIVE;
      hints.ai_family = AF_UNSPEC;
      hints.ai_socktype = SOCK_STREAM;
```

769

```c
    /* Call getaddrinfo() for the server hostname or IP address.
     * Note that the res returned by getaddrinfo() contains a linked list
     * of the server's addresses found. So one could potentially try the
     * next one in the list if the current one fails.
     */
    ret = getaddrinfo(srvhost, service, &hints, &res);
    if (ret != 0)
    {
       fprintf(stderr, "Error: getaddrinfo() failed, error %d, %s\n", ret,
          gai_strerror(ret));
#if !WINDOWS
       if (ret == EAI_SYSTEM)
          fprintf(stderr,"System error: errno=%d, %s\n", errno, strerror(errno));
#endif
       ret = (-3);
       break;
    }


    /* Loop through all addresses returned until one succeeds. */
    success = 0;
    for (aip = res; aip; aip = aip->ai_next)
    {
      /* Print the server's IP address */
      switch (aip->ai_family)
      {
        case AF_INET6:
          addrFam = AF_INET6;
          /* Without NI_NUMERIC*, it returns hostname & text service name */
          ret = getnameinfo(aip->ai_addr, sizeof(struct sockaddr_in6),
            hostaddr, IPADDRSZ, NULL, 0,  niflags);
          if (ret == 0)
             fprintf(stdout, "Server IPv6 address is %s.\n", hostaddr);
          else
             fprintf(stderr, "Error: getnameinfo() failed, error %d, %s\n",
               ret, gai_strerror(ret));
         break;
        case AF_INET:
          addrFam = AF_INET;
          ret = getnameinfo(aip->ai_addr, sizeof(struct sockaddr_in),
            hostaddr, IPADDRSZ, NULL, 0,  niflags);
          if (ret == 0)
             fprintf(stdout, "Server IPv4 address is %s.\n", hostaddr);
          else
             fprintf(stderr, "Error: getnameinfo() failed, error %d, %s\n",
               ret, gai_strerror(ret));
         break;
        default:
          fprintf(stdout, "Server address family unexpected = %d\n",
            aip->ai_family);
         break;
      }   /* switch */


      /* Create the server's listener socket. */
      if ((lsnr = socket(addrFam, SOCK_STREAM, 0)) < 0)
      {
         fprintf(stderr, "socket() failed, errno=%d, %s\n", ERRNO, ERRNOSTR);
```

```
            continue;
        } else {
          /* Set the flag and exit the for loop. */
          success = 1;
          printSockType(addrFam);
          break;
        }
    }   /* for */

    /* Exit if no success in creating the server socket. */
    if (!success)
    {
      fprintf(stderr, "Failed to create the server socket.\n");
      ret = (-4);
      break;
    }
  }   /* if (!LOCALHOST) */

  /* We have a listener socket to work with. */

  if (setsockopt(lsnr, SOL_SOCKET, SO_REUSEADDR, (char *)&on, sizeof(on)) < 0)
  {
    fprintf(stderr, "setsockopt(SO_REUSEADDR) failed, errno=%d, %s\n", ERRNO,
      ERRNOSTR);
    ret = (-5);
    break;
  }

  /* If IPv6, turn off IPV6_V6ONLY socket option. Default is on in Windows. */
  if (addrFam == AF_INET6)
  {
    if (setsockopt(lsnr, IPPROTO_IPV6, IPV6_V6ONLY, (char*)&v6only,
      sizeof(v6only)) != 0)
    {
      fprintf(stderr, "Error: setsockopt(IPV6_V6ONLY) failed, errno=%d, %s\n",
        ERRNO, ERRNOSTR);
      ret = (-6);
      break;
    }
  }

  /* Bind the server socket. */
  memset(&srvaddr4, 0, sizeof(srvaddr4));
  memset(&srvaddr6, 0, sizeof(srvaddr6));
  if (addrFam == AF_INET6)
  {
    srvaddr6.sin6_family = AF_INET6;
    srvaddr6.sin6_port   = htons(srvport);
    srvaddr6.sin6_addr   = in6addr_any;
  } else {
    srvaddr4.sin_family = AF_INET;
    srvaddr4.sin_port   = htons(srvport);
    srvaddr4.sin_addr.s_addr = INADDR_ANY;
  }

  if (addrFam == AF_INET6)
```

```
      ret = bind(lsnr, (struct sockaddr *)&srvaddr6, sizeof(srvaddr6));
   else
      ret = bind(lsnr, (struct sockaddr *)&srvaddr4, sizeof(srvaddr4));

   if (ret < 0)
   {
     fprintf(stderr, "bind() failed, errno=%d, %s\n", ERRNO, ERRNOSTR);
     ret = (-7);
     break;
   }


   /* Listen for client connection requests. Set queue length. */
   if (listen(lsnr, BACKLOG) < 0)
   {
     fprintf(stderr, "listen() failed, errno=%d, %s\n", ERRNO, ERRNOSTR);
     ret = (-8);
     break;
   }


   fprintf(stdout, "Ready for client to connect.\n");


   /* Accept the next client connection.
    * We could have let accept() return client's address by doing
    * accept(lsnr, (struct sockaddr *)&clntaddr, &addrlen).
    * To demonstrate how to get that separately, we use getpeername below.
    */
   if ((clntsk = accept(lsnr, NULL, NULL)) < 0)
   {
     fprintf(stderr, "accept() failed, errno=%d, %s\n", ERRNO, ERRNOSTR);
     ret = (-9);
     break;
   }
   else
   {
     /* Display the client address.  Note that if the client is an IPv4
      * client, the address will be shown as an IPv4 Mapped IPv6 address.
      */
     getpeername(clntsk, (struct sockaddr *)&clntaddr, &addrlen);
     ret = getnameinfo((struct sockaddr *)&clntaddr, addrlen,
          clntipaddr, NI_MAXHOST, NULL, 0,  niflags);
     if (ret == 0)
       fprintf(stdout, "Client address is %s.\n", clntipaddr);
   }


   /* Receive the data the client sends */
   ret = recv(clntsk, buf, sizeof(buf), 0);
   if (ret < 0)
   {
     fprintf(stderr, "recv() failed, errno=%d, %s\n", ERRNO, ERRNOSTR);
     ret = (-10);
     break;
   }


   fprintf(stdout, "%d bytes of data were received.\n", ret);
   if (ret == 0)
   {
```

```
        fprintf(stdout, "The client has closed the connection.\n");
        break;
    }
    buf[ret] = '\0';

    /* Send the client data back to the client */
    ret = send(clntsk, buf, ret, 0);
    if (ret < 0)
    {
        fprintf(stderr, "send() failed, errno=%d, %s\n", ERRNO, ERRNOSTR);
        ret = (-11);
        break;
    }
    fprintf(stdout, "Server echoed the message back to the client.\n");
    ret = 0;

#if WINDOWS
    /* On Windows, server closing its socket may fail client's recv() */
    Sleep(1);
#endif
    break;
} while (0);

fprintf(stdout, "Program terminated.\n");

/* Free the memory allocated by getaddrinfo() */
if (res)
    freeaddrinfo(res);

/* Close the listener and client sockets */
if (clntsk != -1)
    CLOSE1(clntsk);
if (lsnr != -1)
    CLOSE1(lsnr);
#if WINDOWS
WSACleanup();
#endif

return(ret);
}

/* Print the type of a socket */
void printSockType(int addrFam)
{
    switch (addrFam)
    {
    case AF_INET6: fprintf(stdout, "Server uses an IPv6 socket.\n"); break;
    case AF_INET:  fprintf(stdout, "Server uses an IPv4 socket.\n"); break;
    default:       fprintf(stdout, "Server uses an unknown socket.\n");
    }
}
```

(b) ip_ag_clnt_all.c

```
/*
 * This is a cross-platform IP-agnostic TCP client program.
```

```
 * It uses getaddrinfo() to find out if the server is a IPv4 or IPv6.
 * If the user provides a server host name or IP address, that is used.
 * Otherwise, localhost is used. 2345 is the default port number.
 * This program allows users to easily test IPv4 and IPv6 combinations
 * using the same program without recompilation.
 * This program also prints the communication partner's IP address.
 * Support for multiple platforms including Linux, Windows, Solaris, AIX, HPUX
 * and Apple Darwin.
 * Usage: ip_ag_clnt_all [srvport [server_hostname_or_IP]]
 * Use -DWINDOWS compiler flag to build in Windows.
 * Authored by Jin-Jwei Chen.
 * Copyright (c) 2005-2018, 2020 Mr. Jin-Jwei Chen. All rights reserved.
 */

#include "mysocket.h"

/*
 * First command line argument is expected to be either the IP address
 * or host name of the server. Second argument is server's port number.
 */
int main(int argc, char *argv[])
{
  /* Variables and structures */
  int     sfd=-1;                          /* socket file descriptor */
  int     ret;                             /* function's return code */
  int     bytesRead=0;                     /* number of bytes received so far */
  char    buffer[BUFLEN1];        /* I/O data buffer */
  char    server[NETDB_MAX_HOST_NAME_LENGTH];  /* server's name or address */
  char    servport[12] = DEFSRVPORTSTR;        /* server's port number */
  struct in6_addr serveraddr;              /* server's socket address */
  struct addrinfo hints;                   /* hints to getaddrinfo() */
  struct addrinfo *res=NULL;               /* results from getaddrinfo() */
  char srvipaddr[INET6_ADDRSTRLEN+1]; /* server's IP address in string format */
  int niflags = (NI_NUMERICHOST|NI_NUMERICSERV);  /* flags for getnameinfo() */
#if WINDOWS
  short          addrFam;                  /* address/protocol family */
#else
  sa_family_t    addrFam;                  /* address/protocol family */
#endif
#if WINDOWS
  WSADATA wsaData;                         /* Winsock data */
  char* GetErrorMsg(int ErrorCode);   /* print error string in Windows */
#endif

  /* Get the server's hostname or IP address and port number from user */
  if (argc > 1)
    strcpy(servport, argv[1]);

  if (argc > 2)
    strcpy(server, argv[2]);
  else
    strcpy(server, SERVER_NAME);

#if WINDOWS
  /* Use at least Winsock version 2.2 */
  if ((ret = WSAStartup(MAKEWORD(2, 2), &wsaData)) != 0) {
```

```
    fprintf(stderr, "WSAStartup failed with error %d: %s\n",
            ret, GetErrorMsg(ret));
    return (-1);
  }
#endif

  do
  {
    memset(&hints, 0x00, sizeof(hints));
    /* AI_NUMERICSERV flag works on AIX but not on Solaris, nor on Windows.
    hints.ai_flags    = AI_NUMERICSERV;
    */
    hints.ai_family   = AF_UNSPEC;
    hints.ai_socktype = SOCK_STREAM;

    /* Look up the server's address information. The input parameter
       'server' can be a host name or IP address. */
    ret = getaddrinfo(server, servport, &hints, &res);
    if (ret != 0)
    {
      fprintf(stderr, "Error: getaddrinfo() failed, error %d, %s\n", ret,
        gai_strerror(ret));
#if !WINDOWS
      if (ret == EAI_SYSTEM)
        fprintf(stderr, "System error: errno=%d, %s\n", errno, strerror(errno));
#endif
      break;
    }

    /* Get and print the server's IP address. */
    if (res->ai_family == AF_INET)
    {
      fprintf(stdout, "Server %s is IPv4.\n", server);
      ret = getnameinfo(res->ai_addr, sizeof(struct sockaddr_in),
          srvipaddr, INET6_ADDRSTRLEN, NULL, 0,  niflags);
    }
    else if (res->ai_family == AF_INET6)
    {
      fprintf(stdout, "Server %s is IPv6.\n", server);
      ret = getnameinfo(res->ai_addr, sizeof(struct sockaddr_in6),
          srvipaddr, INET6_ADDRSTRLEN, NULL, 0,  niflags);
    }
    else
    {
      fprintf(stderr, "Unexpected address family %u\n", res->ai_family);
      break;
    }

    if (ret == 0)
      fprintf(stdout, "Server IP address is %s.\n", srvipaddr);
    else
      fprintf(stderr, "Error: getnameinfo() failed, error %d, %s\n", ret,
        gai_strerror(ret));

    addrFam = res->ai_family;
```

```
  /* Create the socket */
  sfd = socket(addrFam, res->ai_socktype, res->ai_protocol);
  if (sfd < 0)
  {
    fprintf(stderr, "First socket() failed with error %d: %s.\n",
            ERRNO, ERRNOSTR);

    /* First IP-type fails. Try another IP type. */
    if (addrFam == AF_INET) {
      addrFam = AF_INET6;
      fprintf(stdout, "Try to switch to IPv6 ...\n");
    } else if (addrFam == AF_INET6) {
      addrFam = AF_INET;
      fprintf(stdout, "Try to switch to IPv4 ...\n");
    } else
      break;

    sfd = socket(addrFam, res->ai_socktype, res->ai_protocol);
    if (sfd < 0)
    {
      fprintf(stderr, "Second socket() failed with error %d: %s\n",
              ERRNO, ERRNOSTR);
      break;
    }
  }
  fprintf(stdout, "Client is using an IPv%ld socket.\n",
      (addrFam == AF_INET6)?6:4);

  /* Connect to the server */
  ret = connect(sfd, res->ai_addr, res->ai_addrlen);
  if (ret < 0)
  {
    /* Note that the res returned by getaddrinfo() contains a linked list
     * of the server's addresses found. So one could potentially try the
     * next one in the list if the current one fails.
     */
    fprintf(stderr, "connect() failed with error %d: %s\n",
            ERRNO, ERRNOSTR);
    break;
  }

  /* Send a message to the server */
  memset(buffer, 'a', sizeof(buffer));
  ret = send(sfd, buffer, sizeof(buffer), 0);
  if (ret < 0)
  {
    fprintf(stderr, "send() failed with error %d: %s\n",
            ERRNO, ERRNOSTR);
    break;
  }
  fprintf(stdout, "A message of %lu bytes was sent to server.\n",
      sizeof(buffer));

  /* Receive the reply from the server */
  while (bytesRead < BUFLEN1)
  {
```

```
      ret = recv(sfd, & buffer[bytesRead], BUFLEN1 - bytesRead, 0);
      if (ret < 0)
      {
        fprintf(stderr, "recv() failed with error %d: %s\n",
            ERRNO, ERRNOSTR);
        break;
      }
      else if (ret == 0)
      {
        fprintf(stdout, "The server may have closed the connection.\n");
        break;
      }

      bytesRead += ret;
    }  /* while */

    buffer[bytesRead] = '\0';
    fprintf(stdout, "Server's reply message:\n%s\n", buffer);

  } while (FALSE);

  /* Close the socket */
  if (sfd != -1)
    CLOSE1(sfd);

  /* Free the results returned from getaddrinfo() */
  if (res != NULL)
    freeaddrinfo(res);

#if WINDOWS
  WSACleanup();
#endif
  return(0);
}
```

12-13 Common Socket Errors and Their Resolutions

This section lists a number of errors that are often seen from running
socket programs. These errors may appear to be confusing and sometimes
very time-consuming to figure out exactly what is wrong for beginners.
We document why these errors occur and how to resolve them. Hopefully,
this will help developers troubleshoot their socket programs faster.

Socket error numbers are normally defined in errno.h.
Note that one should try to use the error macros (e.g. EADDRINUSE) or error
strings because they are more portable across platforms. The error numbers
shown below are the Linux ones. They usually differ from one operating system
to the next.

1. Error: bind() failed, errno=98

    #define EADDRINUSE   98   /* **Address already in use** */

Error EADDRINUSE or "Address already in use" means the port number the
program tries to bind or use is already being used by another process.

```
$ mytcpsrv
Error: bind() failed, errno=98
```

Resolution:

A program can get this error under a couple of situations.

If this is due to the previous process has terminated but
the socket bound to the port number is still in the TIME_WAIT state,
then turn on the SO_REUSEADDR socket option in your program so it can
reuse the same port number before that wait time period expires.
Note that turning on the SO_REUSEADDR socket option must be done before
the bind() function call, or it won't be effective. For further details,
please see sections 13-6 and 13-7.

If this is due to another running process is using the same port number,
then either you choose to use a different port number or find the process
that is using it and get the port back from it if your application has
reserved it. Use tools like lsof or netstat to identify the other process.

2. Error: bind() failed, errno=99

```
#define EADDRNOTAVAIL    99      /* Cannot assign requested address */
```

Error EADDRNOTAVAIL means the IP address used in the bind() call is either
not set or wrong. The IP address specified is not the local host's address.

```
$ mytcpsrv
Connection-oriented server program ...
Error: bind() failed, errno=99

$  ./multicast_snd
Error: setsockopt(IP_MULTICAST_IF) failed, errno=99
```

IP address specified is not the local host's IP address.

Resolution: Check the IP address you are using and make sure it is
correct.

3. Error: bind() failed, errno=13

```
#define EACCES           13      /* Permission denied */
```

Getting error EACCES (Permission denied) (value 13 in Linux) usually means
a non-root process tries to bind to a port number less than 1024
which requires the super-user privilege.

```
$ tcpsrv_async_io_all 1 5
Connection-oriented server program ...
Error: bind() failed, errno=13
```

Resolution: Either run the program as the root user or use a port number
greater than 1024.

4. Client connect error: Error: connect() failed, errno=101

```
    #define ENETUNREACH      101      /* Network is unreachable */
```

When a client trying to connect to a server gets error ENETUNREACH
(101 in Linux), it usually means the server's address used is wrong.

```
$ tcpclnt 2345 ::2
Connection-oriented client, connect to ::2, port 2345
Error: connect() failed, errno=101
```

Resolution: Make sure the IP address you are using is correct.
Try to ping that IP address or host and make sure ping can reach it.

5. Client connect error: Error: connect() failed, errno=111

```
    #define ECONNREFUSED     111      /* Connection refused */
```

When a client trying to connect to a server gets error ECONNREFUSED
(Connection refused) (value 111 in Linux), it usually means the server
program is not running. It could also mean the client is using a wrong
server's IP address or server's port number, too.

```
$ tcpclnt 2345 ::1
Connection-oriented client, connect to ::1, port 2345
Error: connect() failed, errno=111
```

Resolution: Make sure the server process that your program tries to
communicate with is up and running. And make sure the client is using
the correct server's IP address and port number.

6. Client connect error: Error: connect() failed, errno=113

```
    #define EHOSTUNREACH     113      /* No route to host */
```

When a client trying to connect to a server gets error EHOSTUNREACH
(errno is 113 in Linux), this usually means the target computer that
the server program is expected to run on either does not exist or
is down.

```
$ ./tcpclnt_all 2345 xyz
Connection-oriented client program ...
Error: connect() failed, errno=113, No route to host
```

This means the target host computer is not reachable or is down.

7. Client recv() error: Error: recv() failed, errno=110

```
    #define ETIMEDOUT        110      /* Connection timed out */
```

If a client program is blocked in the recv() call waiting to receive
a message from the server and the network cable is unplugged,
eventually after the configured timeout period expires, the client's
recv() call will return with error ETIMEDOUT (110 in Linux).

```
$ ./tcpclnt_all 2345 mysrv
  Error: recv() failed, errno=110
```

12-14 Local Communication -- Unix Domain Sockets

Computer network communication, especially that happens over the Internet, typically occurs between two different computer systems connected via a computer network of some sort. In this type of communication, two computer programs running on two different computer systems are exchanging information with each other and the information is physically sent out of the computer sending the information, travels through some network cable or communication media, and then arrives at the computer receiving the information.
At either computer, the information also travels through the network protocol stack within the operating system, which includes TCP or UDP at the transport layer, IP at the network layer, and perhaps Ethernet at the Data Link layer.

The sections above have shown exactly this type of communications.
It's for inter-computer communications -- communications between separate computer systems using Internet sockets, although they also work equally well should the two communicating programs run on the same computer.

Here in this section, we introduce a third type of sockets, which works for communications between programs running locally on the same computer only.
It's Unix domain sockets.

You may ask why use Unix domain sockets?

Well, communications between processes running on the same computer do not have to go through any computer network. Therefore, the information being exchanged does not have to flow through the computer network protocol stack inside the operating system. Rather, file system files or memory can instead be used because they are all accessible by processes running on the same computer. Unix domain sockets use files as the communication media in this scenario.

For software developers, Unix domain sockets is just another type of sockets similar to Stream sockets using the TCP protocol or Datagram sockets using the UDP protocol. The layout of the client and server programs using UNIX domain sockets is almost exactly the same as that of using Internet sockets. Therefore, you program it the same way whether it's using Internet sockets or Unix domain sockets. The only differences are the following:

1. Your program includes the following header file to use Unix domain sockets.

    #include <sys/un.h>

2. For Unix domain sockets, the socket's address family is AF_UNIX.

3. In Unix domain sockets, the address of a socket is a file pathname.

    That is, instead of being identified by a unique combination of an
    IP address and a port number as in an Internet socket, **a Unix domain
    socket is identified by a unique file system pathname.**
    This also means a server socket has its own unique file pathname and
    a client socket does, too.

    Be aware that the maximum length of the file pathname used for identifying

a Unix domain socket is hardwired to be 108 in the definition of
'struct sockaddr_un' in <sys/un.h>. The program will fail if the pathname
used is longer than that.

```
struct sockaddr_un
{
    __SOCKADDR_COMMON (sun_);
    char sun_path[108];            /* Path name. Length is limited. */
};
```

I have seen a product that heavily uses Unix domain sockets for client
server communications on the same system and it uses very long pathnames.
It breaks from time to time because the file pathname gets too long and
exceeds the limit of 108 characters. So, bear in mind that this type of
local socket communication won't work if the pathname used exceeds
108 characters. In general, you want to pick a naming mechanism that
will produce short file names and use a base directory whose name is also
short so that the resulted full pathname does not exceed the limit.

4. With Unix domain sockets, both client and server programs need to invoke
   the bind() function to bind its socket with its own unique file pathname.

Note that just like the Internet sockets, Unix Domain sockets support both
connection-oriented and connectionless communications as well.

For instance, to use Unix domain Datagram sockets, pass in AF_UNIX in the
first argument and SOCK_DGRAM in the second argument when you make the
socket() call to create the socket.

There is no need to worry about which port number to use for the server.
All you need to do is to pick a unique file pathname for your server
program and bind to it. And do the same for the client program, too.
The unique file pathname serves a role similar to the unique port number
combined with an IP address.

Figure 12-17 shows a pair of client and server programs communicating using
Unix Domain sockets.

Figure 12-17 Client-server communication using Unix Domain socket --
udsclnt_all.c and udssrv_all.c

(a) udssrv_all.c

```
/*
 * A connection-oriented server program using Unix domain stream socket.
 * Support of multiple platforms including Linux, Solaris, AIX, HPUX, Windows
 * and Apple Darwin.
 * Usage: udssrv_all
 * Authored by Mr. Jin-Jwei Chen.
 * Copyright (c) 1993-2018, 2020 Mr. Jin-Jwei Chen. All rights reserved.
 */

#include "mysocket.h"

int main(int argc, char *argv[])
{
```

```c
  int     ret;                        /* return code */
  int     sfd;                        /* file descriptor of the listener socket */
  int     newsock;                    /* file descriptor of client data socket */
  struct sockaddr_un    srvaddr;      /* server socket structure */
  int     srvaddrsz = sizeof(struct sockaddr_un);
  struct sockaddr_un    clntaddr;     /* client socket structure */
  socklen_t    clntaddrsz = sizeof(struct sockaddr_un);
  char    inbuf[BUFLEN];              /* input message buffer */
  char    outbuf[BUFLEN];             /* output message buffer */
  size_t msglen;                      /* length of reply message */
  unsigned int  msgcnt;               /* message count */

#if WINDOWS
  WSADATA wsaData;                    /* Winsock data */
  char* GetErrorMsg(int ErrorCode);  /* print error string in Windows */
#endif

  fprintf(stdout, "Connection-oriented server program using Unix Domain "
    "socket...\n");

#if WINDOWS
  /* Initiate use of the Winsock DLL. Ask for Winsock version 2.2 at least. */
  if ((ret = WSAStartup(MAKEWORD(2, 2), &wsaData)) != 0)
  {
    fprintf(stderr, "WSAStartup() failed with error %d: %s\n",
      ret, GetErrorMsg(ret));
    return (-1);
  }
#endif

  /* Create the Stream server socket. */
  if ((sfd = socket(AF_UNIX, SOCK_STREAM, 0)) < 0)
  {
    fprintf(stderr, "Error: socket() failed, errno=%d, %s\n", ERRNO, ERRNOSTR);
#if WINDOWS
    WSACleanup();
#endif
    return(-2);
  }

  /* Fill in the server socket address. */
  memset((void *)&srvaddr, 0, (size_t)srvaddrsz); /* clear the address buffer */
  srvaddr.sun_family = AF_UNIX;
  strcpy(srvaddr.sun_path, SERVER_PATH);

  /* Bind the server socket to its address. */
  unlink(SERVER_PATH);
  if ((ret = bind(sfd, (struct sockaddr *)&srvaddr, srvaddrsz)) != 0)
  {
    fprintf(stderr, "Error: bind() failed, errno=%d, %s\n", ERRNO, ERRNOSTR);
    CLOSE(sfd);
    return(-3);
  }

  /* Set maximum connection request queue length that we can fall behind. */
  if (listen(sfd, BACKLOG) == -1) {
```

```
      fprintf(stderr, "Error: listen() failed, errno=%d, %s\n", ERRNO, ERRNOSTR);
      CLOSE(sfd);
      return(-4);
}

/* Wait for incoming connection requests from clients and service them. */
while (1) {

    fprintf(stdout, "\nListening for client connect request ...\n");
    newsock = accept(sfd, (struct sockaddr *)&clntaddr, &clntaddrsz);
    if (newsock < 0)
    {
      fprintf(stderr, "Error: accept() failed, errno=%d, %s\n", ERRNO, ERRNOSTR);
      CLOSE(sfd);
      return(-5);
    }

    fprintf(stdout, "Client Connected. Client file path=%s\n",
      clntaddr.sun_path);

    msgcnt = 1;
    /* Receive and service requests from the current client. */
    while (1)
    {
      /* Receive a request from a client. */
      errno = 0;
      inbuf[0] = '\0';
      ret = recv(newsock, inbuf, BUFLEN, 0);
      if (ret > 0)
      {
        /* Process the request. We simply print the request message here. */
        inbuf[ret] = '\0';
        fprintf(stdout, "\nReceived the following request from client:\n%s\n",
          inbuf);

        /* Construct a reply */
        sprintf(outbuf, "This is reply #%3u from the server program.", msgcnt++);
        msglen = strlen(outbuf);

        /* Send a reply. */
        errno = 0;
        ret = send(newsock, outbuf, msglen, 0);
        if (ret == -1)
          fprintf(stderr, "Error: send() failed, errno=%d, %s\n", ERRNO,
            ERRNOSTR);
        else
          fprintf(stdout, "%u of %lu bytes of the reply was sent.\n", ret, msglen);
      }
      else if (ret < 0)
      {
        fprintf(stderr, "Error: recv() failed, errno=%d, %s\n", ERRNO,
          ERRNOSTR);
        break;
      }
      else
      {
```

```
            /* The client may have disconnected. */
            fprintf(stdout, "The client may have disconnected.\n");
            break;
        }
    } /* while - inner */

    CLOSE1(newsock);
    } /* while - outer */

    CLOSE(sfd);
    return(0);
}
```

(b) udsclnt_all.c

```
/*
 * A connection-oriented client program using Unix domain stream socket.
 * Support for Linux, Solaris, AIX, HPUX, Apple Darwin and Windows.
 * Usage: udsclnt_all
 * Authored by Mr. Jin-Jwei Chen.
 * Copyright (c) 1993-2018, 2020 Mr. Jin-Jwei Chen. All rights reserved.
 */

#include "mysocket.h"

int main(int argc, char *argv[])
{
  int     ret;
  int     sfd;                         /* socket file descriptor */
  struct sockaddr_un    server;   /* server socket structure */
  int     srvaddrsz = sizeof(struct sockaddr_un);
  struct sockaddr_un    client;   /* client socket structure */
  int     clntaddrsz = sizeof(struct sockaddr_un);
  struct sockaddr_un    fromaddr; /* socket structure */
  socklen_t     fromaddrsz = sizeof(struct sockaddr_un);
  char    inbuf[BUFLEN];               /* input message buffer */
  char    outbuf[BUFLEN];              /* output message buffer */
  size_t msglen;                       /* length of reply message */
  size_t msgnum=0;                     /* count of request message */
  size_t len;

#if WINDOWS
  WSADATA wsaData;                        /* Winsock data */
  char* GetErrorMsg(int ErrorCode);    /* print error string in Windows */
#endif

  fprintf(stdout, "Connection-oriented client program using Unix domain socket"
    " ...\n");

#if WINDOWS
  /* Initiate use of the Winsock DLL. Ask for Winsock version 2.2 at least. */
  if ((ret = WSAStartup(MAKEWORD(2, 2), &wsaData)) != 0)
  {
    fprintf(stderr, "Error: WSAStartup() failed with error %d: %s\n",
      ret, GetErrorMsg(ret));
    return (-1);
```

```
  }
#endif

  /* Create a socket. */
  sfd = socket(AF_UNIX, SOCK_STREAM, 0);
  if (sfd < 0)
  {
    fprintf(stderr,"Error: socket() failed, errno=%d, %s\n", ERRNO, ERRNOSTR);
#if WINDOWS
    WSACleanup();
#endif
    return (-2);
  }

  /* Set up the client's address. */
  client.sun_family = AF_UNIX;
  strcpy(client.sun_path, CLIENT_PATH);

  /* Unlink the file and bind client socket to its address. */
  unlink(CLIENT_PATH);
  ret = bind(sfd, (struct sockaddr *) &client, clntaddrsz);
  if (ret == -1)
  {
    fprintf(stderr, "Error: connect() failed, errno=%d, %s\n", ERRNO,
      ERRNOSTR);
    CLOSE(sfd);
    return(-3);
  }

  /* Set up the server's address. */
  server.sun_family = AF_UNIX;
  strcpy(server.sun_path, SERVER_PATH);

  /* Connect to the server. */
  ret = connect(sfd, (struct sockaddr *) &server, srvaddrsz);
  if (ret == -1)
  {
    fprintf(stderr, "Error: connect() failed, errno=%d, %s\n", ERRNO, ERRNOSTR);
    CLOSE(sfd);
    return(-4);
  }

  /* Get server's address. */
  ret = getpeername(sfd, (struct sockaddr *) &fromaddr, &fromaddrsz);
  if (ret == -1)
    fprintf(stderr, "Error: getpeername() failed, errno=%d, %s\n", ERRNO,
      ERRNOSTR);
  else
    fprintf(stdout, "Connected to server. Server socket filepath: %s\n",
      fromaddr.sun_path);

  fprintf(stdout, "Send request messages to server\n");

  /* Send request messages to the server and process the reply messages. */
  while (msgnum < MAXMSGS)
  {
```

```c
      /* Send a request message to the server. */
      sprintf(outbuf, "%s%4lu%s", "This is request message ", ++msgnum,
      " from the client program.");
      msglen = strlen(outbuf);
      errno = 0;

      ret = send(sfd, outbuf, msglen, 0);
      if (ret >= 0)
      {
        /* Print a warning if not entire message was sent. */
        if (ret == msglen)
          fprintf(stdout, "\n%lu bytes of message were successfully sent.\n",
            msglen);
        else if (ret < msglen)
          fprintf(stderr, "Warning: only %u of %lu bytes were sent.\n",
            ret, msglen);

        if (ret > 0)
        {
          /* Receive a reply from the server. */
          errno = 0;
          inbuf[0] = '\0';
          ret = recv(sfd, inbuf, BUFLEN, 0);

          if (ret > 0)
          {
            /* Process the reply. */
            inbuf[ret] = '\0';
            fprintf(stdout, "Received the following reply from server:\n%s\n",
              inbuf);
          }
          else if (ret == 0)
            fprintf(stdout, "Warning: Zero bytes were received.\n");  .
          else
          {
            fprintf(stderr, "Error: recv() failed, errno=%d, %s\n", ERRNO,
              ERRNOSTR);
            break;
          }
        }
      }
      else
      {
        fprintf(stderr, "Error: send() failed, errno=%d, %s\n", ERRNO, ERRNOSTR);
        break;
      }

#if WINDOWS
    Sleep(1000); /* Unit is ms. For demo only. Remove this in real code. */
#else
    sleep(1);   /* For demo only. Remove this in real code. */
#endif
  } /* while */

  CLOSE(sfd);
  return(0);
```

Remember that the socket address structure for a Unix Domain socket is 'struct sockaddr_un'. Also each program must call bind().

Binding to a File Pathname

In order to identify the different clients connected to the server on the same system, you can add the client's process id to its file pathname. That way, you can place all of this type of files used by all client and server processes employing Unix domain sockets for a given application in the same directory. For multithreaded programs, you might want to use thread id as well.

When the bind() call is executed, a file system file corresponding to the file pathname specified in the client or server's socket address will be actually created. If the file already exists when the bind() call is executed, the bind() call will fail with the following error:

    Error: bind() failed, errno=98, Address already in use

That's why the standard practice of using Unix domain socket is to either remove the associated file when a process terminates or remove the file right before calling the bind() by invoking the unlink() call on the file name.

Support for Unix domain sockets in Windows

Although Unix domain sockets have been supported in Unix for decades and they are also available in Linux, Windows has not supported it until very recent time. And as of 2018, Windows still does not support it out of box. Developers must first join Windows Insider program, download the Windows Insiders SDK and install it to get the support for Unix domain sockets in Windows. And you will have to use Windows 10 or a later version. You also need to include the header file
    #include <afunix.h>   /* Unix domain socket in Windows */
to get the definition of "struct sockaddr_un" and get your program to compile.

12-15 Asynchronous Socket Operations

12-15-1 Asynchronous Socket I/O

In socket programming, it's very often that one process needs to communicate with multiple data sources or destinations. One way of doing it is to create a separate thread to handle each data source or destination. Yet a very common approach is to have a single thread dealing with all of them using asynchronous socket I/O.

The default behavior of a socket is **synchronous**, meaning a socket read is blocked until data is available for read. If there is no data available, the reading process/thread will block forever until either data is available or some event happens. Similarly, a socket write will block until the data

is sent. This means a thread or process can handle only one data source
or destination at a time and must work through all of them serially.

In contrast, **asynchronous socket I/O** involves making each socket
non-blocking. Instead of blocking and waiting on a particular socket,
the process or thread is hand-off on all and sits back and watches
whichever becomes ready first. Whichever socket(s) becomes ready for read
or write, that's the one that the process or thread works on next.
Comparing with being blocked on one socket which may or may not have data to
read or write, this asynchronous approach is more responsive, effective,
and productive. In summary, using asynchronous I/O, the process or thread
does not get blocked on any socket anymore, it sits back and watches,
and works on whichever socket that has data ready to send or receive first.

12-15-1-1 Using select() Function

How does a process or thread know which socket is ready for I/O?
It's the select() call! The **select()** system call allows the caller to
poll multiple sockets at the same time and get back how many and which of
them are ready for I/O. Please note that the select() function works for all
types of file descriptors, not just socket file descriptors.

The synopses of the select() and other related functions are listed below:

```
#include <sys/select.h>

int select(int nfds, fd_set *restrict readfds,
      fd_set *restrict writefds, fd_set *restrict errorfds,
      struct timeval *restrict timeout);

void FD_CLR(int fd, fd_set *fdset);
int FD_ISSET(int fd, fd_set *fdset);
void FD_SET(int fd, fd_set *fdset);
void FD_ZERO(fd_set *fdset);
```

There are three file descriptor sets, which are actually bit maps, that
the select() function can take as inputs. These parameters are actually
both input and output. On input, if present (i.e. the pointer is not NULL),
each file descriptor set indicates to the operating system kernel that
which file descriptors you like to poll for a particular operation.
On output, the values of these parameters indicate to caller which file
descriptors are indeed ready for performing the operation being polled.
The three operations supported for polling are ready for read, ready for
write, and error pending. The use of these three parameters is explained
below:

```
readfds - read file descriptor set
  On input, this specifies the set of file descriptors you like
    to poll for being ready to read (has data ready for read).
  On output, this contains the set of file descriptors that are
    ready for read.

writefds - write file descriptor set
  On input, this is the set of file descriptors you like to poll
    for being ready to write/send.
```

On output, this has the set of file descriptors that are
ready for write/send.

errorfds - error file descriptor set
On input, this contains the set of file descriptors you like
to check for error conditions pending.
On output, this returns the set of file descriptors that
have error conditions pending.

We said earlier that each of the file descriptor sets is used as a bit map.
If you peek into it, each file descriptor set is of type fd_set,
which is 32 4-byte integers (that is, 128 bytes long). Therefore, there are
total 1024 bits in this data.

When you create a socket, you get back a socket file descriptor which is
an integer, say 8 or 10. To poll this socket for ready for read, this is
how you do it (assuming the socket file descriptor is sfd):

```
fd_set  readfds;        /* declare a variable for the file descriptor set */
FD_ZERO(&readfds);      /* initialize all bits to zero */
FD_SET(sfd, &readfds);  /* set the bit corresponding to socket file
                           descriptor sfd to poll */
```

For instance, if sfd is 8, then the 8th bit in readfds will be set to 1.
This indicates to the select() system call and the operating system
that the caller likes to poll the socket whose file descriptor is 8
and see if it's ready for read.

This means a select() call can poll at most 1024 file descriptors at once
for a particular operation.

The write and error file descriptor sets are handled similarly.
Simply replace the readfds above with writefds or errorfds.

After the setup above, then you pass the readfds to the select() system call
as below.

```
ret = select(maxsfd + 1, &readfds, NULL, NULL, &timeout);
```

Here we pass in a value NULL to both writefds and errorfds arguments because
we don't care about the writing operation and error conditions.

When the select() call returns, this is how you check if a particular
socket is ready for read:

```
if (FD_ISSET(sfd, &readfds))
  /* Yes, the socket sfd is ready for read */
else
  /* No, the socket sfd is not ready for read yet */
```

If you need to poll all sockets for ready to read only, then you just need
to pass in the readfds pointer, with NULL in the writefds and errorfds
positions. However, for example, if you also like to poll some of the
sockets you have for ready for write, then you will need to set up the
writefds parameter in a similar fashion and pass the address of writefds
in the third argument to the select() function as well.

According to POSIX standard, a socket file descriptor is ready for read shall mean the socket really has some data that can be read, or it is an end-of-file condition, or there is an error other than one indicating that it is blocked. A socket file descriptor is ready for write means a blocking output function call would not be blocked. That is all. It does not guarantee the call would transfer data successfully.

The first parameter of the select() function is worth further explanation. It's a bit confusing to many people. This number actually specifies a **range**. It specifies **the upper bound of file descriptors** that the operating system needs to examine or test. Hence, its value should always be the maximum socket file descriptor your program uses plus one. For instance, if you pass in a value n in the first argument, the operating system will test file descriptors in the range of [0 ... n-1].

For example, if your program creates three sockets and the values of the socket file descriptors are 8, 12 and 17. Then you will need to pass 17+1=18 in the first argument. This tells the operating system that it only needs to test file descriptors in the range from 0 to 17.

The 5th and last parameter in the select() call allows you to specify a timeout value. This timeout parameter specifies the maximum amount of time that the caller wants the select() call to block/wait if none of the selected descriptors are ready for the requested operation. This timeout period is of type "struct timeval" and the timeout value is given in seconds and microseconds. The select() function will block until at least one of the requested operations becomes ready, until the timeout occurs, or until it is interrupted by a signal.

The select() function returns the **total number of ready descriptors in all of the three file descriptor sets**. If the return value is 0, it means no data source or target is ready.

Upon successful completion, the select() function will modify the three file descriptor sets arguments to indicate which file descriptors are ready for reading, ready for writing, or have an error condition pending, respectively. The timeout parameter will contain time left until timeout occurs.

It's almost always true that a program has to run select() in a loop in order to keep monitoring the readiness of all of the sockets. There is a decision to make if you would like to take a little pause in between two consecutive calls to select() or just keep trying without any pause. The decision of if and how long depends on how busy the load is. Take into consideration of the timeout value you provide to the select() call as well.

Figure 12-18 is an example program that does asynchronous socket input from multiple sources concurrently without using threads.

Figure 12-18 Asynchronous socket I/O -- tcpclnt_async_io_all.c and tcpsrv_async_io_all.c

(a) tcpsrv_async_io_all.c

```c
/*
 * A connection-oriented server program using Stream socket.
 * Single-threaded server.
 * This version is for testing async client doing async recv().
 * Support for multiple platforms including Linux, Windows, Solaris, AIX, HPUX
 * and Apple Darwin.
 * Usage: tcpsrv_async_io_all [port# [myid [#messages-to-send]]]
 * Authored by Mr. Jin-Jwei Chen.
 * Copyright (c) 2002, 2014, 2017-8, 2020 Mr. Jin-Jwei Chen. All rights reserved.
 */

#include "mysocket.h"

#undef    SLEEPMS
#define   SLEEPMS        5    /* number of milliseconds to sleep */

int main(int argc, char *argv[])
{
  int     ret;
  int     sfd;                        /* file descriptor of the listener socket */
  int     newsock;                    /* file descriptor of client data socket */
  struct sockaddr_in    srvaddr;      /* socket structure */
  int     srvaddrsz=sizeof(struct sockaddr_in);
  struct sockaddr_in    clntaddr;     /* socket structure */
  socklen_t   clntaddrsz=sizeof(struct sockaddr_in);
  in_port_t   portnum=DEFSRVPORT;     /* port number */
  int     portnum_in = 0;             /* port number entered by user */
  char    outbuf[BUFLEN];             /* output message buffer */
  size_t  msglen;                     /* length of reply message */
  int     myid = 1;                   /* my id number */
  int     messages = 2;               /* number of message to send */
  int     i, on=1;
#if !WINDOWS
  struct timespec  sleeptm;           /* sleep time - seconds and nanoseconds */
#endif

#if WINDOWS
  WSADATA wsaData;                    /* Winsock data */
  int winerror;                       /* error in Windows */
  char* GetErrorMsg(int ErrorCode);   /* print error string in Windows */
#endif

  fprintf(stdout, "Connection-oriented server program ...\n");

  /* Get the server port number from user, if any. */
  if (argc > 1)
  {
    portnum_in = atoi(argv[1]);
    if (portnum_in <= 0)
    {
      fprintf(stderr, "Port number %d invalid, set to default value %u\n",
        portnum_in, DEFSRVPORT);
      portnum = DEFSRVPORT;
    }
    else
      portnum = (in_port_t)portnum_in;
```

```
    }

    /* Get my id number. */
    if (argc > 2)
      myid = atoi(argv[2]);
    if (argc > 3)
      messages = atoi(argv[3]);

#if WINDOWS
    /* Ask for Winsock version 2.2 at least. */
    if ((ret = WSAStartup(MAKEWORD(2, 2), &wsaData)) != 0)
    {
      fprintf(stderr, "WSAStartup() failed with error %d: %s\n",
        ret, GetErrorMsg(ret));
      return (-1);
    }
#endif

    /* Create the Stream server socket. */
    if ((sfd = socket(AF_INET, SOCK_STREAM, 0)) < 0)
    {
      fprintf(stderr, "Error: socket() failed, errno=%d, %s\n", ERRNO, ERRNOSTR);
#if WINDOWS
      WSACleanup();
#endif
      return(-2);
    }

    /* Turn on SO_REUSEADDR socket option so that the server can restart
       right away before the required wait time period expires. */
    if (setsockopt(sfd, SOL_SOCKET, SO_REUSEADDR, (char *)&on, sizeof(on)) < 0)
    {
      fprintf(stderr, "setsockopt(SO_REUSEADDR) failed, errno=%d, %s", ERRNO,
        ERRNOSTR);
    }

    /* Fill in the server socket address. */
    memset((void *)&srvaddr, 0, (size_t)srvaddrsz); /* clear the address buffer */

    srvaddr.sin_family = AF_INET;                    /* Internet socket */
    srvaddr.sin_addr.s_addr = htonl(INADDR_ANY);     /* server's IP address */
    srvaddr.sin_port = htons(portnum);               /* server's port number */

    /* Bind the server socket to its address. */
    if ((ret = bind(sfd, (struct sockaddr *)&srvaddr, srvaddrsz)) != 0)
    {
      fprintf(stderr, "Error: bind() failed, errno=%d, %s\n", ERRNO, ERRNOSTR);
      CLOSE(sfd);
      return(-3);
    }

    /* Set maximum connection request queue length that we can fall behind. */
    if (listen(sfd, BACKLOG) == -1) {
      fprintf(stderr, "Error: listen() failed, errno=%d, %s\n", ERRNO, ERRNOSTR);
      CLOSE(sfd);
      return(-4);
```

```
    }

  /* Set sleep time to be 5 ms. */
#if !WINDOWS
  sleeptm.tv_sec = 0;
  sleeptm.tv_nsec = (SLEEPMS*1000000);
#endif

  /* Wait for incoming connection requests from clients and service them. */
  while (1) {

    fprintf(stdout, "\nListening at port number %u ...\n", portnum);
    newsock = accept(sfd, (struct sockaddr *)&clntaddr, &clntaddrsz);
    if (newsock < 0)
    {
      fprintf(stderr, "Error: accept() failed, errno=%d, %s\n", ERRNO, ERRNOSTR);
      CLOSE(sfd);
      return(-5);
    }

    fprintf(stdout, "Client Connected.\n");

    /* Wait for a little bit so that all data sources can fire at same time.
       This is for demo only. */
#if WINDOWS
    Sleep(SLEEPMS);   /* Unit is ms. */
#else
    nanosleep(&sleeptm, (struct timespec *)NULL);
#endif

    /* Send a number of messages to the client. */
    i = 1;
    while (messages--)
    {
      /* Construct the message to send. */
      sprintf(outbuf, "%s%2d%s%2d%s", "This is message ", i++, " from server ",
        myid, ".\n");
      msglen = strlen(outbuf);

      /* Send the message. */
      errno = 0;
      ret = send(newsock, outbuf, msglen, 0);
      if (ret == -1)
        fprintf(stderr, "Error: send() failed, errno=%d, %s\n", ERRNO, ERRNOSTR);
      else
        fprintf(stdout, "%u of %lu bytes of the message was sent.\n", ret, msglen);
    }   /* while - inner */

    CLOSE1(newsock);

    /* The following statement is for test only */
    break;
  }   /* while - outer */

  CLOSE(sfd);
  return(0);
```

```
}

    (b)  tcpclnt_async_io_all.c

/*
 * A connection-oriented client program using Stream socket and
 * making asynchronous recv().
 * A single thread handling inputs from multiple data sources at the same time.
 * Run multiple servers and a single client to test.
 * This version works on Linux, Solaris, AIX, HPUX, Apple Darwin and Windows.
 * Usage: tcpclnt_async_io_all nsources hostname1/IP1 port1 hostname2/IP2 port2 ..
 * Authored by Mr. Jin-Jwei Chen.
 * Copyright (c) 2002, 2014, 2017-8, 2020 Mr. Jin-Jwei Chen. All rights reserved.
 */

#include "mysocket.h"

int main(int argc, char *argv[])
{
  int      ret;
  int      sfd[MAXSOURCES];              /* file descriptors of the sockets */
  struct sockaddr_in     server;      /* socket structure */
  int      srvaddrsz=sizeof(struct sockaddr_in);
  in_port_t      portnum=DEFSRVPORT; /* port number */
  char     inbuf[BUFLEN];                /* input message buffer */
  size_t     len;
  unsigned int addr;
  char     server_name[NAMELEN+1];
  int      socket_type = SOCK_STREAM;
  struct hostent *hp;
  int      nsources;                     /* number of message sources */
  unsigned int  done_cnt = 0, i;
  int     maxsfd = 0;                    /* maximum socket file descriptor */
  int     status[MAXSOURCES];            /* remember if each input is done */
  int     dataRead = 0;                  /* Did we read any data from any input? */
#if !WINDOWS
  struct timespec   sleeptm;             /* time to sleep - seconds and nanoseconds */
#endif
#if WINDOWS
  WSADATA wsaData;                       /* Winsock data */
  char* GetErrorMsg(int ErrorCode); /* print error string in Windows */
  unsigned long opt = 1;
#endif

  fprintf(stdout, "Connection-oriented client program reading n data
sources...\n\n");

  /* Get the number of data sources. */
  if (argc > 1)
  {
    nsources = atoi(argv[1]);
    if ((nsources <= 0) || (nsources > MAXSOURCES))
    {
      fprintf(stderr, "Maximum number of sources %d out of range\n", nsources);
      return(-1);
    }
```

```
    }

    /* Make sure enough arguments are provided. */
    if (argc < (2+(nsources*2)))
    {
      fprintf(stderr, "Usage: %s nsources IP1 Port1 IP2 Port2 ...\n", argv[0]);
      return(-2);
    }

#if WINDOWS
    /* Ask for Winsock version 2.2 at least. */
    if ((ret = WSAStartup(MAKEWORD(2, 2), &wsaData)) != 0)
    {
      fprintf(stderr, "Error: WSAStartup() failed with error %d: %s\n",
        ret, GetErrorMsg(ret));
      return (-3);
    }
#endif

    /* Clear the file descriptor and status arrays. */
    for (i = 0; i < nsources; i++)
    {
      sfd[i] = 0;
      status[i] = 0;
    }

    /* Connect to all data sources, one at a time. */
    for (i = 0; i < nsources; i++)
    {
      /* Get the host names or IP addresses of next data source. */
      len = strlen(argv[2+(i*2)]);
      if (len > NAMELEN)
        len = NAMELEN;
      strncpy(server_name, argv[2+(i*2)], len);
      server_name[len] = '\0';

      /* Get the port number of next data source. */
      portnum = atoi(argv[3+(i*2)]);
      if (portnum <= 0)
      {
        fprintf(stderr,"Error: invalid port number %s\n", argv[3+(i*2)]);
        continue;
      }

      /* Translate the host name or IP address into server socket address. */
      if (isalpha(server_name[0]))
      {  /* A host name is given. */
        hp = gethostbyname(server_name);
      }
      else
      {  /* Convert the n.n.n.n IP address to a number. */
        addr = inet_addr(server_name);
        hp = gethostbyaddr((char *)&addr, sizeof(addr), AF_INET);
      }
      if (hp == NULL )
      {
```

```
        fprintf(stderr,"Error: cannot get address for [%s], errno=%d, %s\n",
            server_name, ERRNO, ERRNOSTR);
#if WINDOWS
      WSACleanup();
#endif
        return(-4);
    }

    /* Copy the resolved information into the sockaddr_in structure. */
    memset(&server, 0, sizeof(server));
    memcpy(&(server.sin_addr), hp->h_addr, hp->h_length);
    server.sin_family = hp->h_addrtype;
    server.sin_port = htons(portnum);

    /* Create a socket for the next data source. */
    sfd[i] = socket(AF_INET, socket_type, 0);
    if (sfd[i] < 0)
    {
      fprintf(stderr,"Error: socket() failed, errno=%d, %s\n", ERRNO,
        ERRNOSTR);
#if WINDOWS
      WSACleanup();
#endif
        return (-5);
    }

    /* Connect to the data source. */
    errno = 0;
    ret = connect(sfd[i], (struct sockaddr *)&server, srvaddrsz);

    /* Continue to next source if connect has failed. */
    if (ret != 0)
    {
      fprintf(stderr, "Error: connect() failed, errno=%d, %s\n", ERRNO,
        ERRNOSTR);
      CLOSE1(sfd[i]);
      sfd[i] = 0;
      continue;
    }
    if (sfd[i] > maxsfd)
      maxsfd = sfd[i];

    /* connect() has succeeded.
       Make the socket non-blocking after connect. O_NONBLOCK=0x0800 */
    fprintf(stdout, "To set socket non-blocking ...\n");
#if WINDOWS
    if (ioctlsocket(sfd[i], FIONBIO, &opt) != 0)
#else
    if (fcntl(sfd[i], F_SETFL, fcntl(sfd[i], F_GETFL, 0) | O_NONBLOCK) != 0)
#endif
    {
      fprintf(stderr, "Error: fcntl() failed to set socket nonblocking, "
        "errno=%d, %s\n", ERRNO, ERRNOSTR);
      fprintf(stderr, "Close the current socket, i=%d.\n", i);
      CLOSE1(sfd[i]);
      sfd[i] = 0;
```

```
      }

   }   /* for */

   /* Now we are connected to all data sources with all sockets asynchronous.
    * Start to receive data from multiple sockets using non-blocking I/O.
    */

   fprintf(stdout, "\nReceive messages from multiple sources ...\n");

   /* Set sleep time. */
#if !WINDOWS
   sleeptm.tv_sec = 0;
   sleeptm.tv_nsec = (SLEEPMS*1000000);   /* unit is nanoseconds */
#endif

   /* Use select() to poll all data sources and wait for next message to arrive. */
   while (done_cnt < nsources)
   {
     /* Check if any socket has messages ready to be read. */
     struct timeval tv = { 1, 0 };   /* one second to timeout */
     fd_set readfds;   /* This is 128 bytes long. 32 4-byte integers. */
     int     ret2;
     int optval = 0;
     socklen_t vallen;

     /* Check the socket for ready to read. */
     FD_ZERO(&readfds);
     for (i = 0; i < nsources; i++)
       if (status[i] == 0)
         FD_SET(sfd[i], &readfds);

     errno = 0;
     /* First argument is always highest fd plus 1. It specifies a range. */
     ret2 = select(maxsfd + 1, &readfds, NULL, NULL, &tv);
     fprintf(stdout, "select() returned %d, errno=%d, %s\n", ret2, ERRNO,
       ERRNOSTR);
     fflush(stdout);

     /* If select() returns positive integer, check which socket is ready. */
     if (ret2 > 0)
     {
       dataRead = 0;   /* Mark we've not read anything yet. */
       /* Loop through all socket file descriptor. */
       for (i = 0; i < nsources; i++)
       {
         if (status[i] == 1)   /* The file descriptor is done. Skip it. */
           continue;

         if (FD_ISSET(sfd[i], &readfds))
         {
           /* This sfd is ready for read. */
           fprintf(stdout, "Data source %2d is ready for read.\n", (i+1));
           fflush(stdout);

           /* Read all of the data that is available at current input. */
```

```
        while(1)
        {
          /* Receive next message. */
          ret = 0;
          errno = 0;
          inbuf[0] = '\0';
          ret = recv(sfd[i], inbuf, BUFLEN, 0);

          /* Break if error occurred during recv(). */
          if (ret < 0)
          {
            fprintf(stderr, "recv() returned %d, errno=%d, %s\n", ret, ERRNO,
              ERRNOSTR);
            fflush(stderr);
            break;
          }

          /* No error during recv(). */
          if (ret > 0)
          {
            dataRead = 1;   /* Remember we've read something. */
            /* Print the message received. */
            inbuf[ret] = '\0';
            fprintf(stdout, "Received the following message:\n%s\n",
              inbuf);
            fflush(stdout);
          }
          else if (ret == 0)
          {
            fprintf(stdout, "Warning: The other end may have closed.\n");
            fflush(stdout);
            /* Mark this data source as 'done'. */
            if (status[i] == 0)
            {
              status[i] = 1;
              done_cnt++;
            }
            break;
          }
        }  /* while (reading current data source) */
      }  /* if (FD ISSET()) */
    }  /* for */

    /* If no data is read from any source, sleep for 10 ms before next poll.
       This sleep is very important for not wasting CPU time. */
    if (!dataRead)
    {
      fprintf(stdout, "To sleep for %2d ms and wait...\n", SLEEPMS);
      fflush(stdout);
#if WINDOWS
      Sleep(SLEEPMS);   /* Unit is ms. */
#else
      nanosleep(&sleeptm, (struct timespec *)NULL);
#endif
    }
  }
```

```
    else if (ret2 < 0)   /* select() returned error */
    {
        fprintf(stderr, "Error on select(): errno=%d, %s\n", ERRNO,
          ERRNOSTR);
        fflush(stderr);
    }

} /* while (done_cnt < nsources) */

/* We're done reading all data sources. Close all sockets and return. */
    for (i = 0; i < nsources; i++)
      CLOSE1(sfd[i]);
#if WINDOWS
  WSACleanup();
#endif
  return(0);
}
```

As you can see, the maximum number of concurrent data sources or targets asynchronous I/O can handle is limited by the size of the data type fd_set, which is 1024. Whether you can actually handle up to that many data sources or targets at the same time and get reasonable performance depends on the data traffic. For scalability, when the number of data sources or targets gets very high, using multiple threads or combining both might be worth considering.

12-15-1-2 The pselect() Function

Note that the POSIX standard defines a variation of the select() function and names it pselect() as shown below:

```
#include <sys/select.h>

int pselect(int nfds, fd_set *restrict readfds,
        fd_set *restrict writefds, fd_set *restrict errorfds,
        const struct timespec *restrict timeout,
        const sigset_t *restrict sigmask);
```

The pselect() function is essentially the same as select() with three differences:

- In pselect(), the timeout period is of type "struct timespec" and the timeout value is given in seconds and nanoseconds.

- pselect() has an additional parameter, the sigmask argument. If this argument is specified (i.e. not NULL), pselect() first replaces the current signal mask by this one, then does the select() function, and then restores the original signal mask before return.

- On return, the select() function may modify the timeout argument to indicate how much time left whereas pselect() does not.

Although all most popular operating systems have implemented the select() function, not all of them implement pselect().

12-15-1-3 Pitfalls of the select() Function

Be careful in using the select() function. One mistake some people sometimes make is resulting into very high CPU utilization from the application. This usually is because select() is normally used within a loop. So, there is a possibility that if there is no data available, the program ends up spinning the select() call and leads to very high CPU usage.

A select() call usually takes about 15 microseconds. Note that the call may actually return before the timeout period expires even if there is no data to be read or written.

There are a number of things to watch out for when using select() function.

First, make sure you **never pass in a zero value** to the first argument, nfds. As we said above, this value should always be the maximum socket file descriptor that you want the select() function to monitor plus one. If you mistakenly pass in 0 here, the select call will end up checking no socket at all and will return after the timeout period you specify in the timeout argument expires. This will also mean that your program will fail to work because none of socket file descriptors that you try to poll will ever get set when select() returns.

Second, watch out the **CPU utilization of your program**. If you don't program it correctly, using select() function in a loop may lead to very high CPU utilization. The general idea is you need a little pause between consecutive select() calls to avoid wasting CPU time.

There are two places to do this. First is the timeout argument of the select() call. This argument is a bit confusing. If present, it specifies a maximum time that can elapse before select() returns. But do not use this as a vehicle for controlling how much time you like to sleep or spend with each select() call for two reasons. First, the implementation of this parameter varies between operating systems. Second, under normal conditions, it's very rare that select() waits that much time before return even when there is no data available. This is true at least in some operating systems. So, it's a good idea to use it to put a cap on how much time select() can take, but don't use it as a means to control how much time you want to pause in between consecutive select() calls.

The second (and best) place is after the select() call. You can add a sleep() call to pause a little bit if the previous select() call ends up with no data being read or written. A common practice is to sleep some milliseconds.

Again, be careful setting the sleep and/or timeout period(s). You need to strike a good balance. The risks are setting it too small may result in unwanted high CPU usage while setting it too big could lead to slow response and performance. Hence, one needs to examine how often there is data available in any of the sockets being monitored and adjust the sleep time accordingly.

One sample data is an application uses 12% of CPU time when it sleeps for 1 millisecond in between consecutive select() calls. The same application uses only 1.3% of CPU time if it sleeps 10 milliseconds in between consecutive select() calls. You see the difference. This is just to give you a rough idea. The actual number varies with systems and applications. You need to measure it yourself (by using tools like top or something similar).

12-15-2 Asynchronous Socket Connect

Similar to doing asynchronous socket read/write, one can do asynchronous socket connect as well.

To do asynchronous connect, a client first creates a socket and then changes its socket into the non-blocking mode by calling the fcntl() function in Linux/Unix or ioctlsocket() function in Windows. It then calls the connect() call. If the connect() has succeeded, it will return 0. If the connection cannot be completed immediately, the connect() call will return with errno being set to EINPROGRESS in Linux/Unix or WSAEWOULDBLOCK in Windows. In that case, the client will then need to invoke the select() function to poll if the socket is ready for I/O. Note that the connect attempt may still fail. So it's important to make a getsockopt() call to try to see if there is a socket error. If there is no error and the socket file descriptor is set, then the socket is ready.

Should the asynchronous connect fail, the best practice is to close the socket and repeat the entire connect effort again from scratch (i.e. from creating the client socket). This is because when a connect() call fails, the socket becomes undefined in Solaris, AIX, and HPUX. Unless you close and then re-create the socket, the connect reattempt will never succeed. In some operating systems (e.g. Linux and Windows), it is OK to re-use the same socket to re-try the connect().

Figure 12-19 is an example client program that employs asynchronous connect() in trying to connect to a server. It creates a socket, sets the socket to non-blocking I/O, invokes the connect() to try to connect to the server. If the connect() succeeds, the program resets the socket back to blocking I/O. And then the client and server communication takes place.

If the connect() call fails, the program sleeps for one second and then reattempts the connect again. It repeats the connect attempt for five times before it gives up.

Figure 12-19 Asynchronous socket connect -- tcpclnt_async_conn_all.c

```
/*
 * A connection-oriented client program using Stream socket and
 * making asynchronous connect.
 * Closing and recreating the socket before re-trying to connect after it fails.
 * This is because when the connect() fails, the socket becomes undefined
 * in Solaris, AIX and HPUX.
 * This version works on Linux, Solaris, AIX, HPUX, Apple Darwin and Windows.
 * Note: The errno on different platforms is different when server is not up.
 * Usage: tcpclnt_async_conn_all [server_hostname or IP_address [server_port#]]
 * Authored by Mr. Jin-Jwei Chen.
 * Copyright (c) 2002, 2014, 2017, 2018, 2020 Mr. Jin-Jwei Chen. All rights reserved.
```

```
*/

#include "mysocket.h"

int main(int argc, char *argv[])
{
  int     ret;
  int     sfd;                        /* file descriptor of the socket */
  struct sockaddr_in    server;       /* socket structure */
  int     srvaddrsz=sizeof(struct sockaddr_in);
  struct sockaddr_in    fromaddr;     /* socket structure */
  int     fromaddrsz=sizeof(struct sockaddr_in);
  in_port_t    portnum=DEFSRVPORT;    /* port number */
  int     portnum_in = 0;             /* port number entered by user */
  char    inbuf[BUFLEN];              /* input message buffer */
  char    outbuf[BUFLEN];             /* output message buffer */
  size_t     msglen;                  /* length of reply message */
  size_t     msgnum=0;                /* count of request message */
  size_t     len;
  unsigned int addr;
  char    server_name[NAMELEN+1] = "localhost";
  int     socket_type = SOCK_STREAM;
  struct hostent *hp;
  int     option;
  socklen_t  optlen;
  unsigned int  trycnt = MAXCONNTRYCNT;

#if WINDOWS
  WSADATA wsaData;                         /* Winsock data */
  int winerror;                            /* error in Windows */
  char* GetErrorMsg(int ErrorCode); /* print error string in Windows */
  unsigned long opt = 1;
#endif

  fprintf(stdout, "Connection-oriented client program ...\n\n");

  /* Get the host name or IP address of the server from command line. */
  if (argc > 1)
  {
    len = strlen(argv[1]);
    if (len > NAMELEN)
      len = NAMELEN;
    strncpy(server_name, argv[1], len);
    server_name[len] = '\0';
  }

  /* Get the port number of the server from command line. */
  if (argc > 2)
  {
    portnum_in = atoi(argv[2]);
    if (portnum_in <= 0)
    {
      fprintf(stderr, "Port number %d invalid, set to default value %u\n",
        portnum_in, DEFSRVPORT);
      portnum = DEFSRVPORT;
    }
```

```
    else
        portnum = (in_port_t)portnum_in;
    }

#if WINDOWS
    /* Ask for Winsock version 2.2 at least. */
    if ((ret = WSAStartup(MAKEWORD(2, 2), &wsaData)) != 0)
    {
        fprintf(stderr, "Error: WSAStartup() failed with error %d: %s\n",
            ret, GetErrorMsg(ret));
        return (-1);
    }
#endif

    /* Translate the host name or IP address into server socket address. */
    if (isalpha(server_name[0]))
    {   /* A host name is given. */
        hp = gethostbyname(server_name);
    }
    else
    {   /* Convert the n.n.n.n IP address to a number. */
        addr = inet_addr(server_name);
        hp = gethostbyaddr((char *)&addr, sizeof(addr), AF_INET);
    }
    if (hp == NULL )
    {
        fprintf(stderr,"Error: cannot get address for [%s], errno=%d, %s\n",
            server_name, ERRNO, ERRNOSTR);
#if WINDOWS
        WSACleanup();
#endif
        return(-2);
    }

    /* Copy the resolved information into the sockaddr_in structure. */
    memset(&server, 0, sizeof(server));
    memcpy(&(server.sin_addr), hp->h_addr, hp->h_length);
    server.sin_family = hp->h_addrtype;
    server.sin_port = htons(portnum);

    /* Connect to the server asynchronously.
     * Close and re-create the socket each time after connect() fails.
     * We must close and re-create socket when connect() fails in Solaris,
     * AIX, and HPUX.
     */
    while (trycnt-- > 0)
    {
        /* Open a socket. */
        sfd = socket(AF_INET, socket_type, 0);
        if (sfd < 0)
        {
            fprintf(stderr,"Error: socket() failed, errno=%d, %s\n", ERRNO, ERRNOSTR);
#if WINDOWS
            WSACleanup();
#endif
            return (-3);
```

```
    }

    /* Make the socket non-blocking before connect. O_NONBLOCK=0x0800 */
    fprintf(stdout, "To set socket non-blocking ...\n");
#if WINDOWS
    if (ioctlsocket(sfd, FIONBIO, &opt) != 0)
#else
    if (fcntl(sfd, F_SETFL, fcntl(sfd, F_GETFL, 0) | O_NONBLOCK) != 0)
#endif
    {
      fprintf(stderr, "Error: fcntl() failed to set socket nonblocking, "
        "errno=%d, %s\n", ERRNO, ERRNOSTR);
      CLOSE(sfd);
      return (-4);
    }

    /* Connect to the server asynchronously. */
    errno = 0;
    ret = connect(sfd, (struct sockaddr *)&server, srvaddrsz);
    fprintf(stdout, "connect() returned %d, errno=%d, %s\n", ret, ERRNO,
      ERRNOSTR);
    /* connect() succeeds */
    if (ret == 0)
      break;
#if WINDOWS
    /* Windows does not return socket connect error (i.e. put error from
       connect() in errno). We have to call WSAGetLastError() to get it. */
    winerror = WSAGetLastError();
    fprintf(stdout, "In Windows, WSAGetLastError() returned %d\n", winerror);
#endif

    /* It (connect()) is in progress. */
#if WINDOWS
    if (winerror == WSAEWOULDBLOCK)
#else
    if (errno == EINPROGRESS)
#endif
    {
      struct timeval tv = { 2, 0 };  /* 2 seconds to timeout */
      fd_set writefds;  /* This is 128 bytes long. 32 4-byte integers. */
      int    ret2;
      int optval = 0;
      socklen_t vallen;

      fprintf(stdout, "connect() returned EINPROGRESS (Windows-WSAEWOULDBLOCK)\n");

      /* Check the socket for ready to write. */
      /* Note: We must do both select() and getsockopt(), and in that order. */
      FD_ZERO(&writefds);
      FD_SET(sfd, &writefds);
      errno = 0;
      /* First argument is always highest fd plus 1. It specifies a range. */
      ret2 = select(sfd + 1, NULL, &writefds, NULL, &tv);
      fprintf(stdout, "select() returned %d, errno=%d, %s\n", ret2, ERRNO,
        ERRNOSTR);
```

```
    /* This is how we determine if connect() has failed. */
    if (ret2 > 0)
    {
        /* Check for error. Note: Doing this before select() doesn't work. */
        /* Note: We must do this after the select() call above. */
        /* This is necessary because connect() could encounter an error. */
        vallen = sizeof(int);
        getsockopt(sfd, SOL_SOCKET, SO_ERROR, (void*)(&optval), &vallen);
        if (optval)
        {
            fprintf(stderr, "Error in connect()/select() %d - %s\n",
                optval, strerror(optval));
            goto tryConnectAgain;
        }

        if (FD_ISSET(sfd, &writefds))
        {
            /* The sfd is ready for write. */
            fprintf(stdout, "select() returned and sfd is set. So it's ready!\n");
            ret = 0;
            break;
        }
    }
    else if (ret2 < 0)
    {
        fprintf(stderr, "Error on select(): errno=%d, %s\n", ERRNO, ERRNOSTR);
    }
    }  /* if INPROGRESS */

tryConnectAgain:
    fprintf(stdout, "Closing the socket before trying to connect again.\n");
    CLOSE1(sfd);

    /* Sleep a second before try again. */
#if WINDOWS
    Sleep(1000); /* Unit is ms. */
#else
    sleep(1);
#endif
    }  /* while */

    /* Return from here if connect has failed */
    if (ret != 0)
    {
        CLOSE(sfd);
        return(-5);
    }

    /* connect() has succeeded. */
    /* Make socket blocking again after connect */
    fprintf(stdout, "To clear socket non-blocking ...\n");
#if WINDOWS
    opt = 0;
    if (ioctlsocket(sfd, FIONBIO, &opt) != 0)
#else
    if (fcntl(sfd, F_SETFL, fcntl(sfd, F_GETFL, 0) & ~O_NONBLOCK) != 0)
```

```
#endif
  {
    fprintf(stderr, "Error: fcntl() failed to set socket blocking, errno=%d,"
      " %s\n", ERRNO, ERRNOSTR);
    CLOSE(sfd);
    return(-6);
  }

  /* Exchange data with the server using blocking I/O. */

  fprintf(stdout, "\nSend request messages to server at port %d\n", portnum);

  /* Send request messages to the server and process the reply messages. */
  while (msgnum < MAXMSGS)
  {
    /* Send a request message to the server. */
    sprintf(outbuf, "%s%4lu%s", "This is request message ", ++msgnum,
      " from the client program.");
    msglen = strlen(outbuf);
    errno = 0;

    /* It could die at this send() in Solaris if socket is not re-created. */
    ret = send(sfd, outbuf, msglen, 0);
    if (ret >= 0)
    {
      /* Print a warning if not entire message was sent. */
      if (ret == msglen)
        fprintf(stdout, "\n%lu bytes of message were successfully sent.\n",
          msglen);
      else if (ret < msglen)
        fprintf(stderr, "Warning: only %u of %lu bytes were sent.\n",
          ret, msglen);

      if (ret > 0)
      {
        /* Receive a reply from the server. */
        errno = 0;
        inbuf[0] = '\0';
        ret = recv(sfd, inbuf, BUFLEN, 0);

        if (ret > 0)
        {
          /* Process the reply. */
          inbuf[ret] = '\0';
          fprintf(stdout, "Received the following reply from server:\n%s\n",
            inbuf);
        }
        else if (ret == 0)
          fprintf(stdout, "Warning: Zero bytes were received.\n");
        else
        {
          fprintf(stderr, "Error: recv() failed, errno=%d, %s\n", ERRNO,
            ERRNOSTR);
          CLOSE(sfd);
          return(-7);
        }
```

```
        }
    }
    else
    {
        fprintf(stderr, "Error: send() failed, errno=%d, %s\n", ERRNO, ERRNOSTR);
        CLOSE(sfd);
        return(-8);
    }

    /* Pause one second between messages. Remove this in real code. */
#if WINDOWS
    Sleep(1000); /* Unit is ms. For demo only. Remove this in real code. */
#else
    sleep(1); /* For demo only. Remove this in real code. */
#endif
} /* while */

    CLOSE(sfd);
    return(0);
}
```

Summary of Behavior

Notice that although using the connect() function call to connect to a server is common, when a connect() call fails, the behavior is different on different platforms in at least two aspects.

First, the error codes returned via the errno variable are different on different platforms. For example, when the client uses asynchronous connect in trying to connect to the server and the server program is not up and running yet, the returned error codes on the most popular platforms are listed below:

Linux:
    Async connect() first returns -1 with errno = 115 (EINPROGRESS)
      (Operation now in progress).
    If connect() fails because server is not up, socket error is 111
      (Connection refused).
    Using select() to poll if socket is ready for write returns 1.

Solaris:
    Async connect() first returns -1 with errno = 150 (EINPROGRESS)
      (Operation now in progress).
    If connect() fails because server is not up, socket error is 146
      (Connection refused).
    Using select() to poll if socket is ready for write returns 1.

AIX:
    Async connect() first returns -1 with errno = 79 (ECONNREFUSED -
      Connection refused) if the server is not up.
    Using select() to poll if socket is ready for write returns 1.

HPUX:
    Async connect() first returns -1 with errno = 239 (ECONNREFUSED -
      Connection refused) if the server is not up.
    Using select() to poll if socket is ready for write returns 1.

```
Apple Mac Darwin;
   Async connect() first returns -1 with errno = 36 (EINPROGRESS -
      Operation now in progress) if the server is not up.
   Using select() to poll if socket is ready for write returns 1.

Windows:
   Async connect() first returns -1 with errno = 0.
   A call to WSAGetLastError() returns 10035 (EINPROGRESS).
   Using select() to poll if socket is ready for write returns 0.
```

Please refer to the errno.h header file in each operating system for these error codes.

As you might have noticed, on Windows, the connect() call does not return error code in the errno global variable. Hence, you need to make a separate WSAGetLastError() call to get the real error on Windows platform.

Second, when a connect() call fails, the socket stays valid in Linux and Windows but it becomes undefined in Solaris, AIX and HPUX operating systems. Because of this, you have to close the socket and create a new one before you try another connect() call.

In other words, in Linux and Windows if a connect() call fails, you can re-use the same socket to try to connect again and it's possible to succeed in subsequent attempts and the send() and recv() operations later will work just fine.

However, this is not the case in AIX, HPUX or Solaris.
Trying to re-use the same socket that has failed in a connect() call will cause the subsequent connect() to get an error of 22 (Invalid argument) in AIX and HPUX Itanium, and although the subsequent connect() call may succeed in Solaris, the subsequent send() or recv() call will kill the program in Solaris.

Therefore, to write a single version of code that works across all these five different operating systems, make sure you always close and re-create the socket before you re-try the connect() call again after it has failed. This approach of re-creating a new socket works fine on Linux, Solaris, AIX, HPUX, Apple Darwin and Windows.

How to Check if the Async Connect Has Succeeded?

The recommended way of detecting whether an asynchronous socket is actually connected and ready for use is to use the select() call to poll whether the socket is ready for write. If that select() call returns a positive number, you then check if the corresponding bit in the write file descriptor set is set (on):

```
if (FD_ISSET(sfd, &writefds))
```

where sfd is the socket's file descriptor. If the condition is true, then it means the socket is connected and ready for use.

However, to be safe and robust across all platforms, it's best to add a getsockopt() call right after the select() call to check if there is any error that has occurred.

```
getsockopt(sfd, SOL_SOCKET, SO_ERROR, (void*)(&optval), &vallen);
```

If the returned optval from this getsockopt(,,SO_ERROR,,) call is not zero, then it means some error has occurred during the connect(). In this case, you should close the socket, re-create a new one and re-try the connect() again.

In other words, the best strategy is to do both: select() and getsockopt(sfd, SOL_SOCKET, SO_ERROR,...), and in that order.

12-16 Detecting Peer Termination and Auto-reconnect

This section talks about how to write more robust, automatic self-fixing socket applications.

From time to time you may find that when a socket program communicates with another, the partner may die, terminate, or restart in the middle of a communication and you want to be able to detect that and do something about it.

For example, if a client registers itself with some server and that server keeps the registry in memory only without persisting it to disk. Then when the server dies or restarts, it will lose the registry data and the client will have to re-register itself again. In situations like this, being able to detect if the server dies or restarts would be very helpful.

We show a way to do exactly that in this section -- the auto_reconnect() function of our own:

```
int auto_reconnect(char *server_name, in_port_t portnum);
```

The auto_reconnect() function connects to the server or peer program running at the computer specified by the server_name parameter (in the form of either a hostname or IP address) and at the port given by the portnum parameter. It detects if the server/peer program has gone away and reconnects to it in case that happens. This function can be used as the start function if you like to run this in a separate thread.

Figure 12-20 and 12-21 shows two pairs of client and server programs in which the client uses auto_reconnect() function to detect if the server program has ever terminated and automatically reconnect with the server in case it restarts.

There is a difference between the two pairs. As shown below, tcpclnt_auto_reconn_all.c uses the newer getaddrinfo() to obtain the server's socket address and tcpsrv_auto_reconn_all.c uses an IPv6 server socket. In contrast, tcpclnt_auto_reconn2_all.c uses the traditional gethostbyname()and gethostbyaddr() functions to convert the server's hostname or IP address into a socket address and tcpsrv_auto_reconn2_all uses an IPv4 server socket. Obviously, the tcpclnt_auto_reconn2_all.c and tcpsrv_auto_reconn2_all.c pair is for IPV4 only. It does not work with IPv6 hostnames or IP addresses.

```
tcpclnt_auto_reconn_all : IPv4 client, getaddrinfo()
tcpsrv_auto_reconn_all  : IPv6 server

tcpclnt_auto_reconn2_all : IPv4 client, gethostbyname(), gethostbyaddr()
tcpsrv_auto_reconn2_all  : IPv4 server
```

This method of detecting if a partner has gone away can be used in a client-server or peer-to-peer situation as long as the two processes are communicating via a Stream socket using TCP protocol.

Figure 12-20 Detecting server death and reconnecting automatically -- tcpclnt_auto_reconn_all.c and tcpsrv_auto_reconn_all.c

(a) tcpsrv_auto_reconn_all.c

```c
/*
 * A connection-oriented server program using Stream socket.
 * This version is for testing client detecting server's death.
 * Support for multiple platforms including Linux, Windows, Solaris, AIX, HPUX
 * and Apple Darwin.
 * Usage: tcpsrv_auto_reconn_all [port#]
 * Authored by Mr. Jin-Jwei Chen.
 * Copyright (c) 2002, 2014, 2017-8, 2020 Mr. Jin-Jwei Chen. All rights reserved.
 */

#include "mysocket.h"

int main(int argc, char *argv[])
{
  int     ret;
  int     sfd;                        /* file descriptor of the listener socket */
  int     newsock;                    /* file descriptor of client data socket */
  struct sockaddr_in6   srvaddr;      /* socket structure */
  int     srvaddrsz=sizeof(struct sockaddr_in6);
  struct sockaddr_in6   clntaddr;     /* socket structure */
  socklen_t    clntaddrsz=sizeof(struct sockaddr_in6);
  in_port_t    portnum=DEFSRVPORT;    /* port number */
  int     portnum_in = 0;             /* port number user provides */
  char    outbuf[BUFLEN];             /* output message buffer */
  size_t msglen;                      /* length of reply message */
  int     myid;                       /* my id number */
  int     messages;                   /* number of message to send */
  int     v6only = 0;                 /* IPV6_V6ONLY socket option off */
  int     i, on=1;
#if !WINDOWS
  struct timespec  sleeptm;           /* sleep time - seconds and nanoseconds */
#endif
#if WINDOWS
  WSADATA wsaData;                    /* Winsock data */
  int winerror;                       /* error in Windows */
  char* GetErrorMsg(int ErrorCode);   /* print error string in Windows */
#endif
```

810

```
    fprintf(stdout, "Connection-oriented server program ...\n");

  /* Get the server port number from user, if any. */
  if (argc > 1)
  {
    portnum_in = atoi(argv[1]);
    if (portnum_in <= 0)
    {
      fprintf(stderr, "Port number %d invalid, set to default value %u\n",
        portnum_in, DEFSRVPORT);
      portnum = DEFSRVPORT;
    }
    else
      portnum = (in_port_t)portnum_in;
  }

#if WINDOWS
  /* Ask for Winsock version 2.2 at least. */
  if ((ret = WSAStartup(MAKEWORD(2, 2), &wsaData)) != 0)
  {
    fprintf(stderr, "WSAStartup() failed with error %d: %s\n",
      ret, GetErrorMsg(ret));
    return (-1);
  }
#endif

  /* Create a Stream server socket. */
  if ((sfd = socket(AF_INET6, SOCK_STREAM, 0)) < 0)
  {
    fprintf(stderr, "Error: socket() failed, errno=%d, %s\n", ERRNO, ERRNOSTR);
#if WINDOWS
    WSACleanup();
#endif
    return(-2);
  }

  /* Turn on SO_REUSEADDR socket option so that the server can restart
     right away before the required wait time period expires. */
  if (setsockopt(sfd, SOL_SOCKET, SO_REUSEADDR, (char *)&on, sizeof(on)) < 0)
  {
    fprintf(stderr, "setsockopt(SO_REUSEADDR) failed, errno=%d, %s\n",
      ERRNO, ERRNOSTR);
  }

  /* Turn off IPV6_V6ONLY socket option. Default is on in Windows. */
  if (setsockopt(sfd, IPPROTO_IPV6, IPV6_V6ONLY, (char*)&v6only,
    sizeof(v6only)) != 0)
  {
    fprintf(stderr, "Error: setsockopt(IPV6_V6ONLY) failed, errno=%d, %s\n",
      ERRNO, ERRNOSTR);
    CLOSE(sfd);
    return(-3);
  }

  /* Fill in the server socket address. */
  memset((void *)&srvaddr, 0, (size_t)srvaddrsz); /* clear the address buffer */
```

```
    srvaddr.sin6_family = AF_INET6;                    /* Internet socket */
    srvaddr.sin6_addr= in6addr_any;                    /* server's IP address */
    srvaddr.sin6_port = htons(portnum);                /* server's port number */

    /* Bind the server socket to its address. */
    if ((ret = bind(sfd, (struct sockaddr *)&srvaddr, srvaddrsz)) != 0)
    {
      fprintf(stderr, "Error: bind() failed, errno=%d, %s\n", ERRNO, ERRNOSTR);
      CLOSE(sfd);
      return(-4);
    }

    /* Set maximum connection request queue length that we can fall behind. */
    if (listen(sfd, BACKLOG) == -1) {
      fprintf(stderr, "Error: listen() failed, errno=%d, %s\n", ERRNO, ERRNOSTR);
      CLOSE(sfd);
      return(-5);
    }

    /* Set sleep time to be 5 ms. */
#if !WINDOWS
    sleeptm.tv_sec = SLEEPS;
    sleeptm.tv_nsec = (SLEEPMS*1000000);
#endif

    /* Wait for incoming connection requests from clients and service them. */
    while (1) {

      fprintf(stdout, "\nListening at port number %u ...\n", portnum);
      newsock = accept(sfd, (struct sockaddr *)&clntaddr, &clntaddrsz);
      if (newsock < 0)
      {
        fprintf(stderr, "Error: accept() failed, errno=%d, %s\n", ERRNO, ERRNOSTR);
        CLOSE(sfd);
        return(-6);
      }

      fprintf(stdout, "Client Connected.\n");

      /* Exchange messages with the client here in real code. Do the real work. */
      /* For demo purposes, we wait a little bit and then exit here. */
#if WINDOWS
      Sleep(SLEEPMS);    /* Unit is ms. */
#else
      nanosleep(&sleeptm, (struct timespec *)NULL);
#endif

      /* For demo purposes, terminate the communication with the client. */
      CLOSE1(newsock);

      /* Simulate server down. For demo only. Remove these 2 lines in real code. */
      CLOSE1(sfd);
      break;
    }  /* while - outer */

#if WINDOWS
```

```
  WSACleanup();
#endif
  return(0);
}
```

(b) tcpclnt_auto_reconn_all.c

```
/*
 * A connection-oriented client program using Stream socket.
 * Detecting the death of a server and reconnecting with it automatically.
 * Using getaddrinfo().
 * This version works on Linux, Solaris, AIX, HPUX, Apple Darwin and Windows.
 * Usage: tcpclnt_auto_reconn_all [port [hostname/IPaddr]]
 * Authored by Mr. Jin-Jwei Chen.
 * Copyright (c) 2002, 2014, 2017-8, 2020 Mr. Jin-Jwei Chen. All rights reserved.
 */

#include "mysocket.h"

#undef    SLEEPMS
#define   SLEEPMS         500      /* number of milliseconds to sleep & wait */

int auto_reconnect(char *server_name, in_port_t portnum);

int main(int argc, char *argv[])
{
  int        ret;
  size_t     len;
  in_port_t  portnum=DEFSRVPORT;      /* port number */
  int        portnum_in = 0;          /* port number user provides */
  char       server_name[NAMELEN+1];  /* hostname or IP address */

  fprintf(stdout, "Connection-oriented client program detecting server
death...\n\n");

  /* Get the server's port number from user, if there is one. */
  if (argc > 1)
  {
    portnum_in = atoi(argv[1]);
    if (portnum_in <= 0)
    {
      fprintf(stderr,"Error: invalid port number %s. Use default port %d.\n",
        argv[1], DEFSRVPORT);
      portnum = DEFSRVPORT;
    }
    else
      portnum = (in_port_t)portnum_in;
  }

  /* Get the server's host name or IP address from user, if there is one. */
  if (argc > 2)
  {
    len = strlen(argv[2]);
    if (len > NAMELEN)
      len = NAMELEN;
    strncpy(server_name, argv[2], len);
```

```
    server_name[len] = '\0';
  } else
    strcpy(server_name, SERVER_NAME);

  ret = auto_reconnect(server_name, portnum);

  return(ret);
}

int auto_reconnect(char *server_name, in_port_t portnum)
{
  int    ret;
  int    sfd;                      /* file descriptor of the socket */
  struct addrinfo hints;           /* address info hints */
  struct addrinfo *res=NULL;       /* address info result */
  char   portnumstr[16];           /* port number in string form */
  char   inbuf[BUFLEN];            /* input message buffer */
#if WINDOWS
  WSADATA wsaData;                          /* Winsock data */
  char* GetErrorMsg(int ErrorCode); /* print error string in Windows */
  unsigned long opt = 1;
#else
  struct timespec  sleeptm;        /* time to sleep - seconds and nanoseconds */
#endif

  if (server_name == NULL || portnum <= 0)
    return(EINVAL);

#if WINDOWS
  /* Ask for Winsock version 2.2 at least. */
  if ((ret = WSAStartup(MAKEWORD(2, 2), &wsaData)) != 0)
  {
    fprintf(stderr, "Error: WSAStartup() failed with error %d: %s\n",
      ret, GetErrorMsg(ret));
    return (-3);
  }
#endif

  /* Translate the server's host name or IP address into socket address.
   * Fill in the hints information.
   */
  sprintf(portnumstr, "%d", portnum);
  memset(&hints, 0x00, sizeof(hints));
    /* This works on AIX but not on Solaris, nor on Windows. */
    /* hints.ai_flags    = AI_NUMERICSERV; */
  hints.ai_family    = AF_UNSPEC;
  hints.ai_socktype = SOCK_STREAM;

  /* Get the address information of the server using getaddrinfo().  */
  ret = getaddrinfo(server_name, portnumstr, &hints, &res);
  if (ret != 0)
  {
    fprintf(stderr, "Error: getaddrinfo() failed, error %d, %s\n", ret,
      gai_strerror(ret));
#if !WINDOWS
    if (ret == EAI_SYSTEM)
```

```
        fprintf(stderr,"System error: errno=%d, %s\n", errno, strerror(errno));
#else
    WSACleanup();
#endif
    return(-4);
  }

  /* Set sleep time. */
#if !WINDOWS
  sleeptm.tv_sec = 0;
  sleeptm.tv_nsec = (SLEEPMS*1000000);
#endif

  /* Try to detect if the server has terminated. If yes, try to re-connect. */
  while (1)
  {
    fprintf(stderr,"Try to (re-)create a new socket and (re-)connect to "
      "the server ...\n");

    /* Create or re-create a socket for the client. */
    errno = 0;
    sfd = socket(res->ai_family, res->ai_socktype, res->ai_protocol);
    if (sfd < 0)
    {
      fprintf(stderr,"Error: socket() failed, errno=%d, %s\n", ERRNO, ERRNOSTR);
#if WINDOWS
      WSACleanup();
#endif
      return (-5);
    }

    /* Connect to the server. */
    errno = 0;
    ret = connect(sfd, res->ai_addr, res->ai_addrlen);

    /* Try it again a bit later if connect has failed. */
    if (ret != 0)
    {
      fprintf(stderr, "Error: connect() failed, errno=%d, %s\n", ERRNO, ERRNOSTR);
      goto tryAgain;;
    }

    /* Connect has succeeded. */
    fprintf(stdout, "\n*** Server is up. Connecting to server is successful.\n\n");

    /* The main loop that exchanges messages with the server. */
    while(1)
    {
      /* Receive next message. */
      ret = 0;
      errno = 0;
      inbuf[0] = '\0';
      ret = recv(sfd, inbuf, BUFLEN, 0);

      /* Break if error occurred during recv(). */
      if (ret < 0)
```

```
      {
        fprintf(stderr, "Error: recv() failed, errno=%d, %s\n", ERRNO, ERRNOSTR);
        break;
      }
      /* No error during recv(). */
      else if (ret > 0)
      {
        /* Print the message received, if any. */
        inbuf[ret] = '\0';
        fprintf(stdout, "Received the following message:\n%s\n",
          inbuf);
      }
      else if (ret == 0)
      {
        fprintf(stdout, "\n*** The server may have terminated.\n\n");
        break;
      }
    }  /* inner while */

tryAgain:
    /* Close the current socket */
    CLOSE1(sfd);
    sfd = 0;

    /* Wait a little bit for the server to restart and be ready. */
    fprintf(stdout, "Sleep for %2d ms and wait for server to be ready...\n",
      SLEEPMS);
#if WINDOWS
    Sleep(SLEEPMS);  /* Unit is ms. */
#else
    nanosleep(&sleeptm, (struct timespec *)NULL);
#endif
  }  /* outer while (1) */

#if WINDOWS
  WSACleanup();
#endif
  return(0);
}
```

Figure 12-21 Detecting server death and reconnecting automatically --
   tcpclnt_auto_reconn2_all.c and tcpsrv_auto_reconn2_all.c

(a) tcpsrv_auto_reconn2_all.c

```
/*
 * A connection-oriented server program using Stream socket.
 * This version is for testing client detecting server's death.
 * Support for multiple platforms including Linux, Windows, Solaris, AIX, HPUX
 * and Apple Darwin.
 * Usage: tcpsrv_auto_reconn2_all [port#]
 * Authored by Mr. Jin-Jwei Chen.
 * Copyright (c) 2002, 2014, 2017, 2018 Mr. Jin-Jwei Chen. All rights reserved.
 */

#include "mysocket.h"
```

```c
int main(int argc, char *argv[])
{
  int    ret;
  int    sfd;                        /* file descriptor of the listener socket */
  int    newsock;                    /* file descriptor of client data socket */
  struct sockaddr_in    srvaddr;     /* socket structure */
  int    srvaddrsz=sizeof(struct sockaddr_in);
  struct sockaddr_in    clntaddr;    /* socket structure */
  socklen_t    clntaddrsz=sizeof(struct sockaddr_in);
  in_port_t    portnum=DEFSRVPORT;   /* port number */
  int    portnum_in = 0;             /* port number entered by user */
  char   outbuf[BUFLEN];             /* output message buffer */
  size_t msglen;                     /* length of reply message */
  int    myid;                       /* my id number */
  int    messages;                   /* number of message to send */
  int    i, on=1;
#if !WINDOWS
  struct timespec  sleeptm;          /* sleep time - seconds and nanoseconds */
#endif
#if WINDOWS
  WSADATA wsaData;                   /* Winsock data */
  int winerror;                      /* error in Windows */
  char* GetErrorMsg(int ErrorCode); /* print error string in Windows */
#endif

  fprintf(stdout, "Connection-oriented server program ...\n");

  /* Get the server port number from user, if any. */
  if (argc > 1)
  {
    portnum_in = atoi(argv[1]);
    if (portnum_in <= 0)
    {
      fprintf(stderr, "Port number %d invalid, set to default value %u\n",
        portnum_in, DEFSRVPORT);
      portnum = DEFSRVPORT;
    }
    else
      portnum = (in_port_t)portnum_in;
  }

#if WINDOWS
  /* Ask for Winsock version 2.2 at least. */
  if ((ret = WSAStartup(MAKEWORD(2, 2), &wsaData)) != 0)
  {
    fprintf(stderr, "WSAStartup() failed with error %d: %s\n",
      ret, GetErrorMsg(ret));
    return (-1);
  }
#endif

  /* Create the Stream server socket. */
  if ((sfd = socket(AF_INET, SOCK_STREAM, 0)) < 0)
  {
    fprintf(stderr, "Error: socket() failed, errno=%d, %s\n", ERRNO, ERRNOSTR);
```

817

```
#if WINDOWS
    WSACleanup();
#endif
    return(-2);
  }

  /* Turn on SO_REUSEADDR socket option so that the server can restart
     right away before the required wait time period expires. */
  if (setsockopt(sfd, SOL_SOCKET, SO_REUSEADDR, (char *)&on, sizeof(on)) < 0)
  {
    fprintf(stderr, "setsockopt(SO_REUSEADDR) failed, errno=%d, %s\n", ERRNO,
      ERRNOSTR);
  }

  /* Fill in the server socket address. */
  memset((void *)&srvaddr, 0, (size_t)srvaddrsz); /* clear the address buffer */
  srvaddr.sin_family = AF_INET;                    /* Internet socket */
  srvaddr.sin_addr.s_addr = htonl(INADDR_ANY);     /* server's IP address */
  srvaddr.sin_port = htons(portnum);               /* server's port number */

  /* Bind the server socket to its address. */
  if ((ret = bind(sfd, (struct sockaddr *)&srvaddr, srvaddrsz)) != 0)
  {
    fprintf(stderr, "Error: bind() failed, errno=%d, %s\n", ERRNO, ERRNOSTR);
    CLOSE(sfd);
    return(-3);
  }

  /* Set maximum connection request queue length that we can fall behind. */
  if (listen(sfd, BACKLOG) == -1) {
    fprintf(stderr, "Error: listen() failed, errno=%d, %s\n", ERRNO, ERRNOSTR);
    CLOSE(sfd);
    return(-4);
  }

  /* Set sleep time to be 5 ms. */
#if !WINDOWS
  sleeptm.tv_sec = SLEEPS;
  sleeptm.tv_nsec = (SLEEPMS*1000000);
#endif

  /* Wait for incoming connection requests from clients and service them. */
  while (1) {

    fprintf(stdout, "\nListening at port number %u ...\n", portnum);
    newsock = accept(sfd, (struct sockaddr *)&clntaddr, &clntaddrsz);
    if (newsock < 0)
    {
      fprintf(stderr, "Error: accept() failed, errno=%d, %s\n", ERRNO, ERRNOSTR);
      CLOSE(sfd);
      return(-5);
    }

    fprintf(stdout, "Client Connected.\n");

    /* Exchange messages with the client here in real code. Do the real work. */
```

```
    /* For demo purposes, we wait a little bit and then exit here. */
#if WINDOWS
    Sleep(SLEEPMS);   /* Unit is ms. */
#else
    nanosleep(&sleeptm, (struct timespec *)NULL);
#endif

    /* For demo purposes, terminate the communication with the client. */
    CLOSE1(newsock);

    /* Simulate server down. For demo only. Remove these 2 lines in real code. */
    CLOSE1(sfd);
    break;
  }   /* while - outer */

#if WINDOWS
  WSACleanup();
#endif
  return(0);
}
```

(b) tcpclnt_auto_reconn2_all.c

```
/*
 * A connection-oriented client program using Stream socket.
 * Detecting death of the server and reconnecting with it automatically.
 * Using gethostbyname() and gethostbyaddr().
 * This version works on Linux, Solaris, AIX, HPUX, Apple Darwin and Windows.
 * Usage: tcpclnt_auto_reconn2_all [port [hostname/IPaddr]]
 * Authored by Mr. Jin-Jwei Chen.
 * Copyright (c) 2002, 2014, 2017-8, 2020 Mr. Jin-Jwei Chen. All rights reserved.
 */

#include "mysocket.h"

#undef    SLEEPMS
#define   SLEEPMS         500     /* number of milliseconds to sleep & wait */

int auto_reconnect(char *server_name, in_port_t portnum);

int main(int argc, char *argv[])
{
  int       ret;
  size_t    len;
  in_port_t portnum=DEFSRVPORT;    /* port number */
  int       portnum_in = 0;        /* port number provided by user */
  char      server_name[NAMELEN+1]; /* hostname or IP address */

  fprintf(stdout, "Connection-oriented client program detecting server
death...\n\n");

  /* Get the server's port number from user, if there is one. */
  if (argc > 1)
  {
    portnum_in = atoi(argv[1]);
    if (portnum_in <= 0)
```

819

```
        {
            fprintf(stderr,"Error: invalid port number %s. Use default port %d.\n",
              argv[1], DEFSRVPORT);
            portnum = DEFSRVPORT;
        }
        else
            portnum = (in_port_t)portnum_in;
    }

    /* Get the server's host name or IP address from user, if there is one. */
    if (argc > 2)
    {
      len = strlen(argv[2]);
      if (len > NAMELEN)
        len = NAMELEN;
      strncpy(server_name, argv[2], len);
      server_name[len] = '\0';
    } else
      strcpy(server_name, "localhost");

    ret = auto_reconnect(server_name, portnum);

    return(ret);
}

int auto_reconnect(char *server_name, in_port_t portnum)
{
    int     ret;
    int     socket_type = SOCK_STREAM;
    int     sfd;                        /* file descriptor of the socket */
    struct sockaddr_in    server;       /* socket structure */
    int     srvaddrsz=sizeof(struct sockaddr_in);
    unsigned int addr;
    struct hostent *hp;
    char    inbuf[BUFLEN];              /* input message buffer */
#if !WINDOWS
    struct timespec   sleeptm;          /* time to sleep - seconds and nanoseconds */
    int     winerror;                  /* socket error in Windows */
#endif
#if WINDOWS
    WSADATA wsaData;                    /* Winsock data */
    int winerror;                      /* error in Windows */
    char* GetErrorMsg(int ErrorCode); /* print error string in Windows */
    unsigned long opt = 1;
#endif

    if (server_name == NULL || portnum <= 0)
      return(EINVAL);

#if WINDOWS
    /* Ask for Winsock version 2.2 at least. */
    if ((ret = WSAStartup(MAKEWORD(2, 2), &wsaData)) != 0)
    {
      fprintf(stderr, "Error: WSAStartup() failed with error %d: %s\n",
        ret, GetErrorMsg(ret));
      return (-3);
```

```
  }
#endif

  /* Translate the host name or IP address into server socket address. */
  if (isalpha(server_name[0]))
  {   /* A host name is given. */
    hp = gethostbyname(server_name);
  }
  else
  {   /* Convert the n.n.n.n IP address to a number. */
    addr = inet_addr(server_name);
    hp = gethostbyaddr((char *)&addr, sizeof(addr), AF_INET);
  }

  if (hp == NULL )
  {
     fprintf(stderr,"Error: cannot get address for [%s], errno=%d, %s\n",
       server_name, ERRNO, ERRNOSTR);
#if WINDOWS
     WSACleanup();
#endif
     return(-4);
  }

  /* Copy the resolved information into the sockaddr_in structure. */
  memset(&server, 0, sizeof(server));
  memcpy(&(server.sin_addr), hp->h_addr, hp->h_length);
  server.sin_family = hp->h_addrtype;
  server.sin_port = htons(portnum);

  /* Set sleep time. */
#if !WINDOWS
  sleeptm.tv_sec = 0;
  sleeptm.tv_nsec = (SLEEPMS*1000000);
#endif

  /* Connect and communicate with the server. Try to detect if the server
     has terminated. If yes, try to re-connect automatically. */
  while (1)
  {
    fprintf(stderr,"Try to (re-)create a new socket and (re-)connect to "
      "the server ...\n");

    /* Create or re-create a socket for the client. */
    sfd = socket(AF_INET, socket_type, 0);
    if (sfd < 0)
    {
      fprintf(stderr,"Error: socket() failed, errno=%d, %s\n", ERRNO, ERRNOSTR);
#if WINDOWS
      WSACleanup();
#endif
      return (-5);
    }

    /* Connect to the server. */
    errno = 0;
```

```
    ret = connect(sfd, (struct sockaddr *)&server, srvaddrsz);

    /* Try it again a bit later if connect has failed. */
    if (ret != 0)
    {
      fprintf(stderr, "Error: connect() failed, errno=%d, %s\n", ERRNO,
        ERRNOSTR);
      goto tryAgain;;
    }

    /* Connect has succeeded. */
    fprintf(stdout, "\n*** Server is up. Connecting to server is successful.\n\n");

    /* The main loop that exchanges messages with the server. */
    while (1)
    {
      /* Receive next message. */
      ret = 0;
      errno = 0;
      inbuf[0] = '\0';
      ret = recv(sfd, inbuf, BUFLEN, 0);

      /* Break if error occurred during recv(). */
      if (ret < 0)
      {
        fprintf(stderr, "recv() returned %d, errno=%d, %s\n", ret, ERRNO,
          ERRNOSTR);
        break;
      }

      /* No error during recv(). */
      if (ret > 0)
      {
        /* Print the message received, if any. */
        inbuf[ret] = '\0';
        fprintf(stdout, "Received the following message:\n%s\n",
          inbuf);
      }
      else if (ret == 0)
      {
        fprintf(stdout, "\n*** The server may have terminated.\n\n");
        break;
      }
    }  /* inner while */

tryAgain:
    /* Close the current socket */
    CLOSE1(sfd);
    sfd = 0;

    /* Wait a little bit for the server to restart and be ready. */
    fprintf(stdout, "Sleep for %2d ms and wait for server to restart...\n",
      SLEEPMS);
#if WINDOWS
    Sleep(SLEEPMS);   /* Unit is ms. */
#else
```

822

```
     nanosleep(&sleeptm, (struct timespec *)NULL);
#endif
  } /* outer while (1) */

#if WINDOWS
  WSACleanup();
#endif
  return(0);
}
```

12-17 Multicasting

The network communications we have illustrated so far have been unicast,
meaning a message sender sends messages to one single receiver.
It's the typical one-to-one communications.

At times, for instances, applications, like those in social networking
environment which is extremely popular now, may wish to send messages to
a group of receivers. It's a kind of "broadcasting" to all people in a
select group. However, it is not real broadcasting, which sends a message
to all on the network. This feature is called 'multicasting'.
With **multicasting,** a single send operation sends the message to multiple
receivers on multiple hosts all at once. We discuss this in current section.

Multicasting is a one-to-many transmission scheme. It is typically done via
a UDP Datagram (SOCK_DGRAM) socket or via a raw (SOCK_RAW) socket if it is
a routing daemon. Note that multicasting cannot be done using a TCP stream
(SOCK_STREAM) socket. (In TCP, a separate connection will be needed
between the message sender and each receiver.)

Multicasting is a hardware and software feature. Namely, it requires
hardware that is capable of and configured for doing multicasting and
programs must also be coded to support multicasting.

12-17-1 Forming a Multicast Group

A group of hosts in a computer network can form a multicast group and
exchange messages between them efficiently in which each message a sender
sends gets delivered to each member in the group.

A **multicast group** is identified by a **multicast group address.**
Certain multicast address blocks in IPv4 and IPv6 are specially reserved
for multicasting. In IPv4, Class D IP addresses are used as multicast IP
addresses. This means IPv4 multicast IPs range from 224.0.0.0 to
239.255.255.255. In IPv6, multicast addresses use the prefix ff00::/8.
For example, a well-known IPv6 multicast address is ff02::1, which is
reserved for doing multicasting for all nodes on the local network segment.

Hosts in the same multicast group may reside on a single subnet or on
different subnets. If they reside in different subnets then they must be
connected by multicast capable routers.

A host can join or leave a multicast group at any time.
There is no restriction on the location or number of members in a group.

Multicast addressing can be used in the network link and network (IP) layers. We discuss IP multicast in this section.

12-17-2 How to Program Multicasting?

To do multicasting, a program creates a normal unicast UDP Datagram socket and then invokes the setsockopt() function to associate various multicasting attributes with the socket. Figure 12-22 lists these **multicast socket options**. Note that different names are used between IPv4 and IPv6 protocols. Also note that each option can be used with getsockopt() or setsockopt() to get or set the option's value.

```
        IPv4                          IPv6
-------------------     ---------------------------------------
IP_MULTICAST_LOOP       IPV6_MULTICAST_LOOP
IP_MULTICAST_IF         IPV6_MULTICAST_IF
IP_MULTICAST_TTL        IPV6_MULTICAST_HOPS
IP_ADD_MEMBERSHIP       IPV6_ADD_MEMBERSHIP, IPV6_JOIN_GROUP
IP_DROP_MEMBERSHIP      IPV6_DROP_MEMBERSHIP, IPV6_LEAVE_GROUP
-------------------------------------------------------------
```
        Figure 12-22 Multicast socket options

Socket options for multicast

The function of each of these socket options is explained below:

1. IP_ADD_MEMBERSHIP / IPV6_ADD_MEMBERSHIP / IPV6_JOIN_GROUP

   Join the socket to the specified multicast group on the specified local network interface. The addresses of the multicast group and the local interface are specified in the setsockopt() call.

   The option value for this socket option is an ip_mreq (IPv4) or ipv6_mreq (IPv6) structure consisting the IP address of the multicast group and the IP address of the local network interface for the multicasting.

   Note that only the receivers of multicast messages need to explicitly join the multicast group using the IP_ADD_MEMBERSHIP socket option.

   Joining-a-group operation is nonblocking. The function call should return immediately with a success or failure.

2. IP_DROP_MEMBERSHIP / IPV6_DROP_MEMBERSHIP / IPV6_LEAVE_GROUP

   This option is the opposite of IP_ADD_MEMBERSHIP and IPV6_JOIN_GROUP. It drops the program from the multicast group specified in the ip_mreq /ipv6_mreq structure.

   Leaving-a-group operation is nonblocking. The function call should return immediately with a success or failure.

3. IP_MULTICAST_IF / IPV6_MULTICAST_IF

This socket option allows you to get or set interface (IF) for multicast. Using this option with setsockopt() function allows a program to specify a local network interface to be used for sending outgoing multicast messages. The IP address specified in this call must be a multicast capable network interface.

Note that this is for setting a local interface for **sending** multicast traffic. It's separate and independent from the interface used in **receiving** multicast datagrams for which you would call bind() to bind your socket to.

Calling getsockopt() with this option returns the current default interface for sending multicast datagrams.

4. IP_MULTICAST_LOOP / IPV6_MULTICAST_LOOP

This option controls whether outgoing multicast messages should be delivered back to the local host so that the sender application itself or other application on the same local host can get the multicast messages.

On Linux, this option is enabled by default. That is, by default, multicast messages sent are delivered back to the local host if there is any application listens to the multicast group.

5. IP_MULTICAST_TTL / IPV6_MULTICAST_HOPS

This option gets or sets the TTL (number of hops) value associated with multicast traffic on the socket.

Typically, this value is 1 by default, preventing the multicast datagrams from being forwarded beyond the local network. This value cannot be greater than 255. Messages are not transmitted on any sub-network if TTL is 0. If multicast routers are attached to the first sub-network and TTL > 1, multicast messages can be delivered to more than one sub-network.

To send multicast messages, a program must do the following:

- Create an Internet Datagram socket

- Set up the multicast group's IP address and port number

- Set the local network interface for outbound multicast messages by using the IP_MULTICAST_IF socket option.

- Call sendto() to send the multicast message to the multicast group's address and port number.

To receive multicast messages, a socket program must do the following:

- Create an Internet Datagram socket

- Bind the socket to the wildcard IP address and multicast port number. This port number must be the same as the port number as specified in the multicast address by the sender.

- Specify a local network interface and join the multicast group,
  via the IP_ADD_MEMBERSHIP socket option.
  The IP_ADD_MEMBERSHIP socket option must be called for every local
  network interface receiving the multicast datagram messages.

  Joining a multicast group must specify two addresses: the multicast
  group address and the IP address of a local network interface
  over which multicast messages will be received.

  This call tells the operating system kernel to deliver the multicast
  messages of the specified multicast group to your program.

- Turn on SO_REUSEADDR or SO_REUSEPORT socket option to allow multiple
  programs, or instances of the same program, running on the same host
  to be able to receive copies of the same multicast datagrams.

- Receive multicast messages

  Note that to be able to receive multicast messages, normally a receiver
  needs to be on the same subnet as the sender.

Figure 12-23a shows a multicast message sender program, multicast_snd_all,
which works for all platforms tested including Linux, AIX, Solaris, HP-UX,
Apple Darwin and Windows.

Figure 12-23b lists a multicast message receiver program, multicast_rcv_all,
which turns on the SO_REUSEADDR socket option and allows multiple instances
of the program on the same host to all receive multicast messages.
It works in Linux, Solaris and Windows.

Figure 12-23c displays a slightly different version of the multicast message
receiver program, multicast_rcv2_all, which turns on the SO_REUSEPORT socket
option and allows multiple instances of the program on the same host to all
receive multicast messages. It works in AIX, HP-UX, Linux and Apple Darwin.

The select group is defined by the MULTICASTGROUP macro, which could be
"224.1.1.1", "224.0.0.251", "225.1.1.1", "226.1.1.1", etc.

Figure 12-23a Multicast message sender -- multicast_snd_all.c (all platforms)

```
/*
 * Multicast message sender
 * This program sends a message via multicasting.
 * Usage: multicast_snd ip_address_of_local_interface
 * Authored by Mr. Jin-Jwei Chen.
 * Copyright (c) 2017-8, Mr. Jin-Jwei Chen. All rights reserved.
 */

#include "mysocket.h"

int main (int argc, char *argv[ ])
{
    struct sockaddr_in mcastgrp;     /* address of the multicast group */
    struct in_addr localintf;        /* IP address of the local interface */
```

```c
  int    sfd;                          /* socket file descriptor */
  char   databuf[BUFLEN];              /* IN/OUT data buffer */
  unsigned char  loopval;             /* value of socket option */
  unsigned int   ttlval;              /* value of socket option */
  socklen_t ttlvalsz = sizeof(ttlval);   /* size of option value */
  char   *localintfaddr = LOCALINTFIPADDR;  /* IP addr of local interface */

#if WINDOWS
  int   ret = 0;
  WSADATA wsaData;
  char* GetErrorMsg(int ErrorCode);    /* print error string in Windows */
#endif

  /* Get local interface IP address from user, if any */
  if (argc > 1)
    localintfaddr = argv[1];

#if WINDOWS
  /* Start up Windows socket. Use at least Winsock version 2.2 */
  if ((ret = WSAStartup(MAKEWORD(2, 2), &wsaData)) != 0)
  {
    fprintf(stderr, "WSAStartup failed with error %d: %s\n",
      ret, GetErrorMsg(ret));
    WSACleanup();
    return (-1);
  }
#endif

  /* Create a Datagram socket */
  sfd = socket(AF_INET, SOCK_DGRAM, 0);
  if (sfd < 0)
  {
    fprintf(stderr, "Error: socket() failed, errno=%d, %s\n", ERRNO, ERRNOSTR);
#if WINDOWS
    WSACleanup();
#endif
    return(-2);
  }

  /* Fill in the multicast group's address */
  memset((char *) &mcastgrp, 0, sizeof(mcastgrp));
  mcastgrp.sin_family = AF_INET;
  mcastgrp.sin_addr.s_addr = inet_addr(MULTICASTGROUP);
  mcastgrp.sin_port = htons(MCASTPORT);

  /* Enable loopback so multicast messages we send get delivered to
   * to this local host as well. */
  /* On Linux, this is sort of redundant because, by default, this is on.
     That is, applications on this same host can receive multicast message. */
  loopval = 1;
  if (setsockopt(sfd, IPPROTO_IP, IP_MULTICAST_LOOP, (char *)&loopval,
    sizeof(loopval)) < 0)
  {
    fprintf(stderr, "Error: setsockopt(IP_MULTICAST_LOOP) failed, "
      "errno=%d, %s\n", ERRNO, ERRNOSTR);
    CLOSE(sfd);
```

```
      return(-3);
    }

    /* Set the local interface for outbound multicast messages. The local IP
       address specified must be a multicast capable interface. */
    localintf.s_addr = inet_addr(localintfaddr);
    if (setsockopt(sfd, IPPROTO_IP, IP_MULTICAST_IF, (char *)&localintf,
        sizeof(localintf)) < 0)
    {
      fprintf(stderr, "Error: setsockopt(IP_MULTICAST_IF) failed, "
        "errno=%d, %s\n", ERRNO, ERRNOSTR);
      CLOSE(sfd);
      return(-4);
    }

    /* Send a message to the multicast group */
    strcpy(databuf, "This is a multicast datagram message.");
    if (sendto(sfd, databuf, BUFLEN, 0, (struct sockaddr*)&mcastgrp,
        sizeof(mcastgrp)) < 0)
    {
      fprintf(stderr, "Error: sendto() failed, errno=%d, %s\n", ERRNO, ERRNOSTR);
      CLOSE(sfd);
      return(-5);
    }
    fprintf(stdout, "The multicast message was successfully sent.\n");

  CLOSE(sfd);
  return(0);
}
```

Figure 12-23b Multicast message receiver -- multicast_rcv_all.c
(for Linux, Solaris and Windows)

```
/*
 * Multicast message receiver
 * This program receives a message through multicasting.
 * Multiple programs running on same host are enabled to receive in same
 * multicast group via turning on the SO_REUSEADDR socket option.
 * This works in Linux, Oracle/Sun Solaris, Apple Darwin and Windows.
 * Usage: multicast_rcv  ip_address_of_local_interface
 * Authored by Mr. Jin-Jwei Chen.
 * Copyright (c) 2017-8, Mr. Jin-Jwei Chen. All rights reserved.
 */

#include "mysocket.h"

int main(int argc, char *argv[])
{
  struct sockaddr_in  rcvraddr;   /* address of the receiving socket */
  struct ip_mreq      mcastgrp;   /* address of the multicast group */
  int     sfd;                    /* socket file descriptor */
  char    inbuf[BUFLEN];          /* input buffer */
  int     optval;                 /* value of socket option */
  char    *localintfaddr = LOCALINTFIPADDR;  /* IP addr of local interface */

#if WINDOWS
```

```
  int   ret = 0;
  WSADATA wsaData;
  char* GetErrorMsg(int ErrorCode);    /* print error string in Windows */
#endif

  /* Get local interface IP address from user, if any */
  if (argc > 1)
    localintfaddr = argv[1];

#if WINDOWS
  /* Start up Windows socket. Use at least Winsock version 2.2 */
  if ((ret = WSAStartup(MAKEWORD(2, 2), &wsaData)) != 0)
  {
    fprintf(stderr, "WSAStartup failed with error %d: %s\n",
      ret, GetErrorMsg(ret));
    WSACleanup();
    return (-1);
  }
#endif

  /* Create a Datagram socket */
  sfd = socket(AF_INET, SOCK_DGRAM, 0);
  if (sfd < 0)
  {
    fprintf(stderr, "Error: socket() failed, errno=%d, %s\n", ERRNO, ERRNOSTR);
#if WINDOWS
    WSACleanup();
#endif
    return(-2);
  }

  /* Turn on SO_REUSEADDR socket option to allow multiple instances of this
     program to be able to receive copies of the multicast datagrams. */
  optval = 1;
  if (setsockopt(sfd, SOL_SOCKET, SO_REUSEADDR, (char *)&optval, sizeof(optval))
    < 0)
  {
    fprintf(stderr, "Error: setsockopt(SO_REUSEADDR) failed, errno=%d, %s\n",
      ERRNO, ERRNOSTR);
    CLOSE(sfd);
    return(-3);
  }
  fprintf(stdout, "The SO_REUSEADDR socket option is turned on.\n");

  /* Bind the Datagram socket to an address */
  memset((char *) &rcvraddr, 0, sizeof(rcvraddr));
  rcvraddr.sin_family = AF_INET;
  rcvraddr.sin_port = htons(MCASTPORT);
  rcvraddr.sin_addr.s_addr = INADDR_ANY;
  if (bind(sfd, (struct sockaddr*)&rcvraddr, sizeof(rcvraddr)))
  {
    fprintf(stderr, "Error: bind() failed, errno=%d, %s\n", ERRNO, ERRNOSTR);
    CLOSE(sfd);
    return(-4);
  }
```

```
  /* Join the multicast group on the specified local host's interface.
   * A multicast datagram receiver must turn on the IP_ADD_MEMBERSHIP
   * socket option.
   */
  mcastgrp.imr_multiaddr.s_addr = inet_addr(MULTICASTGROUP);
  mcastgrp.imr_interface.s_addr = inet_addr(localintfaddr);
  if (setsockopt(sfd, IPPROTO_IP, IP_ADD_MEMBERSHIP, (char *)&mcastgrp,
    sizeof(mcastgrp)) < 0)
  {
    fprintf(stderr, "Error: setsockopt(IP_ADD_MEMBERSHIP) failed, "
      "errno=%d, %s\n", ERRNO, ERRNOSTR);
    CLOSE(sfd);
    return(-5);
  }

  /* Read the multicast message. Windows requires using recvfrom() here. */
  if (recvfrom(sfd, inbuf, BUFLEN, 0, (struct sockaddr *)NULL,
      (socklen_t *)NULL) < 0)
  {
    fprintf(stderr, "Error: recvfrom() failed, errno=%d, %s\n", ERRNO, ERRNOSTR);
    CLOSE(sfd);
    return(-6);
  }

  fprintf(stdout, "The following multicast message was successfully received:"
    "\n%s\n", inbuf);

  CLOSE(sfd);
  return(0);
}
```

Figure 12-23c Multicast message receiver -- multicast_rcv2_all.c
(for AIX, HP-UX, Linux and Apple Darwin)

```
/*
 * Multicast message receiver
 * This program receives a message through multicasting.
 * Multiple programs running on same host are enabled to receive in same
 * multicast group via turning on the SO_REUSEPORT socket option.
 * This works in Linux, IBM AIX, HP HPUX and Apple Darwin.
 * Usage: multicast_rcv2  ip_address_of_local_interface
 * Authored by Mr. Jin-Jwei Chen.
 * Copyright (c) 2017-8, Mr. Jin-Jwei Chen. All rights reserved.
 */

#include "mysocket.h"

int main(int argc, char *argv[])
{
  struct sockaddr_in  rcvraddr;   /* address of the receiving socket */
  struct ip_mreq      mcastgrp;   /* address of the multicast group */
  int     sfd;                    /* socket file descriptor */
  char    inbuf[BUFLEN];          /* input buffer */
  int     optval;                 /* value of socket option */
  char    *localintfaddr = LOCALINTFIPADDR;  /* IP addr of local interface */
```

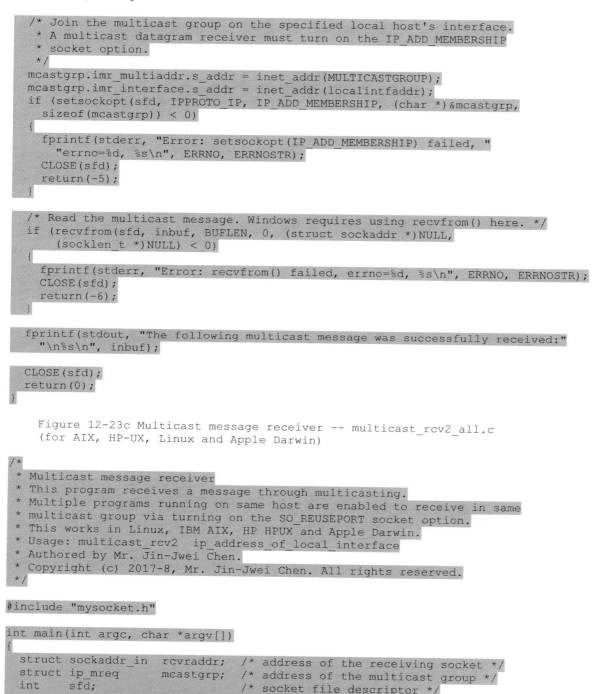

```c
#if WINDOWS
  int   ret = 0;
  WSADATA wsaData;
  char* GetErrorMsg(int ErrorCode);    /* print error string in Windows */
#endif
```

```c
  /* Get local interface IP address from user, if any */
  if (argc > 1)
    localintfaddr = argv[1];
```

```c
#if WINDOWS
  /* Start up Windows socket. Use at least Winsock version 2.2 */
  if ((ret = WSAStartup(MAKEWORD(2, 2), &wsaData)) != 0)
  {
    fprintf(stderr, "WSAStartup failed with error %d: %s\n",
      ret, GetErrorMsg(ret));
    WSACleanup();
    return (-1);
  }
#endif
```

```c
  /* Create a Datagram socket */
  sfd = socket(AF_INET, SOCK_DGRAM, 0);
  if (sfd < 0)
  {
    fprintf(stderr, "Error: socket() failed, errno=%d, %s\n", ERRNO, ERRNOSTR);
#if WINDOWS
    WSACleanup();
#endif
    return(-2);
  }
```

```c
  /* Turn on SO_REUSEPORT socket option to allow multiple instances of this
     program to be able to receive copies of the multicast datagrams. */
  optval = 1;
  if (setsockopt(sfd, SOL_SOCKET, SO_REUSEPORT, (char *)&optval, sizeof(optval))
    < 0)
  {
    fprintf(stderr, "Error: setsockopt(SO_REUSEPORT) failed, errno=%d, %s\n",
      ERRNO, ERRNOSTR);
    CLOSE(sfd);
    return(-3);
  }
  fprintf(stdout, "The SO_REUSEPORT socket option is turned on.\n");
```

```c
  /* Bind the Datagram socket to an address */
  memset((char *) &rcvraddr, 0, sizeof(rcvraddr));
  rcvraddr.sin_family = AF_INET;
  rcvraddr.sin_port = htons(MCASTPORT);
  rcvraddr.sin_addr.s_addr = INADDR_ANY;
  if (bind(sfd, (struct sockaddr*)&rcvraddr, sizeof(rcvraddr)))
  {
    fprintf(stderr, "Error: bind() failed, errno=%d, %s\n", ERRNO, ERRNOSTR);
    CLOSE(sfd);
    return(-4);
  }
```

```
/* Join the multicast group on the specified local host's interface.
 * A multicast datagram receiver must turn on the IP_ADD_MEMBERSHIP
 * socket option.
 */
mcastgrp.imr_multiaddr.s_addr = inet_addr(MULTICASTGROUP);
mcastgrp.imr_interface.s_addr = inet_addr(localintfaddr);
if (setsockopt(sfd, IPPROTO_IP, IP_ADD_MEMBERSHIP, (char *)&mcastgrp,
    sizeof(mcastgrp)) < 0)
{
    fprintf(stderr, "Error: setsockopt(IP_ADD_MEMBERSHIP) failed, "
      "errno=%d, %s\n", ERRNO, ERRNOSTR);
    CLOSE(sfd);
    return(-5);
}
```

```
/* Read the multicast message. Windows requires using recvfrom() here. */
if (recvfrom(sfd, inbuf, BUFLEN, 0, (struct sockaddr *)NULL,
    (socklen_t *)NULL) < 0)
{
    fprintf(stderr, "Error: recvfrom() failed, errno=%d, %s\n", ERRNO, ERRNOSTR);
    CLOSE(sfd);
    return(-6);
}
```

```
fprintf(stdout, "The following multicast message was successfully received:"
  "\n%s\n", inbuf);
```

```
CLOSE(sfd);
return(0);
}
```

Below are some sample outputs of the multicast example programs.
The two receivers are run on two separate hosts.
First, this is a sample output from Linux or Solaris.

```
$ ./multicast_rcv_all  192.168.1.26
The SO_REUSEADDR socket option is turned on.
The following multicast message was successfully received:
This is a multicast datagram message.

$ ./multicast_rcv_all  192.168.1.31
The SO_REUSEADDR socket option is turned on.
The following multicast message was successfully received:
This is a multicast datagram message.

$ ./multicast_snd_all  192.168.1.31
The multicast message was successfully sent.
```

Below is the output of the multicast programs from AIX or HP-UX.

```
$ ./multicast_rcv2_all 192.168.1.61
The SO_REUSEPORT socket option is turned on.
The following multicast message was successfully received:
This is a multicast datagram message.
```

```
$ ./multicast_rcv2_all 192.168.1.60
The SO_REUSEPORT socket option is turned on.
The following multicast message was successfully received:
This is a multicast datagram message.

$ ./multicast_snd_all 192.168.1.61
The multicast message was successfully sent.
```

12-17-3 Multiple Multicast Receivers on Same Host

Sometimes, there is a need to let multiple programs or multiple instances of the same program running on the same host to be able to all receive multicast messages sent to the same address and port number.
As we mentioned it before, a multicast message receiver must bind its socket to an IP address and port number in order to receive multicast messages. However, normally only one process is allowed to use a port number at a time on a given host. This prevents multiple processes from binding to the same address and port number to receive multicast messages all at the same time. This problem can be solved by enabling the SO_REUSEADDR option.

Below is how a multicast message receiver enables the SO_REUSEADDR socket option:

```
int reuse = 1;
if (setsockopt(sfd, SOL_SOCKET, SO_REUSEADDR, (char *)&reuse, sizeof(reuse)) < 0)
```

Enabling the SO_REUSEADDR option allows more than one process running on the same host at the same time to bind to the same IP address and port number so that they can all receive the multicast messages sent to that address and port number.

Without enabling this option, only one receiver process can bind to that port number and receive the multicast messages sent to that address. The second process (for instance, a second instance of the same receiver program) will fail to even start because its bind() call will fail and get this following error:

```
    Error: bind() failed, errno=98
  or
    bind() error: Address already in use
```

Hence, in addition to all the multicast-specific socket options introduced above, SO_REUSEADDR socket option is a generic option that you may often see in multicast applications.

But this feature is operating system dependent.
Turning on the **SO_REUSEADDR option** to enable multiple receivers of the same multicast messages on a single host works in Linux, Solaris and Windows. In AIX, HP-UX and Apple Darwin, the option you need to turn on is the **SO_REUSEPORT option** instead of the SO_REUSEADDR, as shown below:

```
int reuse = 1;
if (setsockopt(sfd, SOL_SOCKET, SO_REUSEPORT, (char *)&reuse, sizeof(reuse)) < 0)
```

In AIX, HP-UX and Apple Darwin, if you turn on the SO_REUSEADDR option, the second process trying to bind to the same address and port number will fail.

In fact, in Linux you can turn on either SO_REUSEADDR or SO_REUSEPORT option. Both of them work.

In Solaris, if you turn on the SO_REUSEPORT option it allows the second process to bind to the same address and port, but only one of them (the first one) gets the multicast message.
Also notice that Solaris 11 supports SO_REUSEPORT option but not Solaris 10.5.

Below is a summary of the option you need to turn on for multiple receivers on the same host to get same multicast messages:

```
Table 12-2 How to enable multiple multicast receivers on same host
-------------------------------------------------------------------
Linux: turn on the SO_REUSEADDR or SO_REUSEPORT socket option
Oracle/Sun Solaris: turn on the SO_REUSEADDR socket option
Windows: turn on the SO_REUSEADDR socket option
AIX:   turn on the SO_REUSEPORT socket option
HPUX: turn on the SO_REUSEPORT socket option
Apple Darwin: turn on the SO_REUSEPORT socket option
-------------------------------------------------------------------
```

12-17-4 Multicasting on Windows

On Windows, the SO_REUSEPORT socket option is not supported at the writing of this book. It is the SO_REUSEADDR socket option that you must turn on for multiple receivers running on the same host to all receive multicast messages.

The main difference between Windows and other platforms for the multicast receiver program is that Windows requires using the Datagram recvfrom() function to read the multicast messages whereas using read() function works just fine in Linux, AIX, Solaris, HP-UX and Apple Darwin. The receiver program will crash if the read() function is used to receive multicast messages in Windows.

Below is a sample output from running the multicast example programs on Windows:

```
C:\myprog\multicast\windows>multicast_rcv_all.exe
The SO_REUSEADDR socket option is turned on.
The following multicast message was successfully received:
This is a multicast datagram message.

C:\myprog\multicast\windows>multicast_rcv_all.exe
The SO_REUSEADDR socket option is turned on.
The following multicast message was successfully received:
This is a multicast datagram message.

C:\myprog\multicast\windows>multicast_snd_all.exe
The multicast message was successfully sent.
```

12-18 Multitasking Server

12-18-1 Single-threaded Server

The simplest connected-oriented server program one can write is a single threaded one, as shown in Figure 12-12a earlier.

Sure, you can have a single-threaded connection-oriented server program that accepts a connection request at a time, carries out the communication with that client, finishes it and then moves on to accept the next client's connection request and service its needs, and so on.
However, such a single-threaded server will perform poorly in most high traffic applications because it can serve only one client at a time -- it handles all clients serially. Some client may take a while to finish its task. This means other clients behind it will have to wait until it finishes. This kind of design is almost unacceptable in a real world because the response time of the server will be slow and its throughput will be low. And this is true regardless the server is connection-oriented or connectionless.

12-18-2 Concurrent or Parallel Processing

Therefore, a typical server program is always **multitasking**, being able to serve multiple clients at the same time. To achieve that, the server program (the main thread) must dedicate itself to handling only the connection requests from all clients and delegate the actual communication with each client to another thread or process. This way the server itself or its main thread won't get tied up, or tied down, in communicating with individual clients and it can quickly respond to connection requests from all clients.

The server main thread's job is solely to listen for and accept connection requests (the connect() call) from all clients. Once a connection request is accepted, the server creates a new socket and hands that new socket over to a child thread or process. It's this child thread's or process's job to take care of the new client and serve all of that client's needs.
The server itself or its main thread can go right back to listen for and accept the next client's connection request. Hence, the jobs of accepting all clients' connection requests and actually servicing each client are separated. The server's main process or thread handles the former and the latter is delegated to other worker processes or threads.

That is, within the server program, once the server gets a client's connection request message, it could create a child thread or spawn a child process, hand the client request and the client's address to it, and let the child thread or process service that request. Or it can even mix in by servicing some simple requests itself and using child threads or processes to handle the longer and more complex tasks if the request processing is known beforehand.

This is the architecture that a server program needs to have, a multitasking server! Modern server programs must be capable of handling thousands of clients at the same time. For instance, all web servers are multitasking servers. They are able to serve hundreds or thousands of simultaneous users.

Some might even need to distribute connect request loads to multiple servers.

There are two main approaches to multitasking: using thread or process.
In the old days, threading was not always available so processes were used.
Nowadays, threading support is available everywhere so it is more popular.
In general, using threads is more light weight than using processes.
The only thing is the maximum number of threads a process can have might
be limited on some platforms. Therefore, mixing the two by having multiple
processes where each process is multithreaded is certainly an option, too.

Figure 12-24 shows a connection-oriented multitasking server program using
child processes and Figure 12-25 lists a similar program using pthreads
(the POSIX threads).

12-18-3 Multiprocess Server

Figure 12-24 A connection-oriented multiprocess server program (tcpsrvp.c)

```
/*
 * A connection-oriented server program using Stream socket.
 * Multi-threaded server using processes.
 * Usage: tcpsrvp [port#]
 * Authored by Mr. Jin-Jwei Chen.
 * Copyright (c) 1993-2017, 2020 Mr. Jin-Jwei Chen. All rights reserved.
 */

#include <stdio.h>
#include <errno.h>
#include <sys/types.h>
#include <sys/socket.h>
#include <netinet/in.h>       /* protocols such as IPPROTO_TCP, ... */
#include <string.h>           /* memset() */
#include <stdlib.h>           /* atoi() */
#include <signal.h>           /* sigaction() */
#include <unistd.h>           /* close(), fork() */

#define   BUFLEN      1024    /* size of message buffer */
#define   DEFSRVPORT  2345    /* default server port number */
#define   BACKLOG     50      /* length of listener queue */

int main(int argc, char *argv[])
{
  int    ret, portnum_in=0, i;
  int    sfd;                      /* file descriptor of the listener socket */
  int    newsock;                  /* file descriptor of client data socket */
  struct sockaddr_in   srvaddr;    /* socket structure */
  int    srvaddrsz=sizeof(struct sockaddr_in);
  struct sockaddr_in   clntaddr;   /* socket structure */
  socklen_t   clntaddrsz=sizeof(struct sockaddr_in);
  in_port_t   portnum=DEFSRVPORT;  /* port number */
  int service_client(int sfd);
  struct sigaction  oldact, newact;

  fprintf(stdout, "Connection-oriented server program ...\n");
```

```
  /* Ignore the SIGCHLD signal so child processes won't become defunct. */
  sigfillset(&newact.sa_mask);
  newact.sa_flags = 0;
  newact.sa_handler = SIG_IGN;
  ret = sigaction(SIGCHLD, &newact, &oldact);
  if (ret != 0)
  {
    fprintf(stderr, "sigaction failed, errno=%d, %s\n", errno, strerror(errno));
    return(-1);
  }

  /* Get the port number from user, if any. */
  if (argc > 1)
    portnum_in = atoi(argv[1]);
  if (portnum_in <= 0)
  {
    fprintf(stderr, "Port number %d invalid, set to default value %u\n",
      portnum_in, DEFSRVPORT);
    portnum = DEFSRVPORT;
  }
  else
    portnum = portnum_in;

  /* Create the Stream server socket. */
  if ((sfd = socket(AF_INET, SOCK_STREAM, 0)) < 0)
  {
    fprintf(stderr, "Error: socket() failed, errno=%d, %s\n", errno,
      strerror(errno));
    return(-2);
  }

  /* Fill in the server socket address. */
  memset((void *)&srvaddr, 0, (size_t)srvaddrsz); /* clear the address buffer */
  srvaddr.sin_family = AF_INET;                    /* Internet socket */
  srvaddr.sin_addr.s_addr = htonl(INADDR_ANY);     /* server's IP address */
  srvaddr.sin_port = htons(portnum);               /* server's port number */

  /* Bind the server socket to its address. */
  if ((ret = bind(sfd, (struct sockaddr *)&srvaddr, srvaddrsz)) != 0)
  {
    fprintf(stderr, "Error: bind() failed, errno=%d, %s\n", errno,
      strerror(errno));
    return(-3);
  }

  /* Set maximum connection request queue length that we can fall behind. */
  if (listen(sfd, BACKLOG) == -1) {
    fprintf(stderr, "Error: listen() failed, errno=%d, %s\n", errno,
      strerror(errno));
    close(sfd);
    return(-4);
  }

  /* Wait for incoming connection requests from clients and service them. */
  while (1) {
```

```
      fprintf(stdout, "\nListening at port number %u ...\n", portnum);
      newsock = accept(sfd, (struct sockaddr *)&clntaddr, &clntaddrsz);
      if (newsock < 0)
      {
        fprintf(stderr, "Error: accept() failed, errno=%d, %s\n", errno,
          strerror(errno));
        close(sfd);
        return(-5);
      }

      fprintf(stdout, "Client Connected.\n");

      /* Service the client's requests. */
      ret = service_client(newsock);
      close(newsock);

  }   /* while - outer */
}

/*
 * This function is called to service the needs of a client by the server
 * after it has accepted a network connection request from a client.
 */
int service_client(int newsock)
{
  int     ret;
  pid_t   pid;
  char    inbuf[BUFLEN];                /* input message buffer */
  char    outbuf[BUFLEN];               /* output message buffer */
  size_t  msglen;                       /* length of reply message */

  /* Create a child process to service the client. */
  pid = fork();

  if (pid == -1)
  {
    fprintf(stderr, "fork() failed, errno=%d, %s\n", errno, strerror(errno));
    return(-7);
  }
  else if (pid == 0)
  {
    /* This is the child process. */
    /* Receive and service requests from the client. */
    while (1)
    {
      /* Receive a request from a client. */
      errno = 0;
      inbuf[0] = '\0';
      ret = recv(newsock, inbuf, BUFLEN, 0);
      if (ret > 0)
      {
        /* Process the request. We simply print the request message here. */
        inbuf[ret] = '\0';
        fprintf(stdout, "\nReceived the following request from client:\n%s\n",
          inbuf);
```

```
      /* Set the reply message */
      sprintf(outbuf, "%s", "This is a reply from the server program.");
      msglen = strlen(outbuf);

      /* Send a reply. */
      errno = 0;
      ret = send(newsock, outbuf, msglen, 0);
      if (ret == -1)
        fprintf(stderr, "Error: send() failed, errno=%d, %s\n", errno,
          strerror(errno));
      else
        fprintf(stdout, "%u of %lu bytes of the reply was sent.\n", ret, msglen);
    }
    else if (ret < 0)
    {
      fprintf(stderr, "Error: recv() failed, errno=%d, %s\n", errno,
        strerror(errno));
      break;
    }
    else
    {
      /* It may come here when the client goes away. */
      fprintf(stdout, "The client may have disconnected.\n");
      break;
    }
  }  /* while */

  close(newsock);
  exit(0);
}
else
{
  /* This is the parent process. */
  /* The parent has nothing to do here. */
  return(0);
}
}
```

Notice that in the multiprocess server program, we set up to **ignore the SIGCHLD signal** at the beginning of the program. The reason for doing this is that the server will be spawning child processes to handle the clients but we don't want the server to be tied up in waiting for the child processes to terminate. The server would instead focus on listening for clients' connection requests. Since if the parent does not wait for its child processes, any and all terminated child processes will become defunct and continue to exist in the system and use up process slots, we do so such that the child processes can go away as soon as they finish without having to be waited for. This is a clean way to do it.

In the multiprocess server program, each time a client connection request is accepted, the server calls the service_client() function. That function does a fork() to create a child process to serve all the needs of the client. This frees up the server's main thread right away.

Notice that the server closes the open file descriptor of new socket after the control returns from the service_client(). This is because

service_client() does a fork() and after the fork() the child process
has a copy of everything the parent process has except the stack.
This means the child process also has a copy of the open file descriptor
for the newly created socket, and it will use that to communicate with
the client to service it. Since the parent also has a copy of the open
file descriptor of the new socket and it won't need to use that socket
at all, it does

```
close(newsock);
```

right after the control returns from service_client().

Scalability of this type of server program will depend on how many concurrent
processes, how many sockets and how many open file descriptors
the operating system can support at the same time.

Performance will depend on the CPU processing power, memory capacity and
I/O bandwidth of the system hardware.

12-18-4 Multithreaded Server

Figure 12-25 A connection-oriented multithreaded server program (tcpsrvt.c)

```c
/*
 * A connection-oriented server program using Stream socket.
 * Multi-threaded server using pthread.
 * You must link this program with pthread library (-lpthread) on all platforms.
 * Usage: tcpsrvt [port#]
 * Authored by Mr. Jin-Jwei Chen.
 * Copyright (c) 1993-2017, 2019-2020 Mr. Jin-Jwei Chen. All rights reserved.
 */

#include <stdio.h>
#include <errno.h>
#include <sys/types.h>
#include <sys/socket.h>
#include <netinet/in.h>      /* protocols such as IPPROTO_TCP, ... */
#include <string.h>          /* memset() */
#include <stdlib.h>          /* atoi() */
#include <signal.h>          /* sigaction() */
#include <unistd.h>          /* close(), fork() */
#include <pthread.h>

#define  BUFLEN     1024     /* size of message buffer */
#define  DEFSRVPORT 2345     /* default server port number */
#define  BACKLOG    50       /* length of listener queue */
#define  STACKSIZE  16384    /* worker thread's stack size */

int main(int argc, char *argv[])
{
  int    ret, portnum_in=0, i;
  int    sfd;                     /* file descriptor of the listener socket */
  int    newsock;                 /* file descriptor of client data socket */
  struct sockaddr_in    srvaddr;  /* socket structure */
  int    srvaddrsz=sizeof(struct sockaddr_in);
```

```
struct sockaddr_in    clntaddr;   /* socket structure */
socklen_t     clntaddrsz=sizeof(struct sockaddr_in);
in_port_t     portnum=DEFSRVPORT; /* port number */
int service_client(int sfd);

fprintf(stdout, "Connection-oriented server program ...\n");

/* Get the port number from user, if any. */
if (argc > 1)
  portnum_in = atoi(argv[1]);
if (portnum_in <= 0)
{
  fprintf(stderr, "Port number %d invalid, set to default value %u\n",
    portnum_in, DEFSRVPORT);
  portnum = DEFSRVPORT;
}
else
  portnum = portnum_in;

/* Create the Stream server socket. */
if ((sfd = socket(AF_INET, SOCK_STREAM, 0)) < 0)
{
  fprintf(stderr, "Error: socket() failed, errno=%d, %s\n", errno,
    strerror(errno));
  return(-2);
}

/* Fill in the server socket address. */
memset((void *)&srvaddr, 0, (size_t)srvaddrsz); /* clear the address buffer */
srvaddr.sin_family = AF_INET;                    /* Internet socket */
srvaddr.sin_addr.s_addr = htonl(INADDR_ANY);    /* server's IP address */
srvaddr.sin_port = htons(portnum);              /* server's port number */

/* Bind the server socket to its address. */
if ((ret = bind(sfd, (struct sockaddr *)&srvaddr, srvaddrsz)) != 0)
{
  fprintf(stderr, "Error: bind() failed, errno=%d, %s\n", errno,
    strerror(errno));
  return(-3);
}

/* Set maximum connection request queue length that we can fall behind. */
if (listen(sfd, BACKLOG) == -1) {
  fprintf(stderr, "Error: listen() failed, errno=%d, %s\n", errno,
    strerror(errno));
  close(sfd);
  return(-4);
}

/* Wait for incoming connection requests from clients and service them. */
while (1) {

  fprintf(stdout, "\nListening at port number %u ...\n", portnum);
  newsock = accept(sfd, (struct sockaddr *)&clntaddr, &clntaddrsz);
  if (newsock < 0)
  {
```

```
      fprintf(stderr, "Error: accept() failed, errno=%d, %s\n", errno,
        strerror(errno));
      close(sfd);
      return(-5);
    }

    fprintf(stdout, "Client Connected.\n");

    /* Service the client's requests. */
    ret = service_client(newsock);
    /* Note: We cannot close the socket here when using thread. */
    if (ret != 0 )
    {
      fprintf(stderr, "Error: service_client() failed, ret=%d\n", ret);
      close(newsock);
    }

  } /* while - outer */
}

/*
 * This function is called to service the needs of a client by the server
 * after it has accepted a network connection request from a client.
 * This function dynamically allocates the memory for argument passing in
 * the heap. The child thread must free that memory after use.
 */
int service_client(int newsock)
{
  int    ret;

  pthread_t      thrd;
  unsigned int  *args;
  pthread_attr_t  attr;  /* thread attributes */
  int worker_thread(void *);

  /* Create a child thread to service the client. */

  /* Dynamically allocate buffer for argument passing. */
  args = (unsigned int *)malloc(sizeof(unsigned int));
  if (args == NULL)
  {
    fprintf(stderr, "Error: malloc() failed\n");
    close(newsock);
    return(-1);
  }

  /* Set the argument to pass on. */
  args[0] = (unsigned int)newsock;

  /* Initialize the pthread attributes. */
  ret = pthread_attr_init(&attr);
  if (ret != 0)
  {
    fprintf(stderr, "Error: failed to init thread attribute, ret=%d\n", ret);
    close(newsock);
    free(args);
```

```
      return(-2);
}

/* Set up to create detached threads. */
ret = pthread_attr_setdetachstate(&attr, PTHREAD_CREATE_DETACHED);
if (ret != 0)
{
    fprintf(stderr, "Error: failed to set detach state, ret=%d\n", ret);
    close(newsock);
    free(args);
    ret = pthread_attr_destroy(&attr);
    return(-3);
}

/* Set thread's stack size. Error 22 is returned if value is wrong. */
ret = pthread_attr_setstacksize(&attr, STACKSIZE);
if (ret != 0)
{
    fprintf(stderr, "Error: failed to set stack size, ret=%d\n", ret);
    close(newsock);
    free(args);
    ret = pthread_attr_destroy(&attr);
    return(-4);
}

/* Create a new thread to run the worker_thread() function. */
ret = pthread_create(&thrd, (pthread_attr_t *)&attr,
        (void *(*)(void *))worker_thread, (void *)args);
if (ret != 0)
{
    fprintf(stderr, "Error: failed to create the worker thread\n");
    close(newsock);
    free(args);
    ret = pthread_attr_destroy(&attr);
    return(-5);
}
fprintf(stdout, "Thread with id=%ul is created to serve the client.\n", thrd);

/* Destroy the pthread attributes. */
ret = pthread_attr_destroy(&attr);
if (ret != 0)
{
    fprintf(stderr, "Error: failed to destroy thread attribute, ret=%d\n", ret);
}

return(0);
}

/*
 * The worker thread.
 * This worker thread gets an open file descriptor of a socket that is already
 * connected to a client and uses it to communicate with and service that
 * client.
 * This worker thread terminates when the client closes the connection.
 */
int worker_thread(void *args)
```

```
{
  unsigned int  *argp;
  int  newsock;
  int  ret;
  char    inbuf[BUFLEN];                  /* input message buffer */
  char    outbuf[BUFLEN];                 /* output message buffer */
  size_t msglen;                          /* length of reply message */

  /* Extract the argument. */
  argp = (unsigned int *)args;
  if (argp != NULL)
  {
    newsock = (int)argp[0];
    free(argp);       /* free the memory used to pass arguments */
  }
  else
    pthread_exit((void *)(-1));

  /* Receive and service requests from the client. */
  while (1)
  {
    /* Receive a request from a client. */
    errno = 0;
    inbuf[0] = '\0';
    ret = recv(newsock, inbuf, BUFLEN, 0);
    if (ret > 0)
    {
      /* Process the request. We simply print the request message here. */
      inbuf[ret] = '\0';
      fprintf(stdout, "\nReceived the following request from client:\n%s\n",
        inbuf);

      /* Set the reply message. */
      sprintf(outbuf, "%s%ul%s", "This is a reply from thread ", pthread_self(),
        " of the server program.");
      msglen = strlen(outbuf);

      /* Send a reply. */
      errno = 0;
      ret = send(newsock, outbuf, msglen, 0);
      if (ret == -1)
        fprintf(stderr, "Error: send() failed, errno=%d, %s\n", errno,
          strerror(errno));
      else
        fprintf(stdout, "%u of %lu bytes of the reply was sent.\n", ret, msglen);
    }
    else if (ret < 0)
    {
      fprintf(stderr, "Error: recv() failed, errno=%d, %s\n", errno,
        strerror(errno));
      break;
    }
    else
    {
      /* It comes here when the client goes away. */
```

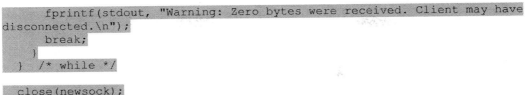

```
      fprintf(stdout, "Warning: Zero bytes were received. Client may have
disconnected.\n");
      break;
   }
}  /* while */

close(newsock);
pthread_exit((void *)0);
}
```

In the multithreaded server program, each time a client connection request
is accepted, the server calls the service_client() function.
That function creates a child thread and passes the newly created client
socket to it. The child thread then takes cares of all the needs of the
client. After creating the child thread, the main thread returns.
That frees up the server's main thread right away so that it can continue
to listen for and accept the next client's connect request.

In the multithreaded server program, each time the service_client() function
is called, it dynamically allocates the memory for passing arguments to
each child thread. In case there is an error in creating the child thread,
that memory is freed before the function returns. If a child thread is
successfully created, that memory is freed by the child thread after the
input arguments are extracted.

Unlike the multiprocess version in which both the parent and the child
processes have a copy of the open file descriptor for the new socket,
there is only one copy of it in the thread model. Therefore, after returning
from the service_client() function, the main thread cannot close the open
file descriptor of the new socket because the child thread needs to use
it to service the client. If the main thread closed the new socket, the
child thread would not have the socket to communicate with the client.
The child thread closes that socket after servicing the client.

Note that to build the tcpsrvt program correctly, you MUST link it with
the pthreads library by specifying "-lpthread" on the compiler/linker command
line. If you don't, you will get undefined symbols for the pthread_xxx()
functions on most platforms. But on HP-UX, it will instead link with the
version of these functions in libc. And that will link the program without
any error. But later when you try to run it, calling the pthread_xxx()
functions will get errno=251 (function not supported). Therefore, make sure
you always link this program with pthreads library (-lpthread).
You can test tcpsrvt using tcpclnt1 or any TCP client program.

Scalability of this type of server program will depend on how many threads
per process, how many concurrent threads per system, how many sockets,
and how many open file descriptors the operating system can support at
the same time.

Performance will depend on the CPU processing power, memory capacity and
I/O bandwidth of the system hardware. In general, the thread model has
less overhead than the process model because all threads within a process
share the code, data, and heap segments except the stack.

This multi-threaded server is a very typical design of a server program.
It dedicates one thread to do the listening for all incoming connection

requests and then passes them over to other threads for processing. This model should work fine in small, medium and high loads, except in most extreme cases. For instance, if you are building a server program that is supposed to handle 30,000 or 40,000 connections per second, then the listening thread itself could become a bottleneck.

In that case, you will have to use other alternatives.
One is to use multiple listening threads where each listening thread uses a distinct socket but all of them bind to the same socket address. This requires support from the operating system. For instance, in Linux 3.9 and after, SO_REUSEPORT socket option is supported. That option allows multiple AF_INET (IPv4) or AF_INET6 (IPv6) sockets to be bound to an identical socket address, which is exactly what is needed here for distributing the load of accept() over multiple threads.
The SO_REUSEPORT socket option will be discussed in next chapter.

The other alternative is to split the accept() load over multiple servers where each server uses a different port number (and perhaps a different IP address).

To further optimize the performance, one can also consider **thread pooling** where a worker thread does not get terminated after it finishes servicing a client. It hangs around to continue to serve next client. These worker threads in the pool could be pre-created or created on-demand until it reaches the pool size. You would need a data structure to organize these worker threads so that you know which are busy and which are available at a given time.

12-18-5 Potential Socket Resource Issue

As we have mentioned before, a socket could be put in the TIME_WAIT state after the application closes it. It will be put in that state if the application does the close before the other end of the connection. And once being in that state, the socket's resources won't be freed up until after at least a few minutes -- this actual time is O.S. dependent.

Because of this, if any application (including the one that has just closed it) tries to use the same address and port number that was used by this socket, it will get this error:

    bind() failed, error "Address already in use"

Many developers probably have seen this error when trying to start an application after just shutting it down. You get this error simply because the address and port number your program tries to bind to is being used by some other socket. It could be another program that is actively running is using that same address and port number, or another closed socket that is in the TIME_WAIT state used that same address and port number and the operating system kernel is not ready to release it and free it up yet.

There are two ways to avoid getting the "Address already in use" error.

First, enable the SO_REUSRADDR socket option in your application before it calls bind(). The SO_REUSRADDR socket option allows a program to use a port that is stuck in the TIME_WAIT state, i.e. a port used by a socket that is closed but its resources have not been released yet.

Note that although this allows the local address to be re-used before the port number is really freed up, it won't allow the program to use that port to establish a connection to the last place it connected to. This is because no two connections are allowed to have the same value of this combination:

{protocol, source_ip_addr, source port, destination_addr, destination_port}

The SO_REUSRADDR option permits reuse of only the local address, that is, the {protocol, source_ip_addr, source port} portion of it.

Some operating systems (e.g. Linux 3.9 and later) have another socket option named SO_REUSEPORT, which does something very similar to what SO_REUSRADDR does. It permits multiple sockets to be bound to the same socket address and port number at the same time. We will talk a little bit more about this option in the next chapter.

Although this strategy of trying to avoid the "Address already in use" error is very easy to do programmatically, it is somewhat operating system and protocol dependent. It may not work in all operating systems or in all cases. However, all operating systems we tested support either SO_REUSRADDR or SO_REUSEPORT. Some (e.g. Linux) even supports both.

Second, since it is always the endpoint which closes a connection before the other end gets to go into and through the TIME_WAIT state, to avoid getting into that state and consequently getting the "Address already in use" error when trying to restart on the same port number right after, you can design your application protocol such that it is always the other end closes the connection first. In other words, if you are writing a server program and want to protect the server, then you design your application such that the client always does the close first.

On some very busy servers, sometimes you may see hundreds or even thousands of sockets stuck in the TIME_WAIT state. If you see this, then it's time to examine the application protocol and see if it can be changed so that the clients always do the close of their sockets first.

12-19 Port Numbers -- Reserve it or not

12-19-1 Introduction to Port Numbers

As stated before, in order to be able to exchange messages with a server, a peer, or another program via sockets, a program needs to know at least the IP address and port number that program runs on.

In this section we give a brief introduction to the socket port number and discuss the common issues software engineers face in choosing port numbers for their applications.

The issue discussed here in this section applies to both connectionless and connection-oriented communication.

In socket programming, each socket has an address that uniquely identifies it. A server program typically has a well-known socket address so that all the clients from all over the world know how to connect to it. As we have said it multiple times, a socket address consists of at least two major components: an IP address which uniquely identifies a computer or device in the world, and a port number which uniquely identifies a process within that computer or device. This ensures the messages a client sends to the server won't go to somewhere else.

In other words, a port number is a number which is part of a socket address and helps identify a process within a computer or device that uses that socket. It's just like the number of your home address that identifies your home on the street you live in.

When the TCP/IP protocols were designed decades ago, a port number was given the C data type of 'unsigned short', which is only 16 bits long. This means a socket port number can be from 0 to 65535. It also means that there can be at most 65536 port numbers in use at any given time on each computer. Some may ask why not use an int? Well, when TCP/IP was designed, perhaps computer scientists thought 64K different ports on a system was plenty. And it proves to be so at least so far.

In Linux/Unix systems, there is a special data type defined for the port numbers. It is in_port_t. However, not every operating system has done so. For instance, Windows does not.

12-19-2 Privileged Port Numbers

One thing to know about the socket port numbers is that the first 1023 port numbers (from 1 to 1023) are reserved for processes that require the super user privilege to run. In order to be able to bind a server socket to a port number in-between 1 and 1023, you must run the program as the root (i.e. super) user. Client programs connecting to it do not need to have root user privilege.

If a running program does not have the super-user privilege, then when it tries to bind a socket to a port number that is in-between 1 and 1023, the bind() call will fail with the EACCESS (Permission denied) error, which is error 13 in Linux.

Note that **0 and 1024 are NOT privileged port numbers** as some web pages on the Internet have said. 1023 is the highest privileged port number. And port 0 is NOT a privileged port number, either. Port 0 is the wild card port number, INADDR_ANY, that any server can bind to.

12-19-3 Look Up Server's Port Number Dynamically -- Service Registration Database

When an operating system starts, there are typically many daemon programs that run in the background to provide various services to applications and end users. Examples include the ftp daemon (ftpd) that provides the

file transfer service, the NFS daemon (nfsd) that provides network file
system service, the Domain Name Service daemon (dnsd) that provides host
name to IP address translation service, Electronic Mail Service (smtpd),
and the Web Service (httpd), etc. The list goes on.

Each of these operating system daemons runs on a different port number
reserved by the operating system. And the reserved port numbers are
"published" in a system registration/configuration file.
This file is /etc/services in Unix and Linux operating systems.
It is C:\Windows\System32\drivers\etc\services in Windows.
This configuration file lists all the port numbers that have been reserved
by various operating system services or user applications.

For instance, a service called "dbm" is usually reserved in a Linux system.

```
$ grep -w dbm /etc/services
dbm              2345/tcp                    # dbm
dbm              2345/udp                    # dbm
```

This means the name of the service (or application) reserving the port is
"dbm". It uses port 2345. Both TCP and UDP protocols are supported.
A service's name is often the name of the application providing the service.

Note that **the port number reservation/registration is an honor system**.
There is no mechanism in place to prevent anyone from stealing a reserved
port number or using a particular port number.

This service registration database file is designed for both vendors and
applications. The way it is meant to be used is this.

1. For computer software vendors, any and all port numbers that a software
   product reserves and uses must be registered (i.e. entered) in this file.
   This is typically done at software installation time. Adding entries to
   this file requires root (super) user privilege.

2. For applications, instead of hardwiring a server's port number in the
   code, all applications should consult this database and look up a server's
   port number dynamically at run time. The C API to use for this purpose
   is the **getservbyname**() function.

   An application looks up a server's port number by calling the
   getservbyname() function and providing the name of the service and the
   name of the protocol the server uses (TCP or UDP).

Figure 12-26 lists an example client program that uses the getservbyname()
function to look up the server's port number and uses that to connect to
the server. It's a slight modification of the tcpclnt_all.c program.
It should work with the tcpsrv_all.c server listed earlier in this chapter.
To test, start the server with the service's port number as the first
argument. Then run the client with the service's name as the first argument.

   Figure 12-26 A client looking up server's reserved port number at run time
   (tcpclnt_getsvc_all.c)

```
/*
 * A connection-oriented client program using Stream socket.
```

```
 * Connecting to a server program on any host using a hostname or IP address.
 * Support for IPv4 and IPv6 and multiple platforms including
 * Linux, Windows, Solaris, AIX, HPUX and Apple Darwin.
 * Usage: tcpclnt_getsvc_all [srvport# [server-hostname | server-ipaddress]]
 * Authored by Mr. Jin-Jwei Chen.
 * Copyright (c) 1993-2018, 2020 Mr. Jin-Jwei Chen. All rights reserved.
 */

#include "mysocket.h"

int main(int argc, char *argv[])
{
  int     ret;
  int     sfd;                        /* socket file descriptor */
  char    portnumstr[12];             /* port number in string format */
  char    *svcname = SVCNAME;         /* pointer to service name */
  struct servent *srvService;         /* server's service */

  char    inbuf[BUFLEN];              /* input message buffer */
  char    outbuf[BUFLEN];             /* output message buffer */
  size_t  msglen;                     /* length of reply message */
  size_t  msgnum=0;                   /* count of request message */
  size_t  len;
  char    server_name[NAMELEN+1] = SERVER_NAME;
  struct addrinfo hints, *res=NULL;   /* address info */

#if WINDOWS
  WSADATA wsaData;                          /* Winsock data */
  char* GetErrorMsg(int ErrorCode);    /* print error string in Windows */
#endif

  fprintf(stdout, "Connection-oriented client program ...\n");

  /* Get the server's service name from command line. */
  if (argc > 1)
    svcname = argv[1];

  /* Get the server's host name or IP address from command line. */
  if (argc > 2)
  {
    len = strlen(argv[2]);
    if (len > NAMELEN)
      len = NAMELEN;
    strncpy(server_name, argv[2], len);
    server_name[len] = '\0';
  }

#if WINDOWS
  /* Initiate use of the Winsock DLL. Ask for Winsock version 2.2 at least. */
  if ((ret = WSAStartup(MAKEWORD(2, 2), &wsaData)) != 0)
  {
    fprintf(stderr, "Error: WSAStartup() failed with error %d: %s\n",
      ret, GetErrorMsg(ret));
    return (-1);
  }
#endif
```

```
    /* Look up server's port number from /etc/services file. */
    srvService = getservbyname(svcname, PROTOCOLNAME);
    if (srvService == NULL)
    {
#if WINDOWS
        ret = WSAGetLastError();
        fprintf(stderr, "Error: getservbyname() failed with error %d: %s\n",
          ret, GetErrorMsg(ret));
#else
        fprintf(stderr, "Error: getservbyname() failed.\n");
#endif
        return(-2);
    }

    if (argc <= 1)
        strcpy(portnumstr, DEFSRVPORTSTR);
    else
        sprintf(portnumstr, "%d", ntohs(srvService->s_port));

    /* Translate the server's host name or IP address into socket address.
     * Fill in the hints information.
     */
    memset(&hints, 0x00, sizeof(hints));
        /* This works on AIX but not on Solaris, nor on Windows. */
        /* hints.ai_flags     = AI_NUMERICSERV; */
    hints.ai_family   = AF_UNSPEC;
    hints.ai_socktype = SOCK_STREAM;
    hints.ai_protocol = IPPROTO_TCP;

    /* Get the address information of the server using getaddrinfo().
     * This function returns errors directly or 0 for success. On success,
     * argument res contains a linked list of addrinfo structures.
     */
    ret = getaddrinfo(server_name, portnumstr, &hints, &res);
    if (ret != 0)
    {
        fprintf(stderr, "Error: getaddrinfo() failed, error %d, %s\n", ret,
          gai_strerror(ret));
#if !WINDOWS
        if (ret == EAI_SYSTEM)
            fprintf(stderr,"System error: errno=%d, %s\n", errno, strerror(errno));
#else
        WSACleanup();
#endif
        return(-3);
    }

    /* Create a socket. */
    sfd = socket(res->ai_family, res->ai_socktype, res->ai_protocol);
    if (sfd < 0)
    {
        fprintf(stderr,"Error: socket() failed, errno=%d, %s\n", ERRNO, ERRNOSTR);
#if WINDOWS
        WSACleanup();
#endif
```

```
    return (-4);
}

/* Connect to the server. */
ret = connect(sfd, res->ai_addr, res->ai_addrlen);
if (ret == -1)
{
  fprintf(stderr, "Error: connect() failed, errno=%d, %s\n", ERRNO, ERRNOSTR);
  CLOSE(sfd);
  return(-5);
}

fprintf(stdout, "Send request messages to server(%s) at port %s\n",
  server_name, portnumstr);

/* Send request messages to the server and process the reply messages. */
while (msgnum < MAXMSGS)
{
  /* Send a request message to the server. */
  sprintf(outbuf, "%s%4lu%s", "This is request message ", ++msgnum,
    " from the client program.");
  msglen = strlen(outbuf);
  errno = 0;

  ret = send(sfd, outbuf, msglen, 0);
  if (ret >= 0)
  {
    /* Print a warning if not entire message was sent. */
    if (ret == msglen)
      fprintf(stdout, "\n%lu bytes of message were successfully sent.\n",
        msglen);
    else if (ret < msglen)
      fprintf(stderr, "Warning: only %u of %lu bytes were sent.\n",
        ret, msglen);

    if (ret > 0)
    {
      /* Receive a reply from the server. */
      errno = 0;
      inbuf[0] = '\0';
      ret = recv(sfd, inbuf, BUFLEN, 0);

      if (ret > 0)
      {
        /* Process the reply. */
        inbuf[ret] = '\0';
        fprintf(stdout, "Received the following reply from server:\n%s\n",
          inbuf);
      }
      else if (ret == 0)
        fprintf(stdout, "Warning: Zero bytes were received.\n");
      else
        fprintf(stderr, "Error: recv() failed, errno=%d, %s\n", ERRNO,
          ERRNOSTR);
    }
}
```

```
    else
        fprintf(stderr, "Error: send() failed, errno=%d, %s\n", ERRNO, ERRNOSTR);

    /* Sleep a second. For demo only. Remove this in real code. */
#if WINDOWS
        Sleep(1000); /* Unit is ms. For demo only. Remove this in real code. */
#else
        sleep(1);   /* For demo only. Remove this in real code. */
#endif
    }   /* while */

    /* Free the memory allocated by getaddrinfo() */
    freeaddrinfo(res);
    CLOSE(sfd);
    return(0);
}
```

Note that to test this example program, you need to either become the super
or root or administrator user and reserve your own service and port number
in the services file whose pathname is mentioned above (that is, edit the
file and insert a new line), or find a service from the services file which
is not being currently used. For example, we use the "dbm" service, which
is typically reserved in the services file in most Linux/Unix systems, in
our test below:

```
$ ./tcpsrv_all 2345
Connection-oriented server program ...

Listening at port number 2345 ...
Client Connected.

Received the following request from client:
This is request message    1 from the client program.
43 of 43 bytes of the reply was sent.

Received the following request from client:
This is request message    2 from the client program.
43 of 43 bytes of the reply was sent.
Warning: Zero bytes were received.

$ ./tcpclnt_getsvc_all dbm
Connection-oriented client program ...
Send request messages to server(localhost) at port 2345

53 bytes of message were successfully sent.
Received the following reply from server:
This is reply #  1 from the server program.

53 bytes of message were successfully sent.
Received the following reply from server:
This is reply #  2 from the server program.
```

On Windows, I added the following two lines to the file
C:\Windows\System32\drivers\etc\services:

```
jjcsvc              9898/tcp
```

```
jjcsvc              9898/udp
```

And then I start the tcpsrv_all.exe with 9898 being port number and
run the "tcpclnt_getsvc_all.exe jjcsvc":

```
C:\myprog\fin3>tcpsrv_all.exe 9898
Connection-oriented server program ...

Listening at port number 9898 ...
Client Connected.

Received the following request from client:
This is request message    1 from the client program.
43 of 43 bytes of the reply was sent.

Received the following request from client:
This is request message    2 from the client program.
43 of 43 bytes of the reply was sent.
Warning: Zero bytes were received.

Listening at port number 9898 ...

C:\myprog\fin3>tcpclnt_getsvc_all.exe jjcsvc
Connection-oriented client program ...
Send request messages to server(localhost) at port 9898

53 bytes of message were successfully sent.
Received the following reply from server:
This is reply #  1 from the server program.

53 bytes of message were successfully sent.
Received the following reply from server:
This is reply #  2 from the server program.
```

12-19-4 Use Fixed Port or Dynamic Port?

For those who have had experience designing distributed applications,
two questions that often come to mind are:

1. Do I use a fixed or dynamic port number?
2. Do I reserve the port number in the operating system or not?

In practice, a server or daemon program, or any program, can run on any
port so long as that port is not being used. It's just that if it always
runs on the same port, a fixed port, it's a lot of easier to use because
of the following reasons:

- The program does not need to hunt for a free port to use at each startup.

- Hopefully everyone knows that port is already reserved and won't try
  to use it for something else so that the server daemon can always have
  its port available and be able to start.

- It's easier for all clients to get to the server because it always uses
  that same port.

In general, it makes life a lot easier if you choose to use a fixed port number and reserve it in the operating system. It simplifies the software a lot and saves a lot of work and troubles. The only downside is you need to do a number of things:

1. You need to do a bit of research and pick a port number that has not been reserved or used by any existing application.

2. You need to reserve this port number by "registering" it in the operating system's network services registration database.
   In Unix and Linux systems, this means becoming the super-user and adding your entry into the /etc/services file during the installation of your software. In Windows, do the same to the services file.

3. In case some other application "steals" your port number, you need to find out what application did it and try to resolve it and get it back from that application.

But as long as you pick a port number that has not been reserved and reserve it in the operation system's network services database, then you have got the "right" to use that number and to kick another application out if it happens to use the same port number you have reserved.

Again, be aware that the port number reservation is an honor system. If some application or service reserves a port number but it is not running and not using that particular port number, another program could grab and use it. The operating system has no mechanism to enforce the reservations.

All applications that run on fixed port numbers should reserve their port numbers in the operating system's services database so that they're publicly known and so that other applications won't try to use those numbers. And client applications should not hardwire the service/server's port number. It should use the getservbyname() function to look up the port number dynamically at run time.

Alternatively, if you decide to use dynamic ports, then since the same server or daemon could be running on a different port each time it starts, there needs to be some dynamic port registrations and lookups at run time. The software application will need to take care of these by itself.

Basically, there needs to have a server/daemon which maintains port number registrations and lookups. This particular server or daemon probably needs to use a fixed port so that all other servers/daemons and clients always know where to go for registrations and lookups. When a server/daemon starts, it grabs whatever port number available at that time and uses it. And it will need to register that port number and a unique name with the registrar server/daemon. Whoever needs to communicate with it will then need to query the registrar by providing the unique name to get its port number.

The dynamic port approach offers some flexibility. But it adds a lot of work, overhead and complexity. And it will run slower. I have seen distributed software that uses this approach and often it just cannot even find itself. That is, a server daemon cannot locate where the other collaborating server daemons are (what port numbers they are currently running on)! So, **whenever possible, the reserved (i.e. fixed) port approach** should be taken. It will simplify your software design a lot!

Port Numbers in a Complex Distributed System

In a complex distributed system software, often there are multiple servers or daemon programs running in the software and they need to communicate with one another. In order to communicate with one another through sockets, these programs need to know what port numbers other server/daemon programs run on. How to design and manage the inter-daemon communications so that they can always find one another could be a challenge. And port number design is the key part of it. Doing it right in the beginning is very crucial and that will simplify the entire software very significantly.

If fixed-port approach is chosen and the ports are reserved in the system, then software becomes much simpler and life gets much easier. There is no need to write extra code to manage the port number registrations and lookups yourself. Each program just simply calls the getservbyname() API to look up the port number of the server daemon it wants to talk to. That's it!

Using fixed-port approach, each server or daemon program runs on its own reserved port. There is no need to hunt a port number at startup. There is no registration work to be done by the server programs. And for the clients, looking up a server's port will be as easy as calling the getservbyname() API, which is very quick and robust, instead of going through very complex lookup procedure through another server/daemon which can often break down and is slower and time-consuming.

When a port number reserved by some application is stolen and being used by some other application, the server/daemon program which has reserved the port won't be able to start on that port. In that case, system administrator will have to hunt down that application, stop it and get it to use a different port.

12-19-5 Quick Recap

In summary, after reading this section, readers should be able to answer at least the following questions:

1. Where are port numbers reserved on a computer system?
2. What port numbers have been reserved?
3. What are the port numbers of typical system services and applications?
4. What services or applications have reserved their port numbers?
5. What do I need to do if I like to reserve fixed port numbers for my application?
6. How to dynamically look up port numbers and avoid hardwiring them?

Readers should also become capable of designing distributed systems that are much simpler, more robust, and using port numbers the correct way in applications.

12-20 Summary

There exist many interprocess communication options.
Using sockets for interprocess communication is one of the most common,

popular, powerful and important IPC mechanisms. It allows two processes residing anywhere in the world, literally they can be physically a whole world apart, to communicate with each other as long as they are connected via a computer network, for example, the Internet.

The Internet which everyone is familiar with is primarily built with socket communications. When you open a browser, type in an URL to access a certain web page from a web site, the web page you are accessing could be residing in a web server physically tens of thousands miles away. The underlying software making this remote communication possible uses sockets -- connection-oriented socket communication using the TCP protocol at the transport layer.

There are essentially two types of network socket communication: connection-oriented communication based on TCP protocol and connectionless communication based on UDP protocol. The former requires a connection being established before message exchanges can begin. It has resources on computers along the network communication path between the two parties reserved for the entire duration of the connection and thus provides a "reliable" communication. Being reliable here means as long as all of the computers, network routers and links on the communication path remain up, the messages one sends are guaranteed to reach their destination due to extra persistent attempts of delivery and error checking. In effect, it's like a message pipe built in-between the two parties. Messages sent are guaranteed to be delivered and delivered in order without error. It's message streaming!

In contrast, connectionless communication requires no connection establishment. Once a socket is created, a message can be sent to any party at any time. It's a bit simpler, more flexible, having no network resources reserved, and the same socket can be used to send to multiple destinations. Each message sent is a separate transaction that can succeed or fail. If certain resource is not available at the time, the message could get discarded and never being delivered.

One advantage of using network socket for inter-process communication is that the exactly same code works regardless of how far or how close the the two processes are. That is, it works whether the two processes reside on the same computer or different computers connected by a network. Besides, the two communicating processes or programs do not have to have any relationship. The only thing needed is the server's IP address and port number. Besides, one can send anything, text or binary, free format. For instance, with Internet, all a user needs to know in web browsing is the URL of the web server it needs to connect to.

Socket communications is at the heart of almost every distributed and networking software. This chapter has shown readers how to write distributed and networking software using sockets.

In the subsequent three chapters, we will further discuss other more advanced topics in socket communications.

Questions

1. What is a network socket? Is it a software or hardware component? How many sockets are needed for a network communication?

2. In the ISO seven-layer architecture, what layer does socket operate in? What is the layer immediately below the socket layer? And what layer is the second layer below?

3. What protocol does a web browser use to communicate with a web server? What layer does that operate in?

4. How many types of network sockets are there? Give a short description of each of them.

5. What data structures are used to represent the address of a socket?

6. How does a program create a socket?

7. What are the two basic types of network communications between software programs over the Internet in terms of connection? What are the differences between them in terms of resources allocation and reliability?

8. What functions can be used to send messages through an unconnected socket? And what functions can be used to send messages through a connected socket?

9. What functions can be used to receive messages from an unconnected socket? And what functions can be used to receive messages from a connected socket?

10. What is INADDR_ANY? What is its IPv6 counterpart?

11. What are htonl() and ntohl()? Why does a network program need to use them?

12. What information is contained in a socket address?

13. What is getaddrinfo() for? What is the function that does the opposite?

14. What kind of server socket supports both IPv4 and IPv6 clients?

15. What type of sockets support local communication on same host only? What does it use to identify a socket? And what limitation does that have?

16. To support asynchronous I/O or connect, what function does a program use?

17. How does a program convert a synchronous socket into an asynchronous (i.e. non-blocking) one?

18. What is multicast? What are the steps to send multicast messages? What are the steps to receive multicast messages?

19. What must a program do to enable multiple multicast receivers on same host?

20. Compare multi-process servers with multithreaded servers.

21. Why does a program get "Address already in use" error?

What are the ways to avoid getting this error?

22. What are privileged port numbers? What are these numbers?

23. Where are reserved port numbers listed? How does a program dynamically look up a server's reserved port number?

24. What are the advantages for a server program to use a reserved, fixed port number?

Programming Assignments

1. Modify the example program udpclnt_conn_all.c so that it invokes the connect() function twice and sends messages to two different servers. To test, run two instances of the udpsrv_all program at different ports.

2. Run the single-threaded connection-oriented server program (tcpsrv) with two or more clients at the same time and verify that it is truly single threaded.

3. Modify the tcpsrvp.c to pre-create a pool of processes. Each time a client comes along, invoke one of them that is free to service that client and keep the worker process around after the service.

4. Modify the tcpsrvt.c to pre-create a pool of threads. Each time a client comes along, invoke one of them that is free to service that client and keep the worker thread around after the service.

5. Convert programs tcpclnt1.c and tcpsrv1.c to use read() and write() functions by replacing send() with write() and recv() with read().

6. Compile and run the multicast example programs. Test two scenarios: one with two receivers running on different hosts and the other with two receivers running on the same host.

7. Write a multithreaded server program using a pool of worker threads. Make the pool size configurable from an input command line argument. The worker threads are pre-created and stick around after servicing each client.

8. Write a multithread server program which employs multiple listener threads to spread out the listening workload. Test it by running hundreds or thousands of clients at the same time.

9. Write a pair of programs to demonstrate the socket SO_RCVLOWAT option. Set the SO_RCVLOWAT option on the receiver and perform two send operations on the sender with a pause in between. The first send operation should send a message smaller than the SO_RCVLOWAT watermark.

10. Write a program that displays the TCP (SOCK_STREAM) socket default send and receive buffer sizes on your system. The program should then increase both parameters by 4096 and query and display the new values.

11. Write a program that displays the UDP (SOCK_DGRAM) socket default send and receive buffer sizes on your system. The program should then increase

both parameters by 4096 and query and display the new values.

12. Write your own pair of file transfer programs that send a file from one system to another using SOCK_STREAM sockets. Test them using a data file of different sizes, for instance, 1 MB, 50 MB and 250 MB. Measure elapsed times with different send and receive buffer sizes. Find out the socket send and receive buffer sizes that deliver the best performance, with the shortest elapsed time.

13. Repeat the file transfer project in the problem above using SOCK_DGRAM sockets.

References

- Computer Networks, Andrew S. Tanenbaum, Prentice Hall, Inc.

- The Open Group Base Specifications Issue 7, POSIX.1-2018 and IEEE Std 1003.1-2017, 2017 Edition

- http://pubs.opengroup.org/onlinepubs/9699919799/

- https://en.wikipedia.org/wiki/IEEE_802

- https://en.wikipedia.org/wiki/List_of_network_protocols_(OSI_model)

13 Socket Performance Tuning and Socket Options

This chapter covers a more advanced network socket programming subject, which involves tuning performance of network socket programs and using socket options. The topics range from tuning socket buffer sizes to TCP Keepalive, to lingering and timeout, as well as enabling socket options of reusing socket address and port number. These are more advanced topics and are for experienced socket programmers. It's OK if novice readers decide to skip some part of this chapter at first read.

13-1 Tuning Basics

Before we delve into how to tune some of the parameters for best performance of network socket applications, here we go over some of the general concepts of tuning first.

In general, tuning application performance often involves changing tunable parameters at different levels:

- **Hardware**, by adding more and/or faster memory and/or CPU power or using network with higher bandwidth
- **Operating system**, by adjusting settings of related O.S. kernel parameters
- **Database system**, by changing database system's tunable parameters, if there is a database system involved.
- **Networking system**, if any
- **Application** itself

The key to tuning is to identify and locate the performance bottleneck(s) first. Sometimes the performance trouble spot is more than one. Once the performance trouble spot is identified, then you find out what can be done to improve it.

Some tunable parameters can be changed only at the operating system level while others can also be tuned at the application level, which normally should override the setting of the operating system kernel parameter just for the application itself. Some parameters may only be available for tuning at only one level, operating system or application but not both. Sometimes tuning may need to be done at more than one level. In many cases, settings at application level can be bounded by settings at the operating system level.

Operating system level tunable parameters can be either static or dynamic. Static parameters require a system reboot for the changes to go into effect. Dynamic parameters can be changed on the fly without rebooting the system and the change takes effect right away. Obviously, dynamic tunable parameters are more flexible, desirable and user-friendly.

A good software design is to make things user configurable, make the tunable parameters dynamic, and also make them tunable at least from the user or application level. The best is to make the software self-tune.

If a tunable parameter is settable at the application level, then the best programming practice is to set or change the parameter from within the application itself. There are two reasons for it. (1) The specific setting will affect only the application itself, not others running on the same system. (2) Normally it's hard for the operating system to find a 'one size fits all' setting that will work best with all applications. Therefore, typically the operating system will set a default value that works reasonably well for most applications. Then it also allows individual applications to be able to change/override it based on their special needs.

Tuning or changing operating system kernel parameters requires root/super user privilege. Changing parameters at the user or application level normally does not require root/super user privilege.

There is no industry standard in terms of what operating system kernel parameters are, if they should be tunable or how to tune them. Parameters bear different names in different operating systems. The way to change them also differs from one operating system to next. Hence, kernel parameter tuning is all operating system specific. Note that even on a given operating system, sometimes the operating system developers change how the tuning is done from one version to next, too. That is bad for users. But it happens. At least Linux does that.

13-2 How to Tune Kernel Parameters in Various Operating Systems

This section goes over how operating system kernel parameters are changed in the most popular operating systems today. Remember that you must have super user privilege to change settings of system kernel parameters.

13-2-1 How to Tune Kernel Parameters in Linux

There are at least three different ways to tune operating system kernel parameters in Linux. Note that Linux operating system developers change how this is done from one version to next, too.

(1) You can directly edit the configuration file **/etc/sysctl.conf** file and put the parameter name and new value in it. For example,

    net.ipv4.ip_forward = 0

Then you run the following command

    # /sbin/sysctl -p /etc/sysctl.conf

to make the change take effect.
The change becomes permanent this way. It not only changes the
parameter's value in memory right away but also the changes
will survive any future system reboots because configuration file
is changed.

(2) Use the '/sbin/sysctl -w' command to change it. But this change is
in memory only. It won't last after the system is rebooted.

To change a parameter's value in memory, run a command like this:

```
# /sbin/sysctl -w net.ipv4.ip_forward=0
```

Changing the parameter value this way is temporary because it
only affects the in-memory copy and does not last beyond system reboot.

To display the current setting of a kernel parameter:

```
# /sbin/sysctl  net.ipv4.ip_forward
net.ipv4.ip_forward = 0
```

To display all kernel parameters currently available:

```
# /sbin/sysctl -a
```

(3) Every kernel tunable parameter has a corresponding file system entry
in the /proc file system. Its pathname is similar to the parameter's
full name except the dot (.) is replaced by forward slash (/) and
the pathname has a prefix of /proc/sys/.

You can modify the value of a parameter by writing the new value into
its corresponding file system entry in the /proc file system.
Use the cat command to display the current value and use the echo
command to change its value. For example, to set the value of the
net.ipv4.ip_forward kernel parameter to 0, you do:

```
# echo 0 > /proc/sys/net/ipv4/ip_forward
```

To query a parameter's current value:

```
# cat /proc/sys/net/ipv4/ip_forward
0
```

To query the TCP socket send buffer sizes:

```
$ cat /proc/sys/net/ipv4/tcp_wmem
4096    16384   4194304
```

The three values represent the min, default and max values of the
parameter.

Again, changing the parameter value this way is temporary because it
only affects the in-memory copy and does not last beyond system reboot.

In summary, directly editing the /etc/sysctl.conf file makes the change
persist through system reboots. But you need to run the

```
'/sbin/sysctl -p /etc/sysctl.conf'
```
command to make the change take effect right away.

Alternatively, altering a parameter's value by either running the
'/sbin/sysctl -w' command or overwriting the corresponding /proc file
system entry takes effect right away. But it's temporary because
the change is made in memory only and is not persisted in the
/etc/sysctl.conf file. As a result, the change will be lost once the
system is rebooted.

13-2-2 How to Tune Kernel Parameters in AIX

In IBM AIX, use the no (no stands for network options) command to tune
network socket parameters in the IBM AIX kernel.

To set a kernel parameter temporarily until reboot:

```
# no -o parameter_name=newValue
```

To set the parameter now and make the change permanent (i.e. last after
reboot):

```
# no -p -o parameter_name=newValue
```

To query the current setting of a parameter:

```
# no -o parameter_name
```

13-2-3 How to Tune Kernel Parameters in Solaris

In Oracle/Sun Solaris, use the ndd or ipadm command to tune the networking
kernel parameters. The ipadm command is recommended.

For example, to change the value of the tcp_max_buf parameter, you do

```
# ndd -set /dev/tcp tcp_max_buf 2097152
```
or
```
# ipadm set-prop -p max_buf=2097152  tcp
```

To query the current setting, you do:

```
# ndd -get /dev/tcp tcp_max_buf
```
or
```
# ipadm show-prop -p max_buf tcp
```

13-2-4 How to Tune Kernel Parameters in HPUX

In HPUX, one can use the ndd command to tune the system kernel parameters
related to sockets.

For example, you can tune the default UDP socket buffer size using the
following ndd command:

```
# ndd -set /dev/sockets socket_udp_rcvbuf_default 65535
```

To monitor the system, use the following commands to get a sense of how the system is performing:

```
# netstat -p tcp
# netstat -p udp
```

13-2-5 How to Tune Kernel Parameters in Apple Darwin and FreeBSD

Many kernel parameters in Apple Darwin and FreeBSD are tuned via the sysctl mechanism. One can run the sysctl command to set a new parameter value or directly edit the /etc/sysctl.conf file.

When a FreeBSD operating system starts and transitions from the single user mode into multi-user mode, the file sysctl.conf is read by the operating system to set default settings for the kernel parameters configured there. This configuration file is the primary tuning and optimization mechanism for FreeBSD and Apple Darwin.

To query the current value of a kernel parameter, do

```
sysctl kernel_parameter_name
```

For instance, to retrieve the maximum number of processes allowed in the entire system, you do:

```
sysctl kern.maxproc
```

Note that in order to support this many processes, some kernel data structures and tables must be pre-allocated. That's why this parameter.

To change a kernel parameter to a new value, you do

```
# sysctl kernel_parameter_name=new_value
```

For example, to set the maximum number of open files allowed, you do:

```
# sysctl kern.maxfiles=15000
```
or

```
$ sudo sysctl kern.maxfiles=15000
```

13-2-6 How to Tune Kernel Parameters in Windows

In Windows, you must have administrator rights/privileges to change kernel parameters.

Tuning Windows kernel parameters involves changing Windows registry. Be careful. If you incorrectly modify Windows registry, serious problems could occur.

You can change Windows registry using the GUI tool, regedit.exe. Once this tool starts, navigate to the registry key or subkey to reset a new value. Some of the TCP related registry keys are located at

```
HKEY_LOCAL_MACHINE\SYSTEM\CurrentControlSet\Services\Tcpip\Parameters\
```

Some of the TCP parameters can be queried or set using the netsh command as well.

In Windows, one can see the current settings of network TCP tunable parameters using the following command:

```
netsh interface tcp show global
```
or
```
netsh int tcp show global
```

To change the settings, you can run the following command:

```
netsh interface tcp set global parameter=value
```

For example, to set receive window autotuning to normal, you run

```
netsh interface tcp set global autotuninglevel=normal
```

13-3 Tuning Socket Buffer Sizes

Many performance issues with network socket applications are a result of inappropriate (often too small) socket buffer sizes used by the applications. This section talks about how to tune socket buffer sizes.

13-3-1 Socket Send and Receive Buffers

In a socket implementation, a network socket has a send buffer and a receive buffer associated with it within the operating system kernel.
The send buffer is used by the operating system to hold the outgoing data that has been sent by the application but has not yet transmitted to the destination yet. Similarly, the receive buffer is used by the operating system to hold the data that is received by the operating system but has not yet been removed by the application via a receive call.
These buffers reside in the operating system kernel space and are separated from the buffers that an application allocates and uses as its input and output buffers within the application.

Figure 13-1 Socket buffers

```
           Process 1                network          Process 2
-------------------------------              -------------------------------

Application      O.S. Kernel              O.S. Kernel       Application
--------------   ---------------          ---------------   ---------------
|output buffer|->|socket send   |-> /\/ ->|socket receive|->| input buffer|
|            |   | buffer       |         | buffer       |   |             |
--------------   ---------------          ---------------   ---------------
| input buffer|<-|socket receive|<- /\/ <-|socket send   |<-|output buffer|
|            |   | buffer       |         | buffer       |   |             |
--------------   ---------------          ---------------   ---------------
```

In other words, as shown in Figure 13-1, the underlying operating system allocates a **send buffer** and a **receive buffer** to support each socket's send and receive operations.

From the diagram, it's not too difficult to figure out that data can be buffered at a minimum of four places when travelling from its source to its destination:

(1) In the application's output buffer at the sending side while the sending application is waiting to get its share of the CPU time and to be executed by the CPU.

(2) In the socket send buffer on the sending system, waiting to be transmitted out of the wire to the destination system or the next router/hop along the way. (There could be a jam somewhere along the way.)

(3) If any, in the buffer of some router(s) between the source and destination systems.

(4) In the socket receive buffer inside the operating system kernel of the receiving system, waiting to be consumed by the receiving application.

13-3-2 Tuning Socket Buffer Sizes

When writing applications that transmit or receive large quantities of data, it may be important to consider the values of socket parameters often referred to as the "socket buffer sizes", namely the SO_SNDBUF and SO_RCVBUF socket options. These options can be examined and set using the **getsockopt()** and **setsockopt()** functions, respectively, which are implemented as system calls into the operating system kernel in most systems.

The design of the SO_RCVBUF and SO_SNDBUF socket options is to allow an application to be able to regulate the amount of data that can be buffered in the pipeline between the sending end and the receiving end. However, be aware that the relationship between the values of the socket buffer size parameters and the amount of data in the pipeline is kind of complicated and dynamic, rather than simple and straightforward. One of the reasons is a network connection may involve multiple hops; data travelling through multiple routers along the way to reach its destination.

Very often engineers find network or distributed applications have a sluggish performance. And from time to time, it turns out that the performance issue is caused, either entirely or at least partly, by socket buffer size being too small. Be aware that, as mentioned above, depending on the actual connection, data may be buffered at multiple places along the way and thus slow performance may not just be caused by insufficient socket buffer space on the sending and receiving ends.

In many operating systems, the default socket send and receive buffer sizes are often 4096 or 8192 bytes. Most real-world applications send data chunks much larger than that size. Therefore, to get better performance, it's very important that you set the socket send and/or receiver buffer size to be equal to or greater than that size. Be aware that it may take some experiments to arrive at the values that produce the best performance for your application.

Usually, tunable parameters can be set at two different levels: at the operating system kernel and at the application level. The settings at the operating system level affect all applications unless applications override them. Settings from within an application should only affect the application itself. However, the maximum settings that can be set at the application level could sometimes be bounded by (i.e. cannot exceed) the maximum set at the operating system level.

Opting to tune these parameters at the operating system kernel level has some advantages and some disadvantages. The advantages are (1) It is done once at one central location. (2) It applies to all applications. (3) Applications don't need to do it themselves individually. The disadvantages are (1) One needs to have the root/super user privilege to tune OS kernel parameters. (2) It's hard to have a one-size-fits-all setting. The setting may be good for some applications but may not be good for all.

Different applications usually have different requirements. In general, it's very difficult to get a "one size fits all" setting at the operating system level that will work well for all different applications. Therefore, in practice, the strategy often is two-folded. First is to have a setting at the operating system level that works reasonably well for most applications. Second, those applications finding this default setting not optimal for them try to override it by changing it from the application level so that it only impacts the application itself and no others.

13-3-3 Tuning Socket Buffer Sizes at Application Level

Socket send and receive buffer sizes are tunable parameters that can be set both at the operating system level and at the application level. Setting them at the application level is standardized; it's done the same way across all different operating systems as long as they support the POSIX standard. For your applications to be portable, you should choose this option.

In contrast, there is no standard for setting these parameters in the operating system kernel, which we will discuss in the next section.

To set socket send or receive buffer size **at the application level**, an application invokes the setsockopt() function with SOL_SOCKET in the second (i.e. level) argument and with **SO_SNDBUF** or **SO_RCVBUF** passed into the third (optname) argument, respectively. To get the current setting, an application invokes the getsockopt() function.

Be aware that when a program calls the setsockopt() function to set or change the socket send and/or receive buffer sizes, it affects only one socket -- the socket whose file descriptor is specified in the first argument of the setsockopt() call.

Figure 13-2 Changing TCP send buffer size -- tcp_bufsz.c

```
/*
 * Get and set socket options related to socket buffer sizes.
 * With TCP socket buffer size options.
 * Authored by Mr. Jin-Jwei Chen.
 * Copyright (c) 1993-2016, 2018 Mr. Jin-Jwei Chen. All rights reserved.
 */

#include <stdio.h>
#include <errno.h>
#include <sys/types.h>
#include <sys/socket.h>
#include <netinet/in.h>        /* protocols such as IPPROTO_TCP, ... */
#include <unistd.h>            /* close() */
#include <netinet/tcp.h>

int main(int argc, char *argv[])
{
  int     ret;
  int     sfd;                        /* file descriptor of the socket */
  int         option;                 /* option value */
  socklen_t   optlen;                 /* length of option value */

  /* Create a Stream socket. */
  if ((sfd = socket(AF_INET, SOCK_STREAM, 0)) < 0)
  {
    fprintf(stderr, "Error: socket() failed, errno=%d\n", errno);
    return(-1);
  }

  /* Get the original setting of the SO_SNDBUF socket option. */
  option = 0;
  optlen = sizeof(option);
  ret = getsockopt(sfd, SOL_SOCKET, SO_SNDBUF, &option, &optlen);
  if (ret < 0)
  {
    fprintf(stderr, "Error: getsockopt(SO_SNDBUF) failed, errno=%d\n", errno);
    close(sfd);
    return(-2);
  }
  fprintf(stdout, "TCP SO_SNDBUF's original setting is %u.\n", option);

  /* Set the SO_SNDBUF socket option. */
  option = option + 2048;
  ret = setsockopt(sfd, SOL_SOCKET, SO_SNDBUF, &option, optlen);
  if (ret < 0)
  {
    fprintf(stderr, "Error: setsockopt(SO_SNDBUF) failed, errno=%d\n", errno);
    close(sfd);
    return(-3);
  }
  fprintf(stdout, "TCP SO_SNDBUF is reset to %u.\n", option);

  /* Get the current setting of the SO_SNDBUF socket option. */
  option = 0;
  ret = getsockopt(sfd, SOL_SOCKET, SO_SNDBUF, &option, &optlen);
```

```
  if (ret < 0)
  {
    fprintf(stderr, "Error: getsockopt(SO_SNDBUF) failed, errno=%d\n", errno);
    close(sfd);
    return(-4);
  }
  fprintf(stdout, "TCP SO_SNDBUF's current setting is %u.\n", option);

  /* Set the SO_SNDBUF option to be above default maximum. This may fail. */
  /* By default, max. value allowed is 2 MB in AIX and 1 MB on Solaris. */
  option = 1024000;
  fprintf(stdout, "Trying to reset TCP SO_SNDBUF to %u.\n", option);
  ret = setsockopt(sfd, SOL_SOCKET, SO_SNDBUF, &option, optlen);
  if (ret < 0)
  {
    fprintf(stderr, "Error: setsockopt(SO_SNDBUF) failed, errno=%d\n", errno);
    close(sfd);
    return(-5);
  }

  /* Get the current setting of the SO_SNDBUF socket option. */
  option = 0;
  ret = getsockopt(sfd, SOL_SOCKET, SO_SNDBUF, &option, &optlen);
  if (ret < 0)
  {
    fprintf(stderr, "Error: getsockopt(SO_SNDBUF) failed, errno=%d\n", errno);
    close(sfd);
    return(-6);
  }
  fprintf(stdout, "TCP SO_SNDBUF's current setting is %u.\n", option);

  /* Make the connection after setting the socket buffer size(s) */

  close(sfd);
}
```

Figure 13-2 is a program which demonstrates how to tune the TCP send
buffer size from within an application. It also demonstrates the
maximum limit. Please notice that by default, the maximum SO_SNDBUF size
an application can set differs from one operating system to another.
For instance, it could be 1 MB on Solaris, 2 MB on AIX and nearly 4 MB
on Linux.

Below is a sample execution of this example application.
First, we check the current kernel setting of these parameters (in Linux):

```
    $ /sbin/sysctl -a |grep net|grep mem
    net.core.wmem_max = 1048576
    net.core.rmem_max = 4194304
    net.core.wmem_default = 262144
    net.core.rmem_default = 262144
    net.core.optmem_max = 20480
    net.ipv4.igmp_max_memberships = 20
    net.ipv4.tcp_mem = 191808      255744    383616
    net.ipv4.tcp_wmem = 4096       16384     4194304
    net.ipv4.tcp_rmem = 4096       87380     4194304
```

```
net.ipv4.udp_mem = 191808          255744   383616
net.ipv4.udp_rmem_min = 4096
net.ipv4.udp_wmem_min = 4096
```

Then we run the application (in Linux):

```
$ ./tcp_bufsz
TCP SO_SNDBUF's original setting is 16384.
TCP SO_SNDBUF is reset to 18432.
TCP SO_SNDBUF's current setting is 36864.
Trying to reset TCP SO_SNDBUF to 4196352.
TCP SO_SNDBUF's current setting is 2097152.
```

The application first creates a socket using TCP protocol (SOCK_STREAM).
It then calls getsockopt() to get the current system setting of the TCP
send buffer size. The value is 16384. This is the middle column value of
the net.ipv4.tcp_wmem kernel parameter, as shown in the output of the
"/sbin/sysctl -a" command above.

The program then invokes the setsockopt() to change the value and increase
it by 2048. (The increase here is small because it is just for demonstration
purpose.) A call to getsockopt() shows the value is now 36864.
As we said it before, Linux tends to double the value.
(16384 + 2048) = 18432. 18432 x 2 = 36864.

Lastly, the application attempts to set the same parameter value to
4196352. Another call to getsockopt() shows the value is now 2097152 in
Linux. This is because the maximum limit is constrained by
net.core.wmem_max, whose value is 1048576 and double of that is exactly
2097152. Please be aware this maximum limit is different on different
platforms. You may have to use a smaller value on some platforms (e.g.
AIX and Solaris).

To change the TCP receive buffer size, you do exactly the same except
replacing the constant SO_SNDBUF with SO_RCVBUF in all of the calls.

To change the same parameters for UDP sockets, you create a UDP Datagram
socket (SOCK_DGRAM) and then invoke the same getsockopt() and setsockopt()
functions with SO_SNDBUF or SO_RCVBUF to do it.

Remember that in Linux when you set the socket send and receive buffer sizes
using the setsockopt() function (SO_SNDBUF and SO_RCVBUF), the Linux
kernel doubles its size to allow space for bookkeeping overhead.
That is why after your application sets these values, if it queries them,
the values returned appear to be doubled.

Figure 13-3 is a pair of TCP client server programs that change send and
receive buffer sizes.

Note that if a program does only send operations, it only needs to call
setsockopt() for the SO_SNDBUF option to tune its socket output buffer size.
Similarly, if a program does only receive operations, it only needs to
change its socket receive buffer size, namely, the SO_RCVBUF option.
For programs performing both send and receive operations, they may need
to change both. Note that to be effective you may need to change buffer sizes
on both ends; send buffer size at sender and receive buffer size at receiver.

Figure 13-3 Applications that change TCP send/receive buffer size
-- tcpclnt_bufsz.c and tcpsrv_bufsz.c

(a) tcpsrv_bufsz.c

```c
/*
 * A connection-oriented server program using Stream socket.
 * Single-threaded server.
 * With socket buffer size options (SO_SNDBUF and SO_RCVBUF).
 * Authored by Mr. Jin-Jwei Chen.
 * Copyright (c) 1993-2016, 2018, 2020 Mr. Jin-Jwei Chen. All rights reserved.
 */

#include <stdio.h>
#include <errno.h>
#include <sys/types.h>
#include <sys/socket.h>
#include <netinet/in.h>        /* protocols such as IPPROTO_TCP, ... */
#include <string.h>            /* memset() */
#include <stdlib.h>            /* atoi() */
#include <unistd.h>            /* close() */

#define  BUFLEN      1024      /* size of message buffer */
#define  DEFSRVPORT  2344      /* default server port number */
#define  BACKLOG     5         /* length of listener queue */
#define  SOCKBUFSZ   1048576   /* socket buffer size */

int main(int argc, char *argv[])
{
  int     ret, portnum_in=0;
  int     sfd;                           /* file descriptor of the listener socket */
  int     newsock;                       /* file descriptor of client data socket */
  struct sockaddr_in    srvaddr;    /* socket structure */
  int     srvaddrsz=sizeof(struct sockaddr_in);
  struct sockaddr_in    clntaddr;   /* socket structure */
  socklen_t   clntaddrsz=sizeof(struct sockaddr_in);
  in_port_t   portnum=DEFSRVPORT;  /* port number */
  char    inbuf[BUFLEN];                 /* input message buffer */
  char    outbuf[BUFLEN];                /* output message buffer */
  size_t  msglen;                        /* length of reply message */
  int     option;
  socklen_t  optlen;

  fprintf(stdout, "Connection-oriented server program ...\n\n");

  /* Get the port number from user, if any. */
  if (argc > 1)
    portnum_in = atoi(argv[1]);
  if (portnum_in <= 0)
  {
    fprintf(stderr, "Port number %d invalid, set to default value %u\n\n",
      portnum_in, DEFSRVPORT);
    portnum = DEFSRVPORT;
  }
  else
```

```
    portnum = portnum_in;

/* Create the Stream server socket. */
if ((sfd = socket(AF_INET, SOCK_STREAM, 0)) < 0)
{
  fprintf(stderr, "Error: socket() failed, errno=%d\n", errno);
  return(-1);
}

/* Get socket input buffer size set by the OS. */
option = 0;
optlen = sizeof(option);
ret = getsockopt(sfd, SOL_SOCKET, SO_RCVBUF, &option, &optlen);
if (ret < 0)
  fprintf(stderr, "Error: getsockopt(SO_RCVBUF) failed, errno=%d\n", errno);
else
  fprintf(stdout, "SO_RCVBUF was originally set to be %u\n", option);

/* Set socket input buffer size. */
option = SOCKBUFSZ;
ret = setsockopt(sfd, SOL_SOCKET, SO_RCVBUF, &option, sizeof(option));
if (ret < 0)
  fprintf(stderr, "Error: setsockopt(SO_RCVBUF) failed, errno=%d\n", errno);
else
  fprintf(stdout, "SO_RCVBUF is set to be %u\n", option);

/* Get socket input buffer size. */
option = 0;
optlen = sizeof(option);
ret = getsockopt(sfd, SOL_SOCKET, SO_RCVBUF, &option, &optlen);
if (ret < 0)
  fprintf(stderr, "Error: getsockopt(SO_RCVBUF) failed, errno=%d\n", errno);
else
  fprintf(stdout, "SO_RCVBUF now is %u\n", option);

/* Turn on SO_KEEPALIVE socket option. */
option = 1;
ret = setsockopt(sfd, SOL_SOCKET, SO_KEEPALIVE, &option, sizeof(option));
if (ret < 0)
{
  fprintf(stderr, "Error: setsockopt(SO_KEEPALIVE) failed, errno=%d\n", errno);
}
else
  fprintf(stdout, "SO_KEEPALIVE socket option is set.\n");

/* Fill in the server socket address. */
memset((void *)&srvaddr, 0, (size_t)srvaddrsz); /* clear the address buffer */
srvaddr.sin_family = AF_INET;                    /* Internet socket */
srvaddr.sin_addr.s_addr = htonl(INADDR_ANY);     /* server's IP address */
srvaddr.sin_port = htons(portnum);               /* server's port number */

/* Bind the server socket to its address. */
if ((ret = bind(sfd, (struct sockaddr *)&srvaddr, srvaddrsz)) != 0)
{
  fprintf(stderr, "Error: bind() failed, errno=%d\n", errno);
  return(-2);
```

```
  }

  /* Set maximum connection request queue length that we can fall behind. */
  if (listen(sfd, BACKLOG) == -1) {
    fprintf(stderr, "Error: listen() failed, errno=%d\n", errno);
    close(sfd);
    return(-3);
  }

  /* Wait for incoming connection requests from clients and service them. */
  while (1) {

    fprintf(stdout, "\nListening at port number %u ...\n", portnum);
    newsock = accept(sfd, (struct sockaddr *)&clntaddr, &clntaddrsz);
    if (newsock < 0)
    {
      fprintf(stderr, "Error: accept() failed, errno=%d\n", errno);
      close(sfd);
      return(-4);
    }

    fprintf(stdout, "Client Connected.\n");

    /* Set the reply message */
    sprintf(outbuf, "%s", "This is a reply from the server program.");
    msglen = strlen(outbuf);

    /* Receive and service requests from the current client. */
    while (1)
    {
      /* Receive a request from a client. */
      errno = 0;
      inbuf[0] = '\0';
      ret = recv(newsock, inbuf, BUFLEN, 0);
      if (ret > 0)
      {
        /* Process the request. We simply print the request message here. */
        inbuf[ret] = '\0';
        fprintf(stdout, "\nReceived the following request from client:\n%s\n",
          inbuf);

        /* Send a reply. */
        errno = 0;
        ret = send(newsock, outbuf, msglen, 0);
        if (ret == -1)
          fprintf(stderr, "Error: send() failed, errno=%d\n", errno);
        else
          fprintf(stdout, "%u of %lu bytes of the reply was sent.\n", ret, msglen);
      }
      else if (ret < 0)
      {
        fprintf(stderr, "Error: recv() failed, errno=%d\n", errno);
        break;
      }
      else
      {
```

```
              /* The client may have disconnected. */
              fprintf(stdout, "The client may have disconnected.\n");
              break;
          }
      }  /* while - inner */
      close(newsock);
  }  /* while - outer */
}
```

   (b) tcpclnt_bufsz.c

```
/*
 * A connection-oriented client program using Stream socket.
 * With socket buffer size options (SO_SNDBUF and SO_RCVBUF).
 * Authored by Mr. Jin-Jwei Chen.
 * Copyright (c) 1993-2016, 2018, 2020 Mr. Jin-Jwei Chen. All rights reserved.
 */

#include <stdio.h>
#include <errno.h>
#include <sys/types.h>
#include <sys/socket.h>
#include <netinet/in.h>         /* protocols such as IPPROTO_TCP, ... */
#include <arpa/inet.h>          /* inet_addr(), inet_ntoa(), inet_ntop() */
#include <string.h>             /* memset() */
#include <stdlib.h>             /* atoi() */
#include <netdb.h>              /* gethostbyname() */
#include <ctype.h>              /* isalpha() */
#include <unistd.h>             /* close() */

#define  BUFLEN      1024       /* size of input message buffer */
#define  DEFSRVPORT  2344       /* default server port number */
#define  MAXMSGS     4          /* Maximum number of messages to send */
#define  NAMELEN     63
#define  SOCKBUFSZ   1048576    /* socket buffer size */

int main(int argc, char *argv[])
{
  int     ret;
  int     sfd;                          /* file descriptor of the socket */
  struct sockaddr_in    server;         /* socket structure */
  int     srvaddrsz=sizeof(struct sockaddr_in);
  struct sockaddr_in    fromaddr;       /* socket structure */
  socklen_t    fromaddrsz=sizeof(struct sockaddr_in);
  in_port_t    portnum=DEFSRVPORT;      /* port number */
  char    inbuf[BUFLEN];                /* input message buffer */
  char    outbuf[BUFLEN];               /* output message buffer */
  size_t    msglen;                     /* length of reply message */
  size_t    msgnum=0;                   /* count of request message */
  size_t    len;
  unsigned int addr;
  char    server_name[NAMELEN+1] = "localhost";
  int     socket_type = SOCK_STREAM;
  struct hostent *hp;
  int     option;
  socklen_t  optlen;
```

875

```c
  fprintf(stdout, "Connection-oriented client program ...\n\n");

  /* Get the host name or IP address from command line. */
  if (argc > 1)
  {
    len = strlen(argv[1]);
    if (len > NAMELEN)
      len = NAMELEN;
    strncpy(server_name, argv[1], len);
    server_name[len] = '\0';
  }

  /* Get the port number from command line. */
  if (argc > 2)
    portnum = atoi(argv[2]);
  if (portnum <= 0)
  {
    fprintf(stderr, "Port number %d invalid, set to default value %u\n",
      portnum, DEFSRVPORT);
    portnum = DEFSRVPORT;
  }

  /* Translate the host name or IP address into server socket address. */
  if (isalpha(server_name[0]))
  {  /* A host name is given. */
    hp = gethostbyname(server_name);
  }
  else
  {  /* Convert the n.n.n.n IP address to a number. */
    addr = inet_addr(server_name);
    hp = gethostbyaddr((char *)&addr, sizeof(addr), AF_INET);
  }
  if (hp == NULL )
  {
    fprintf(stderr,"Error: cannot get address for [%s], errno=%d\n",
      server_name, errno);
    return(-1);
  }

  /* Copy the resolved information into the sockaddr_in structure. */
  memset(&server, 0, sizeof(server));
  memcpy(&(server.sin_addr), hp->h_addr, hp->h_length);
  server.sin_family = hp->h_addrtype;
  server.sin_port = htons(portnum);

  /* Open a socket. */
  sfd = socket(AF_INET, socket_type, 0);
  if (sfd < 0)
  {
    fprintf(stderr,"Error: socket() failed, errno=%d\n", errno);
    return (-2);
  }

  /* Get socket output buffer size set by the OS. */
  option = 0;
```

```
  optlen = sizeof(option);
  ret = getsockopt(sfd, SOL_SOCKET, SO_SNDBUF, &option, &optlen);
  if (ret < 0)
  {
    fprintf(stderr, "Error: getsockopt(SO_SNDBUF) failed, errno=%d\n", errno);
  }
  else
    fprintf(stdout, "originally, SO_SNDBUF was set to be %u\n", option);

  /* Set socket output buffer size. */
  option = SOCKBUFSZ;
  ret = setsockopt(sfd, SOL_SOCKET, SO_SNDBUF, &option, sizeof(option));
  if (ret < 0)
  {
    fprintf(stderr, "Error: setsockopt(SO_SNDBUF) failed, errno=%d\n", errno);
  }
  else
    fprintf(stdout, "SO_SNDBUF is set to be %u\n", option);

  /* Get socket output buffer size. */
  option = 0;
  optlen = sizeof(option);
  ret = getsockopt(sfd, SOL_SOCKET, SO_SNDBUF, &option, &optlen);
  if (ret < 0)
  {
    fprintf(stderr, "Error: getsockopt(SO_SNDBUF) failed, errno=%d\n", errno);
  }
  else
    fprintf(stdout, "SO_SNDBUF now is %u\n", option);

  fprintf(stdout, "\nSend request messages to server at port %d\n", portnum);

  /* Connect to the server. */
  ret = connect(sfd, (struct sockaddr *)&server, srvaddrsz);
  if (ret == -1)
  {
    fprintf(stderr, "Error: connect() failed, errno=%d\n", errno);
    close(sfd);
    return(-3);
  }

  /* Send request messages to the server and process the reply messages. */
  while (msgnum < MAXMSGS)
  {
    /* Send a request message to the server. */
    sprintf(outbuf, "%s%4lu%s", "This is request message ", ++msgnum,
      " from the client program.");
    msglen = strlen(outbuf);
    errno = 0;

    ret = send(sfd, outbuf, msglen, 0);
    if (ret >= 0)
    {
      /* Print a warning if not entire message was sent. */
      if (ret == msglen)
        fprintf(stdout, "\n%lu bytes of message were successfully sent.\n",
```

```
            msglen);
      else if (ret < msglen)
        fprintf(stderr, "Warning: only %u of %lu bytes were sent.\n",
            ret, msglen);

      if (ret > 0)
      {
        /* Receive a reply from the server. */
        errno = 0;
        inbuf[0] = '\0';
        ret = recv(sfd, inbuf, BUFLEN, 0);

        if (ret > 0)
        {
          /* Process the reply. */
          inbuf[ret] = '\0';
          fprintf(stdout, "Received the following reply from server:\n%s\n",
              inbuf);
        }
        else if (ret == 0)
          fprintf(stdout, "Warning: Zero bytes were received.\n");
        else
          fprintf(stderr, "Error: recv() failed, errno=%d\n", errno);
      }
    }
    else
      fprintf(stderr, "Error: send() failed, errno=%d\n", errno);

  } /* while */

  close(sfd);
}
```

Note that increasing the socket buffer sizes increases the consumption of memory space by an application, but it may reduce the amount of time that the application has to be blocked and wait while sending or receiving data (to and from the operating system kernel).

In addition, **setting the buffer sizes should be done before the connection is made.**

For a TCP (SOCK_STREAM) socket, the values of socket send and receive buffers have an impact on TCP congestion control. TCP protocol uses these values in negotiating the TCP receive window. If the value is large, a window scaling option value may be negotiated.
The receive window size of the peer, in combination with the SO_SNDBUF set by a sending application and TCP congestion control algorithms, limit the total amount of data that can be buffered in a single direction over a given connection.

Summary

Again, just to recap, as for tuning socket send and receive buffer sizes, application developers should attempt to write POSIX compliant applications and invoke setsockopt() with SO_SNDBUF and/or SO_RCVBUF options to set these values to achieve best performance for the application itself.

The code is the same across all POSIX-complaint operating systems as being illustrated in this section. The only thing is that the maximum value an application can set may be limited by the maximum value set inside the operating system kernel by the system administrator.

For system administrators, it's also important to set the values of the system kernel parameters related to the socket buffer sizes to some that will work reasonably well for most, if not all, applications. The default values set in the operating system kernel will be used by applications that do not specifically set these values. Also, the maximum value set in the kernel will impose a limit on how high applications can set the value to. We will discuss how to set these kernel parameters in the next section.

Be aware that exactly what settings allow you to get best throughput out of your network connection depends on at least a number of factors: the socket buffer sizes, the bandwidth (speed) of your network, the network latency (the RTT value - the Round Trip Time), the kernel implementation of the network protocols, and potentially others as well. It may take some experiments and measurements to find out.

13-3-4 Tuning Socket Buffer Sizes at Operating System Kernel Level

Different operating systems use different system kernel parameters for the socket send and receive buffer sizes. In addition, the way to reconfigure them is also different from one operating system to next. Most operating systems also have separate set of parameters for TCP and UDP protocols. The precise behavior of these parameters may also vary between implementations, too.

In this section we introduce these parameters and discuss how to set them in various operating systems.

Please be aware that changing kernel parameter settings requires root, super or administrator user privilege in all operating systems.

13-3-4-1 Linux

Compared to other operating systems, Linux has more kernel parameters involved in socket buffer size tuning.

Auto-tuning

In newer versions of Linux kernel, socket send and receive buffer sizes are automatically tuned by the operating system kernel for all TCP sockets. Starting from Linux 2.4, TCP send buffer size is automatically tuned. And starting from Linux 2.6.7, TCP receive buffer size is also automatically tuned. This means normally an application does not need to change the TCP send and receive buffer sizes anymore.

However, an application program can take the matter into its own hand by invoking the setsockopt() function and setting the buffer size(s) it likes, which effectively disables the auto-tuning.

When the auto-tuning is in effect, the minimum, default and maximum
values for a TCP (SOCK_STREAM) socket are defined by the following
kernel tunable parameters:

net.ipv4.tcp_wmem

This Linux kernel tunable parameter is a vector of three integers
representing the minimum, default (i.e. initial) and maximum send buffer
sizes in bytes for TCP sockets.

Note that this parameter is automatically tuned by the Linux kernel.
The value in the middle is the default send buffer size for a TCP
(SOCK_STREAM) socket. Linux will auto-adjust it between the minimum
value on the left and the maximum value on the right.

net.ipv4.tcp_rmem

This Linux kernel tunable parameter is a vector of three integers
defining the minimum, default (i.e. initial) and maximum receive buffer
sizes in bytes for TCP sockets.

Note that this parameter is automatically tuned by the Linux kernel.
The value in the middle is the default receive buffer size for a TCP
(SOCK_STREAM) socket. Linux will auto-adjust it between the minimum
value on the left and the maximum value on the right.

Note that if an application calls setsockopt() with SO_SNDBUF, then
it disables automatic tuning of that socket's send buffer size.
In this case, the maximum value of the net.ipv4.tcp_wmem parameter
is ignored. Similarly, if an application calls setsockopt() with
SO_RCVBUF, then it disables automatic tuning of that socket's receive
buffer size. In that case, the maximum value of the net.ipv4.tcp_rmem
parameter is ignored.

Also note that the maximum send or receive socket buffer size for
automatically tuned TCP sockets does not override net.core.wmem_max or
net.core.rmem_max, respectively.

For example,

```
$ sysctl -q net.ipv4.tcp_wmem net.ipv4.tcp_rmem
net.ipv4.tcp_wmem = 4096    16384    4194304
net.ipv4.tcp_rmem = 4096    87380    4194304
```

With these settings, if an application does not call setsockopt() to alter
any of its socket buffer sizes, a SOCK_STREAM socket will initially get
16384 bytes for its send buffer and 87380 bytes for its receive buffer.

Note that there is another parameter named net.ipv4.tcp_mem.
Try not to touch that one because it's already automatically tuned based
on the amount of memory the system has. Besides, that parameter uses
memory pages, rather than bytes, as the unit. Hence, it can be confusing.
The Linux kernel uses this parameter to determine when to pressure memory
usage down. When the memory usage exceeds the default (middle column)
value, that's when the system starts to do so. The maximum value indicates
the maximum number of memory pages that can be used by TCP sockets

system-wide.

Other Protocols

For other protocols that do not have its own tunable parameters, the default socket send and receive buffer sizes are defined by the following two parameters at the net.core level:

net.core.wmem_default

This Linux kernel parameter defines the default size of send buffers used by sockets. A protocol that does not have its own tunable parameter gets this value.

net.core.rmem_default

This Linux kernel parameter defines the default size of receive buffers used by sockets. A protocol that does not have its own tunable parameter gets this value.

Below is an example of the default values for these parameters:

```
net.core.wmem_default = 262144
net.core.rmem_default = 262144
```

Note that UDP protocol does not have separate kernel tunable parameters for send or receive buffer. It has only the following:

```
net.ipv4.udp_mem = 185955      247942   371910
net.ipv4.udp_rmem_min = 4096
net.ipv4.udp_wmem_min = 4096
```

Therefore, when an application creates a SOCK_DGRAM socket, the default send and receive buffer sizes will be defined by the net.core.wmem_default and net.core.rmem_default parameters, respectively.

```
net.core.rmem_default = 212992
net.core.rmem_max = 212992
net.core.wmem_default = 212992
net.core.wmem_max = 212992
```

The parameter net.core.rmem_max sets the max OS receive buffer size for all types of connections. One can use the 'sysctl -w' command to change it. Similarly, net.core.wmem_max sets the max OS send buffer size for all types of connections.

Note on Application Tuning

As we said it before, when your socket program invokes the setsockopt() function to change the socket send or receive buffer size, it disables the auto-tuning for your application. In this case, the maximum value of the tcp_wmem or tcp_rmem parameter is ignored and the maximum buffer sizes that an application can set are instead limited by parameters at the net.core level.

The maximum socket send buffer size an application can set is defined

by the net.core.wmem_max kernel parameter for both TCP and UDP protocols.
The maximum socket receive buffer size an application can set is defined
by the net.core.rmem_max kernel parameter for both TCP and UDP protocols.

In other words, the maximum values of socket send and receive buffer sizes
that applications can set by using the setsockopt() SO_SNDBUF and
SO_RCVBUF options are defined by the following Linux kernel parameters,
respectively:

net.core.wmem_max

  defines the maximum socket send buffer size in bytes which a socket
  application program may set by using the setsockopt() SO_SNDBUF option.

net.core.rmem_max

  defines the maximum socket receive buffer size in bytes which a socket
  application program may set by using the setsockopt() SO_RCVBUF socket
  option.

These maximum limits apply to both SOCK_STREAM and SOCK_DGRAM sockets.

How to Tune

Use the '/sbin/sysctl -q' command to get the current value of a parameter.
For example:

```
# sysctl -q net.core.wmem_max net.core.rmem_max
net.core.wmem_max = 1048576
net.core.rmem_max = 4194304
```

To change the parameter value for the entire system or all applications,
use the '/sbin/sysctl -w' command to tune or change a parameter's value.
For instance,

```
# /sbin/sysctl -w net.core.wmem_max=2097152
```

Summary

As we mentioned above, an application can invoke the setsockopt()
function to disable the auto-tuning and manually set the socket send
and/or receive buffer sizes, just for the application itself.
In this case, the maximum buffer size an application can set will be
bounded by the maximum value set at the bottom net.core level, rather
than by the maximum value of the net.ipv4.tcp_wmem or net.ipv4.tcp_rmem,
respectively. That is, the upper bound is then instead defined by the
net.core.wmem_max (for SO_SNDBUF) and net.core.rmem_max (for SO_RCVBUF)
parameters, respectively.

If an application does not invoke the setsockopt() function to change
the socket send or receive buffer size, then these parameters are
automatically set by the Linux kernel. The send and receive buffer
sizes an application gets are defined by the default value (the middle
column one) of the net.ipv4.tcp.wmem and net.ipv4.tcp.rmem kernel
parameters, respectively.

Linux tunable kernel parameters that are related to socket buffer sizes
include the following:

```
net.core.wmem_max = 1048576
net.core.wmem_default = 262144
net.core.rmem_max = 4194304
net.core.rmem_default = 262144

net.ipv4.tcp_wmem = 4096        16384    4194304
net.ipv4.tcp_rmem = 4096        87380    4194304
net.ipv4.tcp_mem = 191808       255744   383616

net.ipv4.udp_wmem_min = 4096
net.ipv4.udp_rmem_min = 4096
net.ipv4.udp_mem = 191808       255744   383616
```

Use the "sysctl -a" or a command like "cat /proc/sys/net/ipv4/tcp_wmem"
to query the current settings.

13-3-4-2 AIX

What to Tune

IBM AIX has the following kernel parameters related to socket buffer sizes:

- tcp_recvspace
  The tcp_recvspace tunable parameter specifies how many bytes of data
  a receiving application can buffer in the kernel on the receiving
  socket's queue. The default value usually is around 16384.

- tcp_sendspace
  The tcp_sendspace tunable parameter specifies how much data a sending
  application can buffer in the kernel before the application is blocked
  on a send call. The default value usually is around 16384.

- sb_max
  The sb_max parameter sets an upper limit on the number of socket buffers
  that are queued to an individual socket, which controls how much buffer
  space is consumed by buffers queued to a sender's socket or to
  a receiver's socket. The default value is usually 1048576.

- udp_sendspace
  The udp_sendspace tunable parameter controls the memory buffer space
  for outgoing data that is queued on a UDP socket.
  Set it to a value that is equal to or greater than the largest UDP
  datagram that will be sent by the application.
  The default value is usually around 42080.

- udp_recvspace
  The udp_recvspace tunable parameter controls the amount of memory buffer
  space for incoming data that is queued on a UDP socket.
  Once the udp_recvspace limit is reached for a socket, incoming packets
  are discarded. The default value is usually around 42080.

- use_sndbufpool = "1"

Specifies whether send buffer pools should be used for sockets.
Default value is 1 (enabled). Setting it to 0 to disable it.

How to Tune

Use the 'no -o' command to tune the socket buffer size parameters.
For example,

To set the tcp_sendspace parameter temporarily until reboot:

    # no -o tcp_sendspace=16384

To set the parameter now and make the change last after reboot:

    # no -p -o tcp_sendspace=16384

To query the current setting:

    # no -o tcp_sendspace

IBM recommends users to set the TCP send and receive space to at least
10 times the MTU size.

The MTU size for 10/100 Mbps Ethernet is 1500. Set tcp_sendspace and
tcp_recvspace to 16384 and sb_max to be 32768.

The MTU size for Gigabit Ethernet can be 1500 or 9000. Set tcp_sendspace
to 131072 and tcp_recvspace to 65536. And set sb_max to 131072 or 262144.

When you change tunable parameters affecting TCP/IP connections
using the 'no -o' command, it only has an effect on connections that
are established after the change is made.
The 'no -o 'command may restart the inetd daemon process when
changes are made that might affect processes for which the inetd daemon
is listening for new connections.

13-3-4-3 Solaris

What to Tune

Note that many Solaris kernel tunable parameters underwent a name
change in Solaris 11.

In older versions of Solaris, network tunable parameters have protocol
name prefix such as tcp or udp. For example, tcp_max_buf.
Solaris 11 breaks the tunable parameters into protocol categories,
gets rid of the protocol name prefix, puts them under the ipadm (as
opposed to ndd) administrative command, and calls them properties.
For instance, TCP parameter tcp_max_buf has become TCP property max_buf.

Oracle/Sun Solaris 11 has the following kernel parameters that are related
to socket buffer sizes.

1. TCP Tunable Parameters (Properties)

send_buf - the default send buffer size in bytes.
      Range of values allowed is 4096 to the current value of max_buf.
      The default value is 49,152.

recv_buf - the default receive buffer size in bytes.
      Range of values allowed is 2048 to the current value of max_buf.
      The default value is 128,000.

max_buf - the maximum send and receive buffer size in bytes.
      This parameter places a limit on how large an application can set
      the send and receive buffers to using setsockopt().
      Range of values allowed is 128,000 to 1,073,741,824.
      The default value is 1,048,576.

      If the network is a high-speed network, you may need to
      increase this value to match the network link speed.

Note that these three new tunables are called TCP properties in Solaris 11.
They correspond to TCP parameters tcp_xmit_hiwat, tcp_recv_hiwat and
tcp_max_buf, respectively, in older versions of Solaris.

2. UDP Tunable Parameters (Properties)

send_buf - the default send buffer size for a UDP socket.
      Range of values allowed is 1024 to the current value of max_buf.
      The default value is 57,344 bytes.

recv_buf - the default receive buffer size for a UDP socket.
      Range of values allowed is 128 to the current value of max_buf.
      The default value is 57,344 bytes.

max_buf - the maximum send and receive buffer size for a UDP socket in bytes.
      This parameter places a limit on how large an application can set
      the send and receive buffers to for a UDP socket using setsockopt().
      Range of values allowed is 65,536 to 1,073,741,824.
      The default value is 2,097,152.

These three UDP properties correspond to udp_xmit_hiwat, udp_recv_hiwat
and udp_max_buf, respectively, in older versions of Solaris.

How to Tune

Use the ndd or ipadm command to tune the networking kernel parameters.
The ipadm command is recommended.
For example,

```
  # ndd -set /dev/tcp tcp_max_buf 2097152
  # ipadm set-prop -p max_buf=2097152  tcp
```

To query the current setting:

```
  # ndd -get /dev/tcp tcp_max_buf
  # ipadm show-prop -p max_buf tcp
```

For example,

```
$ ipadm show-prop -p send_buf,recv_buf,max_buf tcp
PROTO  PROPERTY    PERM  CURRENT   PERSISTENT   DEFAULT    POSSIBLE
tcp    send_buf    rw    49152     --           49152      4096-1048576
tcp    recv_buf    rw    128000    --           128000     2048-1048576
tcp    max_buf     rw    1048576   --           1048576    128000-1073741824
```

13-3-4-4 HP-UX

What to Tune

HP-UX has the following operating system kernel parameters related to socket buffer sizes.

(a) For TCP (SOCK_STREAM type) sockets

Socket send buffer parameters:

- tcp_xmit_hiwater_def: default value for SO_SNDBUF socket option
- tcp_xmit_hiwater_max: maximum value applications may set for SO_SNDBUF socket option

  By setting the TCP socket send socket buffer default (tcp_xmit_hiwater_def) sufficiently large for a given bandwidth-delay product, the transport is better positioned to taking full advantage of the remote TCP's advertised window.

In addition to these "high water mark" parameters, the transmit side also has a related "low water mark" tunable:

- tcp_xmit_lowater_def: the amount of unsent data that relieves write-side flow control

Socket receive buffer parameters:

- tcp_recv_hiwater_def: default value for SO_RCVBUF socket option
- tcp_recv_hiwater_max: maximum value applications may set for SO_RCVBUF socket option

(b) For UDP (SOCK_DGRAM type) sockets

- socket_udp_sndbuf_default parameter:

  Default send buffer size for UDP sockets. Default value is 65535 bytes.

- socket_udp_rcvbuf_default parameter:

  Default receive buffer size for UDP sockets. Default value is 65535 bytes. The value of this tunable parameter should not exceed the value of the ndd parameter udp_recv_hiwater_max. Otherwise a socket() call to create UDP socket will fail and return the errno value EINVAL.

  Note: If the command 'netstat -p udp' shows socket overflows, it might be useful to increase the value of this tunable parameter. However, increasing the size of this parameter helps only if the overload condition is short-lived and the burst of traffic is less

than the size of the socket buffer. Increasing the socket buffer size
will not help if the overload condition is sustained.

- udp_recv_hiwater_max parameter:

   Maximum limit of the receive buffer size for UDP sockets specified in
   a SO_RCVBUF option of a setsockopt() call.

   A setsockopt() call with a SO_RCVBUF option exceeding the corresponding
   kernel parameter (xxx_recv_hiwater_max) value will fail and return the
   errno value EINVAL.

   A socket() call to create a UDP socket will fail and return
   the errno value EINVAL if the value of the socket_udp_rcvbuf_default
   parameter exceeds the value of udp_recv_hiwater_max.
   Default value is 2147483647 (2^31) bytes. Range of values allowed is
   [1024-2147483647].

(c) For UNIX Domain (AF_UNIX) sockets

   socket_buf_max:
      Specifies the maximum socket buffer size for AF_UNIX sockets.
      Default: 262144 bytes. Range of values allowed: [1024, 2147483647]

How to Tune

   As long as you have the super user privilege, you can use the ndd command
   to tune the system kernel parameters related to sockets.

   For example, you can tune the default UDP socket receive buffer size using
   the following ndd command:

      # ndd -set /dev/sockets socket_udp_rcvbuf_default 65535

   To monitor the system, use the following commands to get a sense of
   how the system is performing:

      # netstat -p tcp
      # netstat -p udp

13-3-4-5 Apple Darwin

In Apple Darwin, OS kernel tunable parameters related to socket send and
receive buffers are listed below:

   net.inet.tcp.sendspace: 131072
   net.inet.tcp.recvspace: 131072

   net.inet.tcp.doautosndbuf: 1
   net.inet.tcp.autosndbufinc: 8192
   net.inet.tcp.autosndbufmax: 2097152

   net.inet.tcp.doautorcvbuf: 1
   net.inet.tcp.autorcvbufmax: 2097152

You can use the "sudo sysctl -w param=newval" command to change any one of these, including the net.inet.tcp.autosndbufmax and net.inet.tcp.autorcvbufmax. By default, net.inet.tcp.doautosndbuf is set to 1, meaning TCP send buffer size is automatically tuned. Setting its value to 0 disabling it. The same applies to net.inet.tcp.doautorcvbuf.

For net.inet.tcp.sendspace and net.inet.tcp.recvspace, I was able to increase them to above 5MB, but not 6MB though.

13-3-4-6 FreeBSD

What to Tune

In FreeBSD, socket buffer related kernel parameters include the following:

net.inet.tcp.recvspace

  - the default socket receive buffer size, in bytes.

net.inet.tcp.sendspace

  - the default socket send buffer size, in bytes.

net.inet.tcp.recvbuf_max

  - the maximum socket receive buffer size in bytes, for autotuning.

net.inet.tcp.sendbuf_max

  - the maximum socket send buffer size in bytes, for autotuning.

net.inet.tcp.recvbuf_auto

  - controls receive window autotuning on or off.

net.inet.tcp.sendbuf_auto

  - controls send window autotuning on or off.

net.inet.tcp.recvbuf_inc

  - size of each increment of the receive window autotuning.

net.inet.tcp.sendbuf_inc

  - size of each increment of the send window autotuning.

For example, below is a snapshot of the settings of these parameters:

```
# Socket buffer kernel parameters in FreeBSD
net.inet.tcp.recvspace=65536
net.inet.tcp.sendspace=32768
net.inet.tcp.sendbuf_max=16777216
net.inet.tcp.recvbuf_max=16777216
net.inet.tcp.sendbuf_auto=1
```

```
net.inet.tcp.recvbuf_auto=1
net.inet.tcp.sendbuf_inc=8192
net.inet.tcp.recvbuf_inc=16384
```

How to Tune

Run the sysctl utility to query or set the value of a parameter.
Or directly edit the /etc/sysctl.conf file and put the new settings there.

13-3-4-7 Windows

What to Tune

The Windows TCP/IP stack is designed to self-tune itself in most
environments.

The socket send and receive buffer sizes are called TCP Window Size in
Microsoft Windows.

The TCP receive window size is the amount of receive data, in bytes,
that can be buffered by Windows kernel during a connection. The sending
host can send only that amount of data before it must wait for an
acknowledgment from the receiving host.

Rather than using a hard-coded default receive window size, TCP adjusts
to even increments of the maximum segment size (MSS), which is negotiated
during connection setup.

The receive window size on Windows is determined in the following manner:

1. The first connection request sent to a remote host advertises a receive
   window size of 16K (16,384 bytes).
2. When the connection is established, the receive window size is rounded
   up to an even increment of the MSS.
3. The window size is adjusted to 4 times the MSS, to a maximum size of
   64K, unless the window scaling option (RFC 1323) is used.

How to Tune

Microsoft documentation says the following:

To set the receive window size to a specific value, add the TcpWindowSize
value to the registry subkey specific to your version of Windows.
Do the following steps:

1. Click Start, click Run, type Regedit, and then click OK.
2. Windows' TCPIP parameters normally are located at the following
   registry subkeys:
   HKEY_LOCAL_MACHINE\SYSTEM\CurrentControlSet\Services\Tcpip\Parameters\
   Navigate to and expand the subkey and select the parameter
   you would like to modify.
3. Right click on the parameter and select 'Modify'.
4. Type in the new value in the New Value (or Value data) box,
   and then press OK.

Note that some of the parameters are located under the Interfaces subkey.

13-3-5 Summary of Socket Options on Send/Receive Buffer Sizes

- Socket send and receive buffer sizes can be tuned at application level
  and at operating system kernel level.

- Changing socket send and receive buffer sizes at application level
  is done by invoking the setsockopt() function with level=SOL_SOCKET
  and optname=SO_SNDBUF or SO_RCVBUF.
  This code is the same across all POSIX-compliant operating systems.

- Changing socket send and receive buffer sizes at operating system
  kernel level differs from one operating system to the next.
  The kernel parameters have different names between operating systems.
  TCP and UDP protocols may have their own parameters on some platforms.
  The user command used to change them differs as well.

- Tuning socket send/receive buffers at application level

      setsockopt(fd, SOL_SOCKET, SO_SNDBUF or SO_RCVBUF)

- Tuning socket send/receive buffers at O.S. kernel level

    Linux:

      Common

          net.core.wmem_max = 1048576
          net.core.rmem_max = 4194304
          net.core.wmem_default = 262144
          net.core.rmem_default = 262144

      TCP

          net.ipv4.tcp_mem = 191808   255744   383616
          net.ipv4.tcp_wmem = 4096   16384   4194304
          net.ipv4.tcp_rmem = 4096   87380   4194304

      UDP

          net.ipv4.udp_mem = 191808   255744   383616
          net.ipv4.udp_rmem_min = 4096
          net.ipv4.udp_wmem_min = 4096

    AIX:
          tcp_sendspace   tcp_recvspace
          udp_sendspace   udp_recvspace

    Solaris:
      TCP: send_buf   recv_buf   max_buf
      UDP: send_buf   recv_buf   max_buf

    HP-UX:
      TCP: tcp_xmit_hiwater_def   tcp_xmit_hiwater_max

```
            tcp_recv_hiwater_def  tcp_recv_hiwater_max
            tcp_xmit_lowater_def
   UDP: socket_udp_sndbuf_default  socket_udp_rcvbuf_default
   Unix Domain socket: socket_buf_max
```

Apple Darwin:

```
   net.inet.tcp.sendspace: 131072
   net.inet.tcp.recvspace: 131072
   net.inet.tcp.doautosndbuf: 1
   net.inet.tcp.autosndbufinc: 8192
   net.inet.tcp.autosndbufmax: 2097152
   net.inet.tcp.doautorcvbuf: 1
   net.inet.tcp.autorcvbufmax: 2097152
```

FreeBSD:

```
   net.inet.tcp.recvspace=65536
   net.inet.tcp.sendspace=32768
   net.inet.tcp.sendbuf_max=16777216
   net.inet.tcp.recvbuf_max=16777216
   net.inet.tcp.sendbuf_auto=1
   net.inet.tcp.recvbuf_auto=1
   net.inet.tcp.sendbuf_inc=8192
   net.inet.tcp.recvbuf_inc=16384
```

13-4 The SO_KEEPALIVE Socket Option

SO_KEEPALIVE socket option offers a way for TCP applications to detect dead peer or broken network connections earlier than a default time set by the operating system.

Many applications use connection-oriented TCP socket connections to exchange data between two programs running on two separate computers connected via a network. After a connection is established between the two ends, if there is no data exchange going on and one of the computers goes down or the network cable in unplugged, the down situation won't be automatically detected for quite some time. And the two programs or the one still alive would have no idea about the situation and would appear to be hung.

Part of this is due to most TCP applications do synchronous input/output, meaning once a program calls the recv() function to try to receive data sent from the other end, it will block forever until some data arrives. If the computer at the other end dies or the cable is unplugged, then there will not be any data arrives for as long as the situation persists. And the application(s) would appear to be hung or unresponsive.

This condition will last for a very long time until a timer preset in each operating system expires. This default time is typically around 1.5 to 2 hours or even longer.

The SO_KEEPALIVE socket option allows you to speed up the detection of these dead peer or broken network conditions.

Three levels of behaviors your application can get in terms of how soon it can detect a broken network connection or a peer death:

1. The default behavior, which typically means SO_KEEPALIVE option off. The peer death or broken network condition may go undetected forever. This time is the default time specified by the TCP protocol.

2. Turning on the SO_KEEPALIVE socket option but changing no parameters. The application is getting the behavior set by the operating system kernel tunable parameters for the SO_KEEPALIVE option.

   The peer death or broken network condition will be detected after the time set in the related operating system kernel parameters for this option expires, which is typically around 2 hours.

3. Turning the SO_KEEPALIVE option on and changing parameters. In this case the application is getting the behavior it defines in the application itself. The peer death or broken network condition will be detected after the time set by the application expires.

We will discuss how to use the SO_KEEPALIVE option in this section.

13-4-1 What Is SO_KEEPALIVE Socket Option?

The TCP keep-alive mechanism is described in RFC 1122.

The SO_KEEPALIVE socket option enables periodic transmission of probing messages over an idle connected socket by the operating system to check if the connection is still alive. If the other end does not respond to the KEEPALIVE probing messages within a certain period of time, the connection is deemed broken and an error value is set internally for the socket. Note that no response from the other end (i.e. not being able to reach to the communicating partner) could mean either the network connection is broken or the other host is down.

The SO_KEEPALIVE socket option allows applications to detect a broken network connection sooner, especially when the application has not transmitted any actual data for some time.

For instance, on a connection-mode socket for which a connection has been established, if SO_KEEPALIVE is enabled and the connected socket fails to respond to the keep-alive messages, the broken connection will be detected. This makes a blocked network send or receive call on the socket return, which would otherwise continue to block and appear to be hung if the SO_KEEPALIVE option were not on.

Remember that **the SO_KEEPALIVE option must be enabled before a socket connection is made.** That is, an application must turn on the option before the accept() call on a TCP server program (do it before and outside the listening loop) or before the connect() call in a TCP client program.

Note that for a TCP server program, the socket that the server uses to communicate with a connected client is automatically created by the accept() call. The value of the SO_KEEPALIVE socket option for this socket is inherited from the parent socket. Therefore, **on a TCP server program,** you want to turn on the SO_KEEPALIVE option on the connection listening socket (the listener socket) -- the one used to make the accept() call.

Also notice that the SO_KEEPALIVE socket option applies to a "connected" socket only, for instance, a TCP SOCK_STREAM socket. It does not apply to UDP Datagram service socket because there is no connection established there.

It is very important for an application to turn on the SO_KEEPALIVE option because otherwise it may have to wait for hours or even longer to detect a broken socket connection. In almost all systems the SO_KEEPALIVE socket option is off by default and the default time for a broken connection to be automatically detected is set to 75 or 90 minutes or even longer.

In many applications, it is very desirable to detect a network outage or remote host failure as early as possible such that measures can be taken to handle the failures. For instance, in a cluster or high availability system or application, failover to a surviving or standby node can be done right away after detecting such a node or network link failure. That's why these systems typically have to implement exchanging heart-beat messages themselves in order to detect such failures at the earliest time. The sooner a failure can be detected, the less down time it will be.

13-4-2 Parameters Implementing the SO_KEEPALIVE Option

This section discusses how the SO_KEEPALIVE socket option works. It talks about the parameters involved and the two different levels at which these parameters can be set and the scope of their impacts.

In most operating systems, when it is enabled, the internal working of the SO_KEEPALIVE option is controlled by a combination of three operating system kernel parameters. These parameters may have different names on different operating systems but they essentially have the following functions:

1. **The time to wait before starting probing an idle connection.**

   When the SO_KEEPALIVE socket option is enabled, the TCP layer within the operating system probes a socket connection that has been idle for some amount of time. When does the operating system start to do the probing? That is, for how long does a socket connection have to be idle before the operating system starts probing into it? This idle time is normally default to 2 hours in most operating systems but it is tunable.

   This is the amount of time that a connection has to be idle before the network protocol layer in the operating system kernel sends the first keepalive probing packet, if the SO_KEEPALIVE option is enabled. **There is no probing if the SO_KEEPALIVE option is disabled**.

   Different operating systems use different names for this kernel parameter. Examples include keepalive_time, KeepAliveTime, keepalive_interval, keepidle, keep_idle, and time_wait_interval.

2. **The time to wait before retrying the probe if previous probe gets no response.**

This is the interval of time between successive keepalive packets sent.

Parameter names used by different operating systems for this tunable include tcp_keepalive_intvl, tcp_keepintvl, tcp_keepalive_interval, KeepAliveInterval and TCPTV_KEEPINTVL.

3. **The maximum number of times to try the probe**

When the SO_KEEPALIVE socket option is enabled, the TCP layer within the operating system probes a socket connection that has been idle for some amount of time. If the remote system does not respond to a keepalive probe message, TCP retransmits the probe message a certain number of times before a connection is deemed broken. This parameter specifies that number of times.

In other words, this parameter specifies the maximum number of keepalive packets to be sent to validate a connection. After this many attempts, the connection will be considered dead if no response is returned.

Different names used for this parameter on various operating systems include tcp_keepalive_probes, tcp_keepcnt, tcp_keepalives_kill, TcpMaxDataRetransmission and TCPTV_KEEPCNT.

Note that some operating systems combine the second and third parameters into a single parameter and name it something like tcp_keepalive_abort_interval or tcp_ip_abort_interval .

So, as a network application developer, your job is to enable the SO_KEEPALIVE socket option at the socket level from within your program. After that, to control how quickly a broken network connection is detected, the related parameters may also need to be tuned.

These parameters can be tuned at two different levels. First, they can be set/tuned at the operating system kernel level by the system administrator. Note that changing them requires super user privilege and the settings apply to all applications running on the system. So be very careful if you are to change them at the operating system kernel level.

Table 13-1 **Operating System Kernel Parameters for SO_KEEPALIVE option**

Operating System	Wait time before probing starts	Time interval between probes	Probing retries	Time unit
Linux	tcp_keepalive_time	tcp_keepalive_intvl	tcp_keepalive_probes	seconds
AIX	tcp_keepidle	tcp_keepintvl	tcp_keepcnt	0.5 sec
Solaris	tcp_keepalive_interval	tcp_keepalive_abort_interval	N/A	seconds
HP-UX	tcp_keepalive_interval	tcp_ip_abort_interval	N/A	ms
Apple Darwin	tcp.keepidle	tcp.keepintvl	tcp.keepcnt	ms
Windows	KeepAliveTime	KeepAliveInterval	TcpMaxDataRetransmission	ms

Note 1: ms: milliseconds
Note 2: tcp_keepalives_kill is always set to 1 on HP-UX.

Second, these parameters can be set or tuned by each individual application too. And this is the recommended way to do it because it only impacts the application. As a software engineer, you can programmatically change the values of these parameters from within your program to override the settings done at the operating system kernel level. This is done via the setsockopt() function call and it impacts only one socket and one application.

Table 13-1 shows these operating system kernel parameters on some of the most popular platforms. Be aware that the time unit for these parameters is different on different operating systems as well. For instance, it is seconds in Linux, Solaris and FreeBSD, half seconds in AIX, and milliseconds in HPUX, Apple Darwin and Windows.

Note that the tunable parameters related to the KEEPALIVE socket option are at the TCP protocol level and they are operating system dependent. You probably have noticed that almost all operating systems tag the tunable parameters with 'tcp'. This is because as we said it earlier, the SO_KEEPALIVE socket option applies to connection-oriented sockets only, which use the TCP protocol at the transport layer.

Here we discuss a specific example.
In the case of Linux, the three operating system kernel parameters controlling the internal working of the SO_KEEPALIVE socket option are named: tcp_keepalive_time, tcp_keepalive_intvl and tcp_keepalive_probes. tcp_keepalive_time specifies the time to wait before the process of probing into an idle connection starts. Its default value is usually 7200 seconds, which is two hours. tcp_keepalive_intvl specifies the time interval between keepalive probe packets. Its default value is 75 seconds. tcp_keepalive_probes specifies the number of tries in sending probe packets. Its default value is 9.

The formula for calculating the maximum time that a dead TCP connection can hang around (keep staying idle) before it is disconnected by the operating system is:

```
net.ipv4.tcp_keepalive_time +
(net.ipv4.tcp_keepalive_intvl x net.ipv4.tcp_keepalive_probes)
```

For example, with the following default settings,

```
net.ipv4.tcp_keepalive_time = 7200
net.ipv4.tcp_keepalive_intvl = 75
net.ipv4.tcp_keepalive_probes = 9
```

the time it takes for the network protocol layer to detect a broken connection is 7200+75*9=7875 seconds (about 2 hours 15 minutes), which is a very long time. This often makes users feel like the application hangs while in fact it's the network cable is pulled or the network connection is broken or the other node went down.

We will introduce the corresponding parameters that can be tuned at the application level in the next section below.

So now you understand that the default time for a broken network connection to be detected is a result of some network protocol tunable parameters that are set within the operating system kernel. In many systems, this default value is two hours or even longer. That means if your socket

program does not specifically turn on the SO_KEEPALIVE socket option,
then it will take at least this long for your socket applications to detect
a broken network connection. Since the default value can be too long for
your applications, it is important that you enable the SO_KEEPALIVE socket
option from within your program and perhaps change the related tunable
parameters as well so that broken connections can be detected sooner
when your application runs.

Note that the default value for SO_KEEPALIVE option is zero, which means
this capability is turned off. This means there will be no automatic idle
connection probing, at least not until the very long default time set in
the operating system kernel expires, if there is one.

In general, it's almost always a good idea to turn on the SO_KEEPALIVE
option to prevent the application from appearing hung for a very long
period of time in case of losing the network connection or a remote node.
However, there is also a flip side of the TCP KEEPALIVE feature.
If the feature is turned on and the settings for detecting dead connections
are too aggressive, it is possible that temporary network outages can be
incorrectly identified as dead connections, resulting in TCP connections
to unexpectedly terminate. Therefore, it is important to carefully examine
the requirements of your applications and strike the right balance.
In some cases, to avoid or reduce the occurrences of such undesired
terminations, you might even want to turn off the KEEPALIVE option.

On many systems, the command

```
# netstat -p tcp
```

displays many information items including the number of keepalive probes
sent and the number of connections dropped by keepalive or retransmission
timeout. From there one can get an idea of whether the keepalive parameter
settings are too aggressive or not. For example,

```
# netstat -p tcp
3 keepalive timeouts
0 keepalive probe sent
0 connections dropped by keepalive

46 connections dropped by rexmit timeout
```

13-4-3 Changing Keepalive Tunable Parameters

As we said it earlier, TCP keepalive related parameters can be tuned at
two different levels: in the application or at the operating system kernel.
Below we introduce how to perform these tunings.

13-4-3-1 Change TCP Keepalive Parameters at Application Level

Changing TCP KEEPALIVE parameters at application level can be done via
IPPROTO_TCP socket options. That is, it can be done by invoking
the setsockopt() function with IPPROTO_TCP in the level (the second)
argument and an appropriate option (i.e. tunable parameter) name in the
optname (the third) argument.

The option names here are usually in capital letters because they are indeed pre-defined C macros. In contrast, their corresponding operating system kernel tunable parameters are usually in lower case.

13-4-3-1-1 Linux and AIX

Linux and AIX share the same way to change keepalive parameters at application level. The level argument to the setsockopt() call is IPPROTO_TCP and the option names are TCP_KEEPIDLE, TCP_KEEPINTVL, and TCP_KEEPCNT, respectively.

```
-----------------------------------------------------------------------
Level        Option name         Description
-----------  ------------        -------------------------------------------
IPPROTO_TCP  TCP_KEEPIDLE        connection idle time before first keepalive probe
IPPROTO_TCP  TCP_KEEPINTVL       time interval between keepalive probe packets
IPPROTO_TCP  TCP_KEEPCNT         maximum number of keepalive probe packets
-----------------------------------------------------------------------
```

Below are the TCP keepalive options and their default values in Linux and AIX which are tunable at application level via setsockopt():

```
TCP_KEEPIDLE (7200 seconds)
TCP_KEEPINTVL (75 seconds)
TCP_KEEPCNT (9 in Linux, 8 in AIX)
```

Figure 13-4 lists a pair of client server programs that get and set the TCP keepalive related parameters at application level. This same pair of programs works in Linux, AIX, HPUX and Apple Darwin. The only thing is that TCP_KEEPIDLE is called TCP_KEEPALIVE in Darwin. The test client program pauses for a few seconds after sending each message so that you can go pull the network cable before the test ends. By default, the test sends only 4 messages. If you need more time to pull the cable, modify the client program to send more messages or sleep a bit longer between sending messages.

These programs enable SO_KEEPALIVE and change parameters from application level.

Figure 13-4 Changing Keepalive Parameters at Application Level
in Linux/AIX/HPUX/Apple Darwin -- tcpsrv_alive.c and tcpclnt_alive.c

(a) tcpsrv_alive.c

```
/*
 * A connection-oriented server program using Stream socket.
 * Single-threaded server.
 * Tune parameters of SO_KEEPALIVE socket option in Linux, AIX, HP-UX, and
 * Apple Darwin.
 * Copyright (c) 2002, 2014, 2018-2020 Mr. Jin-Jwei Chen. All rights reserved.
 */

#include <stdio.h>
#include <errno.h>
```

```c
#include <sys/types.h>
#include <sys/socket.h>
#include <netinet/in.h>        /* protocols such as IPPROTO_TCP, ... */
#include <string.h>            /* memset() */
#include <stdlib.h>            /* atoi() */
#include <unistd.h>            /* close() */
#include <netinet/tcp.h>       /* TCP_KEEPIDLE, TCP_KEEPCNT, TCP_KEEPINTVL */

#define   BUFLEN      1024     /* size of message buffer */
#define   DEFSRVPORT  2344     /* default server port number */
#define   BACKLOG     5        /* length of listener queue */

int main(int argc, char *argv[])
{
  int     ret, portnum_in=0;
  int     sfd;                            /* file descriptor of the listener socket */
  int     newsock;                        /* file descriptor of client data socket */
  struct sockaddr_in    srvaddr;   /* socket structure */
  int     srvaddrsz=sizeof(struct sockaddr_in);
  struct sockaddr_in    clntaddr;  /* socket structure */
  socklen_t   clntaddrsz=sizeof(struct sockaddr_in);
  in_port_t   portnum=DEFSRVPORT; /* port number */
  char    inbuf[BUFLEN];                  /* input message buffer */
  char    outbuf[BUFLEN];                 /* output message buffer */
  size_t msglen;                          /* length of reply message */
  int     option;

  fprintf(stdout, "Connection-oriented server program ...\n");

  /* Get the port number from user, if any. */
  if (argc > 1)
    portnum_in = atoi(argv[1]);
  if (portnum_in <= 0)
  {
    fprintf(stderr, "Port number %d invalid, set to default value %u\n",
      portnum_in, DEFSRVPORT);
    portnum = DEFSRVPORT;
  }
  else
    portnum = portnum_in;

  /* Create the Stream server socket. */
  if ((sfd = socket(AF_INET, SOCK_STREAM, 0)) < 0)
  {
    fprintf(stderr, "Error: socket() failed, errno=%d\n", errno);
    return(-1);
  }

  /* Turn on SO_KEEPALIVE socket option. */
  option = 1;
  ret = setsockopt(sfd, SOL_SOCKET, SO_KEEPALIVE, &option, sizeof(option));
  if (ret < 0)
  {
    fprintf(stderr, "Error: setsockopt(SO_KEEPALIVE) failed, errno=%d\n", errno);
    close(sfd);
    return(-2);
```

```
   }
   else
     fprintf(stdout, "SO_KEEPALIVE socket option is enabled.\n");

   /* Set the TCP_KEEPIDLE (called TCP_KEEPALIVE in Apple Darwin) socket option. */
   option = 300;   /* 5 minutes */
#ifdef __APPLE__
   ret = setsockopt(sfd, IPPROTO_TCP, TCP_KEEPALIVE, &option, sizeof(option));
#else
   ret = setsockopt(sfd, IPPROTO_TCP, TCP_KEEPIDLE, &option, sizeof(option));
#endif
   if (ret < 0)
   {
#ifdef __APPLE__
     fprintf(stderr, "Error: setsockopt(TCP_KEEPALIVE) failed, errno=%d\n", errno);
#else
     fprintf(stderr, "Error: setsockopt(TCP_KEEPIDLE) failed, errno=%d\n", errno);
#endif
     close(sfd);
     return(-3);
   }
#ifdef __APPLE__
   fprintf(stdout, "TCP_KEEPALIVE is reset to (%d)\n", option);
#else
   fprintf(stdout, "TCP_KEEPIDLE is reset to (%d)\n", option);
#endif

   /* Set the TCP_KEEPCNT socket option. */
   option = 2;
   ret = setsockopt(sfd, IPPROTO_TCP, TCP_KEEPCNT, &option, sizeof(option));
   if (ret < 0)
   {
     fprintf(stderr, "Error: setsockopt(TCP_KEEPCNT) failed, errno=%d\n", errno);
     close(sfd);
     return(-4);
   }
   fprintf(stdout, "TCP_KEEPCNT is reset to (%d)\n", option);

   /* Set the TCP_KEEPINTVL socket option. */
   option = 30;
   ret = setsockopt(sfd, IPPROTO_TCP, TCP_KEEPINTVL, &option, sizeof(option));
   if (ret < 0)
   {
     fprintf(stderr, "Error: setsockopt(TCP_KEEPINTVL) failed, errno=%d\n", errno);
     close(sfd);
     return(-5);
   }
   fprintf(stdout, "TCP_KEEPINTVL is reset to (%d)\n", option);

   /* Fill in the server socket address. */
   memset((void *)&srvaddr, 0, (size_t)srvaddrsz); /* clear the address buffer */
   srvaddr.sin_family = AF_INET;                    /* Internet socket */
   srvaddr.sin_addr.s_addr = htonl(INADDR_ANY);     /* server's IP address */
   srvaddr.sin_port = htons(portnum);               /* server's port number */

   /* Bind the server socket to its address. */
```

```c
  if ((ret = bind(sfd, (struct sockaddr *)&srvaddr, srvaddrsz)) != 0)
  {
    fprintf(stderr, "Error: bind() failed, errno=%d\n", errno);
    close(sfd);
    return(-6);
  }

  /* Set maximum connection request queue length that we can fall behind. */
  if (listen(sfd, BACKLOG) == -1) {
    fprintf(stderr, "Error: listen() failed, errno=%d\n", errno);
    close(sfd);
    return(-7);
  }

  /* Wait for incoming connection requests from clients and service them. */
  while (1) {

    fprintf(stdout, "\nListening at port number %u ...\n", portnum);
    newsock = accept(sfd, (struct sockaddr *)&clntaddr, &clntaddrsz);
    if (newsock < 0)
    {
      fprintf(stderr, "Error: accept() failed, errno=%d\n", errno);
      close(sfd);
      return(-8);
    }

    fprintf(stdout, "Client Connected.\n");

    /* Set the reply message */
    sprintf(outbuf, "%s", "This is a reply from the server program.");
    msglen = strlen(outbuf);

    /* Receive and service requests from the current client. */
    while (1)
    {
      /* Receive a request from a client. */
      errno = 0;
      inbuf[0] = '\0';
      ret = recv(newsock, inbuf, BUFLEN, 0);
      if (ret > 0)
      {
        /* Process the request. We simply print the request message here. */
        inbuf[ret] = '\0';
        fprintf(stdout, "\nReceived the following request from client:\n%s\n",
          inbuf);

        /* Send a reply. */
        errno = 0;
        ret = send(newsock, outbuf, msglen, 0);
        if (ret == -1)
          fprintf(stderr, "Error: send() failed, errno=%d\n", errno);
        else
          fprintf(stdout, "%u of %lu bytes of the reply was sent.\n", ret, msglen);
      }
      else if (ret < 0)
      {
```

```
            fprintf(stderr, "Error: recv() failed, errno=%d\n", errno);
            break;
        }
        else
        {
            /* The client may have disconnected. */
            fprintf(stdout, "The client may have disconnected.\n");
            break;
        }
    } /* while - inner */
    close(newsock);

    /* The following two statements are for test only */
    close(sfd);
    break;

  } /* while - outer */
}
```

    (b) tcpclnt_alive.c

```
/*
 * A connection-oriented client program using Stream socket.
 * Tune parameters of SO_KEEPALIVE socket option in Linux, AIX, HP-UX and
 * Apple Darwin.
 * Copyright (c) 2002, 2014, 2018-2020 Mr. Jin-Jwei Chen. All rights reserved.
 */

#include <stdio.h>
#include <errno.h>
#include <sys/types.h>
#include <sys/socket.h>
#include <netinet/in.h>        /* protocols such as IPPROTO_TCP, ... */
#include <string.h>            /* memset() */
#include <stdlib.h>            /* atoi() */
#include <netdb.h>             /* gethostbyname() */
#include <unistd.h>            /* close() */
#include <netinet/tcp.h>       /* TCP_KEEPIDLE, TCP_KEEPCNT, TCP_KEEPINTVL */
#include <arpa/inet.h>         /* inet_addr() */
#include <ctype.h>             /* isalpha() */

#define  BUFLEN       1024     /* size of input message buffer */
#define  DEFSRVPORT   2344     /* default server port number */
#define  MAXMSGS         4     /* Maximum number of messages to send */
#define  NAMELEN        63

int main(int argc, char *argv[])
{
  int     ret;
  int     sfd;                        /* file descriptor of the socket */
  struct sockaddr_in     server;      /* socket structure */
  int     srvaddrsz=sizeof(struct sockaddr_in);
  struct sockaddr_in     fromaddr;    /* socket structure */
  socklen_t     fromaddrsz=sizeof(struct sockaddr_in);
  in_port_t     portnum=DEFSRVPORT;   /* port number */
  char    inbuf[BUFLEN];              /* input message buffer */
```

```c
  char    outbuf[BUFLEN];              /* output message buffer */
  size_t    msglen;                    /* length of reply message */
  size_t    msgnum=0;                  /* count of request message */
  size_t    len;
  unsigned int addr;
  char    server_name[NAMELEN+1] = "localhost";
  int    socket_type = SOCK_STREAM;
  struct hostent *hp;
  int    option;
#ifdef HPUX
  int   optlen;
#else
  socklen_t  optlen;
#endif

  fprintf(stdout, "Connection-oriented client program ...\n\n");

  /* Get the host name or IP address from command line. */
  if (argc > 1)
  {
    len = strlen(argv[1]);
    if (len > NAMELEN)
      len = NAMELEN;
    strncpy(server_name, argv[1], len);
    server_name[len] = '\0';
  }

  /* Get the port number from command line. */
  if (argc > 2)
    portnum = atoi(argv[2]);
  if (portnum <= 0)
  {
    fprintf(stderr, "Port number %d invalid, set to default value %u\n",
      portnum, DEFSRVPORT);
    portnum = DEFSRVPORT;
  }

  /* Translate the host name or IP address into server socket address. */
  if (isalpha(server_name[0]))
  {  /* A host name is given. */
    hp = gethostbyname(server_name);
  }
  else
  {  /* Convert the n.n.n.n IP address to a number. */
    addr = inet_addr(server_name);
    hp = gethostbyaddr((char *)&addr, sizeof(addr), AF_INET);
  }
  if (hp == NULL )
  {
    fprintf(stderr,"Error: cannot get address for [%s], errno=%d\n",
      server_name, errno);
    return(-1);
  }

  /* Copy the resolved information into the sockaddr_in structure. */
  memset(&server, 0, sizeof(server));
```

```
  memcpy(&(server.sin_addr), hp->h_addr, hp->h_length);
  server.sin_family = hp->h_addrtype;
  server.sin_port = htons(portnum);

  /* Open a socket. */
  sfd = socket(AF_INET, socket_type, 0);
  if (sfd < 0)
  {
    fprintf(stderr,"Error: socket() failed, errno=%d\n", errno);
    return (-2);
  }

  /* Get the SO_KEEPALIVE socket option. */
  option = 0;
  optlen = sizeof(option);
  ret = getsockopt(sfd, SOL_SOCKET, SO_KEEPALIVE, &option, &optlen);
  if (ret < 0)
  {
    fprintf(stderr, "Error: getsockopt(SO_KEEPALIVE) failed, errno=%d\n", errno);
    close(sfd);
    return(-3);
  }
  if (option == 0)
    fprintf(stdout, "SO_KEEPALIVE socket option was not set (%d) by default.\n",
      option);

  /* Set the SO_KEEPALIVE socket option. Do this before connect. */
  option = 1;
  ret = setsockopt(sfd, SOL_SOCKET, SO_KEEPALIVE, &option, sizeof(option));
  if (ret < 0)
  {
    fprintf(stderr, "Error: setsockopt(SO_KEEPALIVE) failed, errno=%d\n", errno);
    close(sfd);
    return(-4);
  }
  else
    fprintf(stdout, "SO_KEEPALIVE socket option is now enabled.\n");

  /* Set the TCP_KEEPIDLE (called TCP_KEEPALIVE in Apple Darwin) socket option. */
  option = 120;   /* 2 minutes */
#ifdef __APPLE__
  ret = setsockopt(sfd, IPPROTO_TCP, TCP_KEEPALIVE, &option, sizeof(option));
#else
  ret = setsockopt(sfd, IPPROTO_TCP, TCP_KEEPIDLE, &option, sizeof(option));
#endif
  if (ret < 0)
  {
#ifdef __APPLE__
    fprintf(stderr, "Error: setsockopt(TCP_KEEPALIVE) failed, errno=%d\n", errno);
#else
    fprintf(stderr, "Error: setsockopt(TCP_KEEPIDLE) failed, errno=%d\n", errno);
#endif
    close(sfd);
    return(-5);
  }
#ifdef __APPLE__
```

```
    fprintf(stdout, "TCP_KEEPALIVE is reset to (%d)\n", option);
#else
    fprintf(stdout, "TCP_KEEPIDLE is reset to (%d)\n", option);
#endif

    /* Set the TCP_KEEPCNT socket option. */
    option = 2;
    ret = setsockopt(sfd, IPPROTO_TCP, TCP_KEEPCNT, &option, sizeof(option));
    if (ret < 0)
    {
      fprintf(stderr, "Error: setsockopt(TCP_KEEPCNT) failed, errno=%d\n", errno);
      close(sfd);
      return(-6);
    }
    fprintf(stdout, "TCP_KEEPCNT is reset to (%d)\n", option);

    /* Set the TCP_KEEPINTVL socket option. */
    option = 30;
    ret = setsockopt(sfd, IPPROTO_TCP, TCP_KEEPINTVL, &option, sizeof(option));
    if (ret < 0)
    {
      fprintf(stderr, "Error: setsockopt(TCP_KEEPINTVL) failed, errno=%d\n", errno);
      close(sfd);
      return(-7);
    }
    fprintf(stdout, "TCP_KEEPINTVL is reset to (%d)\n", option);

    /* Connect to the server. */
    ret = connect(sfd, (struct sockaddr *)&server, srvaddrsz);
    if (ret == -1)
    {
      fprintf(stderr, "Error: connect() failed, errno=%d\n", errno);
      close(sfd);
      return(-8);
    }

    fprintf(stdout, "\nSend request messages to server at port %d\n", portnum);

    /* Send request messages to the server and process the reply messages. */
    while (msgnum < MAXMSGS)
    {
      /* Send a request message to the server. */
      sprintf(outbuf, "%s%4ld%s", "This is request message ", ++msgnum,
        " from the client program.");
      msglen = strlen(outbuf);
      errno = 0;

      ret = send(sfd, outbuf, msglen, 0);
      if (ret >= 0)
      {
        /* Print a warning if not entire message was sent. */
        if (ret == msglen)
          fprintf(stdout, "\n%lu bytes of message were successfully sent.\n",
            msglen);
        else if (ret < msglen)
          fprintf(stderr, "Warning: only %u of %lu bytes were sent.\n",
```

```
            ret, msglen);

     if (ret > 0)
     {
        /* Receive a reply from the server. */
        errno = 0;
        inbuf[0] = '\0';
        ret = recv(sfd, inbuf, BUFLEN, 0);

        if (ret > 0)
        {
           /* Process the reply. */
           inbuf[ret] = '\0';
           fprintf(stdout, "Received the following reply from server:\n%s\n",
             inbuf);
        }
        else if (ret == 0)
           fprintf(stdout, "Warning: Zero bytes were received.\n");
        else
           fprintf(stderr, "Error: recv() failed, errno=%d\n", errno);
     }
     else
        fprintf(stderr, "Error: send() failed, errno=%d\n", errno);

     sleep(5);  /* Pause so we can pull the cable. For testing only. */
  }  /* while */

  close(sfd);
}
```

Notes

In AIX, a connection-oriented socket program, both TCP server and TCP client,
detects the network outage at the time set by the program itself
as long as the program enables SO_KEEPALIVE socket option and sets the
related timeout parameters at the application level.

In Linux, when the TCP server program enables SO_KEEPALIVE option
but does not change the timeout period, the TCP server program times out
at the time set by the O.S. kernel keepalive parameters.
However, a TCP client program's timeout period seems somehow always 4 minutes
longer than the time set by the OS kernel parameters!

13-4-3-1-2 Solaris

Solaris recommends users not to change the tcp_keepalive_interval
and tcp_keepalive_abort_interval parameters in the operating system kernel.
We will discuss these two kernel parameters in the next section.

Instead, applications should use the setsockopt() function with
TCP_KEEPALIVE_THRESHOLD and TCP_KEEPALIVE_ABORT_THRESHOLD options,
as shown above, to change the keepalive related parameters just for
the application itself.

Note that the TCP_KEEPALIVE_THRESHOLD option in Solaris is similar to the TCP_KEEPIDLE option in Linux and AIX.
Besides, the TCP_KEEPALIVE_ABORT_THRESHOLD option in Solaris is sort of equivalent to the product of TCP_KEEPINTVL and TCP_KEEPCNT in Linux/AIX.

Level	Option name	Description
IPPROTO_TCP	TCP_KEEPALIVE_THRESHOLD	connection idle time before probe. This overrides tcp_keepalive_interval setting in O.S. kernel for a socket.
IPPROTO_TCP	TCP_KEEPALIVE_ABORT_THRESHOLD	time threshold to abort a connection after probe fails

If an application has the SO_KEEPALIVE socket option enabled, it can then use the TCP_KEEPALIVE_THRESHOLD socket option to change the time interval for initial probe and TCP_KEEPALIVE_ABORT_THRESHOLD socket option to change the time interval for aborting the connection.

So below are the keepalive options and their default values in Solaris which are tunable at application level via setsockopt():

```
TCP_KEEPALIVE_THRESHOLD (7200000 milliseconds = 2 hours)
TCP_KEEPALIVE_ABORT_THRESHOLD (480000 milliseconds = 8 minutes)
```

Figure 13-5 is a pair of client-server programs illustrating how to change the keepalive parameters at the application level in Solaris. These programs enable SO_KEEPALIVE and change parameters from application level.

Figure 13-5 Changing Keepalive Parameters at Application Level in Solaris -- tcpsrv_alive_sun.c and tcpclnt_alive_sun.c

(a) tcpsrv_alive_sun.c

```
/*
 * A connection-oriented server program using Stream socket.
 * Single-threaded server.
 * Tune parameters of SO_KEEPALIVE socket option in Oracle/Sun Solaris.
 * Copyright (c) 2002, 2014, 2018-2020 Mr. Jin-Jwei Chen. All rights reserved.
 */

#include <stdio.h>
#include <errno.h>
#include <sys/types.h>
#include <sys/socket.h>
#include <netinet/in.h>     /* protocols such as IPPROTO_TCP, ... */
#include <string.h>         /* memset() */
#include <stdlib.h>         /* atoi() */
#include <unistd.h>         /* close() */
#include <netinet/tcp.h>    /* TCP_KEEPIDLE, TCP_KEEPCNT, TCP_KEEPINTVL */

#define  BUFLEN       1024    /* size of message buffer */
#define  DEFSRVPORT   2344    /* default server port number */
#define  BACKLOG         5    /* length of listener queue */
```

```c
int main(int argc, char *argv[])
{
  int    ret, portnum_in=0;
  int    sfd;                          /* file descriptor of the listener socket */
  int    newsock;                      /* file descriptor of client data socket */
  struct sockaddr_in    srvaddr;       /* socket structure */
  int    srvaddrsz=sizeof(struct sockaddr_in);
  struct sockaddr_in    clntaddr;      /* socket structure */
  socklen_t    clntaddrsz=sizeof(struct sockaddr_in);
  in_port_t    portnum=DEFSRVPORT;     /* port number */
  char   inbuf[BUFLEN];                /* input message buffer */
  char   outbuf[BUFLEN];               /* output message buffer */
  size_t msglen;                       /* length of reply message */
  int    option;

  fprintf(stdout, "Connection-oriented server program ...\n");

  /* Get the port number from user, if any. */
  if (argc > 1)
    portnum_in = atoi(argv[1]);
  if (portnum_in <= 0)
  {
    fprintf(stderr, "Port number %d invalid, set to default value %u\n",
      portnum_in, DEFSRVPORT);
    portnum = DEFSRVPORT;
  }
  else
    portnum = portnum_in;

  /* Create the Stream server socket. */
  if ((sfd = socket(AF_INET, SOCK_STREAM, 0)) < 0)
  {
    fprintf(stderr, "Error: socket() failed, errno=%d\n", errno);
    return(-1);
  }

  /* Turn on SO_KEEPALIVE socket option. */
  option = 1;
  ret = setsockopt(sfd, SOL_SOCKET, SO_KEEPALIVE, &option, sizeof(option));
  if (ret < 0)
  {
    fprintf(stderr, "Error: setsockopt(SO_KEEPALIVE) failed, errno=%d\n", errno);
    close(sfd);
    return(-2);
  }
  else
    fprintf(stdout, "SO_KEEPALIVE socket option is enabled.\n");

  /* Set the TCP_KEEPALIVE_THRESHOLD socket option. This overrides the
   * tcp_keepalive_interval setting in Solaris kernel for the current socket.
   */
  option = 120000;   /* unit is ms */
  ret = setsockopt(sfd, IPPROTO_TCP, TCP_KEEPALIVE_THRESHOLD, &option,
sizeof(option));
  if (ret < 0)
```

```
  {
    fprintf(stderr, "Error: setsockopt(TCP_KEEPALIVE_THRESHOLD) failed, errno=%d\n",
errno);
    close(sfd);
    return(-4);
  }
  fprintf(stdout, "TCP_KEEPALIVE_THRESHOLD is reset to (%d)\n", option);

  /* Set the TCP_KEEPALIVE_ABORT_THRESHOLD socket option. */
  option = 60000;  /* unit is ms */
  ret = setsockopt(sfd, IPPROTO_TCP, TCP_KEEPALIVE_ABORT_THRESHOLD, &option,
       sizeof(option));
  if (ret < 0)
  {
    fprintf(stderr, "Error: setsockopt(TCP_KEEPALIVE_ABORT_THRESHOLD) failed,"
      " errno=%d\n", errno);
    close(sfd);
    return(-5);
  }
  fprintf(stdout, "TCP_KEEPALIVE_ABORT_THRESHOLD is reset to (%d)\n", option);

  /* Fill in the server socket address. */
  memset((void *)&srvaddr, 0, (size_t)srvaddrsz); /* clear the address buffer */
  srvaddr.sin_family = AF_INET;                    /* Internet socket */
  srvaddr.sin_addr.s_addr = htonl(INADDR_ANY);    /* server's IP address */
  srvaddr.sin_port = htons(portnum);              /* server's port number */

  /* Bind the server socket to its address. */
  if ((ret = bind(sfd, (struct sockaddr *)&srvaddr, srvaddrsz)) != 0)
  {
    fprintf(stderr, "Error: bind() failed, errno=%d\n", errno);
    close(sfd);
    return(-6);
  }

  /* Set maximum connection request queue length that we can fall behind. */
  if (listen(sfd, BACKLOG) == -1) {
    fprintf(stderr, "Error: listen() failed, errno=%d\n", errno);
    close(sfd);
    return(-7);
  }

  /* Wait for incoming connection requests from clients and service them. */
  while (1) {

    fprintf(stdout, "\nListening at port number %u ...\n", portnum);
    newsock = accept(sfd, (struct sockaddr *)&clntaddr, &clntaddrsz);
    if (newsock < 0)
    {
      fprintf(stderr, "Error: accept() failed, errno=%d\n", errno);
      close(sfd);
      return(-8);
    }

    fprintf(stdout, "Client Connected.\n");
```

```
  /* Set the reply message */
  sprintf(outbuf, "%s", "This is a reply from the server program.");
  msglen = strlen(outbuf);

  /* Receive and service requests from the current client. */
  while (1)
  {
    /* Receive a request from a client. */
    errno = 0;
    inbuf[0] = '\0';
    ret = recv(newsock, inbuf, BUFLEN, 0);
    if (ret > 0)
    {
      /* Process the request. We simply print the request message here. */
      inbuf[ret] = '\0';
      fprintf(stdout, "\nReceived the following request from client:\n%s\n",
        inbuf);

      /* Send a reply. */
      errno = 0;
      ret = send(newsock, outbuf, msglen, 0);
      if (ret == -1)
        fprintf(stderr, "Error: send() failed, errno=%d\n", errno);
      else
        fprintf(stdout, "%u of %u bytes of the reply was sent.\n", ret, msglen);
    }
    else if (ret < 0)
    {
      fprintf(stderr, "Error: recv() failed, errno=%d\n", errno);
      break;
    }
    else
    {
      /* The client may have disconnected. */
      fprintf(stdout, "The client may have disconnected.\n");
      break;
    }
  }  /* while - inner */
  close(newsock);

  /* The following two statements are for test only */
  close(sfd);
  break;

}  /* while - outer */
}
```

(b) tcpclnt_alive_sun.c

```
/*
 * A connection-oriented client program using Stream socket.
 * Tune parameters of SO_KEEPALIVE socket option in Oracle/Sun Solaris.
 * Copyright (c) 2002, 2014, 2018-2020 Mr. Jin-Jwei Chen. All rights reserved.
 */

#include <stdio.h>
```

```c
#include <errno.h>
#include <sys/types.h>
#include <sys/socket.h>
#include <netinet/in.h>        /* protocols such as IPPROTO_TCP, ... */
#include <string.h>            /* memset() */
#include <stdlib.h>            /* atoi() */
#include <netdb.h>             /* gethostbyname() */
#include <unistd.h>            /* close() */
#include <netinet/tcp.h>       /* TCP_KEEPIDLE, TCP_KEEPCNT, TCP_KEEPINTVL */
#include <arpa/inet.h>
#include <ctype.h>

#define    BUFLEN        1024      /* size of input message buffer */
#define    DEFSRVPORT    2344      /* default server port number */
#define    MAXMSGS          4      /* Maximum number of messages to send */
#define    NAMELEN         63

int main(int argc, char *argv[])
{
  int      ret;
  int      sfd;                                /* file descriptor of the socket */
  struct sockaddr_in      server;       /* socket structure */
  int      srvaddrsz=sizeof(struct sockaddr_in);
  struct sockaddr_in      fromaddr;  /* socket structure */
  socklen_t      fromaddrsz=sizeof(struct sockaddr_in);
  in_port_t      portnum=DEFSRVPORT; /* port number */
  char     inbuf[BUFLEN];                     /* input message buffer */
  char     outbuf[BUFLEN];                    /* output message buffer */
  size_t      msglen;                         /* length of reply message */
  size_t      msgnum=0;                       /* count of request message */
  size_t      len;
  unsigned int addr;
  char     server_name[NAMELEN+1] = "localhost";
  int      socket_type = SOCK_STREAM;
  struct hostent *hp;
  int      option;
  socklen_t  optlen;

  fprintf(stdout, "Connection-oriented client program ...\n\n");

  /* Get the host name or IP address from command line. */
  if (argc > 1)
  {
    len = strlen(argv[1]);
    if (len > NAMELEN)
      len = NAMELEN;
    strncpy(server_name, argv[1], len);
    server_name[len] = '\0';
  }

  /* Get the port number from command line. */
  if (argc > 2)
    portnum = atoi(argv[2]);
  if (portnum <= 0)
  {
    fprintf(stderr, "Port number %d invalid, set to default value %u\n",
```

```
        portnum, DEFSRVPORT);
    portnum = DEFSRVPORT;
}

/* Translate the host name or IP address into server socket address. */
if (isalpha(server_name[0]))
{   /* A host name is given. */
    hp = gethostbyname(server_name);
}
else
{   /* Convert the n.n.n.n IP address to a number. */
    addr = inet_addr(server_name);
    hp = gethostbyaddr((char *)&addr, sizeof(addr), AF_INET);
}
if (hp == NULL )
{
    fprintf(stderr,"Error: cannot get address for [%s], errno=%d\n",
      server_name, errno);
    return(-1);
}

/* Copy the resolved information into the sockaddr_in structure. */
memset(&server, 0, sizeof(server));
memcpy(&(server.sin_addr), hp->h_addr, hp->h_length);
server.sin_family = hp->h_addrtype;
server.sin_port = htons(portnum);

/* Open a socket. */
sfd = socket(AF_INET, socket_type, 0);
if (sfd < 0)
{
    fprintf(stderr,"Error: socket() failed, errno=%d\n", errno);
    return (-2);
}

/* Get the SO_KEEPALIVE socket option. */
option = 0;
optlen = sizeof(option);
ret = getsockopt(sfd, SOL_SOCKET, SO_KEEPALIVE, &option, &optlen);
if (ret < 0)
{
    fprintf(stderr, "Error: getsockopt(SO_KEEPALIVE) failed, errno=%d\n", errno);
    close(sfd);
    return(-3);
}
if (option == 0)
    fprintf(stdout, "SO_KEEPALIVE socket option was not set (%d) by default.\n",
      option);

/* Set the SO_KEEPALIVE socket option. Do this before connect. */
option = 1;
ret = setsockopt(sfd, SOL_SOCKET, SO_KEEPALIVE, &option, sizeof(option));
if (ret < 0)
{
    fprintf(stderr, "Error: setsockopt(SO_KEEPALIVE) failed, errno=%d\n", errno);
    close(sfd);
```

```
      return(-4);
   }
   else
     fprintf(stdout, "SO_KEEPALIVE socket option is now enabled.\n");

   /* Get the TCP_KEEPALIVE_THRESHOLD socket option. */
   option = 0;
   optlen = sizeof(option);
   ret = getsockopt(sfd, IPPROTO_TCP, TCP_KEEPALIVE_THRESHOLD, &option, &optlen);
   if (ret < 0)
   {
     fprintf(stderr, "Error: getsockopt(TCP_KEEPALIVE_THRESHOLD) failed, errno=%d\n",
errno);
     close(sfd);
     return(-5);
   }
   fprintf(stdout, "TCP_KEEPALIVE_THRESHOLD's original setting is (%d)\n", option);

   /* Set the TCP_KEEPALIVE_THRESHOLD socket option. This overrides the
    * tcp_keepalive_interval setting in Solaris kernel for the current socket.
    */
   option = 300000;   /* unit is ms */
   ret = setsockopt(sfd, IPPROTO_TCP, TCP_KEEPALIVE_THRESHOLD, &option, optlen);
   if (ret < 0)
   {
     fprintf(stderr, "Error: setsockopt(TCP_KEEPALIVE_THRESHOLD) failed, errno=%d\n",
errno);
     close(sfd);
     return(-6);
   }
   fprintf(stdout, "TCP_KEEPALIVE_THRESHOLD is reset to (%d)\n", option);

   /* Get the TCP_KEEPALIVE_THRESHOLD socket option. */
   option = 0;
   ret = getsockopt(sfd, IPPROTO_TCP, TCP_KEEPALIVE_THRESHOLD, &option, &optlen);
   if (ret < 0)
   {
     fprintf(stderr, "Error: getsockopt(TCP_KEEPALIVE_THRESHOLD) failed, errno=%d\n",
errno);
     close(sfd);
     return(-7);
   }
   fprintf(stdout, "TCP_KEEPALIVE_THRESHOLD's current setting is (%d)\n", option);

   /* Get the TCP_KEEPALIVE_ABORT_THRESHOLD socket option. */
   option = 0;
   ret = getsockopt(sfd, IPPROTO_TCP, TCP_KEEPALIVE_ABORT_THRESHOLD, &option,
&optlen);
   if (ret < 0)
   {
     fprintf(stderr, "Error: getsockopt(TCP_KEEPALIVE_ABORT_THRESHOLD) failed,
errno=%d\n", errno);
     close(sfd);
     return(-8);
   }
```

```
  fprintf(stdout, "TCP_KEEPALIVE_ABORT_THRESHOLD's original setting is (%d)\n",
option);

  /* Set the TCP_KEEPALIVE_ABORT_THRESHOLD socket option. */
  option = 60000;   /* unit is ms */
  ret = setsockopt(sfd, IPPROTO_TCP, TCP_KEEPALIVE_ABORT_THRESHOLD, &option, optlen);
  if (ret < 0)
  {
    fprintf(stderr, "Error: setsockopt(TCP_KEEPALIVE_ABORT_THRESHOLD) failed,
errno=%d\n", errno);
    close(sfd);
    return(-9);
  }
  fprintf(stdout, "TCP_KEEPALIVE_ABORT_THRESHOLD is reset to (%d)\n", option);

  /* Get the TCP_KEEPALIVE_ABORT_THRESHOLD socket option. */
  option = 0;
  ret = getsockopt(sfd, IPPROTO_TCP, TCP_KEEPALIVE_ABORT_THRESHOLD, &option,
&optlen);
  if (ret < 0)
  {
    fprintf(stderr, "Error: getsockopt(TCP_KEEPALIVE_ABORT_THRESHOLD) failed,
errno=%d\n", errno);
    close(sfd);
    return(-10);
  }
  fprintf(stdout, "TCP_KEEPALIVE_ABORT_THRESHOLD's current setting is (%d)\n",
option);

  /* Connect to the server. */
  ret = connect(sfd, (struct sockaddr *)&server, srvaddrsz);
  if (ret == -1)
  {
    fprintf(stderr, "Error: connect() failed, errno=%d\n", errno);
    close(sfd);
    return(-11);
  }

  fprintf(stdout, "\nSend request messages to server at port %d\n", portnum);

  /* Send request messages to the server and process the reply messages. */
  while (msgnum < MAXMSGS)
  {
    /* Send a request message to the server. */
    sprintf(outbuf, "%s%4d%s", "This is request message ", ++msgnum,
      " from the client program.");
    msglen = strlen(outbuf);
    errno = 0;

    ret = send(sfd, outbuf, msglen, 0);
    if (ret >= 0)
    {
      /* Print a warning if not entire message was sent. */
      if (ret == msglen)
        fprintf(stdout, "\n%u bytes of message were successfully sent.\n",
          msglen);
```

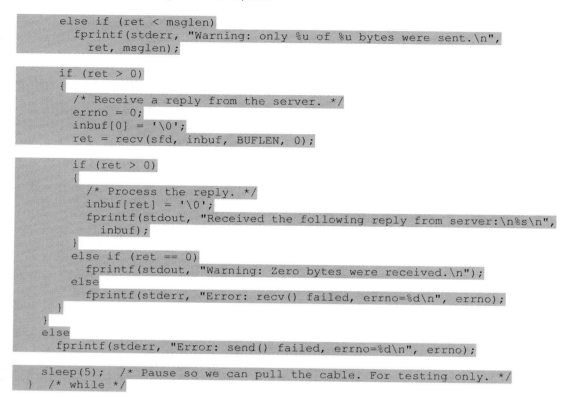

```
        else if (ret < msglen)
          fprintf(stderr, "Warning: only %u of %u bytes were sent.\n",
            ret, msglen);

      if (ret > 0)
      {
        /* Receive a reply from the server. */
        errno = 0;
        inbuf[0] = '\0';
        ret = recv(sfd, inbuf, BUFLEN, 0);

        if (ret > 0)
        {
          /* Process the reply. */
          inbuf[ret] = '\0';
          fprintf(stdout, "Received the following reply from server:\n%s\n",
            inbuf);
        }
        else if (ret == 0)
          fprintf(stdout, "Warning: Zero bytes were received.\n");
        else
          fprintf(stderr, "Error: recv() failed, errno=%d\n", errno);
      }
      else
        fprintf(stderr, "Error: send() failed, errno=%d\n", errno);

    sleep(5);  /* Pause so we can pull the cable. For testing only. */
  } /* while */

  close(sfd);
}
```

Summary

In Oracle/Sun Solaris, a program, a TCP server or a TCP client,
detects the network outage at the time set by the program itself
as long as the program enables SO_KEEPALIVE socket option and sets the
related timeout parameters at the application level.

13-4-3-1-3 HP-UX

HP-UX 11i Version 3 has the following three SO_KEEPALIVE parameters that
can be tuned from the application level. An application can enable the
SO_KEEPALIVE socket option and alter these parameters to control the
timeout period for a lost connection on a per socket basis.

```
------------------------------------------------------------------------
Level          Option name     Description
----------     -----------     -------------------------------------------
IPPROTO_TCP    TCP_KEEPIDLE    connection idle time before first keepalive probe
IPPROTO_TCP    TCP_KEEPINTVL   time interval between keepalive probe packets
IPPROTO_TCP    TCP_KEEPCNT     maximum number of keepalive probe packets
IPPROTO_TCP    TCP_KEEPINIT    connection establishment timeout, unit is seconds.
------------------------------------------------------------------------
```

TCP_KEEPIDLE

When the SO_KEEPALIVE option is enabled, TCP probes a connection that
has been idle for an amount of time specified by this parameter.
The default value for this idle period is 2 hours.

This option takes an int value, with a range of 1 to 32767.
The time unit is seconds.

TCP_KEEPINTVL

When the SO_KEEPALIVE option is enabled, TCP starts probing an idle
connection after the connection has been idle for TCP_KEEPIDLE seconds.
If the remote system does not respond to a keepalive probe,
TCP retransmits the probe packet after TCP_KEEPINTVL seconds.
Range of integer values allowed for this option is 1 to 32767.

TCP_KEEPCNT

This option controls how many times TCP retransmits the probe packet
before declaring the connection dead if the remote system does not
respond to a keepalive probe.
This option takes an integer value, with a range of 1 to 32767.

Hence, once TCP starts probing into an idle connection, if the remote
system does not respond to any of the probe, then after
(TCP_KEEPINTVL * TCP_KEEPCNT) seconds, the connection will be deemed
broken.

Note that these three parameters are the same as those used in
Linux and AIX. Therefore, the example programs listed in Figure 13-4
for Linux and AIX work for HP-UX 11i V3 and on as well.

It's probably worth mentioning that as you will see in the section below,
at the operating system kernel level, the tunable parameters in HP-UX
are tcp_keepalive_interval and tcp_ip_abort_interval, which is different
than Linux and AIX.

In addition to the above three parameters, HP-UX also supports
a parameter for tuning connection establishment timeout.

TCP_KEEPINIT

If a TCP connection cannot be established within some amount of time,
TCP will time out the connect attempt. The default value for this
initial connection establishment timeout is 75 seconds.
The TCP_KEEPINIT socket option can be used to change this initial
timeout period for a given socket. The value this option is set to
represents the number of seconds to wait before a connect attempt
is timed out. The range of this value is 1 to 32767.

Note that the TCP_KEEPINIT option is a bit tricky.
When you call getsockopt() function to get the value set by the
operating system by default, you get back 75000. But the values that
you can use to set this parameter is from 1 to 32767.

The TCP_KEEPINIT option is supported in HP-UX only.
It is not supported in Linux, AIX or Solaris.

13-4-3-1-4 Apple Darwin and FreeBSD Unix

Apple Darwin on Mac Pro supports the SO_KEEPALIVE socket option, too.
The tunable parameters at application level are the same as Linux, AIX and
HPUX except that the TCP_KEEPIDLE parameter is called TCP_KEEPALIVE in Darwin
at the application level. Note that it is called net.inet.tcp.keepidle inside
the Darwin O.S. kernel! Don't know why this inconsistency inside Darwin.

The three tunable parameters that can be changed from the application
level in Apple Darwin and their usual default values are as below:

```
TCP_KEEPALIVE : 7200 seconds (This is called TCP_KEEPIDLE in other platforms.)
TCP_KEEPINTVL : 75 seconds
TCP_KEEPCNT   : 8
```

These parameters are explained below:

TCP_KEEPALIVE (TCP_KEEPIDLE)

This is the amount of time, in seconds, that the connection must be
idle before keepalive probes (if enabled) are sent to the peer.

The corresponding kernel tunable parameter is net.inet.tcp.keepidle
which sets a global default value for all applications that do not
change this value. The time unit here is in milliseconds.

TCP_KEEPINTVL

This is the time interval, in seconds, between keepalive probe packets
are sent to a peer.

The corresponding kernel tunable parameter is net.inet.tcp.keepintvl
which sets a global default value for all applications that do not
change this value.

TCP_KEEPCNT

After this number of probes are sent, if no response, then the TCP
connection will be dropped. That is, the system will kill the
connection.

The operating system kernel parameter net.inet.tcp.keepcnt sets the
global default value for all applications that do not change this value.

If any of these three values is set on a listening socket, the value is
inherited by the newly created socket upon accept().

Note that there doesn't seem to be a tunable parameter at the application
level corresponding to the kernel tunable parameter net.inet.tcp.keepinit.

The programs listed in Figure 13-4 above work for Linux, AIX, HPUX and

```
Apple Darwin.
```

13-4-3-1-5 Windows

Windows does not implement the IPPROTO_TCP Socket Options that enable changing of the keepalive tunable parameters at application level.

13-4-3-2 Change TCP Keepalive Parameters at Operating System Kernel Level

Please be very cautious about changing the TCP keepalive related parameters in any operating system kernel because the change will impact all applications running on the system unless an application has overridden these settings from within the application itself.

Lowering the socket connection abort/timeout value might cause unnecessary network traffic and also increase the chance of premature termination of the connection in case of a transient network problem.

13-4-3-2-1 Linux

What to Tune

Linux kernel has the following three keepalive tunable parameters:

```
net.ipv4.tcp_keepalive_time (7200 seconds)
   (This is the time a TCP socket must have been idle before the first
    Keep-Alive packet is sent by the operating system.)
net.ipv4.tcp_keepalive_probes (9)
   (This is the number of Keep-Alive probes that will be sent.)
net.ipv4.tcp_keepalive_intvl (75 seconds)
   (This is the time in-between successive Keep-Alive probes.)
```

The values in parentheses are the default values.

The currently configured TCP Keep-Alive settings in a Linux kernel can be found by displaying the contents of these files:

```
$ cat /proc/sys/net/ipv4/tcp_keepalive_time
$ cat /proc/sys/net/ipv4/tcp_keepalive_probes
$ cat /proc/sys/net/ipv4/tcp_keepalive_intvl
```

How to Tune

To make permanent changes that will persist through a reboot, do the following:

Become the super user and edit the /etc/sysctl.conf file.
Set the parameters in the file. For example,

```
net.ipv4.tcp_keepalive_time = 600
net.ipv4.tcp_keepalive_probes = 4
net.ipv4.tcp_keepalive_intvl = 30
```

Run the following command to make the change go into effect:

```
# /sbin/sysctl -p /etc/sysctl.conf
```

To change the parameters' values in memory only, do:

```
# /sbin/sysctl -w net.ipv4.tcp_keepalive_time=600
net.ipv4.tcp_keepalive_probes=4 net.ipv4.tcp_keepalive_intvl=30
```

or
```
# echo 600 > /proc/sys/net/ipv4/tcp_keepalive_time
# echo   4 > /proc/sys/net/ipv4/tcp_keepalive_probes
# echo  30 > /proc/sys/net/ipv4/tcp_keepalive_intvl
```

The example commands above change the TCP keepalive timeout to 12 minutes (600+30*4=720 seconds). With it, your application will detect dead TCP connections at or after 12 minutes.

Notice that the changes made through the 'sysctl -w' command is not persistent.

Note that if an application does not turn on SO_KEEPALIVE option, or it turns on the option but does not change any of the keepalive related parameters, then whatever keepalive settings the operating system has will determine how soon a broken network connection gets detected. For instance, in a Linux system, if the operating system has the kernel parameter settings as shown above, then even if the application does not turn on the SO_KEEPALIVE socket option, a broken connection can be detected in around 12 minutes or so. This is just for illustration purpose. This value is probably way too small for most applications.

Be aware that Linux does not implement a separate set of these parameters for IPV6. So the above network TCP IPv4 settings apply to IPv6 as well.

13-4-3-2-2 AIX

What to Tune

AIX kernel has the following three keepalive tunable parameters:

tcp_keepidle:
  Specifies the length of time that a TCP connection must be idle before the TCP protocol layer sends the first keepalive probe packet to validate the connection. The unit of time is measured in half-seconds.

tcp_keepintvl:
  Specifies the time interval between keepalive probe packets sent to validate the TCP connection. The unit is half-seconds.

tcp_keepcnt:
  Specifies the maximum number of keepalive packets to be sent to validate a connection.

Note that if a socket is a child socket, such as the one created by the accept() call of a TCP listening server socket, the values of these parameters are inherited from its parent socket.

Below are the names of these keepalive kernel parameters and their default values (in parentheses) in AIX:

```
tcp_keepidle (14400 half seconds = 7200 seconds)
tcp_keepcnt (8)
tcp_keepintvl (150 half seconds = 75 seconds)
```

How to Tune

IBM AIX uses the no command to set networking parameters.
To set the parameters temporarily until reboot:

```
# no -o tcp_keepidle=1200
# no -o tcp_keepintvl=60
# no -o tcp_keepcnt=4
```

Note that the time unit is half-seconds.

To set the parameters now and make the changes last after reboot:

```
# no -p -o tcp_keepidle=1200
# no -p -o tcp_keepintvl=60
# no -p -o tcp_keepcnt=4
```

To query the current setting:

```
# no -o tcp_keepidle
# no -a |grep tcp_keepidle
```

13-4-3-2-3 Solaris

What to Tune

Solaris has the following two keepalive tunable parameters in its kernel:

tcp_keepalive_interval:

The TCP keep-alive mechanism is enabled by setting the SO_KEEPALIVE socket option on a TCP socket.

The tcp_keepalive_interval parameter specifies the time interval that a TCP connection must have been idle before the system starts probing the connection for an outage. If the peer does not respond to the probe after eight minutes, the TCP connection is aborted.
The default value for this parameter is 7200000 milliseconds (2 hours). The range of values allowed for this parameter is from 10 seconds to 10 days.

Note that Solaris recommends against changing this parameter. Instead, applications should use the TCP_KEEPALIVE_THRESHOLD socket option to override this system level setting for each individual socket used by the applications.

tcp_keepalive_abort_interval:

919

This ndd parameter sets a default time threshold to abort a TCP connection after the keepalive probing has failed.
This parameter's value is an unsigned integer measured in milliseconds. A value of zero means that TCP should never time out and abort the connection when probing. The default value is 480000 ms (8 minutes). Range of values allowed for this parameter is 0 to 8 minutes.

This abort time threshold can also be changed from within an application on a per socket basis by calling the setsockopt() function with the TCP_KEEPALIVE_ABORT_THRESHOLD option.

Solaris recommends against changing the value of this kernel parameter. Instead, the tuning should be done at the application level.

Notice that Solaris differs from Linux and AIX in that the retry probe period is determined by a single parameter tcp_keepalive_abort_interval, instead of the product of two parameters. Therefore, there are no corresponding kernel parameters for retry interval or retry count.

Below are the keepalive kernel parameters and their default values in Solaris:

    tcp_keepalive_interval (7200000 milliseconds = 2 hours)
    tcp_keepalive_abort_interval (480000 milliseconds = 8 minutes)

How to Tune

Oracle/Sun Solaris uses the ndd command with the -set option to tune networking parameters. For example, to tune the tcp_keepalive_interval parameter, you do:

    # ndd -set /dev/tcp tcp_keepalive_interval 600000

The time unit is milliseconds.

To query the current setting:

    # ndd -get /dev/tcp tcp_keepalive_interval

13-4-3-2-4 HP-UX

What to Tune

The algorithm of sending TCP keepalive packets has been changed between HP HP-UX 10 and HP-UX 11.

HP HP-UX 11 has the following operating system kernel parameters related to TCP KEEPALIVE feature:

    tcp_keepalive_interval - idle time before starting keepalive probe packets

    tcp_ip_abort_interval - wait time before declaring connection is dead
                            if keepalive probe is not ack-ed

The parameter tcp_keepalive_interval defines the amount of time that

TCP waits for an idle connection before sending keepalive probing packets. The default is 7200000 ms = 2 hours.

The parameter tcp_ip_abort_interval defines the total amount of time that the system will continue keepalive probing before declaring the connection dead. The default is 600000 ms = 10 minutes.

If the keepalive packet is not ACK-ed by the remote TCP, the retransmission time-out will eventually exceed tcp_ip_abort_interval. The connection will be terminated at that time.

This means in HP-UX by default an idle TCP connection is terminated in 2 hours 10 minutes.

The parameters and their default values in HP-UX are as follows:

```
tcp_keepalive_interval (7200000 ms = 2 hours)
tcp_ip_abort_interval  (600000 ms = 10 minutes)
```

Note that once an application invokes the close() function on a socket, the keepalive mechanism will be automatically enabled for the connection, regardless of the setting of SO_KEEPALIVE. In this case, keepalive probe packets will be sent after tcp_keepalive_detached_interval milliseconds for the detached connection.

Note that you do not set the value of the tcp_ip_abort_interval parameter to be lower than tcp_time_wait_interval, which specifies the time connections need to be in the TIME_WAIT state before closing down. In addition, you should not set this parameter to be less than four minutes (240000 ms); otherwise the port number may be prematurely re-used.

How to Tune

Similar to Solaris, HP-UX uses the ndd command with the -set option to tune TCP parameters:

```
# ndd -set [network] [device] [parameter] [value]
```

For example:

To set tcp_keepalive_interval to 10 minutes:

```
# ndd -set /dev/tcp tcp_keepalive_interval 600000
```

The time unit is milliseconds.

To query the current setting:

```
# ndd -get /dev/tcp tcp_keepalive_interval
7200000
```

```
# ndd -get /dev/tcp tcp_ip_abort_interval
600000
```

13-4-3-2-5 Apple Darwin and FreeBSD Unix

What to Tune

In Apple Darwin and FreeBSD, the operating system kernel has the following tunable parameters which may be changed via sysctl for tuning KEEPALIVE behavior. Note that these settings affect all socket applications unless an application makes its own settings.

net.inet.tcp.keepidle

This is the amount of time in milliseconds that a connection must be idle before keepalive probes (if enabled) are sent. The default is 7200000 msec (2 hours).

net.inet.tcp.keepintvl

This is the time interval in milliseconds between keepalive probes are sent to the remote machine when no response is received on a keepalive probe. The default is 75000 msec.

net.inet.tcp.keepcnt

This is the total number of probes that will be sent to the remote machine before the system drops (kills) the connection when the remote machine does not respond to the probes. The default is 8 probe packets.

net.inet.tcp.always_keepalive

This is the system-wide switch to enable (1) or disable (0) keepalive probes. Default to 0. It can be changed via 'sysctl -w' command.

If this is turned on, then for all TCP connections, the operating system kernel will periodically send a probe packet to the remote host of the connection to verify the connection is still alive.

net.inet.tcp.keepinit

Timeout period in milliseconds for new, non-established TCP connections. The default is 75000 msec.

Below are the default settings usually seen on an Apple Mac Pro:

```
net.inet.tcp.keepinit: 75000
net.inet.tcp.keepidle: 7200000
net.inet.tcp.keepintvl: 75000
net.inet.tcp.keepcnt: 8
net.inet.tcp.always_keepalive: 0
```

Unlike other operating systems, Apple Darwin and BSD Unix have a kernel tunable parameter, net.inet.tcp.always_keepalive, to centrally control whether the TCP KEEPALIVE feature is turned on or off for all socket applications. By default, the value of this parameter is 0 (disabled). This means the operating system kernel by default doesn't attempt to detect dead TCP connections by transmitting "keepalives" probing messages over a connection.

In addition, unlike Linux which uses seconds for the unit of these times, in Apple Darwin and BSD Unix, the unit of these time values is milliseconds. It is a bit confusing that Apple Darwin uses seconds as unit for SO_KEEPALIVE parameters tunable at application level but milliseconds for parameters in the O.S. kernel.

How to Tune

All of the parameters listed above can be changed by the sysctl command. To make your changes permanent (persistent through reboots), you should add them to the /etc/sysctl.conf file.
Note that when I use the sudo command to try to change the parameters in Apple Darwin kernel, only net.inet.tcp.keepinit works.
net.inet.tcp.keepidle and net.inet.tcp.keepintvl don't seem to change.

```
jim@Jims-MacBook-Air mac % sysctl -q net.inet.tcp.keepidle
net.inet.tcp.keepidle: 7200000
jim@Jims-MacBook-Air mac % sudo sysctl -w net.inet.tcp.keepidle=7000000
net.inet.tcp.keepidle: 7200000 -> 7200000
jim@Jims-MacBook-Air mac % sysctl -q net.inet.tcp.keepidle
net.inet.tcp.keepidle: 7200000
==> It won't change!

jim@Jims-MacBook-Air mac % sysctl -q net.inet.tcp.keepintvl
net.inet.tcp.keepintvl: 75000
jim@Jims-MacBook-Air mac % sudo sysctl -w net.inet.tcp.keepintvl=3000
net.inet.tcp.keepintvl: 75000 -> 75000
jim@Jims-MacBook-Air mac % sysctl -q net.inet.tcp.keepintvl
net.inet.tcp.keepintvl: 75000
==> This does not change either!

jim@Jims-MacBook-Air mac % sysctl -q net.inet.tcp.keepcnt
net.inet.tcp.keepcnt: 8
jim@Jims-MacBook-Air mac % sudo sysctl -w  net.inet.tcp.keepcnt=2
net.inet.tcp.keepcnt: 8 -> 2
jim@Jims-MacBook-Air mac % sysctl -q net.inet.tcp.keepcnt
net.inet.tcp.keepcnt: 2
==>This one changed!
```

The currently configured settings can be viewed via the sysctl command:

```
$ sysctl -a | grep net.inet.tcp
```
or
```
$ sysctl net.inet.tcp | grep -E "keepidle|keepintvl|keepcnt"
```

The formula for calculating the maximum time that a dead TCP connection can hang around before it is disconnected by the operating system is

    net.inet.tcp.keepidle + (net.inet.tcp.keepintvl x net.inet.tcp.keepcnt)

13-4-3-2-6 Windows

Microsoft Windows uses registry keys for tunable parameters.

TCP/IP parameters are located in the following registry location:

\HKEY_LOCAL_MACHINE\System\CurrentControlSet\Services\TCPIP\Parameters

If the KeepAliveTime parameter does not exist, you will need to create it.
Set the value after the KeepAliveTime parameter exists.
The time specified is in milliseconds.

To set or get the parameter value, click Start button, run regedit.exe,
and then navigate to the above registry key location.
After setting the parameter(s), you may have to reboot your system
for your changes to take effect.

Parameter name	Data Type	Description	Default Value (in ms)
KeepAliveTime	REG_DWORD	wait time (ms) before probe	7200000 (2 hours)
KeepAliveInterval	REG_DWORD	time between probe packets	1000 (1 second)
TcpMaxDataRetransmissions	REG_DWORD	number of retries	5

13-4-3-3 Summary of SO_KEEPALIVE Socket Option

- Enabling the SO_KEEPALIVE socket option from within your application
  allows for faster detection of a network connection outage resulted
  from losing either a network link or a remote node.
  This is a socket option at the SOL_SOCKET level.

- There is one socket option to turn on from within an application.
  And there are up to three tunable parameters to change at the
  application level and also at the operating system kernel level.

- Enabling the SO_KEEPALIVE option is done via a call to setsockopt()
  with level=SOL_SOCKET and optname=SO_KEEPALIVE. This is so that your
  application won't hang "forever", or days, in case the network connection
  is lost and does not come back. Turning on or off the SO_KEEPALIVE option
  must be done before a connection is made on the socket. This code is
  identical across all POSIX-compliant operating systems. Enabling
  SO_KEEPALIVE option from within an application impacts only one
  socket and one application.

- Changing the keepalive tunable parameters at application level is done by
  calling setsockopt() with level=IPPROTO_TCP. This allows your application
  to have its own timeout period independent from whatever set in the
  operating system. The default timeout period set in the operating system
  kernel is usually two hours, which may be too long for some applications.
  Again, changing these parameters from within an application impacts only
  one socket and one application.

  Changing the SO_KEEPALIVE tunable parameters should be done before a
  connection is made on the socket.

  This part of code is almost the same across all POSIX-compliant operating
  systems. As our example programs show, the code is identical between

Linux, AIX and HPUX. It also true for Apple Darwin except it uses a different name for one of the three tunable parameters. Unfortunately, Solaris goes its own way on this.

- **Keepalive tunable parameters at application level**
  These are socket options at the IPPROTO_TCP level.

  ```
  Linux: TCP_KEEPIDLE   TCP_KEEPINTVL   TCP_KEEPCNT
  AIX:   TCP_KEEPIDLE   TCP_KEEPINTVL   TCP_KEEPCNT
  HP-UX: TCP_KEEPIDLE   TCP_KEEPINTVL   TCP_KEEPCNT
  Apple Darwin: TCP_KEEPALIVE   TCP_KEEPINTVL   TCP_KEEPCNT
  Solaris: TCP_KEEPALIVE_THRESHOLD   TCP_KEEPALIVE_ABORT_THRESHOLD
  ```

  These are the keepalive tunable parameters at application level that can be tuned by each application via the setsockopt() function call.

- The tunable parameters at operating system kernel level affect all applications unless an application has overridden them.
  These parameters have different names in different operating systems. Their meanings might differ as well. The operating system command used to change them is different too. The need to change these is rare. Super user privilege is required to make these changes.

- **Keepalive tunable parameters at O.S. kernel level**

  ```
  Linux: tcp_keepalive_time tcp_keepalive_intvl  tcp_keepalive_probes
  AIX:   tcp_keepidle        tcp_keepintvl           tcp_keepcnt
  Solaris: tcp_keepalive_interval  tcp_keepalive_abort_interval
  HP-UX:  tcp_keepalive_interval  tcp_ip_abort_interval
  Apple Darwin: net.inet.tcp.keepidle net.inet.tcp.keepintvl net.inet.tcp.keepcnt
  Windows: KeepAliveTime     KeepAliveInterval      TcpMaxDataRetransmissions
  ```

- The SO_KEEPALIVE option applies to connected sockets only.

- As for detecting network connection outage, an application program gets three different kinds of behavior depending on what the application and the operating system do.

  (a)
  By default, the SO_KEEPALIVE socket option is turned off in most operating systems.

  When the SO_KEEPALIVE option is off, applications are getting the default behavior of the TCP protocol specification, not the local OS kernel settings as specified by the OS kernel parameters related to the SO_KEEPALIVE option.

  This means a socket program may just hang forever or for days if the network connection is lost. This is especially true for a TCP server program (blocking on recv()). AIX, Solaris and Linux all have this behavior.

  (b)
  If the application itself turns on the SO_KEEPALIVE option but without changing any parameters related to this option, then it will get the operating system kernel's settings of parameters for this option.

For example, in a Linux system, very often the default settings in the
OS kernel will be the following:

```
net.ipv4.tcp_keepalive_time = 7200
net.ipv4.tcp_keepalive_probes = 2
net.ipv4.tcp_keepalive_intvl = 30
```

This means the peer death or broken network will be detected after
7200+2*30 = 7260 seconds = 121 minutes.

Note that this time may be still too long for some applications.

(c)
If an application program turns on the SO_KEEPALIVE option and further
tunes the option's application level parameters from within the application
itself, then the broken network condition will be detected after the time
that the application has set in itself has elapsed.

For instance, if a server program turns on the SO_KEEPALIVE option and
also sets the following parameter values using the setsockopt() call,

```
TCP_KEEPIDLE   = 300
TCP_KEEPCNT    = 2
TCP_KEEPINTVL  = 30
```

Then the network outage will be detected after 300+2*30=360 seconds = 6 minutes.

- A socket program (client or server) must enable the SO_KEEPALIVE socket
  option first before it changes the keepalive tunable parameters.
  Simply changing the tunable parameters with the SO_KEEPALIVE socket
  option disabled will have no effect! The enabling and tuning must be
  done before a connection is made.

- A client program can do this alone without the server doing the same.
  It works for the client.

13-5 The SO_LINGER Socket Option

The SO_LINGER option controls how to deal with unsent buffered data
queued on a socket when a close() function is called on the socket.
The options are attempting to deliver it or discarding it.
The behavior of this option is protocol specific.

Turning on the SO_LINGER option on a socket allows the calling thread or
process to indicate that when a close() is called on the socket, the
system should attempt to deliver the remaining unsent data up to the
specified timeout period, or simply discard it. If the specified timeout
period expires and there is still some unsent buffered data, then discard it.

The SO_LINGER option is controlled via a structure of two elements -- the
"struct linger", as shown below:

```
/* Structure used to manipulate the SO_LINGER option.  */
struct linger
```

```
{
  int l_onoff;              /* Nonzero means to linger on close.  */
  int l_linger;             /* Time to linger.  */
};
```

Setting the value of the l_onoff member of the structure to zero is to turn SO_LINGER option off. Setting its value to a non-zero value is to turn SO_LINGER option on. While the option is on, the value of the l_linger field is the number of seconds the close() call should wait before it returns in case not all data is sent.

To query or change the setting of the SO_LINGER option, the option value (i.e. the fourth) argument of the getsockopt() or setsockopt() call must be a linger structure (i.e. of type "struct linger"). A getsockopt() call on the SO_LINGER option returns two values in the linger structure while a setsockopt() call for the same option must provide these two values.

By default, the SO_LINGER socket option is turned off according to the POSIX Standard. This means the value of the l_onoff member of the 'struct linger' is zero, lingering off. And the value of the l_linger member of the linger structure is also zero.

Figure 13-6 is a pair of client server programs that get the current SO_LINGER setting and then turn it on with a 15 seconds timeout. The example programs are only for demonstration. It is written in a way such that it demonstrates the potential issue with the close() call and the way to avoid it.

Figure 13-6 Turn on SO_LINGER socket option (tcpsrv_bufsz_linger.c and tcpclnt_bufsz_linger.c)

(a) tcpsrv_bufsz_linger.c

```
/*
 * A connection-oriented server program using Stream socket.
 * Single-threaded server.
 * With socket buffer size options (SO_SNDBUF and SO_RCVBUF).
 * Also turning on SO_KEEPALIVE and SO_LINGER socket options.
 * Usage: tcpsrv_bufsz_linger port_num bigbuf linger
 * Authored by Mr. Jin-Jwei Chen.
 * Copyright (c) 1993-2016, 2018, 2020 Mr. Jin-Jwei Chen. All rights reserved.
 */

#include <stdio.h>
#include <errno.h>
#include <sys/types.h>
#include <sys/socket.h>
#include <netinet/in.h>       /* protocols such as IPPROTO_TCP, ... */
#include <string.h>           /* memset() */
#include <stdlib.h>           /* atoi() */
#include <sys/time.h>         /* gettimeofday *//* TEST ONLY */
#include <unistd.h>           /* close() */

#define BUFLEN      1024      /* size of message buffer */
#define DEFSRVPORT  2344      /* default server port number */
```

```
#define   BACKLOG        5      /* length of listener queue */
#define   SOCKBUFSZ   1048576   /* socket buffer size */
#define   INBUFSZ     1048576   /* socket input buffer size */

int main(int argc, char *argv[])
{
  int     ret, portnum_in=0;
  int     sfd;                       /* file descriptor of the listener socket */
  int     newsock;                   /* file descriptor of client data socket */
  struct sockaddr_in    srvaddr;     /* socket structure */
  int     srvaddrsz=sizeof(struct sockaddr_in);
  struct sockaddr_in    clntaddr;    /* socket structure */
  socklen_t    clntaddrsz=sizeof(struct sockaddr_in);
  in_port_t    portnum=DEFSRVPORT;   /* port number */
  char    *inbufp = NULL;            /* pointer to input message buffer */
  char    outbuf[BUFLEN];            /* output message buffer */
  size_t msglen;                     /* length of reply message */
  int     option;
  socklen_t  optlen;
  int     bigbuf = 0;            /* increase socket buffer size (off by default) */
  int     lingeron = 0;          /* socket linger option (off by default) */
  struct linger    solinger;     /* for SO_LINGER option */
  int     totalBytes = 0;        /* total # of bytes received */

  fprintf(stdout, "Connection-oriented server program ...\n\n");

  /* Get the port number from user, if any. */
  if (argc > 1)
    portnum_in = atoi(argv[1]);
  if (portnum_in <= 0)
  {
    fprintf(stderr, "Port number %d invalid, set to default value %u\n\n",
       portnum_in, DEFSRVPORT);
    portnum = DEFSRVPORT;
  }
  else
    portnum = portnum_in;

  /* Get switch to increase socket receive buffer size. */
  if (argc > 2)
    bigbuf = atoi(argv[2]);
  if (bigbuf < 0)
  {
    fprintf(stderr, "%s is an invalid switch value, use 1 or 0.\n", argv[2]);
    bigbuf = 0;   /* By default, do not increase socket buffer size. */
  }

  /* Get switch to turn on/off linger option. */
  if (argc > 3)
    lingeron = atoi(argv[3]);
  if (lingeron < 0)
  {
    fprintf(stderr, "%s is an invalid switch value, use 1 or 0.\n", argv[3]);
    lingeron = 0;   /* By default, socket linger option off. */
  }
```

```
  /* Allocate input buffer */
  inbufp = (char *)malloc(INBUFSZ+1);
  if (inbufp == NULL)
  {
    fprintf(stdout, "malloc() failed to allocate input buffer memory.\n");
    return(ENOMEM);
  }

  /* Create the Stream server socket. */
  if ((sfd = socket(AF_INET, SOCK_STREAM, 0)) < 0)
  {
    fprintf(stderr, "Error: socket() failed, errno=%d\n", errno);
    return(-1);
  }

  /* Get socket input buffer size set by the OS. */
  option = 0;
  optlen = sizeof(option);
  ret = getsockopt(sfd, SOL_SOCKET, SO_RCVBUF, &option, &optlen);
  if (ret < 0)
    fprintf(stderr, "Error: getsockopt(SO_RCVBUF) failed, errno=%d\n", errno);
  else
    fprintf(stdout, "SO_RCVBUF was originally set to be %u\n", option);

  if (bigbuf)
  {
    /* Set socket input buffer size. */
    option = SOCKBUFSZ;
    ret = setsockopt(sfd, SOL_SOCKET, SO_RCVBUF, &option, sizeof(option));
    if (ret < 0)
      fprintf(stderr, "Error: setsockopt(SO_RCVBUF) failed, errno=%d\n", errno);
    else
      fprintf(stdout, "SO_RCVBUF is set to be %u\n", option);

    /* Get socket input buffer size. */
    option = 0;
    optlen = sizeof(option);
    ret = getsockopt(sfd, SOL_SOCKET, SO_RCVBUF, &option, &optlen);
    if (ret < 0)
      fprintf(stderr, "Error: getsockopt(SO_RCVBUF) failed, errno=%d\n", errno);
    else
      fprintf(stdout, "SO_RCVBUF now is %u\n", option);
  }

  /* Turn on SO_KEEPALIVE socket option. */
  option = 1;
  ret = setsockopt(sfd, SOL_SOCKET, SO_KEEPALIVE, &option, sizeof(option));
  if (ret < 0)
  {
    fprintf(stderr, "Error: setsockopt(SO_KEEPALIVE) failed, errno=%d\n", errno);
  }
  else
    fprintf(stdout, "SO_KEEPALIVE socket option is set.\n");

  /* Turn on SO_LINGER option. */
  if (lingeron)
```

```
{
  solinger.l_onoff = 1;
  solinger.l_linger = 15;
  ret = setsockopt(sfd, SOL_SOCKET, SO_LINGER, &solinger, sizeof(solinger));
  if (ret < 0)
  {
    fprintf(stderr, "Error: setsockopt(SO_LINGER) failed, errno=%d\n", errno);
    close(sfd);
    return(-4);
  }
  else
    fprintf(stdout, "SO_LINGER socket option is successfully turned on.\n");
}

/* Fill in the server socket address. */
memset((void *)&srvaddr, 0, (size_t)srvaddrsz);  /* clear the address buffer */
srvaddr.sin_family = AF_INET;                    /* Internet socket */
srvaddr.sin_addr.s_addr = htonl(INADDR_ANY);     /* server's IP address */
srvaddr.sin_port = htons(portnum);               /* server's port number */

/* Bind the server socket to its address. */
if ((ret = bind(sfd, (struct sockaddr *)&srvaddr, srvaddrsz)) != 0)
{
  fprintf(stderr, "Error: bind() failed, errno=%d\n", errno);
  return(-2);
}

/* Set maximum connection request queue length that we can fall behind. */
if (listen(sfd, BACKLOG) == -1) {
  fprintf(stderr, "Error: listen() failed, errno=%d\n", errno);
  close(sfd);
  return(-3);
}

/* Wait for incoming connection requests from clients and service them. */
while (1) {

  fprintf(stdout, "\nListening at port number %u ...\n", portnum);
  newsock = accept(sfd, (struct sockaddr *)&clntaddr, &clntaddrsz);
  if (newsock < 0)
  {
    fprintf(stderr, "Error: accept() failed, errno=%d\n", errno);
    close(sfd);
    return(-4);
  }

  fprintf(stdout, "Client Connected.\n");

  /* Set the reply message */
  sprintf(outbuf, "%s", "This is a reply from the server program.");
  msglen = strlen(outbuf);
  totalBytes = 0;

  /* Receive and service requests from the current client. */
  while (1)
  {
```

```c
      /* Receive a request from a client. */
      errno = 0;
      inbufp[0] = '\0';
      /* Note: recv() may return with buffer partially filled. */
      ret = recv(newsock, inbufp, INBUFSZ, 0);
      if (ret > 0)
      {
        /* Process the request. We simply print the request message here. */
        inbufp[ret] = '\0';
        fprintf(stdout, "\n%u bytes of data received at the server.\n", ret);
        totalBytes = totalBytes + ret;

        /* Send a reply. */
        errno = 0;
        ret = send(newsock, outbuf, msglen, 0);
        if (ret == -1)
          fprintf(stderr, "Error: send() failed, errno=%d\n", errno);
        else
          fprintf(stdout, "%u of %lu bytes of the reply was sent.\n", ret, msglen);
      }
      else if (ret < 0)
      {
        fprintf(stderr, "Error: recv() failed, errno=%d\n", errno);
        break;
      }
      else
      {
        /* The client may have disconnected. */
        fprintf(stdout, "The client may have disconnected.\n");
        break;
      }
    }  /* while - inner */
    close(newsock);

    fprintf(stdout, "Total number of bytes received is %d.\n", totalBytes);

    break; /* TEST ONLY */

  }  /* while - outer */
}
```

(b) `tcpclnt_bufsz_linger.c`

```c
/*
 * A connection-oriented client program using Stream socket.
 * With socket buffer size options (SO_SNDBUF and SO_RCVBUF).
 * Turn on SO_LINGER socket option.
 * Usage: tcpclnt_bufsz_linger srvname srvport linger
 * Authored by Mr. Jin-Jwei Chen.
 * Copyright (c) 1993-2016, 2018, 2020 Mr. Jin-Jwei Chen. All rights reserved.
 */

#include <stdio.h>
#include <errno.h>
#include <sys/types.h>
#include <sys/socket.h>
```

931

```c
#include <netinet/in.h>      /* protocols such as IPPROTO_TCP, ... */
#include <arpa/inet.h>       /* inet_addr(), inet_ntoa(), inet_ntop() */
#include <string.h>          /* memset() */
#include <stdlib.h>          /* atoi() */
#include <netdb.h>           /* gethostbyname() */
#include <sys/time.h>        /* gettimeofday *//* TEST ONLY */
#include <ctype.h>           /* isalpha() */
#include <unistd.h>          /* close() */

#define   BUFLEN      1024      /* size of input message buffer */
#define   DEFSRVPORT  2344      /* default server port number */
#define   MAXMSGS     4         /* Maximum number of messages to send */
#define   NAMELEN     63
#define   SOCKBUFSZ   1048576   /* socket buffer size */
#define   OUTBUFSZ    1048576   /* socket output buffer size */

int main(int argc, char *argv[])
{
  int     ret, i;
  int     sfd;                           /* file descriptor of the socket */
  struct sockaddr_in    server;          /* socket structure */
  int     srvaddrsz=sizeof(struct sockaddr_in);
  struct sockaddr_in    fromaddr;        /* socket structure */
  socklen_t    fromaddrsz=sizeof(struct sockaddr_in);
  in_port_t    portnum=DEFSRVPORT;       /* port number */
  char    inbuf[BUFLEN];                 /* input message buffer */
  char    *outbufp = NULL;               /* pointer to output message buffer */
  size_t    msglen;                      /* length of reply message */
  size_t    msgnum=0;                    /* count of request message */
  size_t    len;
  unsigned int addr;
  char    server_name[NAMELEN+1] = "localhost";
  int     socket_type = SOCK_STREAM;
  struct hostent *hp;
  int     option;
  socklen_t  optlen;
  int     bigbuf = 1;               /* increase socket buffer size (on by default) */
  struct linger    solinger;       /* for SO_LINGER option */
  int     lingeron = 0;            /* socket linger option (off by default) */
  int     totalBytes = 0;          /* total # of bytes received */

  fprintf(stdout, "Connection-oriented client program ...\n\n");

  /* Get the host name or IP address from command line. */
  if (argc > 1)
  {
    len = strlen(argv[1]);
    if (len > NAMELEN)
      len = NAMELEN;
    strncpy(server_name, argv[1], len);
    server_name[len] = '\0';
  }

  /* Get the port number from command line. */
  if (argc > 2)
    portnum = atoi(argv[2]);
```

```
if (portnum <= 0)
{
  fprintf(stderr, "Port number %d invalid, set to default value %u\n",
    portnum, DEFSRVPORT);
  portnum = DEFSRVPORT;
}

/* Get switch to turn on/off linger option. */
if (argc > 3)
  lingeron = atoi(argv[3]);
if (lingeron < 0)
{
  fprintf(stderr, "%s is an invalid switch value, use 1 or 0.\n", argv[3]);
  lingeron = 0;  /* By default, socket linger option off. */
}

/* Allocate output buffer */
outbufp = (char *)malloc(OUTBUFSZ);
if (outbufp == NULL)
{
  fprintf(stderr, "malloc() failed to allocate output buffer memory.\n");
  return(ENOMEM);
}

/* Translate the host name or IP address into server socket address. */
if (isalpha(server_name[0]))
{  /* A host name is given. */
  hp = gethostbyname(server_name);
}
else
{  /* Convert the n.n.n.n IP address to a number. */
  addr = inet_addr(server_name);
  hp = gethostbyaddr((char *)&addr, sizeof(addr), AF_INET);
}
if (hp == NULL )
{
  fprintf(stderr,"Error: cannot get address for [%s], errno=%d\n",
    server_name, errno);
  return(-1);
}

/* Copy the resolved information into the sockaddr_in structure. */
memset(&server, 0, sizeof(server));
memcpy(&(server.sin_addr), hp->h_addr, hp->h_length);
server.sin_family = hp->h_addrtype;
server.sin_port = htons(portnum);

/* Open a socket. */
sfd = socket(AF_INET, socket_type, 0);
if (sfd < 0)
{
  fprintf(stderr,"Error: socket() failed, errno=%d\n", errno);
  return (-2);
}

/* Get socket output buffer size set by the OS. */
```

```
  option = 0;
  optlen = sizeof(option);
  ret = getsockopt(sfd, SOL_SOCKET, SO_SNDBUF, &option, &optlen);
  if (ret < 0)
  {
    fprintf(stderr, "Error: getsockopt(SO_SNDBUF) failed, errno=%d\n", errno);
  }
  else
    fprintf(stdout, "originally, SO_SNDBUF was set to be %u\n", option);

  if (bigbuf)
  {
    /* Set socket output buffer size. */
    option = SOCKBUFSZ;
    ret = setsockopt(sfd, SOL_SOCKET, SO_SNDBUF, &option, sizeof(option));
    if (ret < 0)
    {
      fprintf(stderr, "Error: setsockopt(SO_SNDBUF) failed, errno=%d\n", errno);
    }
    else
      fprintf(stdout, "SO_SNDBUF is set to be %u\n", option);

    /* Get socket output buffer size. */
    option = 0;
    optlen = sizeof(option);
    ret = getsockopt(sfd, SOL_SOCKET, SO_SNDBUF, &option, &optlen);
    if (ret < 0)
    {
      fprintf(stderr, "Error: getsockopt(SO_SNDBUF) failed, errno=%d\n", errno);
    }
    else
      fprintf(stdout, "SO_SNDBUF now is %u\n", option);
  }

  fprintf(stdout, "\nSend request messages to server at port %d\n", portnum);

  /* Turn on SO_LINGER option if user says so. */
  if (lingeron)
  {
    solinger.l_onoff = 1;
    solinger.l_linger = 15;
    ret = setsockopt(sfd, SOL_SOCKET, SO_LINGER, &solinger, sizeof(solinger));
    if (ret < 0)
    {
      fprintf(stderr, "Error: setsockopt(SO_LINGER) failed, errno=%d\n", errno);
      close(sfd);
      return(-4);
    }
    else
      fprintf(stdout, "SO_LINGER socket option was successfully turned on.\n");
  }

  /* Connect to the server. */
  ret = connect(sfd, (struct sockaddr *)&server, srvaddrsz);
  if (ret == -1)
  {
```

```
        fprintf(stderr, "Error: connect() failed, errno=%d\n", errno);
        close(sfd);
        return(-3);
    }

    /* Fill up output message buffer */
    for (i = 0; i < OUTBUFSZ; i++)
        outbufp[i] = 'A';

    /* Send request messages to the server and process the reply messages. */
    while (msgnum < MAXMSGS)
    {
        /* Send a request message to the server. */
        msgnum++;
        msglen = OUTBUFSZ;
        errno = 0;

        ret = send(sfd, outbufp, msglen, 0);
        if (ret >= 0)
        {
            totalBytes = totalBytes + ret;
            /* Print a warning if not entire message was sent. */
            if (ret == msglen)
            {
                fprintf(stdout, "\n%lu bytes of message were successfully sent.\n",
                    msglen);
                /* For testing linger option only */
                if (msgnum >= MAXMSGS)
                {
                    close(sfd);
                    fprintf(stdout, "Total number of bytes sent is %d.\n", totalBytes);
                    return(0);
                }
            }
            else if (ret < msglen)
                fprintf(stderr, "Warning: only %u of %lu bytes were sent.\n",
                    ret, msglen);

            if (ret > 0)
            {
                /* Receive a reply from the server. */
                errno = 0;
                inbuf[0] = '\0';
                ret = recv(sfd, inbuf, BUFLEN, 0);

                if (ret > 0)
                {
                    /* Process the reply. */
                    inbuf[ret] = '\0';
                    fprintf(stdout, "Received the following reply from server:\n%s\n",
                        inbuf);
                }
                else if (ret == 0)
                    fprintf(stdout, "Warning: Zero bytes were received.\n");
                else
                    fprintf(stderr, "Error: recv() failed, errno=%d\n", errno);
```

```
        }
    }
    else
        fprintf(stderr, "Error: send() failed, errno=%d\n", errno);

}  /* while */

close(sfd);
}
```

The example client program sends four messages of size 1 MB to the server.
By default, the client increases the send buffer size to 1 MB while the
server does not. This creates a buffer size imbalance situation.
The client purposely closes its socket immediately right after it sends
all data. Under most operating systems, with SO_LINGER socket option off,
this will cause data loss -- the server does not receive all of the data
that the client has just sent. You will likely be able to see this on
most systems if you run the programs the following way in two separate
windows:

```
$ ./tcpsrv_bufsz_linger
$ ./tcpclnt_bufsz_linger
```

By default, SO_LINGER option is turned off on both client and server.
Besides, the client uses a much bigger socket send buffer than the server's
receive buffer. This creates a buffer size imbalance situation which
should lead to data loss given the client closes its socket immediately.

In this situation, the error that the server program may get differs from
one operating system to another:

    Error: recv() failed, errno=104 (Linux x86) (Connection reset by peer)

    Error: send() failed, errno=104 (Linux x86) (Connection reset by peer)

    Error: recv() failed, errno=131 (Oracle/Sun SPARC Solaris)

    Error: recv() failed, errno=73 (IBM AIX)

After seeing the data loss, if you then run the same programs the following
way, with the SO_LINGER socket option turned on at both ends of the
connection, you will see the data loss issue disappears:

```
$ ./tcpsrv_bufsz_linger 2344 1 1
$ ./tcpclnt_bufsz_linger jvmx 2344 1
```

The input argument jvmx is the host name of the server. 2344 is the port
number of the server. Third argument 1 is to turn on the SO_LINGER option.

Therefore, to prevent data loss resulted from closing a connection,
both applications at the two ends of a connection should turn on the
SO_LINGER socket option!

Note that for a SOCK_STREAM socket, in many simple cases turning on
SO_LINGER option or not may not really make a difference.
This could be because the data exchanged is very small or the socket

buffer sizes on both ends of the connection are not way out of balance.

Ideally, applications should be very carefully designed and coded in a way such that the sender does not close its socket until after it has received confirmation from the receiver indicating that all data sent has been received. We mentioned this in the previous chapter. Alternatively, turning on SO_LINGER socket option may get you covered.

But bear in mind that the behavior of the SO_LINGER socket option is somewhat protocol and operating system implementation dependent.

For instance, on IBM AIX, for sockets using a connection-oriented transport service with an address family of AF_TELEPHONY, by default the SO_LINGER option is on (opposite of the POSIX's default behavior) with a linger time of one second. This means that the system will wait up to one second to try to send buffered data before actually closing the telephone connection.

As another example, for the data loss issue the example programs above demonstrate, it can sometimes be avoided by just turning on the SO_LINGER option only on the server side on some platforms. But the safest thing to do is to turn on the option at both ends. On some platforms, unless you turn on the SO_LINGER option on both ends of the communication, the problem continues to occur.

Besides, we use a very long linger period of 15 seconds. This is just for the purpose of clear observation in demonstration.

13-6 What Happens at Closing a TCP Socket Connection

This section looks into the details of the TCP protocol and describes what happens during closing a TCP socket connection. Understanding this low level of details helps readers understand why the SO_LINGER socket option as discussed above as well as the SO_REUSEADDR and SO_REUSEPORT options which we will talk about in the next section.

The states a TCP connection goes through are described in RFC 793. Readers are encouraged to read it. Here we focus on only the states that a closed TCP connection goes through.

At the first glance, lingering on with a timeout value of zero does not seem to make much sense. However, under certain rare circumstances, it may be desirable to do that.

First, a little background on the termination of a TCP connection.

When an application invokes the close() call on a socket to tear down a connection-oriented network connection, in a nutshell, below is what happens.

The network TCP layer uses a modified three-way handshake to close connections. TCP connections are full-duplex, allowing information to flow in both directions.

Since the TCP protocol implements a reliable service, when a close() function is invoked on a socket using such a service, the TCP layer will

first ensure the remaining buffered data is sent and it is received and
acknowledged.

```
                   Figure 13-7 Closing a TCP connection
-------------------------------------------------------------------
   socket program P1                     socket program P2
-------------------------------   -------------------------------
call close()

   finish sending remaining data  ---->
                                              receive remaining data
                                      <----  send ACK
   receive ACK (of last piece of data)

   send segment with FIN bit set  ---->
   enter FIN_WAIT_1 state
                                              receive FIN
                                      <----  send ACK
                                              enter CLOSE_WAIT state
   receive ACK
   enter FIN_WAIT_2 state


                                      <---- potentially more data

                                              call close()
                                      <----  send FIN + ACK
                                              enter LAST_ACK state
   receive FIN + ACK
   send ACK                          ---->
   enter TIME_WAIT state
                                              receive ACK
                                              FIN in both directions are ACK-ed
                                              enter CLOSED state
   timeout after 2 segment lifetimes
   enter CLOSED state
-------------------------------------------------------------------
```

Then the TCP layer starts a procedure of closing the connection in one
direction. It starts by transmitting a TCP segment with the FIN bit set.
The receiving program responds by sending back an acknowledgement (ACK).
After receiving this ACK for FIN, the socket initiating the close() enters
the FIN_WAIT_2 state.

Remember that a TCP connection is full-duplex and bi-directional.
At this time, the other direction is not being closed yet. So potentially
it's possible that data is still flowing in the other direction.

The socket initiating the close sits in the FIN_WAIT_2 state until the
other end also issues the close() call. When it finally receives the FIN
message from the other end, it will send the ACK and enter the
TIME_WAIT state.

At the other end, the socket enters the CLOSED state when it sees its FIN
segment is also acknowledged by the initiating socket.

Normally, as long as a socket sees the FIN segments flowing in both

directions are ack-ed, it can enter the CLOSED state.
However, to account for some of the problems incurred with unreliable delivery, the socket initiating the close() call is put in the TIME_WAIT state first. The TIME_WAIT state is designed to prevent TCP segments from a previous connection from interfering with a current connection. The initiating socket stays in the TIME_WAIT state for a duration of two TCP segment lifetimes. Then it transitions into the final CLOSED state in which all resources of the connection are deleted.

TIME_WAIT is the state that typically ties up the port resource for several minutes after a socket has been closed or even the process has been terminated. The length of the associated timeout varies on different operating systems. It may be even dynamic on some operating systems. Typically, the value of this timeout is in the range of one to four minutes. What we'll discuss in Section 13-7 is also related to this.

Remember that a system has only (2^16)=65536 ports available.
It can be a problem if there are too many sockets in the TIME_WAIT state in a system, especially on a server because it may end up with running out of resources and the server is not being able to accept connections anymore.

Because of this, when designing socket applications, it is always a good idea to design your applications such that the client always initiates the close() call, rather than the server. By letting the client close first, the server can avoid the TIME_WAIT state. It is whoever does the close() call first that needs to go through the TIME_WAIT state which could take time.

When a socket program turns on the SO_LINGER option with a zero timeout value, the termination process is a little different from what is described above. It results in the RST (reset) message being sent instead of FIN. And the close() operation becomes an abortive close. The other side responds to a reset TCP segment immediately by aborting the connection.
In order to prevent it from getting into the situation where thousands of client connections are in the TIME_WAIT or CLOSE_WAIT state and not being able to accept any more connections or not being able to restart, a server program may sometimes consider using this option of turning on the SO_LINGER option with a timeout value of zero.

But keep in mind that making the timeout too short might have a negative side-effect when the network is congested.

13-6-1 TCP TIME_WAIT state

As it can be seen from Figure 13-7 above, the process which closes a TCP connection first gets to enter the TCP TIME_WAIT state. This TCP TIME_WAIT state is what ties up a network port for one or more minutes before it can be re-used even after its owning process has terminated. We will introduce a way to avoid this wait in next section.

There are two purposes to have the TCP TIME_WAIT state.
First, it prevents delayed TCP segments from one connection from being accidently accepted by a later connection. Second, it is to ensure the other end of the communication has also closed the connection.

13-7 The SO_REUSEADDR and SO_REUSEPORT Socket Options

13-7-1 The SO_REUSEADDR Socket Option

The SO_REUSEADDR socket option has at least two uses.

First, as we mentioned earlier in the multicast section (12-17), turning on the SO_REUSEADDR socket option allows multiple processes in a single computer system to bind to the same socket address and be able to receive the same multicast messages.

Second, a more common use of the SO_REUSEADDR socket option is to allow a socket program to avoid getting the "Address already in use" error from bind() during its start or restart, or reduce the chances of getting it.

Sometimes you may find that after a server program terminates, if you try to start the same program right away then you get this following error:

    Error: bind() failed, errno=98, Address already in use

The actual value of errno is different on different operating systems. It is 98 in Linux, 67 in AIX, 125 in Solaris, 226 in HP-UX and 48 in Apple Darwin. The error number could be 10013 or 10048 in Windows. But they all mean the same -- the socket address the program tries to bind to is already in use. In fact, it normally means the port number is already in use.

Sometimes the error really indicates that the address/port number is actually being actively used by another active process, but most of the time socket programs get this error because of the design of TCP.

As just said, to ensure reliability, the design of the TCP protocol is such that under certain circumstances, when a socket is closed, its resources are not released right away. Instead, it enters the so-called TIME_WAIT state to prevent packets from a previous TCP connection from interfering with a current connection, or packets from current connection to interfere with the next connection using the same address and port number.

When a socket is closed but still in the TIME_WAIT state, if another process tries to use the same port number that socket used, it will get the **"Address already in use" error** because that previous socket is not completely closed yet. In this case, turning on the SO_REUSEADDR socket option allows the port number associated with a closed socket still in the TIME_WAIT state to be able to be reused immediately.

Hence, when you try to start a socket program and the start gets the "Address already in use" error, this is what you need to do.

First, you need to make sure no other process is actively using that same port number. The lsof utility in Linux can usually help you do that.

Second, if you find no other process is using it, then the error is probably

due to the fact that that same port number was used by a closed socket
still in the TIME_WAIT state. In this case, if you turn on the
SO_REUSEADDR socket option in your program, the error should go away.
The "Address already in use" error usually comes from the bind() function.
So **make sure you turn on the SO_REUSEADDR option before calling bind()**.

In short, turning on the SO_REUSEADDR socket option allows a process to be
able to bind to a port that is in the TIME_WAIT state. This will let a
server program that just terminates be able to re-start and bind to the
same port again right away without having to wait until the TIME_WAIT period
expires. Notice that there is still only one process that is allowed to
to be bound to that port though.

Be aware that the actual implementation of the SO_REUSEADDR option differs
slightly in different operating systems. Specifically, in most operating
systems, as long as you turn on the SO_REUSEADDR option on the current
socket instance, the feature will work regardless of whether the other
conflicting socket still in the TIME_WAIT state turns on the same option
or not. **However, on some other operating systems (e.g. Linux), it requires
all involved socket instances, including the other conflicting socket
still in the TIME_WAIT state, to all turn on the option for it to work**.

AIX 6.1, Solaris 11, HP-UX 11.31 and Apple Darwin 19.3 are in the first camp.
Linux 4.1.12 and Windows are in the second (stricter) camp.

Besides, the behavior of turning on the SO_REUSEADDR socket option is also
different between TCP and UDP protocols.

For a connection-oriented socket using the TCP protocol, only one process
is allowed to bind to a particular port at a given time even when the
SO_REUSEADDR option is enabled. But for connectionless sockets using the
UDP protocol, turning on the SO_REUSEADDR option does allow more than one
process to bind to the same port. We have shown this in the multicasting
section in the previous chapter.

Figure 13-8 Turn on/off SO_REUSEADDR option -- tcpsrv_reuseaddr_all.c
and tcpclnt_reuse_all.c (**Demo only**)

(a) tcpsrv_reuseaddr_all.c

```
/*
 * A connection-oriented server program using Stream socket.
 * Demonstrating use of SO_REUSEADDR socket option.
 * Support for multiple platforms including Linux, Windows, Solaris, AIX, HPUX.
 * Usage: tcpsrv_reuseaddr_all [port#] [reuseAddr]
 * Authored by Mr. Jin-Jwei Chen.
 * Copyright (c) 2002, 2014, 2017, 2018, 2020 Mr. Jin-Jwei Chen. All rights reserved.
 */

#include "mysocket.h"

int main(int argc, char *argv[])
{
    int     ret;        /* return code */
    int     sfd;        /* file descriptor of the listener socket */
    int     newsock;    /* file descriptor of client data socket */
```

```
    struct sockaddr_in6    srvaddr;    /* socket structure */
    int    srvaddrsz=sizeof(struct sockaddr_in6);
    struct sockaddr_in6    clntaddr;    /* socket structure */
    socklen_t clntaddrsz = sizeof(struct sockaddr_in6);
    in_port_t portnum = DEFSRVPORT;    /* port number */
    int    portnum_in;                 /* port number entered by user */
    char    inbuf[BUFLEN];             /* input message buffer */
    char    outbuf[BUFLEN];            /* output message buffer */
    size_t msglen;                     /* length of reply message */
    unsigned int  msgcnt = 1;          /* message count */
    int    reuseAddr = 0;              /* SO_REUSEADDR option off by default */
    int    sw;                         /* value of option */
    int    v6only = 0;                 /* IPV6_V6ONLY socket option off */
#if !WINDOWS
    struct timespec  sleeptm;          /* sleep time */
#endif
#if WINDOWS
    WSADATA wsaData;                   /* Winsock data */
    char* GetErrorMsg(int ErrorCode);  /* print error string in Windows */
#endif
    int        option;                 /* option value */
    socklen_t  optlen;                 /* length of option value */

    fprintf(stdout, "Connection-oriented server program ...\n");

    /* Get the server's port number from user, if any. */
    if (argc > 1)
    {
      portnum_in = atoi(argv[1]);
      if (portnum_in <= 0)
      {
        fprintf(stderr, "Port number %d invalid, set to default value %u\n",
           portnum_in, DEFSRVPORT);
        portnum = DEFSRVPORT;
      }
      else
        portnum = portnum_in;
    }

    /* Get switch on SO_REUSEADDR. */
    if (argc > 2)
      reuseAddr = atoi(argv[2]);

#if WINDOWS
    /* Initiate use of the Winsock DLL. Ask for Winsock version 2.2 at least. */
    if ((ret = WSAStartup(MAKEWORD(2, 2), &wsaData)) != 0)
    {
      fprintf(stderr, "WSAStartup() failed with error %d: %s\n",
        ret, GetErrorMsg(ret));
      return (-1);
    }
#endif

    /* Create the Stream server socket. */
    if ((sfd = socket(AF_INET6, SOCK_STREAM, 0)) < 0)
    {
```

942

```
    fprintf(stderr, "Error: socket() failed, errno=%d, %s\n", ERRNO, ERRNOSTR);
#if WINDOWS
    WSACleanup();
#endif
    return(-2);
  }

  /* If instructed, turn on SO_REUSEADDR socket option so that the server can
     restart right away before the required TCP wait time period expires. */
  if (reuseAddr)
    sw = 1;
  else
    sw = 0;

  errno = 0;
  if (setsockopt(sfd, SOL_SOCKET, SO_REUSEADDR, (char *)&sw, sizeof(sw)) < 0)
  {
    fprintf(stderr, "setsockopt(SO_REUSEADDR) failed, errno=%d, %s\n", ERRNO,
      ERRNOSTR);
  }
  else
  {
    if (sw)
      fprintf(stdout, "SO_REUSEADDR socket option is turned on.\n");
    else
      fprintf(stdout, "SO_REUSEADDR socket option is turned off.\n");
  }

  /* Get the current setting of the SO_SNDBUF socket option. */
  optlen = sizeof(option);
  option = 0;
  ret = getsockopt(sfd, SOL_SOCKET, SO_REUSEADDR, &option, &optlen);
  if (ret < 0)
  {
    fprintf(stderr, "Error: getsockopt(SO_REUSEADDR) failed, errno=%d\n", errno);
  }
  fprintf(stdout, "TCP SO_REUSEADDR's current setting is %u.\n", option);

  /* Fill in the server socket address. */
  memset((void *)&srvaddr, 0, (size_t)srvaddrsz); /* clear the address buffer */
  srvaddr.sin6_family = AF_INET6;                  /* Internet socket */
  srvaddr.sin6_addr= in6addr_any;                  /* server's IP address */
  srvaddr.sin6_port = htons(portnum);              /* server's port number */

  /* Turn off IPV6_V6ONLY socket option. Default is on in Windows. */
  if (setsockopt(sfd, IPPROTO_IPV6, IPV6_V6ONLY, (char*)&v6only,
    sizeof(v6only)) != 0)
  {
    fprintf(stderr, "Error: setsockopt(IPV6_V6ONLY) failed, errno=%d, %s\n",
      ERRNO, ERRNOSTR);
    CLOSE(sfd);
    return(-3);
  }

  /* Bind the server socket to its address. */
  if ((ret = bind(sfd, (struct sockaddr *)&srvaddr, srvaddrsz)) != 0)
```

```
  {
    fprintf(stderr, "Error: bind() failed, errno=%d, %s\n", ERRNO, ERRNOSTR);
    CLOSE(sfd);
    return(-4);
  }

  /* Set maximum connection request queue length that we can fall behind. */
  if (listen(sfd, BACKLOG) == -1) {
    fprintf(stderr, "Error: listen() failed, errno=%d, %s\n", ERRNO, ERRNOSTR);
    CLOSE(sfd);
    return(-5);
  }

  /* Wait for incoming connection requests from clients and service them. */
  while (1) {

    fprintf(stdout, "\nListening at port number %u ...\n", portnum);
    newsock = accept(sfd, (struct sockaddr *)&clntaddr, &clntaddrsz);
    if (newsock < 0)
    {
      fprintf(stderr, "Error: accept() failed, errno=%d, %s\n", ERRNO, ERRNOSTR);
      CLOSE(sfd);
      return(-6);
    }

    fprintf(stdout, "Client Connected.\n");

    while (1)
    {
      /* Receive a request from a client. */
      errno = 0;
      inbuf[0] = '\0';
      ret = recv(newsock, inbuf, BUFLEN, 0);
      if (ret > 0)
      {
        /* The three lines below are FOR TEST ONLY */
        CLOSE1(newsock);
        CLOSE(sfd);
        return(-1);

      /* Process the request. We simply print the request message here. */
      inbuf[ret] = '\0';
      fprintf(stdout, "\nReceived the following request from client:\n%s\n",
        inbuf);

      /* Construct a reply */
      sprintf(outbuf, "This is reply #%3u from the server program.", msgcnt++);
      msglen = strlen(outbuf);

      /* Send a reply. */
      errno = 0;
      ret = send(newsock, outbuf, msglen, 0);
      if (ret == -1)
        fprintf(stderr, "Error: send() failed, errno=%d, %s\n", ERRNO,
          ERRNOSTR);
      else
```

```
            fprintf(stdout, "%u of %lu bytes of the reply was sent.\n", ret, msglen);
        /* Break here to create a situation where the server close first. */
        break;
    }
    else if (ret < 0)
    {
        fprintf(stderr, "Error: recv() failed, errno=%d, %s\n", ERRNO,
            ERRNOSTR);
        break;
    }
    else
    {
        /* The client may have disconnected. */
        fprintf(stdout, "The client may have disconnected.\n");
        break;
    }
    } /* while - inner */

    CLOSE1(newsock);
    } /* while - outer */

    CLOSE(sfd);
    return(0);
}
```

(b) tcpclnt_reuse_all.c

```
/*
 * A connection-oriented client program using Stream socket.
 * Demonstrating use of SO_REUSEADDR socket option.
 * This version works on Linux, Solaris, AIX, HPUX and Windows.
 * Usage: tcpclnt_reuse_all portnum server_hostname/IP
 * Authored by Mr. Jin-Jwei Chen.
 * Copyright (c) 2002, 2014, 2017, 2018, 2020 Mr. Jin-Jwei Chen. All rights reserved.
 */

#include "mysocket.h"

int main(int argc, char *argv[])
{
    int     ret;
    int     sfd;                            /* socket file descriptor */
    in_port_t  portnum=DEFSRVPORT;   /* port number */
    char    *portnumstr  = DEFSRVPORTSTR; /* port number in string format */
    char    inbuf[BUFLEN];                  /* input message buffer */
    char    outbuf[BUFLEN];                 /* output message buffer */
    size_t msglen;                          /* length of reply message */
    size_t msgnum=0;                        /* count of request message */
    size_t len;
    char    server_name[NAMELEN+1] = "localhost";
    struct addrinfo hints, *res=NULL;    /* address info */

#if WINDOWS
    WSADATA wsaData;                         /* Winsock data */
    int winerror;                            /* error in Windows */
    char* GetErrorMsg(int ErrorCode);    /* print error string in Windows */
```

945

```c
#endif

  fprintf(stdout, "Connection-oriented client program ...\n");

  /* Get the server's port number from command line. */
  if (argc > 1)
  {
    portnum = atoi(argv[1]);
    portnumstr = argv[1];
  }
  if (portnum <= 0)
  {
    fprintf(stderr, "Port number %d invalid, set to default value %u\n",
      portnum, DEFSRVPORT);
    portnum = DEFSRVPORT;
    portnumstr = DEFSRVPORTSTR;
  }

  /* Get the server's host name or IP address from command line. */
  if (argc > 2)
  {
    len = strlen(argv[2]);
    if (len > NAMELEN)
      len = NAMELEN;
    strncpy(server_name, argv[2], len);
    server_name[len] = '\0';
  }

#if WINDOWS
  /* Ask for Winsock version 2.2 at least. */
  if ((ret = WSAStartup(MAKEWORD(2, 2), &wsaData)) != 0)
  {
    fprintf(stderr, "Error: WSAStartup() failed with error %d: %s\n",
      ret, GetErrorMsg(ret));
    return (-1);
  }
#endif

  /* Translate the server's host name or IP address into socket address.
   * Fill in the hint information.
   */
  memset(&hints, 0x00, sizeof(hints));
    /* This works on AIX but not on Solaris, nor on Windows. */
    /* hints.ai_flags    = AI_NUMERICSERV; */
  hints.ai_family   = AF_UNSPEC;
  hints.ai_socktype = SOCK_STREAM;

  /* Get the address information of the server using getaddrinfo().  */
  ret = getaddrinfo(server_name, portnumstr, &hints, &res);
  if (ret != 0)
  {
    fprintf(stderr, "Error: getaddrinfo() failed, error %d, %s\n", ret,
      gai_strerror(ret));
#if !WINDOWS
    if (ret == EAI_SYSTEM)
      fprintf(stderr,"System error: errno=%d, %s\n", errno, strerror(errno));
```

```c
#else
    WSACleanup();
#endif
    return(-2);
  }

  /* Create a socket. */
  sfd = socket(res->ai_family, res->ai_socktype, res->ai_protocol);
  if (sfd < 0)
  {
    fprintf(stderr,"Error: socket() failed, errno=%d, %s\n", ERRNO, ERRNOSTR);
#if WINDOWS
    WSACleanup();
#endif
    return (-3);
  }

  /* Connect to the server. */
  ret = connect(sfd, res->ai_addr, res->ai_addrlen);
  if (ret == -1)
  {
    fprintf(stderr, "Error: connect() failed, errno=%d, %s\n", ERRNO, ERRNOSTR);
    CLOSE(sfd);
    return(-4);
  }

  fprintf(stdout, "Send request messages to server(%s) at port %d\n",
   server_name, portnum);

  /* Send request messages to the server and process the reply messages. */
  while (msgnum < MAXMSGS)
  {
    /* Send a request message to the server. */
    sprintf(outbuf, "%s%4lu%s", "This is request message ", ++msgnum,
     " from the client program.");
    msglen = strlen(outbuf);
    errno = 0;

    ret = send(sfd, outbuf, msglen, 0);
    if (ret >= 0)
    {
      /* Print a warning if not entire message was sent. */
      if (ret == msglen)
        fprintf(stdout, "\n%lu bytes of message were successfully sent.\n",
          msglen);
      else if (ret < msglen)
        fprintf(stderr, "Warning: only %u of %lu bytes were sent.\n",
          ret, msglen);

      if (ret > 0)
      {
        /* Receive a reply from the server. */
        errno = 0;
        inbuf[0] = '\0';
        ret = recv(sfd, inbuf, BUFLEN, 0);
```

```
        if (ret > 0)
        {
            /* Process the reply. */
            inbuf[ret] = '\0';
            fprintf(stdout, "Received the following reply from server:\n%s\n",
                inbuf);
        }
        else if (ret == 0)
        {
            fprintf(stdout, "Warning: Zero bytes were received.\n");
            /* FOR TEST ONLY */
            if (msgnum == 1)
            {
#if WINDOWS
                Sleep(15000);
#else
                sleep(15);
#endif
                exit(0);
            }
        }
        else
            fprintf(stderr, "Error: recv() failed, errno=%d, %s\n", ERRNO,
                ERRNOSTR);
    }
    else
        fprintf(stderr, "Error: send() failed, errno=%d, %s\n", ERRNO, ERRNOSTR);

    /* Client waits a bit to ensure server closes its socket first. */
#if WINDOWS
    Sleep(1000); /* Unit is ms. For demo only. Remove this in real code. */
#else
    sleep(1);   /* For demo only. Remove this in real code. */
#endif
  }  /* while */

  /* Free the memory allocated by getaddrinfo() and close the socket. */
  freeaddrinfo(res);
  CLOSE(sfd);
  return(0);
}
```

Figure 13-8 lists a pair of client and server programs that demonstrate
the problem of and the solution to the "Address already in use" socket error.

Note that this pair of example programs is for demonstration only.
In order to create the scenario to demonstrate the problem,
we alter the server program to close its socket and break out of its
service loop as soon as it receives the first message from the client.
This is so that the server socket will enter the TIME_WAIT state.
Besides, we also change the client program to sleep and wait a little bit
to ensure that the server program closes its socket before the client does.

To facilitate demonstration of the error and the implementation differences
between different operating systems, we program the example server program

in Fig 13-8 to take an additional argument by which you can use to turn on
or off the SO_REUSEADDR option when the server starts. If you do two
consecutive server restarts after the server receives the first client
message and exits, one with the SO_REUSEADDR option off (argument value 0)
followed by another with the SO_REUSEADDR option on (argument value 1),
you will find out which implementation camp the operating system you are
using belongs to. If both scenarios work for you, then it is the less strict
one. Otherwise, it is the stricter one, requiring turning the option on for
all socket instances involved.

Because of the implementation discrepancy, in order for your program
to work on all operating systems without changes, you should always
turn on the SO_REUSEADDR option up-front!

13-7-2 Testing the SO_REUSEADDR Option

(A) See the "Address already in use" error

To test the example programs, start the server program first, then
run the client program. After the client sends its first message and the
server exits, try to start the server again.

Perform the test first with the default option, i.e. SO_REUSEADDR option off.
During the restart of the server program, it should get the error.

```
$ ./tcpsrv_reuseaddr_all
Connection-oriented server program ...
SO_REUSEADDR socket option is turned off.
TCP SO_REUSEADDR's current setting is 0.

Listening at port number 2345 ...
Client Connected.

$ ./tcpclnt_reuse_all
Connection-oriented client program ...
Send request messages to server(localhost) at port 2345

53 bytes of message were successfully sent.
Warning: Zero bytes were received.

$ ./tcpsrv_reuseaddr_all
Connection-oriented server program ...
SO_REUSEADDR socket option is turned off.
TCP SO_REUSEADDR's current setting is 0.
Error: bind() failed, errno=98, Address already in use
```

(The server restart gets the "Address already in use" error.)

Note that on stricter platforms such as Linux, even if you instead do

```
$ ./tcpsrv_reuseaddr_all 2345 1
```

here on the server restart, you would still get the same error!

(B) See turning on the option get rid of the error

Then repeat the same test steps, but with SO_REUSEADDR option on this time. You should see the restart of the server program succeeds without getting the "Address already in use" error.

(Running both client and server on the same host.)

```
$ ./tcpsrv_reuseaddr_all 2345 1
Connection-oriented server program ...
SO_REUSEADDR socket option is turned on.
TCP SO_REUSEADDR's current setting is 1.

Listening at port number 2345 ...
Client Connected.
```

   (Argument 2345 is server's port number. Argument 1 means turning
   SO_REUSEADDR option on.)
   (Starting the server initially by running
      $ ./tcpsrv_reuseaddr_all 2345
   instead would let you find out which implementation your O.S. has.)

```
$ ./tcpclnt_reuse_all
Connection-oriented client program ...
Send request messages to server(localhost) at port 2345

53 bytes of message were successfully sent.
Warning: Zero bytes were received.
```

   (Inserting one additional step here in-between as follows:
      $ ./tcpsrv_reuseaddr_all
   will let you verify that you would get the error without turning on
   the option.)

```
$ ./tcpsrv_reuseaddr_all 2345 1
Connection-oriented server program ...
SO_REUSEADDR socket option is turned on.
TCP SO_REUSEADDR's current setting is 1.

Listening at port number 2345 ...
```

(The server restart does not get the "Address already in use" error!)

Note that for the sole purpose of demonstrating the problem and how to fix the problem, we set the default to be SO_REUSEADDR option off in our example programs. **Though in practice, it is a very good idea to always turn on this option by default so that restarting your application won't unnecessarily get the "address already in use" error.**

Besides, on the security front, to prevent socket hijacking, the effective user ID may be checked in some platforms (e.g. Linux) when multiple processes try to bind to the same socket address to ensure that they are all the same as the user who first binds its socket to the same address and port number.

Another note to add is that although turning on SO_REUSEADDR option permits a socket program to use a port that is stuck in the TIME_WAIT state, the program still cannot use that port to establish a connection to the last place it connected to. In other words, using the port to try to establish a connection with exactly the same destination

<source IP, source port, destination IP, destination port, protocol>

as the previous port was connected to is still not allowed until the TIME_WAIT period expires. This is to ensure packet interference as mentioned previously does not occur.

13-7-3 The SO_REUSEADDR and SO_EXCLUSIVEADDRUSE Socket Options in Windows

The actual implementation of the SO_REUSEADDR socket option is sometimes a bit dangerous in Windows. It allows two processes (for instances, two server programs) running on the same host to bind their respective TCP sockets to exactly the same source address and port number if both of them turn on the SO_REUSEADDR option. At least this is the behavior in Windows 7. Although it may facilitate load sharing, it could be a security issue because you could have a normal server listening on a particular port and some other piece of malware or application can come along, bind to the same address and port number, and silently steal the same port intercepting many of the connections. This behavior is not permitted at all in Linux or Unix, especially when the wild card address is used with a specific port.

The test and output below show this behavior in Windows:

```
C:\sock> tcpsrv_reuseaddr_all.exe 2345 1
Connection-oriented server program ...
SO_REUSEADDR socket option is turned on.
TCP SO_REUSEADDR's current setting is 1.

Listening at port number 2345 ...

C:\sock> tcpsrv_reuseaddr_all.exe 2345 1
Connection-oriented server program ...
SO_REUSEADDR socket option is turned on.
TCP SO_REUSEADDR's current setting is 1.

Listening at port number 2345 ...
```

However, if one of them does not turn on the SO_REUSEADDR option, then the second or later one that tries to bind to the same source address and port number will fail with error 10048:

```
C:\sock> tcpsrv_reuseaddr_all.exe 2345 1
Connection-oriented server program ...
SO_REUSEADDR socket option is turned on.
TCP SO_REUSEADDR's current setting is 1.

Listening at port number 2345 ...

C:\sock> tcpsrv_reuseaddr_all.exe
Connection-oriented server program ...
SO_REUSEADDR socket option is turned off.
```

```
TCP SO_REUSEADDR's current setting is 0.
Error: bind() failed, errno=10048, Only one usage of each socket address
    (protocol/network address/port) is normally permitted.
```

Or

```
C:\sock> tcpsrv_reuseaddr_all
Connection-oriented server program ...
SO_REUSEADDR socket option is turned off.
TCP SO_REUSEADDR's current setting is 0.

Listening at port number 2345 ...

C:\sock> tcpsrv_reuseaddr_all 2345 1
Connection-oriented server program ...
SO_REUSEADDR socket option is turned on.
TCP SO_REUSEADDR's current setting is 1.
Error: bind() failed, errno=10013, An attempt was made to access a socket
    in a way forbidden by its access permissions.
```

Remember that BOTH processes must all turn on the SO_REUSEADDR option
for binding to the same address and port number to work.

By the way, Windows documentation states that when multiple sockets
are successfully bound to the same source address and port number by
all enabling the SO_REUSEADDR options, the behavior is non-deterministic.

The SO_EXCLUSIVEADDRUSE Option in Windows

After realizing this might be a problem, Microsoft Windows supports another
socket option named SO_EXCLUSIVEADDRUSE, which is not available in Linux
or Unix. If the first socket that is bound to a particular source address
and port number has the SO_EXCLUSIVEADDRUSE socket option turned on, then
no other socket can be bound to the same source address and port number,
not even if it turns on the SO_REUSEADDR option. This ensures that a port
number that is already used by a process won't get stolen or reused by
another process that comes later.

So SO_EXCLUSIVEADDRUSE option is what you want to turn on in Windows
unless you are doing load distribution/balancing over multiple servers.
Note that in Windows you as a developer must explicitly turn on the
SO_EXCLUSIVEADDRUSE socket option to prevent the port number your application
binds to from being stolen behind the scene.

Figure 13-9 Turn on exclusive port use option in Windows and Solaris --
tcpsrv_exclu_bind_all.c (**for demo in Windows and Solaris only**)

```
/*
 * A connection-oriented server program using Stream socket.
 * Demonstrating use of Exclusive Bind socket option (Windows, Solaris).
 * Support for multiple platforms including Windows, Solaris.
 * Usage: tcpsrv_exclu_bind_all [port#] [excluBind]
 * How to build:
 *   Solaris: gcc -DSOLARIS -o tcpsrv_exclu_bind_all.sun tcpsrv_exclu_bind_all.c -lnsl
-lsocket
 *   Windows: cl -DWINDOWS tcpsrv_exclu_bind_all.c ws2_32.lib kernel32.lib
```

```
 * Authored by Mr. Jin-Jwei Chen.
 * Copyright (c) 2002, 2014, 2017-9 Mr. Jin-Jwei Chen. All rights reserved.
 */

#include "mysocket.h"

/* Exclusive Bind socket option -- not all platforms support this. */
#if WINDOWS
#define SOCKET_OPTION SO_EXCLUSIVEADDRUSE
#elif SOLARIS
#define SOCKET_OPTION SO_EXCLBIND
#else
#define SOCKET_OPTION SO_NOTSUPPORTED
#endif

int main(int argc, char *argv[])
{
  int     ret;                        /* return code */
  int     sfd;                        /* file descriptor of the listener socket */
  int     newsock;                    /* file descriptor of client data socket */
  struct sockaddr_in6   srvaddr;      /* socket structure */
  int     srvaddrsz=sizeof(struct sockaddr_in6);
  struct sockaddr_in6   clntaddr;     /* socket structure */
  socklen_t clntaddrsz = sizeof(struct sockaddr_in6);
  in_port_t portnum = DEFSRVPORT;     /* port number */
  int     portnum_in;                 /* port number entered by user */
  char    inbuf[BUFLEN];              /* input message buffer */
  char    outbuf[BUFLEN];             /* output message buffer */
  size_t msglen;                      /* length of reply message */
  unsigned int  msgcnt = 1;           /* message count */
  int     excluBind = 0;              /* socket option off by default */
  int     sw;                         /* value of option */
  int     v6only = 0;                 /* IPV6_V6ONLY socket option off */
#if !WINDOWS
  struct timespec  sleeptm;           /* sleep time */
#endif
#if WINDOWS
  WSADATA wsaData;                    /* Winsock data */
  char* GetErrorMsg(int ErrorCode);   /* print error string in Windows */
#endif
  int         option;                 /* option value */
  socklen_t   optlen;                 /* length of option value */

  fprintf(stdout, "Connection-oriented server program ...\n");

  /* Get the server's port number from user, if any. */
  if (argc > 1)
  {
    portnum_in = atoi(argv[1]);
    if (portnum_in <= 0)
    {
      fprintf(stderr, "Port number %d invalid, set to default value %u\n",
        portnum_in, DEFSRVPORT);
      portnum = DEFSRVPORT;
    }
    else
```

953

```
        portnum = portnum_in;
  }

  /* Get switch on the socket option. */
  if (argc > 2)
    excluBind = atoi(argv[2]);

#if WINDOWS
  /* Initiate use of the Winsock DLL. Ask for Winsock version 2.2 at least. */
  if ((ret = WSAStartup(MAKEWORD(2, 2), &wsaData)) != 0)
  {
    fprintf(stderr, "WSAStartup() failed with error %d: %s\n",
      ret, GetErrorMsg(ret));
    return (-1);
  }
#endif

  /* Create the Stream server socket. */
  if ((sfd = socket(AF_INET6, SOCK_STREAM, 0)) < 0)
  {
    fprintf(stderr, "Error: socket() failed, errno=%d, %s\n", ERRNO, ERRNOSTR);
#if WINDOWS
    WSACleanup();
#endif
    return(-2);
  }

  /* Get the current setting of the exclusive bind socket option. */
  optlen = sizeof(option);
  option = 0;
  ret = getsockopt(sfd, SOL_SOCKET, SOCKET_OPTION, &option, &optlen);
  if (ret < 0)
  {
    fprintf(stderr, "Error: getsockopt(Exclusive Bind) failed, errno=%d, %s\n",
      ERRNO, ERRNOSTR);
  }
  fprintf(stdout, "TCP Exclusive Bind's original setting is %u.\n", option);

  /* If requested, enable exclusive bind socket option on the server socket */
  if (excluBind)
    sw = 1;
  else
    sw = 0;

  errno = 0;
  if (setsockopt(sfd, SOL_SOCKET, SOCKET_OPTION, (char *)&sw, sizeof(sw)) < 0)
  {
    fprintf(stderr, "setsockopt(Exclusive Bind) failed, errno=%d, %s\n", ERRNO,
      ERRNOSTR);
  }
  else
  {
    if (sw)
      fprintf(stdout, "Exclusive Bind socket option is turned on.\n");
    else
      fprintf(stdout, "Exclusive Bind socket option is turned off.\n");
```

```
  }

  /* Fill in the server socket address. */
  memset((void *)&srvaddr, 0, (size_t)srvaddrsz); /* clear the address buffer */

  srvaddr.sin6_family = AF_INET6;                 /* Internet socket */
  srvaddr.sin6_addr= in6addr_any;                 /* server's IP address */
  srvaddr.sin6_port = htons(portnum);             /* server's port number */

  /* Turn off IPV6_V6ONLY socket option. Default is on in Windows. */
  if (setsockopt(sfd, IPPROTO_IPV6, IPV6_V6ONLY, (char*)&v6only,
    sizeof(v6only)) != 0)
  {
    fprintf(stderr, "Error: setsockopt(IPV6_V6ONLY) failed, errno=%d, %s\n",
      ERRNO, ERRNOSTR);
    CLOSE(sfd);
    return(-3);
  }

  /* Bind the server socket to its address. */
  if ((ret = bind(sfd, (struct sockaddr *)&srvaddr, srvaddrsz)) != 0)
  {
    fprintf(stderr, "Error: bind() failed, errno=%d, %s\n", ERRNO, ERRNOSTR);
    CLOSE(sfd);
    return(-4);
  }

  /* Set maximum connection request queue length that we can fall behind. */
  if (listen(sfd, BACKLOG) == -1) {
    fprintf(stderr, "Error: listen() failed, errno=%d, %s\n", ERRNO, ERRNOSTR);
    CLOSE(sfd);
    return(-5);
  }

  /* Wait for incoming connection requests from clients and service them. */
  while (1) {

    fprintf(stdout, "\nListening at port number %u ...\n", portnum);
    newsock = accept(sfd, (struct sockaddr *)&clntaddr, &clntaddrsz);
    if (newsock < 0)
    {
      fprintf(stderr, "Error: accept() failed, errno=%d, %s\n", ERRNO, ERRNOSTR);
      CLOSE(sfd);
      return(-6);
    }

    fprintf(stdout, "Client Connected.\n");

    while (1)
    {
      /* Receive a request from a client. */
      errno = 0;
      inbuf[0] = '\0';
      ret = recv(newsock, inbuf, BUFLEN, 0);
      if (ret > 0)
      {
```

```
        /* Process the request. We simply print the request message here. */
        inbuf[ret] = '\0';
        fprintf(stdout, "\nReceived the following request from client:\n%s\n",
            inbuf);

        /* Construct a reply */
        sprintf(outbuf, "This is reply #%3u from the server program.", msgcnt++);
        msglen = strlen(outbuf);

        /* Send a reply. */
        errno = 0;
        ret = send(newsock, outbuf, msglen, 0);
        if (ret == -1)
          fprintf(stderr, "Error: send() failed, errno=%d, %s\n", ERRNO,
            ERRNOSTR);
        else
          fprintf(stdout, "%u of %u bytes of the reply was sent.\n", ret, msglen);
      }
      else if (ret < 0)
      {
        fprintf(stderr, "Error: recv() failed, errno=%d, %s\n", ERRNO,
          ERRNOSTR);
        break;
      }
      else
      {
        /* The client may have disconnected. */
        fprintf(stdout, "The client may have disconnected.\n");
        break;
      }
    } /* while - inner */

    CLOSE1(newsock);
  } /* while - outer */

  CLOSE(sfd);
  return(0);
}
```

Figure 13-9 shows an example of how to turn on the SO_EXCLUSIVEADDRUSE
option on Windows. Remember to add -DWINDOWS to the compiler command line
when you build in Windows.

As shown below, the SO_EXCLUSIVEADDRUSE socket option in Windows does not
allow more than one process to bind to the same source address and port number.

```
C:\myprog>tcpsrv_exclu_bind_all.exe 2345 1
Connection-oriented server program ...
TCP Exclusive Bind's current setting is 0.
Exclusive Bind socket option is turned on.

Listening at port number 2345 ...

C:\myprog>tcpsrv_exclu_bind_all.exe 2345 0
Connection-oriented server program ...
TCP Exclusive Bind's current setting is 0.
```

Exclusive Bind socket option is turned off.
Error: bind() failed, errno=10048, Only one usage of each socket address
(protocol/network address/port) is normally permitted.

The test and output below show that the SO_EXCLUSIVEADDRUSE option in
Windows works the way similar to what SO_REUSEADDR option does in Linux/Unix
as far as immediately reusing a port number stuck in TIME_WAIT state is
concerned.

```
C:\myprog>tcpsrv_exclu_bind_all.exe 2345 1
Connection-oriented server program ...
TCP Exclusive Bind's current setting is 0.
Exclusive Bind socket option is turned on.

Listening at port number 2345 ...
Client Connected.

Received the following request from client:
This is request message    1 from the client program.
43 of 43 bytes of the reply was sent.
The client may have disconnected.

Listening at port number 2345 ...
```

Press Ctrl-C to quit the server, and then restart immediately:

```
C:\myprog>tcpsrv_exclu_bind_all.exe 2345 1
Connection-oriented server program ...
TCP Exclusive Bind's current setting is 0.
Exclusive Bind socket option is turned on.

Listening at port number 2345 ...
```

13-7-4 The SO_EXCLBIND Socket Option in Solaris

Solaris supports the exclusive bind option too but it's called SO_EXCLBIND.

In Solaris the SO_EXCLBIND option enables or disables the exclusive binding
of a socket. It overrides the use of the SO_REUSEADDR option to reuse an
address on bind. If a program turns on the SO_EXCLBIND option, then after it
binds a socket to certain address and port number, no other process/thread
on the same host will be able to bind its socket to the same address and
port number at the same time.

In other words, if an application does not want to allow another socket
using the SO_REUSEADDR or SO_REUSEPORT option to bind to a port its socket
is already bound to, it can do so by turning on the SO_EXCLBIND option
on its socket before calling bind(). That is, the SO_EXCLBIND option
supersedes the SO_REUSEADDR or SO_REUSEPORT option.

The actual semantics of the SO_EXCLBIND option depends on the underlying
protocol (TCP or UDP).

The same program in Figure 13-9 can be built and run on Oracle/Sun
Solaris as well. As mentioned above, the name of the option changes to

SO_EXCLBIND in Solaris, as defined at the top of the program. Remember to add -DSOLARIS to the compiler command line when you build the example program in SOLARIS.

Note that as of this writing neither SO_EXCLUSIVEADDRUSE nor SO_EXCLBIND is supported in Apple Darwin.

13-7-5 The SO_REUSEPORT Socket Option

In recent years, after POSIX 2018 Standard, most operating systems have added the SO_REUSEPORT socket option, mostly to enable server load sharing. The functionality of the SO_REUSEPORT socket option overlaps with the SO_REUSEADDR option.

The SO_REUSEPORT socket option allows multiple (two or more) sockets, especially TCP sockets, to bind to exactly the same source address and port number. In almost all implementations it requires all involved sockets to turn on the same option before binding.

Again, the actual behavior of the SO_REUSEPORT socket option is operating system dependent. In particular, as we will describe below, Solaris has a special restriction on the option that no other platforms have and Linux has a feature that no other operating systems have implemented. The common thing is that when supported they seem to all require all involved sockets turn on the option for it to work.
That is, both the binding and existing bound socket(s) must all turn the option on.

The SO_REUSEPORT option works slightly different than SO_REUSEADDR in AIX 6.1. While the SO_REUSEADDR option works as soon as it gets turned on, not requiring the prior bound socket to turn the same option on, the SO_REUSEPORT option does require prior bound socket(s) to turn the option on for it to work.

The SO_REUSEPORT option also works in HP-UX 11.31 but has a different behavior than the SO_REUSEADDR option. It requires all sockets prior bound to the same address and port number also turn the option on for it to work.

The behavior of the SO_REUSEPORT option in Oracle/Sun Solaris is a bit different from other operating systems. When both involved sockets turn on the SO_REUSEPORT option and the two processes have the same user ID, they are allowed to bind to the same address and port number.
But only one of the two sockets (the first one) can become a listener socket. This restriction is different from other platforms.
This means if the first socket is already bound to the address and port number and already listening on the port, the second socket trying to do the same will be allowed to bind but when it tries to listen on the same port, its listen() call will fail with errno=122.

In Apple Darwin, as long as the current program turns on the SO_REUSEPORT or SO_REUSEADDR option, it works regardless of whether the option was turned on or not on the conflicting socket that is in the TIME_WAIT state.

Microsoft Windows does not support SO_REUSEPORT socket option as of the writing of this book.

In Linux, the SO_REUSEPORT socket option is supported only from Linux 3.9 and on. It allows multiple IPv4 (AF_INET) or IPv6 (AF_INET6) sockets to be bound to the same socket address and port number. And it's supported for both TCP and UDP protocols in Linux 3.9. The SO_REUSEPORT option also requires all conflicting sockets involved to turn on the option.

In Linux, the SO_REUSEPORT option enables a server program to distribute the load of listening and accepting incoming connection requests (i.e. the accept() call) over multiple processes or threads where each listener process or thread uses a distinct socket but all of them are bound to an identical socket address and port number. This allows a server to be able to handle even higher load, say, tens of thousands of incoming connections per second.

Figure 13-10 displays a server program tcpsrv_reuseport_all.c that works with the client program tcpclnt_reuse_all.c shown in Figure 13-8b.

Figure 13-10 Example server program for SO_REUSEPORT option – tcpsrv_reuseport_all.c (for demo only)

```c
/*
 * A connection-oriented server program using Stream socket.
 * Demonstrating use of SO_REUSEPORT socket option.
 * Test this in Linux 3.9 or later.
 * Support for multiple platforms including Linux, Windows, Solaris, AIX, HPUX.
 * Usage: tcpsrv_reuseport_all [port#] [reusePort]
 * Authored by Mr. Jin-Jwei Chen.
 * Copyright (c) 2002, 2014, 2017, 2018, 2020 Mr. Jin-Jwei Chen. All rights reserved.
 */

#include "mysocket.h"

int main(int argc, char *argv[])
{
  int     ret;                          /* return code */
  int     sfd;                          /* file descriptor of the listener socket */
  int     newsock;                      /* file descriptor of client data socket */
  struct sockaddr_in6  srvaddr;         /* socket structure */
  int     srvaddrsz=sizeof(struct sockaddr_in6);
  struct sockaddr_in6  clntaddr;        /* socket structure */
  socklen_t clntaddrsz = sizeof(struct sockaddr_in6);
  in_port_t portnum = DEFSRVPORT;       /* port number */
  int     portnum_in;                   /* port number entered by user */
  char    inbuf[BUFLEN];                /* input message buffer */
  char    outbuf[BUFLEN];               /* output message buffer */
  size_t  msglen;                       /* length of reply message */
  unsigned int  msgcnt = 1;             /* message count */
  int     reusePort = 0;                /* SO_REUSEPORT option off by default */
  int     sw;                           /* value of option */
  int     v6only = 0;                   /* IPV6_V6ONLY socket option off */
#if !WINDOWS
  struct timespec  sleeptm;             /* sleep time */
#endif
#if WINDOWS
```

```
  WSADATA wsaData;                      /* Winsock data */
  char* GetErrorMsg(int ErrorCode);     /* print error string in Windows */
#endif
  int        option;                    /* option value */
  socklen_t  optlen;                    /* length of option value */

  fprintf(stdout, "Connection-oriented server program ...\n");

  /* Get the server's port number from user, if any. */
  if (argc > 1)
  {
    portnum_in = atoi(argv[1]);
    if (portnum_in <= 0)
    {
      fprintf(stderr, "Port number %d invalid, set to default value %u\n",
        portnum_in, DEFSRVPORT);
      portnum = DEFSRVPORT;
    }
    else
      portnum = portnum_in;
  }

  /* Get switch on SO_REUSEPORT. */
  if (argc > 2)
    reusePort = atoi(argv[2]);

#if WINDOWS
  /* Initiate use of the Winsock DLL. Ask for Winsock version 2.2 at least. */
  if ((ret = WSAStartup(MAKEWORD(2, 2), &wsaData)) != 0)
  {
    fprintf(stderr, "WSAStartup() failed with error %d: %s\n",
      ret, GetErrorMsg(ret));
    return (-1);
  }
#endif

  /* Create the Stream server socket. */
  if ((sfd = socket(AF_INET6, SOCK_STREAM, 0)) < 0)
  {
    fprintf(stderr, "Error: socket() failed, errno=%d, %s\n", ERRNO, ERRNOSTR);
#if WINDOWS
    WSACleanup();
#endif
    return(-2);
  }

  /* If instructed, turn on SO_REUSEPORT socket option so that the server can
     restart right away before the required TCP wait time period expires. */
  if (reusePort)
    sw = 1;
  else
    sw = 0;

  errno = 0;
  if (setsockopt(sfd, SOL_SOCKET, SO_REUSEPORT, (char *)&sw, sizeof(sw)) < 0)
  {
```

```
        fprintf(stderr, "setsockopt(SO_REUSEPORT) failed, errno=%d, %s\n", ERRNO,
          ERRNOSTR);
}
else
{
   if (sw)
     fprintf(stdout, "SO_REUSEPORT socket option is turned on.\n");
   else
     fprintf(stdout, "SO_REUSEPORT socket option is turned off.\n");
}

/* Get the current setting of the SO_SNDBUF socket option. */
optlen = sizeof(option);
option = 0;
ret = getsockopt(sfd, SOL_SOCKET, SO_REUSEPORT, &option, &optlen);
if (ret < 0)
{
   fprintf(stderr, "Error: getsockopt(SO_REUSEPORT) failed, errno=%d\n", errno);
}
fprintf(stdout, "TCP SO_REUSEPORT's current setting is %u.\n", option);

/* Fill in the server socket address. */
memset((void *)&srvaddr, 0, (size_t)srvaddrsz); /* clear the address buffer */
srvaddr.sin6_family = AF_INET6;                  /* Internet socket */
srvaddr.sin6_addr= in6addr_any;                  /* server's IP address */
srvaddr.sin6_port = htons(portnum);              /* server's port number */

/* Turn off IPV6_V6ONLY socket option. Default is on in Windows. */
if (setsockopt(sfd, IPPROTO_IPV6, IPV6_V6ONLY, (char*)&v6only,
     sizeof(v6only)) != 0)
{
   fprintf(stderr, "Error: setsockopt(IPV6_V6ONLY) failed, errno=%d, %s\n",
       ERRNO, ERRNOSTR);
   CLOSE(sfd);
   return(-3);
}

/* Bind the server socket to its address. */
if ((ret = bind(sfd, (struct sockaddr *)&srvaddr, srvaddrsz)) != 0)
{
   fprintf(stderr, "Error: bind() failed, errno=%d, %s\n", ERRNO, ERRNOSTR);
   CLOSE(sfd);
   return(-4);
}

/* Set maximum connection request queue length that we can fall behind. */
if (listen(sfd, BACKLOG) == -1) {
   fprintf(stderr, "Error: listen() failed, errno=%d, %s\n", ERRNO, ERRNOSTR);
   CLOSE(sfd);
   return(-5);
}

/* Wait for incoming connection requests from clients and service them. */
while (1) {

   fprintf(stdout, "\nListening at port number %u ...\n", portnum);
```

```
  newsock = accept(sfd, (struct sockaddr *)&clntaddr, &clntaddrsz);
  if (newsock < 0)
  {
    fprintf(stderr, "Error: accept() failed, errno=%d, %s\n", ERRNO, ERRNOSTR);
    CLOSE(sfd);
    return(-6);
  }

  fprintf(stdout, "Client Connected.\n");

  while (1)
  {
    /* Receive a request from a client. */
    errno = 0;
    inbuf[0] = '\0';
    ret = recv(newsock, inbuf, BUFLEN, 0);
    if (ret > 0)
    {
      /* The 3 lines below are FOR TEST ONLY */
      CLOSE1(newsock);
      CLOSE(sfd);
      return(-1);

      /* Process the request. We simply print the request message here. */
      inbuf[ret] = '\0';
      fprintf(stdout, "\nReceived the following request from client:\n%s\n",
        inbuf);

      /* Construct a reply */
      sprintf(outbuf, "This is reply #%3u from the server program.", msgcnt++);
      msglen = strlen(outbuf);

      /* Send a reply. */
      errno = 0;
      ret = send(newsock, outbuf, msglen, 0);
      if (ret == -1)
        fprintf(stderr, "Error: send() failed, errno=%d, %s\n", ERRNO,
          ERRNOSTR);
      else
        fprintf(stdout, "%u of %lu bytes of the reply was sent.\n", ret, msglen);
      /* To create a situation where the server close first. */
      break;
    }
    else if (ret < 0)
    {
      fprintf(stderr, "Error: recv() failed, errno=%d, %s\n", ERRNO,
        ERRNOSTR);
      break;
    }
    else
    {
      /* The client may have disconnected. */
      fprintf(stdout, "The client may have disconnected.\n");
      break;
    }
  } /* while - inner */
```

```
    CLOSE1(newsock);
}   /* while - outer */

CLOSE(sfd);
return(0);
}
```

One potential use of the SO_REUSEPORT option is to allow multiple servers to bind to the same socket address and port number so that they can share the load from the clients. But this would need the operating system kernel's support to evenly distribute incoming connect requests over the servers.

It is worth mentioning that to prevent port hijacking, in Linux, it requires the second user and on to be the same user if it wants to use the REUSEPORT option to bind to the same port number. It is true even if the first user is non-root and the second user is root. At the time of this writing, AIX6.1 and HPUX 11.31 don't require that.

Summary

- Turning on the SO_REUSEPORT socket option allows two or more processes running on the same host to all bind to the same address and port number and even listen on it.

- All sockets involved must all turn on the SO_REUSEPORT option for it to work. If the very first one bound to the same address and port number does not turn the option on, then no others can bind to the same address and port number.

  However, there are exceptions to this general behavior.
  In Oracle/Solaris 11, with TCP protocol, even if all sockets turn on the SO_REUSEPORT option, all sockets are allowed to bind to the same address and port, but only the very first socket is allowed to listen on it.
  In this same platform, with UDP protocol, there is no requirement of all sockets must all turn on the option. That is, even if the first socket does not turn on the SO_REUSEPORT option, a second socket will be allowed to bind to the same address and port number and listen on it as long as it turns on the SO_REUSEPORT option.

- Some platforms (e.g. Linux) check and make sure all processes trying to bind to the same address and port number are running as the same user to prevent port hijacking while others (e.g. AIX and HPUX) don't.

- In Apple Darwin, to re-use a port in TIME_WAIT state, a server program must turn on either the SO_REUSEADDR or SO_REUSEPORT socket option. As long as the program trying to start does that, it will allow the same port to be reused even if the previous program that used it did not turn on the option. In Apple Darwin, the behavior of SO_REUSEADDR option is different from SO_REUSEPORT in one area. Turning on the SO_REUSEPORT option allows two TCP server programs to be able to bind to the same port number and run side by side at the same time on the same system, but turning on the SO_REUSEADDR option does not.

  In contrast, in Linux, a server program must turn on either the SO_REUSEADDR or SO_REUSEPORT socket option in order to reuse a port in

TIME_WAIT state. This is the same as in Apple Darwin. But Linux requires the same option was also turned on on the socket in the TIME_WAIT state for this to work. Just as in Apple Darwin, in Linux, turning on SO_REUSEPORT option allows two TCP server programs to be able to bind to the same port number and run side by side at the same time on the same system, but turning on the SO_REUSEADDR option does not.

13-7-6 Tuning the SO_REUSEADDR Option

Tuning at Operating System Kernel Level

As you know already, the solution stated above affects only the socket that the setsockopt(.., SO_REUSEADDR,..) is invoked on.
Some operating systems allow you to set some kernel parameters and set a default behavior for all applications for the SO_REUSEADDR socket option. Linux is one example. Note that tuning these SO_REUSEADDR related O.S. kernel parameters affects the default behavior all socket applications get whereas using the setsockopt() API to enable the option affects only one socket.

In Linux, there are a number of kernel parameters which are related to this. They are listed below.

  net.ipv4.tcp_fin_timeout

    This specifies the time (in seconds) to wait for a final FIN
    packet before the socket is forcibly closed. The default value is
    usually 60.

    $ /sbin/sysctl -a | grep net.ipv4.tcp_fin_timeout
    net.ipv4.tcp_fin_timeout = 60

  net.ipv4.tcp_tw_reuse

    Setting this parameter allows the system to reuse TIME_WAIT sockets
    for new connections when it is safe from protocol viewpoint.
    Default value is 0 (disabled).

    The 'tw' in the parameter name stands for TIME_WAIT.

    Setting both net.ipv4.tcp_tw_reuse and net.ipv4.tcp_tw_recycle to 1
    reduces the number of entries in the TIME_WAIT state.

    $ /sbin/sysctl -a | grep net.ipv4.tcp_tw_reuse
    net.ipv4.tcp_tw_reuse = 0

  net.ipv4.tcp_tw_recycle

      $ /sbin/sysctl -q -a |grep recycle
      net.ipv4.tcp_tw_recycle = 0

    This value is set to 0 (disabled) by default.
    Setting this parameter enables fast recycling of TIME_WAIT sockets.
    However, enabling this option is not recommended because it causes
    problems for public-facing servers when working with Network Address

Translation (NAT) devices, as it won't handle connections from two different computers behind the same NAT device, as stated by tcp(7) manual page.

In Linux, to turn on the SO_REUSEADDR socket option for all applications from within the operating system kernel, you must turn on the following two kernel parameters. By default, these two parameters are off (with a value 0).

```
# sysctl -a |grep tcp_tw_
net.ipv4.tcp_tw_recycle = 0
net.ipv4.tcp_tw_reuse = 0

# sysctl -w net.ipv4.tcp_tw_recycle=1 net.ipv4.tcp_tw_reuse=1
net.ipv4.tcp_tw_recycle = 1
net.ipv4.tcp_tw_reuse = 1
```

Doing this is sufficient in Linux 4.1.12. However, in older Linux, for example, 2.6.32, in addition to this, you must also change and increase the net.ipv4.tcp_fin_timeout parameter. This parameter usually has a default value of 60. For example,

```
# sysctl -q net.ipv4.tcp_fin_timeout
net.ipv4.tcp_fin_timeout = 60

# sysctl -w net.ipv4.tcp_fin_timeout=90
net.ipv4.tcp_fin_timeout = 90
```

Please be warned that the kernel implementations of this feature have changed a little bit in Linux over time.
As of September of 2017, net.ipv4.tcp_tw_recycle has been removed from Linux 4.12. Note: It is still in Linux 4.1.12.

Please be aware that changing these system-wide tunable parameters must be done with extreme caution because it affects all socket applications. Besides, there are some software products or networking devices which might reject the SYN packet if it reuses the same connection (i.e. source/destination IP address and source/destination port combinations are the same) too quickly. In those cases, changing these kernel parameters may actually break things.

Remember that the safest thing to do is to always change this from within an application by using the setsockopt() call so that it won't affect any other software products or applications running on the same system.

Test Output

(a) Do not turn on SO_REUSEADDR from within the O.S. kernel

Below is a sample output of not tuning SO_REUSEADDR option's kernel parameters:

```
# /sbin/sysctl -a |grep net.ipv4.tcp_fin_timeout
net.ipv4.tcp_fin_timeout = 60
# /sbin/sysctl -a |grep tcp_tw_
net.ipv4.tcp_tw_recycle = 0
```

```
 net.ipv4.tcp_tw_reuse = 0

$ uname -a
 Linux jvmy 4.1.12-124.19.2.el7.x86_64 #2 SMP Fri Sep 14 08:59:15 PDT 2018 x86_64
x86_64 x86_64 GNU/Linux
 $ date ; ./tcpsrv_reuse_all.lin4
 Sun Jan 27 09:06:43 PST 2019
 Connection-oriented server program ...
 SO_REUSEADDR socket option is turned off.
 TCP SO_REUSEADDR's current setting is 0.

 Listening at port number 2345 ...
 Client Connected.

 $ date ; ./tcpsrv_reuse_all.lin4
 Sun Jan 27 09:07:03 PST 2019
 Connection-oriented server program ...
 SO_REUSEADDR socket option is turned off.
 TCP SO_REUSEADDR's current setting is 0.
 Error: bind() failed, errno=98, Address already in use
 $ date ; ./tcpsrv_reuse_all.lin4
 Sun Jan 27 09:07:19 PST 2019
 Connection-oriented server program ...
 SO_REUSEADDR socket option is turned off.
 TCP SO_REUSEADDR's current setting is 0.
 Error: bind() failed, errno=98, Address already in use
 $ date ; ./tcpsrv_reuse_all.lin4
 Sun Jan 27 09:07:54 PST 2019
 Connection-oriented server program ...
 SO_REUSEADDR socket option is turned off.
 TCP SO_REUSEADDR's current setting is 0.
 Error: bind() failed, errno=98, Address already in use
 $ date ; ./tcpsrv_reuse_all.lin4
 Sun Jan 27 09:08:03 PST 2019
 Connection-oriented server program ...
 SO_REUSEADDR socket option is turned off.
 TCP SO_REUSEADDR's current setting is 0.

 Listening at port number 2345 ...

 (The server restarted successfully 60 seconds after client exited.)

 $ uname -a
 Linux jvmy 4.1.12-124.19.2.el7.x86_64 #2 SMP Fri Sep 14 08:59:15 PDT 2018 x86_64
x86_64 x86_64 GNU/Linux
 $ date ; ./tcpclnt_reuse_all.lin4 ; date
 Sun Jan 27 09:06:47 PST 2019
 Connection-oriented client program ...
 Send request messages to server(localhost) at port 2345

 53 bytes of message were successfully sent.
 Warning: Zero bytes were received.
 Sun Jan 27 09:07:02 PST 2019
 $
```

(b) Turn on SO_REUSEADDR from within the O.S. kernel

Below is a sample output of tuning SO_REUSEADDR option's
kernel parameters:

```
# /sbin/sysctl -w net.ipv4.tcp_tw_recycle=1 net.ipv4.tcp_tw_reuse=1
net.ipv4.tcp_tw_recycle = 1
net.ipv4.tcp_tw_reuse = 1
```

```
# /sbin/sysctl -a |grep net.ipv4.tcp_fin_timeout
net.ipv4.tcp_fin_timeout = 60
# /sbin/sysctl -a |grep tcp_tw_
net.ipv4.tcp_tw_recycle = 1
net.ipv4.tcp_tw_reuse = 1
```

```
$ uname -a
Linux jvmy 4.1.12-124.19.2.el7.x86_64 #2 SMP Fri Sep 14 08:59:15 PDT 2018 x86_64
x86_64 x86_64 GNU/Linux
$ date ; ./tcpsrv_reuse_all.lin4
Sun Jan 27 09:16:03 PST 2019
Connection-oriented server program ...
SO_REUSEADDR socket option is turned off.
TCP SO_REUSEADDR's current setting is 0.

Listening at port number 2345 ...
Client Connected.

$ date ; ./tcpsrv_reuse_all.lin4
Sun Jan 27 09:16:13 PST 2019
Connection-oriented server program ...
SO_REUSEADDR socket option is turned off.
TCP SO_REUSEADDR's current setting is 0.
Error: bind() failed, errno=98, Address already in use
$ date ; ./tcpsrv_reuse_all.lin4
Sun Jan 27 09:16:22 PST 2019
Connection-oriented server program ...
SO_REUSEADDR socket option is turned off.
TCP SO_REUSEADDR's current setting is 0.

Listening at port number 2345 ...

(The server restarted successfully as soon as the client exited.)

$ uname -a
Linux jvmy 4.1.12-124.19.2.el7.x86_64 #2 SMP Fri Sep 14 08:59:15 PDT 2018 x86_64
x86_64 x86_64 GNU/Linux
$ date ; ./tcpclnt_reuse_all.lin4 ; date
Sun Jan 27 09:16:05 PST 2019
Connection-oriented client program ...
Send request messages to server(localhost) at port 2345

53 bytes of message were successfully sent.
Warning: Zero bytes were received.
Sun Jan 27 09:16:20 PST 2019
$
```

13-7-7 Summary

There are different ways for a socket application to avoid the TCP TIME_WAIT trouble and avoid getting the "bind(): address already in use" error.

1. Operating System Independent

   At the network socket API level, a program can invoke the setsockopt() function to turn on the SO_REUSEADDR socket option, or the SO_REUSEPORT option in some cases. This tells the operating system that it is OK to re-use a port number in the TCP TIME_WAIT state, or is being used by another process. This is done from within an application itself and it affects only one socket.

2. Operating System Dependent

   There are some protocol-specific parameters inside the operating system kernel that can be tuned to change the behavior. This is operating system dependent. Also tuning these kernel parameters affects all socket applications on the system.

   For instance, in Linux, there are two kernel parameters one can tune:

   ```
   net.ipv4.tcp_tw_recycle = 1
   net.ipv4.tcp_tw_reuse = 1
   ```

   to enable the SO_REUSEADDR option.
   Contrary to the names, these parameters work for both IPv4 and IPv6.

13-8 The SO_RCVTIMEO and SO_SNDTIMEO options

Network socket I/O typically has two styles: synchronous and asynchronous. Synchronous I/O is blocking, meaning a receive call will block until some data has arrived or the other end terminates. This means the blocking wait could potentially last a very long time. In contrast, asynchronous calls return immediately and require the caller to go back and check the progress or completeness of the operation. Sometimes some application may find it cannot afford to wait too long or forever and need to set a limit on the amount of time it can block on an I/O operation.

The SO_RCVTIMEO option is used to set a timeout value for input operations on a socket. It takes a timeval structure with the number of seconds and microseconds specifying the limit on how long to wait for an input operation to complete. If a receive operation has blocked for this amount of time without receiving additional data, it will return. At that point, if no data were received, errno will be set to [EAGAIN] or [EWOULDBLOCK]. If partial data is received, it will return the partial count.

The SO_SNDTIMEO option works in a similar way for a socket send operation. It sets a limit on the amount of time a socket send operation would block.

By default, the value for SO_RCVTIMEO or SO_SNDTIMEO is zero second, meaning there is no timeout when a receive operation waits for data to be received or when a send operation waits data to be sent. That is, the default behavior is blocking forever potentially -- the synchronous mode behavior.

If you set the timeout value to, say, 15 seconds, then if no data is received or sent in that period of time, the receive or send function call will return with errno set to be EAGAIN (11 in Linux), meaning it has timed out.

Note that as of this writing, almost all operating systems tested support these options except HPUX.

Figure 13-11 lists a pair of programs that set the SO_RCVTIMEO option. The client sends a message to the server. The server deliberately waits for 15 seconds before sending a reply. Since the client has set the SO_RCVTIMEO to 10 seconds, its recv() call will time out and return with errno=EAGAIN ("try again") when the SO_RCVTIMEO time expires. Without setting the SO_RCVTIMEO option, the client's recv() call would have patiently waited until the server reply arrives.

Please notice that this pair of example programs are for the purpose of demonstrating what the SO_RCVTIMEO option does only. It inserts a long delay on the server side and chooses to exit the client when the timeout happens. These behaviors are not for real applications.

Figure 13-11 Programs demonstrating the SO_RCVTIMEO option (tcpsrv_timeo_all.c and tcpclnt_timeo_all.c)(For Demo only)

(a) tcpsrv_timeo_all.c

```
/*
 * A connection-oriented server program using Stream socket.
 * Demonstration of SO_RCVTIMEO socket option.
 * Support for IPv4 and IPv6. Default to IPV6. Compile with -DIPV4 to get IPV4.
 * Support for multiple platforms including Linux, Windows, Solaris, AIX, HPUX.
 * Usage: tcpsrv_timeo_all [port#]
 * Authored by Mr. Jin-Jwei Chen.
 * Copyright (c) 1993-2020, Mr. Jin-Jwei Chen. All rights reserved.
 */

#include "mysocket.h"
#define   DELAYTIME      15     /* inserted delay in seconds before a reply */

int main(int argc, char *argv[])
{
    int     ret;                     /* return code */
    int     sfd;                     /* file descriptor of the listener socket */
    int     newsock;                 /* file descriptor of client data socket */
#if IPV4
    struct sockaddr_in     srvaddr;  /* socket structure */
    int     srvaddrsz=sizeof(struct sockaddr_in);
    struct sockaddr_in     clntaddr; /* socket structure */
    socklen_t    clntaddrsz=sizeof(struct sockaddr_in);
#else
    struct sockaddr_in6    srvaddr;  /* socket structure */
    int     srvaddrsz=sizeof(struct sockaddr_in6);
    struct sockaddr_in6    clntaddr; /* socket structure */
```

```
  socklen_t      clntaddrsz=sizeof(struct sockaddr_in6);
  int     v6only = 0;                  /* IPV6_V6ONLY socket option off */
#endif
  in_port_t      portnum=DEFSRVPORT; /* port number */
  int     portnum_in = 0;              /* port number entered by user */
  char    inbuf[BUFLEN];               /* input message buffer */
  char    outbuf[BUFLEN];              /* output message buffer */
  size_t msglen;                       /* length of reply message */
  unsigned int  msgcnt;                /* message count */
  int     option;
  socklen_t optlen;

#if WINDOWS
  WSADATA wsaData;                     /* Winsock data */
  char* GetErrorMsg(int ErrorCode); /* print error string in Windows */
#endif

  fprintf(stdout, "Connection-oriented server program ...\n");

  /* Get the port number from user, if any. */
  if (argc > 1)
  {
    portnum_in = atoi(argv[1]);
    if (portnum_in <= 0)
    {
      fprintf(stderr, "Port number %d invalid, set to default value %u\n",
        portnum_in, DEFSRVPORT);
      portnum = DEFSRVPORT;
    }
    else
      portnum = (in_port_t)portnum_in;
  }

#if WINDOWS
  /* Initiate use of the Winsock DLL. Ask for Winsock version 2.2 at least. */
  if ((ret = WSAStartup(MAKEWORD(2, 2), &wsaData)) != 0)
  {
    fprintf(stderr, "WSAStartup() failed with error %d: %s\n",
      ret, GetErrorMsg(ret));
    return (-1);
  }
#endif

  /* Create the Stream server socket. */
  if ((sfd = socket(ADDR_FAMILY, SOCK_STREAM, 0)) < 0)
  {
    fprintf(stderr, "Error: socket() failed, errno=%d, %s\n", ERRNO, ERRNOSTR);
#if WINDOWS
    WSACleanup();
#endif
    return(-2);
  }

  /* Fill in the server socket address. */
  memset((void *)&srvaddr, 0, (size_t)srvaddrsz); /* clear the address buffer */
#if IPV4
```

```c
  srvaddr.sin_family = ADDR_FAMILY;                /* Internet socket */
  srvaddr.sin_addr.s_addr = htonl(INADDR_ANY);     /* server's IP address */
  srvaddr.sin_port = htons(portnum);               /* server's port number */
#else
  srvaddr.sin6_family = ADDR_FAMILY;               /* Internet socket */
  srvaddr.sin6_addr = in6addr_any;                 /* server's IP address */
  srvaddr.sin6_port = htons(portnum);              /* server's port number */
#endif

  /* If IPv6, turn off IPV6_V6ONLY socket option. Default is on in Windows. */
#if !IPv4
  if (setsockopt(sfd, IPPROTO_IPV6, IPV6_V6ONLY, (char*)&v6only,
    sizeof(v6only)) != 0)
  {
    fprintf(stderr, "Error: setsockopt(IPV6_V6ONLY) failed, errno=%d, %s\n",
      ERRNO, ERRNOSTR);
    CLOSE(sfd);
    return(-3);
  }
#endif

  /* Bind the server socket to its address. */
  if ((ret = bind(sfd, (struct sockaddr *)&srvaddr, srvaddrsz)) != 0)
  {
    fprintf(stderr, "Error: bind() failed, errno=%d, %s\n", ERRNO, ERRNOSTR);
    CLOSE(sfd);
    return(-4);
  }

  /* Set maximum connection request queue length that we can fall behind. */
  if (listen(sfd, BACKLOG) == -1) {
    fprintf(stderr, "Error: listen() failed, errno=%d, %s\n", ERRNO, ERRNOSTR);
    CLOSE(sfd);
    return(-5);
  }

  /* Wait for incoming connection requests from clients and service them. */
  while (1) {

    fprintf(stdout, "\nListening at port number %u ...\n", portnum);
    newsock = accept(sfd, (struct sockaddr *)&clntaddr, &clntaddrsz);
    if (newsock < 0)
    {
      fprintf(stderr, "Error: accept() failed, errno=%d, %s\n", ERRNO, ERRNOSTR);
      CLOSE(sfd);
      return(-6);
    }

    fprintf(stdout, "Client Connected.\n");

    msgcnt = 1;
    /* Receive and service requests from the current client. */
    while (1)
    {
      /* Receive a request from a client. */
      errno = 0;
```

```
      inbuf[0] = '\0';
      ret = recv(newsock, inbuf, BUFLEN, 0);
      if (ret > 0)
      {
        /* Process the request. We simply print the request message here. */
        inbuf[ret] = '\0';
        fprintf(stdout, "\nReceived the following request from client:\n%s\n",
          inbuf);

        /* Construct a reply */
        sprintf(outbuf, "This is reply #%3u from the server program.", msgcnt++);
        msglen = strlen(outbuf);

        /* TEST ONLY. Add this delay to test SO_RCVTIMEO on the client side. */
#if WINDOWS
        Sleep(1000*DELAYTIME); /* Unit ms. For demo only. Remove if real code. */
#else
        sleep(DELAYTIME);   /* For demo only. Remove this in real code. */
#endif

        /* Send a reply. */
        errno = 0;
        ret = send(newsock, outbuf, msglen, 0);
        if (ret == -1)
          fprintf(stderr, "Error: send() failed, errno=%d, %s\n", ERRNO,
            ERRNOSTR);
        else
          fprintf(stdout, "%u of %lu bytes of the reply was sent.\n", ret, msglen);
      }
      else if (ret < 0)
      {
        fprintf(stderr, "Error: recv() failed, errno=%d, %s\n", ERRNO,
          ERRNOSTR);
        break;
      }
      else
      {
        /* The client may have disconnected. */
        fprintf(stdout, "The client may have disconnected.\n");
        break;
      }
    }   /* while - inner */
    CLOSE1(newsock);
    break;   /* TEST ONLY */
  }   /* while - outer */

  CLOSE(sfd);
  return(0);
}
```

(b) tcpclnt_timeo_all.c

```
/*
 * A connection-oriented client program using Stream socket.
 * Demonstration of SO_RCVTIMEO socket option.
 * Connecting to a server program on any host using a hostname or IP address.
```

```
 * Support for IPv4 and IPv6 and multiple platforms including
 * Linux, Windows, Solaris, AIX and HPUX.
 * Usage: tcpclnt_timeo_all [srvport# [server-hostname | server-ipaddress]]
 * Authored by Mr. Jin-Jwei Chen.
 * Copyright (c) 1993-2019, 2020 Mr. Jin-Jwei Chen. All rights reserved.
 */

#include "mysocket.h"
#define TOSECONDS  10

int main(int argc, char *argv[])
{
  int     ret;
  int     sfd;                        /* socket file descriptor */
  in_port_t  portnum=DEFSRVPORT;   /* port number */
  int     portnum_in = 0;             /* port number user provides */
  char    *portnumstr = DEFSRVPORTSTR; /* port number in string format */
  char    inbuf[BUFLEN];              /* input message buffer */
  char    outbuf[BUFLEN];             /* output message buffer */
  size_t msglen;                      /* length of reply message */
  size_t msgnum=0;                    /* count of request message */
  size_t len;
  char    server_name[NAMELEN+1] = SERVER_NAME;
  struct addrinfo hints, *res=NULL;   /* address info */
  int     option;
  socklen_t optlen;
  struct timeval tmout;               /* timeout value */

#if WINDOWS
  WSADATA wsaData;                      /* Winsock data */
  char* GetErrorMsg(int ErrorCode);     /* print error string in Windows */
#endif

  fprintf(stdout, "Connection-oriented client program ...\n");

  /* Get the server's port number from command line. */
  if (argc > 1)
  {
    portnum_in = atoi(argv[1]);
    if (portnum_in <= 0)
    {
      fprintf(stderr, "Port number %d invalid, set to default value %u\n",
        portnum_in, DEFSRVPORT);
      portnum = DEFSRVPORT;
      portnumstr = DEFSRVPORTSTR;
    }
    else
    {
      portnum = (in_port_t)portnum_in;
      portnumstr = argv[1];
    }
  }

  /* Get the server's host name or IP address from command line. */
  if (argc > 2)
  {
```

```
    len = strlen(argv[2]);
    if (len > NAMELEN)
      len = NAMELEN;
    strncpy(server_name, argv[2], len);
    server_name[len] = '\0';
  }

#if WINDOWS
  /* Initiate use of the Winsock DLL. Ask for Winsock version 2.2 at least. */
  if ((ret = WSAStartup(MAKEWORD(2, 2), &wsaData)) != 0)
  {
    fprintf(stderr, "Error: WSAStartup() failed with error %d: %s\n",
      ret, GetErrorMsg(ret));
    return (-1);
  }
#endif

  /* Translate the server's host name or IP address into socket address.
   * Fill in the hint information.
   */
  memset(&hints, 0x00, sizeof(hints));
  /* This works on AIX but not on Solaris, nor on Windows. */
  /* hints.ai_flags    = AI_NUMERICSERV; */
  hints.ai_family   = AF_UNSPEC;
  hints.ai_socktype = SOCK_STREAM;
  hints.ai_protocol = IPPROTO_TCP;

  /* Get the address information of the server using getaddrinfo().
   * This function returns errors directly or 0 for success. On success,
   * argument res contains a linked list of addrinfo structures.
   */
  ret = getaddrinfo(server_name, portnumstr, &hints, &res);
  if (ret != 0)
  {
    fprintf(stderr, "Error: getaddrinfo() failed, error %d, %s\n", ret,
      gai_strerror(ret));
#if !WINDOWS
    if (ret == EAI_SYSTEM)
      fprintf(stderr,"System error: errno=%d, %s\n", errno, strerror(errno));
#else
    WSACleanup();
#endif
    return(-2);
  }

  /* Create a socket. */
  sfd = socket(res->ai_family, res->ai_socktype, res->ai_protocol);
  if (sfd < 0)
  {
    fprintf(stderr,"Error: socket() failed, errno=%d, %s\n", ERRNO, ERRNOSTR);
#if WINDOWS
    WSACleanup();
#endif
    return (-3);
  }
```

```c
  /* Connect to the server. */
  ret = connect(sfd, res->ai_addr, res->ai_addrlen);
  if (ret == -1)
  {
    fprintf(stderr, "Error: connect() failed, errno=%d, %s\n", ERRNO, ERRNOSTR);
    CLOSE(sfd);
    return(-4);
  }

  /* Get the socket receive timeout value set by the OS. */
  optlen = sizeof(tmout);
  memset((void *)&tmout, 0, optlen);
  ret = getsockopt(sfd, SOL_SOCKET, SO_RCVTIMEO, &tmout, &optlen);
  if (ret < 0)
  {
    fprintf(stderr, "Error: getsockopt(SO_RCVTIMEO) failed, errno=%d, %s\n",
      ERRNO, ERRNOSTR);
  }
  else
    fprintf(stdout, "SO_RCVTIMEO was originally set to be %lu:%u\n",
      tmout.tv_sec, tmout.tv_usec);

  /* Set the socket receive timeout value. */
#if WINDOWS
  tmout.tv_sec = TOSECONDS*1000;   /* Unit is milliseconds in Windows */
#else
  tmout.tv_sec = TOSECONDS;  /* Unit is seconds in Linux and Unix */
#endif
  tmout.tv_usec = 0;
  ret = setsockopt(sfd, SOL_SOCKET, SO_RCVTIMEO, &tmout, optlen);
  if (ret < 0)
  {
    fprintf(stderr, "Error: setsockopt(SO_RCVTIMEO) failed, errno=%d, %s\n",
      ERRNO, ERRNOSTR);
  }
  else
    fprintf(stdout, "SO_RCVTIMEO is set to be %lu:%u\n",
      tmout.tv_sec, tmout.tv_usec);

  /* Get the socket receive timeout value. */
  memset((void *)&tmout, 0, optlen);
  ret = getsockopt(sfd, SOL_SOCKET, SO_RCVTIMEO, &tmout, &optlen);
  if (ret < 0)
  {
    fprintf(stderr, "Error: getsockopt(SO_RCVTIMEO) failed, errno=%d, %s\n",
      ERRNO, ERRNOSTR);
  }
  else
    fprintf(stdout, "SO_RCVTIMEO now is %lu:%u\n",
      tmout.tv_sec, tmout.tv_usec);

  fprintf(stdout, "Send request messages to server(%s) at port %d\n",
    server_name, portnum);

  /* Send request messages to the server and process the reply messages. */
  while (msgnum < MAXMSGS)
```

```
   {
       /* Send a request message to the server. */
       sprintf(outbuf, "%s%4lu%s", "This is request message ", ++msgnum,
         " from the client program.");
       msglen = strlen(outbuf);
       errno = 0;

       ret = send(sfd, outbuf, msglen, 0);
       if (ret >= 0)
       {
         /* Print a warning if not entire message was sent. */
         if (ret == msglen)
           fprintf(stdout, "\n%lu bytes of message were successfully sent.\n",
             msglen);
         else if (ret < msglen)
           fprintf(stderr, "Warning: only %u of %lu bytes were sent.\n",
             ret, msglen);

         if (ret > 0)
         {
           /* Receive a reply from the server. */
           errno = 0;
           inbuf[0] = '\0';
           ret = recv(sfd, inbuf, BUFLEN, 0);

           if (ret > 0)
           {
             /* Process the reply. */
             inbuf[ret] = '\0';
             fprintf(stdout, "Received the following reply from server:\n%s\n",
               inbuf);
           }
           else if (ret == 0)
             fprintf(stdout, "Warning: Zero bytes were received.\n");
           else
           {
             fprintf(stderr, "Error: recv() failed, errno=%d, %s\n", ERRNO,
               ERRNOSTR);
             break;   /* For demo only. Remove this in real code. */
           }
         }
       }
       else
         fprintf(stderr, "Error: send() failed, errno=%d, %s\n", ERRNO, ERRNOSTR);

       /* Sleep a second. For demo only. Remove this in real code. */
#if WINDOWS
       Sleep(1000); /* Unit is ms. For demo only. Remove this in real code. */
#else
       sleep(1);   /* For demo only. Remove this in real code. */
#endif
   }   /* while */

   /* Free the memory allocated by getaddrinfo() */
   freeaddrinfo(res);
   CLOSE(sfd);
```

```
    return(0);
}
```

As you can see from running the programs, a recv() call returns with error
when the SO_RCVTIMEO time limit expires and no response has been received.
This could be due to the other side is slow but the network is working
or it could be the network is broken.

Below is the output of running the example programs.

```
    $ ./tcpsrv_timeo_all
    Connection-oriented server program ...

    Listening at port number 2345 ...
    Client Connected.

    Received the following request from client:
    This is request message    1 from the client program.
    43 of 43 bytes of the reply was sent.
    The client may have disconnected.

    $ ./tcpclnt_timeo_all 2345 jvmx
    Connection-oriented client program ...
    SO_RCVTIMEO was originally set to be 0:0
    SO_RCVTIMEO is set to be 10:0
    SO_RCVTIMEO now is 10:0
    Send request messages to server(jvmx) at port 2345

    53 bytes of message were successfully sent.
    Error: recv() failed, errno=11, Resource temporarily unavailable
```

HP-UX

Note that as of the writing of this book, the SO_RCVTIMEO and SO_SNDTIMEO
socket options are not yet supported in HP-UX 11, at least not in HP-UX 11.31.
You can compile your program but the timeout option just does not work
and has no effect.

Or if you link your application with the X/Open (-lxnet) library,
then the setsockopt() call to turn on the SO_RCVTIMEO option will get an
error 220 (ENOPROTOOPT), signaling it is not supported.

13-9 The SO_RCVLOWAT and SO_SNDLOWAT options

The SO_RCVLOWAT option sets the minimum number of bytes to process for socket
input operations. In general, receive calls block until any (non-zero)
amount of data is received, then return the smaller of the amount available
or the amount requested. The default value for SO_RCVLOWAT is 1, and
does not affect the general case. If SO_RCVLOWAT is set to a larger value,
blocking receive calls normally wait until they have received the smaller
of the low water mark value or the requested amount.

Receive calls may still return less than the low water mark if an error
occurs, a signal is caught, or the type of data next in the receive queue
is different from that returned (for example, out-of-band data).

977

As mentioned previously, the default value for SO_RCVLOWAT is 1 byte. It is implementation-defined whether the SO_RCVLOWAT option can be set.

Do the programming exercise on the SO_RCVLOWAT socket option to familiarize yourself with how the option works.

Review Questions/Exercises

1. What are the operating system kernel parameters related to socket buffer send and receive sizes on the system you are using? Are they common to both TCP and UDP sockets or separate?

2. What socket options can potentially be used to improve performance?

3. How do you find out what the default and maximum send and receive socket buffer sizes are on the system you are using? How can you change them?

4. What is the SO_KEEPALIVE socket option for? By default, is it enabled or disabled on the system you are using?

5. How do you enable the SO_KEEPALIVE socket option from within a program?

6. What are the keepalive tunable parameters at application level on the system you are using? What are their default values?

7. How do you change the keepalive tunable parameters at application level on the system you are using?

8. What are the keepalive tunable parameters at operating system kernel level on the system you are using? What are their default values?

9. How do you change the keepalive tunable parameters at operating system kernel level on the system you are using?

10. What happens if a program does not enable the SO_KEEPALIVE socket option?

11. What happens if a program does enable the SO_KEEPALIVE socket option but does not alter any of the keepalive tunable parameters?

12. What happens if a program enables the SO_KEEPALIVE socket option and also changes some or all of the keepalive tunable parameters?

13. What is SO_LINGER socket option?

14. Use example programs tcpsrv_reuse_all.c and tcpclnt_reuse_all.c to create the following error

```
$ ./tcpsrv_reuse_all 2345
Connection-oriented server program ...
SO_REUSEADDR socket option is turned off.
Error: bind() failed, errno=98, Address already in use
```

and measure how long you have to wait for that state to be cleared and the same server can restart successfully again.

15. What is SO_REUSEADDR socket option for?

16. Find out if the SO_REUSEPORT socket option is supported in the platform(s) you have access to. How is it different from and similar to SO_REUSEADDR option?

17. What does SO_RCVTIMEO option do?

18. What is SO_RCVLOWAT option?

Programming Assignments/Projects

1. Write a pair of client-server programs which enable the SO_KEEPALIVE option and change the keepalive tunable parameters at application level. Execute these programs, break the network connection and observe the behavior of the programs. Repeat with a node failure if you can.

2. Modify the example programs tcpsrv1.c and tcpclnt1.c from previous chapter so that you can test the SO_LINGER option. Turn on that option. Specifically, create the following sequence of events:

```
---------------------------------------------------------------
    tcpclnt                         tcpsrv
------------------------------  -------------------------------
Send first message
                                Receive first message from client
                                Send first reply to client
Receive first reply from server
Pause for a few seconds
Unplug the network cable at client side

Send second message & return right away
Call close() on the socket
Exit and terminate

Wait for some time
Plug the network cable back in

Wait for some time
                                Anything happens at the server side?
---------------------------------------------------------------
```

(a) What do you observe on the server side?

(b) Does the TCP server program get the second client message after the client program has terminated and then the network is restored? Can you explain why?

(c) Do the test once with SO_LINGER option on and another with the option off. Do you see the same or different behavior? Can you explain what you have observed?

(d) Try to wait for a much longer time before you restore the network.

Do you see a different behavior? Explain what you observe.

(e) Try the same experiment but instead unplug the network cable on server side this time. Do you observe any differences in behavior?

3. Perform the same SO_LINGER tests as described in the previous problem but with SO_KEEPALIVE option on and shortening the keepalive timeout period. Vary keepalive timeout period and your wait time. What do you observe? Explain the behavior you observe.

4. Change the pair of programs tcpclnt_bufsz.c and tcpsrv_bufsz.c to send a big file or files of different sizes. And set the send and receive buffers to different sizes. Measure and record the elapsed time of each experiment. What are the socket buffer sizes that deliver the best performance?

   Run the two programs on the same host and on two different hosts. Try to explain the performance data you obtain.

5. Find out if the platform you use supports the SO_EXCLUSIVEADDRUSE or SO_EXCLBIND socket option. Try to compile and run the example program in this chapter if it does.

6. Explain the similarities and differences between the SO_REUSEADDR and SO_REUSEPORT socket options. Find out and describe the behavior of the operating system's implementation you have access to.

7. Develop three TCP server programs which turn on SO_REUSEADDR, SO_REUSEPORT, and Exclusive Bind socket option, respectively. Then run these programs against each other competing on binding to the same port. Try to start these programs in different orders. Explain what you observe.

8. Write a pair of client-server programs to demonstrate the SO_SNDLOWAT and SO_RCVLOWAT options.

9. If your operating system is not Linux, find out if there are any kernel tunable parameters that allow you to tune the behavior of SO_REUSEADDR and SO_REUSEPORT socket options. Describe what they are and what each does. For those using Linux, find out if the behavior or implementation of these options has changed.

References

- Linux man pages
- RedHat Linux Documentations
- http://lartc.org/howto/lartc.kernel.obscure.html
- https://www.suse.com/documentation/sles11/book_sle_tuning/data/sec_tuning_network_buffers.html
- http://stackoverflow.com/questions/5907527/application-control-of-tcp-retransmission-on-linux
- http://www.linuxweblog.com/tuning-tcp-sysctlconf
- http://pubs.opengroup.org/onlinepubs/9699919799/
- http://www.cs.unc.edu/~jeffay/dirt/FAQ/sobuf.html

- http://www.cyberciti.biz/faq/linux-tcp-tuning/
- http://www.tldp.org/HOWTO/TCP-Keepalive-HOWTO/usingkeepalive.html
- Solaris Tunable Parameters Reference Manual (Solaris 11)
- Oracle Solaris 11.1 Tunable Parameters Reference Manual
- http://docs.oracle.com/cd/B10191_01/calendar.903/b10093/kernels.htm
- Oracle Solaris Administration: Network Interfaces and Network Virtualization
- http://www.symantec.com/docs/HOWTO64304
- http://docs.oracle.com/cd/E26502_01/html/E29022/appendixa-2.html
- http://www.onlamp.com/pub/a/onlamp/2005/11/17/tcp_tuning.html
- IBM AIX man pages
- IBM AIX 6.1 Documentations
- IBM AIX 7.1 Documentations
- IBM AIX 7.1 Reference Communications
- IBM AIX Network Communication Management Guide
- Tuning AIX Network Performance
- IBM AIX 6.1 Networks and communication Management
- IBM Tivoli Directory Server Documentation
- IBM Security Directory Server Documentation
- Microsoft MSDN
- http://www.ibmsystemsmag.com/aix/administrator/networks/network_tuning/
- http://publib.boulder.ibm.com/iseries/v5r2/ic2928/index.htm?info/apis/ssocko.htm
- http://www01.ibm.com/support/knowledgecenter/SSTVLU_7.0.0/
  com.ibm.websphere.extremescale.admin.doc/rxsopchecklist.html
- https://publib.boulder.ibm.com/infocenter/tsminfo/v6/index.jsp?topic=%2Fcom.ibm.
  itsm.perf.doc%2Fc_network_aix_srv_clnt.html
- HP-UX 11i man pages
- HP-UX 11i TCP/IP Performance White Paper
- HP-UX Documentations
- http://docs.hp.com
- http://h30499.www3.hp.com/t5/Networking/How-to-enable-TCP-Keepalive-on-a-
  system/td-p/3671660#.VIRshGex18E
- http://h30499.www3.hp.com/t5/System-Administration/Configuring-TCP-KeepAlive-
  Parameters/td-p/4751119#.VIRqsGex18E
- FreeBSD Tuning and Optimization
- https://wiki.freebsd.org/SystemTuning
- https://www.freebsd.org/doc/handbook/configtuning-kernel-limits.html
- https://www.freebsd.org/doc/handbook/config-tuning.html
- https://calomel.org/freebsd_network_tuning.html
- http://rerepi.wordpress.com/2008/04/19/tuning-freebsd-sysoev-rit/
- http://www.starquest.com/Supportdocs/techStarLicense/SL002_TCPKeepAlive.shtml
- StarQuest Technical Documents
- http://knowledgebase.progress.com/articles/Article/20017
- Microsoft Windows Server TCP/IP Implementation Details
- Winsock ProgrammerÂ's FAQ
- http://tangentsoft.net/wskfaq/articles/lame-list.html
- http://technet.microsoft.com/en-us/library/cc957549.aspx
- http://smallvoid.com/article/winnt-winsock-buffer.html
- http://msdn.microsoft.com/en-
  us/library/windows/desktop/ms740476%28v=vs.85%29.aspx
- http://www-01.ibm.com/support/docview.wss?uid=swg21190501
- http://www.analyticalsystems.com.au/confluence/display/PUB04/
  Configure+Windows+Keep+Alive+network+setting
- http://www.gnugk.org/keepalive.html
- https://hea-www.harvard.edu/~fine/Tech/addrinuse.html
  (Bind: Address Already in Use)
- RFC 1122

- RFC 2525
- https://tools.ietf.org/html/rfc793 (RFC 793) (TIME-WAIT state)
- http://wwwx.cs.unc.edu/~sparkst/howto/network_tuning.php
- http://stackoverflow.com/questions/3757289/tcp-option-so-linger-zero-when-its-required
- http://support.esri.com/ja/knowledgebase/techarticles/detail/25129
- http://www.ccplusplus.com/2011/09/solinger-example.html
- http://blog.netherlabs.nl/articles/2009/01/18/the-ultimate-so_linger-page-or-why-is-my-tcp-not-reliable
- http://en.wikipedia.org/wiki/Keepalive
- http://www.tldp.org/HOWTO/TCP-Keepalive-HOWTO/usingkeepalive.html
- http://www.tldp.org/HOWTO/TCP-Keepalive-HOWTO/overview.html
- http://ltxfaq.custhelp.com/app/answers/detail/a_id/1512/~/tcp-keepalives-explained
- https://www.freebsd.org/cgi/man.cgi?query=tcp
- https://www.kernel.org/doc/Documentation/networking/ip-sysctl.txt
- https://docstore.mik.ua/manuals/hp-ux/en/B2355-60130/TCP.7P.html
- http://www.serverframework.com/asynchronousevents/2011/01/time-wait-and-its-design-implications-for-protocols-and-scalable-servers.html (TIME_WAIT)

References for TIME_WAIT state and "Address already in use" error

- https://hea-www.harvard.edu/~fine/Tech/addrinuse.html
- https://stackoverflow.com/questions/14388706/socket-options-so-reuseaddr-and-so-reuseport-how-do-they-differ-do-they-mean-t
- http://man7.org/linux/man-pages/man7/socket.7.html
- https://lwn.net/Articles/542629/
- http://man7.org/linux/man-pages/man7/socket.7.html
- http://alas.matf.bg.ac.rs/manuals/lspe/snode=104.html
- https://medium.com/uckey/the-behaviour-of-so-reuseport-addr-1-2-f8a440a35af6
- https://qiita.com/SHUAI/items/07573e8a2be37bf3e8d1
- https://docs.microsoft.com/en-us/windows/desktop/winsock/using-so-reuseaddr-and-so-exclusiveaddruse
- https://my.oschina.net/miffa/blog/390932

14 Design of Distributed Software

We talk about how to design and implement a real distributed application in this chapter. Issues normally encountered in the design of a distributed application are discussed.

When you design and implement a real distributed application, the following are the issues you will typically face or encounter:

- **Endian**
- **Alignment**
- **Mixing 32-bit and 64-bit modes**
- **Versioning**
- **Backward and forward compatibility**
- **Interoperability**
- **Security, such as authentication and preventing DOS attacks**

We will discuss how to solve these issues in this chapter.

14-1 Endian

14-1-1 What Is Endian?

Endianness is one of many attributes of a computer CPU's architecture. It has to do with in what order a computer processor stores the individual bytes of a multi-byte integer in memory or in storage media. Therefore, **endianness** is all about **byte ordering**.

Different computer central processors store multi-byte integers in memory or storage media in different orders. Although there could be other possible variations, there are essentially two types of computer processors in this regard:

1. little endian
2. big endian

Little endian CPU architecture stores the least significant byte of a multi-byte integer at the lowest memory address whereas a big-endian CPU stores the most significant byte of the integer at the lowest memory address location.

Figure 14-1 shows how the 32-bit integer 0x01020304 in hexadecimal is stored on little-endian and big-endian computers.

As you can see from the figure, the bytes of the integer are stored in exactly opposite order on little-endian and big-endian computers.

(a) little-endian

memory locations

```
address   contents
          |-----|
10000     |  4  |
          |-----|
10001     |  3  |
          |-----|
10002     |  2  |
          |-----|
10003     |  1  |
          |-----|
```

(b) big-endian

memory locations

```
address   contents
          |-----|
10000     |  1  |
          |-----|
10001     |  2  |
          |-----|
10002     |  3  |
          |-----|
10003     |  4  |
          |-----|
```

Figure 14-1 Little-endian and big-endian (storing integer 0x01020304)

Modern computer processors that use little endian format include Intel x86 architecture and the DEC/HP Alpha processor. In the old days, the once very popular DEC VAX computers used in so many colleges around the world were also little-endian.

Computer processors such as IBM POWER/PowerPC, Oracle/SUN SPARC, HP PARISC are big endian. So are processors from SGI and Fujitsu.

14-1-2 Why Endianness Matters?

Why endianness matters? It matters because for binary integer data, endianness is like a type of encoding. Different endianness is like different encodings. If you don't know about the encoding (endianness) of the data, you could end up with interpreting the data in a completely wrong way.

For example, if you give me the integer 0x01020304 in little endian format and I do not know it's in little endian and try to interpret it as-is on a big-endian machine, then I would get the number 0x04030201, which would be completely wrong!

That is, it is **a correctness issue** for binary integer data!
Therefore, it is absolutely paramount that you know the endian format of
a binary integer data before interpreting or using the data.

14-1-3 When Endianness Matters?

Endianness matters when you try to **interpret or use** a **multiple-byte integer**
represented or stored **in binary format.**

Note that it's only the integer data that you need to be concerned about
its endianness. String data does not have this concern.
Not only that, it's also only if you store the integers in binary format
and if each integer occupies more than one byte of memory or storage.
Integers represented in string form or single-byte integers do not
have endianness issue either.

For example, if you have integer data but all of them are all one byte
long, then you have nothing to worry about. This is because byte ordering
issue doesn't exist when data is a single byte. Or if you have integer data
but all of them are represented or encoded in ASCII format, then you have
nothing to worry about either. This is because in ASCII, each individual
digit in an integer is separately encoded in a single byte. As a result,
there is no byte-ordering, and thus no endianness, involved in ASCII data.
In other words, ASCII data and single-byte binary integer data are portable
across computers with different endian. Unicode data is considered string
data too because although each character is encoded into multiple bytes,
the multiple bytes are not interpreted as one integer. For these types of
data, endianness is not an issue and absolutely no conversion is ever needed.

If your program produces and computes binary integer data and that data
is never transported or used outside that same computer, then you don't
need to worry about endian issues, either.

CPU endianness matters only if you produce binary integer data on one
computer and try to use it on another. This includes at least two situations.

First, a very common application is that a program such as a database system
generates binary integer data, writes the data into a file and that data
file is then read and used by another computer. If the computer consuming
the file has a different endian format than the computer creating the file,
then endian issue arises.

Second, a networking application tries to send binary integer data across
the network to another computer of a different endianness.

In both of these situations, a piece of binary integer data is produced
or written by a computer with a certain endian format and that data is
then interpreted and used by another computer with a different endian
format. This is when problems occur because the data can be interpreted
wrong due to the different endianness. In other words, endian issue surfaces
only when you try to interpret and use a piece of binary integer data
and the endian format of the writing computer is different from that of
the reading computer.

Different endianness becomes a problem only when you create or produce the

binary integer data on a computer of one endianness and try to interpret or use that data on a computer of different endianness.
For example, if the binary integer data is generated on an IBM POWER AIX or Oracle/SUN SPARC Solaris system, which is big endian, and is then consumed on a Windows system on Intel CPU, which is little endian, or vice versa.

It's the interpretation or use of the binary integer data on a different endianness environment that the endianness issue comes into play.
So, if it's on a different computer that you try to interpret the data but it has the same endianness as the computer where the data was created, then no problem at all. Or if you move the data to another computer that has a different endianness but just store it there and not trying to interpret or use it, then there is no problem either, as long as you ensure the moving, copying, or transporting process is done in binary mode and the data is not altered during that process.

For example, you can send or ftp a file created on a little-endian computer with all of your integer data in it across the network to another big-endian computer and then again send it to a third computer with a little-endian CPU. Then you can still interpret that data just fine at the destination as long as you ensure the data is not altered during the transport.
In other words, just storing the data as-is or sending it through a computer of different endianness is not a problem as long as you do not try to interpret or use it on a different endianness computer.

CPU endianness matters only if you are transporting integer data stored in binary format from one computer to another and the two have different endian formats, or exchanging/sharing this type of data between two computers and the two computers involved are of different endianness.

Summary

It's only integer data that is in binary form that is endian sensitive.
Integer data in ASCII or Unicode format is not endian sensitive.
It's only multi-byte integer data that is endian sensitive.
Single-byte integer data is not endian sensitive even in binary form.
Character or text data is not endian sensitive either.

Also, it is the interpretation or use of the binary integer data that touches the nerve of the endianness. If you are just storing the data or simply transporting it from one computer to another without actually trying to use or interpret it, you don't need to worry about the different endianness either.

14-1-4 How to Determine the Endianness of a Computer

Since if you do not handle endianness properly your program may produce wrong results, as a software engineer, it's your job to know how to determine the endianness of a computer.

You can determine the endianness of a computer programmatically.
The endian() function in Figure 14-2 does exactly that.

Figure 14-2 shows a program that displays the endian format of a computer.
It stores a 4-byte integer in memory and then checks the value of the byte

location with the lowest address to determine whether it's a little-endian or big-endian CPU.

Figure 14-2 Program that displays the endianness of the local computer -- get_my_endian.c

```c
/*
 * Get the endian format of this local computer.
 * Authored by Jin-Jwei Chen
 * Copyright (c) 2010-2019 Mr. Jin-Jwei Chen. All rights reserved.
 */

#include <stdio.h>
#include "mydistsys.h"

/* Find the endian type of this local CPU */
int endian()
{
  unsigned int        x = 0x01020304;
  unsigned char       *px = (unsigned char *)&x;

  if (px[0] == 0x01)
    return(BIG_ENDIAN);
  else if (px[0] == 0x04)
    return(LITTLE_ENDIAN);
  else
    return(UNKNOWN_ENDIAN);
}

int main(int argc, char *argv[])
{
  int    myendian;

  myendian = endian();
  if (myendian == LITTLE_ENDIAN)
    printf("This is a little endian processor.\n");
  else if (myendian == BIG_ENDIAN)
    printf("This is a big endian processor.\n");
  else
    printf("This is not a little or big endian processor.\n");
}
```

14-1-5 Different Ways to Solve the Cross-Endian Problem

Let's say you have some multi-byte binary integer data that you have to transport between computers that have different endianness.
How do you make sure after the transport, your data gets interpreted correctly at the receiving end which has a different endianness?

There are a number of ways to solve the cross-endian problem.

First, put all binary integer data in transit in one and only one format. Just pick one, whether it's big-endian or little-endian does not really matter. Then on the sender side, you make sure the data is always in that endian format before sending it. If necessary, you convert the data into that

endian format. On the receiver side, you know what endian format you are
getting the data in. Hence, if necessary, you convert the data into the local
endian format. This way, you don't need to know the endianness of the
computers involved in the transporting or communications because you know
the data in transit is always in a known endian format. You do the
conversion to that known endian format, if necessary, on the sender side
before sending and you do the conversion from that known endian format
to your local format at the receiver side if necessary.

Note that each computer can call the endian() function presented above to
know its own endian format and determine if it needs to do the endian
conversion or not.

The scheme we just described above is actually the way that the Internet
(the TCP/IP) protocol does it. It always makes sure that the sending computer
always puts the binary integer data in the so-called **"network byte order"**
before it is being sent across the network so that the receiving computer
always knows exactly what endian format it is getting.
The actual implementation of the Internet chooses the big-endian format
as the network byte order. So today all applications sending binary integer
data across Internet all convert the data to big-endian format first
and all applications receiving binary integer data from the Internet
convert it from big-endian format to the local host's endian format.

Second, another approach is that right after a network connection is
established, the two computers exchange information of their respective
endianness. The sender which produces the data always sends the data in
its endianness without doing any conversion. The receiver compares its
own endianness with the sender's endianness, and if they are different,
then the receiver does the necessary endian conversion after receiving the
data. This approach requires building the endian information exchange into
the application protocol and only the receiving end does the conversion
when necessary, as opposed to potentially converting every piece of binary
integer data at both ends as the Internet protocol does.

A third approach is to make the data being transported or exchanged self
identifying in terms of endianness, which we will discuss in the next
section.

14-1-6 Writing/Reading Binary Files Portable Across Different Endian Formats

In this section, we introduce a technique of creating portable data file.

It's very common that data generated from one computer is written into a
data file in binary format and later used by another computer.
And it is very likely that the two computers could have different endian
formats.

Let's say you need to produce and send a binary file containing binary
multi-byte integer data between computers having different endian formats.
The file is written in the endianness of the computer that creates it.

To ensure the binary data file is portable across different hardware
platforms, one must write the data file in a self-describing manner.
This is typically done by **having a file header record at the very beginning**

of the data file where different data fields in the header describe different attributes of the file such as endian format of the data, how many data records in the file, size of each data record, name of this data file, etc.

One way to do this is to have a file header and put the endianness of the computer creating the file in the file header. That way the consumer of the file can read the endian format stored in the file header, check it, and then decide whether or not to do endian conversions of the integer data fields read from the file.

By doing this, the writer of the data file does not need to do any endian format conversion before writing the data. And the reader of the file will have to perform the endian conversion only if it has a different endian format than the writer.

Note that, the endian format must be represented as a **single-byte data,** that is, of type 'char' or 'unsigned char' in C language. This is so that it is endian independent by itself and is guaranteed to be portable across all platforms.

```
 ---------------------------- \
| endian format: little endian | |
| number of records: n1        | | file header (record)
| record size:  n2             | |
| file name: XYZ               | |
|   :                          | |
|------------------------------|/
| first data record            |\
|------------------------------| |
| second data record           | |
|------------------------------| | actual file data
|   :                          | |
 ---------------------------- /
```

Figure 14-3 Layout of a portable data file

Figure 14-4 is a program that illustrates how to create a data file in a format that is portable across all processors of different endian. It records the endian format of the computer that creates the data file in a single-byte data field in the file header so that the consumer of the file can read it and know how to interpret the binary integer fields in each of the data record.

Figure 14-5 shows the three small header files that are used in the example program.

Figure 14-4 Exchange data between computers with different endian using portable file -- exchange_rec.c

```
/*
 * Writing or reading portable data records.
 * Writing portable binary output file that can be correctly read on any
 * machines with different endian or reading it.
 * Authored by Mr. Jin-Jwei Chen.
 * Copyright (c) 2008-2019, 2020 Mr. Jin-Jwei Chen. All rights reserved.
```

```
 */

#ifdef WINDOWS
#include <fcntl.h>
#include <sys/types.h>
#include <sys/stat.h>
#include <io.h>
#include <stdio.h>
typedef int    ssize_t;
typedef unsigned int   mode_t;
#endif


#include "mystdhdr.h"
#include "myerrors.h"
#include "mydistsys.h"


#define   READF         1           /* read file */
#define   WRITEF        2           /* write file */
#define   READ          "read"
#define   Write         "write"
#define   FNAME_LEN     32          /* Max. length of file name */
#define   NRECORDS      2           /* number of records */
#define   DEF_FILE_NAME  "portable_recs"  /* default file name */

/* Write actual data records */
int write_data_rec(int fd)
{
  data_rec_t   datarec;           /* data record */
  ssize_t      recsz;             /* record size in byes */
  ssize_t      bytes;             /* number of bytes written */

  /* Write first data record */
  strcpy(datarec.name, "Jennifer Johnson");
  datarec.birthyear = 1980;
  datarec.salary = 224000;
  datarec.bonus = 1234500;
  recsz = sizeof(datarec);
  bytes = write(fd, (void *)&datarec, recsz);
  if (bytes == -1)
  {
    fprintf(stderr, "Error: write_data_rec() failed to write data record "
      "to file, errno=%d\n", errno);
    close(fd);
    return(PROD_ERR_WRITE);
  }

  if (bytes != recsz)
  {
    fprintf(stderr, "Error: write_data_rec() failed to write data record "
      "to file, only %ld of %ld bytes written.\n", bytes, recsz);
    close(fd);
    return(PROD_ERR_WRITE);
  }

  /* Write second data record */
  strcpy(datarec.name, "Allan Smith");
```

```c
  datarec.birthyear = 1970;
  datarec.salary = 448000;
  datarec.bonus = 2469000;
  recsz = sizeof(datarec);
  bytes = write(fd, (void *)&datarec, recsz);
  if (bytes == -1)
  {
    fprintf(stderr, "Error: write_data_rec() failed to write data record "
      "to file, errno=%d\n", errno);
    close(fd);
    return(PROD_ERR_WRITE);
  }

  if (bytes != recsz)
  {
    fprintf(stderr, "Error: write_data_rec() failed to write data record "
      "to file, only %ld of %ld bytes written.\n", bytes, recsz);
    close(fd);
    return(PROD_ERR_WRITE);
  }
  return(SUCCESS);
}

/* Write data records to a file */
int write_rec_file(char *filename)
{
  int       ret;               /* return code */
  int       fd;                /* file descriptor */
  ssize_t   recsz;             /* record size in byes */
  ssize_t   bytes;             /* number of bytes written */
  int       myendian;          /* this CPU's endian type */
  mode_t    mode = 0644;       /* file permissions */
  portable_data_hdr_t  hdr;    /* header of data file */

  if (filename == (char *)NULL)
    return(EINVAL);

  /* Open the output file */
  fd = open(filename, O_CREAT|O_WRONLY|O_TRUNC, mode);
  if (fd == (-1))
  {
    fprintf(stderr, "Error: write_rec_file() failed to open file %s, "
      "errno=%d\n", filename, errno);
    return(PROD_ERR_OPEN);
  }

  /* Write the file header record */
  hdr.endian = endian();
  hdr.version = 1;
  hdr.magic = DATA_MAGIC;
  hdr.nrecs = NRECORDS;
  recsz = sizeof(hdr);
  bytes = write(fd, (void *)&hdr, recsz);
  if (bytes == -1)
  {
    fprintf(stderr, "Error: write_rec_file() failed to write file header "
```

```
        "to file %s, errno=%d\n", filename, errno);
      close(fd);
      return(PROD_ERR_WRITE);
    }

  if (bytes != recsz)
    {
      fprintf(stderr, "Error: write_rec_file() failed to write file header "
        "to file %s, only %ld of %ld bytes written.\n", filename, bytes, recsz);
      close(fd);
      return(PROD_ERR_WRITE);
    }

  /* Write actual data records */
  ret = write_data_rec(fd);
  if (ret == SUCCESS)
    fprintf(stdout, "The data file was successfully created.\n");
  else
    fprintf(stderr, "Creating the data file was unsuccessful.\n");

  close(fd);
  return(ret);
}

/* Print the contents of the file header */
void print_hdr(portable_data_hdr_t *hdr)
{
  if (hdr == (portable_data_hdr_t *)NULL)
    return;
  fprintf(stdout,"\nContents of the file header:\n");
  fprintf(stdout, "  hdr->endian = %d\n", hdr->endian);
  if (endian() == hdr->endian)
    {
      fprintf(stdout, "  hdr->version = %d\n", hdr->version);
      fprintf(stdout, "  hdr->magic = %d\n", hdr->magic);
      fprintf(stdout, "  hdr->nrecs = %llu\n", hdr->nrecs);
    }
  else
    {
      fprintf(stdout, "  hdr->version = %d\n", myByteSwap4(hdr->version));
      fprintf(stdout, "  hdr->magic = %d\n", myByteSwap4(hdr->magic));
      fprintf(stdout, "  hdr->nrecs = %llu\n", myByteSwap8(hdr->nrecs));
    }
  return;
}

/* Print the contents of a data record */
void print_data_rec(data_rec_t *datarec, portable_data_hdr_t *hdr)
{
  if (datarec == (data_rec_t *)NULL || hdr == (portable_data_hdr_t *)NULL)
    return;

  fprintf(stdout, "\n  name = %s\n", datarec->name);

  /* For the binary integer data items, if the endian type is the same,
   * print what is read.  Otherwise, byte swap the value before printing it.
```

```c
*/
  if (endian() == hdr->endian)
  {
    fprintf(stdout, "  birthyear = %u\n", datarec->birthyear);
    fprintf(stdout, "  salary = %u\n", datarec->salary);
    fprintf(stdout, "  bonus = %u\n", datarec->bonus);
  }
  else
  {
    fprintf(stdout, "  birthyear = %u\n", myByteSwap4(datarec->birthyear));
    fprintf(stdout, "  salary = %u\n", myByteSwap4(datarec->salary));
    fprintf(stdout, "  bonus = %u\n", myByteSwap4(datarec->bonus));
  }
  return;
}

/* Read records from a binary data file */
int read_rec_file(char *filename)
{
  int        ret;                   /* return code */
  int        fd;                    /* file descriptor */
  ssize_t    recsz;                 /* record size in byes */
  ssize_t    bytes;                 /* number of bytes read */
  int        myendian;             /* this CPU's endian type */
  portable_data_hdr_t  hdr;        /* header of data file */
  int        i;                     /* loop index */
  data_rec_t  datarec;             /* data record */
  unsigned int hdrmagic;           /* magic number in the file header */

  if (filename == (char *)NULL)
    return(EINVAL);

  /* Open the data file */
  fd = open(filename, O_RDONLY);
  if (fd == (-1))
  {
    fprintf(stderr, "Error: read_rec_file() failed to open file %s, "
      "errno=%d\n", filename, errno);
    return(PROD_ERR_OPEN);
  }

  /* Read the file header record */
  recsz = sizeof(hdr);
  bytes = read(fd, (void *)&hdr, recsz);
  if (bytes == -1)
  {
    fprintf(stderr, "Error: read_rec_file() failed to read file header "
      "from file %s, errno=%d\n", filename, errno);
    close(fd);
    return(PROD_ERR_READ);
  }

  if (bytes != recsz)
  {
    fprintf(stderr, "Error: read_rec_file() failed to read file header "
      "from file %s, only %ld of %ld bytes read.\n", filename, bytes, recsz);
```

```
      close(fd);
      return(PROD_ERR_READ);
   }

   /* Get the magic number from the file header and do a sanity check */
   if (endian() == hdr.endian)
      hdrmagic = hdr.magic;
   else
      hdrmagic = myByteSwap4(hdr.magic);
   if (hdrmagic != DATA_MAGIC)
   {
      fprintf(stderr, "Error: read_rec_file() found magic number mismatch.\n");
      close(fd);
      return(PROD_ERR_WRONGMAGIC);
   }

   print_hdr(&hdr);

   /* Read and print actual data records */
   fprintf(stdout, "\nContents of the data records follow:\n");
   for (i = 0; i < NRECORDS; i++)
   {
      recsz = sizeof(datarec);
      bytes = read(fd, (void *)&datarec, recsz);
      if (bytes == -1)
      {
         fprintf(stderr, "Error: read_rec_file() failed to read data record "
            "from file %s, errno=%d\n", filename, errno);
         close(fd);
         return(PROD_ERR_READ);
      }
      if (bytes != recsz)
      {
         fprintf(stderr, "Error: read_rec_file() failed to read data record "
            "from file %s, only %ld of %ld bytes read.\n", filename, bytes, recsz);
         close(fd);
         return(PROD_ERR_READ);
      }

      print_data_rec(&datarec, &hdr);
   }

   close(fd);
   return(SUCCESS);
}

int main(int argc, char *argv[])
{
   int     action = READF;
   char    action_str[8] = READ;
   char    filename[FNAME_LEN+1] = DEF_FILE_NAME;
   int     len = 0;

   if (argc > 1)
   {
      if (argv[1][0] == 'r' || argv[1][0] == 'R')
```

```
    {
      action = READF;
      strcpy(action_str, "read");
    }
    else if (argv[1][0] == 'w' || argv[1][0] == 'W')
    {
      action = WRITEF;
      strcpy(action_str, "write");
    }
    else
    {
      fprintf(stderr, "Usage: %s [r|w|R|W] filename\n", argv[0]);
      return(PROD_ERR_BAD_SYNTAX);
    }
  }

  if (argc > 2)
  {
    len = strlen(argv[2]);
    if (len > FNAME_LEN)
    {
      fprintf(stderr, "Error, file name %s is too long.\n", argv[2]);
      return(PROD_ERR_NAME_TOOLONG);
    }
    else
    {
      strncpy(filename, argv[2], len);
      filename[len] = '\0';
    }
  }

  fprintf(stdout, "To %s portable binary file %s ...\n", action_str, filename);

  if (action == READF)
    return(read_rec_file(filename));
  else if (action == WRITEF)
    return(write_rec_file(filename));

  return(SUCCESS);
}
```

Figure 14-5 Header files: mystdhdr.h, myerrors.h and mydistsys.h

(a) mystdhdr.h

```
/*
 * My cross-platform standard include file.
 * Copyright (c) 2002, 2014-2019 Mr. Jin-Jwei Chen. All rights reserved.
 */

#include <stdio.h>
#include <errno.h>
#include <string.h>          /* memset(), strerror() */
#include <stdlib.h>          /* atoi() */

#ifdef WINDOWS
```

```
#define WIN32_LEAN_AND_MEAN
#include <Winsock2.h>
#include <ws2tcpip.h>
#include <mstcpip.h>
#include <Windows.h>          /* Sleep() - link Kernel32.lib */

/* Needed for the Windows 2000 IPv6 Tech Preview. */
#if (_WIN32_WINNT == 0x0500)
#include <tpipv6.h>
#endif

#define STRICMP _stricmp
typedef unsigned short in_port_t;
typedef unsigned int in_addr_t;

#else   /* ! WINDOWS */

/* Unix and Linux */
#include <sys/types.h>
#include <sys/socket.h>
#include <netinet/in.h>       /* protocols such as IPPROTO_TCP, ... */
#include <arpa/inet.h>        /* inet_pton(), inet_ntoa() */
#include <netdb.h>            /* struct hostent, gethostbyaddr() */
#include <time.h>             /* nanosleep() */
/* The next few are for async I/O and file I/O. */
#include <unistd.h>
#include <fcntl.h>
#include <sys/time.h>
#include <sys/select.h>
#include <sys/stat.h>
/* Below is for Unix Domain socket */
#include <sys/un.h>

#endif
```

(b) myerrors.h

```
/*
 * All error codes defined by the application.
 * Supported operating systems: Linux, Unix (AIX, Solaris, HP-UX),
 * Apple Darwin and Windows.
 * Copyright (c) 1995, 2014, 2019-2020 Mr. Jin-Jwei Chen. All rights reserved.
 */

#include <errno.h>           /* system-defined errors */

/*
 * Error codes defined by applications
 */

/* Success */
#define SUCCESS 0

/* Base value of all error codes defined. */
#define BASE_ERROR_NUM 5000
```

```
/* All error codes from component 1. */
#define PROD_ERR_WINSOCK_INIT        (BASE_ERROR_NUM+1)
#define PROD_ERR_GETADDRINFO         (BASE_ERROR_NUM+2)
#define PROD_ERR_SOCKET_CREATE       (BASE_ERROR_NUM+3)
#define PROD_ERR_BIND                (BASE_ERROR_NUM+4)
#define PROD_ERR_LISTEN              (BASE_ERROR_NUM+5)
#define PROD_ERR_ACCEPT              (BASE_ERROR_NUM+6)
#define PROD_ERR_CONNECT             (BASE_ERROR_NUM+7)
#define PROD_ERR_SOCKET_SEND         (BASE_ERROR_NUM+8)
#define PROD_ERR_SOCKET_RECV         (BASE_ERROR_NUM+9)
#define PROD_ERR_SETSOCKETOPT        (BASE_ERROR_NUM+10)
#define PROD_ERR_GETSOCKETOPT        (BASE_ERROR_NUM+11)
#define PROD_ERR_WRONGMAGIC          (BASE_ERROR_NUM+12)
#define PROD_ERR_READ                (BASE_ERROR_NUM+13)
#define PROD_ERR_WRITE               (BASE_ERROR_NUM+14)
#define PROD_ERR_OPEN                (BASE_ERROR_NUM+15)

/* The base value and all error codes from component 2. */
#define BASE_ERROR_NUM2 (BASE_ERROR_NUM+1000)
#define PROD_ERR_BAD_OPCODE          (BASE_ERROR_NUM2+1)
#define PROD_ERR_NO_MEMORY           (BASE_ERROR_NUM2+2)
#define PROD_ERR_BAD_SYNTAX          (BASE_ERROR_NUM2+3)
#define PROD_ERR_NAME_TOOLONG        (BASE_ERROR_NUM2+4)
```

(c) mydistsys.h

```
/*
 * Include file for distributed system applications
 * Supported operating systems: Linux, Unix (AIX, Solaris, HP-UX),
 * Apple Darwin and Windows.
 * Copyright (c) 1996, 2002, 2014, 2019-2020 Mr. Jin-Jwei Chen. All rights reserved.
 */

/*
 * Defines for Endianness.
 */
#undef  LITTLE_ENDIAN
#undef  BIG_ENDIAN
#define LITTLE_ENDIAN       1
#define BIG_ENDIAN          2
#define UNKNOWN_ENDIAN      3

/*
 * Endian utility functions.
 */
int endian();
unsigned long long myhtonll(unsigned long long num64bit);
unsigned long long myntohll(unsigned long long num64bit);
unsigned short myByteSwap2(unsigned short num16bit);
unsigned int myByteSwap4(unsigned int num32bit);
unsigned long long myByteSwap8(unsigned long long num64bit);

/* Alternative names for the bytes swap functions */
#define swap2bytes myByteSwap2
#define swap4bytes myByteSwap4
```

```
#define swap8bytes myByteSwap8

/*
 * Use our own version on platforms not supporting htonll()/ntohll().
 * Remove the O.S. from this list once it has native support.
 */
#if (WINDOWS || LINUX || HPUX)
#define htonll  myhtonll
#define ntohll  myntohll
#endif

/*
 * Application protocol version numbers
 */
#define VERSION1   1
#define CURRENT_VER VERSION1   /* always keep this line last */

/* Magic number */
#define PROTO_MAGIC   3923850741
#define REQ_MAGIC     3749500826
#define REPLY_MAGIC   2814594375
#define DATA_MAGIC    1943724308

/* Client request operations */
#define REQ_OPCODE1   1       /* do multiplication */

/*
 * Initial connection packet.
 */
#define AUTH_ID_LEN     32
#define INIT_PKT_LEN   256
typedef struct {
    unsigned int        version;    /* app. protocol version number */
    unsigned int        magic;      /* app. protocol magic number */
    unsigned int        flags;
    char                auth[AUTH_ID_LEN];    /* auth data */
    char                reserved[INIT_PKT_LEN-AUTH_ID_LEN];
} init_pkt_t;

/*
 * Request/Reply header packet.
 */
typedef struct {
    unsigned int        version;    /* App. data version number */
    unsigned int        magic;      /* app. data packet magic number */
    int                 operation;  /* operation to be performed */
    int                 status;     /* status of the operation */
    unsigned long long  datasz;     /* size of data */
    char                reserved[64];
} req_pkt_t;

/*
 * Portable data file header.
 */
typedef struct {
    char                endian;     /* endian format of the data */
```

```
    char                    padding[3];    /* pad it for alignment */
    unsigned int            version;       /* version number */
    unsigned int            magic;         /* magic number of data record header */
    unsigned int            padding2;      /* pad it to 8-byte boundary */
    unsigned long long      nrecs;         /* number of records */
    char                    reserved[24];
} portable_data_hdr_t;

/*
 * Data record.
 */
#define NAME_LEN  32
typedef struct {
    char                    name[NAME_LEN];
    unsigned int            birthyear;
    unsigned int            salary;
    unsigned int            bonus;
} data_rec_t;
```

The example program simply creates a data file containing two employee records. For simplicity, we hardwire in the employees' data.

The same program can be used to create a data file or consume (read) data files created by others. Try to run the program to consume a data file created by a computer with a different endian format. As you can see, the program correctly reads and prints the employee records from the data file regardless of the endian format of the data file.

This program was tested to work in any combinations of IBM PowerPC AIX, Oracle/Sun SPARC Solaris, HP IA64 HPUX, Intel x86 Linux and Apple Mac Pro with x86 CPU platforms, 32-bit and 64-bit modes.

Figure 14-6 shows a sample output of the exchange-data-using-file program. As you can see, running the program in Intel Linux can read the data files produced by running the same program on IBM POWER AIX and Oracle/Sun SPARC Solaris computers without any problem. In this sample run, the file reader runs on a little-endian computer and the input data files were created on big-endian computers. (Input data files portable_recs.sun64 and portable_recs.aix32 were created by running the same exchange_rec program on Oracle/Sun SPARC and IBM PowerPC computers, respectively.)

Figure 14-6 Sample output of exchange_rec program

```
$ ./exchange_rec w portable_recs.lin64
  To write portable binary file portable_recs.lin64 ...
  sizeof(hdr) = 48
  sizeof(datarec) = 44
  The data file was successfully created.

$ ./exchange_rec r portable_recs.lin64
  To read portable binary file portable_recs.lin64 ...

  Contents of the file header:
    hdr->endian = 1
    hdr->version = 1
```

```
        hdr->magic = 1943724308
        hdr->nrecs = 2

    Contents of the data records follow:

        name = Jennifer Johnson
        birthyear = 1980
        salary = 224000
        bonus = 1234500

        name = Allan Smith
        birthyear = 1970
        salary = 448000
        bonus = 2469000

    $ ./exchange_rec r portable_recs.sun64
    To read portable binary file portable_recs.sun64 ...

    Contents of the file header:
        hdr->endian = 2
        hdr->version = 1
        hdr->magic = 1943724308
        hdr->nrecs = 2

    Contents of the data records follow:

        name = Jennifer Johnson
        birthyear = 1980
        salary = 224000
        bonus = 1234500

        name = Allan Smith
        birthyear = 1970
        salary = 448000
        bonus = 2469000

    $ ./exchange_rec r portable_recs.aix32
    To read portable binary file portable_recs.aix32 ...

    Contents of the file header:
        hdr->endian = 2
        hdr->version = 1
        hdr->magic = 1943724308
        hdr->nrecs = 2

    Contents of the data records follow:

        name = Jennifer Johnson
        birthyear = 1980
        salary = 224000
        bonus = 1234500

        name = Allan Smith
        birthyear = 1970
        salary = 448000
        bonus = 2469000
```

14-1-7 How to Do Endian Conversion -- The Endian Utility Functions

In computer network communication, typically applications send an entire
structure of data across the wire. In the data exchange using file case,
data records in the file are typically represented as a C structure too.
Normally only some of the data fields in the structure are binary integer
data. Only these binary integer fields need to be endian converted.
So, you will need to know the definition of the structure and what fields
need to be converted. Depending on your solution, you may need to do the
conversion at both writing and reading ends or just at the reading end.

So how would I do the conversion from one endian to another?

The answer is to use endian conversion functions. The POSIX Standard defines
some endian conversion functions for network communications.
Unfortunately, it's not complete. Therefore, we also define some
conversion functions of our own to fill in the gap. We introduce these
functions in this section.

The endian format conversion functions defined in the POSIX standards
are listed below. They cover endian conversions of 16-bit and 32-bit integers.
We use these functions in the Socket Programming chapter. They come very
handy in writing socket programs.

   htons() - convert a 16-bit integer from host to network byte order
   htonl() - convert a 32-bit integer from host to network byte order
   ntohs() - convert a 16-bit integer from network to host byte order
   ntohl() - convert a 32-bit integer from network to host byte order

Unfortunately, the original POSIX Standard does not include endian
conversion functions for 64-bit integers. And as of the writing of this
book, some platforms have implemented these 64-bit endian conversion
functions, htonll() and ntohll(), while others still don't.
For instances, IBM AIX and Oracle/Sun Solaris have whereas Linux, HPUX and
Windows have not. Windows' support comes in Windows 8.1 and after.

To supplement the POSIX Standard, we define the following conversion
functions. The first group of functions myhtonll() and myntohll() are the
64-bit version of htonl() and ntohl(), respectively. These fill the gap
in the POSIX Standard and can be used on platforms that have not supported
these functions yet.

```
/* Perform endian conversions for 64-bit integers */
unsigned long long myhtonll(unsigned long long num64bit)
unsigned long long myntohll(unsigned long long num64bit)
```

The second group of endian conversion functions we introduce here is
more generic. They are not specific to converting to and from network
(i.e. big-endian) byte order only. They can do the conversions to and
from either endian. And they can be used in any applications including
database, rather than just networking only. They simply reverse the
order of the bytes.

There are two sets of names for these. You could use either myByteSwap2(), myByteSwap4() and myByteSwap8(), or swap2bytes(), swap4bytes() and swap8bytes(), depending on your preferences. We name them myByteSwapx() to avoid potential name conflicts.

These supplemental functions are declared in "mydistsys.h" and defined in the source module mydistlib.c, as shown in Figure 14-7.

```
/* Perform bytes swap for 16-, 32- and 64-bit integers */
unsigned short myByteSwap2(unsigned short num16bit)
unsigned int myByteSwap4(unsigned int num32bit)
unsigned long long myByteSwap8(unsigned long long num64bit)

#define swap2bytes myByteSwap2
#define swap4bytes myByteSwap4
#define swap8bytes myByteSwap8
```

Figure 14-7 Endian conversion utility functions -- mydistlib.c

```
/*
 * Some library functions for distributed applications.
 * Authored by Mr. Jin-Jwei Chen.
 * Copyright (c) 2010-2019, Mr. Jin-Jwei Chen. All rights reserved.
 */

#include "mydistsys.h"

/* Find the endian type of this local CPU */
int endian()
{
  unsigned int      x = 0x01020304;
  unsigned char     *px = (unsigned char *)&x;

  if (px[0] == 0x01)
    return(BIG_ENDIAN);
  else if (px[0] == 0x04)
    return(LITTLE_ENDIAN);
  else
    return(UNKNOWN_ENDIAN);
}

/* Convert an integer of "unsigned long long" type from local host byte order
 * to network byte order.
 * Industry implementations use big endian as the network byte order.
 */
unsigned long long myhtonll(unsigned long long num64bit)
{
  int   i;
  unsigned long long  result;
  unsigned char       n = sizeof(unsigned long long);
  unsigned char       *pin = (unsigned char *)&num64bit;
  unsigned char       *pout = (unsigned char *)&result;

  if (endian() == LITTLE_ENDIAN)
  {
    for (i = 0; i < n; i++)
      pout[n-1-i] = pin[i];
```

```
      return(result);
   }
  else
     return(num64bit);
}


/* Convert an integer of "unsigned long long" type from network byte order
 * to local host byte order.
 * Industry implementations use big endian as the network byte order.
 */
unsigned long long myntohll(unsigned long long num64bit)
{
  int  i;
  unsigned long long  result;
  unsigned char        n = sizeof(unsigned long long);
  unsigned char        *pin = (unsigned char *)&num64bit;
  unsigned char        *pout = (unsigned char *)&result;

  if (endian() == LITTLE_ENDIAN)
   {
    for (i = 0; i < n; i++)
      pout[n-1-i] = pin[i];
    return(result);
   }
  else
     return(num64bit);
}


/*
 * Byte swap a short integer.
 */
unsigned short myByteSwap2(unsigned short num16bit)
{
  int  i;
  unsigned short       result;
  unsigned char        n = sizeof(unsigned short);
  unsigned char        *pin = (unsigned char *)&num16bit;
  unsigned char        *pout = (unsigned char *)&result;

  for (i = 0; i < n; i++)
     pout[n-1-i] = pin[i];
  return(result);
}


/*
 * Byte swap an integer.
 */
unsigned int myByteSwap4(unsigned int num32bit)
{
  int  i;
  unsigned int         result;
  unsigned char        n = sizeof(unsigned int);
  unsigned char        *pin = (unsigned char *)&num32bit;
  unsigned char        *pout = (unsigned char *)&result;

  for (i = 0; i < n; i++)
```

```
    pout[n-1-i] = pin[i];
  return(result);
}

/*
 * Byte swap a "long long" integer.
 */
unsigned long long myByteSwap8(unsigned long long num64bit)
{
    int i;
    unsigned long long result;
    unsigned char      n = sizeof(unsigned long long);
    unsigned char      *pin = (unsigned char *)&num64bit;
    unsigned char      *pout = (unsigned char *)&result;

  for (i = 0; i < n; i++)
    pout[n-1-i] = pin[i];
  return(result);
}
```

14-1-8 Summary

- Endian is about ordering of bytes in a multi-byte integer stored in binary format. It's a processor attribute. Modern computer processors are either little-endian or big-endian.

- A CPU's endianness can be programmatically determined at run time. There is no need to do it at compile time. We provide a very simple function named endian() that does exactly that.

- The issue of endianness surfaces at the time of data interpretation/use.

- When writing binary integer data in a file, to make it portable across different endian platforms, make sure you make the file self-describing by writing the endianness of the file format in the header of the file and storing it in a single-byte data field so that that field is always independent of endianness and thus can always be correctly interpreted by the consumer of the file.

- When sending binary integer data across network, make sure you address the cross-endian issue by making necessary endian conversions at the sending side, receiving side or both. We presented three techniques. A client-server application can exchange endian information with its communication partner at connection time before further exchanging data, include the endianness of the data in a single-byte field in the header of the data, or convert the data to a particular endian format known to both parties.

- We supplement the endian conversion functions defined in POSIX Standard.

As you can see, if you really understand it and do it the right way, cross-endian issues only take tens, or at most a couple of hundreds, of lines of code to solve, rather than thousands or even tens of thousands.

14-2 Design of Distributed Applications

In this section, we give an example of a very simple distributed application and show readers how to design the application to address most, if not all, of the issues listed at the beginning of this chapter.

The example is a client-server application where the client provides a number (the multiplicand) and the server multiplies that number by a multiplier it chooses and returns the product.

14-2-1 Design of General Communication Protocol

A very typical design of distributed applications always includes the design of network messages exchanged. In general, to facilitate data exchange, a network message sent across the network usually includes two parts: the header and the data itself. The header always comes before the actual data and it describes the data.

Besides, many or most distributed applications use connection-oriented protocols. For security purposes, as soon as a connection is made, most application protocols typically require that there is an initial packet sent from the client or initiator which contains information for authentication or security check purposes.

The example distributed application we are providing in this chapter uses both initial connection packet and data header.

14-2-1-1 Initial Connection Packet

It is a very good practice for a server program to require a client to send an initial connection packet right after a connection is made. It is not absolutely required but it brings a number of benefits.

As briefly mentioned before, the benefits include security measures that a server can implement to protect the server from some unwanted attacks including the Denial of Service (DOS) attacks.

Common data fields within an initial connection packet include version number, magic number, flags, some security information such as authentication, and others. **Make sure you always reserve some enough additional space for adding new features in the future without ever having to change the total size of the overall structure**.

```
#define AUTH_ID_LEN    32
#define INIT_PKT_LEN  256
typedef struct {
  unsigned int      version;     /* app. protocol version number */
  unsigned int      magic;       /* app. protocol magic number */
  unsigned int      flags;
  char              auth[AUTH_ID_LEN];   /* auth data */
  char              reserved[INIT_PKT_LEN-AUTH_ID_LEN-(3*sizeof(int))];
} init_pkt_t;
```

The structure definition of the initial connection packet for our example application is listed above, with reserved space at end.

14-2-1-2 Dealing with Denial of Service (DOS) Attacks

The Internet is a public network. Servers on the Internet are exposed to the whole world. It's not hard for hackers to find out the IP address of a server and write a program to connect to a server and flood the server with network messages. Because of this, every server program you design must contain some mechanism to avoid or stop this kind of Denial of Service (DOS) attacks or at least to minimize the impact of attacks.

There are at least two things one can do in this regard.

The first is to **use and check a magic number**. Make sure your communication protocol always requires a client to send an initial connection packet after a connection is made. If the magic number in the initial connection packet does not match, the server should immediately close the connection. Besides, if the size of the initial connection packet does not match, the server should also close the connection right away for security reason.

In our example, we use two different magic numbers, one for client request and the other for server reply. The server should close the connection immediately if the magic number in a client request does not match. The client should throw away the response message it gets if the magic number in a server reply does not match.

This magic number security check should be performed at the earliest time possible so that no or at least minimum damage is done in case of a malicious attack.

Second, in addition to checking the magic number, the server should require the client sending some authentication information. And if the authentication step fails, the server should tear down the connection as well.

These should help defend against some of the security attacks. Additionally, a server can also consider rejecting suspicious repeated connection requests from a same client.

14-2-1-3 Data Header

Depending upon the application and what information needs to be communicated, you may need to define a structure for the request messages and another structure for reply messages. However, in a simple application like our example, you may be able to use a single structure for both request and reply messages because the information being communicated is very simple and/or similar. Hence, we use the same structure for both in our example.

It's a very common practice that when a program sends data, it sends a header, which is often defined in a C structure, with it. The header is used to describe some properties of the data, such as its size in bytes, version, endianness, or even another magic number, and so on.

Although the header information is typically defined as a C structure, the data itself may or may not. It all depends on the application.

In the simplest case, if the actual data to be sent is small and has a
pre-known size, then the data can even be included in the header
structure itself. In this case, the header information and the data together
can be defined in the same structure:

```
-----------------------------------------
| Header information |    Actual Data    |
-----------------------------------------
|<---------  struct  mydata  ---------->|

struct mydata
{
  header information field 1
  header information field 2
     :
  data
};
```

A most common case is the data is of some moderate size, say within a few
MBs, and its size and/or contents may vary. In that case, an application
usually defines a data header structure describing the data, separated
from the actual data.

```
-----------------------------------------------------------
|    Data    Header    |   Actual Data (variable in size )  |
-----------------------------------------------------------
|<- struct mydatahdr ->|

struct mydatahdr
{
  data header field 1
  data header field 2
     :
};
```

In some cases, an application may even want to send three pieces of
information together:

```
------------------------------------------------------------------
| Protocol Header |  Data header  | Actual Data (variable in size) |
------------------------------------------------------------------
|<- myprotohdr -->|<- mydatahdr ->|

struct myprotohdr
{
  protocol header field 1
  protocol header field 2
     :
};

struct mydatahdr
{
  data header field 1
  data header field 2
```

```
        :
    };
```

It's worth mentioning that to send both the header(s) and the data in one
operation, an application will need to allocate one contiguous buffer
so that both the header and the data can fit in the buffer. This is because
the standard operating system output APIs usually take a single contiguous
buffer for the data you like to send. Hence, the application will have to
fill in the header information in the buffer first, followed by the actual
data before sending it.

In some rare cases, the actual data to be sent is very large.
In that case, the application may choose to send the header first, followed
by the actual data itself. This may take two or more write operations.
On the receiving end, the receiver will attempt to receive the header first,
then peek into the header to know how many bytes of data can be expected,
and then receive the actual data. Again, this may take two or more
read operations in some cases.

Besides, the messages exchanged in both directions may be of the same or
similar format, or may be not. If yes, then the request and response
messages may share the same header structure. If not, one may have to define
one separate structure for each.

Our Example

For simplicity, our example uses a single data header structure for both
request and response messages.

Besides, as Figure 14-8 shows, the data follows the header in the messages.
Well, this is true in version 1 and version 2. But in version 3, we add
a new data item within the header structure just to demonstrate changing the
data header structure between versions without breaking anything.

```
-------------------------------------------------
| Header information |     Actual Data         |
-------------------------------------------------
```

Figure 14-8 Layout of a message buffer containing header and data

The data header structure for our example distributed application is
shown below:

```
/*
 * Request/Reply header packet.
 */
typedef struct {
  unsigned int        version;   /* App. data version number */
  unsigned int        magic;     /* app. data packet magic number */
  int                 operation; /* operation to be performed */
  int                 status;    /* status of the operation */
  unsigned long long  datasz;    /* size of data */
  char                reserved[64]; /* reserve space for future growth */
} req_pkt_t;
```

As you can see, the data header structure includes a version number, a magic number, an opcode field, a status field (obviously, this is for reply messages), and a field for size of the actual data following the header. The version field allows both sides to exchange their version information. The magic number is used for a sanity check in both directions. The operation field is the request opcode. The datasz field indicates the size of the data following the header in each direction.

Lastly but not least importantly, there is a space reserved at end of the structure. This is extremely important. It is a true nightmare if you have to change the size of a header structure during the lifetime of the software you develop. That itself could break the interoperability even if you have versioning. To avoid that nightmare, **you always want to leave some head room for future growth in your structure. So always remember to reserve some enough space for future use at the end of your structure.** This will enable you to add more data fields to the structure as needed in the future and yet at the same time keep the size of the structure unchanged throughout all of the versions without breaking backward compatibility and interoperability! This applies to both the request/reply header and the initial connection packet.

14-2-1-4 Avoid Alignment Snag

There is one very important hidden issue in defining a structure for communication data and it affects interoperability between different platforms, especially in an environment of 32-bit and 64-bit mixing together. And you may get bitten unless you are extremely careful in constructing your structure. That is **alignment**.

What Is Alignment?

Each computer has a basic "word" size. This is the size of information that each computer typically computes in one operation. For instance, the word size of a 32-bit computer is typically 4 bytes (32 bits).

Note that the "word" size is also the amount of information that a typical CPU instruction moves data in or out of computer memory.

For efficiency reason, when a computer accesses its memory, it typically reads or writes not only in units of its word size but also on word boundary. This has two meanings. First, it means to read a single byte from the computer memory, the computer hardware may actually read four bytes. Second, if a piece of 4-byte information is not aligned and it spreads across two words, then to read or write that information, the computer hardware will have to perform two reads or writes to get it. This slows down the operation. In other words, **data being unaligned has a performance penalty and to align is to improve performance**.

This concept of arranging data in memory in increments of the basic "word size" of the computer to improve performance is called "alignment". If a piece of information is not stored from or within a word boundary, it is called "unaligned". And being unaligned incurs a performance hit because that usually takes one additional memory access to read or write.

Compiler Automatic Padding

Because of this performance penalty in accessing unaligned data, compilers on many computers typically try to "fix" this by automatically adding padding bytes inside a structure to make data aligned. This is called **compiler padding**.

First, almost all compilers align a structure with word boundary. This means when a compiler compiles your code, it usually does not put a structure at an odd-numbered memory address. The starting address of a structure typically is multiple of four or eight.

Second, compilers typically align the integer data fields (those of types int, long, or long long) within a structure with word boundary as well. This means if you do not very carefully align all of the data fields inside a structure, a compiler will do that for you behind the scene by padding your structure with some padding bytes in between data fields.

When compilers find these unalignments in your structure and automatically pad them to make them aligned, the **actual size of a structure changes**. This could cause problems when a computer sends the data of the structure from one machine to another.

This is something that many people don't know and you absolutely want to avoid in developing a distributed application because it will open up opportunities for your structure to have different sizes in different platforms or environments.

Remember, for your program to run successfully across different platforms and environments, the #1 thing is **the size of your structure MUST remain the same across all these platforms, environments and versions**! The communication will break if not.

Thus, in constructing a structure whose data will be sent across network, please always do the following:

1. Make sure the size of your structure remains the same across all platforms you want to support. Always compile your program in all of the different platforms (including different modes) you want to support and verify the size is always the same. If not, try to adjust your structure until it is.

2. Make sure the size of your structure is always a multiple of eight. Sometimes a multiple of four does not even do it.

3. Don't let the compiler pad your structure. Pad your structure yourself whenever necessary.

This applies to any and all structures whose data is to be sent across network. For our example, it includes both the data header structure and the initial connection packet.

14-2-1-5 Guidelines for Header Structure Definition

Here we summarize the techniques anyone should employ in defining any headers used in a communication protocol to make the distributed application you design become completely portable and run all the time without breaking.

Therefore, in defining any header structures,

- You want to ensure the total size of the structure always remains the same and unchanged anywhere and anytime.

- You don't want to use any data type that has different sizes in different platforms. For instance, avoid using data of 'long int' type because it is 4 bytes long in a 32-bit computer and 8 bytes in a 64-bit one. And that will cause your communication protocol to break in that mixed environment. As you can see, our example header structures use only **'int'** and **'long long'** because their sizes remain the same across all 32-bit and 64-bit platforms. 'int' is 4 bytes and 'long long' is 8 bytes.

- You always want to reserve some enough space at end of the structure for future growth such that adding more data fields in the future won't have to change the size of the structure.

- You want the data fields in the structure to be aligned, especially the numeric fields.

- You want to avoid compiler padding.

- Having a data field for version number and another for magic number in the header structure is kind of standard. Make sure you pick a good random number for the magic.

14-2-2 Versioning, Backward Compatibility and Interoperability

There are at least five issues that almost every distributed application will always encounter: cross-endian, unalignment, inconsistent data size, backward compatibility and cross-version interoperability.

Remember in a distributed application, the two programs communicating with each other, whether they are client and server or peer-to-peer, often reside on two different computers and usually very far apart. Not only one program could be running on a little-endian computer and the other on a big-endian, one is 32-bit and the other is 64-bit, but also one can be running an older or newer version of the software than the other. Therefore, it's extremely important to make a distributed application work under all of these combinations of scenarios. And this is entirely feasible!

We have discussed cross-endian, alignment and structure size in the sections above. We will talk about how to use versioning to achieve backward compatibility and cross-version interoperability in this section.

Computer software has a long life cycle. Each computer software product evolves and changes in its life time. New features are added and implementation may change over time. When new versions of the product are released, many customers continue to use some older versions. Even within a single customer/company, it's not uncommon that multiple versions of the same software co-exist. Therefore, interoperability between different versions of the same software becomes a requirement. Meeting this requirement requires the software to be version sensitive, which is what most software products lack because the engineers who designed them did not have the needed experience to design it in and do it right.

Supposedly, different versions of the same software should be able
to co-exist and inter-operate without any problem. Upgrade or downgrade
to a different version should work without any problem, too.
This requires the product be designed and implemented correctly.
And very often this means having versioning built in.
Versioning means in the code, you use and check the version of the product
or code and do different processing based on versions such that it
always works properly and seamlessly. And this is completely doable.

Designing a software to be version sensitive and making sure old and new
versions can interoperate correctly is what versioning is all about.
Versioning involves tagging your software components (in particular,
application protocols) with a version number, increasing the version number
each time meaningful changes are made, and making the code be able to
properly handle interactions with all different versions.

In addition to interoperability, versioning helps achieve backward
compatibility too.

This means when you are making new changes in a new version,
it's not just ripping out the old code and replacing it with new one.
Instead, it usually means **keeping the existing old code intact and
expanding it to include the new version code.** That is, unless it's not
impacting behavior at all, **you don't just yank and/or replace code.**
In fact, as you will find out, you never just rip off any code from the
old versions. You keep them. All you do is just adding the code implementing
the behavior of the new version. This makes the software remains fully
backward compatible and interoperable with old versions.

Note that this version number we are talking about here typically is
separate and different from the version of the entire product.
This version is about internal implementation of some component(s)
communicating with outside world. That is, it is versioning of the product's
communication protocol, which may not always change each time when
the product version changes.

In summary, the key to the design of a product's communication protocol
is that **both client and server (especially the server) must be coded such
that it can properly handle requests and/or responses from older,
current and future versions at the same time.** And in order to achieve
that, version number must be used and perhaps included in every request
and/or response, or at least being exchanged at the beginning of a session.

We demonstrate how to do software versioning right such that a software
product is always backward compatible and interoperable between all
versions in this section.

To show readers how to do versioning, we do three different versions of the
same software. The differences between the three versions are described
below.

14-2-2-1 Version Numbers

In a most flexible implementation, one could use three different version numbers for maximum flexibility.

1. Protocol version.

   This is for potential changes to be made in the initial connection packet structure in the future, which is usually unlikely.

2. Client version.

   This is so that the client program can change by itself without rebuilding and re-distributing the server.

3. Server version.

   This is so that the server program can change by itself without rebuilding and re-distributing the client.

In a typical application, you can consolidate all these version numbers into two or even one. For example, if you always distribute the client and the server software together, then you can consider using a single version number for both components. Using just one version number is sufficient for most applications. Here we illustrate a typical application using only a single version number.

14-2-2-2 Changes Between Versions

The example application is a client-server application where the client provides and sends a number (a 4-byte integer) to the server. The server multiplies that number by a factor and then sends the product back to the client.

In the initial version of the software (i.e. version 1), the server multiplies the number the client provides by a multiplier of 100 and returns the result:

    version 1: result = (input number * 100)

From version 1 to version 2, everything stays the same except the semantics or internal implementation of the multiply operation REQ_OPCODE1 changes. That is, the server has changed the multiplier from 100 to 1000 in version 2:

    version 2: result = (input number * 1000)

From version 2 to version 3, it involves a bit more changes. The contents of the req_pkt_t structure change. There is one more data field added. Besides, the semantics and internal implementation of the operation REQ_OPCODE1 changes again. Now the server multiplies the input number by 1000 and then adds the second number provided by client to it. Therefore, the returned result from the server will be:

    version 3: result = (input number1 * 1000) + input number2

14-2-2-3 Actual Code Changes

(1) V1 -> V2

Every time you change the implementation, you bump up the version umber by
one. You add the definition of the version macro of the new version
and make that the latest version.

The header file changes from version 1 to version 2 are shown below.
As you can see, we add definition of VERSION2 and make that the CURRENT_VER.

```
$ diff mydistsys.h.v1 mydistsys.h.v2
39c39,40
< #define   CURRENT_VER   VERSION1   /* always keep this line last */
---
> #define   VERSION2   2
> #define   CURRENT_VER   VERSION2   /* always keep this line last *
```

The server-side code changes are the following:

Note that the version 2 server now must have both version 1 and version 2's
code so that it knows how to handle the old clients and the new clients.
As we said earlier, you always keep the old code and add the new code for
the new version.

Hence, the server code must always check the version of the client first before
it knows how to correctly handle the client's request. And the trick here is
it always checks the latest version first and then in decreasing order of
the rest of the versions. This way, each client request will be handled
only once and in the version that exactly matches.

Note that you always check the latest version first. And if the client's
version does not match, then you check the next version down and so on.
This is the order you check in servicing different versions of clients.
You keep all of the old versions' code around and do not delete it so that
if there are still old versions of clients out there they can still
talk to this newer version of server and get services from it.

```
if (clntVersion >= CURRENT_VER) /* latest version */
{
   :   (new version2 implementation)
}
else if (clntVersion >= VERSION1) /* previous version */
{
   :   (previous implementation in version1)
}
```

(2) V2 -> V3

The header file changes from V2 to V3 are shown below.
Here we again bump up the client and server's versions to 3 and make that
the current version. Besides, we add a new data field named addend to the
req_pkt_t without actually changing the size of the entire structure
by taking space from the reserved space.

Remember to update (reduce) the number of reserved bytes in the request
structure when you add the new field. This is so that the size of the
request/reply structure remains constant across all versions so that
the different versions are interoperable. We reduce the number by 4.
You could decrease the size by sizeof(int) too instead of 4 if you like.

```
$ diff mydistsys.h.v2 mydistsys.h.v3
40c40,41
< #define   CURRENT_VER   VERSION2   /* always keep this line last */
---
> #define   VERSION3   3
> #define   CURRENT_VER   VERSION3   /* always keep this line last */
73c74,75
<     char                 reserved[64];
---
>     int                  addend;    /* number to be addded to MUL product */
>     char                 reserved[60];
```

The client-side code changes are the following:

```
$ diff tcpclnt_dist_all_v2.c tcpclnt_dist_all_v3.c
34a35
>    int         addend = 50;       /* the number to be added to the product */
75a77,79
>    /* Get the addend to be added to the product */
>    if (argc > 4)
>      addend = atoi(argv[4]);
165a170
>    reqmsg->addend = htonl(addend);
```

The server-side code changes are shown below:

```
if (clntVersion >= CURRENT_VER) /* latest version3 */
{
  :  (new version3 implementation)
}
else if (clntVersion >= VERSION2) /* previous version */
{
  :  (previous implementation in version2)
}
else if (clntVersion >= VERSION1) /* first version */
{
  :  (first implementation in version1)
}
```

Figures 14-9, 14-10 and 14-11 show the version 1, 2, and 3 of the example
distributed application that implements versioning and demonstrates
all versions of the client and server programs can interoperate across
versions and across platforms without any problem.

Figure 14-9 Example distributed application (version1)
 -- mydistsys.h.v1, tcpclnt_dist_all.c and tcpsrv_dist_all.c

(a) mydistsys.h.v1

```
 * Include file for distributed system applications
 * Supported operating systems: Linux, Unix (AIX, Solaris, HP-UX), Windows.
 * Copyright (c) 1996, 2002, 2014, 2019 Mr. Jin-Jwei Chen. All rights reserved.
 */

/*
 * Defines for Endianness.
 */
#undef  LITTLE_ENDIAN
#undef  BIG_ENDIAN
#define LITTLE_ENDIAN       1
#define BIG_ENDIAN          2
#define UNKNOWN_ENDIAN      3

/*
 * Endian utility functions.
 */
int endian();
unsigned long long myhtonll(unsigned long long num64bit);
unsigned long long myntohll(unsigned long long num64bit);
unsigned short myByteSwap2(unsigned short num16bit);
unsigned int myByteSwap4(unsigned int num32bit);
unsigned long long myByteSwap8(unsigned long long num64bit);

/*
 * Use our own version on platforms not supporting htonll()/ntohll().
 * Remove the O.S. from this list once it has native support.
 */
#if (WINDOWS || LINUX || HPUX)
#define htonll  myhtonll
#define ntohll  myntohll
#endif

/*
 * Application protocol version numbers
 */
#define  VERSION1  1
#define  CURRENT_VER  VERSION1  /* always keep this line last */

/* Magic number */
#define PROTO_MAGIC   3923850741
#define REQ_MAGIC     3749500826
#define REPLY_MAGIC   2814594375
#define DATA_MAGIC    1943724308

/* Client request operations */
#define REQ_OPCODE1   1        /* do multiplication */

/*
 * Initial connection packet.
 */
#define AUTH_ID_LEN    32
#define INIT_PKT_LEN   256
typedef struct {
    unsigned int       version;    /* app. protocol version number */
    unsigned int       magic;      /* app. protocol magic number */
```

```c
    unsigned int         flags;
    char                 auth[AUTH_ID_LEN];        /* auth data */
    char                 reserved[INIT_PKT_LEN-AUTH_ID_LEN];
} init_pkt_t;

/*
 * Request/Reply header packet.
 */
typedef struct {
    unsigned int         version;      /* App. data version number */
    unsigned int         magic;        /* app. data packet magic number */
    int                  operation;    /* operation to be performed */
    int                  status;       /* status of the operation */
    unsigned long long   datasz;       /* size of data */
    char                 reserved[64];
} req_pkt_t;

/*
 * Portable data file header.
 */
typedef struct {
    char                 endian;       /* endian format of the data */
    char                 padding[3];   /* pad it for alignment */
    unsigned int         version;      /* version number */
    unsigned int         magic;        /* magic number of data record header */
    unsigned int         padding2;     /* pad it to 8-byte boundary */
    unsigned long long   nrecs;        /* number of records */
    char                 reserved[24];
} portable_data_hdr_t;

/*
 * Data record.
 */
#define  NAME_LEN  32
typedef struct {
    char                 name[NAME_LEN];
    unsigned int         birthyear;
    unsigned int         salary;
    unsigned int         bonus;
} data_rec_t;
```

(b) tcpclnt_dist_all.c

```c
/*
 * A connection-oriented client program using Stream socket.
 * Connecting to a server program on any host using a hostname or IP address.
 * Demonstrating design of distributed applications.
 * Support for IPv4 and IPv6 and multiple platforms including
 * Linux, Windows, Solaris, AIX and HPUX.
 * Usage: tcpclnt_dist_all [srvport# [server-hostname | server-ipaddress]]
 * Authored by Mr. Jin-Jwei Chen.
 * Copyright (c) 1993-2020, Mr. Jin-Jwei Chen. All rights reserved.
 */

#include "mysocket.h"
#include "mydistsys.h"
```

```c
#include "myerrors.h"

int send_init_pkt(int sfd);

int main(int argc, char *argv[])
{
  int      ret = 0;
  int      sfd;                        /* socket file descriptor */
  in_port_t portnum=DEFSRVPORT;        /* port number */
  int      portnum_in = 0;             /* port number user provides */
  char     *portnumstr = DEFSRVPORTSTR; /* port number in string format */
  char     *inbuf = NULL;              /* pointer to input message buffer */
  char     *outbuf = NULL;             /* pointer to output message buffer */
  size_t   msglen;                     /* length of reply message */
  size_t   len;
  char     server_name[NAMELEN+1] = SERVER_NAME;
  struct addrinfo hints;               /* address info hints*/
  struct addrinfo *res=NULL;           /* pointer to address info */
  req_pkt_t    *reqmsg = NULL;         /* pointer to client request message */
  int          anumber = 15;           /* the number to be multiplied at server */
  int          *dataptr = NULL;        /* pointer to input data */
  unsigned long long *result_ptr = NULL;   /* pointer to multiplication result */
  req_pkt_t    *reply = NULL;          /* pointer to server reply message */

#if WINDOWS
  WSADATA wsaData;                             /* Winsock data */
  char* GetErrorMsg(int ErrorCode);    /* print error string in Windows */
#endif

  fprintf(stdout, "Connection-oriented client program, version %u ...\n",
    CURRENT_VER);

  /* Get the server's port number from command line. */
  if (argc > 1)
  {
    portnum_in = atoi(argv[1]);
    if (portnum_in <= 0)
    {
      fprintf(stderr, "Port number %d invalid, set to default value %u\n",
        portnum_in, DEFSRVPORT);
      portnum = DEFSRVPORT;
      portnumstr = DEFSRVPORTSTR;
    }
    else
    {
      portnum = (in_port_t)portnum_in;
      portnumstr = argv[1];
    }
  }

  /* Get the server's host name or IP address from command line. */
  if (argc > 2)
  {
    len = strlen(argv[2]);
    if (len > NAMELEN)
      len = NAMELEN;
```

```
    strncpy(server_name, argv[2], len);
    server_name[len] = '\0';
  }

  /* Get the number to be multiplied from the user*/
  if (argc > 3)
    anumber = atoi(argv[3]);


#if WINDOWS
  /* Initiate use of the Winsock DLL. Ask for Winsock version 2.2 at least. */
  if ((ret = WSAStartup(MAKEWORD(2, 2), &wsaData)) != 0)
  {
    fprintf(stderr, "Error: WSAStartup() failed with error %d: %s\n",
      ret, GetErrorMsg(ret));
    return (PROD_ERR_WINSOCK_INIT);
  }
#endif

  /* Translate the server's host name or IP address into socket address.
   * Fill in the hint information.
   */
  memset(&hints, 0x00, sizeof(hints));
    /* This works on AIX but not on Solaris, nor on Windows. */
    /* hints.ai_flags    = AI_NUMERICSERV; */
  hints.ai_family   = AF_UNSPEC;
  hints.ai_socktype = SOCK_STREAM;
  hints.ai_protocol = IPPROTO_TCP;


  /* Get the address information of the server using getaddrinfo().
   * This function returns errors directly or 0 for success. On success,
   * argument res contains a linked list of addrinfo structures.
   */
  ret = getaddrinfo(server_name, portnumstr, &hints, &res);
  if (ret != 0)
  {
    fprintf(stderr, "Error: getaddrinfo() failed, error %d, %s\n", ret,
      gai_strerror(ret));
#if !WINDOWS
    if (ret == EAI_SYSTEM)
      fprintf(stderr,"System error: errno=%d, %s\n", errno, strerror(errno));
#else
    WSACleanup();
#endif
    return(PROD_ERR_GETADDRINFO);
  }


  /* Create a socket. */
  sfd = socket(res->ai_family, res->ai_socktype, res->ai_protocol);
  if (sfd < 0)
  {
    fprintf(stderr,"Error: socket() failed, errno=%d, %s\n", ERRNO, ERRNOSTR);
#if WINDOWS
    WSACleanup();
#endif
    ret = PROD_ERR_SOCKET_CREATE;
```

```
    goto return1;
}

/* Connect to the server. */
ret = connect(sfd, res->ai_addr, res->ai_addrlen);
if (ret == -1)
{
    fprintf(stderr, "Error: connect() failed, errno=%d, %s\n", ERRNO, ERRNOSTR);
    ret = PROD_ERR_CONNECT;
    goto return1;
}

/* Send initial packet */
ret = send_init_pkt(sfd);
if (ret != SUCCESS)
{
    fprintf(stderr, "Error: send_init_pkt() failed, ret=%d\n", ret);
    goto return1;
}

fprintf(stdout, "Send request messages to server(%s) at port %d\n",
    server_name, portnum);

/*
 * Send a request message to the server
 */
/* Allocate output buffer */
msglen = (sizeof(req_pkt_t) + sizeof(int));
outbuf = (char *)malloc(msglen);
if (outbuf == NULL)
{
    fprintf(stderr, "malloc() failed.\n");
    ret = PROD_ERR_NO_MEMORY;
    goto return1;
}

/* Fill in request */
memset(outbuf, 0, msglen);
reqmsg = (req_pkt_t *)outbuf;
reqmsg->version = htonl(CURRENT_VER);
reqmsg->magic = htonl(REQ_MAGIC);
reqmsg->operation = htonl(REQ_OPCODE1);
reqmsg->datasz = htonll(sizeof(int));
dataptr = (int *)(outbuf + sizeof(req_pkt_t));
*dataptr = htonl(anumber);

/* Send the request */
errno = 0;
ret = send(sfd, outbuf, msglen, 0);
if (ret < 0)
{
    fprintf(stderr, "Error: send() failed, errno=%d, %s\n", ERRNO, ERRNOSTR);
    ret = PROD_ERR_SOCKET_SEND;
    goto return1;
}
else if (ret != msglen)
```

```
   {
     fprintf(stderr, "Error: send() failed. Only %d out of %lu bytes were sent.\n"
       , ret, msglen);
     ret = PROD_ERR_SOCKET_SEND;
     goto return1;
   }

   /* Receive a reply from the server. */
   /* Allocate input buffer */
   msglen = (sizeof(req_pkt_t) + sizeof(unsigned long long));
   inbuf = (char *)malloc(msglen);
   if (inbuf == NULL)
   {
     fprintf(stderr, "malloc() failed.\n");
     ret = PROD_ERR_NO_MEMORY;
     goto return1;
   }
   memset(inbuf, 0, msglen);

   /* Receive the reply from the server */
   errno = 0;
   ret = recv(sfd, inbuf, msglen, 0);
   if (ret < 0)
   {
     fprintf(stderr, "Error: recv() failed, errno=%d, %s\n", ERRNO, ERRNOSTR);
     ret = PROD_ERR_SOCKET_RECV;
     goto return1;
   }
   else if (ret != msglen)
   {
     fprintf(stderr, "Error: recv() failed. Only %d out of %lu bytes were "
       "received.\n", ret, msglen);
   . ret = PROD_ERR_SOCKET_RECV;
     goto return1;
   }
   reply = (req_pkt_t *)inbuf;
   fprintf(stdout, "The client received %d bytes of reply from a server"
     " of version %u.\n", ret, ntohl(reply->version));

   if (ntohl(reply->status == SUCCESS))
   {
     result_ptr = (unsigned long long *)(inbuf + sizeof(req_pkt_t));
     fprintf(stdout, "The multiplied result of %d is %llu.\n", anumber,
       ntohll(*result_ptr));
   }
   else
   {
     fprintf(stderr, "Requested operation %u failed, status=%d\n",
       ntohl(reply->operation), ntohl(reply->status));
   }

return1:
   /* Free the memory allocated by getaddrinfo() and others */
   if (res != NULL) freeaddrinfo(res);
   if (inbuf != NULL) free(inbuf);
   if (outbuf != NULL) free(outbuf);
```

```
    CLOSE(sfd);
    return(ret);
}

/* Send initial packet */
int send_init_pkt(int sfd)
{
    init_pkt_t   initmsg;
    int          ret;

    memset((void *)&initmsg, 0, sizeof(init_pkt_t));
    initmsg.version = htonl(CURRENT_VER);
    initmsg.magic = htonl(PROTO_MAGIC);
    initmsg.flags = htonl(0);

    errno = 0;
    ret = send(sfd, (void *)&initmsg, sizeof(init_pkt_t), 0);
    if (ret < 0)
    {
      fprintf(stderr, "Error: send_init_pkt(), send() failed, errno=%d, %s\n",
        ERRNO, ERRNOSTR);
      return(PROD_ERR_SOCKET_SEND);
    }
    else if (ret != sizeof(init_pkt_t))
    {
      fprintf(stderr, "Error: send_init_pkt(), send() failed. Only %d out of"
        " %lu bytes of data sent.\n", ret, sizeof(init_pkt_t));
      return(PROD_ERR_SOCKET_SEND);
    }

    return(SUCCESS);
}
```

        (c) tcpsrv_dist_all.c

```
/*
 * A connection-oriented server program using Stream socket.
 * Demonstrating design of distributed applications.
 * Support for multiple platforms including Linux, Windows, Solaris, AIX, HPUX.
 * Usage: tcpsrv_dist_all [port#]
 * Authored by Mr. Jin-Jwei Chen.
 * Copyright (c) 2002, 2014, 2017-2020 Mr. Jin-Jwei Chen. All rights reserved.
 */

#include "mysocket.h"
#include "mydistsys.h"
#include "myerrors.h"

int receive_init_pkt(int sfd);
int service_client(int newsock);

int main(int argc, char *argv[])
{
    int    ret;                    /* return code */
    int    sfd;                    /* file descriptor of the listener socket */
    int    newsock;                /* file descriptor of client data socket */
```

```
  struct sockaddr_in6   srvaddr;    /* socket structure */
  int    srvaddrsz=sizeof(struct sockaddr_in6);
  struct sockaddr_in6   clntaddr;   /* socket structure */
  socklen_t clntaddrsz = sizeof(struct sockaddr_in6);
  in_port_t portnum = DEFSRVPORT;   /* port number */
  int    portnum_in;                /* port number entered by user */
  int    sw;                        /* value of option */
  int    v6only = 0;                /* IPV6_V6ONLY socket option off */
#if !WINDOWS
  struct timespec  sleeptm;         /* sleep time */
#endif
#if WINDOWS
  WSADATA wsaData;                  /* Winsock data */
  char* GetErrorMsg(int ErrorCode);  /* print error string in Windows */
#endif

  fprintf(stdout, "Connection-oriented server program, version %u ...\n",
    CURRENT_VER);

  /* Get the server's port number from user, if any. */
  if (argc > 1)
  {
    portnum_in = atoi(argv[1]);
    if (portnum_in <= 0)
    {
      fprintf(stderr, "Port number %d invalid, set to default value %u\n",
        portnum_in, DEFSRVPORT);
      portnum = DEFSRVPORT;
    }
    else
      portnum = portnum_in;
  }

#if WINDOWS
  /* Initiate use of the Winsock DLL. Ask for Winsock version 2.2 at least. */
  if ((ret = WSAStartup(MAKEWORD(2, 2), &wsaData)) != 0)
  {
    fprintf(stderr, "WSAStartup() failed with error %d: %s\n",
      ret, GetErrorMsg(ret));
    return (PROD_ERR_WINSOCK_INIT);
  }
#endif

  /* Create the Stream server socket. */
  if ((sfd = socket(AF_INET6, SOCK_STREAM, 0)) < 0)
  {
    fprintf(stderr, "Error: socket() failed, errno=%d, %s\n", ERRNO, ERRNOSTR);
#if WINDOWS
    WSACleanup();
#endif
    return(PROD_ERR_SOCKET_CREATE);
  }

  /* Always turn on SO_REUSEADDR socket option on the server. */
  sw = 1;
  errno = 0;
```

```
  if (setsockopt(sfd, SOL_SOCKET, SO_REUSEADDR, (char *)&sw, sizeof(sw)) < 0)
  {
    fprintf(stderr, "setsockopt(SO_REUSEADDR) failed, errno=%d, %s\n", ERRNO,
      ERRNOSTR);
  }
  else
    fprintf(stdout, "SO_REUSEADDR socket option is turned on.\n");

  /* Fill in the server socket address. */
  memset((void *)&srvaddr, 0, (size_t)srvaddrsz); /* clear the address buffer */
  srvaddr.sin6_family = AF_INET6;                  /* Internet socket */
  srvaddr.sin6_addr= in6addr_any;                  /* server's IP address */
  srvaddr.sin6_port = htons(portnum);              /* server's port number */

  /* Turn off IPV6_V6ONLY socket option. Default is on in Windows. */
  if (setsockopt(sfd, IPPROTO_IPV6, IPV6_V6ONLY, (char*)&v6only,
    sizeof(v6only)) != 0)
  {
    fprintf(stderr, "Error: setsockopt(IPV6_V6ONLY) failed, errno=%d, %s\n",
      ERRNO, ERRNOSTR);
    CLOSE(sfd);
    return(PROD_ERR_SETSOCKETOPT);
  }

  /* Bind the server socket to its address. */
  if ((ret = bind(sfd, (struct sockaddr *)&srvaddr, srvaddrsz)) != 0)
  {
    fprintf(stderr, "Error: bind() failed, errno=%d, %s\n", ERRNO, ERRNOSTR);
    CLOSE(sfd);
    return(PROD_ERR_BIND);
  }

  /* Set maximum connection request queue length that we can fall behind. */
  if (listen(sfd, BACKLOG) == -1) {
    fprintf(stderr, "Error: listen() failed, errno=%d, %s\n", ERRNO, ERRNOSTR);
    CLOSE(sfd);
    return(PROD_ERR_LISTEN);
  }

  /* Wait for incoming connection requests from clients and service them. */
  while (1) {

    fprintf(stdout, "\nListening at port number %u ...\n", portnum);
    newsock = accept(sfd, (struct sockaddr *)&clntaddr, &clntaddrsz);
    if (newsock < 0)
    {
      fprintf(stderr, "Error: accept() failed, errno=%d, %s\n", ERRNO, ERRNOSTR);
      CLOSE(sfd);
      return(PROD_ERR_ACCEPT);
    }

    fprintf(stdout, "Client Connected.\n");

    ret = service_client(newsock);
    CLOSE1(newsock);
  }  /* while - outer */
```

```
  CLOSE(sfd);
  return(SUCCESS);
}

/* Receive initial packet from a newly connected client.
 * Perform some security checks or authentication.
 */
int receive_init_pkt(int sfd)
{
  init_pkt_t  initmsg;
  int         ret;

  memset((void *)&initmsg, 0, sizeof(init_pkt_t));
  errno = 0;
  ret = recv(sfd, (void *)&initmsg, sizeof(init_pkt_t), 0);
  if (ret < 0)
  {
    fprintf(stderr, "Error: receive_init_pkt(), recv() failed, errno=%d, %s\n",
      ERRNO, ERRNOSTR);
    return(PROD_ERR_SOCKET_RECV);
  }
  else if (ret != sizeof(init_pkt_t))
  {
    fprintf(stderr, "Error: receive_init_pkt(), recv() failed. Only %d out of"
      " %lu bytes of data received.\n", ret, sizeof(init_pkt_t));
    return(PROD_ERR_SOCKET_RECV);
  }

  /* Make sure the magic number always matches. */
  if (ntohl(initmsg.magic) != PROTO_MAGIC)
  {
    fprintf(stderr, "Error: receive_init_pkt(), wrong magic number.\n");
    return(PROD_ERR_WRONGMAGIC);
  }

  /* Perform protocol version-specific operations here if it applies. */
  if (ntohl(initmsg.version >= CURRENT_VER))
  {
    /* Perform some authentication here ... */

    return(SUCCESS);
  }
  return(0);
}


/*
 * This function is called by the server to service the needs of a client
 * after it has accepted a network connection request from a client.
 */
int service_client(int newsock)
{
  int     ret;
  char    *inbuf = NULL;                /* pointer to input data buffer */
  char    *outbuf = NULL;               /* pointer to output message buffer */
  int     *indata_ptr = NULL;           /* pointer to input data from client */
```

```c
int      indata = 0;            /* input data from client */
size_t               msglen;            /* length of client request message */
unsigned long long   buflen = 0L;       /* length of input data buffer */
unsigned long long   result = 0L;       /* output result of multiplication */
unsigned long long   *result_ptr;       /* pointer to result */
req_pkt_t request;                      /* client's request */
req_pkt_t *reqmsg=NULL;                 /* pointer to client's request msg */
req_pkt_t *rplymsg = NULL;              /* pointer to reply to client */
int                  bytes;             /* number of bytes read */
unsigned long long   total_bytes;       /* total number of bytes read */
int                  opcode;            /* operation requested by client */
int                  status;            /* status of operation */

/* Receive initial packet. Close the connection if it fails.
 * Make sure we always terminate the connection right away in case of magic
 * number mismatch or others to prevent denial-of-service (DOS) attacks.
 */
ret = receive_init_pkt(newsock);
if (ret != SUCCESS)
{
  fprintf(stderr, "Error: service_client(), receive_init_pkt() failed, "
    "ret=%d\n", ret);
  CLOSE1(newsock);
  return(ret);
}

/* Service the connected client until it is done.
 * Receive a request and service the request in each iteration.
 */
while (1)
{
  /* Receive the request header from the connected client. */
  msglen = sizeof(request);
  reqmsg = &request;
  memset(reqmsg, 0, msglen);
  errno = 0;
  ret = recv(newsock, reqmsg, msglen, 0);
  if (ret < 0)
  {
    fprintf(stderr, "Error: recv() failed, errno=%d, %s\n", ERRNO, ERRNOSTR);
    ret = (PROD_ERR_SOCKET_RECV);
    goto return1;
  }
  else if (ret == 0)
  {
    fprintf(stderr, "The client has closed.\n");
    ret = (PROD_ERR_SOCKET_RECV);
    goto return1;
  }
  else if (ret != msglen)
  {
    fprintf(stderr, "Error: recv() failed. Only %d out of %lu bytes were "
      "received.\n", ret, msglen);
    ret = (PROD_ERR_SOCKET_RECV);
    goto return1;
  }
```

```
    fprintf(stdout, "Client version=%d\n", ntohl(reqmsg->version));

    /* Perform some sanity check */
    if (ntohl(reqmsg->magic) != REQ_MAGIC)
    {
      fprintf(stderr, "Error: service_client(), wrong magic number.\n");
      ret = (PROD_ERR_WRONGMAGIC);
      goto return1;
    }

    /* Receive the request data if any */
    buflen = ntohll(reqmsg->datasz);
    if (buflen > 0)
    {
      /* Allocate buffer for the input data */
      inbuf = (char *)malloc(buflen);
      if (inbuf == NULL)
      {
        fprintf(stderr, "malloc() failed.\n");
        ret = (PROD_ERR_NO_MEMORY);
        goto return1;
      }

      /* Read all input data */
      errno = 0;
      total_bytes = 0L;
      do {
        bytes = read(newsock, inbuf+total_bytes, (buflen-total_bytes));
        if (bytes < 0)
        {
          fprintf(stderr, "Error: read() failed, errno=%d, %s\n", ERRNO, ERRNOSTR);
          ret = (PROD_ERR_SOCKET_RECV);
          goto return1;
        }
        else if (bytes == 0)
        {
          fprintf(stderr, "The client has closed.\n");
          ret = (PROD_ERR_SOCKET_RECV);
          goto return1;
        }
        total_bytes = total_bytes + (unsigned long long)bytes;
      } while (total_bytes < buflen);
    }

    /* Extract the input data and perform the requested operation
       which is version specific. Hence versioning is done here. */
    opcode = ntohl(reqmsg->operation);
    if (ntohl(reqmsg->version >= CURRENT_VER))
    {
      switch(opcode)
      {
        case REQ_OPCODE1:
          indata_ptr = (int *)(inbuf);
          indata =  ntohl(*indata_ptr);
          fprintf(stdout, "Client input data is %d\n", indata);
```

1027

```
        result = ((unsigned long long)indata * 100);
        status = SUCCESS;
        fprintf(stdout, "Multiplication result is %llu\n", result);
      break;
      default:
        status = PROD_ERR_BAD_OPCODE;
        result = 0L;
        fprintf(stdout, "Operation code %d is not supported.\n", opcode);
      break;
    }
  }

  /* Send a reply */
  msglen = (sizeof(req_pkt_t) + sizeof(unsigned long long));
  if (outbuf == NULL)
  {
    outbuf = (char *)malloc(msglen);
    if (outbuf == NULL)
    {
      fprintf(stderr, "malloc() failed.\n");
      ret = (PROD_ERR_NO_MEMORY);
      goto return1;
    }
  }
  memset(outbuf, 0, msglen);

  /* Fill in the reply message */
  rplymsg = (req_pkt_t *)outbuf;
  rplymsg->version = htonl(CURRENT_VER);
  rplymsg->magic = htonl(REPLY_MAGIC);
  rplymsg->operation = reqmsg->operation;
  rplymsg->status = htonl(status);
  rplymsg->datasz = htonll(sizeof(unsigned long long));
  result_ptr = (unsigned long long *)(outbuf + sizeof(req_pkt_t));
  *result_ptr = htonll(result);

  /* Send the reply message */
  errno = 0;
  ret = send(newsock, outbuf, msglen, 0);
  if (ret < 0)
  {
    fprintf(stderr, "Error: send() failed, errno=%d, %s\n", ERRNO, ERRNOSTR);
    ret = (PROD_ERR_SOCKET_SEND);
    goto return1;
  }
  else if (ret != msglen)
  {
    fprintf(stderr, "Error: send() failed. Only %d out of %lu bytes were sent.\n"
      , ret, msglen);
    ret = (PROD_ERR_SOCKET_SEND);
    goto return1;
  }

  fprintf(stdout, "Result %llu was successfully sent back to the client.\n",
    result);
}
```

```
return1:
  if (inbuf != NULL)
    free(inbuf);
  if (outbuf != NULL)
    free(outbuf);
  CLOSE1(newsock);
  return(ret);
}
```

Figure 14-10 Example distributed application (version2)
-- mydistsys.h.v2, tcpclnt_dist_all_v2.c and tcpsrv_dist_all_v2.c

(a) mydistsys.h.v2

```
/*
 * Include file for distributed system applications
 * Supported operating systems: Linux, Unix (AIX, Solaris, HP-UX), Windows.
 * Copyright (c) 1996, 2002, 2014, 2019 Mr. Jin-Jwei Chen. All rights reserved.
 */

/*
 * Defines for Endianness.
 */
#undef  LITTLE_ENDIAN
#undef  BIG_ENDIAN
#define LITTLE_ENDIAN     1
#define BIG_ENDIAN        2
#define UNKNOWN_ENDIAN    3

/*
 * Endian utility functions.
 */
int endian();
unsigned long long myhtonll(unsigned long long num64bit);
unsigned long long myntohll(unsigned long long num64bit);
unsigned short myByteSwap2(unsigned short num16bit);
unsigned int myByteSwap4(unsigned int num32bit);
unsigned long long myByteSwap8(unsigned long long num64bit);

/*
 * Use our own version on platforms not supporting htonll()/ntohll().
 * Remove the O.S. from this list once it has native support.
 */
#if (WINDOWS || LINUX || HPUX)
#define htonll  myhtonll
#define ntohll  myntohll
#endif

/*
 * Application protocol version numbers
 */
#define   VERSION1  1
#define   VERSION2  2
#define   CURRENT_VER  VERSION2  /* always keep this line last */
```

```c
/* Magic number */
#define PROTO_MAGIC   3923850741
#define REQ_MAGIC     3749500826
#define REPLY_MAGIC   2814594375
#define DATA_MAGIC    1943724308

/* Client request operations */
#define REQ_OPCODE1   1       /* do multiplication */

/*
 * Initial connection packet.
 */
#define AUTH_ID_LEN    32
#define INIT_PKT_LEN   256
typedef struct {
    unsigned int        version;      /* app. protocol version number */
    unsigned int        magic;        /* app. protocol magic number */
    unsigned int        flags;
    char                auth[AUTH_ID_LEN];      /* auth data */
    char                reserved[INIT_PKT_LEN-AUTH_ID_LEN];
} init_pkt_t;

/*
 * Request/Reply header packet.
 */
typedef struct {
    unsigned int        version;      /* App. data version number */
    unsigned int        magic;        /* app. data packet magic number */
    int                 operation;    /* operation to be performed */
    int                 status;       /* status of the operation */
    unsigned long long  datasz;       /* size of data */
    char                reserved[64];
} req_pkt_t;

/*
 * Portable data file header.
 */
typedef struct {
    char                endian;       /* endian format of the data */
    char                padding[3];   /* pad it for alignment */
    unsigned int        version;      /* version number */
    unsigned int        magic;        /* magic number of data record header */
    unsigned int        padding2;     /* pad it to 8-byte boundary */
    unsigned long long  nrecs;        /* number of records */
    char                reserved[24];
} portable_data_hdr_t;

/*
 * Data record.
 */
#define  NAME_LEN  32
typedef struct {
    char                name[NAME_LEN];
    unsigned int        birthyear;
    unsigned int        salary;
```

```
    unsigned int          bonus;
} data_rec_t;
```

(b) tcpclnt_dist_all_v2.c

```c
/*
 * A connection-oriented client program using Stream socket.
 * Connecting to a server program on any host using a hostname or IP address.
 * Demonstrating design of distributed applications.
 * Support for IPv4 and IPv6 and multiple platforms including
 * Linux, Windows, Solaris, AIX and HPUX.
 * Usage: tcpclnt_dist_all_v2 [srvport# [server-hostname | server-ipaddress]]
 * Authored by Mr. Jin-Jwei Chen.
 * Copyright (c) 1993-2020, Mr. Jin-Jwei Chen. All rights reserved.
 */

#include "mysocket.h"
#include "mydistsys.h"
#include "myerrors.h"

int send_init_pkt(int sfd);

int main(int argc, char *argv[])
{
  int      ret = 0;
  int      sfd;                      /* socket file descriptor */
  in_port_t  portnum=DEFSRVPORT;     /* port number */
  int      portnum_in = 0;           /* port number user provides */
  char    *portnumstr = DEFSRVPORTSTR; /* port number in string format */
  char    *inbuf = NULL;             /* pointer to input message buffer */
  char    *outbuf = NULL;            /* pointer to output message buffer */
  size_t msglen;                     /* length of reply message */
  size_t len;
  char    server_name[NAMELEN+1] = SERVER_NAME;
  struct addrinfo hints;             /* address info hints*/
  struct addrinfo *res=NULL;         /* pointer to address info */
  req_pkt_t    *reqmsg = NULL;       /* pointer to client request message */
  int          anumber = 15;         /* the number to be multiplied at server */
  int          *dataptr = NULL;      /* pointer to input data */
  unsigned long long *result_ptr = NULL;   /* pointer to multiplication result */
  req_pkt_t    *reply = NULL;        /* pointer to server reply message */

#if WINDOWS
  WSADATA wsaData;                   /* Winsock data */
  char* GetErrorMsg(int ErrorCode);  /* print error string in Windows */
#endif

  fprintf(stdout, "Connection-oriented client program, version %u ...\n",
    CURRENT_VER);

  /* Get the server's port number from command line. */
  if (argc > 1)
  {
    portnum_in = atoi(argv[1]);
    if (portnum_in <= 0)
    {
```

1031

```
            fprintf(stderr, "Port number %d invalid, set to default value %u\n",
                portnum_in, DEFSRVPORT);
            portnum = DEFSRVPORT;
            portnumstr = DEFSRVPORTSTR;
        }
        else
        {
            portnum = (in_port_t)portnum_in;
            portnumstr = argv[1];
        }
    }

    /* Get the server's host name or IP address from command line. */
    if (argc > 2)
    {
        len = strlen(argv[2]);
        if (len > NAMELEN)
            len = NAMELEN;
        strncpy(server_name, argv[2], len);
        server_name[len] = '\0';
    }

    /* Get the number to be multiplied from the user*/
    if (argc > 3)
        anumber = atoi(argv[3]);


#if WINDOWS
    /* Initiate use of the Winsock DLL. Ask for Winsock version 2.2 at least. */
    if ((ret = WSAStartup(MAKEWORD(2, 2), &wsaData)) != 0)
    {
        fprintf(stderr, "Error: WSAStartup() failed with error %d: %s\n",
            ret, GetErrorMsg(ret));
        return (PROD_ERR_WINSOCK_INIT);
    }
#endif

    /* Translate the server's host name or IP address into socket address.
     * Fill in the hint information.
     */
    memset(&hints, 0x00, sizeof(hints));
    /* This works on AIX but not on Solaris, nor on Windows. */
    /* hints.ai_flags     = AI_NUMERICSERV; */
    hints.ai_family     = AF_UNSPEC;
    hints.ai_socktype   = SOCK_STREAM;
    hints.ai_protocol   = IPPROTO_TCP;

    /* Get the address information of the server using getaddrinfo().
     * This function returns errors directly or 0 for success. On success,
     * argument res contains a linked list of addrinfo structures.
     */
    ret = getaddrinfo(server_name, portnumstr, &hints, &res);
    if (ret != 0)
    {
        fprintf(stderr, "Error: getaddrinfo() failed, error %d, %s\n", ret,
            gai_strerror(ret));
```

```
#if !WINDOWS
    if (ret == EAI_SYSTEM)
       fprintf(stderr,"System error: errno=%d, %s\n", errno, strerror(errno));
#else
    WSACleanup();
#endif
    return(PROD_ERR_GETADDRINFO);
    }

  /* Create a socket. */
  sfd = socket(res->ai_family, res->ai_socktype, res->ai_protocol);
  if (sfd < 0)
    {
     fprintf(stderr,"Error: socket() failed, errno=%d, %s\n", ERRNO, ERRNOSTR);
#if WINDOWS
    WSACleanup();
#endif
    ret = PROD_ERR_SOCKET_CREATE;
    goto return1;
    }

  /* Connect to the server. */
  ret = connect(sfd, res->ai_addr, res->ai_addrlen);
  if (ret == -1)
    {
     fprintf(stderr, "Error: connect() failed, errno=%d, %s\n", ERRNO, ERRNOSTR);
     ret = PROD_ERR_CONNECT;
     goto return1;
    }

  /* Send initial packet */
  ret = send_init_pkt(sfd);
  if (ret != SUCCESS)
    {
     fprintf(stderr, "Error: send_init_pkt() failed, ret=%d\n", ret);
     goto return1;
    }

  fprintf(stdout, "Send request messages to server(%s) at port %d\n",
     server_name, portnum);

  /*
   * Send a request message to the server
   */
  /* Allocate output buffer */
  msglen = (sizeof(req_pkt_t) + sizeof(int));
  outbuf = (char *)malloc(msglen);
  if (outbuf == NULL)
    {
     fprintf(stderr, "malloc() failed.\n");
     ret = PROD_ERR_NO_MEMORY;
     goto return1;
    }

  /* Fill in request */
  memset(outbuf, 0, msglen);
```

```
reqmsg = (req_pkt_t *)outbuf;
reqmsg->version = htonl(CURRENT_VER);
reqmsg->magic = htonl(REQ_MAGIC);
reqmsg->operation = htonl(REQ_OPCODE1);
reqmsg->datasz = htonll(sizeof(int));
dataptr = (int *)(outbuf + sizeof(req_pkt_t));
*dataptr = htonl(anumber);

/* Send the request */
errno = 0;
ret = send(sfd, outbuf, msglen, 0);
if (ret < 0)
{
  fprintf(stderr, "Error: send() failed, errno=%d, %s\n", ERRNO, ERRNOSTR);
  ret = PROD_ERR_SOCKET_SEND;
  goto return1;
}
else if (ret != msglen)
{
  fprintf(stderr, "Error: send() failed. Only %d out of %lu bytes were sent.\n"
    , ret, msglen);
  ret = PROD_ERR_SOCKET_SEND;
  goto return1;
}

/* Receive a reply from the server. */
/* Allocate input buffer */
msglen = (sizeof(req_pkt_t) + sizeof(unsigned long long));
inbuf = (char *)malloc(msglen);
if (inbuf == NULL)
{
  fprintf(stderr, "malloc() failed.\n");
  ret = PROD_ERR_NO_MEMORY;
  goto return1;
}
memset(inbuf, 0, msglen);

/* Receive the reply from the server */
errno = 0;
ret = recv(sfd, inbuf, msglen, 0);
if (ret < 0)
{
  fprintf(stderr, "Error: recv() failed, errno=%d, %s\n", ERRNO, ERRNOSTR);
  ret = PROD_ERR_SOCKET_RECV;
  goto return1;
}
else if (ret != msglen)
{
  fprintf(stderr, "Error: recv() failed. Only %d out of %lu bytes were "
    "received.\n", ret, msglen);
  ret = PROD_ERR_SOCKET_RECV;
  goto return1;
}
reply = (req_pkt_t *)inbuf;
fprintf(stdout, "The client received %d bytes of reply from a server"
  " of version %u.\n", ret, ntohl(reply->version));
```

```
 if (ntohl(reply->status == SUCCESS))
   {
     result_ptr = (unsigned long long *)(inbuf + sizeof(req_pkt_t));
     fprintf(stdout, "The multiplied result of %d is %llu.\n", anumber,
       ntohll(*result_ptr));
   }
 else
   {
     fprintf(stderr, "Requested operation %u failed, status=%d\n",
       ntohl(reply->operation), ntohl(reply->status));
   }

return1:
  /* Free the memory allocated by getaddrinfo() and others */
  if (res != NULL) freeaddrinfo(res);
  if (inbuf != NULL) free(inbuf);
  if (outbuf != NULL) free(outbuf);
  CLOSE(sfd);
  return(ret);
}


/* Send initial packet */
int send_init_pkt(int sfd)
{
  init_pkt_t  initmsg;
  int         ret;

  memset((void *)&initmsg, 0, sizeof(init_pkt_t));
  initmsg.version = htonl(CURRENT_VER);
  initmsg.magic = htonl(PROTO_MAGIC);
  initmsg.flags = htonl(0);

  errno = 0;
  ret = send(sfd, (void *)&initmsg, sizeof(init_pkt_t), 0);
  if (ret < 0)
    {
      fprintf(stderr, "Error: send_init_pkt(), send() failed, errno=%d, %s\n",
        ERRNO, ERRNOSTR);
      return(PROD_ERR_SOCKET_SEND);
    }
  else if (ret != sizeof(init_pkt_t))
    {
      fprintf(stderr, "Error: send_init_pkt(), send() failed. Only %d out of"
        " %lu bytes of data sent.\n", ret, sizeof(init_pkt_t));
      return(PROD_ERR_SOCKET_SEND);
    }

  return(SUCCESS);
}


    (c) tcpsrv_dist_all_v2.c


/*
 * A connection-oriented server program using Stream socket.
 * Demonstrating design of distributed applications.
```

```c
 * Support for multiple platforms including Linux, Windows, Solaris, AIX, HPUX.
 * Usage: tcpsrv_dist_all_v2 [port#]
 * Authored by Mr. Jin-Jwei Chen.
 * Copyright (c) 2002, 2014, 2017-2020 Mr. Jin-Jwei Chen. All rights reserved.
 */

#include "mysocket.h"
#include "mydistsys.h"
#include "myerrors.h"

int receive_init_pkt(int sfd);
int service_client(int newsock);

int main(int argc, char *argv[])
{
  int    ret;                    /* return code */
  int    sfd;                    /* file descriptor of the listener socket */
  int    newsock;                /* file descriptor of client data socket */
  struct sockaddr_in6    srvaddr;    /* socket structure */
  int    srvaddrsz=sizeof(struct sockaddr_in6);
  struct sockaddr_in6    clntaddr;   /* socket structure */
  socklen_t clntaddrsz = sizeof(struct sockaddr_in6);
  in_port_t portnum = DEFSRVPORT;   /* port number */
  int    portnum_in;             /* port number entered by user */
  int    sw;                     /* value of option */
  int    v6only = 0;             /* IPV6_V6ONLY socket option off */
#if !WINDOWS
  struct timespec  sleeptm;          /* sleep time */
#endif
#if WINDOWS
  WSADATA wsaData;                   /* Winsock data */
  char* GetErrorMsg(int ErrorCode);  /* print error string in Windows */
#endif

  fprintf(stdout, "Connection-oriented server program, version %u ...\n",
    CURRENT_VER);

  /* Get the server's port number from user, if any. */
  if (argc > 1)
  {
    portnum_in = atoi(argv[1]);
    if (portnum_in <= 0)
    {
      fprintf(stderr, "Port number %d invalid, set to default value %u\n",
        portnum_in, DEFSRVPORT);
      portnum = DEFSRVPORT;
    }
    else
      portnum = portnum_in;
  }

#if WINDOWS
  /* Initiate use of the Winsock DLL. Ask for Winsock version 2.2 at least. */
  if ((ret = WSAStartup(MAKEWORD(2, 2), &wsaData)) != 0)
  {
    fprintf(stderr, "WSAStartup() failed with error %d: %s\n",
```

1036

```
      ret, GetErrorMsg(ret));
    return (PROD_ERR_WINSOCK_INIT);
  }
#endif

  /* Create the Stream server socket. */
  if ((sfd = socket(AF_INET6, SOCK_STREAM, 0)) < 0)
  {
    fprintf(stderr, "Error: socket() failed, errno=%d, %s\n", ERRNO, ERRNOSTR);
#if WINDOWS
    WSACleanup();
#endif
    return(PROD_ERR_SOCKET_CREATE);
  }

  /* Always turn on SO_REUSEADDR socket option on the server. */
  sw = 1;
  errno = 0;
  if (setsockopt(sfd, SOL_SOCKET, SO_REUSEADDR, (char *)&sw, sizeof(sw)) < 0)
  {
    fprintf(stderr, "setsockopt(SO_REUSEADDR) failed, errno=%d, %s\n", ERRNO,
      ERRNOSTR);
  }
  else
    fprintf(stdout, "SO_REUSEADDR socket option is turned on.\n");

  /* Fill in the server socket address. */
  memset((void *)&srvaddr, 0, (size_t)srvaddrsz);  /* clear the address buffer */
  srvaddr.sin6_family = AF_INET6;                  /* Internet socket */
  srvaddr.sin6_addr= in6addr_any;                  /* server's IP address */
  srvaddr.sin6_port = htons(portnum);              /* server's port number */

  /* Turn off IPV6_V6ONLY socket option. Default is on in Windows. */
  if (setsockopt(sfd, IPPROTO_IPV6, IPV6_V6ONLY, (char*)&v6only,
    sizeof(v6only)) != 0)
  {
    fprintf(stderr, "Error: setsockopt(IPV6_V6ONLY) failed, errno=%d, %s\n",
      ERRNO, ERRNOSTR);
    CLOSE(sfd);
    return(PROD_ERR_SETSOCKETOPT);
  }

  /* Bind the server socket to its address. */
  if ((ret = bind(sfd, (struct sockaddr *)&srvaddr, srvaddrsz)) != 0)
  {
    fprintf(stderr, "Error: bind() failed, errno=%d, %s\n", ERRNO, ERRNOSTR);
    CLOSE(sfd);
    return(PROD_ERR_BIND);
  }

  /* Set maximum connection request queue length that we can fall behind. */
  if (listen(sfd, BACKLOG) == -1) {
    fprintf(stderr, "Error: listen() failed, errno=%d, %s\n", ERRNO, ERRNOSTR);
    CLOSE(sfd);
    return(PROD_ERR_LISTEN);
  }
```

```c
  /* Wait for incoming connection requests from clients and service them. */
  while (1) {

    fprintf(stdout, "\nListening at port number %u ...\n", portnum);
    newsock = accept(sfd, (struct sockaddr *)&clntaddr, &clntaddrsz);
    if (newsock < 0)
    {
      fprintf(stderr, "Error: accept() failed, errno=%d, %s\n", ERRNO, ERRNOSTR);
      CLOSE(sfd);
      return(PROD_ERR_ACCEPT);
    }

    fprintf(stdout, "Client Connected.\n");

    ret = service_client(newsock);
    CLOSE1(newsock);
  }  /* while - outer */

  CLOSE(sfd);
  return(SUCCESS);
}

/* Receive initial packet from a newly connected client.
 * Perform some security checks or authentication.
 */
int receive_init_pkt(int sfd)
{
  init_pkt_t  initmsg;
  int         ret;

  memset((void *)&initmsg, 0, sizeof(init_pkt_t));
  errno = 0;
  ret = recv(sfd, (void *)&initmsg, sizeof(init_pkt_t), 0);
  if (ret < 0)
  {
    fprintf(stderr, "Error: receive_init_pkt(), recv() failed, errno=%d, %s\n",
      ERRNO, ERRNOSTR);
    return(PROD_ERR_SOCKET_RECV);
  }
  else if (ret != sizeof(init_pkt_t))
  {
    fprintf(stderr, "Error: receive_init_pkt(), recv() failed. Only %d out of"
      " %lu bytes of data received.\n", ret, sizeof(init_pkt_t));
    return(PROD_ERR_SOCKET_RECV);
  }

  /* Make sure the magic number always matches. */
  if (ntohl(initmsg.magic) != PROTO_MAGIC)
  {
    fprintf(stderr, "Error: receive_init_pkt(), wrong magic number.\n");
    return(PROD_ERR_WRONGMAGIC);
  }

  /* Perform protocol version-specific operations here if it applies. */
  if (ntohl(initmsg.version >= CURRENT_VER))
```

```
   {
      /* Perform some authentication here ... */

      return(SUCCESS);
   }
   return(0);
}


/*
 * This function is called by the server to service the needs of a client
 * after it has accepted a network connection request from a client.
 */
int service_client(int newsock)
{
   int       ret;
   char      *inbuf = NULL;             /* pointer to input data buffer */
   char      *outbuf = NULL;            /* pointer to output message buffer */
   int       *indata_ptr = NULL;        /* pointer to input data from client */
   int       indata = 0;                /* input data from client */
   size_t                 msglen;       /* length of client request message */
   unsigned long long     buflen = 0L;  /* length of input data buffer */
   unsigned long long     result = 0L;  /* output result of multiplication */
   unsigned long long     *result_ptr;  /* pointer to result */
   req_pkt_t request;                   /* client's request */
   req_pkt_t *reqmsg=NULL;              /* pointer to client's request msg */
   req_pkt_t *rplymsg = NULL;           /* pointer to reply to client */
   int                    bytes;        /* number of bytes read */
   unsigned long long     total_bytes;  /* total number of bytes read */
   int                    opcode;       /* operation requested by client */
   int                    status;       /* status of operation */
   int                    clntVersion;  /* client's version */


   /* Receive initial packet. Close the connection if it fails.
    * Make sure we always terminate the connection right away in case of magic
    * number mismatch or others to prevent denial-of-service (DOS) attacks.
    */
   ret = receive_init_pkt(newsock);
   if (ret != SUCCESS)
   {
      fprintf(stderr, "Error: service_client(), receive_init_pkt() failed, "
         "ret=%d\n", ret);
      CLOSE1(newsock);
      return(ret);
   }


   /* Service the connected client until it is done.
    * Receive a request and service the request in each iteration.
    */
   while (1)
   {
      /* Receive the request header from the connected client. */
      msglen = sizeof(request);
      reqmsg = &request;
      memset(reqmsg, 0, msglen);
      errno = 0;
      ret = recv(newsock, reqmsg, msglen, 0);
```

```
    if (ret < 0)
    {
      fprintf(stderr, "Error: recv() failed, errno=%d, %s\n", ERRNO, ERRNOSTR);
      ret = (PROD_ERR_SOCKET_RECV);
      goto return1;
    }
    else if (ret == 0)
    {
      fprintf(stderr, "The client has closed.\n");
      ret = (PROD_ERR_SOCKET_RECV);
      goto return1;
    }
    else if (ret != msglen)
    {
      fprintf(stderr, "Error: recv() failed. Only %d out of %lu bytes were "
        "received.\n", ret, msglen);
      ret = (PROD_ERR_SOCKET_RECV);
      goto return1;
    }

    clntVersion = ntohl(reqmsg->version);
    fprintf(stdout, "Client version=%d\n", clntVersion);

    /* Perform some sanity check */
    if (ntohl(reqmsg->magic) != REQ_MAGIC)
    {
      fprintf(stderr, "Error: service_client(), wrong magic number.\n");
      ret = (PROD_ERR_WRONGMAGIC);
      goto return1;
    }

    /* Receive the request data if any */
    buflen = ntohll(reqmsg->datasz);
    if (buflen > 0)
    {
      /* Allocate buffer for the input data */
      inbuf = (char *)malloc(buflen);
      if (inbuf == NULL)
      {
        fprintf(stderr, "malloc() failed.\n");
        ret = (PROD_ERR_NO_MEMORY);
        goto return1;
      }

      /* Read all input data */
      errno = 0;
      total_bytes = 0L;
      do {
        bytes = read(newsock, inbuf+total_bytes, (buflen-total_bytes));
        if (bytes < 0)
        {
          fprintf(stderr, "Error: read() failed, errno=%d, %s\n", ERRNO, ERRNOSTR);
          ret = (PROD_ERR_SOCKET_RECV);
          goto return1;
        }
        else if (bytes == 0)
```

```
        {
           fprintf(stderr, "The client has closed.\n");
           ret = (PROD_ERR_SOCKET_RECV);
           goto return1;
        }
        total_bytes = total_bytes + (unsigned long long)bytes;
    } while (total_bytes < buflen);
}

/* Extract the input data and perform the requested operation
   which is version specific. Hence versioning is done here. */
opcode = ntohl(reqmsg->operation);
if (clntVersion >= CURRENT_VER) /* latest version */
{
  switch(opcode)
  {
    case REQ_OPCODE1:
      indata_ptr = (int *)(inbuf);
      indata =  ntohl(*indata_ptr);
      fprintf(stdout, "Client input data is %d\n", indata);
      result = ((unsigned long long)indata * 1000);
      status = SUCCESS;
      fprintf(stdout, "Multiplication result is %llu\n", result);
    break;
    default:
      status = PROD_ERR_BAD_OPCODE;
      result = 0L;
      fprintf(stdout, "Operation code %d is not supported.\n", opcode);
    break;
  }
}
else if (clntVersion >= VERSION1) /* my previous version */
{
  switch(opcode)
  {
    case REQ_OPCODE1:
      indata_ptr = (int *)(inbuf);
      indata =  ntohl(*indata_ptr);
      fprintf(stdout, "Client input data is %d\n", indata);
      result = ((unsigned long long)indata * 100);
      status = SUCCESS;
      fprintf(stdout, "Multiplication result is %llu\n", result);
    break;
    default:
      status = PROD_ERR_BAD_OPCODE;
      result = 0L;
      fprintf(stdout, "Operation code %d is not supported.\n", opcode);
    break;
  }
}

/* Send a reply */
msglen = (sizeof(req_pkt_t) + sizeof(unsigned long long));
if (outbuf == NULL)
{
  outbuf = (char *)malloc(msglen);
```

```
        if (outbuf == NULL)
        {
            fprintf(stderr, "malloc() failed.\n");
            ret = (PROD_ERR_NO_MEMORY);
            goto return1;
        }
    }
    memset(outbuf, 0, msglen);

    /* Fill in the reply message */
    rplymsg = (req_pkt_t *)outbuf;
    rplymsg->version = htonl(CURRENT_VER);
    rplymsg->magic = htonl(REPLY_MAGIC);
    rplymsg->operation = reqmsg->operation;
    rplymsg->status = htonl(status);
    rplymsg->datasz = htonll(sizeof(unsigned long long));
    result_ptr = (unsigned long long *)(outbuf + sizeof(req_pkt_t));
    *result_ptr = htonll(result);

    /* Send the reply message */
    errno = 0;
    ret = send(newsock, outbuf, msglen, 0);
    if (ret < 0)
    {
        fprintf(stderr, "Error: send() failed, errno=%d, %s\n", ERRNO, ERRNOSTR);
        ret = (PROD_ERR_SOCKET_SEND);
        goto return1;
    }
    else if (ret != msglen)
    {
        fprintf(stderr, "Error: send() failed. Only %d out of %lu bytes were sent.\n"
          , ret, msglen);
        ret = (PROD_ERR_SOCKET_SEND);
        goto return1;
    }

    fprintf(stdout, "Result %llu was successfully sent back to the client.\n",
        result);
}

return1:
  if (inbuf != NULL)
    free(inbuf);
  if (outbuf != NULL)
    free(outbuf);
  CLOSE1(newsock);
  return(ret);
}
```

Figure 14-11 Example distributed application (version3)
-- mydistsys.h.v3, tcpclnt_dist_all_v3.c and tcpsrv_dist_all_v3.c

(a) mydistsys.h.v3

```
/*
 * Include file for distributed system applications
```

1042

```
 * Supported operating systems: Linux, Unix (AIX, Solaris, HP-UX), Windows.
 * Copyright (c) 1996, 2002, 2014, 2019 Mr. Jin-Jwei Chen. All rights reserved.
 */


/*
 * Defines for Endianness.
 */
#undef  LITTLE_ENDIAN
#undef  BIG_ENDIAN
#define LITTLE_ENDIAN    1
#define BIG_ENDIAN       2
#define UNKNOWN_ENDIAN   3


/*
 * Endian utility functions.
 */
int endian();
unsigned long long myhtonll(unsigned long long num64bit);
unsigned long long myntohll(unsigned long long num64bit);
unsigned short myByteSwap2(unsigned short num16bit);
unsigned int myByteSwap4(unsigned int num32bit);
unsigned long long myByteSwap8(unsigned long long num64bit);


/*
 * Use our own version on platforms not supporting htonll()/ntohll().
 * Remove the O.S. from this list once it has native support.
 */
#if (WINDOWS || LINUX || HPUX)
#define htonll  myhtonll
#define ntohll  myntohll
#endif


/*
 * Application protocol version numbers
 */
#define  VERSION1    1
#define  VERSION2    2
#define  VERSION3    3
#define  CURRENT_VER  VERSION3  /* always keep this line last */


/* Magic number */
#define PROTO_MAGIC    3923850741
#define REQ_MAGIC      3749500826
#define REPLY_MAGIC    2814594375
#define DATA_MAGIC     1943724308


/* Client request operations */
#define REQ_OPCODE1  1       /* do multiplication */


/*
 * Initial connection packet.
 */
#define AUTH_ID_LEN     32
#define INIT_PKT_LEN    256
typedef struct {
    unsigned int      version;     /* app. protocol version number */
```

```
    unsigned int          magic;          /* app. protocol magic number */
    unsigned int          flags;
    char                  auth[AUTH_ID_LEN];      /* auth data */
    char                  reserved[INIT_PKT_LEN-AUTH_ID_LEN];
} init_pkt_t;

/*
 * Request/Reply header packet.
 */
typedef struct {
    unsigned int          version;     /* App. data version number */
    unsigned int          magic;       /* app. data packet magic number */
    int                   operation;   /* operation to be performed */
    int                   status;      /* status of the operation */
    unsigned long long    datasz;      /* size of data */
    int                   addend;      /* number to be addded to MUL product */
    char                  reserved[60];
} req_pkt_t;

/*
 * Portable data file header.
 */
typedef struct {
    char                  endian;      /* endian format of the data */
    char                  padding[3];  /* pad it for alignment */
    unsigned int          version;     /* version number */
    unsigned int          magic;       /* magic number of data record header */
    unsigned int          padding2;    /* pad it to 8-byte boundary */
    unsigned long long    nrecs;       /* number of records */
    char                  reserved[24];
} portable_data_hdr_t;

/*
 * Data record.
 */
#define  NAME_LEN   32
typedef struct {
    char                  name[NAME_LEN];
    unsigned int          birthyear;
    unsigned int          salary;
    unsigned int          bonus;
} data_rec_t;
```

(b) tcpclnt_dist_all_v3.c

```
/*
 * A connection-oriented client program using Stream socket.
 * Connecting to a server program on any host using a hostname or IP address.
 * Demonstrating design of distributed applications.
 * Support for IPv4 and IPv6 and multiple platforms including
 * Linux, Windows, Solaris, AIX and HPUX.
 * Usage: tcpclnt_dist_all_v3 [srvport# [server-hostname | server-ipaddress]]
 * Authored by Mr. Jin-Jwei Chen.
 * Copyright (c) 1993-2020, Mr. Jin-Jwei Chen. All rights reserved.
 */
```

```c
#include "mysocket.h"
#include "mydistsys.h"
#include "myerrors.h"

int send_init_pkt(int sfd);

int main(int argc, char *argv[])
{
  int     ret = 0;
  int     sfd;                         /* socket file descriptor */
  in_port_t  portnum=DEFSRVPORT;       /* port number */
  int     portnum_in = 0;              /* port number user provides */
  char    *portnumstr = DEFSRVPORTSTR; /* port number in string format */
  char    *inbuf = NULL;               /* pointer to input message buffer */
  char    *outbuf = NULL;              /* pointer to output message buffer */
  size_t msglen;                       /* length of reply message */
  size_t len;
  char    server_name[NAMELEN+1] = SERVER_NAME;
  struct addrinfo hints;               /* address info hints*/
  struct addrinfo *res=NULL;           /* pointer to address info */
  req_pkt_t    *reqmsg = NULL;         /* pointer to client request message */
  int          anumber = 15;           /* the number to be multiplied at server */
  int          *dataptr = NULL;        /* pointer to input data */
  unsigned long long *result_ptr = NULL;   /* pointer to multiplication result */
  req_pkt_t    *reply = NULL;          /* pointer to server reply message */
  int          addend = 50;            /* the number to be added to the product */

#if WINDOWS
  WSADATA wsaData;                         /* Winsock data */
  char* GetErrorMsg(int ErrorCode);    /* print error string in Windows */
#endif

  fprintf(stdout, "Connection-oriented client program, version %u ...\n",
    CURRENT_VER);

  /* Get the server's port number from command line. */
  if (argc > 1)
  {
    portnum_in = atoi(argv[1]);
    if (portnum_in <= 0)
    {
      fprintf(stderr, "Port number %d invalid, set to default value %u\n",
        portnum_in, DEFSRVPORT);
      portnum = DEFSRVPORT;
      portnumstr = DEFSRVPORTSTR;
    }
    else
    {
      portnum = (in_port_t)portnum_in;
      portnumstr = argv[1];
    }
  }

  /* Get the server's host name or IP address from command line. */
  if (argc > 2)
  {
```

```
    len = strlen(argv[2]);
    if (len > NAMELEN)
      len = NAMELEN;
    strncpy(server_name, argv[2], len);
    server_name[len] = '\0';
  }

  /* Get the number to be multiplied from the user*/
  if (argc > 3)
    anumber = atoi(argv[3]);

  /* Get the addend to be added to the product */
  if (argc > 4)
    addend = atoi(argv[4]);

#if WINDOWS
  /* Initiate use of the Winsock DLL. Ask for Winsock version 2.2 at least. */
  if ((ret = WSAStartup(MAKEWORD(2, 2), &wsaData)) != 0)
  {
    fprintf(stderr, "Error: WSAStartup() failed with error %d: %s\n",
      ret, GetErrorMsg(ret));
    return (PROD_ERR_WINSOCK_INIT);
  }
#endif

  /* Translate the server's host name or IP address into socket address.
   * Fill in the hint information.
   */
  memset(&hints, 0x00, sizeof(hints));
    /* This works on AIX but not on Solaris, nor on Windows. */
    /* hints.ai_flags    = AI_NUMERICSERV; */
  hints.ai_family   = AF_UNSPEC;
  hints.ai_socktype = SOCK_STREAM;
  hints.ai_protocol = IPPROTO_TCP;

  /* Get the address information of the server using getaddrinfo().
   * This function returns errors directly or 0 for success. On success,
   * argument res contains a linked list of addrinfo structures.
   */
  ret = getaddrinfo(server_name, portnumstr, &hints, &res);
  if (ret != 0)
  {
    fprintf(stderr, "Error: getaddrinfo() failed, error %d, %s\n", ret,
      gai_strerror(ret));
#if !WINDOWS
    if (ret == EAI_SYSTEM)
      fprintf(stderr,"System error: errno=%d, %s\n", errno, strerror(errno));
#else
    WSACleanup();
#endif
    return(PROD_ERR_GETADDRINFO);
  }

  /* Create a socket. */
  sfd = socket(res->ai_family, res->ai_socktype, res->ai_protocol);
  if (sfd < 0)
```

```
  {
    fprintf(stderr,"Error: socket() failed, errno=%d, %s\n", ERRNO, ERRNOSTR);
#if WINDOWS
    WSACleanup();
#endif
    ret = PROD_ERR_SOCKET_CREATE;
    goto return1;
  }

  /* Connect to the server. */
  ret = connect(sfd, res->ai_addr, res->ai_addrlen);
  if (ret == -1)
  {
    fprintf(stderr, "Error: connect() failed, errno=%d, %s\n", ERRNO, ERRNOSTR);
    ret = PROD_ERR_CONNECT;
    goto return1;
  }

  /* Send initial packet */
  ret = send_init_pkt(sfd);
  if (ret != SUCCESS)
  {
    fprintf(stderr, "Error: send_init_pkt() failed, ret=%d\n", ret);
    goto return1;
  }

  fprintf(stdout, "Send request messages to server(%s) at port %d\n",
    server_name, portnum);

  /*
   * Send a request message to the server
   */
  /* Allocate output buffer */
  msglen = (sizeof(req_pkt_t) + sizeof(int));
  outbuf = (char *)malloc(msglen);
  if (outbuf == NULL)
  {
    fprintf(stderr, "malloc() failed.\n");
    ret = PROD_ERR_NO_MEMORY;
    goto return1;
  }

  /* Fill in request */
  memset(outbuf, 0, msglen);
  reqmsg = (req_pkt_t *)outbuf;
  reqmsg->version = htonl(CURRENT_VER);
  reqmsg->magic = htonl(REQ_MAGIC);
  reqmsg->operation = htonl(REQ_OPCODE1);
  reqmsg->addend = htonl(addend);
  reqmsg->datasz = htonll(sizeof(int));
  dataptr = (int *)(outbuf + sizeof(req_pkt_t));
  *dataptr = htonl(anumber);

  /* Send the request */
  errno = 0;
  ret = send(sfd, outbuf, msglen, 0);
```

```c
if (ret < 0)
{
  fprintf(stderr, "Error: send() failed, errno=%d, %s\n", ERRNO, ERRNOSTR);
  ret = PROD_ERR_SOCKET_SEND;
  goto return1;
}
else if (ret != msglen)
{
  fprintf(stderr, "Error: send() failed. Only %d out of %lu bytes were sent.\n"
    , ret, msglen);
  ret = PROD_ERR_SOCKET_SEND;
  goto return1;
}

/* Receive a reply from the server. */
/* Allocate input buffer */
msglen = (sizeof(req_pkt_t) + sizeof(unsigned long long));
inbuf = (char *)malloc(msglen);
if (inbuf == NULL)
{
  fprintf(stderr, "malloc() failed.\n");
  ret = PROD_ERR_NO_MEMORY;
  goto return1;
}
memset(inbuf, 0, msglen);

/* Receive the reply from the server */
errno = 0;
ret = recv(sfd, inbuf, msglen, 0);
if (ret < 0)
{
  fprintf(stderr, "Error: recv() failed, errno=%d, %s\n", ERRNO, ERRNOSTR);
  ret = PROD_ERR_SOCKET_RECV;
  goto return1;
}
else if (ret != msglen)
{
  fprintf(stderr, "Error: recv() failed. Only %d out of %lu bytes were "
    "received.\n", ret, msglen);
  ret = PROD_ERR_SOCKET_RECV;
  goto return1;
}
reply = (req_pkt_t *)inbuf;
fprintf(stdout, "The client received %d bytes of reply from a server"
  " of version %u.\n", ret, ntohl(reply->version));

if (ntohl(reply->status == SUCCESS))
{
  result_ptr = (unsigned long long *)(inbuf + sizeof(req_pkt_t));
  fprintf(stdout, "The multiplied result of %d is %llu.\n", anumber,
    ntohll(*result_ptr));
}
else
{
  fprintf(stderr, "Requested operation %u failed, status=%d\n",
    ntohl(reply->operation), ntohl(reply->status));
```

```
    }

return1:
  /* Free the memory allocated by getaddrinfo() and others */
  if (res != NULL) freeaddrinfo(res);
  if (inbuf != NULL) free(inbuf);
  if (outbuf != NULL) free(outbuf);
  CLOSE(sfd);
  return(ret);
}

/* Send initial packet */
int send_init_pkt(int sfd)
{
  init_pkt_t  initmsg;
  int         ret;

  memset((void *)&initmsg, 0, sizeof(init_pkt_t));
  initmsg.version = htonl(CURRENT_VER);
  initmsg.magic = htonl(PROTO_MAGIC);
  initmsg.flags = htonl(0);

  errno = 0;
  ret = send(sfd, (void *)&initmsg, sizeof(init_pkt_t), 0);
  if (ret < 0)
  {
    fprintf(stderr, "Error: send_init_pkt(), send() failed, errno=%d, %s\n",
      ERRNO, ERRNOSTR);
    return(PROD_ERR_SOCKET_SEND);
  }
  else if (ret != sizeof(init_pkt_t))
  {
    fprintf(stderr, "Error: send_init_pkt(), send() failed. Only %d out of"
      " %lu bytes of data sent.\n", ret, sizeof(init_pkt_t));
    return(PROD_ERR_SOCKET_SEND);
  }

  return(SUCCESS);
}
```

    (c) tcpsrv_dist_all_v3.c

```
/*
 * A connection-oriented server program using Stream socket.
 * Demonstrating design of distributed applications.
 * Support for multiple platforms including Linux, Windows, Solaris, AIX, HPUX.
 * Usage: tcpsrv_dist_all_v3 [port#]
 * Authored by Mr. Jin-Jwei Chen.
 * Copyright (c) 2002, 2014, 2017-2020 Mr. Jin-Jwei Chen. All rights reserved.
 */

#include "mysocket.h"
#include "mydistsys.h"
#include "myerrors.h"

int service_client(int newsock);
```

```c
int main(int argc, char *argv[])
{
  int     ret;                         /* return code */
  int     sfd;                         /* file descriptor of the listener socket */
  int     newsock;                     /* file descriptor of client data socket */
  struct sockaddr_in6     srvaddr;     /* socket structure */
  int     srvaddrsz=sizeof(struct sockaddr_in6);
  struct sockaddr_in6     clntaddr;    /* socket structure */
  socklen_t clntaddrsz = sizeof(struct sockaddr_in6);
  in_port_t portnum = DEFSRVPORT;      /* port number */
  int     portnum_in;                  /* port number entered by user */
  int     sw;                          /* value of option */
  int     v6only = 0;                  /* IPV6_V6ONLY socket option off */
#if !WINDOWS
  struct timespec   sleeptm;           /* sleep time */
#endif
#if WINDOWS
  WSADATA wsaData;                     /* Winsock data */
  char* GetErrorMsg(int ErrorCode);    /* print error string in Windows */
#endif

  fprintf(stdout, "Connection-oriented server program, version %u ...\n",
    CURRENT_VER);

  /* Get the server's port number from user, if any. */
  if (argc > 1)
  {
    portnum_in = atoi(argv[1]);
    if (portnum_in <= 0)
    {
      fprintf(stderr, "Port number %d invalid, set to default value %u\n",
        portnum_in, DEFSRVPORT);
      portnum = DEFSRVPORT;
    }
    else
      portnum = portnum_in;
  }

#if WINDOWS
  /* Initiate use of the Winsock DLL. Ask for Winsock version 2.2 at least. */
  if ((ret = WSAStartup(MAKEWORD(2, 2), &wsaData)) != 0)
  {
    fprintf(stderr, "WSAStartup() failed with error %d: %s\n",
      ret, GetErrorMsg(ret));
    return (PROD_ERR_WINSOCK_INIT);
  }
#endif

  /* Create the Stream server socket. */
  if ((sfd = socket(AF_INET6, SOCK_STREAM, 0)) < 0)
  {
    fprintf(stderr, "Error: socket() failed, errno=%d, %s\n", ERRNO, ERRNOSTR);
#if WINDOWS
    WSACleanup();
#endif
```

```
    return(PROD_ERR_SOCKET_CREATE);
}

/* Always turn on SO_REUSEADDR socket option on the server. */
sw = 1;
errno = 0;
if (setsockopt(sfd, SOL_SOCKET, SO_REUSEADDR, (char *)&sw, sizeof(sw)) < 0)
{
  fprintf(stderr, "setsockopt(SO_REUSEADDR) failed, errno=%d, %s\n", ERRNO,
    ERRNOSTR);
}
else
  fprintf(stdout, "SO_REUSEADDR socket option is turned on.\n");

/* Fill in the server socket address. */
memset((void *)&srvaddr, 0, (size_t)srvaddrsz); /* clear the address buffer */
srvaddr.sin6_family = AF_INET6;                  /* Internet socket */
srvaddr.sin6_addr= in6addr_any;                  /* server's IP address */
srvaddr.sin6_port = htons(portnum);              /* server's port number */

/* Turn off IPV6_V6ONLY socket option. Default is on in Windows. */
if (setsockopt(sfd, IPPROTO_IPV6, IPV6_V6ONLY, (char*)&v6only,
  sizeof(v6only)) != 0)
{
  fprintf(stderr, "Error: setsockopt(IPV6_V6ONLY) failed, errno=%d, %s\n",
    ERRNO, ERRNOSTR);
  CLOSE(sfd);
  return(PROD_ERR_SETSOCKETOPT);
}

/* Bind the server socket to its address. */
if ((ret = bind(sfd, (struct sockaddr *)&srvaddr, srvaddrsz)) != 0)
{
  fprintf(stderr, "Error: bind() failed, errno=%d, %s\n", ERRNO, ERRNOSTR);
  CLOSE(sfd);
  return(PROD_ERR_BIND);
}

/* Set maximum connection request queue length that we can fall behind. */
if (listen(sfd, BACKLOG) == -1) {
  fprintf(stderr, "Error: listen() failed, errno=%d, %s\n", ERRNO, ERRNOSTR);
  CLOSE(sfd);
  return(PROD_ERR_LISTEN);
}

/* Wait for incoming connection requests from clients and service them. */
while (1) {

  fprintf(stdout, "\nListening at port number %u ...\n", portnum);
  newsock = accept(sfd, (struct sockaddr *)&clntaddr, &clntaddrsz);
  if (newsock < 0)
  {
    fprintf(stderr, "Error: accept() failed, errno=%d, %s\n", ERRNO, ERRNOSTR);
    CLOSE(sfd);
    return(PROD_ERR_ACCEPT);
  }
```

```c
      fprintf(stdout, "Client Connected.\n");

      ret = service_client(newsock);
      CLOSE1(newsock);
   }  /* while - outer */

   CLOSE(sfd);
   return(SUCCESS);
}

/* Receive initial packet from a newly connected client.
 * Perform some security checks or authentication.
 */
int receive_init_pkt(int sfd)
{
   init_pkt_t   initmsg;
   int          ret;

   memset((void *)&initmsg, 0, sizeof(init_pkt_t));
   errno = 0;
   ret = recv(sfd, (void *)&initmsg, sizeof(init_pkt_t), 0);
   if (ret < 0)
   {
      fprintf(stderr, "Error: receive_init_pkt(), recv() failed, errno=%d, %s\n",
         ERRNO, ERRNOSTR);
      return(PROD_ERR_SOCKET_RECV);
   }
   else if (ret != sizeof(init_pkt_t))
   {
      fprintf(stderr, "Error: receive_init_pkt(), recv() failed. Only %d out of"
         " %lu bytes of data received.\n", ret, sizeof(init_pkt_t));
      return(PROD_ERR_SOCKET_RECV);
   }

   /* Make sure the magic number always matches. */
   if (ntohl(initmsg.magic) != PROTO_MAGIC)
   {
      fprintf(stderr, "Error: receive_init_pkt(), wrong magic number.\n");
      return(PROD_ERR_WRONGMAGIC);
   }

   /* Perform protocol version-specific operations here if it applies. */
   if (ntohl(initmsg.version >= CURRENT_VER))
   {
      /* Perform some authentication here ... */

      return(SUCCESS);
   }
   return(0);
}

/*
 * This function is called by the server to service the needs of a client
 * after it has accepted a network connection request from a client.
 */
```

```
int service_client(int newsock)
{
  int     ret;
  char    *inbuf = NULL;                  /* pointer to input data buffer */
  char    *outbuf = NULL;                 /* pointer to output message buffer */
  int     *indata_ptr = NULL;             /* pointer to input data from client */
  int     indata = 0;                     /* input data from client */
  size_t              msglen;             /* length of client request message */
  unsigned long long  buflen = 0L;        /* length of input data buffer */
  unsigned long long  result = 0L;        /* output result of multiplication */
  unsigned long long  *result_ptr;        /* pointer to result */
  req_pkt_t request;                      /* client's request */
  req_pkt_t *reqmsg=NULL;                 /* pointer to client's request msg */
  req_pkt_t *rplymsg = NULL;              /* pointer to reply to client */
  int                 bytes;              /* number of bytes read */
  unsigned long long  total_bytes;        /* total number of bytes read */
  int                 opcode;             /* operation requested by client */
  int                 status;             /* status of operation */
  int                 clntVersion;        /* client's version */

  /* Receive initial packet. Close the connection if it fails.
   * Make sure we always terminate the connection right away in case of magic
   * number mismatch or others to prevent denial-of-service (DOS) attacks.
   */
  ret = receive_init_pkt(newsock);
  if (ret != SUCCESS)
  {
    fprintf(stderr, "Error: service_client(), receive_init_pkt() failed, "
      "ret=%d\n", ret);
    CLOSE1(newsock);
    return(ret);
  }


  /* Service the connected client until it is done.
   * Receive a request and service the request in each iteration.
   */
  while (1)
  {
    /* Receive the request header from the connected client. */
    msglen = sizeof(request);
    reqmsg = &request;
    memset(reqmsg, 0, msglen);
    errno = 0;
    ret = recv(newsock, reqmsg, msglen, 0);
    if (ret < 0)
    {
      fprintf(stderr, "Error: recv() failed, errno=%d, %s\n", ERRNO, ERRNOSTR);
      ret = (PROD_ERR_SOCKET_RECV);
      goto return1;
    }
    else if (ret == 0)
    {
      fprintf(stderr, "The client has closed.\n");
      ret = (PROD_ERR_SOCKET_RECV);
      goto return1;
    }
```

```
    else if (ret != msglen)
    {
      fprintf(stderr, "Error: recv() failed. Only %d out of %lu bytes were "
        "received.\n", ret, msglen);
      ret = (PROD_ERR_SOCKET_RECV);
      goto return1;
    }

    clntVersion = ntohl(reqmsg->version);
    fprintf(stdout, "Client version=%d\n", clntVersion);

    /* Perform some sanity check */
    if (ntohl(reqmsg->magic) != REQ_MAGIC)
    {
      fprintf(stderr, "Error: service_client(), wrong magic number.\n");
      ret = (PROD_ERR_WRONGMAGIC);
      goto return1;
    }

    /* Receive the request data if any */
    buflen = ntohll(reqmsg->datasz);
    if (buflen > 0)
    {
      /* Allocate buffer for the input data */
      inbuf = (char *)malloc(buflen);
      if (inbuf == NULL)
      {
        fprintf(stderr, "malloc() failed.\n");
        ret = (PROD_ERR_NO_MEMORY);
        goto return1;
      }

      /* Read all input data */
      errno = 0;
      total_bytes = 0L;
      do {
        bytes = read(newsock, inbuf+total_bytes, (buflen-total_bytes));
        if (bytes < 0)
        {
          fprintf(stderr, "Error: read() failed, errno=%d, %s\n", ERRNO, ERRNOSTR);
          ret = (PROD_ERR_SOCKET_RECV);
          goto return1;
        }
        else if (bytes == 0)
        {
          fprintf(stderr, "The client has closed.\n");
          ret = (PROD_ERR_SOCKET_RECV);
          goto return1;
        }
        total_bytes = total_bytes + (unsigned long long)bytes;
      } while (total_bytes < buflen);
    }

    /* Extract the input data and perform the requested operation
       which is version specific. Hence versioning is done here. */
    opcode = ntohl(reqmsg->operation);
```

```
if (clntVersion >= CURRENT_VER) /* latest version */
{
  switch(opcode)
  {
    case REQ_OPCODE1:
      indata_ptr = (int *)(inbuf);
      indata = ntohl(*indata_ptr);
      fprintf(stdout, "Client input data is %d\n", indata);
      result = ((unsigned long long)indata * 1000);
      result = result + ntohl(reqmsg->addend);
      status = SUCCESS;
      fprintf(stdout, "Multiplication result is %llu\n", result);
    break;
    default:
      status = PROD_ERR_BAD_OPCODE;
      result = 0L;
      fprintf(stdout, "Operation code %d is not supported.\n", opcode);
    break;
  }
}
else if (clntVersion >= VERSION2) /* previous version */
{
  switch(opcode)
  {
    case REQ_OPCODE1:
      indata_ptr = (int *)(inbuf);
      indata = ntohl(*indata_ptr);
      fprintf(stdout, "Client input data is %d\n", indata);
      result = ((unsigned long long)indata * 1000);
      status = SUCCESS;
      fprintf(stdout, "Multiplication result is %llu\n", result);
    break;
    default:
      status = PROD_ERR_BAD_OPCODE;
      result = 0L;
      fprintf(stdout, "Operation code %d is not supported.\n", opcode);
    break;
  }
}
else if (clntVersion >= VERSION1) /* first version */
{
  switch(opcode)
  {
    case REQ_OPCODE1:
      indata_ptr = (int *)(inbuf);
      indata = ntohl(*indata_ptr);
      fprintf(stdout, "Client input data is %d\n", indata);
      result = ((unsigned long long)indata * 100);
      status = SUCCESS;
      fprintf(stdout, "Multiplication result is %llu\n", result);
    break;
    default:
      status = PROD_ERR_BAD_OPCODE;
      result = 0L;
      fprintf(stdout, "Operation code %d is not supported.\n", opcode);
    break;
```

```
      }
   }

   /* Send a reply */
   msglen = (sizeof(req_pkt_t) + sizeof(unsigned long long));
   if (outbuf == NULL)
   {
     outbuf = (char *)malloc(msglen);
     if (outbuf == NULL)
     {
       fprintf(stderr, "malloc() failed.\n");
       ret = (PROD_ERR_NO_MEMORY);
       goto return1;
     }
   }
   memset(outbuf, 0, msglen);

   /* Fill in the reply message */
   rplymsg = (req_pkt_t *)outbuf;
   rplymsg->version = htonl(CURRENT_VER);
   rplymsg->magic = htonl(REPLY_MAGIC);
   rplymsg->operation = reqmsg->operation;
   rplymsg->status = htonl(status);
   rplymsg->datasz = htonll(sizeof(unsigned long long));
   result_ptr = (unsigned long long *)(outbuf + sizeof(req_pkt_t));
   *result_ptr = htonll(result);

   /* Send the reply message */
   errno = 0;
   ret = send(newsock, outbuf, msglen, 0);
   if (ret < 0)
   {
     fprintf(stderr, "Error: send() failed, errno=%d, %s\n", ERRNO, ERRNOSTR);
     ret = (PROD_ERR_SOCKET_SEND);
     goto return1;
   }
   else if (ret != msglen)
   {
     fprintf(stderr, "Error: send() failed. Only %d out of %lu bytes were sent.\n"
       , ret, msglen);
     ret = (PROD_ERR_SOCKET_SEND);
     goto return1;
   }

   fprintf(stdout, "Result %llu was successfully sent back to the client.\n",
     result);
}

return1:
  if (inbuf != NULL)
    free(inbuf);
  if (outbuf != NULL)
    free(outbuf);
  CLOSE1(newsock);
  return(ret);
}
```

14-2-2-4 Making the Server Program Robust

There are a couple of little things we must point out here regarding writing a very robust server program.

Using a Read Loop

To be most generic and for it to work in all cases, especially when there is a very large amount of data to be transferred, we use a loop consisting of the read() system call instead of recv() in the server program to read the client's data. The read loop will read until the amount of data specified in the client request's header (in the 'datasz' field) is all received or an error has occurred before it ends.

In the case of very large amount of data, using a single recv() or read() call to try to read the entire data is no longer guaranteed to work because it may take a number of read/recv calls to get it all. Consequently, the read loop we use here is a more robust way to receive data especially when the data is large amount.

Let the Client Close

If it's a server program, you don't want to just close the socket right after it sends the reply because the client may not receive the reply message yet and if you close the server socket, the client may never get the reply.

Hence, it's always very important to let the client close the socket connection, not the server!

To prevent some malicious clients from purposely consuming server resources, a server could potentially consider closing client connections after them being idle for a certain amount of time.

14-2-2-5 Sample output

As demonstrated by our example distributed application, through carefully designing the header structures and building in versioning, a distributed application can interoperate between different versions and become both backward and forward compatible. It does not have to break simply because it evolves and changes over time!

Below is a sample output of running the example distributed application across different platforms (both little and big endian), across mixed environments (mixing 32-bit and 64-bit modes), and across several different versions. As shown, all version combinations work just fine.

    Figure 14-12 sample output of example distributed application

Case 1:
  Server: V1 64-bit Server on Oracle/Sun SPARC Solaris
  Client: V1 32-bit client on IBM Power AIX
          V2 32-bit client on HP IA64 HPUX

```
              V3 32-bit client on x86 Linux

  bash-4.1$ ./ver1/tcpsrv_dist_all.sun64
  Connection-oriented server program, version 1 ...
  SO_REUSEADDR socket option is turned on.

  Listening at port number 2345 ...
  Client Connected.
  Client version=1
  Client input data is 398765421
  Multiplication result is 39876542100
  Result 39876542100 was successfully sent back to the client.
  The client has closed.

  Listening at port number 2345 ...
  Client Connected.
  Client version=2
  Client input data is 398765421
  Multiplication result is 39876542100
  Result 39876542100 was successfully sent back to the client.
  The client has closed.

  Listening at port number 2345 ...
  Client Connected.
  Client version=3
  Client input data is 398765421
  Multiplication result is 39876542100
  Result 39876542100 was successfully sent back to the client.
  The client has closed.

  bash-4.2$ ./ver1/tcpclnt_dist_all.aix32 2345 jvmtku 398765421
  Connection-oriented client program, version 1 ...
  Send request messages to server(jvmtku) at port 2345
  The client received 96 bytes of reply from a server of version 1.
  The multiplied result of 398765421 is 39876542100.

  bash-4.3$ ./ver2/tcpclnt_dist_all_v2.hpux32 2345 jvmtku 398765421
  Connection-oriented client program, version 2 ...
  Send request messages to server(jvmtku) at port 2345
  The client received 96 bytes of reply from a server of version 1.
  The multiplied result of 398765421 is 39876542100.

  $ ./ver3/tcpclnt_dist_all_v3.lin32 2345 jvmtku 398765421 22
  Connection-oriented client program, version 3 ...
  Send request messages to server(jvmtku) at port 2345
  The client received 96 bytes of reply from a server of version 1.
  The multiplied result of 398765421 is 39876542100.

Case 2:
  Server: V2 64-bit server on x86 Linux
  Client: V1 32-bit client on HP IA64 HPUX
          V2 32-bit client on IBM Power AIX
          V3 32-bit client on Oracle/Sun SPARC Solaris

  $ ./ver2/tcpsrv_dist_all_v2.lin64
  Connection-oriented server program, version 2 ...
```

```
SO_REUSEADDR socket option is turned on.

   Listening at port number 2345 ...
   Client Connected.
   Client version=1
   Client input data is 398765421
   Multiplication result is 39876542100
   Result 3987654210 was successfully sent back to the client.
   The client has closed.

   Listening at port number 2345 ...
   Client Connected.
   Client version=2
   Client input data is 398765421
   Multiplication result is 398765421000
   Result 398765421000 was successfully sent back to the client.
   The client has closed.

   Listening at port number 2345 ...
   Client Connected.
   Client version=3
   Client input data is 398765421
   Multiplication result is 398765421000
   Result 398765421000 was successfully sent back to the client.
   The client has closed.

   bash-4.3$ ./ver1/tcpclnt_dist_all.hpux32 2345 jvmx 398765421
   Connection-oriented client program, version 1 ...
   Send request messages to server(jvmx) at port 2345
   The client received 96 bytes of reply from a server of version 2.
   The multiplied result of 398765421 is 39876542100.

   bash-4.2$ ./ver2/tcpclnt_dist_all_v2.aix32 2345 jvmx 398765421
   Connection-oriented client program, version 2 ...
   Send request messages to server(jvmx) at port 2345
   The client received 96 bytes of reply from a server of version 2.
   The multiplied result of 398765421 is 398765421000.

   bash-4.1$  ./ver3/tcpclnt_dist_all_v3.sun32 2345 jvmx 398765421 22
   Connection-oriented client program, version 3 ...
   Send request messages to server(jvmx) at port 2345
   The client received 96 bytes of reply from a server of version 2.
   The multiplied result of 398765421 is 398765421000.
```

```
Case 3:
   Server: V3 32-bit server on IBM Power AIX
   Client: V1 64-bit client on HP IA64 HPUX
           V2 64-bit client on Oracle/Sun SPARC Solaris
           V3 64-bit client on x86 Linux
```

```
   bash-4.2$ uname -a
   AIX jvmdv 1 6 00F634684C00
   bash-4.2$ ./ver3/tcpsrv_dist_all_v3.aix32
   Connection-oriented server program, version 3 ...
   SO_REUSEADDR socket option is turned on.
```

```
Listening at port number 2345 ...
Client Connected.
Client version=1
Client input data is 398765421
Multiplication result is 39876542100
Result 39876542100 was successfully sent back to the client.
The client has closed.
```

```
Listening at port number 2345 ...
Client Connected.
Client version=2
Client input data is 398765421
Multiplication result is 398765421000
Result 398765421000 was successfully sent back to the client.
The client has closed.
```

```
Listening at port number 2345 ...
Client Connected.
Client version=3
Client input data is 398765421
Multiplication result is 398765421050
Result 398765421050 was successfully sent back to the client.
The client has closed.
```

```
bash-4.3$ ./ver1/tcpclnt_dist_all.hpux64 2345 jvmdv 398765421
Connection-oriented client program, version 1 ...
Send request messages to server(jvmdv) at port 2345
The client received 96 bytes of reply from a server of version 3.
The multiplied result of 398765421 is 39876542100.
```

```
bash-4.1$  ./ver2/tcpclnt_dist_all_v2.sun64 2345 jvmdv 398765421
Connection-oriented client program, version 2 ...
Send request messages to server(jvmdv) at port 2345
The client received 96 bytes of reply from a server of version 3.
The multiplied result of 398765421 is 398765421000.
```

```
$ ./ver3/tcpclnt_dist_all_v3.lin64 2345 jvmdv 398765421
Connection-oriented client program, version 3 ...
Send request messages to server(jvmdv) at port 2345
The client received 96 bytes of reply from a server of version 3.
The multiplied result of 398765421 is 398765421050.
```

14-3 Summary

In this chapter, we talk about endianness and various other issues of distributed software. We also give examples on how to solve these problems.

First example demonstrates how to create a data file that is self-described and portable across all platforms regardless of their endianness.

Second example illustrates how to design and develop a software product so that it not only always works across all different platforms and environments but also is always 100% backward compatible and fully interoperable across different versions and different platforms.

Review Questions

1. What issues can a distributed application normally encounter?

2. What is little endian? What computer processors are little endian?

3. What is big endian? What computer processors are big endian?

4. To what data types endian format matters? When does its impact surface?

5. What is alignment? What penalty does unalignment incur?

6. Give an example of structure declaration that will lead to automatic compiler padding.

7. Why you should avoid automatic compiler padding?

8. What are the potential issues that could break a distributed application when it is run across platforms?

Programming Assignments

1. Compile and run the program exchange_rec.c on the platforms you have access to. Run it in the write mode to create data files in each platform. Then run the same program in read mode to read data generated on all platforms.

2. Define a C structure which will result in different sizes in different environments, e.g. in 32-bit and 64-bit modes. Write a little program that prints the size of the structure.

3. Test all version combinations of the client and server programs in Figures 14-9, 14-10 and 14-11. Are all results correct?

4. Change the tcpsrv_dist_all.c server program and make it multi-threaded by creating a thread to execute the service_client() function for each client.

5. Build and test tcpclnt_dist_all*.c and tcpsrv_dist_all*.c on combinations of 32-bit and 64-bit modes on different hardware platforms you have access to and verify they work in every scenario.

6. Modify tcpclnt_dist_all_v3.c and tcpsrv_dist_all_v3.c to create version 4 of the application. In this new version, make the client pass over a multiplier to the server and the server does the multiplication as follows:

       result = (input number * multiplier) + addend

   where all three numbers used in the computation come from the client.

    (a) Do it by modifying the req_pkt_t structure in mydistsys.h and placing the multiplier in the data header.

    (b) Do this without changing mydistsys.h. Hint: Put the multiplier in data portion of the message.

7. Write a pair of client-server programs to demonstrate endian issue. Let the client sends a multi-byte binary integer to the server and the server prints out the received number. Run the client and the server on two computers with different endian formats to test them.

8. Write a pair of client-server programs. Define a structure with unaligned data fields in it. Compile and run them on different platforms or environments to showcase its total size changes.

15 Computer Network Security

With the ubiquitousness of Internet, distributed systems are more prevalent and pervasive than ever. As a result, security becomes more increasingly important and challenging every day. Just to understand some of the day-to-day conversations, to understand how some of the existing products work, and to build more secure systems, one needs to know a lot about what network security is all about and what technologies are in use today.

This chapter intends to give you just that. It aims at a very brief introduction to security in computer network communication and prepares the readers with a very clear understanding of the security concepts and solid programming skills in computer network security.

This chapter talks about the basics of computer network communication security. It discusses aspects involved in securing communications between two systems across network. It touches upon authentication, encryption, data integrity, denial of service attacks, Public Key Infrastructure (PKI), certificates, SSL, and TLS. The information presented here will enable you to make sense out of security discussions and assess technologies, products and designs in computer security.

Note that the subject of computer security itself warrants multiple books, from theories to practices. There have been enormous researches into the theoretical aspects of it and tons of papers and books have been written. Here we aim to give readers just a very brief and general overview of the theories in computer security. We then focus on practices, presenting the technologies and demonstrating how to solve various computer network security problems with real program examples.

After reading through this chapter, readers should be familiar with the major aspects and issues, terminologies, concepts, technologies, and basic building blocks of computer security. And they should be knowledgeable enough to comprehend the day-to-day conversations in computer security and be able to assess various designs and products. Engineers should also feel well-equipped and confident to solve various computer security problems with an excellent architecture, design and implementation using the fundamentals presented in the program examples given here in this chapter.

15-1 OpenSSL

Note that our program examples listed in this chapter are all based on OpenSSL. In order to be able to actually compile and run the example programs in this chapter, readers need to have access to the OpenSSL software.

Example programs in this chapter were tested in OpenSSL 3.3.0, 3.1.0, 3.0.0, 1.1.1g and 1.0.2.

If you already have access to OpenSSL software, you may choose to skip this section.

15-1-1 What Is OpenSSL?

OpenSSL is an open source software. It's free. OpenSSL provides a general-purpose cryptography library that enables applications to perform security operations such as encryption, decryption, message digest, digital signature, as well as exchange information using the standard Secure Sockets Layer (SSL) and Transport Layer Security (TLS) protocols. It provides a set of Application Programming Interfaces (APIs) that perform various security operations. OpenSSL is written in C.

You could download the OpenSSL source code and build the OpenSSL software yourself for your computer. This section below tells you how to do that. There is also pre-built OpenSSL software for certain platforms available for download over the Internet.

After you install the OpenSSL software, among others you get mainly two libraries and one tool. The libraries allow you to write your own security programs to carry out various security operations.
The tool lets you perform a large number of security operations without having to write any program.

The names of the two OpenSSL libraries are the following:

(1) libcrypto.so and libcrypto.a
(2) libssl.so and libssl.a

The **crypto library**, libcrypto.so or libcrypto.a, contains the implementation of the OpenSSL cryptographic API functions. They include the low-level functions like ASN1_xxx(), BIO_xxx(), BN_xxx(), CRYPTO_xxx(), d2i_xxx(), and i2d_xxx(), generic functions like ENGINE_xxx() and OPENSSL_xxx(), encryption functions DES_xxx(), message digest functions using MD2, MD4, MD5, and SHA algorithms, HMAC_xxx(), DH_xxx(), DSA_xxx(), certificate functions X509_xxx(), PEM_xxx() and PKCSx_xxx(), error handling functions ERR_xxx(), and the high-level generic cryptographic wrapper functions EVP_xxx(), many of which our example programs use.

The **SSL library**, libssl.so or libssl.a, contains the implementation of all of the OpenSSL SSL_xxx() and TLS_xxx() library functions that actually implement the SSL and TLS protocols. If you write programs that communicate using the SSL or TLS protocol, they will have to link with this library. And if the build does a dynamic linking instead of static, then the library file libssl.so must be present on the system when the application runs. libssl.a is for applications wanting to link statically.

The main OpenSSL tool you get is the **openssl** command which is very useful. It enables you to perform many security functions including generating keys, encrypting and decrypting using different cipher algorithms, creating, signing and verifying digital certificates, performing SSL/TLS tests and many others. You will see some openssl usage examples in this chapter.

For the documentation and man pages of all OpenSSL APIs in OpenSSL,
please go to https://www.openssl.org/docs/manpages.html.
They may also exist in the ./share/doc/openssl/html/ directory under the
root directory where OpenSSL is installed on your local machine.
For example:

   /opt/openssl/share/doc/openssl/html/man3/OPENSSL_init_ssl.html

15-1-2 Download and Build OpenSSL Software

In order to build and/or run the application programs given in this chapter,
you will need the OpenSSL Toolkit installed on your system.
This section shows you how to download the OpenSSL source code, build OpenSSL
and install it yourself.

Please feel free to skip this section if you already have access to an
installed OpenSSL or know how to do this.

Download and Build OpenSSL

Be aware that building OpenSSL requires a specific version of Perl.
If you find your system does not have the right version of Perl, please
go to the section below to download and build Perl yourself.

It's very easy to download the OpenSSL source code, build and then install
it yourself. Below are the steps.

- Download the OpenSSL source from https://www.openssl.org/source
  Open a web browser and go to the link.
  Click on the version of the software you choose and you will get a
  compressed file, e.g. openssl-3.3.0.tar.gz, downloaded to your computer.

- unzip and then untar the source

  $ gunzip openssl-3.3.0.tar.gz
  $ tar xvf openssl-3.3.0.tar

- Do the following to build the OpenSSL

On Unix or Linux

  $ cd openssl-3.3.0

  $ ./config   (or ./Configure)

     This will later install OpenSSL to the /usr/local/ directory.

     If you want to install it anywhere else, run config like this:

       $ ./config --prefix=/opt/openssl --openssldir=/usr/local/ssl

     This will instead install OpenSSL executables, libraries, include files
     and man pages to the /opt/openssl directory and install miscellaneous

files to the /usr/local/ssl directory. OpenSSL libraries will be
installed in /opt/openssl/lib64/ directory.

```
$ make
```

This step compiles and builds the entire OpenSSL software.
On my Linux system, it did it in 10 minutes or so without any hiccup.

```
$ make test
```

This runs many of the OpenSSL tests that come with the source to
make sure the build is good.

If it goes well, at this moment you are ready to install the OpenSSL
software you just built.

To prepare for the installation, you need to create the install destination
directory and give it appropriate ownership and permissions.
For instance,

```
$ su root
# mkdir /opt/openssl ; chown jim:oinstall /opt/openssl
or
# mkdir /usr/local/ssl ; chown jim:oinstall /usr/local/ssl

# exit

$ make install
```

On Apple Mac Pro (Darwin)

In Apple Darwin, you may do the following to build OpenSSL:

```
$ ./Configure --prefix=/opt/openssl --openssldir=/usr/local/ssl  or
$ ./Configure darwin64-x86_64-cc shared enable-ec_nistp_64_gcc_128 no-ssl2 no-
ssl3 no-comp --openssldir=/usr/local/ssl --api=1.1.0 no-deprecated
$ make depend
$ make
$ sudo make install
```

Please remember to add the path of the OpenSSL libraries to your
environment variable LD_LIBRARY_PATH or equivalent before you run the
example programs in this chapter that use OpenSSL libraries.
For instance, in bash or Bourne shell, do

```
$ export LD_LIBRARY_PATH=/opt/openssl/lib64:$LD_LIBRARY_PATH
```

or do the following in C shell:

```
$ setenv LD_LIBRARY_PATH /opt/openssl/lib64:$LD_LIBRARY_PATH
```

assuming OpenSSL is installed in the /opt/openssl directory.
Note that some version of OpenSSL installs its libraries in the
/opt/openssl/lib directory instad of /opt/openssl/lib64.

Download and Build Perl

Note that building OpenSSL depends on Perl. Therefore, you may have to
download and build the version of Perl required by OpenSSL first.
Follow the instructions below to download and build your own Perl.

For most platforms, you could opt to download the binary version of the Perl
tool. If you choose to download the source version, then you will have to
build and install it yourself. Please follow the steps below to build it
yourself.

- Download the Perl source from https://www.perl.org
- unzip and untar the source
- Do the following to build the Perl

On Unix or Linux:

 Assuming you want to install Perl to the /usr/local/perl536 directory.

```
$ mkdir /usr/local/perl536
$ ./Configure -des -Dprefix=/usr/local/perl536
$ make
$ make test
$ make install
```

How to use your own Perl

Set both PATH and PERL5LIB environment variables to point to your own Perl.

PATH

 For Korn shell or bash:

```
$ PATH="/usr/local/perl536/bin":$PATH ; export PATH
```

 For C shell:

```
% setenv PATH '/usr/local/perl536/bin:/bin:/usr/bin'
```

PERL5LIB

 This environment variable contains a colon-separated list of directories
 in which to look for Perl library files before looking in the standard
 library and the current directory.

 If PERL5LIB is not defined, PERLLIB is used for backward compatibility
 with older releases. If PERL5LIB is defined, PERLLIB is not used.

 For Korn shell or bash:

```
$ PERL5LIB="/usr/local/perl536/lib"; export PERL5LIB
```

 For C shell:

```
% setenv PERL5LIB "/usr/local/perl536/lib"
```

15-1-3 Building and Running SSL/TLS Applications Using OpenSSL

Building Cryptographic or SSL/TLS Applications with OpenSSL

Assuming OpenSSL is already built and installed in the /opt/openssl/ directory of the system you are using.

To build your application using OpenSSL, do:

```
$ cc -o myprog myprog.c -I/opt/openssl/include -L/opt/openssl/lib64
  -lssl -lcrypto -ldl
```

"-I/opt/openssl/include" tells the compiler where to find the SSL/TLS include files. "-L/opt/openssl/lib64" tells the compiler/linker where to find the SSL/TLS related libraries. "-lssl -lcrypto -ldl" tells it to look for library functions your application uses in the libssl.so or libssl.a, libcrypto.so or libcrypto.a, and libdl.so or libdl.a. The linker will find libdl.* in the default standard library directory /usr/lib and find libssl.* and libcrypto.* in the /opt/openssl/lib64/ directory. In some version of OpenSSL, it's named /opt/openssl/lib instead.

If you use Makefile, please add the following two lines to it:

```
LDFLAGS = -L/opt/openssl/lib64
LDLIBS = -lssl -lcrypto -ldl
```

Running Cryptographic or SSL/TLS Applications with OpenSSL

To run your application set the LD_LIBRARY_PATH environment variable or its equivalent in the platform you use for the run-time loader to locate the OpenSSL libraries code. For instance, in Bourne/Korn/bash shell:

```
$ export LD_LIBRARY_PATH=$LD_LIBRARY_PATH:/opt/openssl/lib64
```

This environment variable differs from platform to platform. To find out the name of the environment variable that you have to set for your platform, please see the library chapter (chapter 3).

This is because by default your application is built with dynamic linking. The external library functions your application references are not actually loaded into the executable file of your application. Therefore, when you try to run (i.e. start) your application, the operating system loader needs to know where those library functions actually reside so that it can physically load them into the computer's memory. LD_LIBRARY_PATH does just that. It tells the operating system where to look for dynamic libraries and functions that your program was dynamically linked with.

If you forget to set the LD_LIBRARY_PATH environment variable, running your application may get this error:

```
$ ./digest_sha256
./digest_sha256: error while loading shared libraries: libssl.so.3:
cannot open shared object file: No such file or directory
```

After correctly setting the LD_LIBRARY_PATH environment variable, the application runs successfully:

```
$ export LD_LIBRARY_PATH=$LD_LIBRARY_PATH:/opt/openssl/lib64
$ ./digest_sha256
Enter a message: This is a test message.
digest=0x86e1de74820a9b252ba33b2eed445b0cd02c445b5f4b8007205aff1762d7301a
```

15-2 Aspects in Computer Network Security

There are different, multiple goals in computer network communication security. A secure communication between two parties connected by a computer network possesses a few properties. These properties include the following:

1. The originator of the message must be legitimate and trustworthy. If this does not hold, then all may be in vain.

2. The message must not incur errors or be tampered with during transit.

3. For sensitive materials, the message must be kept secret.

4. The message must get to exactly the intended recipient(s).

5. The communication channel must be available and working normally.

Based on these, computer network communication security involves at least five major aspects:

- **Authentication**

  This includes sender authentication, recipient authentication and message authentication. The sender authentication and message authentication aim to achieve origin integrity, i.e. authenticity of origin.

- **Message integrity**

- **Confidentiality (Secrecy)**

- **Non-repudiation**

- **Denial-Of-Service (DOS) attacks** (Attacks on availability)

First, authentication. **Authentication** is about making sure you are communicating with the true, intended entity who is trustworthy. When you send something, you want to make sure it gets to the exact recipient you intend, not a hacker or someone else. This is recipient authentication. When you are receiving, you want to ensure the message comes from the true sender, not a hacker or someone else. This is sender authentication. And you want the message to be trustworthy too, which is message authentication.

The goal of authentication is to prevent that anyone can originate the message and ensure that only those legitimate and trustworthy can. However, if a hacker finds a way to break in (say, by stealing a username

and password) it's very difficult to detect whether an originator is
a hacker or not.

Unless you can be certain that you are communicating with the party intended,
you cannot really trust what you receive or be certain that what you sent
has safely arrived its destination. Hence, authentication is extremely
important, or perhaps the most important aspect of all.

Second, when you send something, you want the recipient to get exactly what
you send, not something that has been altered. That is, you don't want anyone
to be able to tamper with your message during the process of communication.
If a hacker can go in and alter your message there wouldn't be any security
at all. In addition, a message should not change during transit for any
reason, be it electrical noises, interferences, or equipment failures.
If it does, you want to be able to detect that. This is **message integrity**.
It is about correctness of the message. It's very important that the
integrity of the message is preserved during the entire communication process.
The message should not be altered or replaced, or incur any errors.
If it does, you want to be able to detect it. Ideally you want to be able
to prevent tampering. But at least you want to be able to detect it.

Note that there are two types of integrity involved in computer
communications: **data integrity**, which is correctness of the message itself
(ensuring a message has not been tampered with during transit),
and **origin integrity**, which is the authenticity and trustworthiness of the
message originator.

Third, when you send something important, you want it to remain secret.
That is, it should be known only by the intended recipient(s) and no one else.
To achieve that you want to encrypt (encipher) the message you send so that
only the intended recipient(s) can successfully decrypt (decipher) and
read it. That's encryption and decryption.

Without encrypting the message, that is, if you send it in plain text,
then hackers or anyone 'peeking' into the communication would be able to
read and understand the message. Then there wouldn't be confidentiality
at all. Therefore, **encrypting the messages provides secrecy for the
communication**.

Lastly, in software development, many software products consist of a server
of some kind listening at a particular network port number for incoming
requests. The HTTP web server is one example. For software server development,
it's very important to build in a capability of dealing with
Denial of Service (DOS, for short) attacks. You certainly don't want these
types of attacks, which can be launched by almost anyone, to run your
server to its knee and effectively shut down your server.

DOS attacks can take down a server and block communications. Therefore,
they are considered part of computer network communication security as well.

A **'Denial of Service' attack** is an attack on availability.
It is some malicious individual or program tries to bring your server down
to its knees by flooding your server (program) with tons of requests.
In theory, it is almost impossible to completely prevent the DOS attacks.
A server program listens at a port number at an IP address. There is really
no way to prevent any program from sending messages to that particular

address and port number. So, the only thing one can do is to deal with it and manage it. The key is to put up a defense wall inside the server program itself such that none of these malicious attacking requests actually get through and they all get rejected at the very beginning at the front door. They can come knocking at your door all the time but you would not ever open it. It could take away some processing time and thus slow down your server but at least you could prevent it from making any further damages such as crashing your server due to ill-format request messages or using up all of your server's time resource. We talked about how to do it in chapter 14 (14-2).

Note that a computer service is always provided by some program running on some computer which often is referred to as a 'server' (i.e. computer server or server computer). Therefore, in the context of DOS, the terms 'server', 'server program', and 'service' all mean the same thing. Denial of Service attack is an attack on availability of a service, server program or server (computer).

This chapter gives an introduction to basic concepts, theories, different technologies, techniques, algorithms and protocols used in the various aspects of network communication security. It also illustrates how to solve various security problems using C programs that employ cryptographic APIs as well as SSL and TLS protocols provided in the OpenSSL open source software.

15-3 Message Integrity

15-3-1 Checksum

Computer engineers recognized the necessity of protecting data integrity very early on. It's wonderful that computers can store and process an incredible amount of data. But if the data aren't correct or the integrity of the data is compromised, it would not be very useful at all.

In the old days, though it still exists today and has being used in many applications, the technique for ensuring data integrity during transit is doing checksum. Verifying checksum is the oldest, simplest and most rudimentary data integrity means.

Due to electrical noises and other reasons, data can be accidently altered in recording, writing to disks, or in transport. To detect errors of this nature, a checksum is computed (usually by simply adding up every one, two, or four bytes of the entire data) and stored or sent with the data. When the reader reads back the data or the receiver gets the data, it uses the same algorithm to re-compute a new checksum and compares that with the original checksum. If they match, it is assumed the data is unchanged and correct. Sum up the entire contents of the data or message and check that. That is checksum verification.

Verifying checksum has been providing enormous values in detecting data errors and unintentional data corruptions in many areas and applications for decades. It is still widely used in programs dealing with transporting/storing data.

Doing checksum for message integrity is still cost-effective in certain applications where the data is transported from one process or place to another on a single system or in a closed environment where electrical noise is the main likely source of errors.

In a sense, doing checksum is compressing. It reduces a much larger amount of information into a shortened, very small-sized representation or fingerprint, which is usually 32 or 64 bits long.

The advantage of doing checksum is simplicity. However, its weakness is not strong enough. It's not that difficult to find another message that sums up to the same checksum and replace both the message and checksum to launch an attack. Therefore, checksum verification is very weak against intentional data corruption attacks. But it is useful in many simple applications like writing data to disk or communicating data between entities within the same system or in a closed environment. However, it won't be very useful in the Internet where the messages are often travelling through many systems, outdoor cables, or even across many continents in many cases where they are more accessible to hackers and malicious attackers. In these environments, it's not difficult for attackers to replace both the message and the checksum and the data consumer wouldn't be able to detect that by just verifying the checksum.

More complicated and much stronger message digest or hash algorithms are used to ensure message integrity during transit across a computer network or Internet. We will discuss some of the most commonly used ones in the next section.

15-3-2 Message Digest Algorithms (Hash Functions)

Message digest algorithms are cryptographic hash functions. (We will use the terms 'message digest algorithms', 'message hash functions' , or just 'hash functions' interchangeably.) They hash, or compress, a message into a very small size fingerprint information called **'digest'** or **'hash'** of the message. In a sense, a message digest or hash is similar to a checksum, but the algorithm used to produce the digest is much more complicated and the result is much, much stronger in security.

A digest or hash captures the characteristics of a message. The goal of a message digest algorithm is to produce an output digest that can uniquely identify the input message (at least that's the intention).

Note that some people loosely use the terms checksum, hash, and digest interchangeably because they are all for message integrity. However, we prefer to reserve the term checksum for the cases where only simple arithmetic/logical functions are used, instead of cryptographic hash functions. If cryptographic hash functions are used, we will call the output hash or digest.

The way it works is before a sender sends a message, it invokes a message digest algorithm on the message and produces a message digest. Then the sender sends both the message and the digest to the receiver. When the receiver receives the message, it runs the same message digest algorithm on the received message to produce a new digest. It then compares the message digest it computes with the message digest it receives. If the two do not match, it then knows the message has been tampered with during the transit. In other words, the integrity of a received message

can be determined by re-computing its digest or hash and comparing that
to a known and expected digest value.

Note that cryptographic hash functions are **one-way functions**; they have the
property of being irreversible. That is, it is impossible, or at least
extremely difficult, to revert the process by deriving the original
message from the very small digest output-ed by these functions.

Message digest algorithms are very complex algorithms.
The strength of a message digest algorithm or hash function rests on
the difficulty of creating a collision. If two different messages
produce the same message digest using an algorithm, that is a **collision**.
And if anyone can create a collision using a message digest algorithm,
then that algorithm is vulnerable; it is not 100% secure anymore.
This is because an attacker would then be able to attack by replacing the
original message with a different one that still produces the same digest
and the message receiver would not be able to detect or discover the
tampering.

Both hash and checksum are for data integrity protection.
The difference between a hash and a checksum is that a checksum is computed
using a very simple arithmetic or logical function such as adding-up the
bytes and the length of a checksum is usually 64 bits or less
while a hash is computed by using a more sophisticated keyless
cryptographic hash function and the output is usually longer than 64 bits.
Consequently, checksum is relatively much easier to break than hash.

There are at least three reasons that a message hash is much stronger in
security than a checksum. (1) A hash is usually bigger in size than checksum.
(2) A hash is generated by a much more complicated hash function which
is impossible, or at least almost impossible, to reverse. (3) Again, due to
the complexity and strength of the hash algorithms, it's very difficult to
create a collision -- that is, to.find another message that reduces to the
same message digest.

Note that an attacker could still try to replace both the message and
the hash, if he/she knows where the boundaries of the message and hash
are as well as what hash algorithm is used. But **if you encrypt the hash**,
that would make it very, very difficult for the hackers to break.

The strength of a message digest algorithm rests on its irreversibility
and collision resistance. The strength against collisions is tied to the
size of the digest. On irreversibility, for a message digest algorithm
producing a 160-bit digest, the probability of finding a message producing
a given digest is $1/(2^{160})$. On collision resistance, the probability of
finding two messages producing the same digest (i.e. a collision) is
$1/(2^{80})$.

In addition to providing the security property of message integrity,
message digests are also used in producing Message Authentication Codes
(MACs) and 'digital signatures', both of which we will discuss later in this
chapter.

Traditionally, there has been two major families of message digest algorithms:
MD (Message Digest) and **SHA** (Secure Hash Algorithm).
The following sections introduce them.

15-3-2-1 MD Family of Message Digest Algorithms

The MD family of message digest algorithms were developed by MIT professor Dr. Ronald Rivest. It includes MD2 (1989), MD4 (1990), MD5 (1992) and MD6 (2008). Some of the MD algorithms, for instance, MD2 and MD5, were widely used in the early days.

All of the MD message digest algorithms produce an output digest of 128 bits (16 bytes).

The security of some of the MD algorithms has been compromised. MD4 was first cracked in 1995. A collision was created in 1996 using MD5 algorithm. In 2009, MD2 was shown to be vulnerable to a collision attack as well.

Multiple researchers and computer scientists have demonstrated weaknesses in MD4 and MD5 algorithms. In some cases, a collision using the MD algorithm can be created in hours, or even minutes. One collision attack can even find collisions within seconds with complexity of (2^{24}).

Because of these, some cryptographers recommend switching to other algorithms like SHA or RIPEMD-160.

Note that the TLS protocol uses MD5. Some applications have also hashed user passwords and stored MD5 hash of the passwords.

MD5 [14]

Here we briefly describe how MD5 algorithm computes a message digest.

Dr. Ronald Rivest designed MD5 to replace MD4 in 1991. It was widely used in many applications for some period of time.

MD5 computes a fixed-size output digest of 128 bits from a variable-length message. The input message is padded at end with the length of the original message and other bits before it, if necessary, so that its new total length becomes a multiple of 512.

The padding proceeds like this. First, a single bit of 1 is appended to the end of the message. Then zeros are appended after that to bring the length of the message up to 64 bits fewer than a multiple of 512. The length of the original message, as a 64-bit value, modulo 2^{64} (2 to power of 64), is then placed at the end of the message.

MD5 algorithm operates on a 128-bit state which is divided into four 32-bit words, denoted as A, B, C and D. They are initialized to certain constants. During the computation, the message is broken up into 512-bit chunks. The algorithm uses each 512-bit message block to change the state. The processing of each message block includes 4 rounds (stages). Each round consists of 16 modular addition and left rotating operations with a non-linear function F. At each round, a different function F is used.

```
F1(B,C,D) = (B&C)v(~B&D)
F2(B,C,D) = (B&D)v(C&~D)
```

```
F3(B,C,D) = B+C+D
F4(B,C,D) = C+(B v ~D)
```

Symbols ^, v, ~, + denote the AND, OR, NOT and XOR logical operations, respectively.

Note that unlike the SHA algorithms, the MD5 algorithm has no limit on the length of the input message.

15-3-2-2 SHA Family of Message Digest Algorithms

Secure Hash Algorithms (SHA)

SHA stands for Secure Hash Algorithm. It is a family of cryptographic hash functions designed and/or published by the National Institute of Standards and Technology (NIST) of the United States as a U.S. Federal Information Processing Standard (FIPS). (Note: Some cryptographic algorithms (e.g. SHA-2) are designed by the National Security Agency (NSA) of the United States or others and published by NIST.)

The SHA family of message digest algorithms includes SHA-0, SHA-1, SHA-2 group and SHA-3 group. SHA-0 is a 160-bit message digest algorithm published by NIST in 1993. After collisions were found, it was replaced by the revised version SHA-1.

Note: For each of secure hash algorithms, some alternate computation methods may exist. For instance, for SHA-1 algorithm, it normally uses a message schedule of eighty 32-bit words. But when memory is limited, an alternate computation method is to use sixteen 32-bit words.

SHA-1 [11]

The SHA-1 hash algorithm can be used to hash a message of up to 2^{64} bits long. It uses a message schedule of eighty 32-bit words and five 32-bit working variables. SHA-1 outputs a 160-bit message hash.

SHA-1 is based on principles similar to those used by the MD4 and MD5 algorithms. SHA-1 uses a 160-bit state and 512-bit block size in its computations. It performs 80 rounds of computations using AND, OR, modular addition and rotate with no carry.

SHA-1 was widely used in many protocols including SSL, TLS, SSH, PGP (Pretty Good Privacy), S/MIME, IPsec and others in early days.
However, since studies have found that it requires less than 2^{69} operations (even less than (2^{80}) needed by a brute-force search), some at around (2^{60}), to create a collision attack, SHA-1 has been recommended not to be used anymore. Applications are recommended to use SHA-2 or SHA-3 now.

SHA-2 [12]

SHA-2 is a group of message digest algorithms designed by the National Security Agency (NSA) of the United States.

The SHA-2 family consists of SHA-224, SHA-256, SHA-384, SHA-512/224, SHA-512/256 and SHA-512. The size of the output digest of these algorithms

is 224, 256, 384, 224, 256 and 512 bits, respectively.
That is, the last number in the names of these algorithms is the length
(in bits) of the digest output by the algorithm.

1. SHA-256 and its variants

SHA-256 produces a 256-bit message digest as output.

SHA-256 can be used to hash a message of up to (2^{64}) bits.
It uses a message schedule of sixty-four 32-bit words and eight 32-bit
working variables. It performs 64 rounds of computation, using a 256-bit
state and 512-bit message block size. Operations include logical AND,
OR and XOR, right logical shift, modular addition (modula 2^{32}), and
rotate with no carry.

SHA-224 is the same as SHA-256 except that different initial hash values are
used and the final hash value is truncated to 224 bits for SHA-224.

2. SHA-512 and its Variants

SHA-512 produces a 512-bit message digest as output.

SHA-512 can be used to hash a message of up to (2^{128}) bits long.
It uses a message schedule of eighty 64-bit words and eight 64-bit working
variables in its computation. SHA-512 performs 80 rounds of computation,
using a 512-bit state and 1024-bit message block size. Operations include
logical AND, OR and XOR, right logical shift, modular addition (modula 2^{64}),
and rotate with no carry.

SHA-512 has the following variants:

   SHA-512/224: The final hash value is truncated to its left-most 224 bits.
   SHA-512/256: The final hash value is truncated to its left-most 256 bits.
   SHA-384: The final hash value is truncated to its left-most 384 bits.

SHA-3 [13]

The SHA-3 standard was published by NIST in August of 2015.
The standard includes these message digest algorithms:
SHA3-224, SHA3-256, SHA3-384, SHA3-512, SHAKE128 and SHAKE256.
They were designed by Guido Bertoni, Joan Daemen, Michael Peeters, and
Gilles Van Assche.

SHA3-224, SHA3-256, SHA3-384, and SHA3-512 output a digest of 224, 256, 384,
and 512 bits, respectively. They use a message block size of 1152, 1088,
832, and 576 bits, respectively.

SHAKE128 and SHAKE256 produce an output digest of arbitrary length.
They use a message block size of 1344 and 1088 bits, respectively.

SHA-3 algorithms do not have a limit on the size of the input message.
They all use a state of 1600 bits and carry out 24 rounds of computation.

SHA3 performs logical AND, NOT, XOR and rotate with no carry operation.

Motivation of SHA-3

Due to the successful attacks on MD5 and SHA-0 and theoretical attacks on SHA-1, NIST thought there may exist a need for different cryptographic hash functions. It thus organized the NIST hash function competition to create new hash standard, SHA-3. SHA-3 was meant to provide an alternate, not as a replacement to SHA-2 because there has been no significant attack on SHA-2 so far.

Length of Message

SHA-0, SHA-1 and SHA-224 and SHA-256 of SHA2 limit the length of the input message to 2^{64} bits. The SHA-2 version of SHA-512/224, SHA-512/256, SHA-384, and SHA-512 limit the input message to 2^{128} bits.
SHA3-224, SHA3-256, SHA3-384 and SHA3-512 place no limit on the length of input message.

Figure 15-1 Message Digest Algorithms [13]

Algorithm	output digest (bits)	Maximum message size(bits)
MD5	128	unlimited
SHA-1	160	$2^{64}-1$
SHA-2		
SHA-224	224	$2^{64}-1$
SHA-256	256	
SHA-512/224	224	$2^{128}-1$
SHA-512/256	256	
SHA-384	384	
SHA-512	512	
SHA3		
SHA3-224	224	unlimited
SHA3-256	256	
SHA3-384	384	
SHA3-512	512	

OpenSSL Implementation

Digest Algorithm	Length of output digest in bits (bytes)
MD4	128 (16)
MD5	128 (16)
SHA1	160 (20)
RMD160	160 (20)
SHA256	256 (32)
SHA512	512 (64)

Figure 15-1 displays the lengths of output digest and the maximum length of input message allowed by some common cryptographic hash functions. [13]

15-3-2-3 RIPEMD-160

RACE Integrity Primitives Evaluation Message Digest (RIPEMD) is a family of cryptographic hash functions developed by Hans Dobbertin, Antoon Bosselaers and Bart Preneel in Leuven, Belgium. It was published in 1996.

There are multiple versions of RIPEMD: RIPEMD-128, RIPEMD-160, RIPEMD-256, and RIPEMD-320. Unfortunately, RIPEMD-128, RIPEMD-256, and RIPEMD-320 all seem to have been found with some security weaknesses. The only one that has not is RIPEMD-160.

RIPEMD-160 is a strengthened version of RIPEMD with a 160-bit hash output. It is intended to be used as a replacement for the 128-bit hash functions MD4, MD5, and RIPEMD-128.

15-3-2-4 Programming Examples

This section demonstrates how to write computer programs computing message digests using OpenSSL.

Below we explain how to do message digest in OpenSSL.

After OpenSSL 3.0.0, the original algorithm-specific digest APIs, XXX_Init(), XXX_Update() and XXX_Final() (for example, MD5_Init(), MD5_Update, MD5_Final(), SHA256_Init(), SHA256_Update(), SHA256_Final() and alike) have been deprecated. Users should not use those anymore.

Starting from version 3.0 and on, OpenSSL has made computing a message's digest a bit easier by providing the EVP_xxx envelope APIs. Using the new set of APIs, now one can easily write a single program to compute the digest of any message using any algorithm supported. The digest_evp.c shown in Figure 15-2 is an example of that. This program computes the digest of a message using any algorithm you provide. By default, it uses the sha256 message digest algorithm.

As you can see from the example, the general steps of computing a message's digest using the new EVP_xxx APIs are the following:

1. EVP_get_digestbyname(algrmName)
2. EVP_MD_CTX_new()
3. EVP_DigestInit_ex2(mdctx, md, NULL)
4. EVP_DigestUpdate(mdctx, msgp, strlen(msgp))
5. EVP_DigestFinal_ex(mdctx, digest, &dgst_len)
6. EVP_MD_CTX_free(mdctx)

These APIs are common to all message digest algorithms.

First, a program calls the EVP_get_digestbyname() function with the string name of a message digest algorithm to get an object representing the algorithm.

It then creates a message digest context object by invoking the
EVP_MD_CTX_new() function. Note that a program using EVP_MD_CTX_new() must
remember to free the space of the context or memory leak will occur.

Then it invokes the EVP_DigestInit_ex2() function to set up the message
digest context object using the selected digest algorithm, which is returned
by the EVP_get_digestbyname() function or a function such as EVP_sha1(),
EVP_sha256(), EVP_sha512(), etc.

The program then calls the EVP_DigestUpdate() function to compute the digest
of each chunk of the message in order. This function can be called multiple
times if the message has more than one chunk.

At end, EVP_DigestFinal_ex() is invoked to wrap up the process. This function
retrieves the digest value from digest context object mdctx and places it in
the second argument 'digest' to return it. The number of bytes in the digest
will be returned in the third argument 'dgst_len'.

After calling EVP_DigestFinal_ex() no additional calls to EVP_DigestUpdate()
can be made, but EVP_DigestInit_ex2() can be called again to initialize a
new digest operation.

Note that a program that has successfully called EVP_MD_CTX_new() must
remember to call EVP_MD_CTX_free() to free the space of the context or
memory leak will occur. There is no need to free the EVP_MD pointer returned
by EVP_get_digestbyname().

Figure 15-2 shows an example of computing message digests using any algorithm
supported by OpenSSL. The print_digest() function used in this program is
defined in mycryptolib.c as shown in Figure 15-39(b).

Below are some sample runs of the digest_evp program:

```
$ ./digest_evp ?
Usage: digest_evp [[digestAlgrmNname] [message]]

$ ./digest_evp
Using default digest algorithm sha256 ...
Compute digest of message: Good morning!
digest=0xc9ebfb6f4b8e880908a737b8d770aa3a518fb6053b327720e8dcc79609c32858

$ ./digest_evp sha256 'Good morning!'
Using specified digest algorithm sha256 ...
Compute digest of message: Good morning!
digest=0xc9ebfb6f4b8e880908a737b8d770aa3a518fb6053b327720e8dcc79609c32858

$ ./digest_evp sha512 'Good morning!'
Using specified digest algorithm sha512 ...
Compute digest of message: Good morning!
```

digest=0x1d1e553f217be13daf568d87f622e82447d575aad3d0541af7068f634411f51c765b7a6dde93
01942452d9e895bcbaab77c6cd1143328ad6de2673b251211768

```
$ ./digest_evp md5 'Good morning!'
Using specified digest algorithm md5 ...
```

```
Compute digest of message: Good morning!
digest=0xd56bf970b2bd8c25ab544c337531c117

$ ./digest_evp sha256  "Hi, how are you doing?"
Using specified digest algorithm sha256 ...
Compute digest of message: Hi, how are you doing?
digest=0xf157b6f7429fe48d20a8d56ff0f0164218973e8e59870206dbaf540d8f0ca83a
```

Figure 15-2 Example program of computing message digest -- digest_evp.c

```c
/*
 * This program computes the digest of a message using any algorithm.
 * Authored by Mr. Jin-Jwei Chen.
 * Copyright (c) 2014-2016, 2020, 2023  Mr. Jin-Jwei Chen. All rights reserved.
 */
#include <stdio.h>
#include <errno.h>
#include <stdlib.h>
#include <string.h>
#include <ctype.h>
#include <openssl/evp.h>

/*
 * Compute the digest of an input message using any digest algorithm..
 */
int main(int argc, char *argv[])
{
  char            *algrmName="sha256";    /* default digest algorithm */
  char            *msgp="Good morning!";  /* default message */
  EVP_MD_CTX      *mdctx;                  /* digest context */
  const EVP_MD    *md;                     /* digest object */
  unsigned char   digest[EVP_MAX_MD_SIZE]; /* value of the message digest */
  unsigned int    dgst_len;                /* length of the message digest */

  /* Process command-line arguments */
  if ((argc > 1) && !strcmp(argv[1], "?"))
  {
    fprintf(stderr, "Usage: %s [[digestAlgrmNname] [message]]\n", argv[0]);
    return(-1);
  }

  if (argc >= 2)
  {
    algrmName = argv[1];
    fprintf(stdout, "Using specified digest algorithm %s ...\n", algrmName);
  }
  else
    fprintf(stdout, "Using default digest algorithm %s ...\n", algrmName);

  if (argc >= 3)
    msgp = argv[2];

  fprintf(stdout, "Compute digest of message: %s\n", msgp);

  /* Get message digest algorithm by name */
  md = EVP_get_digestbyname(algrmName);
```

1080

```
   if (md == NULL) {
      fprintf(stderr, "EVP_get_digestbyname(): Unknown message digest algorithm"
        " %s\n", algrmName);
      return(-2);
   }

   /* Create a message digest context */
   mdctx = EVP_MD_CTX_new();
   if (!EVP_DigestInit_ex2(mdctx, md, NULL))
   {
      fprintf(stderr, "EVP_DigestInit_ex2(): Message digest initialization failed.\n");
      EVP_MD_CTX_free(mdctx);
      return(-3);
   }

   /* Hash the next chunk of the message into the digest context.
    * Call this once for every chunk of the message. */
   if (!EVP_DigestUpdate(mdctx, msgp, strlen(msgp))) {
      fprintf(stderr, "EVP_DigestUpdate(): Message digest update failed.\n");
      EVP_MD_CTX_free(mdctx);
      return(-4);
   }

   /* Retrieve the digest value from mdctx and place it in digest.
    * Also return length of digest in dgst_len. */
   if (!EVP_DigestFinal_ex(mdctx, digest, &dgst_len)) {
      fprintf(stderr, "EVP_DigestFinal_ex(): Message digest finalization failed.\n");
      EVP_MD_CTX_free(mdctx);
      return(-5);
   }
   EVP_MD_CTX_free(mdctx);

   print_digest(digest, dgst_len);

   return(0);
}
```

The get_digest() Function

Since computing the digest of a message is such a common operation, we've made it a subroutine, named **get_digest**(), which is defined in mycryptolib.c as shown in 15-39(b). The file mycryptolib.c has our own security library functions used by example programs in this chapter.

Figure 15-3 shows a program employing the get_digest() function to compute the digest of any message using any algorithm.

Below are some sample runs of the getdigest program:

```
$ ./getdigest ?
Usage: ./getdigest [[digestAlgrmName] [message]]

$ ./getdigest
Using default digest algorithm sha256 ...
Compute digest of message: Good morning!
digest=0xc9ebfb6f4b8e880908a737b8d770aa3a518fb6053b327720e8dcc79609c32858
```

```
$ ./getdigest sha512
Using specified digest algorithm sha512 ...
Compute digest of message: Good morning!

digest=0x1d1e553f217be13daf568d87f622e82447d575aad3d0541af7068f634411f51c765b7a6dde93
01942452d9e895bcbaab77c6cd1143328ad6de2673b251211768

$ ./getdigest sha512 'Good morning!'
Using specified digest algorithm sha512 ...
Compute digest of message: Good morning!

digest=0x1d1e553f217be13daf568d87f622e82447d575aad3d0541af7068f634411f51c765b7a6dde93
01942452d9e895bcbaab77c6cd1143328ad6de2673b251211768
```

Figure 15-3 Computing message digest using the get_digest() function -- getdigest.c

```c
/*
 * This program computes the digest of a message using any algorithm.
 * It uses the get_digest() library function.
 * Authored by Mr. Jin-Jwei Chen.
 * Copyright (c) 2014-2016, 2020, 2023 Mr. Jin-Jwei Chen. All rights reserved.
 */
#include <stdio.h>
#include <errno.h>
#include <stdlib.h>
#include <string.h>
#include <ctype.h>
#include <openssl/evp.h>

/*
 * Compute the digest of an input message using any digest algorithm.
 */
int main(int argc, char *argv[])
{
  char            *dgstAlgrm="sha256";    /* default digest algorithm */
  char            *msgp="Good morning!";  /* default message */
  unsigned char   digest[EVP_MAX_MD_SIZE]; /* value of the message digest */
  unsigned int    dgstlen = 0;            /* length of the message digest */
  int             ret = 0;

  /* Process command-line arguments */
  if ((argc > 1) && !strcmp(argv[1], "?"))
  {
    fprintf(stderr, "Usage: %s [[digestAlgrmName] [message]]\n", argv[0]);
    return(-1);
  }

  if (argc >= 2)
  {
    dgstAlgrm = argv[1];
    fprintf(stdout, "Using specified digest algorithm %s ...\n", dgstAlgrm);
  }
  else
    fprintf(stdout, "Using default digest algorithm %s ...\n", dgstAlgrm);
```

```
if (argc >= 3)
   msgp = argv[2];

fprintf(stdout, "Compute digest of message: %s\n", msgp);

/* Compute the digest of the message */
ret = get_digest(msgp, strlen(msgp), dgstAlgrm, digest, &dgstlen);
if (ret != 0)
{
   fprintf(stderr, "get_digest() failed, ret=%d\n", ret);
   return(-2);
}

/* Print the digest of the message */
print_digest(digest, dgstlen);

return(0);
}
```

15-4 Message Secrecy -- Encryption and Decryption

15-4-1 What Is Encryption?

```
              key                        key
               |                          |
               v                          v
          ---------                   ---------
  plaintext -->|encrypt|--> ciphertext --> |decrypt|--> plaintext
          ---------                   ---------
```

Figure 15-4 Encryption and decryption

The goal of encryption is to ensure that the message being sent or stored
is kept confidential during transit or storage.

Encryption is a process of transforming a message into secret form so that
it stays confidential and can later be read only by the intended recipient.
Decryption is the reverse process that converts an encrypted message back to
its original. The purpose of encryption is to provide confidentiality
(or secrecy).

Encrypting is sometimes called enciphering and decrypting is also called
deciphering.

We say a piece of data or message is in 'plaintext' or 'cleartext' when
it is unencrypted. A plaintext becomes a 'ciphertext', 'codetext',
'cryptogram', or simply 'cipher' after it is encrypted.

Encryption is done using an encryption algorithm with an encryption **'key'**.
An **encryption key** is a second input to the encryption and decryption process
that gives users more control and helps provide randomness and strength
of the encryption. A key is usually just a random string that is usually
one to two dozen bytes long.

The encryption key is a critical element of the entire encryption/decryption process. It makes an encryption difficult to break. To decrypt something that has been encrypted, one would need to know both the algorithm and the key used. Therefore, an encryption key must be kept secret. And for security sake you want to pick an encryption key that is difficult to guess.

15-4-2 Symmetric and Asymmetric Cryptography

15-4-2-1 How Symmetric and Asymmetric Cryptography works

In terms of key used, there are two types of cryptography: secret key cryptography and public key cryptography.

Secret key cryptography uses a single key (that is, the same key) in both encryption and decryption. The key is shared between the message sender and recipient and it must be kept secret. The sender uses the shared secret key to encrypt the message and the recipient uses the same key to decrypt it. The key must be kept secret or other people knowing the key would be able to decrypt the message as well.

With secret key encryption, a single secret key is shared between the sender and receiver and used in both encryption and decryption.

Because the same key is used in both encryption and decryption, secret key cryptography is also referred to as **'symmetric cryptography'**.

Secret key encryption and decryption is used in situations where it's easy to share the secret key. For instance, the message sender and recipient are all within the same organization or software.

In contrast, **public key cryptography** uses a pair of keys: one private key and one public key. These keys are generated and used in pair: one in encryption and the other in decryption. A message encrypted with one key can be decrypted by the other.

The two keys that public key cryptography uses are generated mathematically. They are related to each other, are linked together and must be used in pair. The private key is supposed to be known only to the owner whereas the public key may be widely disseminated.

Because different keys are used in encryption and decryption, public key cryptography is also referred to as **'asymmetric cryptography'**.

Please remember that the defining property of asymmetric or public-key cryptography is that encryption and decryption use different keys! In symmetric or classical cryptography, both encryption and decryption use the same key and thus the message sender and recipient must share a common key.

Below is how public key cryptography works.

Each party creates its own pair of private and public keys.

All parties keep their own private keys secret to themselves.
All parties make their public keys available to recipients or the public.
To send a message using **public key encryption** (**PKE**), the sender of the
message uses the public key of the recipient to encrypt the contents of
the message. The encrypted message is then transmitted electronically to
the recipient. The recipient then uses its private key to decrypt
the message. As long as the recipient's private key is not compromised,
this guarantees only the recipient can decrypt and understand the message.

Note that as with secret key cryptography, public key cryptography works
in both directions, too. That is, alternatively, the message sender Bob can
encrypt a message he wants to send using his private key (thus this is
private key encryption) and send his message to Mary. Mary can then
use Bob's public key to decrypt the message from Bob. However, doing it this
way means anyone knows Bob's public key can decrypt and understand the
message. This may defeat the purpose of doing encryption in the first place
in some cases, especially if Bob has made his public key available to the
entire world. Hence, it is not used that often although it works as long as
the distribution of the sender's public key is controlled.
This usage is normally done for the purpose of **sender authentication**,
which we will talk about in a later section, instead of message secrecy.

Therefore, when public or asymmetric key cryptography is applied in
encryption/decryption, it is typically used as public key encryption.
That is, the message recipient's public key is used to encrypt the message
being sent by the sender for the purpose of message secrecy.
Sending a message this way ensures only the intended recipient can read
the message because only he or she knows the private key and can use that
to decrypt the encrypted message, assuming the private key is not
compromised.

In contrast, private key encryption is used for sender authentication.
In that usage, the sender uses its private key to sign a message being sent
for **non-repudiation**. We will further discuss digital signature in a later
section.

In other words, depending on applications and your purposes, there are two
ways to use public key cryptography during encryption/decryption. In certain
communications such as providing digital signature, you may want to use
a private key (the sender's) to encrypt the message and the public key to
decrypt it. While in other applications, for instance, you want only one
person to be able to read the message, you use a public key (the recipient's)
to encrypt the message and the corresponding private key to decrypt it.
And yet some applications **may need to do both**. In that case, one way of
doing it is to use the sender's private key to sign the message digest
for sender authentication and also use the recipient's public key to
encrypt the message itself for confidentiality. Wonderful, isn't it?

Of course, we assume that Bob's private key really represents Bob
and Mary's private key really represents Mary. No impersonation has occurred
and neither Bob's nor Mary's private and public keys have been compromised.

Notice that **public key cryptography provides a solution not only in
confidentiality, but also in authentication.** The two-key system helps
identify the sender and recipient of a message.

15-4-2-2 Strength of Encryption Algorithms

The way to attack a symmetric cipher is to search through all the possible keys until you find one that works. Hence, the strength of a symmetric cipher mainly depends on the length of the key. However, remember that the key length is not the only factor that affects the strength. Ciphers produced using a longer key are not always stronger than those with a shorter key.

As for strength from the key length itself, for a key of length 48 bits, there are 2^{48} different keys to try and therefore it takes that many cryptographic operations to search through all of them.
And for a key of 56-bit long, it would take 2^{56} operations.
It takes 2^8 (256) times longer than the 48-bit case.
Notice that the strength increases **exponentially**, rather than linearly, with the key length.

Research has found that keys shorter than 64 bits may be vulnerable. **Keys of 80 bits or longer are more appropriate.** Given computers get faster almost every day, these numbers may need to be adjusted upward as time goes on. The longer the lifetime of the data is, the longer the key length should be.

Strength of asymmetric ciphers is a bit different because much longer keys are already required just to make asymmetric ciphers work.
In general, **1024 or so is about the minimal acceptable key length for asymmetric ciphers.** A 1024-bit asymmetric key is roughly as strong as a 80-bit symmetric key. You get the idea.

As far as security strength is concerned, remember that something that is strong today may become weak years later for different reasons. It could be computers get faster and it becomes more feasible to apply a brute-force attack or attackers may find a new way to crack the algorithm.

The security of public key cryptography also relies on that it is computationally infeasible to derive the private key from the corresponding public key. (Otherwise, the whole thing would be broken, isn't it?)

15-4-2-3 Performance and Use of Encryption Algorithms

In general, symmetric encryption algorithms work faster than asymmetric ones. The time difference between the two types of algorithms increases **linearly** as the amount of data increases. Therefore, in practice, **symmetric encryption algorithms are often used in encrypting the messages** themselves, which are usually long. And **asymmetric encryption is used to encrypt shorter data such as message digest** in digital signatures and other applications because they tend to be slower due to use of quite large keys.

15-4-3 Symmetric Encryption (Secret Key Cryptographic) Algorithms

15-4-3-1 Key, Block, IV and Padding

There are some basic general concepts about cryptographic algorithms.

Before we dig into these algorithms, we first introduce a few concepts.

Key

Every encryption/decryption operation needs a key. A key is an additional input besides the message itself into the encryption/decryption process to make the encryption random and difficult to guess.

The strength of security (i.e. secrecy) that cryptosystems provide depends on the selection of the cryptographic key.
If an attacker can guess the key, he or she will be able to decrypt the ciphertext using that key and read all messages or even impersonate.
In that case, encrypting a message wouldn't provide secrecy.
Therefore, appropriately selecting an encryption key is extremely important. It has a great impact on the security.

A key is a fixed-length random value chosen to provide randomness of a cryptographic operation. It is an input to a cryptographic operation (e.g. encryption or decryption or hashing), in addition to the message to be operated on.

Different cryptographic algorithms use different key sizes.

The length of a key usually indicates the strength of a cryptographic algorithm because it represents the upper bound of how hard it is to break it by brute force; that is, to enumerate through all possible keys. Computers get faster all the time. As a result, if all else stays the same, cryptographic algorithms get relatively weaker over time as computers grow faster and more powerful because it takes less and less time to break an algorithm by brute force attack as time goes on.

The length of the key used in encryption/decryption usually affects the strength of the encryption security. Normally, the longer the key, the stronger it is because it takes longer for attackers to search through the entire value space to find a matched one.

Block

Most encryption/decryption algorithms work on encrypting and decrypting the data a small chunk at a time. Each chunk is called a block.
Different algorithms use different block sizes. Note that each block is encrypted or decrypted with the same key.

The block size is the size of data that is encrypted/decrypted at a time. In general, block sizes are from 1 to 16 bytes, mostly 8 or 16.

Initialization Vector (IV)

In addition to taking the data and encryption key as input, most encryption/ decryption algorithms also take a third piece of information as input. That is initialization vector.

An **initialization vector (IV)** is a small block of data used as a random starting input in several encryption algorithms to randomize the encryption output so that when the same plaintext is encrypted multiple times with the same key, they result in distinct ciphertexts without re-keying.

Hence, an IV is like a starting variable used in an encryption process.
It has to be non-repeating and, for some modes, random as well.
The purpose of IV is to make an encryption more random and harder to break.
It aims to increase security.

Initialization vector should be **non-repeating**. For security sake, it is very
important that an initialization vector is not reused with the same key.

Since the initialization vector (IV) is used to perform an XOR
operation with the very first block of the message in many algorithms,
**the size of the initialization vector (IV) is usually the same as the
block size.**

Padding

As we said it earlier, most encryption/decryption algorithms work on
encrypting or decrypting a fixed-length block of data at a time.
But we all know messages come at different lengths. This means the last
block of data can be a partial block. Is it OK or good to encrypt a partial
block?

In fact, most algorithms require padding the last non-full block!

Different padding schemes exist. The simplest one is to pad the block with
null (all zero) bytes. However, that has the disadvantage of message length
may be recovered. The original DES method uses a padding scheme recommended
by NIST, which is to pad by adding a single one bit followed by all zero
bits to fill the block. This means if the last block is one byte short, then
pad it with a 0x80 byte. If it's three bytes short, then pad it with 0x80
0x00 0x00. At the decryption end, after decrypting the message, the message
recipient would start at the end of the decrypted output and remove from the
end all zero bytes if any until it sees the first 0x80 byte. Remove that byte
as well and then the rest should be the message itself. This works even
if the last byte of the message is 0x80. For instance, assuming a 8-byte
block size, if the last block of the message is
   0x11 0x22 0x33 0x44 0x55 0x66 0x80
then after padding the last block would become
   0x11 0x22 0x33 0x44 0x55 0x66 0x80 0x80

This padding scheme also works even in another extreme case where the message
happens to end with bytes 0x80 0x00 and also on the block boundary.
For example, let's say the message's last block is
   0x11 0x22 0x33 0x44 0x55 0x66 0x80 0x00
This would result in a pad of an extra block like the following:
   0x80 0x00 0x00 0x00 0x00 0x00 0x00 0x00
After decrypting the message, the entire padding block would be removed
which gives the original message.

As will be introduced below, some of block cipher modes, including
Cipher FeedBack (CFB), Output FeedBack (OFB), and Counter (CTR), do not
require padding because they always XOR the plaintext with the output
of the block cipher.

15-4-3-2 *Stream Ciphers and Block Ciphers* [16][2][1][18]

There are two major types of symmetric ciphers: stream cipher and block cipher. We talk about these in this section.

1. Stream Ciphers

A stream cipher processes a message as a byte stream. It encrypts one byte of the message at a time. A stream cipher algorithm takes two byte streams as input: the message byte stream and a pseudorandom cipher digit stream called the keystream. In other words, both of the message and the key are broken into byte streams. It combines the ith byte from the message with the ith byte from the keystream to produce the ith byte on the ciphertext. The function or operation used to combine the two bytes together usually is very simple. For instance, in many cases, it's just the exclusive-or (XOR) function.

Note that because the function used is very simple, it would be easy to launch an attack on a symmetric stream cipher if the attacker knows either the keystream or the message.

RC4

There are dozens of stream ciphers. Among them the most widely used is RC4. RC4 stands for Rivest Cipher 4. It was designed by Ron Rivest of RSA Security in 1987.

RC4 started as a trade secret. Unfortunately, there was a leak in 1994. It was anonymously posted and then spread onto many Internet web sites.

RC4 supports variable-length keys. A key can be from a couple of bytes to 2048 bits.

The advantages of RC4 are its simplicity and very high performance. RC4 has been used in various protocol standards including WEP, SSL and TLS. However, as of this writing, a number of vulnerabilities have been discovered in RC4, rendering it insecure.

Since the name RC4 was trademarked, RC4 is also referred to as ARCFOUR or ARC4 (meaning alleged RC4) to avoid trademark problems.

2. Block Ciphers

Block cipher algorithms are by far the most popular symmetric encryption algorithms.

Block ciphers encrypt/decrypt a block of data (typically 8 or 16 bytes) at a time, as opposed to one byte at a time in stream ciphers. Because of this, block ciphers are faster than stream ciphers.

In most block ciphers, since each block of data is encrypted independently using the same key, generally (except those using chaining) errors in one block do not affect other blocks, and if two plaintext message blocks are identical the output ciphertext blocks are identical too.

There are many block cipher algorithms. Different algorithms are designed based on different concepts.

For instance, the design of some modern block ciphers is based on the concept of an iterated product cipher which realizes encryption in multiple rounds, with each using a different subkey derived from the original key. Many other implementations also exist.

In this section we briefly talk about a few popular block ciphers.

DES

DES stands for Data Encryption Standard.
The DES cipher was designed by IBM in 1970s. It was later published by the National Institute of Standards and Technology (NIST) of the United States in 1977. NIST used to be the U.S. National Bureau of Standards (NBS).

DES uses a 56-bit key and a 64-bit block size, meaning the input text is encrypted 8 bytes at a time. In fact, a DES key is 64-bit long. It is effectively 56-bit because the least significant bit of each byte is used as a parity bit for error detection.

DES operates on 8-byte input blocks.

DES in Encrypt-Decrypt-Encrypt (EDE) mode (which we will describe very shortly below) is very popular in financial industry.

3DES

3DES means Triple DES. It stands for Triple Data Encryption Algorithm (TDEA or Triple DEA). Notice that Triple DES, 3DES, Triple DEA, and TDEA basically all mean the same thing.

3DES is a symmetric block cipher that applies DES cipher algorithm three times to each input data block. The motivation for 3DES is that with computer getting faster and more powerful all the time, it has become more and more feasible to launch a brute-force attack on DES ciphers. 3DES is a simple answer to that increasing threat. It essentially increases the key length of DES without re-designing the algorithm.

3DES uses a key bundle that consists of three DES keys. As stated above, each of DES keys is 56 bits long, excluding the parity bits.
Though the strength of 3DES ciphers, as designated by NIST, is only about 80 bits, instead of 56x3=168 bits. This is mainly due to meet-in-the-middle attacks and some known-plaintext attacks it is subject to.

3DES is used in many products, including some Microsoft products and electronic payment systems.

At one point in time, 3DES was the recommended standard and perhaps the most widely used symmetric encryption algorithm in the computer industry. However, it may be slowly fading.

AES

AES stands for Advanced Encryption Standard.

AES was adopted and published by NIST and the U.S. government in November of 2001 and is now a United States Federal Standard (FIPS 197). It supersedes DES.

This adoption was the result of a five-year standardization process and competition in which the original designers of AES submitted a proposal and won.

AES is based on the Rijndael cipher co-developed by Belgian cryptographers Joan Daemen and Vincent Rijmen.

Rijndael is a family of ciphers with different key and block sizes. NIST selected three members of the Rijndael family for the AES standard. They all use a 128-bit block size with a key length of 128, 192 and 256 bits, respectively. Keys of 192 and 256 bits can be used for heavy duty encryption purposes.

AES cipher algorithm is based on the so-called 'substitution-permutation network' design. The design uses a combination of substitution and permutation.

AES's performance is extremely fast, especially with 128-bit keys. The use of AES is on rise.

RC2

RC2 block cipher was designed by Ronald Rivest. It uses a 64-bit block size. RC2's key length is variable. RC2 is used in SSL. Unfortunately, just like RC4, RC2 was initially a trade secret but was leaked by some anonymous posting.

RC5

RC5 block cipher was designed by Ronald Rivest in 1994. It's flexible in that it uses variable-length of blocks, keys and rounds. RC5's block size can be 32, 64 or 128 bits. Its key size can be from 0 to 2040 bits. And its computation can be carried out in 0 to 255 rounds.

One of the features of RC5 is its use of data-dependent rotations. RC5 uses an algorithm that is similar to Feistel network, which is an iterated product cipher.

Blowfish

Blowfish is yet another algorithm designed to replace DES. It was designed by computer security expert Bruce Schneier in 1993. Blowfish uses 64-bit blocks and a variable-length key of from 32 to 448 bits in its encryption.

Blowfish is known for its high speed. It is freely available.

Blowfish is utilized in software products ranging from e-commerce platforms for securing payments to password management tools.

Twofish

Twofish is related to Blowfish. It is one of the five finalists in the Advanced Encryption Standard contest.

Twofish uses 128-bit blocks and keys of up to 256 bits long.
Like Blowfish, Twofish is freely available. Since it is free, it is bundled in encryption programs such as PhotoEncrypt, GPG and TrueCrypt.

Twofish is considered one of the fastest symmetric key block ciphers. It is ideal for use in both hardware and software environments.

IDEA

The International Data Encryption Algorithm (IDEA), originally called Improved Proposed Encryption Standard (IPES), is a symmetric-key block cipher designed by James Massey of ETH Zurich and Xuejia Lai in 1991. IDEA was used in Pretty Good Privacy (PGP) v2.0.

IDEA uses a block size of 8 bytes and a key of 16 bytes.
IDEA encryption and decryption uses 8.5 rounds of transformations.
Each round operates on two bytes of data by interleaving three different operators: XOR (Exclusive OR), addition modulo 2^{16}, and multiplication modulo $(2^{16})+1$.

IDEA was broken in 2011 to 2012.

CAST

CAST is a family of cipher algorithms.
CAST-128 (also known as CAST-5) was designed by Carlisle Adams and Stafford Tavares in 1996. CAST-256 was derived from CAST-128.

CAST-128 uses an 8-byte block size. Its key can be from 5 to 16 bytes long. Its transformation can be 12 or 16 rounds. 16 rounds is used when the key is longer than 10 bytes. Operations performed include XOR, modular addition and subtraction, and rotation.

CAST-128 was used in GNU Privacy Guard (GPG) and Pretty Good Privacy (PGP).

Notice that as it has happened in the past already, in general, as time goes on, some algorithms may get cracked and they will gradually fade away. It's also expected that key length may get longer and longer in order to avoid being broken by ever increasingly more powerful computers.

15-4-3-3 Modes of Block Cipher Operation [17]

We will briefly talk about different modes of operation for symmetric key cryptographic block ciphers in this section. For further details, readers can read the Wikipedia's web page on this topic:
[17] https://en.wikipedia.org/wiki/Block_cipher_mode_of_operation
Some of the diagrams in this section are a courtesy of that web page.

A block cipher can operate in many different modes. Below is a list of some of these modes:

```
ECB (Electronic Code Book)
CBC (Cipher Block Chaining)
PCBC (Propagating Cipher Block Chaining)
CFB (Cipher FeedBack)
OFB (Output FeedBack)
EDE (Encrypt-Decrypt-Encrypt)
GCM (Galois/Counter Mode)
CTR (Counter)
```

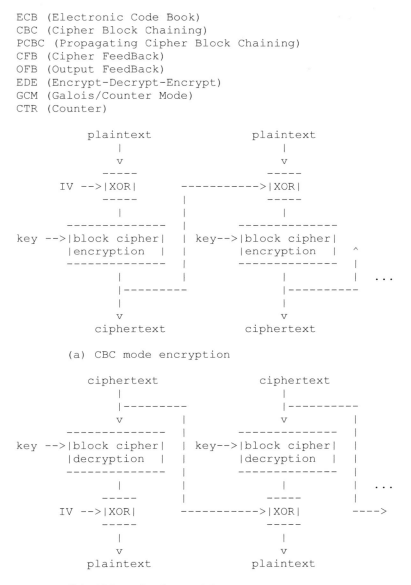

(a) CBC mode encryption

(b) CBC mode decryption

Figure 15-5 How Cipher Block Chaining (CBC) mode works [17]

We briefly introduce some of the commonly used ones below.

1. ECB

Electronic Codebook (ECB) mode is the simplest encryption mode.
In ECB mode, the message is divided into blocks and each block is encrypted and decrypted separately.

The main disadvantage of ECB mode is that identical plaintext blocks are encrypted into identical ciphertext blocks. Obviously, it does not hide data patterns well at all. Therefore, ECB is not recommended for use in encryption.

2. CBC

To encrypt, cipher block chaining (CBC) uses a chaining mechanism in which each plaintext block is first XORed with the immediately previous ciphertext block before it is encrypted using the key.
The first block of the message is XORed with an initialization vector (IV) because there is no previous ciphertext block available at that time. This means the current block of ciphertext depends not only on the current block of input plaintext but also on the preceding ciphertext block. That's where the "chaining" in the name of this mode comes from.

Figure 15-5a shows how the encryption in CBC mode works. [17]

To decrypt, the current ciphertext block is first decrypted using the key. The result is then XOR-ed with the previous ciphertext block to create the current plaintext block. The initialization vector, instead of the previous ciphertext block, is used in the XOR operation that creates the first plaintext block.

Figure 15-5b explains how the decryption in CBC mode works. [17]

3. CFB

The Cipher Feedback (CFB) mode is similar to CBC.
CFB decryption is almost identical to CBC encryption performed in reverse.

In CFB mode, the preceding block of ciphertext is encrypted using the encryption key. This output is then XOR-ed with current block of input plaintext to produce the current block of ciphertext.
For the very first block of data, since there is no preceding block of ciphertext, the initialization vector (IV) is encrypted and its output is XOR-ed with the first block of plaintext.
The XOR operation conceals plaintext patterns.

To decrypt the current block, the preceding block of ciphertext is decrypted. The output is then XOR-ed with the current block of ciphertext to derive the current block of plaintext. In decrypting the first block, the initialization vector is encrypted since there is no previous block of ciphertext.

The goal of CFB is to make a block cipher into a self-synchronizing stream cipher. In case part of the ciphertext is lost, after processing certain amount of input data, the message recipient should be able to continue decrypting the rest of the message and not losing the entire message.

What's special about CFB mode is that it is block cipher with some characteristics of a stream cipher.

4. OFB

Output Feedback (OFB) mode is very similar to the CFB mode.
The OFB mode makes a block cipher into a synchronous stream cipher.
It generates keystream blocks, which are then XORed with the plaintext
blocks to produce the ciphertext.

The OFB mode does not chain the ciphertext.
To encrypt the first block, the initialization vector is block cipher
encrypted using the key. The output is XOR-ed with plaintext to produce
the first block of ciphertext. To encrypt the second block of data,
the encrypted initialization vector from the previous block is used as the
IV input. It is encrypted again using the key. This output is then XOR-ed
with the second block of plaintext to create the second block of
ciphertext. The rest of blocks are encrypted the same way as the second
block.

Figure 15-6 shows how encryption in Output Feedback (OFB) mode
works [17].

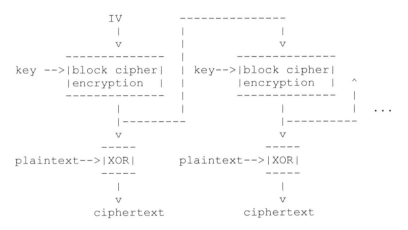

Figure 15-6 How encryption in Output Feedback (OFB) mode works [17]

Notice that the output of the encryption block function is not the
ciphertext but used as the feedback. The XOR (exclusive OR) value of each
plaintext block is created independently of both previous plaintext and
ciphertext. It is this mode that is used when there can be no tolerance
for error propagation, as there are no chaining dependencies.

Like the ciphertext feedback mode, it uses an initialization vector (IV).
Changing the IV in the same plaintext block results in different
ciphertext.

OFB permits encryption of differing block sizes.

5. EDE

The (EDE) mode is used in DES algorithm.
Using the DES algorithm in Encrypt-Decrypt-Encrypt (EDE) mode is popular
because if a single key is used for all 3 operations it is equivalent to
regular 56-bit DES. This means a 56-bit DES implementation can decrypt
the message. It makes this version of 3DES backwards compatible with DES.

Using triple DES in EDE mode provides an advantage because it is backward compatible with the regular DES if you use the same key three times. When you use the same key three times, the first two operations (i.e. Decrypt-Encrypt) cancel each other out. Therefore, it will be the same as just using that same key with DES. Backward compatibility is thus achieved.

When you use three different keys, you get triple DES.

DES in EDE mode is defined in standards ISO 8732 and ANSI X9.17. It is very popular in the financial sector. It may be used for DEK and MIC encryption when symmetric key management is employed.

6. GCM

Galois/Counter Mode (GCM) is a mode of operation that has been getting increasingly popular recently due to its efficiency and performance.

GCM uses a block size of 128 bits (16 bytes).

In GCM mode, to encrypt, data blocks are numbered. The block number is encrypted using a block cipher. The result is then XOR-ed with the plaintext to create the ciphertext. Like other counter modes, this is effectively a stream cipher. Therefore, it's very important that different initialization vectors are used for different streams.

The operation then combines the ciphertext with an authentication code to create an authentication tag, which can be used for integrity check. Because of this, GCM also offers what HMAC offers. The output of the encryption consists of the ciphertext, the authentication tag, and the IV.

7. CTR (Counter)

Just as OFB, Counter (CTR) mode turns a block cipher into a stream cipher. It generates the next keystream block by encrypting successive values of a counter. The counter can be any function that produces a sequence which does not repeat, or at least does not repeat for a long time.

In a way, CTR mode is very similar to the OFB mode. One thing different is that the initialization vector input is now replaced by a counter value and the encrypted counter value output is not a feed into the next block. Each block gets its own different counter value as the input into the the block cipher encryption function.

Which mode to choose?

Studies have found that for CBC and CFB, reusing an IV leaks information about the first block of plaintext. For OFB and CTR, reusing an IV completely destroys security. In CBC mode, the IV must be unpredictable at encryption time. Otherwise, it may be subject to the so-called TLS CBC IV attack.

If you have to choose the mode of block ciphers yourself, it would be a good idea to pick CBC, EDE or GCM. Don't use ECB.

15-4-3-4 Block and Key Sizes of Encryption/Decryption Algorithms

```
Figure 15-7 Key and block sizes of cipher algorithms
--------------------------------------------------------------------------
Algorithm         Block Size             Key Size                  Rounds
-------------     ---------------------  -------------------------  -------
AES               16 bytes (128 bits)    128, 192 or 256 bits       10,12,14
DES               8 bytes (64 bits)      56 bits (+8 parity bits)   16
Triple DES        8 bytes (64 bits)      168, 112 or 56 bits        48
Blowfish          8 bytes (64 bits)      32 to 448 bits             16
Twofish           16 bytes (128 bits)    128, 192 or 256 bits       16
CAST-128          8 bytes (64 bits)      40 to 128 bits             12,16
IDEA              8 bytes (64 bits)      128 bits                   8.5
RC2               8 bytes (64 bits)      8-1024 bits,incr by 8,(defa 64) 16,2
RC5               4, 8 or 16 bytes (8)   0 to 2040 bits (128 suggested) 1-255
RC4               1 - stream cipher      40 to 2048 bits            1
SEED              16 bytes (128 bits)    16 bytes (128 bits)        16
Camellia          16 bytes (128 bits)    128, 192 or 256 bits       18,24
--------------------------------------------------------------------------
```

```
Different ciphers use different block and key sizes.
```

```
Figure 15-7 lists the block and key sizes and number of rounds for
various encryption/decryption algorithms. Make sure you use the correct sizes
for the key and IV. Notice that the IV size usually is the same as the block
size.
```

15-4-4 Asymmetric Encryption (Public Key Cryptographic) Algorithms [3][2][1]

```
Two most well-known asymmetric cipher algorithms today are RSA and
Diffie-Hellman. They are introduced below.
```

15-4-4-1 Diffie-Hellman

```
The Diffie-Hellman cryptographic algorithm is the first publicly known
public key cryptosystem that was published by Whitfield Diffie and Martin
Hellman in 1976. A U.S. patent listing Martin E. Hellman, Bailey W. Diffie
and Ralph C. Merkle as the inventors was filed on September 6 of 1977.
The patent has since expired in 1997.
```

```
Interestingly, it was later known that indeed James H. Ellis, Clifford Cocks
and Malcolm J. Williamson of the British Signals Intelligence Agency had
previously demonstrated how public-key cryptography could be achieved in
1975. Unfortunately, their work was kept secret until 1997.
```

```
Diffie-Hellman cryptographic algorithm is based on modulo arithmetic in
the discrete logarithm problem.
```

```
  In Diffie-Hellman cryptosystem, the two parties choose and share a common
  modulus p, which is a prime number, and another number g, which cannot be
  0, 1 or p-1. g is a primitive root modulo p.
```

```
  The base common value g and the modulus p are what the two parties
  agree upon to begin with. Then the Diffie-Hellman public key cryptosystem
```

works as follows:

First, each party chooses a private key and computes its public key:

Party 1	Party 2
choose private key a	choose private key b
compute public key X = (g^a) mod p	compute public key Y = (g^b) mod p

Second, the two parties exchange their public keys.

```
    Party 1                    Party 2
    -------                    -------
          X ------------->
          <------------- Y
```

Third, each party computes the shared secret key using the value received from the partner and the private key it has chosen.

Party 1	Party 2
compute shared secret key=(Y^a) mod p	compute shared secret key= (X^b) mod p

Indeed, the shared secret key can also be computed by encrypting the other party's public key using the party's private key.

The two parties arrive at the same shared secret key because the following:

(g^(ab)) mod p = (g^(ba)) mod p = (Y^a) mod p = (X^b) mod p

where the number a is the private key party 1 chooses and b is the private key party 2 chooses. ab means multiply a by b. (a^b) means take a to the bth power or a raised to exponential of b. mod means modulo. mod p means to divide by p and take the remainder.

Fourth, if party 1 wants to send a message to party 2, he or she enciphers the message using the shared secret key. Since party 2 has the shared secret key, he or she just uses it to decrypt and get the message.

It is simple, isn't it? Of course, for this to be practically secure, very big values of a, b, and p would be needed.

Note that only a, b, and ((g^(ab)) mod p = (g^(ba)) mod p) are kept secret. All the other values, including p, g, (g^a mod p), and (g^b mod p), are sent in the clear.

**The magic of this is that in the end both parties arrive at the same secret key value. Each party kind of owns one half of a complete circle and each is able to make the whole circle because each knows its partner's half as well as its own half which is private to them.
An attack would not be able to make the complete circle and get the shared secret because it wouldn't know the secret values picked by each party -- the secrets they pick are never sent across the network.**

The Diffie-Hellman protocol is considered secure against eavesdroppers as long as p and g are appropriately chosen.

The security of the Diffie-Hellman public key algorithm is based on the mathematical difficulty of the discrete logarithm problem.
For the Diffie-Hellman algorithm to be secure, the key has to be very long, from 1024 to 2048 bits.

The Network File System developed by Oracle/Sun Microsystems used the Diffie-Hellman algorithm with 192-bit keys.

Although Diffie-Hellman can be used as a public-key cryptography, traditionally public-key cryptography has been dominated by RSA.

15-4-4-2 RSA

RSA is a cryptosystem for public-key encryption.

The RSA public key cryptographic algorithm was invented by Rivest, Shamir, and Adleman at MIT in 1978. The RSA algorithm was patented in the U.S. However, since it was published before it was patented, it cannot be patented outside the U.S. The designers of the algorithm licensed it from MIT and used it in commercial products in 1982. Since then RSA algorithm has been very widely used in so many products.

RSA cipher is an exponentiation cipher. It is based on factoring two very large prime numbers. The math RSA ciphers are based on is described below. [1]

RSA public key algorithm involves four numbers:
   the public exponent e,
   the modulus n,
   and **two very large prime numbers p and q**,
where **n=pq**. Both p and q need to be kept secret.

Let's define totient t(n) of n to be the number of numbers less than n with no factors in common with n. Select an integer e < n that is relatively prime to t(n). Find a second integer d such that the following holds:

   ed mod t(n) = 1

Here d is the private key and (e,n) is the public key.

Let m be a message. Then the ciphertext of m is computed as

   c = (m^e) mod n

and the original message is computed as

   m = (c^d) mod n

In other words, you take m to the eth power and then divide it by n to take the remainder to encrypt the message m. To decrypt the message, you take the encrypted message to the dth power and then divide by n to get the remainder.

The two large prime numbers, p and q, are normally generated using the Rabin-Miller algorithm. A modulus n is calculated as the product of p and q. This modulus is used by both the private and public keys and provides the link between the two. When we talk about the key length of an RSA key, we are referring to the length of the modulus n.

The public key consists of a public exponent e and the modulus n. The exponent e is usually set to be 65537 or a small prime number. Since the public key is made known to all, the exponent e does not need to be secret.

The private key is the exponent d, which is calculated using the Extended Euclidean algorithm to find the multiplicative inverse with respect to the totient of n.

Notes on RSA

The security of RSA rests in the computational difficulty of factoring n to get two very large prime numbers, p and q. The strength of encryption using RSA is tied to the key length. RSA algorithm typically uses keys of 1024, 2048 or 4096 bits. A key length of 2048-bits or longer is very desirable now as it may become more likely that RSA using 1024-bit keys could be cracked someday as computers become more powerful every day.

Note that RSA is a very versatile cryptography solution. It can be used in encryption/decryption in **asymmetric cryptography**. In addition, it can also be used in encryption/decryption in **symmetric cryptography** as well as key exchange and digital signatures which we will discuss a bit later in this chapter. That is, RSA provides security in **confidentiality** as well as **origin authentication** and **key exchange**.

Summary of Encryption Algorithms

In a quick summary, we have provided a brief introduction to the following algorithms in this section.

Symmetric: DES 3DES AES RC2 RC5 Blowfish Twofish IDEA CAST-5
Asymmetric: DH RSA

15-4-5 Programming Examples

15-4-5-1 Encryption and Decryption using OpenSSL

Doing encryption and decryption using OpenSSL is made easy by the EVP_xxx() API functions OpenSSL provides. EVP_*() is a set of OpenSSL APIs that simplify programming in encryption and decryption. Regardless of which cryptographic algorithm you choose, the steps to encrypt and decrypt a message are the same or similar.

There are two different approaches to doing encryption and decryption in OpenSSL. First approach uses different functions for encryption and decryption while the second approach uses the same set of functions for both encryption and decryption. We will introduce both of them in this section.

15-4-5-1-1 Using Different APIs for Encryption and Decryption

When you use different functions for encryption and decryption operations, the APIs are below:

Encryption:

```
int EVP_EncryptInit_ex(EVP_CIPHER_CTX *ctx, const EVP_CIPHER *type,
        ENGINE *impl, unsigned char *key, unsigned char *iv);
int EVP_EncryptUpdate(EVP_CIPHER_CTX *ctx, unsigned char *out,
        int *outl, unsigned char *in, int inl);
int EVP_EncryptFinal_ex(EVP_CIPHER_CTX *ctx, unsigned char *out,
        int *outl);
```

Decryption:

```
int EVP_DecryptInit_ex(EVP_CIPHER_CTX *ctx, const EVP_CIPHER *type,
        ENGINE *impl, unsigned char *key, unsigned char *iv);
int EVP_DecryptUpdate(EVP_CIPHER_CTX *ctx, unsigned char *out,
        int *outl, unsigned char *in, int inl);
int EVP_DecryptFinal_ex(EVP_CIPHER_CTX *ctx, unsigned char *outm,
        int *outl);
```

Note that there is an old version of the EVP_XXXInit_ex() and EVP_XXXFinal_ex() APIs. They are EVP_EncryptInit(), EVP_EncryptFinal(), EVP_DecryptInit() and EVP_DecryptFinal(). These are deprecated but they remain in OpenSSL just for backward compatibility. Try not to use these anymore.

A. Steps for Encryption

We discuss how to do encryption using the first set of OpenSSL's EVP_xxx() APIs here. Below are the steps:

1. Create a cipher context

   ctx = **EVP_CIPHER_CTX_new**()

   A cipher context is needed to use ciphers.
   The EVP_CIPHER_CTX_new() function creates and returns a cipher context.

2. Set up the cipher context with a specific cipher algorithm

   EVP_EncryptInit_ex(ctx, algrm, impl, key, iv)

   The EVP_EncryptInit_ex() function initializes the cipher context ctx with the algorithm algrm you choose and provide in the second argument, with the symmetric key you pick and provide in the fourth argument, and with initial vector (IV) of your choice as given in the fifth argument. The third parameter impl allows you to specify an implementation.

   If impl is NULL then the default implementation is used.
   The algorithm, referred to as type in OpenSSL documentation, is normally

supplied by a function such as EVP_aes_256_cbc().
The actual lengths of the key and IV depend on the cipher.

EVP_EncryptInit_ex() returns 1 for success and 0 for failure.

The most common practice is to supply all arguments at the same time.
But it is also possible to set all arguments except the algorithm/type
to NULL in an initial call and supply the remaining arguments
in subsequent calls.

The old version of this API EVP_EncryptInit(ctx, algrm, key, iv) is
deprecated. It uses the default cipher implementation.

EVP_EncryptInit_ex() should be used because it can reuse an existing
context without allocating and freeing it up on each call.

3. Encrypt the next chunk of input data

   EVP_EncryptUpdate(ctx, outbuf, &outlen, inbuf, inlen)

The EVP_EncryptUpdate() function encrypts inlen bytes from the input data
buffer (inbuf), writes the encryption output to outbuf, and returns the
number of bytes written in outlen.

This step should be repeatedly called until end of input data. That is,
for very large input data, you can break the input into smaller pieces
and call EVP_EncryptUpdate() once for each of the pieces in order.

EVP_EncryptUpdate() returns 1 for success and 0 for failure.

4. Wrap up the encryption by handling the last remaining part

   EVP_EncryptFinal_ex(ctx, outbuf, &outlen)

EVP_EncryptFinal_ex() wraps up the entire encryption process.
If padding is enabled (this is the default) then EVP_EncryptFinal_ex()
encrypts the "final" block of data, any data that remains in a
partial block. In one extreme case, this could be the entire padding block.
The EVP_EncryptFinal_ex() function writes the last remaining output bytes
to the output buffer and returns the number of bytes so written in outlen.
Only after this call is the encryption process considered complete.
No further calls to EVP_EncryptUpdate() should be made after this step.

EVP_EncryptFinal_ex() returns 1 for success and 0 for failure.

The old version of this API is EVP_EncryptFinal(). It's obsolete but is
retained for compatibility with existing code. It takes exactly the same
arguments as EVP_EncryptFinal_ex().

EVP_EncryptFinal_ex() should be used because it can reuse an existing
context without allocating and freeing it up on each call.

5. Free the cipher context

   EVP_CIPHER_CTX_free(ctx)

This step frees the cipher context created early in step 1.

The OpenSSL documentation says that EVP_CIPHER_CTX_free() clears all information from a cipher context and frees up any allocated memory associated with it, including ctx itself. This function should be called after all operations using a cipher are complete so sensitive information does not remain in memory.

In cases where a cipher context is to be reused, EVP_CIPHER_CTX_reset() can be called instead. The OpenSSL documentation says this: EVP_CIPHER_CTX_reset() clears all information from a cipher context and frees up any allocated memory associated with it, except the ctx itself. This function should be called anytime ctx is to be reused for another EVP_XXXInit_ex() / EVP_XXXUpdate() / EVP_XXXFinal_ex() series of calls.

Notice the difference between the two. EVP_CIPHER_CTX_free() frees up all associated memory including the cipher context itself. EVP_CIPHER_CTX_reset() frees up all associated memory except the cipher context itself.

B. Steps for Decryption

The steps for decryption operation are same as above with one difference. The only thing different is the word Encrypt in the encryption APIs listed above needs to be changed to Decrypt. And that's it!

Figure 15-8 is an example program that does encryption and decryption using the aes-256-cbc algorithm, which is a symmetric cryptography.

This program illustrates the basic sequence of steps needed to encrypt and decrypt a message. The example uses aes-256-cbc algorithm. However, it can be easily changed into using other cipher algorithms. Just replace the second argument EVP_aes_256_cbc() in the call to EVP_EncryptInit_ex() with whatever cipher algorithm you like that is supported, for instance, EVP_bf_cbc().

The basic sequence of steps is all the same for using other cipher algorithms. The only thing you need to remember is that the **lengths of IV and key vary** from one algorithm to another. Therefore, if you use a different algorithm, make sure you adjust the lengths, and values, of the key and IV accordingly. The AES algorithm uses 128 bits (16 bytes) of IV and it uses a key of either 128, 192 or 256 bits. If you change the algorithm to, for instance, bf-cbc, then that algorithm uses an 8-byte IV and a 16-byte key.

In addition, the example program assumes the input message is 1024 bytes at most. If the actual input message is longer than that (i.e. than whatever the input buffer can hold), then the program must split the input into multiple chunks and invoke the EVP_EncryptUpdate() or EVP_DecryptUpdate() function multiple times in succession, once for each input chunk.

Figure 15-8 Basic encryption/decryption -- enc_aes_256_cbc.c

```
/*
 * A simple encryption and decryption program -- basic sequence of steps.
 * Authored by Mr. Jin-Jwei Chen.
 * Copyright (c) 2014-2016, 2020-2023 Mr. Jin-Jwei Chen. All rights reserved.
```

```
 */

#include <stdio.h>
#include <errno.h>
#include <string.h>           /* memset(), strlen() */
#include <openssl/evp.h>
#include <openssl/err.h>
#include <openssl/blowfish.h>

#define  OPENSSL_SUCCESS     1     /* Openssl functions return 1 as success */

/* Note: KEYLEN and IVLEN vary from one algorithm to another */
#define IVLEN    16           /* length of IV (number of bytes) */
#define KEYLEN   16           /* key length (number of bytes) */

/* sizes of chunks this program works on */
#define INSIZE 1024
#define OUTSIZE (INSIZE+IVLEN)

/* These are shared by the encryption and decryption. */
unsigned char iv[IVLEN+1] = "0000000000000001";
unsigned char key[KEYLEN+1] = "Axy3pzLk%8q#0)yH";

/* Print the ciphertext stored in 'buf'. Note that data is unsigned. */
void print_ciphertext(unsigned char *buf, unsigned int buflen)
{
  int   i;

  if (buf == NULL) return;
  fprintf(stdout, "ciphertext=0x");
  for (i = 0; i < buflen; i++)
    fprintf(stdout, "%02x", buf[i]);
  printf("\n");
}

/* Encrypt the message in 'inbuf' and put the results in 'outbuf'.
 * The length of output cipher text is returned in 'outlen'.
 * Make sure the 'outbuf' is large enough to hold the results.
 */
int encrypt(unsigned char *inbuf, int inlen, unsigned char *outbuf, int *outlen)
{
  EVP_CIPHER_CTX *ctx = NULL;          /* cipher context */
  int       outlen1, outlen2;          /* length of output cipher text */
  int       totallen = 0;              /* total length of output cipher text */
  int       ret;

  if (inbuf == NULL || outbuf == NULL || outlen == NULL)
    return(EINVAL);
  *outlen = 0;

  /* Create a cipher context */
  ctx = EVP_CIPHER_CTX_new();
  if (ctx == NULL)
  {
    fprintf(stderr, "Error: encrypt(), EVP_CIPHER_CTX_new() failed\n");
    return(-1);
```

```
    }

    /* Set up the cipher context with a specific cipher algorithm */
    ret = EVP_EncryptInit_ex(ctx, EVP_aes_256_cbc(), NULL, key, iv);
    if (!ret)
    {
      fprintf(stderr, "Error: encrypt(), EVP_EncryptInit_ex() failed\n");
      EVP_CIPHER_CTX_free(ctx);
      return(-2);
    }

    /* Encrypt the input message */
    /* If the inlen is wrong, it may result in no error but outlen1 is 0. */
    outlen1 = 0;
    if (EVP_EncryptUpdate(ctx, outbuf, &outlen1, inbuf, inlen) != OPENSSL_SUCCESS)
    {
      fprintf(stderr, "Error: encrypt(), EVP_EncryptUpdate() failed\n");
      EVP_CIPHER_CTX_free(ctx);
      return(-3);
    }
    totallen = totallen + outlen1;
    *outlen = totallen;

    /* Wrap up the encryption by handling the last remaining part */
    outlen2 = 0;
    if (EVP_EncryptFinal_ex(ctx, outbuf+totallen, &outlen2) != OPENSSL_SUCCESS)
    {
      fprintf(stderr, "Error: encrypt(), EVP_EncryptFinal_ex() failed\n");
      EVP_CIPHER_CTX_free(ctx);
      return(-4);
    }
    totallen = totallen + outlen2;
    *outlen = totallen;

    EVP_CIPHER_CTX_free(ctx);

    return(0);
}

/* Decrypt the message in 'inbuf' and put the results in 'outbuf'.
 * The length of output is returned in 'outlen'.
 * Make sure the 'outbuf' is large enough to hold the results.
 */
int decrypt(unsigned char *inbuf, int inlen, unsigned char *outbuf, int *outlen)
{
    EVP_CIPHER_CTX *ctx = NULL;        /* cipher context */
    int      outlen1, outlen2;         /* length of output plain text */
    int      totallen = 0;             /* total length of output plain text */
    int      ret;

    if (inbuf == NULL || outbuf == NULL || outlen == NULL)
       return(EINVAL);
    *outlen = 0;

    /* Create a cipher context */
    ctx = EVP_CIPHER_CTX_new();
```

```c
if (ctx == NULL)
{
   fprintf(stderr, "Error: decrypt(), EVP_CIPHER_CTX_new() failed\n");
   return(-1);
}

/* Set up the cipher context with a specific cipher algorithm */
ret = EVP_DecryptInit_ex(ctx, EVP_aes_256_cbc(), NULL, key, iv);
if (!ret)
{
   fprintf(stderr, "Error: decrypt(), EVP_DecryptInit_ex() failed\n");
   EVP_CIPHER_CTX_free(ctx);
   return(-2);
}

/* Decrypt the input message */
outlen1 = 0;
if (EVP_DecryptUpdate(ctx, outbuf, &outlen1, inbuf, inlen) != OPENSSL_SUCCESS)
{
   fprintf(stderr, "Error: decrypt(), EVP_DecryptUpdate() failed\n");
   EVP_CIPHER_CTX_free(ctx);
   return(-3);
}
totallen = totallen + outlen1;
*outlen = totallen;

/* Wrap up the decryption by handling the last remaining part */
outlen2 = 0;
if (EVP_DecryptFinal_ex(ctx, outbuf+totallen, &outlen2) != OPENSSL_SUCCESS)
{
   fprintf(stderr, "Error: decrypt(), EVP_DecryptFinal_ex() failed\n");
   EVP_CIPHER_CTX_free(ctx);
   return(-4);
}
totallen = totallen + outlen2;
*outlen = totallen;

EVP_CIPHER_CTX_free(ctx);

return(0);
}

/* A simple encryption and decryption program */
int main(int argc, char *argv[])
{
   int      outlen = 0;            /* length of output cipher text */
   int      ret;

   /* Buffer of the original plain text to be encrypted */
   unsigned char  inbuf[INSIZE]="This is the original message.";
   /* Buffer of the output of encryption */
   unsigned char  outbuf[OUTSIZE];
   /* Buffer of the output of decryption */
   unsigned char  outbuf2[OUTSIZE];
   int      outlen2 = 0;           /* length of output cipher text */
```

```
    fprintf(stdout, "Encryption/decryption using enc_aes_256_cbc algorithm.\n");
    fprintf(stdout, "plaintext=%s\n", inbuf);

    /* Encrypt the message */
    ret = encrypt(inbuf, strlen((char *)inbuf), outbuf, &outlen);
    if (ret != 0)
    {
      fprintf(stderr, "Error: main(), encrypt() failed, ret=%d\n", ret);
      return(ret);
    }
    print_ciphertext(outbuf, outlen);

    /* Decrypt the message */
    ret = decrypt(outbuf, outlen, outbuf2, &outlen2);
    if (ret != 0)
    {
      fprintf(stderr, "Error: main(), decrypt() failed, ret=%d\n", ret);
      return(ret);
    }
    outbuf2[outlen2] = '\0';
    fprintf(stdout, "decrypted output=%s\n", outbuf2);

    return(0);
}
```

Figure 15-9 is a more generic encryption/decryption program.
It demonstrates encryption and decryption of an arbitrary message provided
by the user using any algorithm chosen by the user, both given on the
command line. Below is a sample output:

```
$ ./enc_evp1 aes-256-cbc "Have a wonderful summer."
Plain text=Have a wonderful summer.
Cipher text=0xcad0a47c1aae42d011e8198a0eac08cd00d50bfb330f605b09a51150a6a39daf
Decrypted message=Have a wonderful summer.
The encryption and decryption have succeeded.
```

The encryption and decryption utility functions, myencrypt1() and mydecrypt1(),
respectively, used in the enc_evp1 program and many others are defined in
mycryptolib.c listed in Figure 15-39(b) at end of this chapter.
The myencrypt1() function employs the EVP_EncryptXXX() APIs for encryption
and the mydecrypt1() function utilizes the EVP_DecryptXXX() APIs for
decryption.

One note here is that the EVP_DecryptFinal_ex() function used in mydecrypt1()
returns 1 on success for almost all algorithms. However, it returns 0 for
success when GCM-mode algorithms are used. For instance, aes-nnn-gcm,
aria-nnn-gcm, and so on. For the enc_evp1 example program to run successfully
on these algorithms, you need to work around it by modifying mycryptolib.c
and checking return code 0 for success instead. This inconsistent behavior
exists in OpenSSL 1.0.2, 1.1.1g, 3.0.0 and up to at least 3.3.0. This looks
like a bug.

   Figure 15-9 Encrypt/decrypt using any algorithm -- enc_evp1.c

```
/*
 * This program encrypts a message given by the user using a cipher algorithm
```

```c
 * chosen by the user and then decrypts the encrypted message.
 * This single program can encrypt and decrypt using different cipher algorithms.
 * The cipher algorithm used is specified by the user on the command line
 * by providing a name like bf-cbc, aes-256-cbc or des-ede3-ofb.
 * Run the 'openssl ?' command to get the list of cipher algorithms available.
 * Authored by Mr. Jin-Jwei Chen.
 * Copyright (c) 2014-2016, 2019-2020 Mr. Jin-Jwei Chen. All rights reserved.
 */

#include <stdio.h>
#include <errno.h>
#include <sys/types.h>      /* open() */
#include <sys/stat.h>
#include <fcntl.h>
#include <unistd.h>         /* read(), write() */
#include <string.h>         /* memset(), strlen() */
#include <strings.h>        /* bzero() */
#include <openssl/evp.h>
#include <openssl/err.h>
#include <openssl/blowfish.h>
#include "myopenssl.h"

/* sizes of chunks this program works on */
#define MAXMSGSZ   1024
#define MAXOUTSZ   (MAXMSGSZ+IVLEN)

/* A simple encryption and decryption program */
int main(int argc, char *argv[])
{
  size_t     inlen;                   /* length of input plain text */
  size_t     outlen = 0;              /* length of output cipher text */
  size_t     textlen;                 /* length of decrypted text */
  int        ret;
  struct cipher     cipher;           /* cipher to be used */

  char  *inmsg;                       /* pointer to original input message */
  unsigned char  outbuf[MAXOUTSZ];    /* buffer for encrypted message */
  char  plaintext[MAXMSGSZ+1];        /* buffer for decrypted message */

  /* User must enter the name of an algorithm and a message to be encrypted */
  if (argc < 3)
  {
    fprintf(stdout, "Usage: %s algorithm message \n", argv[0]);
    return(-1);
  }

  /* Check to make sure the input message is not too large */
  inmsg = argv[2];
  inlen = strlen(inmsg);
  if (inlen > MAXMSGSZ)
  {
    fprintf(stderr, "Error: input message is too long, max size=%u\n",
      MAXMSGSZ);
    return(-2);
  }
  fprintf(stdout, "Plain text=%s\n", inmsg);
```

```
/* Fill in the name, key and IV for the cipher to be used */
strcpy(cipher.name, argv[1]);
strcpy((char *)cipher.key, DEFAULT_KEY);
strcpy((char *)cipher.iv, DEFAULT_IV);

/* Encrypt the message */
bzero(outbuf, MAXOUTSZ);
ret = myencrypt1(inmsg, inlen, outbuf, &outlen, &cipher);
if (ret != 0)
{
  fprintf(stderr, "Error: main(), myencrypt1() failed, ret=%d\n", ret);
  return(ret);
}
print_cipher_text(outbuf, outlen);

/* Decrypt the message */
ret = mydecrypt1(outbuf, outlen, plaintext, &textlen, &cipher);
if (ret != 0)
{
  fprintf(stderr, "Error: main(), mydecrypt1() failed, ret=%d\n", ret);
  return(ret);
}
plaintext[textlen] = '\0';
fprintf(stdout, "Decrypted message=%s\n", plaintext);

/* Compare the decrypted output with the original input message */
if (!strcmp(inmsg, plaintext))
  fprintf(stdout, "The encryption and decryption have succeeded.\n");
else
  fprintf(stdout, "The encryption and decryption have failed.\n");

return(0);
}
```

Figure 15-10 shows another example program which encrypts and decrypts a very big message such as the contents of an entire file. It handles files of arbitrary length. In this example, the EVP_EncryptUpdate() and EVP_DecryptUpdate() functions are called in a loop until the entire file is encrypted or decrypted, respectively. After that, EVP_EncryptFinal_ex() or EVP_DecryptFinal_ex() is called only once to wrap up the encryption or decryption process. This call encrypts or decrypts the last portion of the input that is left over.

The encryption/decryption algorithm used is des-ede3-cbc. Putting input clear text (just a random text) in the file named 'encindata', which you can create yourself, below are the commands to run to test this program:

  $ ./enc_des_ede3_cbc encindata encoutdata1 encoutdata2

  $ diff encindata encoutdata2

If the program works correctly, the original clear text input file encindata should be identical to the decrypted output file encoutdata2.

The program encrypts the input text messages stored in file 'encindata'
and writes the encrypted result in file 'encoutdata1'. It then reads
the contents from file 'encoutdata1', decrypts it and writes the
output in file 'encoutdata2'. As you can see, the decrypted output
is exactly the same as the original clear text.

Figure 15-10 Encrypt/decrypt an entire file -- enc_des_ede3_cbc.c

```c
/*
 * This program encrypts the contents of a file and writes the encrypted
 * output to another file. It then reads the output file of the encryption,
 * decrypts it and writes the decrypted plain text to a third file.
 * If the third file is identical to the first, then the encryption and
 * decryption have succeeded.
 * The algorithm used here is des-ede3-cbc.
 * Authored by Mr. Jin-Jwei Chen.
 * Copyright (c) 2014-2016, 2019-2023 Mr. Jin-Jwei Chen. All rights reserved.
 */

#include <stdio.h>
#include <errno.h>
#include <sys/types.h>       /* open() */
#include <sys/stat.h>
#include <fcntl.h>
#include <unistd.h>          /* read(), write() */
#include <string.h>          /* memset(), strlen() */
#include <strings.h>         /* bzero() */
#include <openssl/evp.h>
#include <openssl/err.h>
#include <openssl/blowfish.h>

/* Note: KEYLEN and IVLEN vary from one algorithm to another */
#define IVLEN     8          /* length of IV (number of bytes) */
#define KEYLEN    16         /* key length (number of bytes) */

/* sizes of chunks this program works on */
#define INSIZE 1024
#define OUTSIZE (INSIZE+IVLEN)

/* These are shared by the encryption and decryption. */
unsigned char iv[IVLEN+1] = "00000001";
unsigned char key[KEYLEN+1] = "Axy3pzLk%8q#0)yH";

#define MYALGRM  "des-ede3-cbc"

/* clean up before return in case of error */
#define ERROR_RTN(n) \
  if (ctx != NULL) EVP_CIPHER_CTX_free(ctx); \
  if (infd) close(infd); \
  if (outfd) close(outfd); \
  return(n);

/*
 * Encrypt the contents of the input file specified by 'infname' and
 * write the encrypted output (i.e. the cipher text) to the output file
 * specified by the 'outfname' parameter.
```

1110

```
 */
int myencryptf(char *infname, char *outfname)
{
  EVP_CIPHER_CTX *ctx = NULL;           /* cipher context */
  ssize_t  inlen, outbytes;             /* bytes read or written */
  int      outlen;                      /* length of output cipher text */
  int      infd=0, outfd=0;             /* file descriptors */
  int      ret;
  unsigned char  inbuf[INSIZE];
  unsigned char  outbuf[OUTSIZE];
  const EVP_CIPHER *cipher = NULL;

  if (infname == NULL || outfname == NULL || infname == outfname)
    return(EINVAL);

  /* Open the input file */
  infd = open(infname, O_RDONLY);
  if (infd == -1)
  {
    fprintf(stderr, "Error: myencryptf() failed to open input file %s, errno=%d\n
",
      infname, errno);
    return(-1);
  }

  /* Open the output file */
  outfd = open(outfname, O_WRONLY|O_CREAT|O_TRUNC, 0640);
  if (outfd == -1)
  {
    fprintf(stderr, "Error: myencryptf() failed to open output file %s, errno=%d\
n"
      , outfname, errno);
    close(infd);
    return(-2);
  }

  /* Create a cipher context */
  ctx = EVP_CIPHER_CTX_new();
  if (ctx == NULL)
  {
    fprintf(stderr, "Error: myencryptf(), EVP_CIPHER_CTX_new() failed\n");
    ERROR_RTN(-3);
  }

  /* Get the algorithm */
  cipher = EVP_get_cipherbyname(MYALGRM);
  if (cipher == NULL)
  {
    fprintf(stderr, "Error: myencryptf(), EVP_get_cipherbyname() failed\n");
    ERROR_RTN(-4);
  }

  /* Set up the cipher context with a specific cipher algorithm */
  ret = EVP_EncryptInit_ex(ctx, cipher, NULL, key, iv);
  if (!ret)
  {
```

```
      fprintf(stderr, "Error: myencryptf(), EVP_EncryptInit_ex() failed\n");
      ERROR_RTN(-5);
   }

   /* Read contents of the entire file and encrypt it chunk by chunk */
   do
   {
     bzero (inbuf, INSIZE);
     /* Read next chunk from the input file */
     inlen = read(infd, inbuf, INSIZE);
     if (inlen <= 0)
     {
       if (inlen < 0)
       {
         fprintf(stderr, "Error: myencryptf() failed to read input file %s, "
           "errno=%d\n", infname, errno);
         ERROR_RTN(-6);
       }
       else
         break;
     }

     /* Encrypt this current chunk */
     bzero (outbuf, OUTSIZE);
     outlen = 0;
     if (EVP_EncryptUpdate(ctx, outbuf, &outlen, inbuf, inlen) != 1)
     {
       fprintf(stderr, "Error: myencryptf(), EVP_EncryptUpdate() failed\n");
       ERROR_RTN(-7);
     }

     /* Write encrypted chunk to the output file */
     if (outlen > 0)
     {
       outbytes = write(outfd, outbuf, outlen);
       if (outbytes < outlen)
       {
         if (outbytes < 0)
           fprintf(stderr, "Error: myencryptf() failed to write output file %s, "
             "errno=%d\n", outfname, errno);
         else
           fprintf(stderr, "Error: myencryptf() failed to write output file %s, "
             "only %ld out of %d were written\n", outfname, outbytes, outlen);
         ERROR_RTN(-8);
       }
     }

   } while (1);

   /* Wrap up the encryption by handling the last remaining part */
   bzero (outbuf, OUTSIZE);
   outlen = 0;
   if (EVP_EncryptFinal_ex(ctx, outbuf, &outlen) != 1)
   {
     fprintf(stderr, "Error: myencryptf(), EVP_EncryptFinal_ex() failed\n");
     ERROR_RTN(-9);
```

```
   }

   /* Write the last encrypted chunk to the output file */
   if (outlen > 0)
   {
     outbytes = write(outfd, outbuf, outlen);
     if (outbytes < outlen)
     {
       if (outbytes < 0)
         fprintf(stderr, "Error: myencryptf() failed to write output file %s, "
           "errno=%d\n", outfname, errno);
       else
         fprintf(stderr, "Error: myencryptf() failed to write output file %s, "
           "only %ld out of %d were written\n", outfname, outbytes, outlen);
       ERROR_RTN(-10);
     }
   }

   EVP_CIPHER_CTX_free(ctx);

   return(0);
}

/*
 * Decrypt the contents of the input file specified by 'infname' and
 * write the decrypted output (i.e. the plain text) to the output file
 * specified by 'outfname' parameter.
 */
int decrypt(char *infname, char *outfname)
{
   EVP_CIPHER_CTX *ctx = NULL;        /* cipher context */
   ssize_t  inlen, outbytes;          /* bytes read or written */
   int      outlen;                   /* length of output cipher text */
   int      infd=0, outfd=0;          /* file descriptors */
   int      ret;
   unsigned char  inbuf[INSIZE];
   unsigned char  outbuf[OUTSIZE];
   EVP_CIPHER *cipher = NULL;

   if (infname == NULL || outfname == NULL || infname == outfname)
     return(EINVAL);

   /* Open the input file */
   infd = open(infname, O_RDONLY);
   if (infd == -1)
   {
     fprintf(stderr, "Error: decrypt() failed to open input file %s, errno=%d\n",
       infname, errno);
     return(-1);
   }

   /* Open the output file */
   outfd = open(outfname, O_WRONLY|O_CREAT|O_TRUNC, 0640);
   if (outfd == -1)
   {
     fprintf(stderr, "Error: decrypt() failed to open output file %s, errno=%d\n"
```

```
             , outfname, errno);
    close(infd);
    return(-2);
}


/* Create a cipher context */
ctx = EVP_CIPHER_CTX_new();
if (ctx == NULL)
{
    fprintf(stderr, "Error: decrypt(), EVP_CIPHER_CTX_new() failed\n");
    ERROR_RTN(-3);
}


/* Fetch the algorithm */
cipher = EVP_CIPHER_fetch(NULL, MYALGRM, NULL);
if (cipher == NULL)
{
    fprintf(stderr, "Error: decrypt(), EVP_CIPHER_fetch() failed\n");
    ERROR_RTN(-4);
}


/* Set up the cipher context with a specific cipher algorithm */
ret = EVP_DecryptInit_ex(ctx, cipher, NULL, key, iv);
if (!ret)
{
    fprintf(stderr, "Error: decrypt(), EVP_DecryptInit_ex() failed\n");
    ERROR_RTN(-5);
}


/* Read contents of the entire file and decrypt it chunk by chunk */
do
{
    bzero (inbuf, INSIZE);
    /* Read next chunk from the input file */
    inlen = read(infd, inbuf, INSIZE);
    if (inlen <= 0)
    {
        if (inlen < 0)
        {
            fprintf(stderr, "Error: decrypt() failed to read input file %s, "
                "errno=%d\n", infname, errno);
            ERROR_RTN(-6);
        }
        else
            break;
    }


    /* Decrypt this current chunk */
    bzero (outbuf, OUTSIZE);
    outlen = 0;
    if (EVP_DecryptUpdate(ctx, outbuf, &outlen, inbuf, inlen) != 1)
    {
        fprintf(stderr, "Error: decrypt(), EVP_DecryptUpdate() failed\n");
        ERROR_RTN(-7);
    }
```

```
    /* Write decrypted chunk to the output file */
    if (outlen > 0)
    {
      outbytes = write(outfd, outbuf, outlen);
      if (outbytes < outlen)
      {
        if (outbytes < 0)
          fprintf(stderr, "Error: decrypt() failed to write output file %s, "
            "errno=%d\n", outfname, errno);
        else
          fprintf(stderr, "Error: decrypt() failed to write output file %s, "
            "only %ld out of %d were written\n", outfname, outbytes, outlen);
        ERROR_RTN(-8);
      }
    }

  } while (1);

  /* Wrap up the decryption by handling the last remaining part */
  bzero (outbuf, OUTSIZE);
  outlen = 0;
  if (EVP_DecryptFinal_ex(ctx, outbuf, &outlen) != 1)
  {
    fprintf(stderr, "Error: decrypt(), EVP_DecryptFinal_ex() failed\n");
    ERROR_RTN(-8);
  }

  /* Write the last decrypted chunk to the output file */
  if (outlen > 0)
  {
    outbytes = write(outfd, outbuf, outlen);
    if (outbytes < outlen)
    {
      if (outbytes < 0)
        fprintf(stderr, "Error: decrypt() failed to write output file %s, "
          "errno=%d\n", outfname, errno);
      else
        fprintf(stderr, "Error: decrypt() failed to write output file %s, "
          "only %ld out of %d were written\n", outfname, outbytes, outlen);
      ERROR_RTN(-9);
    }
  }

  EVP_CIPHER_CTX_free(ctx);

  return(0);
}


/* A simple encryption and decryption program */
int main(int argc, char *argv[])
{
  int       outlen = 0;              /* length of output cipher text */
  int       ret;

  char      *infname = "encindata";
```

```
char     *outfname1 = "encoutdata1";
char     *outfname2 = "encoutdata2";

/* Get the names of input and output files from user, if any */
if (argc < 4)
{
  fprintf(stderr, "Usage: %s infile outfile1 outfile2\n", argv[0]);
  return(-1);
}
if (argc > 1) infname = argv[1];
if (argc > 2) outfname1 = argv[2];
if (argc > 3) outfname2 = argv[3];

/* Encrypt the message */
ret = myencryptf(infname, outfname1);
if (ret != 0)
{
  fprintf(stderr, "Error: main(), myencryptf() failed, ret=%d\n", ret);
  return(ret);
}

/* Decrypt the message */
ret = decrypt(outfname1, outfname2);
if (ret != 0)
{
  fprintf(stderr, "Error: main(), decrypt() failed, ret=%d\n", ret);
  return(ret);
}

return(0);
}
```

15-4-5-1-2 Using Same APIs for Encryption and Decryption

As we mentioned above, the second approach to doing encryption and decryption using OpenSSL is to use exactly the same set of APIs for both encryption and decryption. Below are the functions to use:

Encryption or Decryption

```
int EVP_CipherInit_ex(EVP_CIPHER_CTX *ctx, const EVP_CIPHER *type,
    ENGINE *impl, unsigned char *key, unsigned char *iv, int enc);
int EVP_CipherUpdate(EVP_CIPHER_CTX *ctx, unsigned char *out,
    int *outl, unsigned char *in, int inl);
int EVP_CipherFinal_ex(EVP_CIPHER_CTX *ctx, unsigned char *outm,
    int *outl);
```

Since exactly the same set of functions is used, to distinguish between the encryption and decryption operations, you set different values in the 'enc' parameter (the last one) when your program calls the EVP_CipherInit_ex() function. A value of 1 in the enc parameter means encryption and 0 means decryption. Setting the value to -1 means the value of this parameter remains unchanged from the previous call to this function.

As you might have noticed, these APIs are almost identical to those
in the first approach. The differences are the word Encrypt or Decrypt in
the first set of APIs is replaced with Cipher and the EVP_CipherInit_ex()
function has one additional parameter (enc) at end.

Figure 15-11 is a program example showing how to do encryption and decryption
using this second approach; that is, using EVP_CipherInit_ex(),
EVP_CipherUpdate() and EVP_CipherFinal_ex() APIs.

Again, the myencrypt2() and mydecrypt2() utility functions used by the
enc_evp2 program are defined in mycryptolib.c which is listed in Figure
15-39(b) at the end of this chapter. These two functions invoke the
EVP_CipherXXX() set of APIs to perform the encryption and decryption tasks.

Please note that unlike other functions, the EVP_CipherFinal_ex() function
used in mydecrypt2() returns 0 for success instead of 1 when an algorithm
in GCM mode is used. For instance, aes-nnn-gcm, aria-nnn-gcm, and so on.
For the enc_evp2 example program to run successfully on these algorithms,
you need to modify mycryptolib.c and check return code 0 for success instead.
This inconsistent behavior exists in OpenSSL 1.0.2, 1.1.1g, 3.0.0 and up to
at least 3.3.0.

Below is a sample output from running the program:

```
$ ./enc_evp2 aes-256-cbc "Have a wonderful summer."
Plain text=Have a wonderful summer.
Cipher text=0x06c2bb740fa2f64ff6a83ceb34d228195f887c524bed5b7ce89170980c06d73f
Decrypted message=Have a wonderful summer.
The encryption and decryption have succeeded.
```

Figure 15-11 Using same APIs for encryption and decryption - enc_evp2.c

```
/*
 * This program encrypts a message given by the user using a cipher algorithm
 * chosen by the user and then decrypts the envrypted message.
 * This single program can encrypt and decrypt using different cipher algorithms.
 * The cipher algorithm used is specified by the user on the command line
 * by providing a name like bf-cbc, aes-256-cbc or des-ede3-ofb.
 * Run the 'openssl ?' command to get the list of cipher algorithms available.
 * This example uses the same set of APIs for both encryption and decryption:
 *   EVP_CipherInit_ex(), EVP_CipherUpdate() and EVP_CipherFinal_ex().
 * Authored by Mr. Jin-Jwei Chen.
 * Copyright (c) 2016-2017, 2019-2020 Mr. Jin-Jwei Chen. All rights reserved.
 */

#include <stdio.h>
#include <errno.h>
#include <sys/types.h>      /* open() */
#include <sys/stat.h>
#include <fcntl.h>
#include <unistd.h>         /* read(), write() */
#include <string.h>         /* memset(), strlen() */
#include <strings.h>        /* bzero() */
#include <openssl/evp.h>
#include <openssl/err.h>
#include <openssl/blowfish.h>
```

```c
#include "myopenssl.h"

#define  OPENSSL_SUCCESS    1     /* Openssl functions return 1 as success */

/* sizes of chunks this program works on */
#define MAXMSGSZ  1024
#define MAXOUTSZ   (MAXMSGSZ+IVLEN)

/* A simple encryption and decryption program */
int main(int argc, char *argv[])
{
  size_t      inlen;                /* length of input plain text */
  size_t      outlen = 0;           /* length of output cipher text */
  size_t      textlen;              /* length of decrypted text */
  int         ret;

  struct cipher  cipher;            /* cipher algorithm */
  char           *cipher_name;      /* string name of the cipher algorithm */

  char   *inmsg;                    /* pointer to original input message */
  unsigned char  outbuf[MAXOUTSZ];       /* buffer for encrypted message */
  char           plaintext[MAXMSGSZ+1];  /* buffer for decrypted message */

  /* User must enter the name of an algorithm and a message to be encrypted */
  if (argc < 3)
  {
    fprintf(stdout, "Usage: %s algorithm message \n", argv[0]);
    return(-1);
  }

  /* Check to make sure the input message is not too large */
  cipher_name = argv[1];
  inmsg = argv[2];
  inlen = strlen(inmsg);
  if (inlen > MAXMSGSZ)
  {
    fprintf(stderr, "Error: input message is too long, max size=%u\n",
      MAXMSGSZ);
    return(-2);
  }
  fprintf(stdout, "Plain text=%s\n", inmsg);

  strcpy(cipher.name, cipher_name);
  strcpy((char *)cipher.key, DEFAULT_KEY2);
  strcpy((char *)cipher.iv, DEFAULT_IV2);

  /* Encrypt the message */
  bzero(outbuf, MAXOUTSZ);
  ret = myencrypt2(inmsg, inlen, outbuf, &outlen, &cipher);
  if (ret != 0)
  {
    fprintf(stderr, "Error: main(), encrypt() failed, ret=%d\n", ret);
    return(ret);
  }
  print_cipher_text(outbuf, outlen);
```

```
/* Decrypt the message */
ret = mydecrypt2(outbuf, outlen, plaintext, &textlen, &cipher);
if (ret != 0)
{
   fprintf(stderr, "Error: main(), mydecrypt2() failed, ret=%d\n", ret);
   return(ret);
}
plaintext[textlen] = '\0';
fprintf(stdout, "Decrypted message=%s\n", plaintext);

/* Compare the decrypted output with the original input message */
if (!strcmp(inmsg, plaintext))
   fprintf(stdout, "The encryption and decryption have succeeded.\n");
else
   fprintf(stdout, "The encryption and decryption have failed.\n");

   return(0);
}
```

15-4-5-1-3 Summary

Main Generic OpenSSL Functions for Encryption and Decryption

In summary, below are the main APIs a C program can call to do encryption
and decryption using OpenSSL.

Init:

EVP_CIPHER_CTX_new()

Encrypt:

old: EVP_EncryptInit(),   EVP_EncryptUpdate(), EVP_EncryptFinal()
new: EVP_EncryptInit_ex(), EVP_EncryptUpdate(), EVP_EncryptFinal_ex()
common: EVP_CipherInit_ex(), EVP_CipherUpdate(), EVP_CipherFinal_ex()

Decrypt:

old: EVP_DecryptInit(),   EVP_DecryptUpdate(), EVP_DecryptFinal()
new: EVP_DecryptInit_ex(), EVP_DecryptUpdate(), EVP_DecryptFinal_ex()
common: EVP_CipherInit_ex(), EVP_CipherUpdate(), EVP_CipherFinal_ex()

At End:

EVP_CIPHER_CTX_free(ctx)
or EVP_CIPHER_CTX_reset() if to repeat and reuse.

Note that EVP_EncryptInit_ex(), EVP_EncryptUpdate() and EVP_EncryptFinal_ex()
return 1 for success and 0 for failure. So are corresponding EVP_DecryptXXX()
and EVP_CipherXXX() APIs. This return code convention is exactly opposite
of traditional Unix/Linux which typically returns 0 for success.

15-4-5-2 Encrypting Client-Server Communications

Figure 15-12 shows a pair of client and server programs (tcpsrvenc1.c and

tcpclntenc1.c) that exchange messages using encryption.
This example invokes our library function myencrypt1() for encryption
and mydecrypt1() for decryption. These two functions employ the OpenSSL
EVP_EncryptXXX() functions for encryption and EVP_DecryptXXX() functions for
decryption.

Messages sent by the client program are encrypted before they are sent.
They are deciphered by the server program after being received by the server.
The cipher suite used is described by the cipher structure.
To use a different cipher suite, just change the cipher.name. Cipher.key and
cipher.iv may also need to be changed to use different key and IV.
To further strengthen security in real applications, you may also want to
change the IV value for each message.

Please note that many example programs in this chapter use our own networking
library functions, for instance, connect_to_server(). They are defined in
netlib.c, which is listed in Figure 15-38(b).

Figure 15-12 Encrypted Client-Server Communication using different APIs
for encryption and decryption (tcpsrvenc1.c and tcpclntenc1.c)

(a) tcpsrvenc1.c

```c
/*
 * Demonstrating secrecy in network communications (myencrypt1 and mydecrypt1).
 * This is a TCP server program which gets a request message from a client
 * and sends back a reply. Both request messages and replies are all encrypted.
 * Incoming request messages and outgoing reply messages are all encrypted.
 * Copyright (c) 2015, 2016, 2020 Mr. Jin-Jwei Chen. All rights reserved.
 */

#include <stdio.h>
#include <errno.h>
#include <sys/types.h>
#include <sys/socket.h>
#include <netinet/in.h>     /* protocols such as IPPROTO_TCP, ... */
#include <string.h>         /* memset(), strlen() */
#include <stdlib.h>         /* atoi() */
#include <openssl/evp.h>
#include <openssl/err.h>
#include "myopenssl.h"
#include "netlib.h"

int main(int argc, char *argv[])
{
  int          sfd;                      /* file descriptor of the listener socket */
  in_port_t    portnum = SRVPORT;        /* port number this server listens on */
  int          portnum_in = 0;           /* port number specified by user */
  struct sockaddr_in    srvaddr;         /* IPv4 socket address structure */
  struct sockaddr_in6   srvaddr6;        /* IPv6 socket address structure */
  struct sockaddr_in6   clntaddr6;       /* client socket address */
  socklen_t             clntaddr6sz = sizeof(clntaddr6);
  int          newsock;                  /* file descriptor of client data socket */
  int          ipv6 = 0;
  int          ret;
  char         reqmsg[MAXREQSZ];    /* request message buffer */
```

```
char        reply[MAXRPLYSZ];      /* buffer for server reply message */
size_t      reqmsgsz;              /* size of client request message */
size_t      replysz;               /* size of server reply message */
size_t      insize;                /* size of encrypted request message */
size_t      outsz;                 /* size of encrypted reply message */
int         done;                  /* done with current client */
int         msgcnt;                /* count of messages from a client */
unsigned char  inbuf[MAXREQSZ];    /* input buffer */
unsigned char  outbuf[MAXRPLYSZ];  /* output buffer */
struct cipher  cipher;             /* cipher algorithm */


/* Get the server port number from user, if any */
if (argc > 1)
{
  if (argv[1][0] == '?')
  {
    fprintf(stderr, "Usage: %s [server_port] [1 (use IPv6)][cipher]\n", argv[0]);
    return(0);
  }

  portnum_in = atoi(argv[1]);
  if (portnum_in <= 0)
  {
    fprintf(stderr, "Error: port number %s invalid\n", argv[1]);
    fprintf(stderr, "Usage: %s [server_port] [1 (use IPv6)][cipher]\n", argv[0]);
    return(-1);
  }
  else
    portnum = portnum_in;
}

/* Get the IPv6 switch from user, if any */
if (argc > 2)
{
  if (argv[2][0] == '1')
    ipv6 = 1;
  else if (argv[2][0] != '0')
  {
    fprintf(stderr, "Usage: %s [server_port] [1 (use IPv6)][cipher]\n", argv[0]);
    return(-2);
  }
}

/* Get the cipher name from user, if any */
if (argc > 3)
  strcpy(cipher.name, argv[3]);
else
  strcpy(cipher.name, DEFAULT_CIPHER);

strcpy((char *)cipher.key, DEFAULT_KEY);
strcpy((char *)cipher.iv, DEFAULT_IV);

fprintf(stdout, "TCP server listening at portnum=%u ipv6=%u cipher=%s\n",
  portnum, ipv6, cipher.name);

/* Create the server listener socket */
```

```
  if (ipv6)
     ret = new_bound_srv_endpt(&sfd, (struct sockaddr *)&srvaddr6, AF_INET6,
        portnum);
  else
     ret = new_bound_srv_endpt(&sfd, (struct sockaddr *)&srvaddr, AF_INET,
        portnum);

  if (ret != 0)
  {
     fprintf(stderr, "Error: new_bound_srv_endpt() failed, ret=%d\n", ret);
     return(-4);
  }

  /* Listen for incoming requests and send replies */
  do
  {
     /* Listen for next client's connect request */
     newsock = accept(sfd, (struct sockaddr *)&clntaddr6, &clntaddr6sz);
     if (newsock < 0)
     {
        fprintf(stderr, "Error: accept() failed, errno=%d\n", errno);
        continue;
     }

     fprintf(stdout, "\nServer got a client connection\n");

     /* Service this current client until done */
     done = 0;
     msgcnt = 1;
     do
     {
        /* Read the request message */
        insize = recv(newsock, inbuf, MAXREQSZ, 0);
        if (insize <= 0)
        {
           fprintf(stderr, "Error: recv() failed, insize=%lu\n", insize);
           break;
        }

        /* Decrypt the requested message */
        reqmsgsz = 0;
        ret = mydecrypt1(inbuf, insize, reqmsg, &reqmsgsz, &cipher);
        if (ret != 0)
        {
           fprintf(stderr, "Error: mydecrypt1() failed, ret=%d\n", ret);
           break;
        }

        reqmsg[reqmsgsz]='\0';
        fprintf(stdout, "Server received: %s\n", reqmsg);

        /* Set reply message */
        if ( !strcmp(reqmsg, BYE_MSG) )
        {
           done = 1;
           strcpy(reply, reqmsg);
```

```
    }
    else
      sprintf(reply, SRVREPLY2, msgcnt++);

    replysz = strlen(reply);

    /* Encrypt the reply message */
    outsz = 0;
    ret = myencrypt1(reply, replysz, outbuf, &outsz, &cipher);
    if (ret != 0)
    {
      fprintf(stderr, "Error: myencrypt1() failed, ret=%d\n", ret);
      break;
    }

    /* Send back an encrypted reply */
    ret = send(newsock, outbuf, outsz, 0);
    if (ret < 0)
      fprintf(stderr, "Error: send() failed to send a reply, errno=%d\n",
        errno);

  } while (!done);

  /* We can close the socket now. */
  close(newsock);

} while (1);
}
```

(b) tcpclntenc1.c

```
/*
 * Demonstrating secrecy in network communications (myencrypt1 and mydecrypt1).
 * This is a simple TCP client program which exchanges messages with
 * a TCP server with the messages encrypted.
 * Copyright (c) 2015, 2016, 2020 Mr. Jin-Jwei Chen. All rights reserved.
 */

#include <stdio.h>
#include <errno.h>
#include <sys/types.h>
#include <sys/socket.h>
#include <netinet/in.h>      /* protocols such as IPPROTO_TCP, ... */
#include <string.h>          /* memset(), strlen() */
#include <stdlib.h>          /* atoi(), malloc() */
#include <openssl/evp.h>
#include <openssl/err.h>
#include <openssl/blowfish.h>
#include "myopenssl.h"
#include "netlib.h"

#define FREEALL        \
    close(sfd);        \
    free(reqmsg);

int main(int argc, char *argv[])
```

1123

```
{
  int            ret;                    /* return value */
  int            sfd=0;                  /* socket file descriptor */
  unsigned char  outbuf[MAXREQSZ];       /* output buffer */
  unsigned char  inbuf[MAXRPLYSZ];       /* input buffer */
  char           replymsg[MAXRPLYSZ];    /* reply message from server */
  size_t         reqbufsz = MAXREQSZ;    /* size of client request buffer */
  char           *reqmsg=NULL;           /* pointer to request message buffer */
  size_t         reqmsgsz;               /* size of client request message */
  size_t         replysz;                /* size of server reply message */
  size_t         outsz;                  /* size of encrypted request message */
  size_t         insize;                 /* size of encrypted reply message */

  in_port_t      srvport = SRVPORT;      /* port number the server listens on */
  int            srvport_in = 0;         /* port number specified by user */
  char           *srvhost = "localhost"; /* name of server host */
  int            done = 0;               /* to end client */

  struct cipher  cipher;                 /* cipher algorithm */

  /* Get the server port number from user, if any */
  if (argc > 1)
  {
    if (argv[1][0] == '?')
    {
      fprintf(stderr, "Usage: %s [server_port_number][server_host][cipher]\n",
        argv[0]);
      return(0);
    }

    srvport_in = atoi(argv[1]);
    if (srvport_in <= 0)
    {
      fprintf(stderr, "Error: port number %s invalid\n", argv[1]);
      fprintf(stderr, "Usage: %s [server_port_number][server_host][cipher]\n",
        argv[0]);
      return(-1);
    }
    else
      srvport = srvport_in;
  }

  /* Get the name of the server host from user, if specified */
  if (argc > 2)
    srvhost = argv[2];

  /* Get the algorithm name from command line, if there is one */
  if (argc > 3)
    strcpy(cipher.name, argv[3]);
  else
    strcpy(cipher.name, DEFAULT_CIPHER);

  strcpy((char *)cipher.key, DEFAULT_KEY);
  strcpy((char *)cipher.iv, DEFAULT_IV);

  /* Allocate input buffer */
```

```
  reqmsg = malloc(MAXREQSZ);
  if (reqmsg == NULL)
  {
    fprintf(stderr, "Error: malloc() failed\n");
    return(-3);
  }

  /* Connect to the server */
  ret = connect_to_server(&sfd, srvhost, srvport);
  if (ret != 0)
  {
    fprintf(stderr, "Error: connect_to_server() failed, ret=%d\n", ret);
    if (sfd) close(sfd);
    free(reqmsg);
    return(-4);
  }

  /* Send a few messages to the server */
  do
  {
    fprintf(stdout, "Enter a message to send ('bye' to end): ");
    reqmsgsz = getline(&reqmsg, &reqbufsz, stdin);
    if (reqmsgsz == -1)
    {
      fprintf(stderr, "Error: getline() failed, ret=%lu\n", reqmsgsz);
      FREEALL
      return(-5);
    }

    /* Remove the newline character at end of input */
    reqmsg[--reqmsgsz] = '\0';

    /* Encrypt the message to be sent */
    ret = myencrypt1(reqmsg, reqmsgsz, outbuf, &outsz, &cipher);
    if (ret != 0)
    {
      fprintf(stderr, "Error: myencrypt1() failed, ret=%d\n", ret);
      FREEALL
      return(-6);
    }

    fprintf(stdout, "Send request:\n");
    print_cipher_text(outbuf, outsz);

    /* Send the encrypted message */
    ret = send_msg(sfd, (unsigned char *)outbuf, outsz, 0);
    if (ret != 0)
    {
      fprintf(stderr, "Error: send_msg() failed, ret=%d\n", ret);
      FREEALL
      return(-7);
    }

    /* Wait for server reply */
    memset((void *)inbuf, 0, MAXRPLYSZ);
    insize = 0;
```

```
    insize = recv(sfd, inbuf, MAXRPLYSZ, 0);
    if (insize <= 0)
    {
      fprintf(stderr, "Error: recv() failed to receive a reply from "
        "server, insize=%lu\n", insize);
      FREEALL
      return(-8);
    }

    /* Decrypt the server reply message */
    memset((void *)replymsg, 0, MAXRPLYSZ);
    replysz = 0;
    ret = mydecrypt1(inbuf, insize, replymsg, &replysz, &cipher);
    if (ret != 0)
    {
      fprintf(stderr, "Error: mydecrypt1() failed, ret=%d\n", ret);
      FREEALL
      return(-9);
    }

    replymsg[replysz]='\0';
    fprintf(stdout, "Got this reply: %s\n", replymsg);

    if (!strcmp(replymsg, reqmsg))
      done = 1;

  } while (!done);

  close(sfd);
  free(reqmsg);
  return(0);
}
```

Figure 15-13 shows a similar example using myencrypt2() function for encryption and mydecrypt2() for decryption. These two functions employ the EVP_CipherXXX() set of APIs, which use the same set of API calls for both encryption and decryption.

Figure 15-13 Encrypted Client-Server Communication using EVP_CipherXXX APIs (tcpsrvenc2.c and tcpclntenc2.c)

(a) tcpsrvenc2.c

```
/*
 * Demonstrating secrecy in network communications (myencrypt2 and mydecrypt2).
 * This is a TCP server program which gets a request message from a client
 * and sends back a reply. Both request messages and replies are all encrypted.
 * Incoming request messages and outgoing reply messages are all encrypted.
 * Copyright (c) 2015, 2016, 2020 Mr. Jin-Jwei Chen. All rights reserved.
 */

#include <stdio.h>
#include <errno.h>
#include <sys/types.h>
#include <sys/socket.h>
#include <netinet/in.h>    /* protocols such as IPPROTO_TCP, ... */
```

```c
#include <string.h>            /* memset(), strlen() */
#include <stdlib.h>            /* atoi() */
#include <openssl/evp.h>
#include <openssl/err.h>
#include "myopenssl.h"
#include "netlib.h"

int main(int argc, char *argv[])
{
  int          sfd;                        /* file descriptor of the listener socket */
  in_port_t  portnum = SRVPORT;          /* port number this server listens on */
  int          portnum_in = 0;             /* port number specified by user */
  struct sockaddr_in    srvaddr;           /* IPv4 socket address structure */
  struct sockaddr_in6   srvaddr6;          /* IPv6 socket address structure */
  struct sockaddr_in6   clntaddr6;         /* client socket address */
  socklen_t             clntaddr6sz = sizeof(clntaddr6);
  int          newsock;                    /* file descriptor of client data socket */
  int          ipv6 = 0;
  int          ret;
  char         reqmsg[MAXREQSZ];       /* request message buffer */
  char         reply[MAXRPLYSZ];       /* buffer for server reply message */
  size_t       reqmsgsz;               /* size of client request message */
  size_t       replysz;                /* size of server reply message */
  size_t       insize;                 /* size of encrypted request message */
  size_t       outsz;                  /* size of encrypted reply message */
  int          done;                   /* done with current client */
  int          msgcnt;                 /* count of messages from a client */
  unsigned char  inbuf[MAXREQSZ];      /* input buffer */
  unsigned char  outbuf[MAXRPLYSZ];    /* output buffer */
  struct cipher  cipher;               /* cipher algorithm */

  /* Get the server port number from user, if any */
  if (argc > 1)
  {
    if (argv[1][0] == '?')
    {
      fprintf(stderr, "Usage: %s [server_port] [1 (use IPv6)][cipher]\n", argv[0]);
      return(0);
    }

    portnum_in = atoi(argv[1]);
    if (portnum_in <= 0)
    {
      fprintf(stderr, "Error: port number %s invalid\n", argv[1]);
      fprintf(stderr, "Usage: %s [server_port] [1 (use IPv6)][cipher]\n", argv[0]);
      return(-1);
    }
    else
      portnum = portnum_in;
  }

  /* Get the IPv6 switch from user, if any */
  if (argc > 2)
  {
    if (argv[2][0] == '1')
      ipv6 = 1;
```

```
  else if (argv[2][0] != '0')
  {
    fprintf(stderr, "Usage: %s [server_port] [1 (use IPv6)][cipher]\n", argv[0]);
    return(-2);
  }
}

/* Get the cipher name from user, if any */
if (argc > 3)
  strcpy(cipher.name, argv[3]);
else
  strcpy(cipher.name, DEFAULT_CIPHER);

strcpy((char *)cipher.key, DEFAULT_KEY2);
strcpy((char *)cipher.iv, DEFAULT_IV2);

fprintf(stdout, "TCP server listening at portnum=%u ipv6=%u cipher=%s\n",
  portnum, ipv6, cipher.name);

/* Create the server listener socket */
if (ipv6)
  ret = new_bound_srv_endpt(&sfd, (struct sockaddr *)&srvaddr6, AF_INET6,
    portnum);
else
  ret = new_bound_srv_endpt(&sfd, (struct sockaddr *)&srvaddr, AF_INET,
    portnum);

if (ret != 0)
{
  fprintf(stderr, "Error: new_bound_srv_endpt() failed, ret=%d\n", ret);
  return(-4);
}

/* Listen for incoming requests and send replies */
do
{
  /* Listen for next client's connect request */
  newsock = accept(sfd, (struct sockaddr *)&clntaddr6, &clntaddr6sz);
  if (newsock < 0)
  {
    fprintf(stderr, "Error: accept() failed, errno=%d\n", errno);
    continue;
  }

  fprintf(stdout, "\nServer got a client connection\n");

  /* Service this current client until done */
  done = 0;
  msgcnt = 1;
  do
  {
    /* Read the request message */
    insize = recv(newsock, inbuf, MAXREQSZ, 0);
    if (insize <= 0)
    {
      fprintf(stderr, "Error: recv() failed, insize=%lu\n", insize);
```

```
        break;
    }

    /* Decrypt the requested message */
    reqmsgsz = 0;
    ret = mydecrypt2(inbuf, insize, reqmsg, &reqmsgsz, &cipher);
    if (ret != 0)
    {
      fprintf(stderr, "Error: mydecrypt2() failed, ret=%d\n", ret);
      break;
    }

    reqmsg[reqmsgsz]='\0';
    fprintf(stdout, "Server received: %s\n", reqmsg);

    /* Set reply message */
    if ( !strcmp(reqmsg, BYE_MSG) )
    {
      done = 1;
      strcpy(reply, reqmsg);
    }
    else
      sprintf(reply, SRVREPLY2, msgcnt++);

    replysz = strlen(reply);

    /* Encrypt the reply message */
    outsz = 0;
    ret = myencrypt2(reply, replysz, outbuf, &outsz, &cipher);
    if (ret != 0)
    {
      fprintf(stderr, "Error: myencrypt2() failed, ret=%d\n", ret);
      break;
    }

    /* Send back an encrypted reply */
    ret = send(newsock, outbuf, outsz, 0);
    if (ret < 0)
      fprintf(stderr, "Error: send() failed to send a reply, errno=%d\n",
        errno);

  } while (!done);

  /* We can close the socket now. */
  close(newsock);

 } while (1);
}
```

  (b) tcpclntenc2.c

```
/*
 * Demonstrating secrecy in network communications (myencrypt2 and mydecrypt2).
 * This is a simple TCP client program which exchanges messages with
 * a TCP server with the messages encrypted.
 * Copyright (c) 2015, 2016, 2020 Mr. Jin-Jwei Chen. All rights reserved.
```

```
*/

#include <stdio.h>
#include <errno.h>
#include <sys/types.h>
#include <sys/socket.h>
#include <netinet/in.h>        /* protocols such as IPPROTO_TCP, ... */
#include <string.h>            /* memset(), strlen() */
#include <stdlib.h>            /* atoi(), malloc() */
#include <openssl/evp.h>
#include <openssl/err.h>
#include <openssl/blowfish.h>
#include "myopenssl.h"
#include "netlib.h"

#define FREEALL        \
    close(sfd);        \
    free(reqmsg);

int main(int argc, char *argv[])
{
    int             ret;                    /* return value */
    int             sfd=0;                  /* socket file descriptor */
    unsigned char   outbuf[MAXREQSZ];       /* output buffer */
    unsigned char   inbuf[MAXRPLYSZ];       /* input buffer */
    char            replymsg[MAXRPLYSZ];    /* reply message from server */
    size_t          reqbufsz = MAXREQSZ;    /* size of client request buffer */
    char            *reqmsg=NULL;           /* pointer to request message buffer */
    size_t          reqmsgsz;               /* size of client request message */
    size_t          replysz;                /* size of server reply message */
    size_t          outsz;                  /* size of encrypted request message */
    size_t          insize;                 /* size of encrypted reply message */

    in_port_t       srvport = SRVPORT;      /* port number the server listens on */
    int             srvport_in = 0;         /* port number specified by user */
    char            *srvhost = "localhost"; /* name of server host */
    int             done = 0;               /* to end client */

    struct cipher   cipher;                 /* cipher algorithm */

    /* Get the server port number from user, if any */
    if (argc > 1)
    {
      if (argv[1][0] == '?')
      {
        fprintf(stderr, "Usage: %s [server_port_number][server_host][cipher]\n",
          argv[0]);
        return(0);
      }

      srvport_in = atoi(argv[1]);
      if (srvport_in <= 0)
      {
        fprintf(stderr, "Error: port number %s invalid\n", argv[1]);
        fprintf(stderr, "Usage: %s [server_port_number][server_host][cipher]\n",
          argv[0]);
```

```
        return(-1);
    }
    else
        srvport = srvport_in;
}

/* Get the name of the server host from user, if specified */
if (argc > 2)
    srvhost = argv[2];

/* Get the algorithm name from command line, if there is one */
if (argc > 3)
    strcpy(cipher.name, argv[3]);
else
    strcpy(cipher.name, DEFAULT_CIPHER);

strcpy((char *)cipher.key, DEFAULT_KEY2);
strcpy((char *)cipher.iv, DEFAULT_IV2);

/* Allocate input buffer */
reqmsg = malloc(MAXREQSZ);
if (reqmsg == NULL)
{
    fprintf(stderr, "Error: malloc() failed\n");
    return(-3);
}

/* Connect to the server */
ret = connect_to_server(&sfd, srvhost, srvport);
if (ret != 0)
{
    fprintf(stderr, "Error: connect_to_server() failed, ret=%d\n", ret);
    if (sfd) close(sfd);
    free(reqmsg);
    return(-4);
}

/* Send a few messages to the server */
do
{
    fprintf(stdout, "Enter a message to send ('bye' to end): ");
    reqmsgsz = getline(&reqmsg, &reqbufsz, stdin);
    if (reqmsgsz == -1)
    {
        fprintf(stderr, "Error: getline() failed, ret=%lu\n", reqmsgsz);
        FREEALL
        return(-5);
    }

    /* Remove the newline character at end of input */
    reqmsg[--reqmsgsz] = '\0';

    /* Encrypt the message to be sent */
    ret = myencrypt2(reqmsg, reqmsgsz, outbuf, &outsz, &cipher);
    if (ret != 0)
    {
```

```
      fprintf(stderr, "Error: myencrypt2() failed, ret=%d\n", ret);
      FREEALL
      return(-6);
    }

    fprintf(stdout, "Send request:\n");
    print_cipher_text(outbuf, outsz);

    /* Send the encrypted message */
    ret = send_msg(sfd, (unsigned char *)outbuf, outsz, 0);
    if (ret != 0)
    {
      fprintf(stderr, "Error: send_msg() failed, ret=%d\n", ret);
      FREEALL
      return(-7);
    }

    /* Wait for server reply */
    memset((void *)inbuf, 0, MAXRPLYSZ);
    insize = 0;
    insize = recv(sfd, inbuf, MAXRPLYSZ, 0);
    if (insize <= 0)
    {
      fprintf(stderr, "Error: recv() failed to receive a reply from "
          "server, insize=%lu\n", insize);
      FREEALL
      return(-8);
    }

    /* Decrypt the server reply message */
    memset((void *)replymsg, 0, MAXRPLYSZ);
    replysz = 0;
    ret = mydecrypt2(inbuf, insize, replymsg, &replysz, &cipher);
    if (ret != 0)
    {
      fprintf(stderr, "Error: mydecrypt2() failed, ret=%d\n", ret);
      FREEALL
      return(-9);
    }

    replymsg[replysz]='\0';
    fprintf(stdout, "Got this reply: %s\n", replymsg);

    if (!strcmp(replymsg, reqmsg))
      done = 1;

  } while (!done);

  close(sfd);
  free(reqmsg);
  return(0);
}
```

15-5 Message Authentication

Authentication is done in many places and in different forms in computer.

When you login to a computer as a particular user, you must enter a password. That's authentication. By entering the user's password, you prove to the system you are who you claim to be because you know the secret password.

When you run an application to access data in a database server, authentication is required too. Typically, it is done through username and password.

These are called **user authentication**. User authentication verifies that a user is really who he or she claims who he or she is. A user has to provide both a user name and that user's secret password in order to gain access to a computer or some data.

The applications mentioned above are all pre-known and set up in advance. Contrary to this, most applications over the Internet, for instance, electronic commerce transactions (getting on to Internet to make a purchase), are mostly not known in advance and cannot be set up ahead of time. In these applications, sharing a secret preset password between the user and the server is typically impossible. Thus, other means of authentication must be employed.

Computer network communications, such as traffic over the Internet, involve exchanging messages between two parties (often called end-points). In these situations, the two parties communicating often do not know each other, nor a pre-arranged setup can be done beforehand for them to share some secret. An example of this type of communication is that a client, which could be anyone from anywhere in this world, needs to communicate with a well-known server (e.g. some company's web site) to get something done, for instance, making a purchase over the Internet.
To achieve security, just protecting message integrity as we have discussed above in this chapter is not enough. Security issues include how do I know whom I'm talking to? How do I know the message is really from who it is supposed to be, not a hacker. Besides, there is also the issue of message authenticity. In fact, message authentication is very important, especially in an open environment like the Internet.

We discuss this issue in this section.

15-5-1 Message Authentication Code (MAC)

We discussed using message hash for data integrity in section 15-3. A potential problem of using hash for message integrity over the Internet is that an attacker could potentially intercept the communication and replace both the message and the hash and the message recipient would not be able to detect that security breach because the new hash would still match the replaced message's re-computed hash at the receiver end.

In order to solve this problem, message integrity needs to take another step up in the ladder by doing, for instance, message authentication code (MAC). To ensure the message really originates from the real sender,

not one from an attacker, sender authenticity or authentication is needed.
To provide message authentication, a message authentication code (MAC) is
used. Please note that MAC sometimes is also referred to as
message integrity check (**MIC**).

A **Message Authentication Code** (**MAC**) is a short piece of message fingerprint
information generated from an input message with a secret key using a
message hash function. Hence, a MAC is also known as a **keyed hash.**

The generation and verification of MAC are similar to those of hash.
The only main difference is that a key is used in the process, in both
generating and verifying the MAC, i.e. the keyed hash.

Note that the main difference between a message hash (which is for integrity)
and a MAC is that **a key is used in computing a MAC.** This key is secret and
it is shared between the message sender and receiver.
Since there is a secret key used in calculating the message hash,
presumably a hacker would not know the key and the afore-mentioned
attack of replacing both the message and hash would not succeed.
A hacker will be able to replace the original message. However, since it
does not know the secret key used in generating the message hash, it would
not be able to compute a correct replacement hash and use that.

Therefore, MAC is for message integrity but not just that.
It is actually one step up -- it's for **message authentication.**
It authenticates the origin of message. As long as the key used in computing
the MAC is not compromised and is known to only the message sender and
receiver, after the MAC is verified, the recipient can be sure that
the message is the original from the sender sharing the secret hash key.
The use of a shared secret key in computing the message hash (i.e. the
keyed hash) allows the authentication of the message origin or sender.

A MAC protects against message forgery by anyone who doesn't know the
secret key.

Assuming the secret key shared between the sender and receiver is not
compromised, when the recipient sees that the MAC it computes matches the
one it receives from the sender, it can be certain of two things:

  1. The message was not altered during transit (because the MAC agrees).
  2. The message comes from the sender. The key helps accomplish this.

MAC is used to verify both the data integrity of a received message and the
authenticity of the sender (origin authentication). Hence, it covers both
authentication and **message integrity** aspects of security.

Note that a message digest or fingerprint is computed and a shared secret
key is used in the computation in getting a MAC.

MAC functions are similar to cryptographic hash functions.

15-5-2 Keyed-Hash Message Authentication Code (HMAC)

Most widely used MACs are **keyed-Hash Message Authentication Code** (**HMAC**).
A HMAC is computed using a secret cryptographic key and a cryptographic hash

function (hence the 'H' in HMAC). The difference between MAC and HMAC is that HMAC always uses a cryptographic hash function in calculating the MAC. In other words, HMAC uses a keyless hash function and a cryptographic key to create a keyed hash function.

As with any MAC, HMAC verifies both data integrity and authenticity of a message.

Any cryptographic hash function can be used in computing an HMAC. The two most widely used cryptographic hash functions are the MD and SHA families. For instance, a HMAC calculated using the SHA-1 cryptographic hash function is named HMAC-SHA1 and one calculated using the MD-5 function is named HMAC-MD5.

The strength of a HMAC depends on the strength of the underlying hash function as well as the length of the secret key, especially the length of the secret key. Most attacks against HMACs are trying to uncover the secret key by brute force.

HMAC is used in the TLS (Transport Layer Security) standard. A variant of HMAC was also used in SSLv3. SSL requires every record being HMAC-ed first before it is encrypted.

You might ask how is the shared key used in HMAC computed?

In a simple communication between two programs, it can be preset so it's known to both parties.

In the Internet, for instance, when you access some web server using the HTTPS protocol, the HTTPS protocol actually deploys the SSL or TLS protocol. In SSL and TLS protocols, the two communicating parties go through a handshake phase to determine the shared key.

Note that MAC/HMAC uses a secret key shared between the sender and the recipient. Hence, it's symmetric cryptography. It does not use public key (i.e. asymmetric) cryptography.

In OpenSSL, HMAC functions are defined in libssl.so and they are referenced by functions in libcrypto.so.

How HMAC Hash is computed

To compute the hash of a message, a HMAC algorithm prepends a block of data to the message. This block contains 64 bytes of 0x36 XOR-ed with the shared secret. The result is hashed. The hash then is appended to another block of data which consists of a block of bytes 0x5C, again XOR-ed with the shared secret. This is hashed again to get the final hash.

How Is HMAC Verified?

The sender of a message computes the HMAC. It sends both the message and the HMAC to the recipient. After receiving the message, the recipient computes the HMAC using exactly the same algorithm and key as the sender did. The recipient compares the HMAC it receives from the sender with the HMAC it has computed independently. If the two HMACs match, then it knows that the message was not altered during transit and it must have come from the sender who knows the shared secret key.

Note that the sender and receiver both compute the HMAC independently using the same shared key and same cryptographic hash function.

An attacker could try to intercept the communication and replace both the message and the HMAC. However, assuming the shared key is not compromised, since the attacker does not know the key used in calculating the HMAC, when the recipient gets the altered message and computes a HMAC from it, that HMAC won't match the replaced HMAC from the attacker because the key used by the recipient is different from the one used by the attacker. The tampering is thus detected.

15-5-3 Programming Examples

Starting from version 3.0 and on, OpenSSL has deprecated its original APIs for HMAC, including HMAC_Init_ex(), HMAC_Update(), HMAC_Final(), HMAC_CTX_new() and HMAC_CTX_free(). In the new versions, EVP_MAC_xxx() APIs are recommended.

Figure 15-14 shows an example program which demonstrates how to compute the HMAC of a big message, which is the contents of a whole file, using OpenSSL.

As you can see from the get_HMAC() function, the major steps are the following:

(1) Fetch the MAC algorithm

  mac = EVP_MAC_fetch(NULL, macAlgrm, NULL);

(2) Creates a HMAC context

  hmac_ctx = EVP_MAC_CTX_new(mac);

(3) Set up the HMAC context with the hash function and key

  ret = EVP_MAC_init(hmac_ctx, key, strlen((char *)key), params);

(4) Compute message authentication code of current input chunk

  EVP_MAC_update(hmac_ctx, inbuf, inlen);

  This step needs to be executed for each chunk of the message.

(5) Wrap up the calculation by handling the last remaining part

  EVP_MAC_final(hmac_ctx, hash, hashlen, EVP_MAX_MD_SIZE);

(6) Free up the context

  EVP_MAC_CTX_free(hmac_ctx);

These functions are described below.

EVP_MAC_fetch() returns a pointer to a newly fetched EVP_MAC which represents a MAC algorithm of the type specified by the macAlgrm parameter, or NULL if allocation failed. This space must be freed after use.

EVP_MAC_CTX_new(mac) creates a new context for the MAC type mac. The memory occupied by the returned pointer must be freed too after use.

EVP_MAC_init() sets up the underlying context hmac_ctx with information given via the key and params arguments. It should be called before EVP_MAC_update() and EVP_MAC_final().

EVP_MAC_update() adds inlen bytes from inbuf to the MAC input.

EVP_MAC_final() does the final computation and stores the result in the memory pointed at by hash whose size is indicated by hashlen on input. The actual number of bytes of the hash value being returned is written into the hashlen parameter on return.

If the parameter hash is NULL or hashlen is too small, then no HMAC computation is done. To dynamically figure out the actual buffer size and allocate space for it, simply make the call with hash being NULL and the size will be returned in hashlen.

Below is a sample output from running hmac_file. The program assumes the message is contained in the file named 'hmacdatain'.

```
$ ./hmac_file sha256
cipher=aes-256-cbc key=!12*4i6(8#a-c+e@0123456789012345 keylen=32 MAC=hmac
HMAC value of the file hmacdatain is:
0x1e10c2627628b7bd4f567bf6d643b0fc281805c16d52ddd9a645e67983b8c06d
$ ./hmac_file sha512
cipher=aes-256-cbc key=!12*4i6(8#a-c+e@0123456789012345 keylen=32 MAC=hmac
HMAC value of the file hmacdatain is:
```

0xbb0e97f62ec3bdc1048e72f4dec351ba7502f965c91ce3a982e15c2623f77a8247fc7f9553ba0fd9589
c6a5f581eb1b9400bf00008a4446b479b67081fa36cb3

The example program hmac_file uses the print_binary_buf() function which is defined in netlib.c displayed in Figure 15-38(b) at end of the chapter. Many example programs in this chapter make use of our own networking library functions in netlib.c.

Figure 15-14 HMAC code example -- hmac_file.c

```
/*
 * This program computes the HMAC value of a big message stored in a file.
 * The entire contents of a file are regarded as a message.
 * Authored by Mr. Jin-Jwei Chen.
 * Copyright (c) 2014-2016, 2020, 2023 Mr. Jin-Jwei Chen. All rights reserved.
 */

#include <stdio.h>
#include <errno.h>
#include <sys/types.h>      /* open() */
#include <sys/stat.h>
#include <fcntl.h>
#include <unistd.h>         /* read(), write() */
```

```c
#include <string.h>            /* memset(), strlen() */
#include <strings.h>           /* bzero() */
#include <openssl/evp.h>
#include <openssl/hmac.h>
#include <openssl/err.h>
#include <openssl/params.h>
#include "myopenssl.h"
#include "netlib.h"

/* Get error */
#define  GET_ERROR  \
    error = ERR_get_error(); \
    ERR_error_string_n(error, errstr, ERRBUFLEN);

/* Free all resources */
#define  FREEALL  \
  EVP_MAC_CTX_free(hmac_ctx); \
  EVP_MAC_free(mac);


/*
 * Compute the HMAC value of the contents of a file using the cryptographic
 * hash function specified by the 'hashfunc_name' parameter.
 * The input file is specified by the 'infname' parameter.
 * The key used in computing the HMAC is given by the 'key' parameter.
 * The resulting HMAC value is returned in the 'hash' parameter.
 * This output buffer must be at least EVP_MAX_MD_SIZE bytes long.
 * The length of the hash value is returned in the 'hashlen' parameter.
 * The input parameter macAlgrm selects a MAC algorithm to use.
 * Supported macAlgrm includes: HMAC, GMAC and CMAC.
 * Cipher is optional.
 */
int get_HMAC(char *infname, char *hashfunc_name, const char *key,
    char *macAlgrm, unsigned char *hash, size_t *hashlen, char *cipher)
{
  int           infd=0;          /* input file descriptors */
  ssize_t       inlen;           /* bytes read */
  int           ret;
  unsigned char inbuf[INSIZE];   /* input buffer */
  EVP_MAC_CTX   *hmac_ctx;       /* HMAC context */
  EVP_MAC       *mac;            /* MAC object */

  unsigned long error = 0L;            /* error code */
  char          errstr[ERRBUFLEN];     /* error string */

  /* Set up OSSL params. 'digest' is required but cipher is not . */
  OSSL_PARAM params[] = {
    OSSL_PARAM_utf8_string("digest", hashfunc_name, sizeof(hashfunc_name)),
    OSSL_PARAM_utf8_string("cipher", cipher, sizeof(cipher)),
    OSSL_PARAM_END
  };

  if (infname == NULL || hashfunc_name == NULL || key == NULL
      || macAlgrm == NULL || hash == NULL || hashlen == NULL || cipher == NULL)
    return(EINVAL);

  /* Fetch the MAC algorithm. */
```

1138

```
mac = EVP_MAC_fetch(NULL, macAlgrm, NULL);
if (mac == NULL)
{
  GET_ERROR
  fprintf(stderr, "Error: get_HMAC(), EVP_MAC_fetch() failed,"
    " error=%lu\n%s\n", error, errstr);
  return(-1);
}

/* Creates a HMAC context */
hmac_ctx = EVP_MAC_CTX_new(mac);
if (hmac_ctx == NULL)
{
  GET_ERROR
  fprintf(stderr, "Error: get_HMAC(), EVP_MAC_CTX_new() failed,"
    " error=%lu\n%s\n", error, errstr);
  EVP_MAC_free(mac);
  return(-2);
}

/* Set up the HMAC context with the hash function and key */
ret = EVP_MAC_init(hmac_ctx, key, strlen((char *)key), params);
if (ret != 1)
{
  GET_ERROR
  fprintf(stderr, "Error: get_HMAC(), EVP_MAC_init() failed,"
    " error=%lu\n%s\n", error, errstr);
  FREEALL
  return(-3);
}

/* Open the input file */
infd = open(infname, O_RDONLY);
if (infd == -1)
{
  fprintf(stderr, "Error: get_HMAC(), open() failed to open input file %s,"
    " errno=%d\n", infname, errno);
  FREEALL
  return(-4);
}

/* Read contents of the entire file and calculate its HMAC */
do
{
  bzero (inbuf, INSIZE);
  /* Read next chunk from the input file */
  inlen = read(infd, inbuf, INSIZE);
  if (inlen <= 0)
  {
    if (inlen < 0)
    {
      fprintf(stderr, "Error: get_HMAC(), read() failed to read input file "
        "%s, errno=%d\n", infname, errno);
      FREEALL
      return(-5);
    }
```

```c
        else
            break;
    }

    /* Compute message authentication code of current input chunk */
    if (EVP_MAC_update(hmac_ctx, inbuf, inlen) != 1)
    {
        GET_ERROR
        fprintf(stderr, "Error: get_HMAC(), EVP_MAC_update() failed,"
            " error=%lu\n%s\n", error, errstr);
        FREEALL
        return(-6);
    }

} while (1);

    /* Wrap up the calculation by handling the last remaining part */
    memset(hash, 0, EVP_MAX_MD_SIZE);
    if (EVP_MAC_final(hmac_ctx, hash, hashlen, EVP_MAX_MD_SIZE) != 1)
    {
        GET_ERROR
        fprintf(stderr, "Error: get_HMAC(), EVP_MAC_final() failed,"
            " error=%lu\n%s\n", error, errstr);
        FREEALL
        return(-7);
    }

    FREEALL
    return(0);
}

/*
 * Compute the HMAC of the contents of a file.
 * Note that the length of key changes with cipher algorithm.
 * For instance, with "aes-128-cbc", keylen = 16.
 * For "aes-256-cbc", keylen = 32.
 */
int main(int argc, char *argv[])
{
    char        *infname = "hmacdatain";    /* file containing the message */
    char        cipherName[] = DEFAULT_CIPHER;  /* default cipher */
    char        *hashfunc_name=HASHFUNC_NAME;   /* name of hash function */
    char        *macAlgrm = MAC_ALGORITHM;      /* MAC algorithm */
    unsigned char  hash[EVP_MAX_MD_SIZE];       /* HMAC hash value */
    size_t      hashlen=0;                   /* length of hash value */
    char    *key = "!12*4i6(8#a-c+e@0123456789012345";  /* 32-bit key */
    int         ret;

    /* Get the names of input file and hash function from user, if any */
    if (argc > 1)
        hashfunc_name = argv[1];

    if (argc > 2)
        infname = argv[2];

    fprintf(stdout, "cipher=%s key=%s keylen=%d MAC=%s\n", cipherName, key,
```

```
    strlen(key), macAlgrm);

/* Calculate the HMAC value of the contents of the input file */
memset(hash, 0, EVP_MAX_MD_SIZE);
ret = get_HMAC(infname, hashfunc_name, key, macAlgrm, hash, &hashlen, cipherName);
if (ret != 0)
{
    fprintf(stderr, "Error: main(), get_HMAC() failed, ret=%d\n", ret);
    return(ret);
}

fprintf(stdout, "HMAC value of the file %s is:\n", infname);
print_binary_buf(hash, hashlen);

return(0);
}
```

15-5-3-1 Encrypted communication with Message Integrity and Authentication

Figure 15-15 displays a client-server program example that demonstrates secrecy using encryption/decryption and message integrity and origin authentication using HMAC. OpenSSL function HMAC() is used here.

What follows is a sample output from running the client and server programs.

```
$ ./tcpsrvhmac
TCP server listening at portnum=7878 ipv6=0

Server got a client connection
Server received: Hi, there! This is a test message.
HMAC of the request message was successfully verified.
Server received: bye
HMAC of the request message was successfully verified.

$ ./tcpclnthmac
Enter a message to send ('bye' to end): Hi, there! This is a test message.
Send request:
Cipher
text=0xd2b6ae1300a17f1830c11949882bc2de95c40ab25e9c3fb4c21fc1080859ec99e166a9b0aefdc5
4ffaad2541f928df9679efcf3964f1ee33524fec2e4070c6a856e100a31f6b3d6dc140ed094de6ff945f0
aaeb581d91f0a5c3ce7ee59090597ed524102ce1a79bb
Got this reply: This is reply message # 1 from the server.
Enter a message to send ('bye' to end): bye
Send request:
Cipher
text=0x39778cc2f0b7c7f6fe95546fa61ad118fa4a1078700f1e0cde57de80f29ae2db90d198c32d6830
97e2f76997208722de6475825cb4a65e80e8041be9cd920bf4ffb0c0b202f607fe
Got this reply: bye
```

Figure 15-15 Client server communication with triple protections

(a) tcpsrvhmac.c

```
/*
 * Demonstrating secrecy, message integrity and origin authentication
```

```
 * in network communications.
 * This is a TCP server program which gets a request message from a client
 * and sends back a reply. Both request messages and replies are all encrypted.
 * HMAC is also verified for message integrity and message authentication.
 * Copyright (c) 2015, 2016, 2020 Mr. Jin-Jwei Chen. All rights reserved.
 */

#include <stdio.h>
#include <errno.h>
#include <sys/types.h>
#include <sys/socket.h>
#include <netinet/in.h>     /* protocols such as IPPROTO_TCP, ... */
#include <string.h>         /* memset(), strlen(), memcmp() */
#include <stdlib.h>         /* atoi() */
#include <openssl/evp.h>
#include <openssl/hmac.h>
#include <openssl/err.h>
#include "myopenssl.h"
#include "netlib.h"

int main(int argc, char *argv[])
{
  int     sfd;                        /* file descriptor of the listener socket */
  struct sockaddr_in    srvaddr;      /* IPv4 socket address structure */
  struct sockaddr_in6   srvaddr6;     /* IPv6 socket address structure */
  in_port_t  portnum = SRVPORT;       /* port number this server listens on */
  int        portnum_in = 0;          /* port number specified by user */
  struct sockaddr_in6   clntaddr6;    /* client socket address */
  socklen_t             clntaddr6sz = sizeof(clntaddr6);
  int     newsock;                    /* file descriptor of client data socket */
  int     ipv6 = 0;
  int     ret;
  unsigned char  inbuf[MAXREQSZ+EVP_MAX_MD_SIZE];    /* input buffer */
  unsigned char  reqmsg[MAXREQSZ];    /* request message buffer */
  char           reply[MAXRPLYSZ];    /* buffer for server reply message */
  unsigned char  outbuf[MAXRPLYSZ];   /* output buffer */
  size_t         reqmsgsz;            /* size of client request message */
  size_t         replysz;             /* size of server reply message */
  size_t         insize;             /* size of encrypted request message */
  size_t         outsz;               /* size of encrypted reply message */
  int            done;                /* done with current client */
  int            msgcnt;              /* count of messages from a client */

  struct cipher  cipher;              /* cipher to be used */
  unsigned char  newiv[EVP_MAX_IV_LENGTH];  /* new IV */

  const EVP_MD   *hashfunc;           /* hash function */
  unsigned int   hashlen = 0;         /* length of hash */
  unsigned char  *hashptr;            /* pointer to output hash */
  unsigned char  hash[EVP_MAX_MD_SIZE];  /* hash of the request message */

  /* Get the server port number from user, if any */
  if (argc > 1)
  {
    portnum_in = atoi(argv[1]);
    if (portnum_in <= 0)
```

1142

```
  {
    fprintf(stderr, "Error: port number %s invalid\n", argv[1]);
    fprintf(stderr, "Usage: %s [server_port] [1 (use IPv6)]\n", argv[0]);
    return(-1);
  }
  else
    portnum = portnum_in;
}

/* Get the IPv6 switch from user, if any */
if (argc > 2)
{
  if (argv[2][0] == '1')
    ipv6 = 1;
  else if (argv[2][0] != '0')
  {
    fprintf(stderr, "Usage: %s [server_port] [1 (use IPv6)]\n", argv[0]);
    return(-2);
  }
}

fprintf(stdout, "TCP server listening at portnum=%u ipv6=%u\n", portnum, ipv6);

/* Get the structure describing the message hash algorithm by name */
hashfunc = EVP_get_digestbyname(HASHFUNC_NAME);
if(hashfunc == NULL)
{
  fprintf(stderr, "Error: unknown hash function %s\n", HASHFUNC_NAME);
  return(-3);
}

/* Create the server listener socket */
if (ipv6)
  ret = new_bound_srv_endpt(&sfd, (struct sockaddr *)&srvaddr6, AF_INET6,
    portnum);
else
  ret = new_bound_srv_endpt(&sfd, (struct sockaddr *)&srvaddr, AF_INET,
    portnum);

if (ret != 0)
{
  fprintf(stderr, "Error: new_bound_srv_endpt() failed, ret=%d\n", ret);
  return(-4);
}

/* Listen for incoming requests and send replies */
do
{
  /* Listen for next client's connect request */
  newsock = accept(sfd, (struct sockaddr *)&clntaddr6, &clntaddr6sz);
  if (newsock < 0)
  {
    fprintf(stderr, "Error: accept() failed, errno=%d\n", errno);
    continue;
  }
```

```
  fprintf(stdout, "\nServer got a client connection\n");

  /* Initialize the cipher */
  strcpy(cipher.name, DEFAULT_CIPHER);
  strcpy((char *)cipher.key, DEFAULT_KEY);
  strcpy((char *)cipher.iv, DEFAULT_IV);

  /* Service this current client until done */
  done = 0;
  msgcnt = 1;
  do
  {
    /* Read the request message */
    insize = recv(newsock, inbuf, MAXREQSZ, 0);
    if (insize <= 0)
    {
      fprintf(stderr, "Error: recv() failed, insize=%lu\n", insize);
      break;
    }

    /* Decrypt the requested message */
    reqmsgsz = 0;
    ret = mydecrypt2(inbuf+EVP_MAX_MD_SIZE, insize-EVP_MAX_MD_SIZE,
        (char *)reqmsg, &reqmsgsz, &cipher);
    if (ret != 0)
    {
      fprintf(stderr, "Error: mydecrypt2() failed, ret=%d\n", ret);
      break;
    }

    reqmsg[reqmsgsz]='\0';
    fprintf(stdout, "Server received: %s\n", reqmsg);

    /* Verify HMAC */
    hashlen = 0;
    hashptr = HMAC(hashfunc, HMACKEY, strlen(HMACKEY),
        reqmsg, reqmsgsz, hash, &hashlen);
    if (hashptr == NULL)
    {
      fprintf(stderr, "Error: HMAC() failed\n");
      break;
    }

    if (memcmp(inbuf, hash, hashlen))
    {
      fprintf(stderr, "Error: verifying HMAC failed\n");
      break;
    }
    fprintf(stdout, "HMAC of the request message was successfully verified.\n");

    /* Set reply message */
    if ( !strcmp((char *)reqmsg, BYE_MSG) )
    {
      done = 1;
      strcpy(reply, (char *)reqmsg);
    }
```

```
    else
        sprintf(reply, SRVREPLY2, msgcnt++);

    replysz = strlen(reply);

    /* Encrypt the reply message */
    outsz = 0;
    ret = myencrypt2(reply, replysz, outbuf, &outsz, &cipher);
    if (ret != 0)
    {
      fprintf(stderr, "Error: myencrypt2() failed, ret=%d\n", ret);
      break;
    }

    /* Send back an encrypted reply */
    ret = send(newsock, outbuf, outsz, 0);
    if (ret < 0)
      fprintf(stderr, "Error: send() failed to send a reply, errno=%d\n",
        errno);

    /* Change the IV */
    ret = increment_iv(cipher.iv, newiv);
    if (ret == 0)
      strcpy((char *)cipher.iv, (char *)newiv);
    else
    {
      fprintf(stderr, "Error: increment_iv() failed, ret=%d\n", ret);
      break;
    }

  } while (!done);

  /* We can close the socket now. */
  close(newsock);

} while (1);
}
```

(b) tcpclnthmac.c

```
/*
 * Demonstrating secrecy, message integrity and origin authentication
 * in network communications.
 * This is a TCP client program which exchanges messages with
 * a TCP server using encryption/decryption for secrecy and HMAC for
 * message integrity and message authentication.
 * Copyright (c) 2015, 2016, 2020 Mr. Jin-Jwei Chen. All rights reserved.
 */

#include <stdio.h>
#include <errno.h>
#include <sys/types.h>
#include <sys/socket.h>
#include <netinet/in.h>        /* protocols such as IPPROTO_TCP, ... */
#include <string.h>            /* memset(), strlen() */
#include <stdlib.h>            /* atoi(), malloc() */
```

```c
#include <openssl/evp.h>
#include <openssl/hmac.h>
#include <openssl/err.h>
#include "myopenssl.h"
#include "netlib.h"

#define FREEALL         \
    close(sfd);         \
    free(reqmsg);

int main(int argc, char *argv[])
{
  int       ret;                      /* return value */
  int       sfd=0;                    /* socket file descriptor */
  char      replymsg[MAXRPLYSZ];      /* reply message from server */
  size_t    reqbufsz = MAXREQSZ;      /* size of client request buffer */
  char      *reqmsg=NULL;             /* pointer to request message buffer */
  size_t    reqmsgsz;                 /* size of client request message */
  size_t    replysz;                  /* size of server reply message */
  size_t    outsz;                    /* size of encrypted request message */
  size_t    insize;                   /* size of encrypted reply message */
  unsigned char  outbuf[MAXREQSZ+EVP_MAX_MD_SIZE];   /* output buffer */
  unsigned char  inbuf[MAXRPLYSZ];                   /* input buffer */

  in_port_t  srvport = SRVPORT;       /* port number the server listens on */
  int        srvport_in = 0;          /* port number specified by user */
  char       *srvhost = "localhost";  /* name of server host */
  int        done = 0;                /* to end client */

  struct cipher  cipher;              /* cipher to be used */
  unsigned char  newiv[EVP_MAX_IV_LENGTH];   /* new IV */

  const EVP_MD   *hashfunc;           /* hash function */
  unsigned int   hashlen = 0;         /* length of hash */
  unsigned char  *hashptr;            /* pointer to output hash */

  /* Get the server port number from user, if any */
  if (argc > 1)
  {
    srvport_in = atoi(argv[1]);
    if (srvport_in <= 0)
    {
      fprintf(stderr, "Error: port number %s invalid\n", argv[1]);
      return(-1);
    }
    else
      srvport = srvport_in;
  }

  /* Get the name of the server host from user, if specified */
  if (argc > 2)
    srvhost = argv[2];

  /* Set the cipher */
  strcpy(cipher.name, DEFAULT_CIPHER);
  strcpy((char *)cipher.key, DEFAULT_KEY);
```

```
    strcpy((char *)cipher.iv, DEFAULT_IV);

    /* Get the structure describing the message hash algorithm by name */
    hashfunc = EVP_get_digestbyname(HASHFUNC_NAME);
    if(hashfunc == NULL)
    {
      fprintf(stderr, "Error: unknown hash function %s\n", HASHFUNC_NAME);
      return(-2);
    }

    /* Connect to the server */
    ret = connect_to_server(&sfd, srvhost, srvport);
    if (ret != 0)
    {
      fprintf(stderr, "Error: connect_to_server() failed, ret=%d\n", ret);
      if (sfd) close(sfd);
      return(-3);
    }

    /* Allocate input buffer */
    reqmsg = malloc(MAXREQSZ);
    if (reqmsg == NULL)
    {
      fprintf(stderr, "Error: malloc() failed\n");
      close(sfd);
      return(-4);
    }

    /* Send a few messages to the server */
    do
    {
      fprintf(stdout, "Enter a message to send ('bye' to end): ");
      reqmsgsz = getline(&reqmsg, &reqbufsz, stdin);
      if (reqmsgsz == -1)
      {
        fprintf(stderr, "Error: getline() failed, ret=%lu\n", reqmsgsz);
        FREEALL
        return(-5);
      }

      /* Remove the newline character at end of input */
      reqmsg[--reqmsgsz] = '\0';

      /* Calculate the HMAC hash of the message */
      hashlen = 0;
      hashptr = HMAC(hashfunc, HMACKEY, strlen(HMACKEY),
          (unsigned char *)reqmsg, reqmsgsz, outbuf, &hashlen);
      if (hashptr == NULL)
      {
        fprintf(stderr, "Error: HMAC() failed\n");
        FREEALL
        return(-6);
      }

      /* Encrypt the message to be sent and place it after the hash in buffer */
      ret = myencrypt2(reqmsg, reqmsgsz, outbuf+EVP_MAX_MD_SIZE, &outsz, &cipher);
```

```
  if (ret != 0)
  {
    fprintf(stderr, "Error: myencrypt2() failed, ret=%d\n", ret);
    FREEALL
    return(-7);
  }

  fprintf(stdout, "Send request:\n");
  print_cipher_text(outbuf, outsz+EVP_MAX_MD_SIZE);

  /* Send the encrypted message, together with HMAC */
  ret = send_msg(sfd, (unsigned char *)outbuf, outsz+EVP_MAX_MD_SIZE, 0);
  if (ret != 0)
  {
    fprintf(stderr, "Error: send_msg() failed, ret=%d\n", ret);
    FREEALL
    return(-8);
  }

  /* Wait for server reply */
  memset((void *)inbuf, 0, MAXRPLYSZ);
  insize = 0;
  insize = recv(sfd, inbuf, MAXRPLYSZ, 0);
  if (insize <= 0)
  {
    fprintf(stderr, "Error: recv() failed to receive a reply from "
      "server, insize=%lu\n", insize);
    FREEALL
    return(-9);
  }

  /* Decrypt the server reply message */
  memset((void *)replymsg, 0, MAXRPLYSZ);
  replysz = 0;
  ret = mydecrypt2(inbuf, insize, replymsg, &replysz, &cipher);
  if (ret != 0)
  {
    fprintf(stderr, "Error: mydecrypt2() failed, ret=%d\n", ret);
    FREEALL
    return(-10);
  }

  replymsg[replysz]='\0';
  fprintf(stdout, "Got this reply: %s\n", replymsg);

  if (!strcmp(replymsg, reqmsg))
    done = 1;

  /* Change the IV */
  ret = increment_iv(cipher.iv, newiv);
  if (ret == 0)
    strcpy((char *)cipher.iv, (char *)newiv);
  else
  {
    fprintf(stderr, "Error: increment_iv() failed, ret=%d\n", ret);
    FREEALL
```

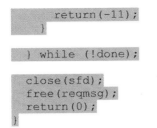

```
        return(-11);
    }

} while (!done);

close(sfd);
free(reqmsg);
return(0);
}
```

15-6 Sender Authentication -- Digital Signatures

Along the line of message integrity and message authentication, there is another step up in the security ladder.

It's good that MAC/HMAC authenticates the message sender, in addition to providing message integrity. However, if there is a litigation, the sender could deny he or she actually sent the message or document under dispute. He or she could claim that since the message recipient also knows the shared secret key, he or she could have created and sent the message. To solve this problem, nonrepudiation is needed in certain applications to ensure that the sender has no way of denying he or she has sent the message. This new step up is the nonrepudiation or sender authentication!

Digital Signature is the technology that provides message integrity, message authentication and nonrepudiation all-in-one. It provides nonrepudiation by adding yet another component to it, which requires use of public key cryptography.

message integrity (using hash/digest)
   |
   v
message/origin authentication (using MAC/HMAC - keyed hash)
   |
   v
sender authentication - nonrepudiation (using digital signature (PKC))

Figure 15-16 Ladder of message integrity and origin authentication

15-6-1 How Digital Signature Works

Digital signature requires using **public key cryptography (PKC)**.

Remember earlier we talked about using public key cryptography for secrecy. Indeed, asymmetric or public key cryptography is useful in sender authentication as well.

When asymmetric key cryptography is used for the purpose of **message secrecy**, it is used as a **public key encryption**. This means the message "recipient's public key" is used to encrypt the message being sent by the sender for the purpose of message secrecy. Secrecy is accomplished this way because by encrypting the message being sent with the recipient's public key, it is guaranteed that only the intended recipient can decrypt it using its own private key, so long as the recipient's private key is not compromised.

In contrast, when asymmetric key cryptography is used for the purpose of **sender authentication**, it is used as a **private key encryption**. That is, the "sender's private key" is used to encrypt the digest of the message being sent as a digital signature for the purpose of sender authentication and non-repudiation! The use of the sender's private key is what provides nonrepudiation.

As we mentioned before, public key cryptography uses a pair of mathematically generated related keys, one private key known only to the owner and no one else and one related public key known to the message recipient and perhaps others. With digital signature, the sender of a message must generate and have a pair of public and private keys.

The way digital signature works is described below.

First, in general, when a digital document or message is signed, it is the digest or hash value of it is signed, not the entire document or message itself. This is because the document or message itself could be huge. Signing (i.e. encrypting) the document or message itself could be very costly in time.

With digital signature, when a sender wants to send a message, it has to sign the message.

To sign a message, the sender of the message computes a digest of the message, encrypts the digest using his/her private key, and then sends the signature (which is the encrypted message digest) with the message.

At the receiving end, to verify the digital signature, the message recipient decrypts the digital signature using the sender's public key to get the received message digest, independently computes the message digest from the message it has received, and compares the two digests. If they match the signature is valid. This is in general how digital signature works if certain signature algorithm (e.g. RSA) is used, although there are some minor variations in details during the signature generation and verification if another signature algorithm (e.g. DSA/DSS) is used.

Because the recipient is able to decrypt the signature (i.e. the encrypted message digest) using the sender's public key, it proves that it must have been signed by the sender using his/her private key, assuming the sender's private key is not compromised. This provides **origin authentication** and **nonrepudiation**.

And then since the decrypted message digest -- the one computed and sent by the sender -- matches the one that the recipient independently computes from the message it has received, it proves that the message is unchanged during transit. This provides **message integrity**.

Therefore, a digital signature authenticates both the origin/sender and contents integrity of a message. It is by far the most advanced and sophisticated message authentication scheme. The nonrepudiation is accomplished by employing the public key cryptography (PKC) technology.

As you can see there are a number of elements involved in signing a message:

a message digest algorithm, the digest/hash of the message, the sender's private key and an encryption algorithm.

Note that in real practice, in addition to doing digital signature to provide message integrity and sender authentication, very often it is also desirable to provide message secrecy as well. In that case before the sender sends the message, the entire message itself is also separately encrypted, typically using a symmetric cryptography for the sake of efficiency. As a result, both asymmetric and symmetric cryptographies are employed. **Asymmetric cryptography is used in digital signature for nonrepudiation to encrypt the much smaller message digest and symmetric cryptography is used to efficiently encrypt the potentially huge message itself for secrecy.**

Summary of Producing and Verifying a Digital Signature

In summary, a "digital signature" is some entity electronically signs a document or message.

Below is how a digital signature is produced.

1. A cryptographic hash algorithm is selected.
2. A hash value or digest is computed from the entire contents of the document or message being signed using the selected hash algorithm.
3. An encryption algorithm is chosen.
4. The hash value from step 2 is encrypted using the encryption algorithm chosen and the signer's private key as the key input.
   The encrypted digest is the digital signature.

Below is how a digital signature is verified.

1. The verifier computes a hash/digest from the document/message using the same cryptographic hash algorithm used by the signer.
2. The signer's signature is decrypted using the same algorithm chosen by the signer and using the signer's public key as key input.
   This recovers the hash value originally computed by the signer.
3. The two hash values (the one computed by the verifier and the one originally computed by the signer) are compared.
   If they match, the signature is considered verified.

15-6-2 Different Digital Signature Algorithms

There are two main digital signature algorithms that are in use today. We provide a brief overview of both in this section.

15-6-2-1 RSA

RSA algorithm can be used for both key establishment and digital signature. The roles of the RSA private and public keys are reversed in these two applications.

Using RSA for digital signature is similar to using it for key exchange except that the roles of the private and public keys are reversed.

The RSA digital signature algorithm and RSA encryption algorithm are essentially the same except that the roles of the keys are reversed and the padding bytes are different.

To sign a message or document, you compute the digest of the message or document to be sent and then encrypt it using your private key.
To verify the signature, the recipient computes its own version of the digest from the message or document received, decrypts the signature it receives using the sender's public key to get the sender's version of the message digest, and compares the two. If they match then the signature is valid. This proves the message is really from the sender and the message has not been tampered with during transit because the two versions of the message digest match.

Notice that RSA digital signature is essentially the same as RSA encryption except that the padding is different and that signing uses a private key while encrypting uses a public key.

The exponential and modular (modulus) math that RSA Digital Signature algorithm is based on is subject to attacks if a message sender encrypts the message first and signs it after. **To be secure, the sender of a message should always sign the message first and then encrypt it after.** This way a hacker won't be able to get access to information needed to construct a new public key and fake the communication.

In addition, to avoid another attack, a message sender should never sign a random message. And when signing a message, it should always sign a cryptographic hash of the message and never sign the entire message itself.

15-6-2-2 DSA/DSS

The **Digital Signature Algorithm** (**DSA**) was invented by David W. Kravitz of U.S. NSA (National Security Agency), an intelligence organization of the United States government, in 1991 and it is patented in the U.S.

DSA was adopted in the Federal Information Processing Standard (FIPS) 186, which is called the **Digital Signature Standard** (**DSS**), by the U.S. National Institute of Standards and Technology (NIST). NIST is a measurement standards laboratory and an agency of the United States Department of Commerce.

There have been at least four revisions to the FIPS-186 standard: FIPS 186-1 in 1996, FIPS 186-2 in 2000, FIPS 186-3 in 2009, and FIPS 186-4 in 2013.

NIST has made the DSA patent royalty free for the whole world.

How DSA works

DSA is also based on modular exponentiation of prime numbers. A DSA signature consists of two elements, called r and s, which are large integers.

DSA signature supports SHA digest only. It works with SHA-1 (which produces a 160-bit digest) and SHA-256 (which produces a 256-bit digest).

Using DSA/DSS involves three stages: key generation, message signing and signature verifying. The key generation has two phases. The first phase involves choosing parameters for the algorithm, which could be shared between the two communicating parties. The second phase involves each party generating a pair of public and private keys for itself.

We describe the DSA signature generation and verification at a high level below.

DSA Signature Generation [3]

A DSA signature generation algorithm takes the message to be signed and four parameters as input and outputs the signature in two elements r and s. The four input parameters are g, p, q and x where x is the sender's private key and g, p and q are part of its public key.

The algorithm is described at a high level as below:

```
h = hash of message, truncated to length of q
j = func1(r, q) where r is a random number of length q
s1 = func2(g, p, q, j)
s2 = func3(q, x, h, j, s1)
```

First, the hash of the message (h) is computed and it is truncated to the length of q. The value of j is computed using a random number r and the input parameter q. The first part of the signature s1 is computed from g, p, q and j. The second part of the signature s2 is calculated from q, x, h, j and s1.

DSA Signature Verification [3]

At receiving end the message recipient has the message itself, together with the DSA parameters g, p, and q, sender's public key y, and the signature elements s1 and s2.

To verify a DSA signature, the message recipient computes the following:

```
h = hash of message, truncated to length of q
d = func4(q, s2)
u1 = (hd) % q
u2 = (s1d) % q
v = func5(g, p, q, y, u1, u2)
```

where % means modulus.

If v equals to s1, the signature is valid. Otherwise, the signature is wrong.

Notice that DSA signature generation and verification are not really doing encrypting and decrypting as RSA algorithm does.

For those readers who are really interested in knowing what the different functions listed above (i.e. func1, func2, func3, ...) are, please refer to the book "Implementing SSL/TLS Using Cryptography and PKI, by Joshua Davies, Wiley Publishing, Inc.".

The maximum length of DSA signature, when parameters p and y are 2048 bits (the variable 'bits' in the DSA example program), is DSA_size(dsa)=72 bytes.

15-6-2-3 Differences Between RSA and DSA Signatures

There are a number of differences between RSA and DSA digital signatures.

First, RSA signature can be used with any message digest (e.g. MD5, SHA) while DSA signature works with SHA digest only (e.g. SHA-1 and SHA-256).

Second, the way signature is verified is slightly different between RSA and DSA. With RSA signature, the message recipient computes a digest from the message it receives and compares that with the digest it has obtained from decrypting the sender's signature. In contrast, DSA's signature verification takes the digital signature from the sender and the digest the recipient computes on its own as input and computes a yes or no answer from those. It does not allow the recipient to recover the message digest that the sender computes. This arguably may have made the DSA a bit harder to break.

Third, the RSA algorithm is relatively simple compared to DSA/DSS. In RSA, the encryption, decryption, signature and verification operations are basically the same except the parameters and padding are different. In DSA/DSS, the signature and verification operations are very different and they are relatively complex.

Fourth, performance-wise, RSA is much faster in signature verification. The two are not far apart in performance of signing.

DSA is an authentication technology only. All it does is digital signature. RSA is not only an authentication technology but also an encryption technology. Because of this, RSA has export restrictions while DSA does not.

15-6-2-4 Caveats of Digital Signatures

There are two tricks in using public key digital signatures. First, researchers have found that messages that are encrypted and signed should be **signed first and then encrypted second,** not in the reverse order. Encrypting a message first and then signing it could allow a malicious recipient to get information such that he or she could generate a different message and re-compute and re-publish a new public key for himself or herself and make it look like the sender has sent the new message.

Second, it is more secure to **sign the digest,** or cryptographic hash, of a message, **rather than the message itself.** Indeed, never sign an entire message or document itself just to protect yourself against attacks. The mathematics is such that if someone tricks you to sign two messages computed from a third message (the real one), then there exists a way to derive your signature for the third message and thus he/she can forge your signature for the third message.

If you are interested in the mathematical foundations that show how these attacks can occur, please refer to references [1] and [2] listed at the end of this chapter.

15-6-2-5 Applications of Digital Signatures

Note that digital signatures provide non-repudiation.
In most network communications where two programs are just exchanging some data and want to be secure, digital signature is not really necessary or useful. In these applications, doing MAC or HMAC is probably the right thing to do. Ultimately, when two programs are exchanging messages, how useful is the nonrepudiation really is? What would you do if you find it is broken? The feature of nonrepudiation is more useful in electronically transporting legal documents than simply exchanging communication data between two different programs.

Another issue is practicality. Digital signatures involve signing messages or documents and the sender's private key MUST be used in doing that (for being able to provide nonrepudiation). This means the recipient has to verify the digital signature using the sender's public key.
In a Web server application, for instance, doing so wouldn't be practical because the client can be anyone from anywhere in the world.
How could the server have the public keys of all or most people in the world?

Therefore, digital signature is invaluable in certain applications such as submitting or transferring legal documents electronically. However, it's inappropriate or impractical for many other applications. This is very important because I have met many people who think signing the message is always the best way to go. It's not really so. In fact, for many other applications, such as, exchanging data between two programs, using MAC/HMAC is probably the top of the ladder where you really want to climb to.

15-6-2-6 MAC/HMAC Versus Digital Signatures

A MAC/HMAC provides message integrity and origin authentication.

A MAC/HMAC is generated and verified using the same secret key. So it is symmetric (or secret-key) cryptography. This means the sender and receiver of a message must share the key and agree upon the same key to use before the communication starts.

In contrast, a digital signature is produced using the private key and is verified using the public key of a key pair. It is asymmetric (or public-key) cryptography. The message sender simply creates the pair of keys and makes its public key accessible by the recipient(s) without having to negotiate anything with the recipient.

Digital signatures provide message integrity, origin authentication and nonrepudiation.

Digital signatures provide nonrepudiation because if one can decrypt a digitally signed message using the public key of someone, then the message must come from him or her because only he or she holds the corresponding private key of the key pair that has been used to sign the message, assuming the private key has not been compromised.

Note that there is no Public Key Infrastructure (PKI) needed or involved in doing MAC/HMAC whereas PKI is needed and used in using digital signatures.

Summary

```
-------------------------------------------------------------------
Technology              Security features accomplished
----------------        -------------------------------------------
checksum, hash          integrity
MAC, HMAC               integrity, origin authentication
Digital signature      integrity, origin authentication, nonrepudiation
-------------------------------------------------------------------
```

15-6-3 Programming Examples

We provide program examples on how to do digital signature using RSA and DSA algorithms in this section.

Starting from version 3.0 and on, OpenSSL deprecates its original APIs for digital signature, including RSA_sign(), RSA_verify(), DSA_sign(), DSA_verify() and many others.

The new set of APIs recommended now is the EVP_PKEY_xxx(). Using this new set of APIs, performing a digital signature using the RSA or DSA algorithm on the sender side involves the following steps:

1. Generate a digest for the message to be signed
   This is because the new APIs do not compute the message digest anymore.
2. Generate an asymmetric cryptographic key pair
3. Allocate buffer space for receiving the digital signature
4. Produce the digital signature (i.e. signing the message (digest))

On the receiving end, it's just verifying the signature:

1. Verify the digital signature.

To simplify, among all of the steps listed above, we create library functions of our own so that the digesting, signing and verifying steps share the same functions between RSA and DSA algorithms. These functions are:

   - get_digest(): compute digest of the message to be signed
   - get_signature(): compute the digital signature (i.e. sign the digest)
   - verify_signature(): verify the digital signature

Obviously, because of the sharing, the signature algorithm to be used is an input parameter to both signing and verifying functions. The name of this parameter is called 'keytype' in our own APIs. Its value is EVP_PKEY_RSA for RSA and EVP_PKEY_DSA for DSA. Besides, the message digest algorithm is also another input parameter. The name of this parameter is 'dgstName'. Its value can be "sha256", "sha512", or "md5", etc.

The only thing that does not share the same routine between the two signature algorithms is the key generation. This is performed by generate_RSAkey() and generate_DSAkey(), respectively. DSA algorithm requires generation of parameters whereas RSA usually does not.

One advantage that the new OpenSSL digital signature APIs provide is simplicity because RSA and DSA algorithms can now share the same functions as introduced above. This sharing does not exist in the old APIs.

15-6-3-1 Shared Functions

Here we introduce the three shared functions. get_digest() was discussed before in Section 15-3-2-4. Hence, we discuss the other two below.

15-6-3-1-1 Signature Signing -- get_signature()

```
int get_signature(EVP_PKEY *pkey, const char *dgstName, unsigned char *digest,
    unsigned int dgstlen, unsigned char *sigbuf, SIZET_BAD *siglen, int keytype);
```

get_signature() generates the digital signature on the input digest using the signature algorithm indicated by the 'keytype' input parameter. The digest algorithm that is used to generate the message digest is specified by the 'dgstName' input parameter. This function returns 0 on success.

The **get_signature**() function includes the following steps:

1. Create a public key context from signer's private key
   EVP_PKEY_CTX_new(pkey, NULL /* no engine */)

2. Initialize the public key algorithm context ctx for signing
   EVP_PKEY_sign_init(ctx)

3. Set RSA padding (for RSA only)
   EVP_PKEY_CTX_set_rsa_padding(ctx, RSA_PKCS1_PADDING)

4. Set signature's digest algorithm
   EVP_PKEY_CTX_set_signature_md(ctx, EVP_get_digestbyname(dgstName))

5. Sign the digest. Return signature and its length in sigbuf and siglen.
   EVP_PKEY_sign(ctx, sigbuf, siglen, digest, dgstlen)

6. Free the memory of the key context
   EVP_PKEY_CTX_free(ctx)

Note that there exists at least two ways of finding out how big the buffer for holding the signature should be.

One way is to invoke the EVP_PKEY_get_size() function with the keypair as input to find out the size and allocate it before calling the get_signature():

```
  siglen = EVP_PKEY_get_size(pkey);
  sigbuf = malloc(siglen);
```

Alternatively, the buffer for signature can be determined and allocated in-between step 4 and 5 within the get_signature() function as below:

```
  if (EVP_PKEY_sign(ctx, NULL, siglen, digest, dgstlen) <= 0) goto err;
  sigbuf = OPENSSL_malloc(*siglen);
```

Calling EVP_PKEY_sign() with the signature buffer parameter (the second one) being NULL indicates the caller just wants to get the size of the signature that would be returned, rather than actually doing the signing.

Our implementation uses the first approach. That is, we've taken care of the business in the caller of get_signature().

Here we provide a very brief introduction to each of the functions used in get_signature(), which produces a digital signature.

(1) Create a public key context from signer's private key

As shown below, there are four different ways to create a public key algorithm context.

```
#include <openssl/evp.h>
EVP_PKEY_CTX *EVP_PKEY_CTX_new(EVP_PKEY *pkey, ENGINE *e);
EVP_PKEY_CTX *EVP_PKEY_CTX_new_id(int id, ENGINE *e);
EVP_PKEY_CTX *EVP_PKEY_CTX_new_from_name(OSSL_LIB_CTX *libctx,
                                         const char *name,
                                         const char *propquery);
EVP_PKEY_CTX *EVP_PKEY_CTX_new_from_pkey(OSSL_LIB_CTX *libctx,
                                         EVP_PKEY *pkey,
                                         const char *propquery);
```

The EVP_PKEY_CTX_new() function allocates public key algorithm context using the pkey key type and ENGINE e. The input argument e can be NULL.

Alternatively, the EVP_PKEY_CTX_new_id() function allocates public key algorithm context using the key type specified by id and ENGINE e. The value of id can be EVP_PKEY_RSA, EVP_PKEY_DSA, EVP_PKEY_RSA_PSS, EVP_PKEY_DH, EVP_PKEY_EC, etc.

The EVP_PKEY_CTX_new_from_name() function allocates a public key algorithm context using the library context 'libctx', the key type specified by 'name' and the property query 'propquery'. The name can be "RSA" or "DSA".

EVP_PKEY_CTX_new_from_pkey() is similar to EVP_PKEY_CTX_new_from_name() except a keypair is used instead of a name.

These functions return either the newly allocated EVP_PKEY_CTX structure or NULL if an error occurred.

(2) Initialize the public key algorithm context ctx for signing

```
#include <openssl/evp.h>
```

```
int EVP_PKEY_sign_init(EVP_PKEY_CTX *ctx);
int EVP_PKEY_sign_init_ex(EVP_PKEY_CTX *ctx, const OSSL_PARAM params[]);
```

EVP_PKEY_sign_init() initializes a public key algorithm context ctx for signing using the algorithm given when the context was created using EVP_PKEY_CTX_new() or its variants. The algorithm is used to fetch a EVP_SIGNATURE method implicitly.

EVP_PKEY_sign_init_ex() is the same as EVP_PKEY_sign_init() except it additionally sets the passed parameters params on the context before returning.

EVP_PKEY_sign_init() and EVP_PKEY_sign_init_ex() return 1 for success and 0 or a negative value for failure. A return value of -2 means the operation is not supported by the public key algorithm.

(3) Set RSA padding (for RSA only)

```
#include <openssl/rsa.h>
int EVP_PKEY_CTX_set_rsa_padding(EVP_PKEY_CTX *ctx, int pad);
```

EVP_PKEY_CTX_set_rsa_padding() sets the padding for RSA. This is RSA only. The padding we set is RSA_PKCS1_PADDING.

(4) Set signature's digest algorithm

```
#include <openssl/evp.h>
int EVP_PKEY_CTX_set_signature_md(EVP_PKEY_CTX *ctx, const EVP_MD *md);
```

EVP_PKEY_CTX_set_signature_md() sets the message digest type used in a signature. It can be used in the RSA, DSA and ECDSA algorithms.

(5) Sign the digest. Return signature and its length in sigbuf and siglen.

```
#include <openssl/evp.h>
int EVP_PKEY_sign(EVP_PKEY_CTX *ctx,
                  unsigned char *sigbuf, size_t *siglen,
                  const unsigned char *tbs, size_t tbslen);
```

The EVP_PKEY_sign() function performs a public key signing operation using ctx. The data to be signed is specified by the tbs and tbslen parameters. If sigbuf is NULL then the maximum size of the output buffer is written to the siglen parameter. If sigbuf is not NULL then before the call the siglen parameter should contain the length of the sigbuf buffer. If the call is successful the signature is written to sigbuf and the length of the signature is written to siglen.

Note that EVP_PKEY_sign() does not hash the data to be signed, and therefore is normally used to sign digests.

The function EVP_PKEY_sign() can be called more than once on the same context if several operations are performed using the same parameters.

EVP_PKEY_sign() returns 1 for success and 0 or a negative value for failure. A return value of -2 means the operation is not supported.

(6) Free the memory of the key context

EVP_PKEY_CTX_free(ctx) frees up the context ctx. It does not return a value.

15-6-3-1-2 Signature Verifying -- verify_signature()

```
int verify_signature(EVP_PKEY *pkey, unsigned char *digest, size_t dgstlen,
    unsigned char *sigbuf, SIZET_BAD siglen, const char *dgstName, int keytype);
```

The **verify_signature**() function verifies a digital signature to see if it's valid. It returns 0 if it is. This function consists of the following steps:

1. Allocates a public key algorithm context
   ctx = EVP_PKEY_CTX_new(pkey, NULL /* no engine */)

2. Initialize the public key algorithm context for verification
   EVP_PKEY_verify_init(ctx)

3. Set RSA padding (for RSA only)
   EVP_PKEY_CTX_set_rsa_padding(ctx, RSA_PKCS1_PADDING)

4. Set the message digest algorithm used
   EVP_PKEY_CTX_set_signature_md(ctx, EVP_get_digestbyname(dgstName))

5. Verify the digital signature
   EVP_PKEY_verify(ctx, sigbuf, siglen, digest, dgstlen)

6. Free the memory of the key context
   EVP_PKEY_CTX_free(ctx)

Below are descriptions of the functions that are used in signature verification. Some of these are the same as in signature generation.

(1) Allocates a public key algorithm context

   See description in (1) in Section 15-6-3-1-1 above.

(2) Initialize the public key algorithm context for verification

   Two functions are available for initializing a public key algorithm context for verification:

   #include <openssl/evp.h>
   int EVP_PKEY_verify_init(EVP_PKEY_CTX *ctx);
   int EVP_PKEY_verify_init_ex(EVP_PKEY_CTX *ctx, const OSSL_PARAM params[]);

   EVP_PKEY_verify_init() initializes a public key algorithm context ctx for verification using the algorithm given in the provided context which was created using EVP_PKEY_CTX_new() or its variants. The algorithm is used to fetch an EVP_SIGNATURE method implicitly.

   EVP_PKEY_verify_init_ex() is same as EVP_PKEY_verify_init() but it also sets the passed parameters params on the context before returning.

   EVP_PKEY_verify_init() and EVP_PKEY_verify_init_ex() return 1 if the initialization was successful and 0 if it failed.

(3) Set RSA padding (for RSA only)

   See description in (3) in Section 15-6-3-1-1 above.

(4) Set the message digest algorithm used

   See description in (4) in Section 15-6-3-1-1 above.

(5) Verify the digital signature

```
int EVP_PKEY_verify(EVP_PKEY_CTX *ctx,
                    const unsigned char *sigbuf, size_t siglen,
                    const unsigned char *tbs, size_t tbslen);
```

The EVP_PKEY_verify() function performs a signature verification operation. The signature to be verified and its length are provided by the sigbuf and siglen parameters. The data believed originally signed is specified by the tbs and tbslen parameters.

EVP_PKEY_verify() returns 1 if the verification was successful and 0 if it failed. Note that EVP_PKEY_verify() returning 0 only means that the signature did not verify successfully; that is, tbs did not match the original data or the signature was of invalid form.

(6) Free the memory of the key context

EVP_PKEY_CTX_free(ctx) frees up the context ctx. It does not return a value.

Note on Portability of Data Type in OpenSSL

One thing worth mentioning here is that the digital signature envelope APIs in OpenSSL 3.0+ unwisely use size_t as the data type for the length of a digital signature. As we have mentioned in Section 14-2-1-5, this data type is not very portable because size_t is defined to be a 'long int', which could be 4- or 8-byte long depending on platforms. Because of this, our example programs calling the EVP_PKEY_sign() and EVP_PKEY_verify() functions run on Linux but break on Apple Darwin. It's all because both of these APIs take 'siglen', which is of type size_t, as an argument.

To overcome this problem, we have defined a new data type named **SIZET_BAD** in myopenssl.h, which is defined to be either size_t or 'unsigned int' depending on whether the macro USE_SIZET is defined or not.

Our programs try to use 'unsigned int' for the length of a digital signature whenever possible (for example, in Linux) and switch to use size_t only if it's necessary (for instance, in Apple Darwin). This is why you see we use SIZET_BAD as the data type of the 'siglen' argument in both of our library functions get_signature() and verify_signature().

By not defining the USE_SIZET macro in the Makefile or compiler line, the example programs compile and run fine in Linux. And by defining this macro in Apple Darwin, the same example programs compile and run fine in Apple Darwin too.

15-6-3-2 Standalone Signature Signing and Verifying

Here in this section, we provide one example on how to do digital signature, including both signing and verifying, in a standalone program.
In the next section, we will give another example of applying digital signature in a client-server application.

Figure 15-17(a) is a program demonstrating how digital signature is done using RSA algorithm, and Figure 15-17(b) is another using DSA algorithm. This is a very simple program just to demonstrate the basic steps of signature signing and verifying using the new APIs recommended in OpenSSL 3.0+. For simplicity we hardwire the message to be signed in the program and store it in a variable called 'data'.

15-6-3-2-1 RSA

As shown in Figure 15-17(a) (rsa.c), performing the RSA digital signature on a message using the new APIs recommended in OpenSSL 3.0+ involves the following four major steps:

- get_digest(): compute the digest of the message

- generate_RSAkey(): generate an RSA key pair

- get_signature(): sign the digest using the signer's private key

- verify_signature(): at the receiving end, verify the signature using the signer's public key

where normally the first three steps are done at the sender of the message and the message receiver does step 1 and 4.

Please note that each of these four functions are our own library functions which are defined in mycryptolib.c as shown in Figure 15-39(b).

The generate_RSAkey() Function

We have described the other three functions shared between RSA and DSA. Here we will describe the steps in the generate_RSAkey() function.

1. Allocates the key context object using the key type
   ctx_kp = EVP_PKEY_CTX_new_id(keytype, NULL);

2. Initialize the public key algorithm context
   ret = EVP_PKEY_keygen_init(ctx_kp);

3. Generate RSA keypair and store the result in keypair
   ret = EVP_PKEY_generate(ctx_kp, keypair);
   /* Alternatively, ret = EVP_PKEY_keygen(ctx_kp, keypair); */

4. EVP_PKEY_CTX_free(ctx_kp);

These steps are explained below.

(1) Allocates the key context object using the key type

 As mentioned above, the EVP_PKEY_CTX_new_id() function allocates public key algorithm context using the key type specified by id and ENGINE e.

(2) Initialize the public key algorithm context

 EVP_PKEY_keygen_init() initializes a public key algorithm context ctx for a key generation operation. It returns 1 for success and 0 or a negative value for failure. A return value of -2 means the operation is not supported.

(3) Generate RSA keypair

```
#include <openssl/evp.h>
int EVP_PKEY_generate(EVP_PKEY_CTX *ctx, EVP_PKEY **ppkey);
```

EVP_PKEY_generate() or EVP_PKEY_keygen() performs the key generation operation and returns the generated key in the ppkey. If *ppkey is NULL when this function is called, it will be allocated, and that memory should be freed using EVP_PKEY_free() after use.

(4) Free the memory of the key context (using EVP_PKEY_CTX_free())

The following is the output from running the rsa program:

```
$ ./rsa
Signing the message digest using RSA was successful (siglen=256). Below is the
signature:

0xa127ba18f622e574fcfd29b8a3f5f7b862fac8d186f1c1093b498118a65cec752cc8d2b6f61fadabf69
70916cc0f5eac1a59018fe400cae162939f953661b19ec486fdf240245474c5eb04b869fc7610933a54dc
591f03c3d337bd5abbb203560b73d1761d319ea913ab7b0d1e5104407f6a275b446fa725702f332487686
fb29e1f192f78e38f80580235b28ca5b9c188e6cd6e9c56e9b7f87c087ab241f8acdc9b1edfce4beaed83
ecc1ea09af46552ee07564f0a4642a0c83954b0511a3d30843ac58e8177b904a0cbe03788ba6b5674750e
08e7bbda1a6f55b086a2f6eb97ff24e78097bf2389ca7ebd0919087c0c0293fa06baaf9de935aed1fe3c2
3442
verify_signature(): signature was successfully verified!
The RSA digital signature was successfully verified.
```

15-6-3-2-2 DSA

As shown in Figure 15-17(b) (dsa.c), performing the DSA digital signature on a message using the new APIs recommended in OpenSSL 3.0+ involves the following four major steps:

- get_digest(): compute the digest of the message

- generate_DSAkey(): generate an DSA key pair

- get_signature(): sign the digest using the signer's private key

- verify_signature(): at the receiving end, verify the signature using the signer's public key

where the first three steps are normally done at the sender of the message and the message receiver does step 1 and 4.

Please note that each of these four functions are our own library functions which are defined in mycryptolib.c as shown in Figure 15-39(b).

The generate_DSAkey() Function

We have described the other three functions shared between RSA and DSA.
Below we will describe the steps in the generate_DSAkey() function.

1. Allocates the key parameter context using the key type
   ctx_params = EVP_PKEY_CTX_new_id(keytype, NULL);

2. Initialize key parameter generation
   ret = EVP_PKEY_paramgen_init(ctx_params);

3. Set DSA key generation parameters - nbits
   ret = EVP_PKEY_CTX_set_dsa_paramgen_bits(ctx_params, keylen);

4. Generate key parameters and store the results in params
   ret = EVP_PKEY_paramgen(ctx_params, &params);

5. Create the public key algorithm context using the generated parameters
   ctx_kp = EVP_PKEY_CTX_new(params, NULL);

6. Initialize the public key algorithm context
   ret = EVP_PKEY_keygen_init(ctx_kp);

7. Generate DSA keypair and store the result in keypair
   ret = EVP_PKEY_generate(ctx_kp, keypair);
   /* Alternatively, ret = EVP_PKEY_keygen(ctx_kp, keypair); */

8. Free all resources
   EVP_PKEY_free(params);
   EVP_PKEY_CTX_free(ctx_params);
   EVP_PKEY_CTX_free(ctx_kp);

Notice that one thing special about generating a DSA key pair is that
(1) you need to generate parameters first before you can actually
generate the key pair, and (2) you need two different contexts: one context
for the parameter generation and the other for the key generation.
The two contexts are represented by ctx_params and ctx_kp, respectively,
in our code.

Because of this, at end, a program needs to free up memory for parameters
generated and for the two contexts as well, as shown in step 8 above.

The EVP_PKEY_CTX_new_id(), EVP_PKEY_CTX_new(), EVP_PKEY_keygen_init(),
and EVP_PKEY_generate() functions are same as what we've described above.
Therefore, we will introduce only the EVP_PKEY_paramgen_init(),
EVP_PKEY_CTX_set_dsa_paramgen_bits(), and EVP_PKEY_paramgen() here.

EVP_PKEY_paramgen_init() initializes key parameter generation.
It returns 1 for success and 0 or a negative value for failure.

EVP_PKEY_CTX_set_dsa_paramgen_bits() sets the number of bits used for DSA
parameter generation to nbits. If not specified, 2048 is used.
It returns a positive value for success and 0 or a negative value for failure.

EVP_PKEY_paramgen() generates key parameters. It returns 1 for success and
0 or a negative value for failure. A return value of -2 means the operation
is not supported.

The following is the output from running the dsa program:

```
$ ./dsa
Signing the message digest using DSA was successful (siglen=63). Below is the
signature:

0x303d021c55cd3cd34b32980ef929decbaf52f8d32d3e32f228d6eda9923e3ae5021d00d8d450b9787bc
82d991bd3bfff8293df2c8cc09dc4b283114918b3cf
verify_signature(): signature was successfully verified!
The DSA digital signature was successfully verified.
```

As you can tell from running the rsa and dsa programs, **dsa is slower than rsa**.

Figure 15-17 Example standalone programs of doing digital signature
-- rsa.c and dsa.c

(a)   rsa.c

```c
/*
 * Doing digital signature using RSA Algorithm in OpenSSL.
 * The new EVP_XXX APIs in OpenSSL 3.0+ are used.
 * Sharing functions of signature signing and verifying between RSA and DSA.
 * Copyright (c) 2015, 2016, 2020, 2023 Mr. Jin-Jwei Chen. All rights reserved.
 */

#include <stdio.h>
#include <errno.h>
#include <string.h>          /* memset(), strlen() */
#include <openssl/evp.h>
#include <openssl/rsa.h>
#include <openssl/dsa.h>
#include <openssl/err.h>
#include <openssl/sha.h>
#include "myopenssl.h"
#include "netlib.h"


#define DGSTBUFLEN    128   /* buffer length (bytes) for message digest */
#define DGSTNAMELEN    32   /* buffer length (bytes) for digest algorithm name */
#define DEFDGSTALGRM "sha256"   /* default digest algorithm */
#define MSGLEN         44        /* length of data */

/* This program demonstrates signing a message using RSA digital signature
 * algorithm and then verifying the signature using EVP APIs in OpenSSL 3.0+.
 */
int main(int argc, char *argv[])
{
  char    data[MSGLEN] = "1234567890axij25F7S4302dhLMyTRs2333333333333";
  unsigned int    datalen = MSGLEN;
  unsigned char   digest[DGSTBUFLEN];
  unsigned int    dgstlen = 0;
  char            dgstName[DGSTNAMELEN]=DEFDGSTALGRM;
  unsigned char   *sigbuf = NULL;     /* digital signature */
  SIZET_BAD       siglen = 0;         /* length of digital signature */
  int             ret;
```

1165

```
EVP_PKEY       *pkey = NULL;          /* public cryptography keypair */
int  bits = RSABITSLEN;  /* length of the prime number p to be generated */

/* The new API EVP_PKEY_sign() doesn't do hashing. Hence, we need to compute
 * the hash ourself.
 */
ret = get_digest(data, datalen, dgstName, digest, &dgstlen);
if (ret != SUCCESS)
{
  fprintf(stderr, "get_digest() failed, ret=%d\n", ret);
  return(ret);
}

/* Generate a RSA keypair */
ret = generate_RSAkey(EVP_PKEY_RSA, bits, &pkey);
if (ret != SUCCESS || pkey == NULL)
{
  fprintf(stderr, "generate_RSAkey() failed, ret=%d.\n", ret);
  if (pkey != NULL)
    EVP_PKEY_free(pkey);
  return(ret);
}

/* Allocate space for receiving the digital signature */
siglen = EVP_PKEY_get_size(pkey);
sigbuf = malloc(siglen);
if (sigbuf == NULL)
{
  fprintf(stderr, "malloc() failed\n");
  EVP_PKEY_free(pkey);
  return(ENOMEM);
}
memset(sigbuf, 0, siglen);

/* Compute the digital signature using RSA */
ret = get_signature(pkey, dgstName, digest, dgstlen, sigbuf, &siglen,
     EVP_PKEY_RSA);
if (ret != SUCCESS)
{
  fprintf(stderr, "get_signature() failed, ret=%d\n", ret);
  EVP_PKEY_free(pkey);
  free(sigbuf);
  return(ret);
}

fprintf(stdout, "Signing the message digest using RSA was successful "
  "(siglen=%lu). Below is the signature:\n", siglen);
print_binary_buf(sigbuf, siglen);

/* Verify the digital signature */
ret = verify_signature(pkey, digest, dgstlen, sigbuf, siglen,
     DEFDGSTALGRM, EVP_PKEY_RSA);
if (ret != SUCCESS)
{
  fprintf(stderr, "verify_signature() failed, ret=%d\n", ret);
  EVP_PKEY_free(pkey);
```

```
      free(sigbuf);
      return(ret);
    }
   fprintf(stdout, "The RSA digital signature was successfully verified.\n");

   EVP_PKEY_free(pkey);
   free(sigbuf);
   return(0);
}
```

(b)　dsa.c

```
/*
 * Doing digital signature using DSA Algorithm in OpenSSL.
 * The new EVP_XXX APIs in OpenSSL 3.0+ are used.
 * Sharing functions of signature signing and verifying between RSA and DSA.
 * Copyright (c) 2015, 2016, 2020, 2023 Mr. Jin-Jwei Chen. All rights reserved.
 */

#include <stdio.h>
#include <errno.h>
#include <string.h>          /* memset(), strlen() */
#include <openssl/evp.h>
#include <openssl/rsa.h>
#include <openssl/dsa.h>
#include <openssl/err.h>
#include <openssl/sha.h>
#include "myopenssl.h"
#include "netlib.h"

#define DGSTBUFLEN   128  /* buffer length (bytes) for message digest */
#define DGSTNAMELEN   32  /* buffer length (bytes) for digest algorithm name */
#define DEFDGSTALGRM "sha256"  /* default digest algorithm */
#define MSGLEN        44       /* length of data */

/* This program demonstrates signing a message using DSA digital signature
 * algorithm and then verifying the signature using EVP APIs in OpenSSL 3.0+.
 */
int main(int argc, char *argv[])
{
  char   data[MSGLEN] = "1234567890axij25F7S4302dhLMyTRs2333333333333";
  unsigned int   datalen = MSGLEN;
  unsigned char  digest[DGSTBUFLEN];
  unsigned int   dgstlen = 0;
  char           dgstName[DGSTNAMELEN]=DEFDGSTALGRM;
  unsigned char  *sigbuf = NULL;    /* digital signature */
  SIZET_BAD      siglen = 0;        /* length of digital signature */
  int            ret;

  EVP_PKEY       *pkey = NULL;      /* public cryptography keypair */
  int bits = DSABITSLEN;   /* length of the prime number p to be generated */

  /* The new API EVP_PKEY_sign() doesn't do hashing. Hence, we need to compute
   * the hash ourself.
   */
  ret = get_digest(data, datalen, dgstName, digest, &dgstlen);
```

1167

```
  if (ret != SUCCESS)
  {
    fprintf(stderr, "get_digest() failed, ret=%d\n", ret);
    return(ret);
  }

  /* Generate a DSA keypair */
  ret = generate_DSAkey(EVP_PKEY_DSA, bits, &pkey);
  if (ret != SUCCESS || pkey == NULL)
  {
    fprintf(stderr, "generate_DSAkey() failed, ret=%d.\n", ret);
    if (pkey != NULL)
      EVP_PKEY_free(pkey);
    return(ret);
  }

  /* Allocate space for receiving the digital signature */
  siglen = EVP_PKEY_get_size(pkey);
  sigbuf = malloc(siglen);
  if (sigbuf == NULL)
  {
    fprintf(stderr, "malloc() failed\n");
    EVP_PKEY_free(pkey);
    return(ENOMEM);
  }
  memset(sigbuf, 0, siglen);

  /* Compute the digital signature using DSA */
  ret = get_signature(pkey, dgstName, digest, dgstlen, sigbuf, &siglen,
        EVP_PKEY_DSA);
  if (ret != SUCCESS)
  {
    fprintf(stderr, "get_signature() failed, ret=%d\n", ret);
    EVP_PKEY_free(pkey);
    free(sigbuf);
    return(ret);
  }

  fprintf(stdout, "Signing the message digest using DSA was successful "
    "(siglen=%lu). Below is the signature:\n", siglen);
  print_binary_buf(sigbuf, siglen);

  /* Verify the digital signature */
  ret = verify_signature(pkey, digest, dgstlen, sigbuf, siglen,
        DEFDGSTALGRM, EVP_PKEY_DSA);
  if (ret != SUCCESS)
  {
    fprintf(stderr, "verify_signature() failed, ret=%d\n", ret);
    EVP_PKEY_free(pkey);
    free(sigbuf);
    return(ret);
  }
  fprintf(stdout, "The DSA digital signature was successfully verified.\n");

  EVP_PKEY_free(pkey);
  free(sigbuf);
```

```
return(0);
}
```

15-6-3-3 Using Digital Signature in Client-server Applications

When applying the digital signature technology between two programs, one extra step is required which is for the message sender to share its public key with the message receiver. This is because in order to verify the digital signature, a message receiver must use the sender/signer's public key.

Writing and Reading Public key

In OpenSSL, an API is provided for the sender to write its public key out to a file or for the receiver to read it in from that file.

The APIs for writing a public key out to a file used to be PEM_write_RSA_PUBKEY() and PEM_write_DSA_PUBKEY(), respectively, for RSA and DSA algorithms.

```
ret = PEM_write_RSA_PUBKEY(fp, rsa);
ret = PEM_write_DSA_PUBKEY(fp, dsa);
```

And the APIs to read a public key in from a file used to be PEM_read_RSA_PUBKEY() and PEM_read_DSA_PUBKEY() respectively for RSA and DSA:

```
ret=PEM_read_RSA_PUBKEY(fp, &rsa, (pem_password_cb *)NULL, (void *)NULL);
ret=PEM_read_DSA_PUBKEY(fp, &dsa, (pem_password_cb *)NULL, (void *)NULL);
```

But from OpenSSL 3.0 and on, these old APIs are deprecated and the new replacements are PEM_write_PUBKEY() and PEM_read_PUBKEY(), respectively, for writing and reading, regardless of the algorithm:

```
ret = PEM_write_PUBKEY(fp, pkey);
ret = PEM_read_PUBKEY(fp, &pkey, pem_password_cb *cb, void *u);
```

In the sender program, after calling get_signature() function to sign the message digest, it could invoke the PEM_write_PUBKEY() function to write out its public key to a file and make it available to the message receiver.

Similarly, in the message receiving program, before calling the verify_signature() function to verify the digital signature, it could invoke the PEM_read_PUBKEY() function to read the sender/signer's public key in from a file.

15-6-3-3-1 RSA

Figure 15-18 shows a pair of client and server programs, tcpclntrsa.c and tcpsrvrsa.c, that deploy RSA digital signature in a client-server communication.

Notice that this particular application provides secrecy because the request messages and replies are all encrypted. In addition, since RSA digital signature is also used, it provides message integrity and sender nonrepudiation as well.

One thing worth of mentioning is that in order for the recipient to be able to always successfully verify a digital signature, the recipient must know how long (i.e. how many bytes) the signature is. To solve this problem, the sender sends the length of the signature to the recipient. The output buffer on the sender side thus contains the following:

```
--------------------------------------------------
|signature length|  signature  |    message      |
--------------------------------------------------
  4 bytes         RSASIGLEN bytes   MAXREQSZ bytes
```

Below is a sample output of running tcpclntrsa and tcpsrvrsa:

```
$ ./tcpsrvrsa
TCP server listening at portnum=7878 ipv6=0
SO_REUSEADDR option is turned on.

Server got a client connection
Server received: Let's go out and have a dinner to celebrate our anniversary
tomorrow.
verify_signature(): signature was successfully verified!
RSA digital signature of the sender was successfully verified.

Server received: bye
verify_signature(): signature was successfully verified!
RSA digital signature of the sender was successfully verified.

$ ./tcpclntrsa
Enter a message to send ('bye' to end): Let's go out and have a dinner to celebrate
our anniversary tomorrow.
Send request:
Cipher
text=0x000001009674987dc1f2c238d8f92fea94bd0e148ef64bf78fbe9b0d3909cd28898884560001d1
ac76e26b6cbf3657244daa918730286f9aff8376235332cd1fb4205e25e68c01c2d412bc3aef9f5218709
dcf72133da793b413dc98d05b913ed78dab58ecf7fd174293302a5aa9274123fcece2d76d814688e9e323
26d74e5fbbf74eb4ce580d50fc95badf6ef5d238924b61dbfc47dd871f2f65375e89a22dcb4ab9f2f25f9
7570129e234e9197c97641dd8966f142554a440c983573ab9316aea183c30231b454bca39be4532136c5a
d22f77dd40b1737d0c2884d70c21a344eb491f5acf460c131ff10f2f20d3c50a9c83439e6eaea92f53b92
86f1abc0801831e2f0000000000000000ff2c4c28516cd08595dbdc18c4d1def7fe67b1cca743a6166b1a
558dd73da968ae45194eaa55b223db38b406afa2754b6353c5e829ffcd4c95f994120b9f476b54d04cd35
9e8f4743271f31f8670082f
Got this reply: This is reply message # 1 from the server.
Enter a message to send ('bye' to end): bye
Send request:
Cipher
text=0x00000100143c11be844ed3f0056b6ba2f1181a74a20e90c123e0989c5924d1fb823f4df22b965a
ef34ebdf220bfc7d0b48ffaf58cc4f9edf2c76277f6fd1656b20f1b813338e554afb60444e0d6e52134ec
2be6520a60df202afcd06f6df2e47b08ac40e1ec60e7b0db4dc12a413b6d05c8494060cc6ce3fc200256c
bcf8dcf5a9cbdb1cb0c8289241ccdd63330ed0040b95184277b6c3f3978a8353db3fbbab87fe8b42956c2
31f0b0d8b50c89eaa61bc51d0d6bc813d372c7340b76ed84fbbbab14a5bdab6f47e58ec4a55e9f314413a
4adb8bb771de37acae2dfbf0c56764d120f70354526398ba03ba8309fd298c4da049dcc18854f7bcdc62d
92c36bfea3d255165000000000000000d8d9e0661c940d67468f18090d2d3477
Got this reply: bye
```

Figure 15-18 Client-server programs using RSA digital signature
-- tcpclntrsa.c and tcpsrvrsa.c

(a) tcpsrvrsa.c

```c
/*
 * Demonstrating secrecy and nonrepudiation in network communications.
 * This is a TCP server program which gets a request message from a client
 * and sends back a reply. Both request messages and replies are all encrypted.
 * RSA digital signature is also used to ensure message integrity and
 * sender nonrepudiation.
 * Copyright (c) 2015, 2016, 2020, 2023 Mr. Jin-Jwei Chen. All rights reserved.
 */

#include <stdio.h>
#include <errno.h>
#include <sys/types.h>
#include <sys/socket.h>
#include <netinet/in.h>      /* protocols such as IPPROTO_TCP, ... */
#include <string.h>          /* memset(), strlen(), memcmp() */
#include <stdlib.h>          /* atoi() */
#include <openssl/evp.h>
#include <openssl/rsa.h>
#include <openssl/pem.h>
#include <openssl/err.h>
#include "myopenssl.h"
#include "netlib.h"

int main(int argc, char *argv[])
{
  int        sfd;                         /* file descriptor of the listener socket */
  struct sockaddr_in     srvaddr;         /* IPv4 socket address structure */
  struct sockaddr_in6    srvaddr6;        /* IPv6 socket address structure */
  in_port_t  portnum = SRVPORT;           /* port number this server listens on */
  int          portnum_in = 0;            /* port number specified by user */
  struct sockaddr_in6    clntaddr6;       /* client socket address */
  socklen_t              clntaddr6sz = sizeof(clntaddr6);
  int    newsock;                         /* file descriptor of client data socket */
  int    ipv6 = 0;
  int    ret;
  unsigned char  inbuf[MAXREQSZ+RSASIGLEN+LENGTHSZ];   /* input buffer */
  char           reqmsg[MAXREQSZ];        /* request message buffer */
  char           reply[MAXRPLYSZ];        /* buffer for server reply message */
  unsigned char  outbuf[MAXRPLYSZ];       /* output buffer */
  size_t         reqmsgsz;                /* size of client request message */
  size_t         replysz;                 /* size of server reply message */
  size_t         insize;                  /* size of encrypted request message */
  size_t         outsz;                   /* size of encrypted reply message */
  int            done;                    /* done with current client */
  int            msgcnt;                  /* count of messages from a client */

  /* variables for encryption/decryption */
  struct cipher  cipher;                  /* cipher to be used */
  unsigned char  newiv[EVP_MAX_IV_LENGTH];  /* new IV */
```

```
/* variables for message digest */
unsigned char   digest[EVP_MAX_MD_SIZE];   /* digest of the request message */
unsigned int    dgstlen = 0;               /* length of hash */

/* variables for RSA */
FILE            *fp = NULL;                 /* file pointer */
unsigned long   error = 0L;                 /* Openssl error code */
unsigned int    siglen = 0;                 /* length of signature */
unsigned int    *siglenp = NULL;            /* pointer to signature length field */
char            dgstName[DGSTNAMELEN]=DEFDGSTALGRM;   /* digest algorithm */
EVP_PKEY        *pkey = NULL;               /* key pair */
EVP_PKEY        *pkeyret = NULL;            /* pley pointer returned */

/* Get the server port number from user, if any */
if (argc > 1)
{
  portnum_in = atoi(argv[1]);
  if (portnum_in <= 0)
  {
    fprintf(stderr, "Error: port number %s invalid\n", argv[1]);
    fprintf(stderr, "Usage: %s [server_port] [1 (use IPv6)]\n", argv[0]);
    return(-1);
  }
  else
    portnum = portnum_in;
}

/* Get the IPv6 switch from user, if any */
if (argc > 2)
{
  if (argv[2][0] == '1')
    ipv6 = 1;
  else if (argv[2][0] != '0')
  {
    fprintf(stderr, "Usage: %s [server_port] [1 (use IPv6)]\n", argv[0]);
    return(-2);
  }
}

fprintf(stdout, "TCP server listening at portnum=%u ipv6=%u\n", portnum, ipv6);

/* Create the server listener socket */
if (ipv6)
  ret = new_bound_srv_endpt(&sfd, (struct sockaddr *)&srvaddr6, AF_INET6,
    portnum);
else
  ret = new_bound_srv_endpt(&sfd, (struct sockaddr *)&srvaddr, AF_INET,
    portnum);

if (ret != 0)
{
  fprintf(stderr, "Error: new_bound_srv_endpt() failed, ret=%d\n", ret);
  return(-4);
}
```

```
/* Listen for incoming requests and send replies */
do
{
  /* Listen for next client's connect request */
  newsock = accept(sfd, (struct sockaddr *)&clntaddr6, &clntaddr6sz);
  if (newsock < 0)
  {
    fprintf(stderr, "Error: accept() failed, errno=%d\n", errno);
    continue;
  }

  fprintf(stdout, "\nServer got a client connection\n");

  /* Initialize the cipher */
  strcpy(cipher.name, DEFAULT_CIPHER);
  strcpy((char *)cipher.key, DEFAULT_KEY);
  strcpy((char *)cipher.iv, DEFAULT_IV);

  /* Service this current client until done */
  done = 0;
  msgcnt = 1;
  pkey = NULL;
  do
  {
    /* Read the request message */
    insize = recv(newsock, inbuf, MAXREQSZ, 0);
    if (insize <= 0)
    {
      fprintf(stderr, "Error: recv() failed, insize=%lu\n", insize);
      break;
    }

    /* Decrypt the requested message */
    reqmsgsz = 0;
    ret = mydecrypt2(inbuf+RSASIGLEN+LENGTHSZ, insize-RSASIGLEN-LENGTHSZ,
         reqmsg, &reqmsgsz, &cipher);
    if (ret != 0)
    {
      fprintf(stderr, "Error: mydecrypt2() failed, ret=%d\n", ret);
      break;
    }

    reqmsg[reqmsgsz]='\0';
    fprintf(stdout, "Server received: %s\n", reqmsg);

    /* Compute message digest from the decrypted message */
    dgstlen = 0;
    ret = get_digest(reqmsg, reqmsgsz, dgstName, digest, &dgstlen);
    if (ret != SUCCESS)
    {
      fprintf(stderr, "Error: get_digest() failed, ret=%d\n", ret);
      break;
    }

    /* Read the sender's RSA public key from the file */
    fp = fopen(RSAPUBKEYFILE, "r");
```

```
    if (fp == NULL)
    {
      fprintf(stderr, "Error: fopen()() failed, errno=%d\n", errno);
      break;
    }

    pkeyret=PEM_read_PUBKEY(fp, &pkey, (pem_password_cb *)NULL, (void *)NULL);
    if (pkeyret == NULL)
    {
      error = ERR_get_error();
      fprintf(stderr, "Error: PEM_read_PUBKEY() failed, error=%lu\n", error);
      fclose(fp);
      break;
    }
    fclose(fp);

    /* Get the length of the actual signature. Do byte order conversion. */
    siglenp = (unsigned int *)inbuf;
    siglen = ntohl(*siglenp);

    /* Verify the RSA signature using the RSA public key read from file */
    ret = verify_signature(pkey, digest, dgstlen, inbuf+LENGTHSZ, siglen,
        dgstName, EVP_PKEY_RSA);
    if (ret != SUCCESS)
    {
      fprintf(stderr, "Error: verify_signature() failed, ret=%d\n", ret);
      break;
    }

    fprintf(stdout, "RSA digital signature of the sender was successfully
verified.\n\n");

    /* Set reply message */
    if ( !strcmp(reqmsg, BYE_MSG) )
    {
      done = 1;
      strcpy(reply, reqmsg);
    }
    else
      sprintf(reply, SRVREPLY2, msgcnt++);

    replysz = strlen(reply);

    /* Encrypt the reply message */
    outsz = 0;
    ret = myencrypt2(reply, replysz, outbuf, &outsz, &cipher);
    if (ret != 0)
    {
      fprintf(stderr, "Error: myencrypt2() failed, ret=%d\n", ret);
      break;
    }

    /* Send back an encrypted reply */
    ret = send(newsock, outbuf, outsz, 0);
    if (ret < 0)
      fprintf(stderr, "Error: send() failed to send a reply, errno=%d\n",
```

```
        errno);

      /* Change the IV for encryption/decryption */
      ret = increment_iv(cipher.iv, newiv);
      if (ret == 0)
        strcpy((char *)cipher.iv, (char *)newiv);
      else
      {
        fprintf(stderr, "Error: increment_iv() failed, ret=%d\n", ret);
        break;
      }

    } while (!done);

    /* We can close the socket now. */
    close(newsock);
    if (pkey != NULL)
      EVP_PKEY_free(pkey);

  } while (1);
}
```

(b) tcpclntrsa.c

```
/*
 * Demonstrating secrecy and nonrepudiation in network communications.
 * This is a TCP client program which exchanges messages with
 * a TCP server using encryption/decryption for secrecy and RSA digital
 * signature for message integrity and sender nonrepudiation.
 * Copyright (c) 2015, 2016, 2020, 2023 Mr. Jin-Jwei Chen. All rights reserved.
 */

#include <stdio.h>
#include <errno.h>
#include <sys/types.h>
#include <sys/socket.h>
#include <netinet/in.h>        /* protocols such as IPPROTO_TCP, ... */
#include <string.h>            /* memset(), strlen() */
#include <stdlib.h>            /* atoi(), malloc() */
#include <openssl/evp.h>
#include <openssl/hmac.h>
#include <openssl/rsa.h>
#include <openssl/pem.h>
#include <openssl/err.h>
#include "myopenssl.h"
#include "netlib.h"

#define FREEALL        \
    close(sfd);        \
    free(reqmsg);      \
    EVP_PKEY_free(pkey);

int main(int argc, char *argv[])
{
  int       ret;             /* return value */
  int       sfd=0;           /* socket file descriptor */
```

```
char        replymsg[MAXRPLYSZ];      /* reply message from server */
size_t      reqbufsz = MAXREQSZ;      /* size of client request buffer */
char        *reqmsg=NULL;             /* pointer to request message buffer */
size_t      reqmsgsz;                 /* size of client request message */
size_t      replysz;                  /* size of server reply message */
size_t      outsz;                    /* size of encrypted request message */
size_t      insize;                   /* size of encrypted reply message */
unsigned char  outbuf[MAXREQSZ+RSASIGLEN+LENGTHSZ];    /* output buffer */
unsigned char  inbuf[MAXRPLYSZ];      /* input buffer */

in_port_t   srvport = SRVPORT;        /* port number the server listens on */
int         srvport_in = 0;           /* port number specified by user */
char        *srvhost = "localhost";   /* name of server host */
int         done = 0;                 /* to end client */

struct cipher  cipher;                /* cipher to be used */
unsigned char  newiv[EVP_MAX_IV_LENGTH];  /* new IV */

unsigned int   dgstlen = 0;           /* length of hash */
unsigned char  digest[EVP_MAX_MD_SIZE];    /* message digest */
char   dgstName[DGSTNAMELEN]=DEFDGSTALGRM;  /* digest algorithm */

int     bits = RSABITSLEN;  /* length of the prime number p to be generated */
unsigned char  seed[RSASEEDLEN+1] = RSASEED;  /* seed */
unsigned int   siglen;                /* actual length of RSA signature */
unsigned int   *siglenp = NULL;       /* pointer to signature length field */
int         dgsttype = RSADGSTTYPE;   /* digest type */
FILE        *fp = NULL;               /* file holding RSA public key */

EVP_PKEY    *pkey = NULL;             /* public cryptography keypair */
unsigned long  error = 0L;            /* error code */
char        errstr[ERRBUFLEN];        /* error string */
unsigned int   keyGenerated = 0;

/* Get the server port number from user, if any */
if (argc > 1)
{
  srvport_in = atoi(argv[1]);
  if (srvport_in <= 0)
  {
    fprintf(stderr, "Error: port number %s invalid\n", argv[1]);
    return(-1);
  }
  else
    srvport = srvport_in;
}

/* Get the name of the server host from user, if specified */
if (argc > 2)
  srvhost = argv[2];

/* Set the cipher */
strcpy(cipher.name, DEFAULT_CIPHER);
strcpy((char *)cipher.key, DEFAULT_KEY);
strcpy((char *)cipher.iv, DEFAULT_IV);
```

```
/* Connect to the server */
ret = connect_to_server(&sfd, srvhost, srvport);
if (ret != 0)
{
  fprintf(stderr, "Error: connect_to_server() failed, ret=%d\n", ret);
  if (sfd) close(sfd);
  return(-2);
}

/* Allocate input buffer */
reqmsg = malloc(MAXREQSZ);
if (reqmsg == NULL)
{
  fprintf(stderr, "Error: malloc() failed\n");
  close(sfd);
  return(-3);
}

/* Send a few messages to the server */
do
{
  fprintf(stdout, "Enter a message to send ('bye' to end): ");
  reqmsgsz = getline(&reqmsg, &reqbufsz, stdin);
  if (reqmsgsz == -1)
  {
    fprintf(stderr, "Error: getline() failed, ret=%lu\n", reqmsgsz);
    close(sfd);
    free(reqmsg);
    return(-4);
  }

  /* Remove the newline character at end of input */
  reqmsg[--reqmsgsz] = '\0';

  /* Calculate the digest of the message */
  memset(digest, 0, EVP_MAX_MD_SIZE);
  memset(outbuf, 0, RSASIGLEN);
  dgstlen = 0;

  /* The new API EVP_PKEY_sign() doesn't do hashing. Hence, we need to
     compute the hash ourself. */
  ret = get_digest(reqmsg, reqmsgsz, dgstName, digest, &dgstlen);
  if (ret != SUCCESS)
  {
    fprintf(stderr, "Error: get_digest() failed, ret=%d\n", ret);
    close(sfd);
    free(reqmsg);
    return(-5);
  }

  /* Generate a RSA keypair */
  if (!keyGenerated)
  {
    ret = generate_RSAkey(EVP_PKEY_RSA, bits, &pkey);
    if (ret != SUCCESS || pkey == NULL)
    {
```

```
      fprintf(stderr, "Error: generate_RSAkey() failed, ret=%d.\n", ret);
      close(sfd);
      free(reqmsg);
      if (pkey != NULL)
        EVP_PKEY_free(pkey);
      return(-6);
    }
  keyGenerated = 1;
}

/* Compute the digital signature using RSA */
ret = get_signature(pkey, dgstName, digest, dgstlen, outbuf+LENGTHSZ,
      &siglen, EVP_PKEY_RSA);
if (ret != SUCCESS)
{
  fprintf(stderr, "Error: get_signature() failed, ret=%d\n", ret);
  FREEALL
  return(-7);
}

/* Place the signature length at beginning of the buffer */
siglenp = (unsigned int *)outbuf;
*siglenp = htonl(siglen);

/* Write the RSA public key out to a file for the recipient */
fp = fopen(RSAPUBKEYFILE, "w");
if (fp == NULL)
{
  fprintf(stderr, "Error: fopen()() failed, errno=%d\n", errno);
  FREEALL
  return(-8);
}

ret = PEM_write_PUBKEY(fp, pkey);
if (ret != OPENSSL_SUCCESS)
{
  error = ERR_get_error();
  ERR_error_string_n(error, errstr, ERRBUFLEN);
  fprintf(stderr, "Error: PEM_write_PUBKEY()() failed,"
    " error=%lu\n%s\n", error, errstr);
  fclose(fp);
  FREEALL
  return(-9);
}
fclose(fp);

/* Encrypt the message to be sent and place it after the hash in buffer */
ret = myencrypt2(reqmsg, reqmsgsz, outbuf+LENGTHSZ+RSASIGLEN, &outsz, &cipher);
if (ret != 0)
{
  fprintf(stderr, "Error: myencrypt2() failed, ret=%d\n", ret);
  FREEALL
  return(-10);
}

fprintf(stdout, "Send request:\n");
```

```
    print_cipher_text(outbuf, outsz+RSASIGLEN+LENGTHSZ);

    /* Send the encrypted message, together with RSA signature */
    ret = send_msg(sfd, (unsigned char *)outbuf, outsz+RSASIGLEN+LENGTHSZ, 0);
    if (ret != 0)
    {
      fprintf(stderr, "Error: send_msg() failed, ret=%d\n", ret);
      FREEALL
      return(-11);
    }

    /* Wait for server reply */
    memset((void *)inbuf, 0, MAXRPLYSZ);
    insize = 0;
    insize = recv(sfd, inbuf, MAXRPLYSZ, 0);
    if (insize <= 0)
    {
      fprintf(stderr, "Error: recv() failed to receive a reply from "
        "server, insize=%lu\n", insize);
      FREEALL
      return(-12);
    }

    /* Decrypt the server reply message */
    memset((void *)replymsg, 0, MAXRPLYSZ);
    replysz = 0;
    ret = mydecrypt2(inbuf, insize, replymsg, &replysz, &cipher);
    if (ret != 0)
    {
      fprintf(stderr, "Error: mydecrypt2() failed, ret=%d\n", ret);
      FREEALL
      return(-13);
    }

    replymsg[replysz]='\0';
    fprintf(stdout, "Got this reply: %s\n", replymsg);

    if (!strcmp(replymsg, reqmsg))
      done = 1;

    /* Change the IV for encryption/decryption */
    ret = increment_iv(cipher.iv, newiv);
    if (ret == 0)
      strcpy((char *)cipher.iv, (char *)newiv);
    else
    {
      fprintf(stderr, "Error: increment_iv() failed, ret=%d\n", ret);
      FREEALL
      return(-14);
    }

  } while (!done);

  FREEALL
  return(0);
}
```

15-6-3-3-2 DSA

Figure 15-19 shows a pair of client and server programs, tcpclntdsa.c and tcpsrvdsa.c, that deploy DSA digital signature in a client-server communication.

Notice that this particular application provides secrecy because the request messages and replies are all encrypted. In addition, since DSA digital signature is also used, it provides message integrity and sender nonrepudiation as well.

The contents of the message buffer sent by the client is similar to what was described in the preceding section for RSA algorithm, except the length of the signature is DSASIGLEN bytes.

Below is a sample output of running tcpclntdsa and tcpsrvdsa:

```
$ ./tcpsrvdsa
TCP server listening at portnum=7878 ipv6=0
SO_REUSEADDR option is turned on.

Server got a client connection
Server received: Let's go out and have a dinner to celebrate our anniversary
tomorrow.
verify_signature(): signature was successfully verified!
DSA digital signature of the sender was successfully verified.

Server received: bye

$ ./tcpclntdsa
Enter a message to send ('bye' to end): Let's go out and have a dinner to celebrate
our anniversary tomorrow.
Signing the message digest using DSA was successful (siglen=64).

0x303e021d00837679d62c52c5a42b855a1f9a264f6d41b99f90ad868c7bbbc3b047021d00b9b3f5840ee
7bcc6ef3638f86a538daee0e95c7e1a65f2ece2cee29e
Send request:
Cipher
text=0x00000040303e021d00837679d62c52c5a42b855a1f9a264f6d41b99f90ad868c7bbbc3b047021d
00b9b3f5840ee7bcc6ef3638f86a538daee0e95c7e1a65f2ece2cee29e000000000000000000000000000
00000ff2c4c28516cd08595dbdc18c4d1def7fe67b1cca743a6166b1a558dd73da968ae45194eaa55b223
db38b406afa2754b6353c5e829ffcd4c95f994120b9f476b54d04cd359e8f4743271f31f8670082f
Got this reply: This is reply message # 1 from the server.
Enter a message to send ('bye' to end): bye
```

Figure 15-19 Client-server programs using DSA digital signature
-- tcpclntdsa.c and tcpsrvdsa.c

(a) tcpsrvdsa.c

```
/*
 * Demonstrating secrecy and nonrepudiation in network communications.
 * This is a TCP server program which gets a request message from a client
```

```
 * and sends back a reply. Both request messages and replies are all encrypted.
 * DSA digital signature is also used to ensure message integrity and
 * sender nonrepudiation.
 * Copyright (c) 2015, 2016, 2020, 2023 Mr. Jin-Jwei Chen. All rights reserved.
 */

#include <stdio.h>
#include <errno.h>
#include <sys/types.h>
#include <sys/socket.h>
#include <netinet/in.h>      /* protocols such as IPPROTO_TCP, ... */
#include <string.h>          /* memset(), strlen(), memcmp() */
#include <stdlib.h>          /* atoi() */
#include <openssl/evp.h>
#include <openssl/dsa.h>
#include <openssl/pem.h>
#include <openssl/err.h>
#include "myopenssl.h"
#include "netlib.h"

int main(int argc, char *argv[])
{
  int     sfd;                          /* file descriptor of the listener socket */
  struct sockaddr_in    srvaddr;        /* IPv4 socket address structure */
  struct sockaddr_in6   srvaddr6;       /* IPv6 socket address structure */
  in_port_t  portnum = SRVPORT;         /* port number this server listens on */
  int        portnum_in = 0;            /* port number specified by user */
  struct sockaddr_in6   clntaddr;       /* client socket address */
  socklen_t             clntaddr6sz = sizeof(clntaddr6);
  int        newsock;                   /* file descriptor of client data socket */
  int        ipv6 = 0;
  int        ret;
  char       reqmsg[MAXREQSZ];     /* request message buffer */
  char       reply[MAXRPLYSZ];     /* buffer for server reply message */
  size_t     reqmsgsz;             /* size of client request message */
  size_t     replysz;              /* size of server reply message */
  size_t     insize;               /* size of encrypted request message */
  size_t     outsz;                /* size of encrypted reply message */
  int        done;                 /* done with current client */
  int        msgcnt;               /* count of messages from a client */
  unsigned char  inbuf[MAXREQSZ+DSASIGLEN+LENGTHSZ];    /* input buffer */
  unsigned char  outbuf[MAXRPLYSZ];  /* output buffer */

  /* variables for encryption/decryption */
  struct cipher    cipher;              /* cipher to be used */
  unsigned char  newiv[EVP_MAX_IV_LENGTH];  /* new IV */

  /* variables for message digest */
  const EVP_MD    *hashfunc;                    /* hash function */
  unsigned char  digest[EVP_MAX_MD_SIZE];  /* digest of the request message */
  unsigned int   dgstlen = 0;                   /* length of hash */

  /* variables for DSA */
  FILE         *fp = NULL;               /* file pointer */
  unsigned long  error = 0L;             /* Openssl error code */
  unsigned int   siglen = 0;             /* length of signature */
```

```c
unsigned int   *siglenp = NULL;        /* pointer to signature length field */
EVP_PKEY       *pkey = NULL;           /* public cryptography keypair */
EVP_PKEY       *pkeyret = NULL;        /* pley pointer returned */
char  dgstName[DGSTNAMELEN]=DEFDGSTALGRM;   /* name of digest algorithm */

/* Get the server port number from user, if any */
if (argc > 1)
{
  portnum_in = atoi(argv[1]);
  if (portnum_in <= 0)
  {
    fprintf(stderr, "Error: port number %s invalid\n", argv[1]);
    fprintf(stderr, "Usage: %s [server_port] [1 (use IPv6)]\n", argv[0]);
    return(-1);
  }
  else
    portnum = portnum_in;
}

/* Get the IPv6 switch from user, if any */
if (argc > 2)
{
  if (argv[2][0] == '1')
    ipv6 = 1;
  else if (argv[2][0] != '0')
  {
    fprintf(stderr, "Usage: %s [server_port] [1 (use IPv6)]\n", argv[0]);
    return(-2);
  }
}

fprintf(stdout, "TCP server listening at portnum=%u ipv6=%u\n", portnum, ipv6);

/* Create the server listener socket */
if (ipv6)
  ret = new_bound_srv_endpt(&sfd, (struct sockaddr *)&srvaddr6, AF_INET6,
    portnum);
else
  ret = new_bound_srv_endpt(&sfd, (struct sockaddr *)&srvaddr, AF_INET,
    portnum);

if (ret != 0)
{
  fprintf(stderr, "Error: new_bound_srv_endpt() failed, ret=%d\n", ret);
  return(-4);
}

/* Listen for incoming requests and send replies */
do
{
  /* Listen for next client's connect request */
  newsock = accept(sfd, (struct sockaddr *)&clntaddr6, &clntaddr6sz);
  if (newsock < 0)
  {
    fprintf(stderr, "Error: accept() failed, errno=%d\n", errno);
    continue;
```

```
    }

    fprintf(stdout, "\nServer got a client connection\n");

    /* Initialize the cipher */
    strcpy(cipher.name, DEFAULT_CIPHER);
    strcpy((char *)cipher.key, DEFAULT_KEY);
    strcpy((char *)cipher.iv, DEFAULT_IV);

    /* Service this current client until done */
    done = 0;
    msgcnt = 1;
    pkey = NULL;
    do
    {
      /* Read the request message */
      insize = recv(newsock, inbuf, MAXREQSZ, 0);
      if (insize <= 0)
      {
        fprintf(stderr, "Error: recv() failed, insize=%lu\n", insize);
        break;
      }

      /* Decrypt the requested message */
      reqmsgsz = 0;
      ret = mydecrypt2(inbuf+DSASIGLEN+LENGTHSZ, insize-DSASIGLEN-LENGTHSZ,
          reqmsg, &reqmsgsz, &cipher);
      if (ret != 0)
      {
        fprintf(stderr, "Error: mydecrypt2() failed, ret=%d\n", ret);
        break;
      }

      reqmsg[reqmsgsz]='\0';
      fprintf(stdout, "Server received: %s\n", reqmsg);

      /* Compute message digest from the decrypted message */
      dgstlen = 0;
      ret = get_digest(reqmsg, reqmsgsz, dgstName, digest, &dgstlen);
      if (ret != SUCCESS)
      {
        fprintf(stderr, "Error: get_digest() failed, ret=%d\n", ret);
        break;
      }

      /* Read the sender's DSA public key from the file */
      fp = fopen(DSAPUBKEYFILE, "r");
      if (fp == NULL)
      {
        fprintf(stderr, "Error: fopen()() failed, errno=%d\n", errno);
        break;
      }

      pkeyret=PEM_read_PUBKEY(fp, &pkey, (pem_password_cb *)NULL, (void *)NULL);
      if (pkeyret == NULL)
      {
```

```
        error = ERR_get_error();
        fprintf(stderr, "Error: PEM_read_PUBKEY() failed, error=%lu\n", error);
        fclose(fp);
        break;
    }
    fclose(fp);

    /* Get the length of the actual signature. Do byte order conversion. */
    siglenp = (unsigned int *)inbuf;
    siglen = ntohl(*siglenp);

    /* Verify the DSA signature using the DSA public key read from file */
    ret = verify_signature(pkey, digest, dgstlen, inbuf+LENGTHSZ, siglen,
        DEFDGSTALGRM, EVP_PKEY_DSA);
    if (ret != SUCCESS)
    {
        fprintf(stderr, "Error: verify_signature() failed, ret=%d\n", ret);
        break;
    }

    fprintf(stdout, "DSA digital signature of the sender was successfully
verified.\n\n");

    /* Set reply message */
    if ( !strcmp(reqmsg, BYE_MSG) )
    {
        done = 1;
        strcpy(reply, reqmsg);
    }
    else
        sprintf(reply, SRVREPLY2, msgcnt++);

    replysz = strlen(reply);

    /* Encrypt the reply message */
    outsz = 0;
    ret = myencrypt2(reply, replysz, outbuf, &outsz, &cipher);
    if (ret != 0)
    {
        fprintf(stderr, "Error: myencrypt2() failed, ret=%d\n", ret);
        break;
    }

    /* Send back an encrypted reply */
    ret = send(newsock, outbuf, outsz, 0);
    if (ret < 0)
        fprintf(stderr, "Error: send() failed to send a reply, errno=%d\n",
          errno);

    /* Change the IV for encryption/decryption */
    ret = increment_iv(cipher.iv, newiv);
    if (ret == 0)
        strcpy((char *)cipher.iv, (char *)newiv);
    else
    {
        fprintf(stderr, "Error: increment_iv() failed, ret=%d\n", ret);
```

```
        break;
    }

  } while (!done);

  /* We can close the socket now. */
  close(newsock);
  if (pkey != NULL)
      EVP_PKEY_free(pkey);

} while (1);
}
```

(b) tcpclntdsa.c

```
/*
 * Demonstrating secrecy and nonrepudiation in network communications.
 * This is a TCP client program which exchanges messages with
 * a TCP server using encryption/decryption for secrecy and DSA digital
 * signature for message integrity and sender nonrepudiation.
 * Copyright (c) 2015, 2016, 2020, 2023 Mr. Jin-Jwei Chen. All rights reserved.
 */

#include <stdio.h>
#include <errno.h>
#include <sys/types.h>
#include <sys/socket.h>
#include <netinet/in.h>      /* protocols such as IPPROTO_TCP, ... */
#include <string.h>          /* memset(), strlen() */
#include <stdlib.h>          /* atoi(), malloc() */
#include <unistd.h>          /* close() */
#include <openssl/evp.h>
#include <openssl/hmac.h> .
#include <openssl/dsa.h>
#include <openssl/pem.h>
#include <openssl/err.h>
#include "myopenssl.h"
#include "netlib.h"

#define FREEALL     \
    close(sfd);     \
    free(reqmsg);   \
    if (pkey != NULL) \
      EVP_PKEY_free(pkey);

int main(int argc, char *argv[])
{
  int      ret;                      /* return value */
  int      sfd=0;                    /* socket file descriptor */
  char     inbuf[MAXRPLYSZ];         /* input buffer */
  char     replymsg[MAXRPLYSZ];      /* reply message from server */
  size_t   reqbufsz = MAXREQSZ;      /* size of client request buffer */
  char     *reqmsg=NULL;             /* pointer to request message buffer */
  size_t   reqmsgsz;                 /* size of client request message */
  size_t   replysz;                  /* size of server reply message */
  size_t   outsz;                    /* size of encrypted request message */
```

1185

```
  size_t      insize;                   /* size of encrypted reply message */
  unsigned char  outbuf[MAXREQSZ+DSASIGLEN+LENGTHSZ];    /* output buffer */

  in_port_t    srvport = SRVPORT;        /* port number the server listens on */
  int          srvport_in = 0;           /* port number specified by user */
  char         *srvhost = "localhost";   /* name of server host */
  int          done = 0;                 /* to end client */

  struct cipher  cipher;                 /* cipher to be used */
  unsigned char  newiv[EVP_MAX_IV_LENGTH];       /* new IV */

  unsigned int   dgstlen = 0;            /* length of hash */
  unsigned char  digest[EVP_MAX_MD_SIZE];   /* message digest */

  int            bits = DSABITSLEN;      /* length of the prime number p to be generated
*/
  unsigned char  seed[DSASEEDLEN+1] = DSASEED;   /* seed */
  unsigned int   siglen;                 /* actual length of DSA signature */
  unsigned int   *siglenp = NULL;        /* pointer to signature length field */
  FILE           *fp = NULL;             /* file holding DSA public key */
  unsigned long  error = 0L;             /* error code */
  char           errstr[ERRBUFLEN];      /* error string */

  char  dgstName[DGSTNAMELEN]=DEFDGSTALGRM;   /* name of digest algorithm */
  EVP_PKEY       *pkey = NULL;           /* public cryptography keypair */
  unsigned int   keyGenerated = 0;

  /* Get the server port number from user, if any */
  if (argc > 1)
  {
    srvport_in = atoi(argv[1]);
    if (srvport_in <= 0)
    {
      fprintf(stderr, "Error: port number %s invalid\n", argv[1]);
      return(-1);
    }
    else
      srvport = srvport_in;
  }

  /* Get the name of the server host from user, if specified */
  if (argc > 2)
    srvhost = argv[2];

  /* Set the cipher */
  strcpy(cipher.name, DEFAULT_CIPHER);
  strcpy((char *)cipher.key, DEFAULT_KEY);
  strcpy((char *)cipher.iv, DEFAULT_IV);

  /* Connect to the server */
  ret = connect_to_server(&sfd, srvhost, srvport);
  if (ret != 0)
  {
    fprintf(stderr, "Error: connect_to_server() failed, ret=%d\n", ret);
    if (sfd) close(sfd);
    return(-2);
```

```
    }

/* Allocate input buffer */
reqmsg = malloc(MAXREQSZ);
if (reqmsg == NULL)
{
  fprintf(stderr, "Error: malloc() failed\n");
  close(sfd);
  return(-3);
}

/* Send a few messages to the server */
do
{
  fprintf(stdout, "Enter a message to send ('bye' to end): ");
  reqmsgsz = getline(&reqmsg, &reqbufsz, stdin);
  if (reqmsgsz == -1)
  {
    fprintf(stderr, "Error: getline() failed, ret=%lu\n", reqmsgsz);
    close(sfd);
    free(reqmsg);
    return(-4);
  }

  /* Remove the newline character at end of input */
  reqmsg[--reqmsgsz] = '\0';

  /* Calculate the digest of the message */
  memset(digest, 0, EVP_MAX_MD_SIZE);
  memset(outbuf, 0, DSASIGLEN);
  dgstlen = 0;

  /* The new API EVP_PKEY_sign() doesn't do hashing. Hence, we need to
     compute the hash ourself.  */
  ret = get_digest(reqmsg, reqmsgsz, dgstName, digest, &dgstlen);
  if (ret != SUCCESS)
  {
    fprintf(stderr, "Error: get_digest() failed, ret=%d\n", ret);
    close(sfd);
    free(reqmsg);
    return(-5);
  }

  /* Generate a DSA keypair -- do it only once */
  if (!keyGenerated)
  {
    ret = generate_DSAkey(EVP_PKEY_DSA, bits, &pkey);
    if (ret != SUCCESS || pkey == NULL)
    {
      fprintf(stderr, "Error: generate_DSAkey() failed, ret=%d.\n", ret);
      FREEALL
      return(-6);
    }
    keyGenerated = 1;
  }
```

```c
/* Set siglen */
siglen = DSASIGLEN;

/* Compute the digital signature using DSA */
ret = get_signature(pkey, dgstName, digest, dgstlen, outbuf+LENGTHSZ,
    &siglen, EVP_PKEY_DSA);
if (ret != SUCCESS)
{
  fprintf(stderr, "Error: get_signature() failed, ret=%d\n", ret);
  FREEALL
  return(-7);
}

fprintf(stdout, "Signing the message digest using DSA was successful "
  "(siglen=%u).\n", siglen);
print_binary_buf(outbuf+LENGTHSZ, siglen);

/* Place the signature length at beginning of the buffer */
siglenp = (unsigned int *)outbuf;
*siglenp = htonl(siglen);

/* Write the DSA public key out to a file for the recipient */
fp = fopen(DSAPUBKEYFILE, "w");
if (fp == NULL)
{
  fprintf(stderr, "Error: fopen()() failed, errno=%d\n", errno);
  FREEALL
  return(-8);
}

ret = PEM_write_PUBKEY(fp, pkey);
if (ret != OPENSSL_SUCCESS)
{
  error = ERR_get_error();
  ERR_error_string_n(error, errstr, ERRBUFLEN);
  fprintf(stderr, "Error: PEM_write_PUBKEY()() failed,"
    " error=%lu\n%s\n", error, errstr);
  fclose(fp);
  FREEALL
  return(-9);
}
fclose(fp);

/* Encrypt the message to be sent and place it after the hash in buffer */
ret = myencrypt2(reqmsg, reqmsgsz, outbuf+LENGTHSZ+DSASIGLEN, &outsz, &cipher);
if (ret != 0)
{
  fprintf(stderr, "Error: myencrypt2() failed, ret=%d\n", ret);
  FREEALL
  return(-10);
}

fprintf(stdout, "Send request:\n");
print_cipher_text(outbuf, outsz+DSASIGLEN+LENGTHSZ);

/* Send the encrypted message, together with the DSA signature */
```

```
    ret = send_msg(sfd, (unsigned char *)outbuf, outsz+DSASIGLEN+LENGTHSZ, 0);
    if (ret != 0)
    {
      fprintf(stderr, "Error: send_msg() failed, ret=%d\n", ret);
      FREEALL
      return(-11);
    }

    /* Wait for server reply */
    memset((void *)inbuf, 0, MAXRPLYSZ);
    insize = 0;
    insize = recv(sfd, inbuf, MAXRPLYSZ, 0);
    if (insize <= 0)
    {
      fprintf(stderr, "Error: recv() failed to receive a reply from "
        "server, insize=%lu\n", insize);
      FREEALL
      return(-12);
    }

    /* Decrypt the server reply message */
    memset((void *)replymsg, 0, MAXRPLYSZ);
    replysz = 0;
    ret = mydecrypt2((unsigned char *)inbuf, insize, replymsg, &replysz, &cipher);
    if (ret != 0)
    {
      fprintf(stderr, "Error: mydecrypt2() failed, ret=%d\n", ret);
      FREEALL
      return(-13);
    }

    replymsg[replysz]='\0';
    fprintf(stdout, "Got this reply: %s\n", replymsg);

    if (!strcmp(replymsg, reqmsg))
      done = 1;

    /* Change the IV for encryption/decryption */
    ret = increment_iv(cipher.iv, newiv);
    if (ret == 0)
      strcpy((char *)cipher.iv, (char *)newiv);
    else
    {
      fprintf(stderr, "Error: increment_iv() failed, ret=%d\n", ret);
      FREEALL
      return(-14);
    }

  } while (!done);

  FREEALL
  return(0);
}
```

15-7 Public Key Infrastructure (PKI)

Some of you may have heard the terminology PKI.

The term **public key infrastructure** (**PKI**) refers to the infrastructure provided to enable and facilitate electronic commerce and communications using computer networks such as the Internet.

The Internet itself is a gigantic computer network spanned the entire world. Because the Internet consists of so many different computer systems, traditional user name and password security mechanism is no longer feasible. It's just impossible to in advance create a user account for anyone around the world who is likely to use a given web server.

In digital commerce, people make purchases remotely.
They use web browsers running on their computers or hand-held devices and connect to some web server of some company somewhere over the Internet. The client (the browser) and the server (the web server) could very well be located in different continents many thousands of miles apart.

Because it's remote over the Internet, there is no personal presence, no verification of driver license or fingerprints or things of that sort. How do people conduct commerce over the Internet without even seeing or talking to each other?

How do you prevent someone from setting up a phony web site and collecting money from the public without actually delivering any goods?
How do companies and people identify themselves?
The answer is it's all relying on digital certificates.

In digital commerce, digital certificates are used to represent and authenticate various entities involved in a communication using computer networks, especially in a situation where the potential clients may not be known in advance, like over the Internet.

Digital certificate is all based on **public key cryptography** (**PKC**) which uses a pair of public and private keys mathematically generated by computer. A **digital certificate** is essentially an electronic document containing some entity's public key signed by an issuer using the issuer's private key.

In other words, **digital commerce relies on using digital certificates to represent and authenticate people and entities. And digital certificates are based on public key cryptography. Hence, digital commerce is built upon public key cryptography.**

As we have discussed in the sections above, public key cryptography is used in multiple aspects of computer security. It's used to provide confidentiality (encryption and decryption), recipient authentication (PKE), as well as sender authentication and nonrepudiation (as in digital signature). In addition, it is also used to facilitate session establishment in distributing the secret session key in protocols such as SSL and TLS. A **session key** is a symmetric encryption key that the two communicating parties agree upon and is to be used for a session.

Public key cryptography makes it much easier to have a secure digital communication over a public computer network such as the Internet with someone or some entity that one never meets and/or is far away because it eliminates the requirement of having to distribute a shared secret key in advance between the two communicating parties. This is a very significant contribution of public key cryptography.

All of the technologies built upon public key cryptography is all part of PKI. But PKI does not include just technologies. It is a set of technologies, rules, roles, protocols and policies. Its components also include certificate authority, certificate repository, certificate registration, certificate validation, certificate revocation, certificate update/renew, key recovery service in case keys are lost, key and certificate life cycle management, etc.

In summary, public key infrastructure is the E-Commerce security infrastructure that is built upon public key cryptography.

15-7-1 Applications of Public Key Cryptography

1. Public Key Encryption - secrecy and recipient authentication

When using public key cryptography in providing secrecy of communication, a message sender encrypts the message being sent using the public key of the receiver. This usage is sometimes called **public key encryption** (**PKE**). This has dual benefits. First, it provides confidentiality because the message is encrypted. Second, since the public key of the receiver is used in encrypting the message, the encrypted message can only be decrypted by using the receiver's private key. This also uniquely identifies the receiver as long as the receiver's private key is not compromised.

2. Digital Signatures - secrecy, integrity and nonrepudiation

The second main use of public key cryptography is in digital signature, which provides secrecy, sender authentication/nonrepudiation and integrity.

In this application, the sender of a message encrypts the message being sent and its digest using the sender's private key. Both are then sent to the receiver. The receiver decrypts them using the sender's public key. If the decryption succeeds, it proves the message must have been encrypted using the sender's private key and thus it must have been sent by the sender as long as the sender's private key has not been compromised. This provides nonrepudiation and secrecy. Besides, when the decrypted digest matches what the receiver has computed on its own from the decrypted message, it shows the message has not been tempered with during transit, which is integrity protection.

3. Digital Certificates - electronic commerce

This is related to what we will discuss in the sections below.

15-8 X.509 Certificates

Before actually jumping into the SSL/TLS protocols themselves, we discuss certificates here in this section because both SSL and TLS depend on use of certificates.

15-8-1 What Is a Certificate?

In SSL/TLS world, every entity, be it a person, company, computer, program (server or client) or device, is always identified by a digital document called certificate.

What is a certificate? Certificates are part of Public Key Infrastructure (PKI). As we've said, in public key cryptography, a pair of public and private keys is generated and used in encryption, decryption and for other purposes such as identification. The pair of keys is generated at the same time by a computer using an algorithm and they uniquely match each other. The private key is supposed to be known only to its owner while the public key is made available to the public. A **certificate** is essentially a digital document containing some entity's **public key** and the information about that entity (such as name, address and company, etc.) in it.

A certificate has an issuer. It is a document digitally signed by the issuer.

In other words, a certificate is a digital document containing some entity A's public key that is signed by some entity B using entity B's private key. Entity A is called the "subject" of the certificate and entity B is called the "issuer" of the certificate. The issuer is also called the **Certificate Authority** (**CA** for short). The issuer is the signer of the certificate.

Here, **signing** means the public key contained within a certificate is actually encrypted by using an encryption/signature algorithm with the signer's private key as input.

The actual contents of a certificate include more than just the public key. It consists of the following information in it:

- Public key: the public key identifying the owner of the certificate
- Subject information: name, address and organization of the owner
- Issuer information: name, address and organization of the certificate signer
- Validity period: the time period that the certificate is valid for
- Certificate's signature algorithm
- Serial number of the X509 certificate
- Version of the X509 certificate
- Whether this is a CA certificate or not

The format of a digital certificate is defined by the **X.509 Standard.** Hence, when we say a certificate we actually refer to an X.509 certificate.

15-8-2 Structure of X.509 Certificates

The structure of a X.509 digital certificate is defined by the X.509 standard and is expressed in a formal language called Abstract Syntax Notation One (ASN.1). The actual format of an X.509 V3 certificate is shown in Figure 15-20.

As shown in Figure 15-20 there are two major components in a X.509 certificate. The first part is the certificate itself which consists of information about the subject and issuer of the certificate. The second part is the certificate signature produced by the certificate issuer when it signs the certificate.

```
 -------------------------------------  --
| Version Number                     |  |
|------------------------------------|  |
| Serial Number                      |  |                      CA's
|------------------------------------|  |                      private key
| Signature Algorithm Id             |  |                         |
|------------------------------------|  |                         v
| Issuer's Name                      |  |   -----------       -----------
|------------------------------------|  |  |hash       |hash |encryption|
| Validity Period                    |  |->|algorithm  |---->|algorithm |
|------------------------------------|  |  |e.g.SHA512 |     |e.g. RSA  |
| Subject's Name                     |  |   -----------       -----------
|------------------------------------|  |                         |
| Subject Public Key Algorithm       |  |                         |
|------------------------------------|  |                         |
| Subject Public Key                 |  |                         |
|------------------------------------|  |                        |certificate
| Issuer Unique Identifier (optional)|  |                        |signature
|------------------------------------|  |                         |
| Subject Unique Identifier (optional)| |                         |
|------------------------------------|  |                         |
| Extensions (optional)              |  --                        |
|------------------------------------|                            |
| Certificate Signature Algorithm    |                            |
|------------------------------------|                            |
| Certificate Signature              |  <-------------------------
 -------------------------------------
```

Figure 15-20 Contents of X.509 certificate and how signature is produced

Each extension has its own ID which is expressed as object identifier. If a critical extension cannot be recognized or its information cannot be processed, then the certificate must be rejected. For a non-critical extension, if it can be recognized it must be processed. It can be ignored if it is not recognized.

Certificate Signature

Note that when the CA signs a certificate, its signature is placed at the end of the certificate. This signature will be verified during the certificate verification phase.

Also notice that, as Figure 15-20 shows, to be exactly precise, when a certificate is signed, it's only the hash or digest of the certificate is signed, not the entire original certificate itself.

To produce the certificate signature, the hash of the first part of a certificate (excluding the certificate signature algorithm and the certificate signature fields) is computed using the hash algorithm contained in the field of certificate signature algorithm. The resulting hash is then

encrypted using the encryption algorithm contained in the second part of the certificate signature algorithm. For instance, one example value of the Certificate's signature algorithm is 'sha512WithRSAEncryption'.
This means SHA512 is the hash algorithm used in computing the hash of the contents of the certificate and RSA encryption algorithm is used to encrypt that hash to produce the certificate signature.

15-8-3 Formats of Certificate Files

There are three possible formats of certificate and key files: PEM, DER, and PKCS #12. They use two different types of encoding: Base64 ASCII encoding and DER binary encoding.

An X.509 digital certificate is usually saved in a file.
There are many different file name extensions used for these certificate files which sometimes cause a lot of confusion.

15-8-3-1 PEM format

The PEM format is the most common format. It's text format.

PEM stands for Privacy-enhanced Electronic Mail. It's actually a protocol designed by the Internet Research Task Force on Privacy to provide security for electronic mails.

PEM-format certificate files are Base64 encoded ACII files.
The contents of a PEM file are readable text but since the contents are encoded, it's not understandable.

A certificate stored in PEM format starts with the header
"-----BEGIN CERTIFICATE-----" and ends with the tail
"-----END CERTIFICATE-----". The actual contents go in-between.
Sometimes you may also see this following pair of header and tail too:
"-----BEGIN X509 CERTIFICATE----"
"-----END X509 CERTIFICATE----"

A PEM file can contain X.509 certificates, private keys (RSA or DSA), and public keys (RSA or DSA).

It's always a good idea to visually inspect a PEM file. A PEM file containing a public key always starts with the following line:

    -----BEGIN PUBLIC KEY-----

and ends with this line:

    -----END PUBLIC KEY-----

A PEM file consisting of an RSA private key starts with the following line:

    -----BEGIN RSA PRIVATE KEY-----

and ends with this line:

```
-----END RSA PRIVATE KEY-----
```

The file name extension of the PEM files is usually ".pem", but they sometimes bear file name extensions such as ".crt", ".cer", or ".key" as well. *.key files usually are PEM-format files containing just private keys.

PEM is the default format for OpenSSL. In OpenSSL, a PEM-format file can contain more than one certificate or private key.
An SSL/TLS program written in C language specifies the PEM file format by using the value SSL_FILETYPE_PEM.

15-8-3-2 DER Format

In contrast to PEM-format certificate files using Base64 ASCII encoding, DER-format certificate files use binary DER encoding.

DER stands for Distinguished Encoding Rules.

DER is an encoding scheme for producing unequivocal transfer syntax for data structures described by ASN.1 notation. A digital certificate is computed on ASN.1 value. ASN stands for Abstract Syntax Notation. ASN.1 is a formal notation used for describing data transmitted by telecommunications protocols, regardless of language implementation and physical representation of the data.

DER format is a binary format. A DER-format certificate file does not contain any text header such as that in a PEM file.

A DER file can contain certificates, private keys and public keys.

DER is the default format for most browsers.

When reading certificates and private keys from files of type SSL_FILETYPE_ASN1 (DER binary encoding), many OpenSSL C APIs support only one certificate or private key per file.

DER-format certificate files use the ".der", ".cer" or ".crt" file name extension.

15-8-3-3 PKCS #12

PKCS #12 is one of the family of standards called Public-Key Cryptography Standards (PKCS) published by RSA Laboratories in 1996.

The **PKCS #12** standard specifies an archive file format for storing multiple cryptography objects in a single file. It is mainly used to bundle an X.509 certificate and its associated private key together in a single file. Since it can contain multiple cryptography objects, it is also often used to bundle all certificates in a chain of trust into a single file too.

The filename extension for PKCS #12 files is ".p12" or ".pfx".
The PFX format and ".pfx" file extension is commonly seen in Windows.
It is predecessor of PKCS#12.

A PKCS #12 file can contain private keys, public keys and certificates. The data in a PKCS #12 format file is stored in a binary format.

15-8-4 Certificate Authority (CA)

How do people get certificates?

Typically, in real commercial deployments, a certificate is "officially" issued by some well-known certificate issuing company. The certificate issuer is called **certificate authority** or **certification authority (CA)**. A certificate authority (CA) is an entity that issues digital certificates.

There are many such companies. Some of the well-known include Symantec, Comodo, GoDaddy, Entrust, GlobalSign, DigiCert, StartCom, Verizon, SwissSign, Verisign and many others. These certificate issuing companies are generally considered trusted. That is, they are considered trusted CAs.

Usually, one seeking to get a certificate generates a pair of keys, creates a certificate signing request, sends that request to one of these companies and has it sign the certificate request into a certificate. Before signing and issuing a digital certificate, a CA has the obligation to verify an applicant's credentials so that the public can really trust the information contained in the certificates it signs and issues.

This certificate application and issuing process takes time and it costs money.

15-8-5 Certificate Chain

As we said it before, a certificate identifies an entity, say, a computer or a web server. In many corporations, there could be dozens or even hundreds or thousands of computers and web servers in a company. It would be very time consuming, inconvenient and costly for these companies to apply and obtain that many different certificates from the trusted CA companies.

Practically, companies apply for one or a very small number of certificates with CA capability from one of these trusted issuers and then use that to further issue other certificates within the company.

When a certificate is issued, it can be marked whether it is a CA certificate or not. A CA certificate can be used to sign and issue other certificates. This creates a chain of CAs as shown below.

```
root CA (some globally trusted certificate issuer organization)
   |
CA of Corporation XYZ
   |
CA of Engineering Department
   |
CA of XXX group
   |
```

```
        end certificate for Web server or computer X
```

In other words, normally a company has a top CA. Typically the subject name of the certificate is the name of the company. The company's top CA certificate is signed by one of these certificate issuers or root CA companies. Then the company's top CA will sign CA certificates used in various departments within that company. The CA at the department level may sign CA certificates used by various groups under it. And a CA in a group may further sign certificates of individual computers and/or engineers, and so on.

In the real world, there are multiple root CAs. Therefore, on a system where certificates can be used, it is very likely to see certificates coming from multiple chains of trust. The well-known certificate issuing companies are playing the role of root CAs. By the way, the certificate of a root CA must be signed by someone too. Hence, they can be self-signed at times.

```
               Root CA 1                      Root CA 2       ...
                  |                               |
        -------------------              ---------------
        |                 |              |             |
     Tier 1            Tier 1         Tier 1   ...   Tier 1
     CA #1             CA #2          CA #7          CA #10
        |                 |              |
    ---------         ---------         ...
    |       |         |       |
  Tier 2  Tier 2    Tier 2  Tier 2
  CA #3   CA #4     CA #5   CA #6
    |
  -------
  | .. |
  End
  Certificate
```

Figure 15-21 Multiple certificate chains is very typical

Note that when a certificate is created, if it is marked as a non-CA certificate, it cannot be used to sign others' certificates. Actually, you may be able to use it to sign other certificates, but later verification of the certificates so issued will fail. That is, you will get caught later during the certificate verification phase. Only those certificates marked as CA certificates can do so. Usually a certificate is marked as a non-CA certificate by default.

15-8-6 Certificate Verification

Note that technically anyone having a computer and knowing how to use some of the security programs can generate a digital certificate himself or herself. But the real matter is the trustworthiness. How many people trust the certificates you sign and issue? That's the real question.

The trust comes into play later at certificate verification stage. In SSL/TLS and other protocols relying on digital certificates, to authenticate entities, when a certificate is presented it has to be verified.

Verifying a certificate essentially involves **decrypting the public key** contained in the certificate which was previously encrypted by the issuer using the issuer's private key. This decrypting operation requires the certificate issuer's public key which is in the issuer's certificate. Therefore, when you use an issuer's (i.e. CA's) certificate to try to verify another certificate, you are trusting that issuer. If you don't trust an issuer then don't use its certificate.

This is why each computer has a certificate store which contains all of the certificates of the trusted CAs. If you don't trust a particular CA, never install that CA's certificate into your computer's trusted CA certificate store. When we buy a Windows PC, many trusted CAs' certificates are already installed on the PC when the Microsoft Windows operating system is installed. If you have certificates from other CAs that you like to trust and they are not already installed on your computer, as a system administrator you can certainly add them to the trusted CA certificate store of your computer so that they will get used in automatic certificate verifications.

A certificate proves the identity of an individual or an entity. Note that when there is a chain of certificates involved, to verify the validity of an end certificate, the identity of the issuer or CA must also be verified. This means verifying the validity of a certificate also includes verifying the validity of the certificate of its issuer. By the same token, we must verify the validity of the certificate of the issuer's issuer (i.e. the CA's CA) too if there is one. This verification process must go on until the ultimate root CA's certificate is verified. Should any certificate in this entire chain is found to be invalid, the verification is considered failed.

Besides verifying the trustworthiness of a certificate's issuer(s), certificate validation should also check if the certificate is valid yet or is still valid. If a certificate has expired or if it has not even become valid yet, then the certificate validation should fail too. Each certificate has a validity period. By comparing the current time against the start and end times of the certificate validity period, it is easy to tell if a certificate is valid or not.

In this chapter, we will demonstrate how to create and use self-signed server certificate and self-signed root CA certificate for our programming examples.

15-8-7 Certificate Revocation List

Each certificate has a validity period which is noted in the certificate itself. However, under certain circumstances a certificate may need to be revoked before it actually reaches its expiration date. This is referred to **certificate revocation**. These situations include the corresponding private key is compromised, the employee owning the certificate has left the company or been terminated, a server machine the certificate represents is retired, information about the certificate subject has changed, and so on.

When a certificate must be revoked, at least two things must be done. First, the certificate authority that issued the certificate must be notified so that it can change the status of the certificate. Second, the certificate revocation must be published/announced to the certificate user community.

The date the certificate is revoked and the reason must also be provided.

A special case of certificate revocation is **certificate suspension** which temporarily puts the certificate on hold. In this case the revocation reason would be Certificate Hold. In other words, certificate revocation has two states: Revoked and Hold.

Reasons for certificate revocation are defined in RFC 5280. They include keyCompromise, CACompromise, aACompromise, privilegeWithdrawn, affiliationChanged, cessationOfOperation, superseded, certificateHold, removeFromCRL and unspecified.

Note that not only end entity certificates but CA certificates may be revoked too.

The list of end (non-CA) certificates that have been revoked form a so-called **certificate revocation list** (**CRL**) whereas the list of revoked CA certificates form an **authority revocation list** (**ARL**).

The CA who issued the certificate being revoked is responsible for publishing the certificate revocation. To prevent spoofing, a revocation usually carries digital signature of the CA who publishes it. Before trusting a revocation, the associated publisher CA's certificate must be verified.

As you can probably imagine, certificate revocations do pose some real problems in practice.

Are CRLs always published promptly? Where are they?
How does a user or system know how many certificates have been revoked?
How many CRLs are out there? And how to access all of the CRLs?
Ideally, certificate verification should also include making sure a certificate is not on any of the CRLs. How can this be done reliably and in a timely fashion?

In practice, many operating systems and applications rely on an installed CRL list. So far that seems to work to certain extent. The question then is how often and timely the installed CRL list gets updated?

There are online revocation services which provide online checking of revocation status of certificates.

An alternative to using CRLs is to use a certificate validation protocol such as Online Certificate Status Protocol (OCSP). OCSP offers benefits of using less network bandwidth and real-time or near real-time status checks for high volume operations.

Some web browsers are moving away from using CRLs and moving toward protocols like OCSP.

15-9 Create X.509 Certificates

As we mentioned before, SSL/TLS was primarily designed for a client-server communication and was mainly to protect the client. Therefore, the protocol always requires server authentication but leaves client authentication optional. This means to test an SSL/TLS communication, at minimum you need to have a server certificate.

A server certificate can be self-signed. That's the simplest case. In that case, you need only one certificate, a self-signed server certificate, for things to work. In a more typical situation, a server certificate is signed by a CA.

In this section, we will show you how to create both types of server certificates using the openssl command. We assume you have access to some OpenSSL installation which is version 1.1 or higher. Among others, an OpenSSL installation comes with a utility command named openssl which is very useful in performing many different kinds of operations.

If you already have all of the certificates you need or know how to create them, you may choose to skip this section.

Configuration File

Creating certificates needs a configuration file which specifies the default values for various attributes so that you don't need to pass in all of them on the command line. These attributes include whether a certificate should be a CA certificate, how many days a certificate should be valid for, what the digest algorithm is, where the certificate directory is, and many others.

When you install OpenSSL on your system, it automatically installs a configuration file named openssl.cnf. This OpenSSL configuration file is used when you invoke the openssl command to perform various operations.

For example, when I installed OpenSSL in /opt/openssl directory, the configuration file /usr/local/ssl/openssl.cnf was automatically created. You can use that or you could create and use your own. We will demonstrate both below.

For further details on how to create openssl.conf, please refer to https://jamielinux.com/docs/openssl-certificate-authority/create-the-root-pair.html

Pay to Get Your Certificates or not

To test a certificate chain, you either have to pay money to get a certificate signed by one of the commercial certificate issuer companies, or you can create your own self-signed root certificate to start with.

For our demo and educational purposes, we will use self-signed certificates here in this book. They work exactly the same way as commercially acquired certificates.

15-9-1 Create a Self-Signed Server Certificate

If you just need a server certificate to test whether your SSL/TLS programs work or not, the simplest thing to do is to create a self-signed server certificate. Then all you need is one certificate. That's it!

Below are the commands to create a self-signed server certificate using the default configuration file from OpenSSL installation.

The common (i.e. owner) name of the certificate is 'mysrv'.

15-9-1-1 Generate a Private Key

To create any certificate, the first step is always to generate a private key. You can choose to create an RSA key by using the 'openssl genrsa' command or a DSA key using the 'openssl gendsa' command. For example, the openssl command below creates a private key that is 4096 bits long using the RSA algorithm and stores the result in a file named mysrv_privkey.pem:

```
$ openssl genrsa -out mysrv_privkey.pem 4096
```

If you omit the "-out mysrv_privkey.pem", the private key will be output to the screen (standard output).

The generated private key will be stored in PEM format.

For security sake, when you generate a private key, you can choose to encrypt the private key with the DES, triple DES, or the IDEA ciphers respectively before outputting it. For instance, the command below generates a 4096-bit RSA private key, encrypts it using the triple DES algorithm and stores the output in the file named rsaprivkey2.pem.

```
$ openssl genrsa -des3 -out rsaprivkey2.pem 4096
```

When you execute this command, it will prompt you to enter a password. An encryption key will be generated from the password you choose and used in the encryption. Later each time when you try to access the private key, you will have to enter the same password again in order to gain access.

Notice that in OpenSSL v1.1.1g if you swap the positions of the 4096 and "-out rsaprivkey2.pem", it will send the output to the standard output instead of the designated file. It would get a syntax error in v3.0.0 and on.

15-9-1-2 Create a Certificate Signing Request and Sign It

The second step is to create a **certificate signing request** (**CSR**) using the 'openssl req -new' and sign it at the same time with the '-x509' option. You can specify attributes that you want to override their default values. In the example below, '-days 14600' specifies the certificate is to be valid for 14600 days, '-key mysrv_privkey.pem' says the private key for this certificate comes from the file named mysrv_privkey.pem, and '-out mysrv_cert.pem' says we want the output certificate to be stored in the file named mysrv_cert.pem. The option '-sha512' says we want the digest algorithm to be SHA512, which is stronger than the usual default SHA256.

```
$ openssl req -new -x509 -nodes -sha512 -days 14600 -key mysrv_privkey.pem
  -out mysrv_cert.pem
```

The '-new' option says you want to create a new certificate request.

The '-x509' option says to sign the certificate request and output a X509 structure instead of a certificate request.

The -nodes option says don't encrypt the output key. If you omit the -nodes option, then the output key will be encrypted and in doing that the command will prompt you for a password and use the password to generate an encryption key.

The command interaction and output on screen are shown below:

```
$ openssl genrsa -out mysrv_privkey.pem 4096
Generating RSA private key, 4096 bit long modulus
.........................................++
...........................++
e is 65537 (0x10001)
$ ls -l mysrv_*
-rw-r--r-- 1 oracle oinstall 3247 Dec 11 16:28 mysrv_privkey.pem

$ openssl req -new -x509 -nodes -sha512 -days 14600 -key mysrv_privkey.pem -out
mysrv_cert.pem
You are about to be asked to enter information that will be incorporated
into your certificate request.
What you are about to enter is what is called a Distinguished Name or a DN.
There are quite a few fields but you can leave some blank
For some fields there will be a default value,
If you enter '.', the field will be left blank.
-----
Country Name (2 letter code) [GB]:US
State or Province Name (full name) [Berkshire]:New Hampshire
Locality Name (eg, city) [Newbury]:Nashua
Organization Name (eg, company) [My Company Ltd]:Chen Systems, Inc.
Organizational Unit Name (eg, section) []:Engineering
Common Name (eg, your name or your server's hostname) []:mysrv
Email Address []:

$ ls -l mysrv_*
-rw-r--r-- 1 oracle oinstall 2260 Dec 11 16:31 mysrv_cert.pem
-rw-r--r-- 1 oracle oinstall 3247 Dec 11 16:28 mysrv_privkey.pem
$ openssl verify -verbose mysrv_cert.pem
mysrv_cert.pem: /C=US/ST=New Hampshire/L=Nashua/O=Chen Systems,
Inc./OU=Engineering/CN=mysrv
error 18 at 0 depth lookup:self signed certificate
OK
```

When you create a server certificate, if it's for a Web (HTTP) server, then **the subject name (i.e. the common name) of the certificate must exactly match the domain name of the server**. For example, www.xyzcompany.com. This is because when a web browser client tries to connect, it typically specifies the domain name of the HTTP server as the target. During the SSL connection handshake, the server sends its certificate to the client and the client verifies it. It compares the common/subject name from the server certificate with the domain name the user has just entered. If they don't match, the connection request will fail. Therefore, **the common name of a certificate is very important**. Don't just enter anything!

15-9-2 Create a Chain of Certificates

We need at least three levels in the hierarchy to demonstrate a certificate chain. Toward that end, we will create a self-signed root CA certificate, an intermediate CA certificate, and then a server (and perhaps a client) certificate. The server certificate will be signed/issued by the intermediate CA, which will in turn be signed/issued by the self-signed root CA, forming a chain of trust.

An intermediate CA is an entity that can sign certificates on behalf of the root CA. The purpose of using an intermediate CA is primarily for security, in addition to convenience and maybe some other. That way the root CA's key can be kept offline and used as infrequently as possible.
If the intermediate CA's key is compromised, the root CA can revoke the intermediate certificate and create a new one.

```
        self-signed root CA
             |
        intermediate CA
             |
     -------------------
     |                 |
  myserver          myclient
```

Figure 15-22 Hierarchy of example certificate chain

In general, creating a digital certificate involves the following three steps:

- Generate a pair of private and public keys for the subject
- Create a certificate signing request (CSR)
- Get the certificate signing request signed by a certificate authority (CA)

This process is the same regardless of who the subject is. The only difference is the information you enter about the subject of the certificate.

When you create a certificate signing request, you will be asked to enter information about the subject which includes the following items, as we have seen in creating our own CA certificate:

```
Country Name (2 letter code) [GB]:US
State or Province Name (full name) [Berkshire]:New Hampshire
Locality Name (eg, city) [Newbury]:Nashua
Organization Name (eg, company) [My Company Ltd]:Chen Systems, Inc.
Organizational Unit Name (eg, section) []:Engineering
Common Name (eg, your name or your server's hostname) []:mysslserver
Email Address []:.
```

The first few items are information about the company and organization that the subject belongs to.

Note that the value you enter for **the Common Name field is very important. This is the "official" name of the subject and it is used in verifying a certificate.** In particular, if the certificate is for a server host, **the Common Name must exactly match the name clients use when they try to connect to the server.** Otherwise, the connection request will fail.

1203

Specifically, the Common Name must be the server host's Fully Qualified Domain Name (FQDN), such as xyzcompany.com.

If you use the openssl command, you can alternatively supply all of the information about the subject on the openssl command line with the '-subj' command argument. For instance,

```
-subj "/C=US/ST=New Hampshire/L=Nashua/O=Chen Systems, Inc/CN=mysslserver"
```

Here we create a certificate that will represent an SSL server program which we will use later in demonstrating our SSL example programs. For SSL/TLS communications, the SSL and TLS specifications require that the server to always have a certificate.

15-9-2-1 Create a Self-Signed Root Certificate

Create Your Own Root CA Certificate

It is indeed very simple to create your own root CA certificate.

The following command generates a pair of keys and stores the private key in a file named rootca_privkey.pem:

```
$ openssl genrsa -out rootca_privkey.pem 4096
Generating RSA private key, 4096 bit long modulus
.......................................................................................++
.......................++
e is 65537 (0x10001)

$ ls -l rootca_privkey.pem
-rw-r--r-- 1 oracle oinstall 3243 Nov 27 11:49 rootca_privkey.pem
```

Note that the argument 4096 tells the openssl command to generate a key that is 4096 bits long. The options are 512, 1024, 2048 and 4096. The longer the key is the stronger, meaning it's harder to crack. In general, 2048 or above is recommended these days.

Once you have the keys, the next step is to create a self-signed root CA certificate by running the following commands:

```
$ openssl req -x509 -new -nodes -sha512 -days 14600 -key rootca_privkey.pem -out
rootca_cert.pem
You are about to be asked to enter information that will be incorporated
into your certificate request.
What you are about to enter is what is called a Distinguished Name or a DN.
There are quite a few fields but you can leave some blank
For some fields there will be a default value,
If you enter '.', the field will be left blank.
-----
Country Name (2 letter code) [GB]:US
State or Province Name (full name) [Berkshire]:New Hampshire
Locality Name (eg, city) [Newbury]:Nashua
Organization Name (eg, company) [My Company Ltd]:Chen Systems, Inc.
```

```
    Organizational Unit Name (eg, section) []:Engineering
    Common Name (eg, your name or your server's hostname) []:rootca
    Email Address []:.

  $ ls -l rootca_cert.pem
  -r--r--r-- 1 oracle oinstall 2179 Nov 27 16:13 rootca_cert.pem
```

This command reads and uses the key from the file named rootca_privkey.pem.
It creates a certificate that is valid for 14600 days (40 years)
and stores the certificate in a file called rootca_cert.pem.

15-9-2-2 Create a Certificate for an Intermediate CA

Figure 15-23 A sample OpenSSL configuration file, openssl-ca.cnf

```
# -------------------------------------------------------------------
[ signing_policy1 ]
countryName              = match
stateOrProvinceName      = match
organizationName         = match
organizationalUnitName   = optional
commonName               = supplied
emailAddress             = optional


[ signing_policy2 ]
countryName              = optional
stateOrProvinceName      = optional
localityName             = optional
organizationName         = optional
organizationalUnitName   = optional
commonName               = supplied
emailAddress             = optional


# -------------------------------------------------------------------
[ signing_req ]
subjectKeyIdentifier=hash
authorityKeyIdentifier=keyid,issuer

basicConstraints = CA:FALSE
keyUsage = digitalSignature, keyEncipherment
default_days    = 10950                  # how long certs valid for, 30 years max


# -------------------------------------------------------------------
[ ca ]
default_ca       = CA_default             # The default CA section


# -------------------------------------------------------------------
[ CA_default ]
wkdir       = .
certificate      = $wkdir/cacert.pem      # The CA certifcate
private_key      = $wkdir/cakey.pem       # The CA private key
new_certs_dir    = $wkdir                 # Location for new certs after signing
database         = $wkdir/index.txt       # Database index file
serial           = $wkdir/serial.txt      # The current serial number
unique_subject   = no                     # Set to 'no' to allow creation of
```

```
                                        # several certificates with same subject.
default_md          = sha512            # use public key default MD
default_days        = 10950             # how long to certify for, 30 years max

# --------------------------------------------------------------------------
[ req ]
# Options for the `req` tool
default_bits            = 2048
default_keyfile         = privkey.pem
distinguished_name      = req_distinguished_name
x509_extensions = v3_ca    # The extensions to add to self-signed certs.

[ req_distinguished_name ]
countryName                     = Country Name (2 letter code)
countryName_default             = US
countryName_min                 = 2
countryName_max                 = 2

stateOrProvinceName             = State or Province Name (full name)
stateOrProvinceName_default     = Massachusetts

localityName                    = Locality Name (e.g. city)

0.organizationName              = Organization Name (e.g. company)
0.organizationName_default      = XYZ Company

organizationalUnitName          = Organizational Unit Name (e.g. department)

commonName                      = Common Name (e.g. your name or server's FQDN)
commonName_max                  = 64

emailAddress                    = Email Address
emailAddress_max                = 64

[ req_attributes ]
challengePassword               = A challenge password
challengePassword_min           = 4
challengePassword_max           = 20

# --------------------------------------------------------------------------
# This is required for TSA certificates.

[ v3_req ]

# Extensions to add to a certificate request
basicConstraints = CA:FALSE
keyUsage = nonRepudiation, digitalSignature, keyEncipherment

[ intermediate_ca ]

# Extensions for an intermediate CA
basicConstraints = CA:true
keyUsage = nonRepudiation, digitalSignature, keyEncipherment, cRLSign, keyCertSign

[ v3_ca ]
```

```
# Extensions for a typical CA
# PKIX recommendation.

subjectKeyIdentifier=hash
authorityKeyIdentifier=keyid:always,issuer
basicConstraints = CA:true
# ----------------------------------------------------------------------
```

Create an Intermediate CA Certificate Signed by the Root CA

The following steps create a certificate for an intermediate CA.

1. Create a configuration file of your own (see Figure 15-23)

   $ vi openssl-ca.cnf

2. Create a private key for the intermediate CA

   $ openssl genrsa 4096 > deptca_privkey.pem

   This creates a private key for the department CA and stores it in the file named deptca_privkey.pem.

3. Create a certificate signing request (CSR) for the intermediate CA

   $ openssl req -config openssl-ca.cnf -new -sha512 -days 14500 -key deptca_privkey.pem -out deptca_csr.pem

   This creates a certificate signing request (CSR) and stores it in the file named deptca_csr.pem.

   $ ls -ltr deptca*
   -rw-r--r-- 1 oracle oinstall 3243 Dec 10 13:43 deptca_privkey.pem
   -rw-r--r-- 1 oracle oinstall 1736 Dec 10 13:50 deptca_csr.pem

   When you create a certificate signing request, the openssl command looks up definitions in the [req] section of the configuration file you specify on the command line to decide what questions to ask the user. Therefore, make sure your configuration file has that section in it.

4. Create the intermediate CA's certificate, signed by the root CA

   Note that the index.txt and serial.txt files specified in the configuration file must exist. So, we do the following to create them:

   $ touch index.txt
   $ echo "01" > serial.txt

   The file index.txt is the so-called "database". Each time a certificate is created, a corresponding entry is written into this file, which includes the value of the expiration date of the certificate (the second column in each entry inside this file) and the information about the subject.

   The file serial.txt keeps track the serial number of the certificate.

Every time a certificate is issued, the value of the serial number is bumped up. Its value is in hexadecimal form.

Just a side note that OpenSSL v1.1 had a bug where the expiration date value (the second column) written into the so-called database, index.txt, could be wrong. This leads to the following error in signing a certificate:

```
entry 5: invalid expiry date
```

The quick fix is to edit the file index.txt and remove the first two digits from the value.

The following command actually creates the certificate:

```
$ openssl ca -config openssl-ca.cnf -extensions intermediate_ca
 -days 14500 -notext -keyfile rootca_privkey.pem -cert rootca_cert.pem
 -in deptca_csr.pem -out deptca_cert.pem -policy signing_policy1
```

The -keyfile option specifies the singer's (root CA) private key and the -cert option specifies the singer's (root CA) certificate. The -config option specifies the configuration file to use. The -policy option specifies which signing policy to use.

5. Verify the Intermediate CA Certificate

```
$ openssl verify -verbose -CAfile rootca_cert.pem deptca_cert.pem
deptca_cert.pem: OK
```

Notice that you must correctly create the intermediate CA certificate. Otherwise, you may find out later that verifying the certificate chain fails with error 24. The key to this is to make sure when you sign the intermediate CA's certificate, you use an extension (as specified in the configuration file) that contains this line:

```
basicConstraints = CA:true
```

This line makes the certificate become a CA certificate so it has authority to sign other certificates. We have used '-extensions intermediate_ca' in our openssl command to sign the intermediate CA's certificate. And in the configuration file openssl-ca.cnf, you will see it does have this line in there.

Normally, the value of the 'basicConstraints' attribute is set to CA:false. In that case, the intermediate CA's certificate will still be created, and you can even use it to sign other certificate signing requests. All will seem to work fine until you actually verify the certificates it signs. The verification will fail with SSL_get_verify_result() returning error of 24. This error typically means some CA certificate in the chain is not a true CA certificate.

15-9-2-3 Bundle All CAs' Certificates into a Single File

To do certificate verification in a C program, normally it's easier if you pack the certificates of all of the CAs in the chain in a single file and use that file. This file typically is of PEM type and has a '.pem' file name extension.

The command below does just that. It bundles the certificates of the root CA and the intermediate CA into a file named myCAchain_cert.pem:

```
$ cat deptca_cert.pem rootca_cert.pem > myCAchain_cert.pem

$ ls -ltr deptca_cert.pem rootca_cert.pem  myCAchain_cert.pem
-r--r--r-- 1 oracle oinstall 2179 Nov 27 16:13 rootca_cert.pem
-rw-r--r-- 1 oracle oinstall 2045 Dec 10 14:15 deptca_cert.pem
-rw-r--r-- 1 oracle oinstall 4224 Dec 10 16:06 myCAchain_cert.pem
```

15-9-2-4 Create Server and Client Certificates Signed by the Intermediate CA

Once you create the certificate of your own certificate authority (CA), you can then use it to sign the certificates of others. For instance, certificates of users, client applications, and server programs. Below we give examples on how to create a certificate for a server and another one for a client so that we can use them in testing SSL communications with our SSL/TLS example programs.

Create a server certificate signed by the intermediate CA

The commands to create a server certificate signed by the intermediate CA are listed below:

```
$ openssl genrsa -out myserver_privkey.pem 4096
$ openssl req -config openssl-ca.cnf -new -sha512 -key myserver_privkey.pem -out myserver_csr.pem
$ openssl ca -config openssl-ca.cnf -keyfile deptca_privkey.pem -cert deptca_cert.pem -in myserver_csr.pem -out myserver_cert.pem -policy signing_policy2
```

The first command creates a private key for the certificate subject, myserver. The second command creates a certificate signing request (CSR) for the subject myserver. The third command signs the CSR for myserver using the department head as the certificate authority (CA). Note that you must specify the signing CA's private key and its certificate in the options as shown below:

```
-keyfile deptca_privkey.pem -cert deptca_cert.pem
```

The interaction output on screen is as shown below:

```
$ openssl genrsa -out myserver_privkey.pem 4096
Generating RSA private key, 4096 bit long modulus
...................................++
......++
e is 65537 (0x10001)
[oracle@jvmx cert]$ ls -l myse*
-rw-r--r-- 1 oracle oinstall 3243 Nov 27 17:39 myserver_privkey.pem

$ openssl req -config openssl-ca.cnf -new -sha512 -key
myserver_privkey.pem -out myserver_csr.pem

You are about to be asked to enter information that will be incorporated
```

```
into your certificate request.
What you are about to enter is what is called a Distinguished Name or a DN.
There are quite a few fields but you can leave some blank
For some fields there will be a default value,
If you enter '.', the field will be left blank.
-----
Country Name (2 letter code) [US]:US
State or Province Name (full name) [California]:New Hampshire
Locality Name (e.g. city) []:Nashua
Organization Name (e.g. company) [XYZ Company]:Chen Systems, Inc.
Organizational Unit Name (e.g. section) []:Engineering
Common Name (e.g. your name or server FQDN) []:myserver
Email Address []:
$ ls -ltr myse*
-rw-r--r-- 1 oracle oinstall 3243 Nov 27 17:39 myserver_privkey.pem
-rw-r--r-- 1 oracle oinstall 1724 Nov 27 17:41 myserver_csr.pem
$ ls -ltr dept*pem
-r--r--r-- 1 oracle oinstall 3239 Nov 27 16:34 deptca_privkey.pem
-r--r--r-- 1 oracle oinstall 1728 Nov 27 17:11 deptca_csr.pem
-r--r--r-- 1 oracle oinstall 6632 Nov 27 17:30 deptca_cert.pem

$ openssl ca -config openssl-ca.cnf -keyfile
deptca_privkey.pem -cert deptca_cert.pem -in myserver_csr.pem -out
myserver_cert.pem -policy signing_policy2
```

```
Using configuration from openssl-ca.cnf
Check that the request matches the signature
Signature ok
The Subject's Distinguished Name is as follows
countryName            :PRINTABLE:'US'
stateOrProvinceName    :PRINTABLE:'New Hampshire'
localityName           :PRINTABLE:'Nashua'
organizationName       :PRINTABLE:'Chen Systems, Inc.'
organizationalUnitName:PRINTABLE:'Engineering'
commonName             :PRINTABLE:'myserver'
Certificate is to be certified until Nov 20 22:44:01 2046 GMT (10950 days)
Sign the certificate? [y/n]:y
```

```
1 out of 1 certificate requests certified, commit? [y/n]y
Write out database with 1 new entries
Data Base Updated
```

```
$ ls -ltr myse*
-rw-r--r-- 1 oracle oinstall 3243 Nov 27 17:39 myserver_privkey.pem
-rw-r--r-- 1 oracle oinstall 1724 Nov 27 17:41 myserver_csr.pem
-rw-r--r-- 1 oracle oinstall 6680 Nov 27 17:44 myserver_cert.pem
```

Create a client certificate signed by the intermediate CA

The procedure for creating a client certificate is exactly the same as that of a server except the value of the common name you enter (and perhaps some other information about the subject of the certificate).

An example of the commands for creating a client certificate are listed below:

```
$ openssl genrsa -out myclient_privkey.pem 4096
```

1210

```
     $ openssl req -config openssl-ca.cnf -new -sha512 -key myclient_privkey.pem -out
myclient_csr.pem
     $ openssl ca -config openssl-ca.cnf -keyfile deptca_privkey.pem -cert
deptca_cert.pem -in myclient_csr.pem -out myclient_cert.pem -policy signing_policy1
```

15-9-3 Verifying Certificates

You can run the 'openssl verify' command to verify a certificate.
To do that, the command needs to specify either a pathname or a filename
that contains certificates of CAs who are in the chain of issuing that
certificate. For example, the following command verifies the intermediate
CA certificate signed by the root CA:

```
     $ openssl verify -verbose -CAfile rootca_cert.pem deptca_cert.pem
     deptca_cert.pem: OK
```

The following command verifies the server certificate signed by the
intermediate CA whose certificate was in turn issued by the root CA:

```
     $ openssl verify -verbose -CAfile <(cat deptca_cert.pem rootca_cert.pem)
myserver_cert.pem
     myserver_cert.pem: OK
```

Figure 15-24 shows a program which displays information of a X.509
certificate. This tool also tells you if a certificate is self-signed and
if it is a CA certificate that has the authority to sign other certificates.
Below is a sample output of the example program get_cert_info.

```
     $ get_cert_info deptca_cert.pem

     This is not a self-signed certificate.
     Subject of the X509 certificate:
     C=US, ST=New Hampshire, O=Chen Systems, Inc., OU=Engineering, CN=IntermediateCA
     Issuer of the X509 certificate:
     C=US, ST=New Hampshire, L=Nashua, O=Chen Systems, Inc., CN=Jim Chen
     Serial number of the X509 certificate: 6
     Validity period: from Dec 10 19:15:32 2016 GMT to Aug 22 19:15:32 2056 GMT
     Version of the X509 certificate: 3
     Certificate's signature algorithm: sha512WithRSAEncryption
     This is a valid CA certificate.
     Public-Key: (4096 bit)
     Modulus:
         :
```

Figure 15-24 Extracting information from a X.509 certificate -- get_cert_info.c

```
/*
 * Print information in an X.509 certificate.
 * Authored by Mr. Jin-Jwei Chen.
 * Copyright (c) 2014-2016, 2020 Mr. Jin-Jwei Chen. All rights reserved.
 */

#include <stdio.h>
#include <errno.h>
#include <sys/types.h>
```

```
#include <string.h>            /* memset(), strlen(), memcmp() */
#include <stdlib.h>            /* atoi() */
#include <unistd.h>
#include <openssl/ssl.h>
#include <openssl/err.h>
#include <openssl/evp.h>
#include <openssl/x509.h>
#include <openssl/x509v3.h>
#include <openssl/pem.h>
#include <openssl/bn.h>
#include <openssl/asn1.h>
#include <openssl/x509_vfy.h>
#include <openssl/bio.h>
#include "myopenssl.h"

/* Peek into a X.509 certificate */
int main(int argc, char *argv[])
{
  char  *certfname;      /* file name of an X.509 certificate */
  FILE  *fp;
  int   ret;
  X509  *cert;           /* pointer to an X.509 object */

  /* Get the name of the file containing the certificate in PEM format */
  if (argc < 2)
  {
    fprintf(stderr, "Usage: %s certificate_file_name (PEM format)\n", argv[0]);
    return(-1);
  }
  certfname = argv[1];

  /* Try to open the certificate file */
  fp = fopen(certfname, "r");
  if (fp == NULL)
  {
    fprintf(stderr, "Error, failed to open certificate file %s, error=%d\n",
      certfname, errno);
    return(-2);
  }

  /* Read the PEM-format certificate into an X.509 object */
  cert = PEM_read_X509(fp, NULL, NULL, NULL);
  if (cert == NULL)
  {
    fprintf(stderr, "Error, PEM_read_X509() failed to read certificate from"
      " file %s\n", certfname);
    fclose(fp);
    return(-3);
  }

  /* Display information contained in the X.509 certificate */
  ret = display_certificate_info(cert);

  X509_free(cert);
  fclose(fp);
  return(0);
```

15-9-4 Converting Between Different Certificate Formats

As we discussed in the beginning of this section, there are different formats of certificate files. Sometimes you may find you need to convert a certificate from one format to another because some applications or web servers may recognize only one format. This can be done by using the 'openssl x509' or 'openssl pkcs12' command. We provide some examples below.

1. PEM -> DER

The command below converts mysrv2's certificate from PEM to DER format:

```
$ openssl x509 -outform der -in mysrv2_cert.pem -out mysrv2_cert.der

$ ls -l mysrv2_cert.*
-rw-r--r-- 1 oracle oinstall 1629 Jan 29 20:07 mysrv2_cert.der
-rw-r--r-- 1 oracle oinstall 2260 Dec 11 16:31 mysrv2_cert.pem
```

2. DER -> PEM

This following command converts a certificate from DER to PEM format:

```
$ openssl x509 -in mysrv2_cert.der -inform DER -out mysrv2_cert.pem
  -outform PEM
```

3. PEM -> PKCS#12

To convert a self-signed, PEM-format certificate file and a private key to PKCS#12 (.p12 or .pfx) format:

```
$ openssl pkcs12 -export -out mysrv2_cert.p12 -inkey mysrv2_privkey.pem -in mysrv2_cert.pem

Enter Export Password:
Verifying - Enter Export Password:
$ ls -ltr mysrv2_cert.*
-rw-r--r-- 1 oracle oinstall 2260 Dec 11 16:31 mysrv2_cert.pem
-rw-r--r-- 1 oracle oinstall 1629 Jan 29 20:07 mysrv2_cert.der
-rw-r--r-- 1 oracle oinstall 4389 Jan 29 20:24 mysrv2_cert.p12
```

The command below converts a certificate file, the corresponding private key and the CA's certificate file, all three of them in PEM format, to a single file in PKCS#12 (.p12 or .pfx) format:

```
$ openssl pkcs12 -export -out mysrv1_cert_bundle.p12 -inkey mysrv1_privkey.pem -in mysrv1_cert.pem -certfile rootca_cert.pem
Enter Export Password:
Verifying - Enter Export Password:
$ ls -l mysrv1_cert_bundle.p12
-rw-r--r-- 1 oracle oinstall 5733 Jan 29 20:51 mysrv1_cert_bundle.p12
```

4. PKCS#12 -> PEM

To convert a bundled PKCS#12 file containing a private key, a certificate and the issuer's certificate to the PEM format:

```
$ openssl pkcs12 -in mysrv1_cert_bundle.p12 -out mysrv1_cert_bundle.pem -nodes
Enter Import Password:
MAC verified OK

$ ls -l mysrv1_cert_bundle.pem
-rw-r--r-- 1 oracle oinstall 7880 Jan 29 20:55 mysrv1_cert_bundle.pem
```

15-10 SSL and TLS

Both SSL and TLS are standard protocols to use for secure network communications, especially over the Internet, these days.

This section provides a very brief introduction to SSL and TLS, their history, where they stand in the entire protocol stack, and how they work. Messages exchanged during the SSL/TLS handshake are also discussed. And, of course, there are many program examples as well.

15-10-1 What Is SSL/TLS?

```
---------------------------------------------
| HTTPS | HTTP | SMTP |...|  DNS   ...       | Application & Presentation layers
|-------|----------------|----------------|
|SSL/TLS|                 |                 | Session layer
|-------------------------|----------------|
|          TCP            |      UDP        | Transport layer
|------------------------------------------|
|          IP or IPsec                     | Network layer
|------------------------------------------|
|      Ethernet, Token-Ring, FDDI          | Data link layer
|------------------------------------------|
|          Hardware (wire)                 | Physical layer
---------------------------------------------
```

Figure 15-25 Where SSL/TLS is in network protocol stack

SSL stands for **Secure Sockets Layer**. It is a network protocol that provides a secure communication channel between two programs running on two separate computers connected by a computer network.

The SSL protocol implements authentication, secrecy, and message integrity aspects of computer security.

TLS stands for **Transport Layer Security**. It is an IETF standard based on SSL protocol. Although there are some minor differences between SSL and TLS, the two are meant for exactly the same purpose -- to provide a secure network communication channel between two computer systems. If you will, it's sort of like SSL is the de facto standard that existed first and TLS is the de jure standard that came later to validate SSL.

SSL/TLS can be used as a client-server or peer-to-peer protocol. Whoever initiates the connection is considered the client.

SSL/TLS is used in the Secure HyperText Transfer Protocol (HTTPS), the secure version of HTTP. In other words, **HTTPS** is **HTTP + SSL/TLS**. When you do online banking or shopping, HTTPS is the secure protocol to use.

In the entire network protocol stack, SSL/TLS is a protocol sitting on top of the TCP protocol. Both SSL and TLS use TCP as transport. Therefore, in the OSI seven-layer model, SSL/TLS belongs to **the Session layer**, layer 5.

15-10-2 SSL/TLS History

SSL was first designed by Netscape in 1994. However, due to serious security flaws in the protocol, SSL Version 1.0 was never publicly released. Its second version, SSLv2, was published in November of 1994. SSLv2 was used in Netscape Navigator 1.1 which was a web browser designed and implemented by Netscape in 1995 and was very popular then.

Due to U.S. government restrictions on exporting very advanced encryption and decryption technologies, SSLv2 has a special export mode in which the encryption security strength was limited to 40 bits.

Since there were some weaknesses in SSLv2, Netscape re-designed it and released SSLv3 in early 1996.

SSLv3 offers a number of new features, including a no encryption but authentication only mode for doing only data authentication, adding DH and DSS as new ciphers, redoing the key expansion transform, support for certificate chains, and adding support for a closure handshake to prevent a truncation attack. In SSLv2, an attacker could forge a TCP connection closure to make it appear as less data was sent. SSLv3 detects such attacks.

Versioning was not very well designed in SSL. Different versions of SSL have limited backward compatibility.

Besides Netscape's efforts on SSL, Microsoft also developed its own version of SSL, named Private Communications Technology (PCT), based on SSLv2 in 1995 , and another version named Secure Transport Layer Protocol (STLP), based on SSLv3 in 1996.

In 1996, the Internet Engineering Task Force (IETF) started the effort to standardize an SSL-like protocol, perhaps an attempt to unify the different designs by the two then rivals Netscape and Microsoft.

The working group received proposals from vendors. Microsoft submitted its STLP, which modified SSLv3 and added support for UDP datagrams and client authentication. The group eventually settled on the name of the protocol and called it Transport Layer Security (TLS), not SSL nor PCT or STLP.

Because SSL had been in use for a couple of years at that time, it was considered the de facto standard by many. As expected, some of the proposed changes met with resistance, largely in the name of backward compatibility. However, in the end, TLS still adopted some changes to SSLv3 which were not fully backward compatible.

Changes in TLS include requiring support of a cipher suite using the DH algorithm for key exchange/agreement, DSS algorithm for authentication, and 3DES (Triple-DES) for encryption. Key expansion and message authentication were also changed.

Since SSL started first and TLS came years later, the number of products supporting SSL exceeds that of TLS as of this writing. However, the landscape is changing. TLS is gradually gaining its popularity. It's conceivable that some day in a not too distant future support of TLS will likely win out.

15-10-3 SSL/TLS Features

As we briefly mentioned above, SSL/TLS offers multiple security features including the following:

- **Authentication**
- **Confidentiality**
- **Message Integrity**

Server authentication is always required in SSL/TLS while client authentication is optional.

Messages sent across a communication channel using SSL/TLS protocols are always encrypted and thus have confidentiality.

Message digest is always computed and verified to ensure the message is not tampered with during transit and thus message integrity is ensured.

In addition, because a "random key" is needed for encryption and that key has to be agreed upon and then shared right after being derived between the two communicating parties, a key exchange/agreement algorithm is also used.

As a result, an SSL/TLS cipher suite includes algorithms used in four security aspects:

- Key Exchange
- Authentication
- Encryption/Decryption
- Message Digest

For example, one of the TLS cipher suites is named TLS_DH_DSS_WITH_3DES_EDE_CBC_SHA. The name tells this cipher suite uses DH for key exchange/agreement, DSS for authentication, 3DES_EDE_CBC for encryption, and SHA algorithm for message digest. This DH/DSS/3DES combination is one of the mandatory cipher suites that TLS has to support.

15-10-4 SSL/TLS Handshake [1]

This section goes over the messages exchanged between the two communicating end points during the establishment of an SSL/TLS connection. Examining these messages gives readers a deeper understanding of the SSL/TLS protocols.

To establish an SSL/TLS network connection, the two parties (usually the client and the server) go through exchanging a number of messages.

To start establishing an SSL/TLS connection, the client first sends a **ClientHello** message. This message contains the cryptographic parameters the client proposes to use, including the ciphers. It also contains a random number to be used to generate an eventual session key that both parties agree upon.

The primary function of the ClientHello message is for the client to communicate its preferences of connection parameters to the server. These parameters are the protocol version, the cipher suites the client supports, and the compression algorithms.

The version number represents the highest SSL version number the client is willing to speak. For SSLv3 protocol, the major version number is 3 and minor version number is 0. For TLS 1.0, the major version number is 3 and minor version number is 1.

The cipher suites are sent in descending order of client's preferences. Each cipher suite is represented by a two-byte number.

The compression algorithm is represented by a one-byte constant. Due to patent considerations, the SSL specification defines no compression algorithm. Thus, this byte is NULL. Nonetheless, OpenSSL and some other implementations implement private compression algorithms.

Besides, the ClientHello message also contains a session id, a timestamp of when the message is generated, and a 28 bytes long random number to be used in creating the master secret.

In response to the ClientHello message, the server sends a **ServerHello** message, which consists of a cipher suite the server selects, a compression algorithm, and a random value the server has generated for creating the master secret later. Doing compression is not mandatory. But if it is done, it must be done before encryption. The server also sends a session id, which is often randomly generated with which the client could later use it to resume the session.

As for how a cipher suite is chosen, the SSL specification does not mandate it. The client sends its preferred cipher suites in the ClientHello message. But the server has no obligation to choose the client's preferred cipher suites. The server could defer to the client's preference or it could select its own. The common practice is for the server to choose the client-supported suite it likes most.

The server sends its certificate to the client after sending the ServerHello message if server authentication is required. (Well, there are a small number of cipher suites where the server is anonymous and thus the server certificate is not sent. But they are rarely used. In all common SSL/TLS cipher suites, a server certificate is sent.) This is done to protect the client such that the client always knows whom it is talking to.

The **Server Certificate** message is just a sequence of X.509 certificates presented in order, with the server certificate coming first, followed by the certificate containing the public key of the CA that signed the server certificate (if the server certificate is not self-signed), and then the next certificate that certifies the immediate CA, and so on, until it reaches the root CA.

The public key in the server certificate will be used a bit later. If the cipher suite selected uses RSA key exchange, then later when the client sends the ClientKeyExchange message, it will use this key to encrypt the pre_master_secret. If the cipher suite selected uses the D-H key exchange then the key will be used to verify the ServerKeyExchange.

After the Server Certificate message, the server sends a **ServerHelloDone** message.

At this point, the client is supposed to do the server authentication, going through verifying the server's certificate. If the server certificate verification fails, the client should terminate the connection. The hello phase ends here.

If the server certificate verification succeeds and the client decides to continue, it then goes into the key exchange and agreement phase. The client first sends a **ClientKeyExchange** message which contains a newly generated key value computed from the two random values separately generated and provided by both the client and the server earlier. This approach of producing the key from random values generated by both parties protects against a hacker from stepping in in the middle and substituting the key. Again, for security reason, this key value is encrypted using the server's public key (extracted from the server's certificate sent by the server) so that only the server can decrypt it using its private key.

The ClientKeyExchange message brings the random number that the client has generated for the creation of the master secret. This random number is carried over as part of a structure named PreMasterSecret which contains a two-byte long version number followed by a 46-byte random number.

To be secure it is very important that this random number is generated by using a cryptographically secure random number generator. If RSA key exchange is used, the client encrypts the PreMasterSecret value using the server's RSA key.

The ClientKeyExchange message is one of the two messages that are different between SSLv3 and TLS. This is because many SSLv3 implementations mistakenly omitting the length bytes when encoding the encrypted pre-master secret.

The client then also sends a **ChangeCipherSpec** message which tells the server that from this point on all messages sent by the client will be encrypted using the just-negotiated cipher and the newly generated key. The ChangeCipherSpec message is not encrypted.

The client then follows up with a Finished message containing a check value (i.e. message digest) for all of the messages exchanged so far (not including the Finished message itself) in the entire session such that the server knows for sure the conversation up to this point has been secure and has not been hacked into. The Finished message is encrypted.

Once the server has received the Finished message from the client, it sends

its own ChangeCipherSpec and Finished messages. This indicates to the client
that the server is ready for getting the real application data.
The application data exchange phase then starts.

```
           Client                                Server
 --------------------------        ------------------------------

 ------------> ClientHello

                                 ServerHello  <---------------
                                 ServerCertificate <----------
                                 ServerHelloDone <-----------
 ---------> ClientKeyExchange
 ---------> ChangeCipherSpec
 ---------> Finished
                                 ChangeCipherSpec <-----------
                                   Finished <-----------------

 -----> client request (application data)

                          server response (application data) <----

                     : (may repeat a few times)

 ----> close_notify Alert
 ----> TCP FIN
                                 close_notify Alert <-----------------
                                     TCP FIN <--------------------
```

   Figure 15-26 Sequence of SSL/TLS messages [1]

As you can see, just for two parties to establish a secure SSL/TLS connection,
so many messages have to be exchanged before any real data can be sent.
And during the phase of exchanging real data, the data is always encrypted
and message digested by the sender, and later decrypted and digest verified
by the recipient. These are the overhead of the SSL/TLS protocols and that
gives you the security.

After sending requests to and receiving responses from the server, when the
client is done with its job, it sends a **close_notify** alert to the server to
tell the server the connection is about to be shut down.
The client then sends a **TCP FIN** message to close the connection.
The server responds with its own TCP FIN. The connection closes.

Figure 15-26 displays the messages exchanged between a client and a server
in a SSL/TLS protocol.

With certain applications, the server may have a need to restrict accesses
to information or resources residing on the server to only certain clients,
as opposed to anyone. In this case, the server can make use of the optional
client authentication feature to do so.

Client authentication in SSL/TLS is always initiated by the server.
To do so the server sends a **CertificateRequest** message right after it sends
its own certificate to the client. In response, the client sends its

certificate before sending the ClientKeyExchange message and also sends
a **CertificateVerify** message after the ClientKeyExchange message. That's it!
Figure 15-27 shows the updated message sequence.

```
              Client                              Server
      --------------------------      -------------------------------

      -------------> ClientHello

                                      ServerHello  <----------------
                                      ServerCertificate <----------
                                      CertificateRequest <----------
                                      ServerHelloDone <------------
      ---------> Certificate
      ---------> ClientKeyExchange
      ---------> CertificateVerify
      ---------> ChangeCipherSpec
      ---------> Finished
                                      ChangeCipherSpec <-----------
                                      Finished <-----------------

      -----> client request (application data)

                          server response (application data) <----

                      : (may repeat a few times)

      ----> close_notify Alert
      ----> TCP FIN
                          close_notify Alert <------------------
                                  TCP FIN <--------------------
```

Figure 15-27 Sequence of SSL/TLS messages with client authentication [1]

15-10-5 Key Establishment/Exchange

Strictly speaking, there are really two ways in establishing a key,
depending on whether the key is established by just one side or both sides.

If the key is computed or established by one side, then it will need to be
transported to the other side, thus there is a 'key exchange' or
'key transport'. In this scheme, one side generates a symmetric key,
encrypts it using the other side's public key, and sends it to the other
party.

If the key is generated by cooperation of both sides, it is called 'key
agreement'. Key agreement establishes a key shared by both parties and
it is jointly computed by the two parties.

The two most commonly used key establishment algorithms are RSA and
Diffie-Hellman (DH). **RSA** is a **key transport** algorithm whereas **Diffie-Hellman**
is a **key agreement** algorithm. However, many people use the terms loosely
and use 'key establishment' and 'key exchange' interchangeably.

15-10-5-1 Why Key Establishment/Exchange?

We all know that to make communications confidential, we need to encrypt the messages. To encrypt, we need a key. To be secure, the key needs to be random and change at each communication session. Besides, the encryption key must also be shared between the message sender and recipient if symmetric encryption is used because the same key used in encryption by the sender must also be used in decryption by the recipient. Hence, a key generation, transport/exchange, and/or agreement is needed at the beginning of a communication for the two parties to agree upon a common key to use in enciphering and deciphering.

As described in the preceding section, a handshake and negotiation phase is carried out in order to establish an SSL/TLS communication channel. During the setup phase, the two parties negotiate and determine the cryptographic algorithms to be used for confidentiality, message integrity and origin authentication. The two parties exchange keys in order to derive the eventual session key shared between them. Therefore, key establishment/exchange constitutes a very important part in the SSL/TLS protocols.

The initial phase of session setup uses a public key cryptosystem for exchanging the initial keys generated by both parties. The messages containing the initial keys are encrypted using a classical cipher and are also checksum-ed. At start, the handshake protocol assumes no key exchange cipher, no classical cipher and no integrity algorithm. The negotiation process selects one algorithm for each.

There are two main algorithms used in key establishment/exchange: Diffie-Hellman and RSA.

15-10-5-2 Key Establishment/Exchange Algorithms

Two most known key establishment/exchange algorithms are Diffie-Hellman and RSA. We talk about these two algorithms in this section.

15-10-5-2-1 Diffie-Hellman (DH)

The Diffie-Hellman key establishment is indeed key agreement.

The Diffie-Hellman key exchange mechanism enables two parties who have no prior knowledge of each other to jointly establish a shared secret key over an insecure public channel. This key can then be used to encrypt subsequent communications using a symmetric key cipher. Because the two parties share a common secret key from that point on, the Diffie-Hellman method is a symmetric key establishment protocol.

Traditionally, secure encrypted communication between two parties required that they first exchange keys by some secure physical channel, such as using a trusted courier. The Diffie-Hellman key establishment method represents a break-through because it enables two parties having no prior knowledge of each other to jointly establish a shared secret key over an insecure communication channel without pre-arrangement of a cipher key.

This makes a tremendous contribution in providing the basis for many protocols in securing today's communications over the Internet, including ephemeral modes support (EDH or DHE) in the Transport Layer Security (TLS) protocol.

The Diffie-Hellman key establishment scheme was patented in U.S., patent number US4200770. The patent was filed on Sep. 6, 1977 and was granted on Apr. 29, 1980. It was invented by Martin E. Hellman, Bailey W. Diffie, Ralph C. Merkle at Stanford University. This patent has expired now.

Note that the Diffie-Hellman scheme was first published by Whitfield Diffie and Martin Hellman in 1976. However, in 1997 it was revealed that Clifford Cocks, James H. Ellis, and Malcolm J. Williamson of the British signals intelligence agency, had previously shown how public-key cryptography could be achieved in 1969.

How the Diffie-Hellman Key Establishment Works

The Diffie-Hellman key establishment process begins by having the two parties agree upon two common values.

Each of them then selects its own private, secret value. A value is computed from combining the common values with the secret values of their choices. Then they exchange the values they so compute. Finally, each of the two computes another value by using the value they received from the partner and their own secret value. This final result is a final secret that is identical to the partner's. And this is the shared secret key to be used in encrypting their subsequent communication!

Below we explain how the Diffie-Hellman key exchange algorithm works.[3][2]

In Diffie-Hellman cryptosystem, the two parties choose and share a common modulus p, which is a large prime number, and another number g, which cannot be 0, 1 or p-1. g is a primitive root modulo p.

The base common value g and the modulus p are what the two parties agree upon to begin with. The two parties agree upon g and p either as part of the key exchange or offline. They don't need to be kept secret. In fact, they are transmitted in clear text in SSL/TLS protocols. After the common value g and modulus p are agreed upon, the Diffie-Hellman key exchange process then proceeds as follows:

First, each party chooses a secret value and computes the first calculated value:

```
     Party 1                    Party 2
     --------------------       ----------------------
     pick secret a              pick secret b

     compute X = (g^a) mod p    compute Y = (g^b) mod p
```

Second, the two parties exchange the first values they compute.

```
     Party 1                    Party 2
     -------                    -------
```

```
X ------------->
            <------------ Y
```

Third, each party computes the final shared secret using the value received
from the partner and the secret value it has chosen.

```
    Party 1                    Party 2
    ------------------         ------------------

compute (Y^a) mod p        compute (X^b) mod p
```

The two parties arrive at the same final value because the following:

$$(g^{(ab)}) \bmod p = (g^{(ba)}) \bmod p = (Y^a) \bmod p = (X^b) \bmod p$$

where the number a is the secret value party 1 chooses and b is the
secret value party 2 chooses. (a^b) means a raised to exponential b.

It's that simple mathematically! Anyone with middle or high school
math understands this.

Of course, for this to be practically secure, very big values of a, b,
and p would be needed.

Note that only a, b, and ((g^(ab)) mod p = (g^(ba)) mod p) are kept secret.
All the other values -- p, g, (g^a mod p), and (g^b mod p) -- are sent
in the clear.

The magic of this is that in the end both parties arrive at the same value.
Each party kind of owns one half of a complete circle and each is able to
make the whole circle because each knows its partner's half, as well as its
own half which is private to them. An attack would not be able to make the
complete circle and get the shared secret because it wouldn't know the secret
values picked by each party -- the secrets they pick are never sent across
the network.

Because the two sides cooperate to generate a shared secret key, the
Diffie-Hellman key exchange algorithm is actually a 'key agreement'
algorithm. It is a non-authenticated key-agreement protocol.

The Diffie-Hellman key exchange algorithm has a property that communications
remain secure even if the private key is uncovered. This property is referred
to as **'perfect forward secrecy'** and is used in SSL/TLS. **Forward Secrecy (FS)**
means that if the long-term private key of the server is leaked, past
communication is still secure.

The Diffie-Hellman protocol is considered secure against eavesdroppers.
It is used to secure a variety of Internet services.
Nonetheless, research found that the parameters in use for many DH Internet
applications in early days may not be strong enough to prevent compromise
by some attackers.

Three Types of Diffie-Hellman Ciphers [2]

When used in protocols like SSL/TLS, there are actually three different
types of Diffie-Hellman ciphers.

The regular 'Diffie-Hellman' cipher means the certificate sent is signed by a proper CA and the parameters to the Diffie-Hellman cipher are contained in it.

The 'Ephemeral Diffie-Hellman' cipher refers to the type of Diffie-Hellman in which an RSA or DSS certificate is used to sign the parameters to the Diffie-Hellman cipher and those parameters will not be reused; thus the name ephemeral. In contrast to static Diffie-Hellman key exchange always uses the same Diffie-Hellman private key, Ephemeral Diffie-Hellman key exchange generates a temporary key for each connection and therefore the same key is never used twice. This enables Forward Secrecy.

The 'Anonymous Diffie-Hellman' cipher uses Diffie-Hellman without either party being authenticated, hence, anonymous. Because of this, the Anonymous Diffie-Hellman is deemed insecure and is not recommended.

15-10-5-2-2 RSA

RSA key exchange/establishment is indeed **key transport.**

When RSA is chosen for key exchange/transport, the sender generates a random session key, makes sure it is properly padded, and then encrypts the session key using the recipient's public key. At receiving end, the recipient decrypts the received message using its own private key and removes the padding to get the shared session key. It's pretty simple.

If RSA cipher is used for key exchange, the server must provide an RSA certificate. But the server then may request the client to provide either an RSA or DSS certificate.

15-10-5-2-3 TLS Support

TLS supports both Diffie-Hellman (DH) and RSA for key exchange/establishment. Due to its fast performance, the Diffie-Hellman key exchange is often chosen.

For key exchange using DH or RSA algorithm, there are only a certain number of encryption and message digest algorithms available. For message digest, both SHA and MD families of algorithms can be used with DH or RSA, but not all possible combinations are supported. For classical cipher, DES, IDEA, RC2 and RC4 are used with RSA and DES and RC4 are used with DH. But again, not all possible combinations of modes are supported. Look at the SSL/TLS implementation you use to find out what are supported.

15-10-5-2-4 Key Establishment/Exchange Message [1]

TLS 1.0 supports two key exchange/establishment methods: RSA and Diffie-Hellman. RSA key exchange is simpler than Diffie-Hellman.

Remember during SSL/TLS handshake, a server sends the server certificate to the client. After the client successfully verifying the server certificate and deciding to trust it, if the server certificate contains enough information for the key exchange method in the cipher suite selected, the client will respond with a ClientKeyExchange message to the server.

Depending on the key exchange method chosen, which is normally driven by
information contained in the server certificate, the ClientKeyExchange
message should contain either an RSA-encrypted premaster secret
or the values used in the Diffie-Hellman key exchange algorithm.

If it is an RSA key exchange, the client generates a random premaster
secret, encrypts the premaster secret using the server's public key
(extracted from the server certificate the server has just sent)
and sends that in the ClientKeyExchange message. The server will then use
its private key to decrypt it.

If Diffie-Hellman key exchange method is chosen, the server must have sent
g, p, and ((g^b) mod p) in the server certificate, where g and p are common
values and b is the secret the server has picked. And the client would
send its g, p and ((g^a) mod p) in the ClientKeyExchange message to the
server.

If you actually dump the SSL/TLS messages exchanged between the server and
the client, you should be able to see the values of g and p.

```
    pre-master secret
          |
          v
    master secret
          |
          v
    final key
```

Figure 15-28 SSL key derivation

The key agreed upon via Diffie-Hellman is normally referred to as the
'premaster secret'. It's not the final key used.
The premaster secret is first expanded into the 'master secret', which
is then expanded into the final key. Both expansion processes take a client
random number and a server random number as input.

15-10-6 Makeup of SSL/TLS Cipher Suites

Figure 15-29 Cipher suite makeup

Cipher suite name	Key Exchange	Digital Signature	Encryption	Digest
TLS_DH_DSS_WITH_3DES_EDE_CBC_SHA	DH	DSS	3DES_EDE_CBC	SHA
TLS_DHE_RSA_WITH_AES_256_CBC_SHA256	DHE	RSA	AES_256_CBC	SHA256
TLS_DHE_DSS_EXPORT_WITH_DES40_CBC_SHA	DHE_EXPORT	DSS	DES_40_CBC	SHA
TLS_RSA_WITH_RC4_128_MD5	RSA	RSA	RC4_128	MD5

As discussed in previous sections, a complete cipher suite needs to include
algorithms used in not only encryption and message integrity but also
digital signature and key exchange. This means a complete cipher suite
consists of multiple algorithms in it for different purposes.

For example, Figure 15-29 shows the makeup of a few SSL/TLS cipher suites. It lists the names of some of the cipher suites supported in the SSL/TLS protocols and the algorithms they use for different operations.

Just as an example, with TLS_DHE_RSA_WITH_AES_256_CBC_SHA256 cipher suite, it means Ephemeral Diffie-Hellman algorithm is used for key exchange (the Server Key Exchange message) and RSA is the algorithm used for digital signature. The AES_256_CBC algorithm is used in encrypting/decrypting the messages to achieve communication secrecy. And the SHA256 algorithm is used for message digest to achieve message integrity protection.

Again, check out the SSL/TLS implementation you use to find out what cipher suites are supported.

15-10-7 Considerations in Using SSL/TLS

These days almost everyone has had experience of using the Internet by entering a URL like this:

    http://www.google.com

into a web browser. As a matter of fact, more and more often people are using the secure version of the web protocol HTTPS instead of the regular HTTP especially when doing online shopping, online banking or financial management:

    https://www.amazon.com/
    https://www.bankofamerica.com/

The secure HTTPS protocol uses the SSL or TLS protocol underneath for secure communications across the Internet. The SSL and TLS protocols implement authentication, encryption and message digest aspects of security.

Note that the SSL and TLS protocols are mainly designed for communications between a web server and a web browser where the server is sitting at a well-known address (like the three URLs given above) waiting for requests from essentially anyone from anywhere in the world using a browser or any program using the HTTPS protocol.

A typical scenario is a user using a browser connects to some company's web site and gives his or her credit card information to purchase something. Since typically it's the client who initiates the communications and gives away important information (credit card number and money) to the server, it's very important to always authenticate the server to try to protect the clients, not the other way around. Because of this, the specifications of SSL and TLS protocols always require server authentication but make client authentication optional.

As we have discussed, in SSL and TLS protocols, a client and a server have to go through a handshaking phase in order to establish a secure connection before they start talking to each other. During this handshaking phase, the server always has to be authenticated. This means the server must send its certificate to the client and the client has to go through verifying that the server certificate is signed by some recognized certificate authority, that it is still valid, that its name matches and that the certificate is trustworthy. If any of these conditions is not true, connection between the two sides won't be established and there won't be further communication at all. On the other hand, a client normally does not send its certificate to the server unless the server explicitly requests that.

Since server authentication is always required in SSL/TLS protocols a server must always have a valid certificate. In contrast, because the client authentication is optional, a client does not need to have a certificate at all. In fact, most of them don't. This means anyone can connect to a server and get information from the server without even proving who he or she is as long as he or she knows the server's address.

Clearly, the SSL and TLS protocols are designed such that its security tilts toward one direction. It's meant to protect the clients more than the server. Essentially, anyone can connect to a web server and get information from it without proving its identity.

It's very important to understand this and keep this in mind when you are considering selecting a security protocol to use for your software and system.

If you are developing your own networking software (e.g. a distributed system) and you like to secure the communications and information exchanges between the two sides, many people might think using SSL or TLS is the way to go. But think that twice. First, SSL/TLS does not require authenticating the clients. Do you really want that? Do you want to protect just the clients? Or indeed what you really want to protect is the server instead? Many software products are actually so. Or is it more peer-to-peer that both sides are equally needing protection? Furthermore, in SSL and TLS, even when the client authentication is turned on, any client from any place in the world is allowed to access a server as long as it has a valid certificate. Do you really want that? I mean do you really want any program with a valid certificate to be able to get information out of your server?

The answer is no for many applications. A lot of applications involving sensitive data need even stronger authentication than just a certificate. In other words, using SSL/TLS with client authentication on may not even be strict or strong enough in security! For some applications, authentication is the weakest link among all three security aspects that SSL/TLS offers. In other words, although SSL/TLS provides very strong security when data travel across network, securing or limiting access to data (especially on the server) may require additional measures for some applications.

An analogy is do you really want to allow anyone with a driver license to access your data? I think the answer is probably no or a big no for many applications! It has got to be more restrictive than that. We've got to know a lot more about the person before granting access. That is, the group of people who should be allowed in should be much, much smaller than that! This means SSL/TLS is not really the correct security protocol to use to guard your data in some applications. And additional authentication is needed beyond SSL/TLS.

Of course, authentication aside, you get encryption and message integrity for free from SSL/TLS. But the authentication part is a very important factor. If you open your door to anyone (with a valid certificate) and let in people you shouldn't, there may not be much point to have secrecy and message integrity in the communications after all. Isn't it? Therefore, make sure

you guard the access first and then do it in secrecy with integrity after!
To be truly secure, you need to do both, not just one half.

Summary

Therefore, there are four things you need to make sure you do it right
when using SSL/TLS. First, you need to ask yourself this question:

- Is SSL/TLS the best security mechanism for my application?

As we have cautioned above, the answer here is probably no for many.

And then if the answer is yes, then you need to do the rest three things
to make sure you do SSL/TLS right.

- Certificate verification. Check to ensure the certificate presented
  is signed by a trusted CA, is still valid, and is not revoked.

- Check to ensure the subject name in the certificate matches.

- Should I require client authentication?
  For normal web applications, the answer is no. But for other applications,
  the answer could be yes if you need to protect your data on server.

Remember that SSL/TLS's strength is that it protects the data in transit,
especially when the data travels through a public network.
It has an advantage when the user can be anyone from anywhere in the world.
As a result, it is best solution for Internet Commerce.
But many other applications do not really have to support such a wide and
random group of users, nor they want to. For those, whether SSL/TLS is the
right or best solution really needs to be thought out.

The down side of using SSL/TLS is that using a certificate may not be a very
strong or strong enough authentication for many applications.
Besides, SSL/TLS has got some overhead, too. That said, SSL/TLS is very
popular and standard in web applications.

15-11 SSL/TLS Programming

In this section, we will talk about how to write a client program and
a server program that communicate with each other using the secure TLS/SSL
protocols. Our examples will base on OpenSSL implementation.

First, we will show you how to establish a TLS/SSL connection and exchange
messages over that.

Then we will show how to do server authentication by verifying a self-signed
server certificate, followed by verifying a server certificate signed by
a chain of CAs. Lastly, we will demonstrate how to do the optional
client authentication. We will provide program examples for each of these.

15-11-1 Basic TLS/SSL Client-Server

Figure 15-30 First SSL/TLS application -- tlsclient1.c and tlsserver1.c

(a) tlsserver1.c

```c
/*
 * A TLS/SSL server.
 * This server program communicates with clients using TLS/SSL protocol.
 * Authored by Mr. Jin-Jwei Chen.
 * Copyright (c) 2014-2016, 2020-2021 Mr. Jin-Jwei Chen. All rights reserved.
 */

#include <stdio.h>
#include <errno.h>
#include <sys/types.h>
#include <sys/socket.h>
#include <netinet/in.h>     /* protocols such as IPPROTO_TCP, ... */
#include <string.h>         /* memset(), strlen(), memcmp() */
#include <stdlib.h>         /* atoi() */
#include <unistd.h>
#include <resolv.h>
#include <netdb.h>
#include <arpa/inet.h>
#include <resolv.h>
#include <openssl/ssl.h>
#include <openssl/err.h>
#include <openssl/x509.h>
#include "myopenssl.h"
#include "netlib.h"

/*
 * This function serves a newly connected SSL client.
 * Parameters:
 *   ctx (input) - SSL context.
 *   clntsock (input) - the child socket to communicate with the client.
 * Function output: return 0 on success, non-zero on failure.
 * Note that Openssl provides different functions to retrieve the actual
 * error. Unfortunately, they return different data types, some 'int'
 * (SSL_get_error()) and some 'unsigned long' (ERR_get_error()).
 * It makes it hard to return both types of errors from a function.
 */
int serve_ssl_client(SSL_CTX *ctx, int clntsock)
{
  SSL           *ssl = NULL;        /* SSL structure/connection */
  char          reqmsg[MAXREQSZ];   /* buffer for incoming request message */
  char          reply[MAXRPLYSZ];   /* buffer for outgoing server reply */
  unsigned char replysz;            /* length in bytes of reply message */
  int           insize;             /* actual number of bytes read */
  int           outsz;              /* actual number of bytes written */
  int           error = 0;          /* error from certain SSL_xxx calls */
  unsigned char msgcnt;             /* count of reply messages to client */
  int           done = 0;           /* done with current client */
  int           ret;

  if (ctx == NULL)
    return(EINVAL);
  ERR_clear_error();
```

```
/* Create a new SSL structure to hold the connection data */
ssl = SSL_new(ctx);
if (ssl == NULL)
{
  fprintf(stderr, "Error: SSL_new() failed:\n");
  ERR_print_errors_fp(stderr);
  return(OPENSSL_ERR_SSLNEW_FAIL);
}

/* Associate the SSL structure with the socket */
ret = SSL_set_fd(ssl, clntsock);
if (ret != OPENSSL_SUCCESS)
{
  fprintf(stderr, "Error: SSL_set_fd() failed:\n");
  ERR_print_errors_fp(stderr);
  SSL_free(ssl);
  return(OPENSSL_ERR_SSLSETFD_FAIL);
}

/* Wait for the TLS/SSL client to initiate the TLS/SSL handshake */
ret = SSL_accept(ssl);
if (ret != OPENSSL_SUCCESS)
{
  error = SSL_get_error(ssl, ret);
  fprintf(stderr, "Error: SSL_accept() failed, error=%d\n", error);
  SSL_free(ssl);
  return(error);
}

/* The service loop */
done = 0;
msgcnt = 1;
do
{
  /* Read the next request message from the TLS/SSL client */
  insize = SSL_read(ssl, reqmsg, MAXREQSZ);
  if (insize <= 0)
  {
    error = SSL_get_error(ssl, insize);
    fprintf(stderr, "Error: SSL_read() failed, error=%d\n", error);
    break;
  }

  reqmsg[insize] = '\0';
  fprintf(stdout, "Server received: %s\n", reqmsg);

  /* Process the request here ... */

  /* Construct a reply message */
  if ( !strcmp(reqmsg, BYE_MSG) )
  {
    done = 1;
    strcpy(reply, reqmsg);
  }
  else
    sprintf(reply, SRVREPLY2, msgcnt++);
```

```
   replysz = strlen(reply);

   /* Send back a reply */
   outsz = SSL_write(ssl, reply, replysz);
   if (outsz != replysz)
   {
     error = SSL_get_error(ssl, outsz);
     fprintf(stderr, "Error: SSL_write() failed, error=%d\n", error);
     break;
   }
 } while (!done);

 /* Free up resources and return */
 SSL_free(ssl);
 return(error);
}

/* TLS/SSL server program */
int main(int argc, char *argv[])
{
  int     sfd;                          /* file descriptor of the listener socket */
  struct sockaddr_in     srvaddr;       /* IPv4 socket address structure */
  struct sockaddr_in6    srvaddr6;      /* IPv6 socket address structure */
  in_port_t  portnum = SRVPORT;         /* port number this server listens on */
  int        portnum_in = 0;            /* port number specified by user */
  struct sockaddr_in6    clntaddr;      /* client socket address */
  socklen_t              clntaddr6sz = sizeof(clntaddr6);
  int     newsock = 0;                  /* file descriptor of client data socket */
  int     ipv6 = 0;                     /* IPv6 mode or not */
  int     ret;                          /* return value */
  SSL_CTX    *ctx;                      /* SSL context */

  /* Print Usage if requested by user */
  if (argc > 1 && argv[1][0] == '?' )
  {
    fprintf(stderr, "Usage: %s [server_port] [1 (use IPv6)]\n", argv[0]);
    return(0);
  }

  /* Get the server port number from user, if any */
  if (argc > 1)
  {
    portnum_in = atoi(argv[1]);
    if (portnum_in <= 0)
    {
      fprintf(stderr, "Error: port number %s invalid\n", argv[1]);
      fprintf(stderr, "Usage: %s [server_port] [1 (use IPv6)]\n", argv[0]);
      return(-1);
    }
    else
      portnum = portnum_in;
  }

  /* Get the IPv6 switch from user, if any */
  if (argc > 2)
```

```
{
  if (argv[2][0] == '1')
    ipv6 = 1;
  else if (argv[2][0] != '0')
  {
    fprintf(stderr, "Usage: %s [server_port] [1 (use IPv6)]\n", argv[0]);
    return(-2);
  }
}

fprintf(stdout, "TLS/SSL server listening at portnum=%u ipv6=%u\n",
  portnum, ipv6);

/* Create the server listener socket */
if (ipv6)
  ret = new_bound_srv_endpt(&sfd, (struct sockaddr *)&srvaddr6, AF_INET6,
    portnum);
else
  ret = new_bound_srv_endpt(&sfd, (struct sockaddr *)&srvaddr, AF_INET,
    portnum);

if (ret != 0)
{
  fprintf(stderr, "Error: new_bound_srv_endpt() failed, ret=%d\n", ret);
  return(-3);
}

/* Create a TLS/SSL context -- a framework enabling TLS/SSL connections. */
ctx = SSL_CTX_new(TLS_server_method());
if (ctx == NULL)
{
  fprintf(stderr, "Error: SSL_CTX_new() failed\n");
  close(sfd);
  return(-4);
}

/* Load the server's certificate and private key */
ret = load_certificate(ctx, SS_SRV_CERT_FILE, SS_SRV_KEY_FILE);
if (ret != SUCCESS)
{
  fprintf(stderr, "Error: load_certificate() failed, ret=%d\n", ret);
  SSL_CTX_free(ctx);
  close(sfd);
  return(-5);
}

/* Server's service loop. Wait for next client and service it. */
while (1)
{
  /* Accept the next client's connection request */
  newsock = accept(sfd, (struct sockaddr *)&clntaddr6, &clntaddr6sz);
  if (newsock < 0)
  {
    fprintf(stderr, "Error: accept() failed, errno=%d\n", errno);
    continue;
  }
```

```
    fprintf(stdout, "\nServer got a client connection\n");

    /* Service the current SSL client */
    ret = serve_ssl_client(ctx, newsock);
    if (ret != 0)
      fprintf(stderr, "Error: serve_ssl_client() failed, ret=%d\n", ret);

    close(newsock);
  }  /* while */

  SSL_CTX_free(ctx);      /* release SSL context */
  close(sfd);             /* close server socket */
  return(0);
}
```

  (b) tlsclient1.c

```
/*
 * A TLS/SSL client.
 * This program communicates with a TLS/SSL server using TLS/SSL protocol.
 * Authored by Mr. Jin-Jwei Chen.
 * Copyright (c) 2014-2016, 2020-2021 Mr. Jin-Jwei Chen. All rights reserved.
 */

#include <stdio.h>
#include <errno.h>
#include <sys/types.h>
#include <sys/socket.h>
#include <netinet/in.h>      /* protocols such as IPPROTO_TCP, ... */
#include <string.h>          /* memset(), strlen(), memcmp() */
#include <stdlib.h>          /* atoi() */
#include <unistd.h>
#include <resolv.h>
#include <netdb.h>
#include <openssl/ssl.h>
#include <openssl/err.h>
#include <openssl/x509.h>
#include "myopenssl.h"
#include "netlib.h"

/* Free all resources */
#define  FREEALL  \
    SSL_free(ssl); \
    SSL_CTX_free(ctx); \
    close(sfd);

/* A TLS/SSL client program */
int main(int argc, char *argv[])
{
  char          *srvhost = "localhost"; /* name of server host */
  in_port_t     srvport = SRVPORT;      /* port number server listens on */
  int           srvport_in = 0;         /* port number specified by user */

  int           ret;        /* return value */
  int           sfd=0;      /* socket file descriptor */
```

```
int          error;              /* return value of SSL_get_error() */

SSL_CTX      *ctx = NULL;  /* SSL/TLS context/framework */
SSL          *ssl = NULL;  /* SSL/TLS connection */

char             replymsg[MAXRPLYSZ];     /* reply message from server */
size_t           reqbufsz = MAXREQSZ;     /* size of client request buffer */
char             *reqmsg=NULL;            /* pointer to request message buffer */
size_t           reqmsgsz;                /* size of client request message */
int              bytes;                   /* number of bytes received */
int              done=0;                  /* done communicating with server */

/* Print Usage if requested by user */
if (argc > 1 && argv[1][0] == '?' )
{
  fprintf(stdout, "Usage: %s [srvportnum] [srvhostname]\n", argv[0]);
  return(0);
}

/* Get the port number of the target server host specified by user */
if (argc > 1)
{
  srvport_in = atoi(argv[1]);
  if (srvport_in <= 0)
  {
    fprintf(stderr, "Error: port number %s invalid\n", argv[1]);
    return(-1);
  }
  else
    srvport = srvport_in;
}

/* Get the name of the target server host specified by user */
if (argc > 2)
  srvhost = argv[2];

/* Connect to the server */
ret = connect_to_server(&sfd, srvhost, srvport);
if (ret != 0)
{
  fprintf(stderr, "Error: connect_to_server() failed, ret=%d\n", ret);
  if (sfd) close(sfd);
  return(-2);
}

/* Create a TLS/SSL context -- a framework enabling TLS/SSL connections. */
ctx = SSL_CTX_new(TLS_client_method());
if (ctx == NULL)
{
  fprintf(stderr, "Error: SSL_CTX_new() failed\n");
  close(sfd);
  return(-3);
}

/* Allocate a new SSL structure to hold SSL connection data */
ssl = SSL_new(ctx);
```

```
  if (ssl == NULL)
  {
    fprintf(stderr, "Error: SSL_new() failed\n");
    SSL_CTX_free(ctx);
    close(sfd);
    return(-4);
  }

  /* Associate the SSL object with the socket file descriptor */
  ret = SSL_set_fd(ssl, sfd);
  if (ret != OPENSSL_SUCCESS)
  {
    fprintf(stderr, "Error: SSL_set_fd() failed, ret=%d\n", ret);
    FREEALL
    return(-5);
  }

  /* Initiate the TLS/SSL handshake with the TLS/SSL server */
  ret = SSL_connect(ssl);
  if (ret != OPENSSL_SUCCESS)
  {
    error = SSL_get_error(ssl, ret);
    fprintf(stderr, "Error: SSL_connect() failed, error=%d\n", error);
    FREEALL
    return(-6);
  }

  /* Connected with TLS/SSL server. Display server certificate info. */
  fprintf(stdout, "Connected with TLS/SSL server, cipher algorithm is %s\n",
    SSL_get_cipher(ssl));
  fprintf(stdout, "Information in the server certificate:\n");
  display_ssl_certificate_info(ssl);

  /* Allocate input buffer */
  reqmsg = malloc(MAXREQSZ);
  if (reqmsg == NULL)
  {
    fprintf(stderr, "Error: malloc() failed\n");
    FREEALL
    return(-7);
  }

  /* Send a message and get a response until done */
  do
  {
    /* Get next message the user wants to send */
    fprintf(stdout, "Enter a message to send ('bye' to end): ");
    reqmsgsz = getline(&reqmsg, &reqbufsz, stdin);
    if (reqmsgsz == -1)
    {
      fprintf(stderr, "Error: getline() failed, ret=%lu\n", reqmsgsz);
      break;
    }

    /* Remove the newline character at end of input */
    reqmsg[--reqmsgsz] = '\0';
```

1235

```
   /* Send a message using SSL -- message automatically encrypted */
   bytes = SSL_write(ssl, reqmsg, reqmsgsz);
   if (bytes != reqmsgsz)
   {
     error = SSL_get_error(ssl, bytes);
     fprintf(stderr, "Error: SSL_write() failed, error=%d\n", error);
     free(reqmsg);
     FREEALL
     return(-8);
   }
```

```
   /* Receive a reply using SSL -- reply automatically decrypted */
   bytes = SSL_read(ssl, replymsg, sizeof(replymsg));
   if (bytes <= 0)
   {
     error = SSL_get_error(ssl, bytes);
     fprintf(stderr, "Error: SSL_read() failed, error=%d\n", error);
     free(reqmsg);
     FREEALL
     return(-9);
   }
   else
   {
     replymsg[bytes] = 0;
     fprintf(stdout, "Received: %s\n", replymsg);
   }
```

```
   if (!strcmp(replymsg, reqmsg))
     done = 1;
```

```
} while (!done);
```

```
/* release all resources */
free(reqmsg);
SSL_free(ssl);         /* release the SSL structure/connection */
SSL_CTX_free(ctx);     /* release the SSL context */
close(sfd);            /* close socket */
return (0);
}
```

Figure 15-30 displays a very first SSL/TLS application where an SSL/TLS client communicates with an SSL/TLS server using the SSL/TLS protocol. Client and server exchange messages over an SSL/TLS connection with the server using a self-signed server certificate.

Note that to run the example programs, make sure you have the server key and certificate files present in the local directory. These are mysrv2_cert.pem and mysrv2_privkey.pem in our example.

Below is a sample output from running the SSL/TLS client and server.

```
$ ./tlsserver1
TLS/SSL server listening at portnum=7878 ipv6=0

Server got a client connection
```

```
Server received: This is a test message from the SSL client.
Server received: bye
```

```
$ ./tlsclient1
Connected with TLS/SSL server, cipher algorithm is ECDHE-RSA-AES256-GCM-SHA384
Information in the server certificate:
   Subject of the X509 certificate:
     C=US, ST=New Hampshire, L=Nashua, O=Chen Systems, Inc., OU=Engineering,
CN=mysrv2
   Issuer of the X509 certificate:
     C=US, ST=New Hampshire, L=Nashua, O=Chen Systems, Inc., OU=Engineering,
CN=mysrv2
```

```
   Enter a message to send ('bye' to end): This is a test message from the SSL
client.
   Received: This is reply message # 1 from the server.
   Enter a message to send ('bye' to end): bye
   Received: bye
```

We introduce the basic outlines of such an application in this section.

15-11-1-1 SSL/TLS Client

An SSL/TLS client application consists of the following major steps:

Major steps for an SSL/TLS client:
  - create a socket and connect to the server (socket, connect)
  - initialize SSL library (OPENSSL_init_ssl)
  - create an SSL context (SSL_CTX_new)
  - create an SSL structure (SSL_new)
  - associate the SSL structure with the socket file descriptor (SSL_set_fd)
  - start SSL handshake with the SSL/TLS server (SSL_connect)
  - send a message (SSL_write)
  - receive a reply (SSL_read)

The first step is to create a client socket and connect to the server. They are accomplished by the socket() and connect() calls, respectively. These are the same as a usual socket client application. We have talked about these in the socket chapter. There is really nothing new here.

The second step is to initialize the SSL library. This step is optional because starting from OpenSSL 1.1.0, it automatically allocates all resources that it needs so no explicit initialization is required. The SSL initialization and deinitialization is all automatic now unless applications have a reason to do them explicitly.

Calling the OPENSSL_init_ssl() function will explicitly initialize both libssl and libcrypto. To explicitly initialize ONLY libcrypto, call the OPENSSL_init_crypto() function instead. In order to perform nondefault initialization, OPENSSL_init_ssl() must be called by applications prior to any other OpenSSL function calls.

The function OPENSSL_init_ssl() returns 1 on success or 0 on error.

The third step is to **create an SSL context object**.

SSL_CTX_new() creates a framework that enables TLS/SSL connection establishment. It initializes the list of ciphers, the session cache setting, the callbacks, the keys and certificates, and the options to their default values.

The SSL_CTX_new() call takes a SSL_METHOD as input argument. This method input parameter can have a value returned by various functions. There are many types of methods, which are listed below. For a SSL/TLS client, normally you want to use **TLS_client_method**().

1. TLS_method(), TLS_server_method(), TLS_client_method()

   These TLS_xxx_method() functions are the general-purpose version-flexible SSL/TLS methods. The actual protocol version used in the SSL connection will be negotiated to the highest version that is mutually supported by both the client and the server. The supported protocols are SSLv3, TLSv1, TLSv1.1 and TLSv1.2. It is highly recommended that applications use these methods instead of the version-specific methods.

2. TLSv1_2_method(), TLSv1_2_server_method(), TLSv1_2_client_method()

   These are methods for the TLSv1.2 protocol only.

3. TLSv1_1_method(), TLSv1_1_server_method(), TLSv1_1_client_method()

   These are methods for the TLSv1.1 protocol only.

4. TLSv1_method(), TLSv1_server_method(), TLSv1_client_method()

   These are methods for the TLSv1.0 protocol only.

5. DTLS_method(), DTLS_server_method(), DTLS_client_method()

   These are the version-flexible DTLS methods.
   DTLS 1.0 and DTLS 1.2 are supported.
   DTLS is Datagram TLS. It is based on the TLS protocol but built on top of UDP protocol.

6. SSLv3_method(), SSLv3_server_method(), SSLv3_client_method()

   These are methods for the SSLv3 protocol, which are deprecated.

7. SSLv23_method(), SSLv23_server_method(), SSLv23_client_method()

   These are methods for the SSLv2.3 protocol, which are deprecated.

The fourth step is to **create an SSL object.**
The SSL_new() function creates a new SSL structure used to hold the data for a TLS/SSL connection. The structure inherits the settings of the underlying SSL context, for instance, connection method, options, verification settings and timeout settings.

Note that you always create an SSL context first and then create an SSL structure out of that context.

The fifth step is to **associate the socket file descriptor created in the**

first step with the SSL object. This is done by the SSL_set_fd(ssl, sfd) call. It sets the socket file descriptor sfd as the input/output facility of the SSL object. This gives the socket identified by sfd SSL/TLS capability as described in the SSL structure.

The sixth step is to **start the SSL/TLS handshaking** with the SSL/TLS server and to establish an SSL/TLS connection. SSL_connect(ssl) does exactly that. Client-side SSL_connect() interacts with the SSL_accept() on the server side. If the handshake fails for some reason, SSL_connect() will return an error and no SSL/TLS connection is established.

If SSL_connect() succeeds then an SSL/TLS connection is established. Once an SSL/TLS connection is established, an SSL/TLS program can then use SSL_write() to send messages and SSL_read() to receive replies.

For debugging and informational purposes, the client calls our library function display_ssl_certificate_subject(SSL *ssl) to display information of the certificate provided by its peer (i.e. the server). This function prints only the following information:

  - who the certificate represents (the Subject of the certificate)
  - who issued/signed the certificate (the Issuer of the certificate)

If you like to examine the certificate in more details, you can invoke the display_certificate_info(X509* cert) function instead, which prints additional information such as a certificate's validity period, signature algorithm and public key. Feel free to expand that function to print more information you want.

15-11-1-2 SSL/TLS Server

The outline of an SSL/TLS server overlaps a bit with an SSL/TLS client.

Major steps of an SSL/TLS server:
  - create a server socket and bind to a well-known port
  - initialize SSL library (OPENSSL_init_ssl)
  - create an SSL context using TLS_server_method (SSL_CTX_new)
  - load the server's certificate and private key
  - loop forever to listen/accept client connection requests and service each client
  - service an SSL client
    -- create a new SSL structure (SSL_new)
    -- associate the SSL structure with the server's client socket file descriptor (SSL_set_fd)
    -- start SSL handshake with the SSL/TLS client (SSL_accept)
    -- receive a client request (SSL_read)
    -- send a reply (SSL_write)

The first step is to create a server socket and bind it to the server's port number. This step is the same as a usual socket server application.

The second and third steps are similar to an SSL/TLS client except that the SSL context is created with a **TLS_server_method()**.

The fourth step is to **load the server's certificate and private key.**

This is for doing server authentication which is required in SSL/TLS.

To use a certificate, an SSL/TLS server (or client) must load its certificate and private key into the SSL context object by calling the following two functions, respectively:

```
SSL_CTX_use_certificate_file(ctx, certfile, SSL_FILETYPE_PEM)
SSL_CTX_use_PrivateKey_file(ctx, keyfile, SSL_FILETYPE_PEM)
```

where the arguments certfile and keyfile specify the pathnames of the files containing the certificate and private key, respectively. The third argument specifies the format of the certificate and key files. We use *.pem file format for both.

We create a library function named **load_certificate**() to do this step just so that it can also be shared by the client later. In load_certificate() we also invoke the

```
SSL_CTX_check_private_key(ctx)
```

function to verify the private key just being loaded into the SSL context to ensure it is correct.

The fifth step is to execute the server's main service loop in which the server listens and accepts a client request and then services that client. This step is similar to a usual socket server program.

In **servicing each SSL/TLS client,** an SSL/TLS server first creates a new SSL structure from the server's SSL context. It then associates the server's client socket with the SSL structure and starts the SSL/TLS handshaking with the client by invoking the SSL_accept() function.

If the SSL handshaking goes well, SSL_accept() returns success and an SSL/TLS connection between the client and server is established. In that case, the server will execute SSL_read() to receive client's requests and SSL_write() to send replies back to the client.

Should the SSL handshake go bad, SSL_accept() will fail and return an error. No connection is established in that case.

15-11-2 Loading Certificates and Private Keys

15-11-2-1 Loading Certificates

To use a certificate, an SSL/TLS program (server or client) must load the certificate identifying the program itself. This means the server must load the server certificate and the client must load the client certificate.

One can load a certificate into either an SSL_CTX object or SSL object. **A certificate loaded into an SSL_CTX object can be shared and used between multiple SSL connections while one loaded into an SSL object is used only by that connection.**

The certificate being loaded can be from a file, a X509 object or a byte array in ASN1 format. Below are the APIs:

```
#include <openssl/ssl.h>

int SSL_CTX_use_certificate(SSL_CTX *ctx, X509 *x);
int SSL_CTX_use_certificate_file(SSL_CTX *ctx, const char *file, int type);
int SSL_CTX_use_certificate_ASN1(SSL_CTX *ctx, int len, unsigned char *d);

int SSL_use_certificate(SSL *ssl, X509 *x);
int SSL_use_certificate_file(SSL *ssl, const char *file, int type);
int SSL_use_certificate_ASN1(SSL *ssl, unsigned char *d, int len);
```

SSL_CTX_use_certificate(SSL_CTX *ctx, X509 *x) loads the certificate
passed in as the second argument into the SSL context specified in the
first argument. SSL_use_certificate() works the same way except it loads
the certificate into an SSL object.

SSL_CTX_use_certificate_file() loads the first certificate found in the
file whose name specified in the second argument into the SSL context
specified in the first argument. The format of the certificate is specified
by the third argument. It must be one of the known types SSL_FILETYPE_PEM,
or SSL_FILETYPE_ASN1. SSL_use_certificate_file() is similar to
SSL_CTX_use_certificate_file() except it loads the certificate into an SSL
object.

SSL_CTX_use_certificate_ASN1() loads the ASN1 encoded certificate from the
memory location specified in the third argument 'd' into the SSL context
provided in the first argument. The length of the certificate data is
given in the second argument. SSL_use_certificate_ASN1() is similar except
it loads the ASN1 encoded certificate into an SSL object.

Note that the SSL_* functions load certificates and keys into a specific
SSL object. The specific information is retained when SSL_clear() is called
to clear the SSL object.

The SSL_CTX_* functions load the certificates and keys into the SSL_CTX
object ctx. The information is copied to all SSL objects created from
this context via the SSL_new() call. This means after an SSL object is
created, changes made to the context object do not get propagated to
existing SSL objects.

These functions return 1 on success. Reason of failure can be found
on the error stack.

Please notice that the order of the "len" and "d" (second and third)
parameters of the SSL_CTX_use_certificate_ASN1() function is a little odd.
It is inconsistent with the order of these two parameters in other
similar functions such as SSL_use_certificate_ASN1(),
SSL_CTX_use_PrivateKey_ASN1() and SSL_use_PrivateKey_ASN1().
The documentation is correct in that it truly reflects the source code of
OpenSSL 1.1.1g thru 3.3.0. It looks like a mistake that OpenSSL has not
had an opportunity to clean up yet! They should make it all consistent
to eliminate the confusion.

15-11-2-2 Loading Private Keys

A X.509 certificate has a subject's public key in it. A public key has a
pairing private key. The matching private key must also be provided for
it to work.

If a certificate and a private key do not match, it won't work.
To set or change/replace a certificate-private-key pair, you need to set/load
the certificate first and then set/load the private key after.

Just like loading a certificate, one can load a private key into either
an SSL_CTX or SSL object. The private key can come from a file,
an EVP_PKEY object or a byte array in ASN1 format. Below are the APIs:

```
#include <openssl/ssl.h>

int SSL_CTX_use_PrivateKey(SSL_CTX *ctx, EVP_PKEY *pkey);
int SSL_CTX_use_PrivateKey_file(SSL_CTX *ctx, const char *file, int type);
int SSL_CTX_use_PrivateKey_ASN1(int pk, SSL_CTX *ctx, unsigned char *d, long
len);

int SSL_use_PrivateKey(SSL *ssl, EVP_PKEY *pkey);
int SSL_use_PrivateKey_file(SSL *ssl, const char *file, int type);
int SSL_use_PrivateKey_ASN1(int pk, SSL *ssl, unsigned char *d, long len);
```

SSL_CTX_use_PrivateKey() loads the key passed in the second argument
as a private key to the SSL context object given in the first argument.
SSL_use_PrivateKey() does the same but to an SSL object.

SSL_CTX_use_PrivateKey_file() loads the first private key found in file
whose name given in the second argument into the SSL context object specified
in the first argument. The file format of the private key is specified in
the third argument. SSL_FILETYPE_PEM and SSL_FILETYPE_ASN1 formats
are supported. SSL_use_PrivateKey_file() does the same except to an SSL
object.

SSL_CTX_use_PrivateKey_ASN1() adds the private key of type pk stored at
memory location d, of length len, to the SSL context ctx.
SSL_use_PrivateKey_ASN1() does the same except to an SSL object.

If the private key is an RSA key (i.e. generated using the RSA algorithm),
then there is a set of similar functions for it. They are listed below.

```
int SSL_CTX_use_RSAPrivateKey(SSL_CTX *ctx, RSA *rsa);
int SSL_CTX_use_RSAPrivateKey_file(SSL_CTX *ctx, const char *file, int type);
int SSL_CTX_use_RSAPrivateKey_ASN1(SSL_CTX *ctx, unsigned char *d, long len);

int SSL_use_RSAPrivateKey(SSL *ssl, RSA *rsa);
int SSL_use_RSAPrivateKey_file(SSL *ssl, const char *file, int type);
int SSL_use_RSAPrivateKey_ASN1(SSL *ssl, unsigned char *d, long len);
```

These functions return 1 on success. Reason of failure can be found
on the error stack.

15-11-2-3 Verify Private Keys

```
#include <openssl/ssl.h>
int SSL_CTX_check_private_key(const SSL_CTX *ctx);
int SSL_check_private_key(const SSL *ssl);
```

It's always a good idea to verify a private key right after it's loaded.
SSL_CTX_check_private_key() checks the consistency of a loaded private key
with the corresponding certificate already loaded into the SSL context.
If there is more than one certificate and key pair installed, the last one
installed will be checked. SSL_check_private_key() does the same but
to an SSL object.

15-11-3 Verifying a Self-Signed Server Certificate

Notice that in our first SSL/TLS program example in the preceding section,
although the SSL/TLS server sends a server certificate to the client
during the SSL/TLS handshake phase right before a connection is established
(an SSL/TLS server always does that because it's required by the protocol),
the client program does not actually try to verify the server's certificate.
Hence, if the server had sent a bogus or expired certificate, the connection
would still have been established and the message exchanges taken place.

This is not what you want to do in a real application.
In a real application, a received certificate should be verified and if it
fails to verify, a connection should not be established.

We discuss how to verify a server certificate in this section.

15-11-3-1 How to verify a certificate

To verify a server's certificate, the client makes three function calls.

```
int SSL_CTX_load_verify_locations(SSL_CTX *ctx, const char *CAfile,
                                  const char *CApath);

void SSL_CTX_set_verify(SSL_CTX *ctx, int mode,
                        int (*verify_callback)(int, X509_STORE_CTX *));

long SSL_get_verify_result(const SSL *ssl);
```

First, the client invokes the SSL_CTX_load_verify_locations() function to
set the trusted CAs in its SSL context object by specifying the name of the
file containing the certificates of the trusted CAs and the directory
where this file resides. These CA certificates will be used in verifying
the server certificate.

Since the server certificate is self-signed, the server certificate is also
the trusted CA's certificate. That's why the client simply loads the
server's certificate in this case.

Note that the second argument, which is supposed to be the name of the file
containing the trusted CAs' certificates, cannot be NULL. However,
the third argument, which is a directory name, can be NULL. If the third

argument is NULL, it is assumed the file resides in the current working
directory.

Be aware that the call to SSL_CTX_load_verify_locations() must be done
after an SSL context is created and before SSL_connect() is invoked
or it won't work.

Second, the client calls

    SSL_CTX_set_verify(ctx, SSL_VERIFY_PEER, NULL)

with the **SSL_VERIFY_PEER flag** set in the second argument, declaring it wants
to verify its peer's (i.e. the server's) certificate.

There are two flavors of SSL_XXX_set_verify() function. One sets it in the
SSL context object which needs to be called only once, and the other sets
it in the SSL object which is on a per-connection basis.

The synopsis of the second flavor (without CTX in its name) is as shown below:

    void SSL_set_verify(SSL *s, int mode,
                    int (*verify_callback)(int, X509_STORE_CTX *));

Third, after the SSL_connect() call, the client executes the

    SSL_get_verify_result(ssl)

function to actually verify the server's certificate and get the result of
the verification. If it returns X509_V_OK, it means the verification of the
server certificate succeeds. If the client has set or loaded wrong trusted
CAs, then the return value will be 20. If the verification fails, the client
has an option to disconnect or proceed as normal.

Alternatively, a client could choose to specify the
SSL_VERIFY_FAIL_IF_NO_PEER_CERT flag as well in addition to SSL_VERIFY_PEER
when it invokes SSL_CTX_set_verify(). Setting this flag will cause the
SSL/TLS to automatically fail the handshake and connect request if the
other end (server in this case) does not even send its certificate.
However, this flag covers only the situation that a peer certificate is
not sent; it does not cover the case where a bad certificate is sent.

If the server sends its certificate, regardless of it's good or bad,
setting the SSL_VERIFY_FAIL_IF_NO_PEER_CERT flag does not make any real
difference. It still comes to SSL_get_verify_result() to detect the failure.
But if the server does not send its certificate, then setting this flag
would prevent a connection from ever being established because both
SSL_connect() and SSL_accept() would fail.

To reemphasize, the SSL_VERIFY_FAIL_IF_NO_PEER_CERT flag covers only the case
of the peer does not send a certificate. It does not cover the case where
a bad certificate is sent or fails to verify!

Besides, since an SSL/TLS server always sends a server certificate to
an SSL/TLS client unless anonymous cipher suite is used, on an SSL/TLS
client, calling SSL_get_verify_result() alone without
SSL_get_peer_certificate() works just fine.

Figure 15-31 is an enhanced version of our client-server SSL/TLS program example with server certificate verification.

Figure 15-31 SSL/TLS client and server with server certificate verification -- tlsclient2.c and tlsserver2.c

(a) tlsserver2.c

```
/*
 * A TLS/SSL server.
 * This server program communicates with clients using TLS/SSL protocol.
 * Using a self-signed server certificate.
 * Authored by Mr. Jin-Jwei Chen.
 * Copyright (c) 2014-2016, 2020-2021 Mr. Jin-Jwei Chen. All rights reserved.
 */

#include <stdio.h>
#include <errno.h>
#include <sys/types.h>
#include <sys/socket.h>
#include <netinet/in.h>      /* protocols such as IPPROTO_TCP, ... */
#include <string.h>          /* memset(), strlen(), memcmp() */
#include <stdlib.h>          /* atoi() */
#include <unistd.h>
#include <resolv.h>
#include <netdb.h>
#include <arpa/inet.h>
#include <resolv.h>
#include <openssl/ssl.h>
#include <openssl/err.h>
#include <openssl/x509.h>
#include "myopenssl.h"
#include "netlib.h"

/*
 * This function serves a newly connected SSL client.
 * Parameters:
 *   ctx (input) - SSL context.
 *   clntsock (input) - the child socket to communicate with the client.
 * Function output: return 0 on success, non-zero on failure.
 * Note that Openssl provides different functions to retrieve the actual
 * error. Unfortunately, they return different data types, some 'int'
 * (SSL_get_error()) and some 'unsigned long' (ERR_get_error()).
 * It makes it hard to return both types of errors from a function.
 */
int serve_ssl_client(SSL_CTX *ctx, int clntsock)
{
  SSL            *ssl = NULL;       /* SSL structure/connection */
  char           reqmsg[MAXREQSZ];  /* buffer for incoming request message */
  char           reply[MAXRPLYSZ];  /* buffer for outgoing server reply */
  unsigned char  replysz;           /* length in bytes of reply message */
  int            insize;            /* actual number of bytes read */
  int            outsz;             /* actual number of bytes written */
  int            error = 0;         /* error from certain SSL_xxx calls */
```

```
unsigned char  msgcnt;                /* count of reply messages to client */
int            done = 0;              /* done with current client */
int            ret;

if (ctx == NULL)
    return(EINVAL);
ERR_clear_error();

/* Create a new SSL structure to hold the connection data */
ssl = SSL_new(ctx);
if (ssl == NULL)
{
    fprintf(stderr, "Error: SSL_new() failed:\n");
    ERR_print_errors_fp(stderr);
    return(OPENSSL_ERR_SSLNEW_FAIL);
}

/* Associate the SSL structure with the socket */
ret = SSL_set_fd(ssl, clntsock);
if (ret != OPENSSL_SUCCESS)
{
    fprintf(stderr, "Error: SSL_set_fd() failed:\n");
    ERR_print_errors_fp(stderr);
    SSL_free(ssl);
    return(OPENSSL_ERR_SSLSETFD_FAIL);
}

/* Wait for the TLS/SSL client to initiate the TLS/SSL handshake */
ret = SSL_accept(ssl);
if (ret != OPENSSL_SUCCESS)
{
    error = SSL_get_error(ssl, ret);
    fprintf(stderr, "Error: SSL_accept() failed, error=%d\n", error);
    SSL_free(ssl);
    return(error);
}

/* The service loop */
done = 0;
msgcnt = 1;
do
{
    /* Read the next request message from the TLS/SSL client */
    insize = SSL_read(ssl, reqmsg, MAXREQSZ);
    if (insize <= 0)
    {
        error = SSL_get_error(ssl, insize);
        fprintf(stderr, "Error: SSL_read() failed, error=%d\n", error);
        break;
    }

    reqmsg[insize] = '\0';
    fprintf(stdout, "Server received: %s\n", reqmsg);

    /* Process the request here ... */
```

```
    /* Construct a reply message */
    if ( !strcmp(reqmsg, BYE_MSG) )
    {
      done = 1;
      strcpy(reply, reqmsg);
    }
    else
      sprintf(reply, SRVREPLY2, msgcnt++);

    replysz = strlen(reply);

    /* Send back a reply */
    outsz = SSL_write(ssl, reply, replysz);
    if (outsz != replysz)
    {
      error = SSL_get_error(ssl, outsz);
      fprintf(stderr, "Error: SSL_write() failed, error=%d\n", error);
      break;
    }
  } while (!done);

  /* Free up resources and return */
  SSL_free(ssl);
  return(error);
}


/* TLS/SSL server program */
int main(int argc, char *argv[])
{
  int     sfd;                         /* file descriptor of the listener socket */
  struct sockaddr_in    srvaddr;       /* IPv4 socket address structure */
  struct sockaddr_in6   srvaddr6;      /* IPv6 socket address structure */
  in_port_t portnum = SRVPORT;         /* port number this server listens on */
  int       portnum_in = 0;            /* port number specified by user */
  struct sockaddr_in6   clntaddr6;     /* client socket address */
  socklen_t             clntaddr6sz = sizeof(clntaddr6);
  int    newsock = 0;                  /* file descriptor of client data socket */
  int    ipv6 = 0;                     /* IPv6 mode or not */
  int    ret;                          /* return value */
  SSL_CTX     *ctx;                    /* SSL context */

  /* Print Usage if requested by user */
  if (argc > 1 && argv[1][0] == '?' )
  {
    fprintf(stderr, "Usage: %s [server_port] [1 (use IPv6)]\n", argv[0]);
    return(0);
  }

  /* Get the server port number from user, if any */
  if (argc > 1)
  {
    portnum_in = atoi(argv[1]);
    if (portnum_in <= 0)
    {
      fprintf(stderr, "Error: port number %s invalid\n", argv[1]);
      fprintf(stderr, "Usage: %s [server_port] [1 (use IPv6)]\n", argv[0]);
```

```
        return(-1);
      }
    else
      portnum = portnum_in;
  }

  /* Get the IPv6 switch from user, if any */
  if (argc > 2)
  {
    if (argv[2][0] == '1')
      ipv6 = 1;
    else if (argv[2][0] != '0')
    {
      fprintf(stderr, "Usage: %s [server_port] [1 (use IPv6)]\n", argv[0]);
      return(-2);
    }
  }

  fprintf(stdout, "TLS/SSL server listening at portnum=%u ipv6=%u\n",
    portnum, ipv6);

  /* Create the server listener socket */
  if (ipv6)
    ret = new_bound_srv_endpt(&sfd, (struct sockaddr *)&srvaddr6, AF_INET6,
      portnum);
  else
    ret = new_bound_srv_endpt(&sfd, (struct sockaddr *)&srvaddr, AF_INET,
      portnum);

  if (ret != 0)
  {
    fprintf(stderr, "Error: new_bound_srv_endpt() failed, ret=%d\n", ret);
    return(-3);
  }

  /* Create a TLS/SSL context -- a framework enabling TLS/SSL connections. */
  ctx = SSL_CTX_new(TLS_server_method());
  if (ctx == NULL)
  {
    fprintf(stderr, "Error: SSL_CTX_new() failed\n");
    close(sfd);
    return(-4);
  }

  /* Load the server's certificate and private key */
  ret = load_certificate(ctx, SS_SRV_CERT_FILE, SS_SRV_KEY_FILE);
  if (ret != SUCCESS)
  {
    fprintf(stderr, "Error: load_certificate() failed, ret=%d\n", ret);
    SSL_CTX_free(ctx);
    close(sfd);
    return(-5);
  }

  /* Server's service loop. Wait for next client and service it. */
  while (1)
```

```
  {
    /* Accept the next client's connection request */
    newsock = accept(sfd, (struct sockaddr *)&clntaddr6, &clntaddr6sz);
    if (newsock < 0)
    {
      fprintf(stderr, "Error: accept() failed, errno=%d\n", errno);
      continue;
    }

    fprintf(stdout, "\nServer got a client connection\n");

    /* Service the current SSL client */
    ret = serve_ssl_client(ctx, newsock);
    if (ret != 0)
      fprintf(stderr, "Error: serve_ssl_client() failed, ret=%d\n", ret);

    close(newsock);
  }   /* while */

  SSL_CTX_free(ctx);     /* release SSL context */
  close(sfd);            /* close server socket */
  return(0);
}
```

    (b) tlsclient2.c

```
/*
 * A TLS/SSL client.
 * This program communicates with a TLS/SSL server using TLS/SSL protocol.
 * The client verifies a self-signed server certificate.
 * Authored by Mr. Jin-Jwei Chen.
 * Copyright (c) 2014-2016, 2020-2021 Mr. Jin-Jwei Chen. All rights reserved.
 */

#include <stdio.h>
#include <errno.h>
#include <sys/types.h>
#include <sys/socket.h>
#include <netinet/in.h>      /* protocols such as IPPROTO_TCP, ... */
#include <string.h>          /* memset(), strlen(), memcmp() */
#include <stdlib.h>          /* atoi() */
#include <unistd.h>
#include <resolv.h>
#include <netdb.h>
#include <openssl/ssl.h>
#include <openssl/err.h>
#include <openssl/x509.h>
#include "myopenssl.h"
#include "netlib.h"

/* Free all resources */
#define  FREEALL  \
    SSL_free(ssl); \
    SSL_CTX_free(ctx); \
    close(sfd);
```

```
/* A TLS/SSL client program */
int main(int argc, char *argv[])
{
  char          *srvhost = "localhost"; /* name of server host */
  in_port_t     srvport = SRVPORT;      /* port number server listens on */
  int           srvport_in = 0;         /* port number specified by user */

  int       ret;             /* return value */
  int       sfd=0;           /* socket file descriptor */
  int       error;           /* return value of SSL_get_error() */
  long      sslret;          /* return value of some SSL calls */

  SSL_CTX   *ctx = NULL;   /* SSL/TLS context/framework */
  SSL       *ssl = NULL;   /* SSL/TLS connection */

  char          replymsg[MAXRPLYSZ];    /* reply message from server */
  size_t        reqbufsz = MAXREQSZ;    /* size of client request buffer */
  char          *reqmsg=NULL;           /* pointer to request message buffer */
  size_t        reqmsgsz;               /* size of client request message */
  int           bytes;                  /* number of bytes received */
  int           done=0;                 /* done communicating with server */

  unsigned char  errstrbuf[ERR_STRING_LEN];  /* error string */

  /* Print Usage if requested by user */
  if (argc > 1 && argv[1][0] == '?' )
  {
    fprintf(stdout, "Usage: %s [srvportnum] [srvhostname]\n", argv[0]);
    return(0);
  }

  /* Get the port number of the target server host specified by user */
  if (argc > 1)
  {
    srvport_in = atoi(argv[1]);
    if (srvport_in <= 0)
    {
      fprintf(stderr, "Error: port number %s invalid\n", argv[1]);
      return(-1);
    }
    else
      srvport = srvport_in;
  }

  /* Get the name of the target server host specified by user */
  if (argc > 2)
    srvhost = argv[2];

  /* Connect to the server */
  ret = connect_to_server(&sfd, srvhost, srvport);
  if (ret != 0)
  {
    fprintf(stderr, "Error: connect_to_server() failed, ret=%d\n", ret);
    if (sfd) close(sfd);
    return(-2);
  }
```

```c
/* Create a TLS/SSL context -- a framework enabling TLS/SSL connections. */
ctx = SSL_CTX_new(TLS_client_method());
if (ctx == NULL)
{
  fprintf(stderr, "Error: SSL_CTX_new() failed\n");
  close(sfd);
  return(-3);
}

/* Allocate a new SSL structure to hold SSL connection data */
ssl = SSL_new(ctx);
if (ssl == NULL)
{
  fprintf(stderr, "Error: SSL_new() failed\n");
  SSL_CTX_free(ctx);
  close(sfd);
  return(-4);
}

/* Set default locations for trusted CA certificates for verification */
if(SSL_CTX_load_verify_locations(ctx, SS_CA_FILE, CA_DIR) < 1)
{
  fprintf(stderr, "Error: SSL_CTX_load_verify_locations() failed to set "
    "verify location\n");
  return(-5);
}

/* Set to do server certificate verification */
SSL_CTX_set_verify(ctx, SSL_VERIFY_PEER, NULL);

/* Associate the SSL object with the socket file descriptor */
ret = SSL_set_fd(ssl, sfd);
if (ret != OPENSSL_SUCCESS)
{
  fprintf(stderr, "Error: SSL_set_fd() failed, ret=%d\n", ret);
  FREEALL
  return(-6);
}

/* Initiate the TLS/SSL handshake with the TLS/SSL server */
ERR_clear_error();
ret = SSL_connect(ssl);
if (ret != OPENSSL_SUCCESS)
{
  error = SSL_get_error(ssl, ret);
  fprintf(stderr, "Error: SSL_connect() failed, error=%d\n", error);
  print_ssl_io_error(error);
  fprintf(stderr, "%s\n", ERR_error_string((unsigned long)error, (char *)NULL));
  FREEALL
  return(-7);
}

/* Connected with TLS/SSL server. Display server certificate info. */
fprintf(stdout, "Connected with TLS/SSL server, cipher algorithm is %s\n",
  SSL_get_cipher(ssl));
```

```
fprintf(stdout, "Information in the server certificate:\n");
display_ssl_certificate_info(ssl);

/* Verify the peer's certificate and get the result */
ERR_clear_error();
if ((sslret = SSL_get_verify_result(ssl)) == X509_V_OK)
{
  /* The server sent a certificate which verified OK. */
  fprintf(stdout, "Verifying server's certificate succeeded.\n");
}
else
{
  fprintf(stderr, "SSL_get_verify_result() failed, ret=%ld\n", sslret);
  fprintf(stderr, "%s\n", ERR_error_string((unsigned long)sslret, (char *)NULL));
  FREEALL
  return(-8);
}

/* Allocate input buffer */
reqmsg = malloc(MAXREQSZ);
if (reqmsg == NULL)
{
  fprintf(stderr, "Error: malloc() failed\n");
  FREEALL
  return(-9);
}

/* Send a message and get a response until done */
do
{
  /* Get next message the user wants to send */
  fprintf(stdout, "Enter a message to send ('bye' to end): ");
  reqmsgsz = getline(&reqmsg, &reqbufsz, stdin);
  if (reqmsgsz == -1)
  {
    fprintf(stderr, "Error: getline() failed, ret=%lu\n", reqmsgsz);
    break;
  }

  /* Remove the newline character at end of input */
  reqmsg[--reqmsgsz] = '\0';

  /* Send a message using SSL -- message automatically encrypted */
  bytes = SSL_write(ssl, reqmsg, reqmsgsz);
  if (bytes != reqmsgsz)
  {
    error = SSL_get_error(ssl, bytes);
    fprintf(stderr, "Error: SSL_write() failed, error=%d\n", error);
    free(reqmsg);
    FREEALL
    return(-10);
  }

  /* Receive a reply using SSL -- reply automatically decrypted */
  bytes = SSL_read(ssl, replymsg, sizeof(replymsg));
  if (bytes <= 0)
```

```
    {
        error = SSL_get_error(ssl, bytes);
        fprintf(stderr, "Error: SSL_read() failed, error=%d\n", error);
        free(reqmsg);
        FREEALL
        return(-11);
    }
    else
    {
        replymsg[bytes] = 0;
        fprintf(stdout, "Received: %s\n", replymsg);
    }

    if (!strcmp(replymsg, reqmsg))
        done = 1;

} while (!done);

/* release all resources */
free(reqmsg);
SSL_free(ssl);          /* release the SSL structure/connection */
SSL_CTX_free(ctx);      /* release the SSL context */
close(sfd);             /* close socket */
return (0);
}
```

Summary

In summary, to do certificate verification in a C program, regardless of whether a certificate is self-signed or signed by a chain of CAs, an SSL/TLS client or server program must do these following three steps:

(1) Call the SSL_CTX_load_verify_locations() function to set the trusted CAs by specifying the name of the file containing all of the trusted CAs' certificates and the directory where that file resides. If the directory name is null, it's assumed the file exists in current working directory. This call must occur after the SSL context object is created and before the client invokes SSL_connect() or the server invokes SSL_accept().

(2) Call the SSL_CTX_set_verify() or SSL_set_verify() function with at least the SSL_VERIFY_PEER flag to specify it wants to verify the peer's certificate. By setting this flag, a client says it wants to verify the server's certificate. Similarly, if setting this flag, then a server says it wants to verify a client's certificate.

(3) Call the SSL_get_verify_result(ssl) to get the verification result. A client does this after an SSL connection is established (i.e. after SSL_connect() returns). A server does this after a client connection is accepted, that is, after the SSL_accept() call returns.

Note that for step 2 and 3, the server side is slightly more complicated than the client side. Please see the section on Client Authentication for details.

Potential Errors in Verifying a Self-signed Certificate

If you use a self-signed certificate, then when you use
SSL_get_verify_result() to get the verification result, it may return
error 18 for a self-signed certificate or error 19 if there is a
certificate chain built up using self-signed certificate.

```
Error    Meaning
-----    ------------------------------------------------------------
18       X509_V_ERR_DEPTH_ZERO_SELF_SIGNED_CERT: self-signed certificate
         The passed certificate is self-signed and the same certificate
         cannot be found in the list of trusted certificates.

19       X509_V_ERR_SELF_SIGNED_CERT_IN_CHAIN: self-signed certificate
         in certificate chain. The certificate chain could be built up using
         untrusted certificates but the root could not be found locally.
         ------------------------------------------------------------
```

15-11-4 Verifying a Server Certificate Signed by a Chain of CAs

OpenSSL has made it easy for developers. In other implementations,
to verify a certificate signed by a chain of CAs, one might have to code
a loop in which it gets and verifies each signing CA's certificate
until the root CA's certificate is verified, all the way from bottom to top.
But in OpenSSL, all a programmer has to do is to put all of
the signing CAs' certificates in a file and load that file using
the SSL_CTX_load_verify_locations() function.

Example programs tlsclient3.c and tlsserver3.c demonstrate how to do SSL/TLS
connections and message exchanges with a server certificate signed by a
chain of CAs using OpenSSL. The client successfully verifies the server's
certificate by using the certificates of the chain of CAs that have directly
or indirectly signed the server's certificate.

As you can see, the client and server programs here are essentially the same
as those in the preceding section where a self-signed server certificate
is used. The only difference is that now the client loads a file that
contains all of the trusted CAs' certificates used to sign the server's
certificate when it calls SSL_CTX_load_verify_locations().
Also, the server loads a different certificate file because the server
certificate now is signed by a chain of CAs rather than being self-signed.

   Figure 15-32 SSL/TLS client and server with verifying server certificates
      signed by a CA chain -- tlsclient3.c and tlsserver3.c

   (a) tlsserver3.c

```
/*
 * A TLS/SSL server.
 * This server program communicates with clients using TLS/SSL protocol.
 * Using a server certificate signed by a chain of CAs.
 * Authored by Mr. Jin-Jwei Chen.
 * Copyright (c) 2014-2016, 2020-2021 Mr. Jin-Jwei Chen. All rights reserved.
 */

#include <stdio.h>
```

```c
#include <errno.h>
#include <sys/types.h>
#include <sys/socket.h>
#include <netinet/in.h>          /* protocols such as IPPROTO_TCP, ... */
#include <string.h>              /* memset(), strlen(), memcmp() */
#include <stdlib.h>              /* atoi() */
#include <unistd.h>
#include <resolv.h>
#include <netdb.h>
#include <arpa/inet.h>
#include <resolv.h>
#include <openssl/ssl.h>
#include <openssl/err.h>
#include <openssl/x509.h>
#include "myopenssl.h"
#include "netlib.h"


/*
 *  This function serves a newly connected SSL client.
 *  Parameters:
 *    ctx (input) - SSL context.
 *    clntsock (input) - the child socket to communicate with the client.
 *  Function output: return 0 on success, non-zero on failure.
 *  Note that Openssl provides different functions to retrieve the actual
 *  error. Unfortunately, they return different data types, some 'int'
 *  (SSL_get_error()) and some 'unsigned long' (ERR_get_error()).
 *  It makes it hard to return both types of errors from a function.
 */
int serve_ssl_client(SSL_CTX *ctx, int clntsock)
{
  SSL             *ssl = NULL;       /* SSL structure/connection */
  char            reqmsg[MAXREQSZ];  /* buffer for incoming request message */
  char            reply[MAXRPLYSZ];  /* buffer for outgoing server reply */
  unsigned char   replysz;           /* length in bytes of reply message */
  int             insize;            /* actual number of bytes read */
  int             outsz;             /* actual number of bytes written */
  int             error = 0;         /* error from certain SSL_xxx calls */
  unsigned char   msgcnt;            /* count of reply messages to client */
  int             done = 0;          /* done with current client */
  int             ret;

  if (ctx == NULL)
     return(EINVAL);
  ERR_clear_error();

  /* Create a new SSL structure to hold the connection data */
  ssl = SSL_new(ctx);
  if (ssl == NULL)
  {
    fprintf(stderr, "Error: SSL_new() failed:\n");
    ERR_print_errors_fp(stderr);
    return(OPENSSL_ERR_SSLNEW_FAIL);
  }

  /* Associate the SSL structure with the socket */
  ret = SSL_set_fd(ssl, clntsock);
```

```
if (ret != OPENSSL_SUCCESS)
{
  fprintf(stderr, "Error: SSL_set_fd() failed:\n");
  ERR_print_errors_fp(stderr);
  SSL_free(ssl);
  return(OPENSSL_ERR_SSLSETFD_FAIL);
}

/* Wait for the TLS/SSL client to initiate the TLS/SSL handshake */
ret = SSL_accept(ssl);
if (ret != OPENSSL_SUCCESS)
{
  error = SSL_get_error(ssl, ret);
  fprintf(stderr, "Error: SSL_accept() failed, error=%d\n", error);
  SSL_free(ssl);
  return(error);
}

/* The service loop */
done = 0;
msgcnt = 1;
do
{
  /* Read the next request message from the TLS/SSL client */
  insize = SSL_read(ssl, reqmsg, MAXREQSZ);
  if (insize <= 0)
  {
    error = SSL_get_error(ssl, insize);
    fprintf(stderr, "Error: SSL_read() failed, error=%d\n", error);
    break;
  }

  reqmsg[insize] = '\0';
  fprintf(stdout, "Server received: %s\n", reqmsg);

  /* Process the request here ... */

  /* Construct a reply message */
  if ( !strcmp(reqmsg, BYE_MSG) )
  {
    done = 1;
    strcpy(reply, reqmsg);
  }
  else
    sprintf(reply, SRVREPLY2, msgcnt++);

  replysz = strlen(reply);

  /* Send back a reply */
  outsz = SSL_write(ssl, reply, replysz);
  if (outsz != replysz)
  {
    error = SSL_get_error(ssl, outsz);
    fprintf(stderr, "Error: SSL_write() failed, error=%d\n", error);
    break;
  }
```

```c
    } while (!done);

    /* Free up resources and return */
    SSL_free(ssl);
    return(error);
}

/* TLS/SSL server program */
int main(int argc, char *argv[])
{
    int     sfd;                            /* file descriptor of the listener socket */
    struct sockaddr_in    srvaddr;          /* IPv4 socket address structure */
    struct sockaddr_in6   srvaddr6;         /* IPv6 socket address structure */
    in_port_t  portnum = SRVPORT;           /* port number this server listens on */
    int        portnum_in = 0;              /* port number specified by user */
    struct sockaddr_in6   clntaddr6;        /* client socket address */
    socklen_t             clntaddr6sz = sizeof(clntaddr6);
    int     newsock = 0;                    /* file descriptor of client data socket */
    int     ipv6 = 0;                       /* IPv6 mode or not */
    int     ret;                            /* return value */
    SSL_CTX      *ctx;                      /* SSL context */

    /* Print Usage if requested by user */
    if (argc > 1 && argv[1][0] == '?' )
    {
        fprintf(stderr, "Usage: %s [server_port] [1 (use IPv6)]\n", argv[0]);
        return(0);
    }

    /* Get the server port number from user, if any */
    if (argc > 1)
    {
        portnum_in = atoi(argv[1]);
        if (portnum_in <= 0)
        {
            fprintf(stderr, "Error: port number %s invalid\n", argv[1]);
            fprintf(stderr, "Usage: %s [server_port] [1 (use IPv6)]\n", argv[0]);
            return(-1);
        }
        else
            portnum = portnum_in;
    }

    /* Get the IPv6 switch from user, if any */
    if (argc > 2)
    {
        if (argv[2][0] == '1')
            ipv6 = 1;
        else if (argv[2][0] != '0')
        {
            fprintf(stderr, "Usage: %s [server_port] [1 (use IPv6)]\n", argv[0]);
            return(-2);
        }
    }

    fprintf(stdout, "TLS/SSL server listening at portnum=%u ipv6=%u\n",
```

```
      portnum, ipv6);

   /* Create the server listener socket */
   if (ipv6)
      ret = new_bound_srv_endpt(&sfd, (struct sockaddr *)&srvaddr6, AF_INET6,
         portnum);
   else
      ret = new_bound_srv_endpt(&sfd, (struct sockaddr *)&srvaddr, AF_INET,
         portnum);

   if (ret != 0)
   {
      fprintf(stderr, "Error: new_bound_srv_endpt() failed, ret=%d\n", ret);
      return(-3);
   }

   /* Create a TLS/SSL context -- a framework enabling TLS/SSL connections. */
   ctx = SSL_CTX_new(TLS_server_method());
   if (ctx == NULL)
   {
      fprintf(stderr, "Error: SSL_CTX_new() failed\n");
      close(sfd);
      return(-4);
   }

   /* Load the server's certificate and private key */
   ret = load_certificate(ctx, SRV_CERT_FILE, SRV_KEY_FILE);
   if (ret != SUCCESS)
   {
      fprintf(stderr, "Error: load_certificate() failed, ret=%d\n", ret);
      SSL_CTX_free(ctx);
      close(sfd);
      return(-5);
   }

   /* Server's service loop. Wait for next client and service it. */
   while (1)
   {
      /* Accept the next client's connection request */
      newsock = accept(sfd, (struct sockaddr *)&clntaddr6, &clntaddr6sz);
      if (newsock < 0)
      {
         fprintf(stderr, "Error: accept() failed, errno=%d\n", errno);
         continue;
      }

   fprintf(stdout, "\nServer got a client connection\n");

      /* Service the current SSL client */
      ret = serve_ssl_client(ctx, newsock);
      if (ret != 0)
         fprintf(stderr, "Error: serve_ssl_client() failed, ret=%d\n", ret);

   close(newsock);
   } /* while */
```

```
  SSL_CTX_free(ctx);      /* release SSL context */
  close(sfd);             /* close server socket */
  return(0);
}
```

    (b) tlsclient3.c

```
/*
 * A TLS/SSL client.
 * This program communicates with a TLS/SSL server using TLS/SSL protocol.
 * The client verifies a server certificate signed by a chain of CAs.
 * Authored by Mr. Jin-Jwei Chen.
 * Copyright (c) 2014-2016, 2020-2021 Mr. Jin-Jwei Chen. All rights reserved.
 */

#include <stdio.h>
#include <errno.h>
#include <sys/types.h>
#include <sys/socket.h>
#include <netinet/in.h>          /* protocols such as IPPROTO_TCP, ... */
#include <string.h>              /* memset(), strlen(), memcmp() */
#include <stdlib.h>              /* atoi() */
#include <unistd.h>
#include <resolv.h>
#include <netdb.h>
#include <openssl/ssl.h>
#include <openssl/err.h>
#include <openssl/x509.h>
#include "myopenssl.h"
#include "netlib.h"

/* Free all resources */
#define  FREEALL  \
    SSL_free(ssl); \
    SSL_CTX_free(ctx); \
    close(sfd);

/* A TLS/SSL client program */
int main(int argc, char *argv[])
{
  char        *srvhost = "localhost"; /* name of server host */
  in_port_t    srvport = SRVPORT;      /* port number server listens on */
  int          srvport_in = 0;         /* port number specified by user */

  int      ret;            /* return value */
  int      sfd=0;          /* socket file descriptor */
  int      error;          /* return value of SSL_get_error() */
  long     sslret;         /* return value of some SSL calls */

  SSL_CTX  *ctx = NULL;    /* SSL/TLS context/framework */
  SSL      *ssl = NULL;    /* SSL/TLS connection */

  char         replymsg[MAXRPLYSZ];    /* reply message from server */
  size_t       reqbufsz = MAXREQSZ;    /* size of client request buffer */
  char         *reqmsg=NULL;           /* pointer to request message buffer */
  size_t       reqmsgsz;               /* size of client request message */
```

1259

```
int              bytes;                    /* number of bytes received */
int              done=0;                   /* done communicating with server */

unsigned char  errstrbuf[ERR_STRING_LEN];  /* error string */

/* Print Usage if requested by user */
if (argc > 1 && argv[1][0] == '?' )
{
  fprintf(stdout, "Usage: %s [srvportnum] [srvhostname]\n", argv[0]);
  return(0);
}

/* Get the port number of the target server host specified by user */
if (argc > 1)
{
  srvport_in = atoi(argv[1]);
  if (srvport_in <= 0)
  {
    fprintf(stderr, "Error: port number %s invalid\n", argv[1]);
    return(-1);
  }
  else
    srvport = srvport_in;
}

/* Get the name of the target server host specified by user */
if (argc > 2)
  srvhost = argv[2];

/* Connect to the server */
ret = connect_to_server(&sfd, srvhost, srvport);
if (ret != 0)
{
  fprintf(stderr, "Error: connect_to_server() failed, ret=%d\n", ret);
  if (sfd) close(sfd);
  return(-2);
}

/* Create a TLS/SSL context -- a framework enabling TLS/SSL connections. */
ctx = SSL_CTX_new(TLS_client_method());
if (ctx == NULL)
{
  fprintf(stderr, "Error: SSL_CTX_new() failed\n");
  close(sfd);
  return(-3);
}

/* Allocate a new SSL structure to hold SSL connection data */
ssl = SSL_new(ctx);
if (ssl == NULL)
{
  fprintf(stderr, "Error: SSL_new() failed\n");
  SSL_CTX_free(ctx);
  close(sfd);
  return(-4);
}
```

```
/* Set default locations for trusted CA certificates for verification */
if(SSL_CTX_load_verify_locations(ctx, CA_FILE, CA_DIR) < 1)
{
  fprintf(stderr, "Error: SSL_CTX_load_verify_locations() failed to set "
    "verify location\n");
  return(-5);
}


/* Set to do server certificate verification */
SSL_CTX_set_verify(ctx, SSL_VERIFY_PEER, NULL);

/* Associate the SSL object with the socket file descriptor */
ret = SSL_set_fd(ssl, sfd);
if (ret != OPENSSL_SUCCESS)
{
  fprintf(stderr, "Error: SSL_set_fd() failed, ret=%d\n", ret);
  FREEALL
  return(-6);
}

/* Initiate the TLS/SSL handshake with the TLS/SSL server */
ERR_clear_error();
ret = SSL_connect(ssl);
if (ret != OPENSSL_SUCCESS)
{
  error = SSL_get_error(ssl, ret);
  fprintf(stderr, "Error: SSL_connect() failed, error=%d\n", error);
  print_ssl_io_error(error);
  fprintf(stderr, "%s\n", ERR_error_string((unsigned long)error, (char *)NULL));
  FREEALL
  return(-7);
}


/* Connected with TLS/SSL server. Display server certificate info. */
fprintf(stdout, "Connected with TLS/SSL server, cipher algorithm is %s\n",
  SSL_get_cipher(ssl));
fprintf(stdout, "Information in the server certificate:\n");
display_ssl_certificate_info(ssl);

/* Verify the peer's certificate and get the result */
ERR_clear_error();
if ((sslret = SSL_get_verify_result(ssl)) == X509_V_OK)
{
  /* The server sent a certificate which verified OK. */
  fprintf(stdout, "Verifying server's certificate succeeded.\n");
}
else
{
  fprintf(stderr, "SSL_get_verify_result() failed, ret=%lu\n", sslret);
  fprintf(stderr, "%s\n", ERR_error_string((unsigned long)sslret, (char *)NULL));
  FREEALL
  return(-8);
}

/* Allocate input buffer */
```

1261

```
  reqmsg = malloc(MAXREQSZ);
  if (reqmsg == NULL)
  {
    fprintf(stderr, "Error: malloc() failed\n");
    FREEALL
    return(-9);
  }

  /* Send a message and get a response until done */
  do
  {
    /* Get next message the user wants to send */
    fprintf(stdout, "Enter a message to send ('bye' to end): ");
    reqmsgsz = getline(&reqmsg, &reqbufsz, stdin);
    if (reqmsgsz == -1)
    {
      fprintf(stderr, "Error: getline() failed, ret=%lu\n", reqmsgsz);
      break;
    }

    /* Remove the newline character at end of input */
    reqmsg[--reqmsgsz] = '\0';

    /* Send a message using SSL -- message automatically encrypted */
    bytes = SSL_write(ssl, reqmsg, reqmsgsz);
    if (bytes != reqmsgsz)
    {
      error = SSL_get_error(ssl, bytes);
      fprintf(stderr, "Error: SSL_write() failed, error=%d\n", error);
      free(reqmsg);
      FREEALL
      return(-10);
    }

    /* Receive a reply using SSL -- reply automatically decrypted */
    bytes = SSL_read(ssl, replymsg, sizeof(replymsg));
    if (bytes <= 0)
    {
      error = SSL_get_error(ssl, bytes);
      fprintf(stderr, "Error: SSL_read() failed, error=%d\n", error);
      free(reqmsg);
      FREEALL
      return(-11);
    }
    else
    {
      replymsg[bytes] = 0;
      fprintf(stdout, "Received: %s\n", replymsg);
    }

    if (!strcmp(replymsg, reqmsg))
      done = 1;

  } while (!done);

  /* release all resources */
```

```
free(reqmsg);
SSL_free(ssl);          /* release the SSL structure/connection */
SSL_CTX_free(ctx);      /* release the SSL context */
close(sfd);             /* close socket */
return (0);
}
```

15-11-4-1 Loading Certificate Chains

There are a couple of functions to load a certificate chain, as opposed to a single certificate. They are listed below.

```
#include <openssl/ssl.h>
int SSL_CTX_use_certificate_chain_file(SSL_CTX *ctx, const char *file);
int SSL_use_certificate_chain_file(SSL *ssl, const char *file);
```

SSL_CTX_use_certificate_chain_file() loads a certificate chain from the file specified in the second argument into an SSL context. The certificates must be in PEM format and have to be sorted in the order of starting with the subject's certificate (actual client or server certificate), followed by intermediate CA certificates if applicable, and ending at the highest level (root) CA.

SSL_use_certificate_chain_file() is similar except it loads the certificate chain into an SSL object, as opposed to an SSL_CTX object.

Note that SSL_CTX_use_certificate_chain_file() or SSL_use_certificate_chain_file() can only be used with PEM-format files (of type SSL_FILETYPE_PEM) because a DER-format file can contain only one certificate or private key at a time.

15-11-4-2 Verify a Certificate Chain Using openssl Command

The commands below verify the ending user certificate of myserver and the intermediate CA certificate. As shown, you need to concatenate the CA certificates together and supply that to the -CAfile option.

```
$ openssl verify -verbose -CAfile <(cat deptca_cert.pem rootca_cert.pem)
myserver_cert.pem
myserver_cert.pem: OK
$ openssl verify -verbose -CAfile rootca_cert.pem deptca_cert.pem
deptca_cert.pem: OK
$ openssl verify -verbose -CAfile rootca_cert.pem rootca_cert.pem
rootca_cert.pem: OK


$ cat deptca_cert.pem rootca_cert.pem > myserver_CAchain_cert.pem
$ openssl verify -verbose -CAfile myserver_CAchain_cert.pem myserver_cert.pem
myserver_cert.pem: OK
```

Note that the following command syntax verifies only the deptca's certificate but not myserver's:

```
$ openssl verify -verbose -CAfile rootca_cert.pem deptca_cert.pem myserver_cert.pem
```

```
deptca_cert.pem: OK
myserver_cert.pem: /C=US/ST=New Hampshire/L=Nashua/O=Chen Systems,
Inc./OU=Engineering/CN=myserver
error 20 at 0 depth lookup:unable to get local issuer certificate
```

15-11-5 Doing Client Authentication

As we said it earlier, the SSL/TLS Standards do not require performing
client authentication during an SSL/TLS handshake. This is because the
SSL/TLS protocols were designed to protect more of the client than the
server in Web applications. However, depending on applications, client
authentication may be needed or even required in some cases.
If the SSL/TLS protocols are used in applications where the server keeps
important information which not everyone is allowed to access, then client
authentication should be required. However, please be aware that using
certificates to authenticate clients may not be strong enough security
for all applications. This is what you need to seriously think about
before deciding on using SSL/TLS.

This section discusses how to do client authentication in SSL/TLS.

As you know it by now, in the SSL/TLS world, every entity is identified by
a certificate. Because of that, the first thing needed in doing client
authentication is that the SSL/TLS client program wishing to communicate
with an SSL/TLS server must have a certificate of its own. In our example,
we use a client certificate that is signed by an intermediate CA and,
therefore, a chain of CA certificates is needed for the server to verify the
client's certificate.

In addition to the client certificate, there are steps both the client and
the server need to take in order to perform client authentication.

15-11-5-1 Client-side Code

On the SSL/TLS client side, the client must now load its certificate and
private key so that its certificate can be sent to the server during the
SSL/TLS handshake phase. These are done by calling the load_certificate()
library function we create.

Notice that a client must load its certificate and private key
before it creates the SSL object (i.e. before SSL_new() is called).
Doing it after SSL_new() would have no effect and accomplish nothing.

If a client does not load its certificate and private key or if it's done
after the SSL object is created (i.e. after SSL_new()), then the client
certificate will NOT get sent to the server. In that case, the SSL
handshake will fail if the SSL/TLS server requires client authentication
(and does it correctly).

15-11-5-2 Server-side Code

On the SSL/TLS server side, the server must now carry out the following
steps to verify the certificate sent by the client. This is very similar

to what an SSL/TLS client does to verify an SSL/TLS server's certificate but with some differences in details.

(1) The server must set the trusted CAs.

This is done by invoking the SSL_CTX_load_verify_locations() function:

    SSL_CTX_load_verify_locations(ctx, CA_FILE, CA_DIR)

The SSL_CTX_load_verify_locations() function specifies the file containing the certificates of the CAs who have signed the client's certificate and in what directory that file exists, via the CA_FILE and CA_DIR arguments, respectively. These CA certificates will be used to verify a client's certificate.

The SSL_CTX_load_verify_locations() function is usually called **right after the SSL context object is created.**

(2) The server must set to verify a client's certificate.

This is done by calling the SSL_CTX_set_verify() function, which declares that the server wants to verify a client's certificate. The best way to do this is to pass in both SSL_VERIFY_PEER and SSL_VERIFY_FAIL_IF_NO_PEER_CERT flags in the call like below:

    SSL_CTX_set_verify(sslctx, SSL_VERIFY_PEER|SSL_VERIFY_FAIL_IF_NO_PEER_CERT
    , NULL);

This way if the client does not even send its certificate, the SSL/TLS connection request from the client will be rejected right away. It will also reject a client's SSL/TLS connection request if the client certificate fails to verify.

If you omit the SSL_VERIFY_FAIL_IF_NO_PEER_CERT flag, then the connection request will continue when the client does not send its certificate. In that case, it will be up to the server to catch it and stop the client later. For instance, after a connection is just established, a SSL/TLS server can invoke the SSL_get_peer_certificate(ssl) function to check if a client has sent its certificate or not. If not (meaning this function returns a null pointer), it can close the connection right away.

With only the SSL_VERIFY_PEER flag, if a client sends its certificate but it fails to verify, then the SSL_accept() call on the server automatically rejects the connection request which will in turn fail the SSL_connect() call on the client side.

Be aware that you have to place the SSL_CTX_set_verify() call at the right place in the SSL/TLS server. Calling this function before the accept() loop is appropriate. But calling it after SSL_new() and before SSL_accept() has no effect at all. In other words, you cannot call it too late. Remember to always **call the SSL_CTX_set_verify() function before the SSL object gets created from the SSL_CTX object,** which is the SSL_new(). Calling SSL_CTX_set_verify() after SSL_new() has no effect at all.

If client authentication is required for all clients, then the SSL_CTX_set_verify() function can be called only once before the server's service loop. If the requirement is client-specific and not being enforced across the board, then its call can be placed inside the server's service loop, before the SSL_new().

Using SSL_get_verify_result() Function in Verification

There are two ways to enforce a required client authentication.

As stated above, the first method is to specify both SSL_VERIFY_PEER and SSL_VERIFY_FAIL_IF_NO_PEER_CERT flags when calling the SSL_CTX_set_verify() function. If the client does not send its certificate or if it sends a certificate but that fails in certificate verification, this will automatically fail the client's connection request. That is, the client's SSL_connect() call and the server's SSL_accept() call will both fail. In general, this is a preferred method.

The second way to enforce a required client authentication is to call the SSL_CTX_set_verify() with only the SSL_VERIFY_PEER flag:

    SSL_CTX_set_verify(ctx, SSL_VERIFY_PEER, NULL);

Then after a client connection is established, invoke the function

    SSL_get_peer_certificate(ssl)

to try to get the certificate sent by the client. If the function returns a null pointer, that means the client has not sent its certificate. The server could decide to close the connection at that point. If the client has sent a certificate (i.e. SSL_get_peer_certificate() returns a non-null pointer), the server can then invoke the

    SSL_get_verify_result(ssl)

function to verify the client certificate. If this function returns X509_V_OK, that means the client certificate verifies OK. Should this function return other value, the server could decide to close the connection as well.

If the client sends a certificate which fails to verify, SSL_accept() will fail and deny the client's connection request.

Note that on the server side the SSL_get_verify_result() function cannot be used alone. It must be used in connection with SSL_get_peer_certificate(). Without pairing with SSL_get_peer_certificate(), SSL_get_verify_result() returns X509_V_OK if the client does not send a certificate, which becomes a hole and is not what you really want!

15-11-5-3 Possible Errors

When the SSL/TLS server requires client authentication and does it correctly, if the client does not send its certificate to the server or if the certificate sent by the client fails to verify, the client's connect request will fail. Specifically, this means the SSL_connect() call on the client side and the SSL_accept() call on the server side shall both fail (both calls return 1).

```
        client                      server
     ------------                 -----------
     SSL_connect() -------> SSL_accept()
```

Figure 15-33 These calls fail if client or server authentication fails
    and SSL_VERIFY_FAIL_IF_NO_PEER_CERT flag is set

The specific errors an SSL/TLS server would get when client authentication
fails are given below:

(a) Server-side error of 'Client does not send its certificate'

   Error: SSL_accept() failed, error=1
   140235133703904:error:1417C0C7:SSL
   routines:tls_process_client_certificate:peer did not return a
   certificate:ssl/statem/statem_srvr.c:2873:

(b) Server-side error of 'Client certificate fails to verify'

   Error: SSL_accept() failed, error=1
   140005507901152:error:1417C086:SSL
   routines:tls_process_client_certificate:certificate verify
   failed:ssl/statem/statem_srvr.c:2887:

15-11-5-4 Program Examples

Figure 15-34 shows a pair of client and server programs that communicate
with each other using SSL/TLS protocol requiring client authentication.

Figure 15-35 shows a slightly different version of an SSL/TLS server
which demonstrates how to use SSL_get_verify_result() together with
SSL_get_peer_certificate() to verify client's certificates.
It works with tlsclient4.

Figure 15-34 SSL/TLS client and server with required client authentication
  -- tlsclient4.c and tlsserver4.c

(a) tlsserver4.c

```c
/*
 * A TLS/SSL server.
 * This server program communicates with clients using TLS/SSL protocol.
 * The server verifies a client certificate signed by a chain of CAs.
 * Requiring client authentication using the SSL_VERIFY_FAIL_IF_NO_PEER_CERT
 * flag.
 * Authored by Mr. Jin-Jwei Chen.
 * Copyright (c) 2014-2016, 2020-2021 Mr. Jin-Jwei Chen. All rights reserved.
 */

#include <stdio.h>
#include <errno.h>
#include <sys/types.h>
#include <sys/socket.h>
#include <netinet/in.h>       /* protocols such as IPPROTO_TCP, ... */
```

```c
#include <string.h>          /* memset(), strlen(), memcmp() */
#include <stdlib.h>          /* atoi() */
#include <unistd.h>
#include <resolv.h>
#include <netdb.h>
#include <arpa/inet.h>
#include <resolv.h>
#include <openssl/ssl.h>
#include <openssl/err.h>
#include <openssl/x509.h>
#include "myopenssl.h"
#include "netlib.h"


/*
 * This function serves a newly connected SSL client.
 * Parameters:
 *    ctx (input) - SSL context.
 *    clntsock (input) - the child socket to communicate with the client.
 * Function output: return 0 on success, non-zero on failure.
 * Note that Openssl provides different functions to retrieve the actual
 * error. Unfortunately, they return different data types, some 'int'
 * (SSL_get_error()) and some 'unsigned long' (ERR_get_error()).
 * It makes it hard to return both types of errors from a function.
 * Note: If SSL_CTX_set_verify() is called in this function, it must be
 * placed before SSL_new().
 */
int serve_ssl_client(SSL_CTX *ctx, int clntsock)
{
    SSL            *ssl = NULL;        /* SSL structure/connection */
    char           reqmsg[MAXREQSZ];   /* buffer for incoming request message */
    char           reply[MAXRPLYSZ];   /* buffer for outgoing server reply */
    unsigned char  replysz;            /* length in bytes of reply message */
    int            insize;             /* actual number of bytes read */
    int            outsz;              /* actual number of bytes written */
    int            error = 0;          /* error from certain SSL_xxx calls */
    unsigned char  msgcnt;             /* count of reply messages to client */
    int            done = 0;           /* done with current client */
    int            ret;
    X509           *clnt_cert = NULL;  /* pointer to peer's certificate */

    if (ctx == NULL)
        return(EINVAL);
    ERR_clear_error();

    /* Create a new SSL structure to hold the connection data.
     * Note that to require client authentication, the call to
     * SSL_CTX_set_verify() must be done BEFORE SSL_new(). Or it has no effect.
     */
    ssl = SSL_new(ctx);
    if (ssl == NULL)
    {
        fprintf(stderr, "Error: SSL_new() failed:\n");
        ERR_print_errors_fp(stderr);
        return(OPENSSL_ERR_SSLNEW_FAIL);
    }
```

```
/* Associate the SSL structure with the socket */
ret = SSL_set_fd(ssl, clntsock);
if (ret != OPENSSL_SUCCESS)
{
  fprintf(stderr, "Error: SSL_set_fd() failed:\n");
  ERR_print_errors_fp(stderr);
  SSL_free(ssl);
  return(OPENSSL_ERR_SSLSETFD_FAIL);
}

/* Wait for the TLS/SSL client to initiate the TLS/SSL handshake */
ret = SSL_accept(ssl);
if (ret != OPENSSL_SUCCESS)
{
  error = SSL_get_error(ssl, ret);
  fprintf(stderr, "Error: SSL_accept() failed, error=%d\n", error);
  ERR_print_errors_fp(stderr);
  SSL_free(ssl);
  return(error);
}

/* Display information about the peer/client certificate */
display_ssl_certificate_info(ssl);

/* The service loop */
done = 0;
msgcnt = 1;
do
{
  /* Read the next request message from the TLS/SSL client */
  insize = SSL_read(ssl, reqmsg, MAXREQSZ);
  if (insize <= 0)
  {
    error = SSL_get_error(ssl, insize);
    fprintf(stderr, "Error: SSL_read() failed, error=%d\n", error);
    break;
  }

  reqmsg[insize] = '\0';
  fprintf(stdout, "Server received: %s\n", reqmsg);

  /* Process the request here ... */

  /* Construct a reply message */
  if ( !strcmp(reqmsg, BYE_MSG) )
  {
    done = 1;
    strcpy(reply, reqmsg);
  }
  else
    sprintf(reply, SRVREPLY2, msgcnt++);

  replysz = strlen(reply);

  /* Send back a reply */
  outsz = SSL_write(ssl, reply, replysz);
```

```
      if (outsz != replysz)
      {
        error = SSL_get_error(ssl, outsz);
        fprintf(stderr, "Error: SSL_write() failed, error=%d\n", error);
        break;
      }
    } while (!done);

    /* Free up resources and return */
    SSL_free(ssl);
    return(error);
}

/* TLS/SSL server program */
int main(int argc, char *argv[])
{
  int      sfd;                        /* file descriptor of the listener socket */
  struct sockaddr_in    srvaddr;       /* IPv4 socket address structure */
  struct sockaddr_in6   srvaddr6;      /* IPv6 socket address structure */
  in_port_t  portnum = SRVPORT;        /* port number this server listens on */
  int        portnum_in = 0;           /* port number specified by user */
  struct sockaddr_in6   clntaddr6;     /* client socket address */
  socklen_t             clntaddr6sz = sizeof(clntaddr6);
  int      newsock = 0;                /* file descriptor of client data socket */
  int      ipv6 = 0;                   /* IPv6 mode or not */
  int      ret;                        /* return value */
  SSL_CTX      *ctx;                   /* SSL context */

  /* Print Usage if requested by user */
  if (argc > 1 && argv[1][0] == '?' )
  {
    fprintf(stderr, "Usage: %s [server_port] [1 (use IPv6)]\n", argv[0]);
    return(0);
  }

  /* Get the server port number from user, if any */
  if (argc > 1)
  {
    portnum_in = atoi(argv[1]);
    if (portnum_in <= 0)
    {
      fprintf(stderr, "Error: port number %s invalid\n", argv[1]);
      fprintf(stderr, "Usage: %s [server_port] [1 (use IPv6)]\n", argv[0]);
      return(-1);
    }
    else
      portnum = portnum_in;
  }

  /* Get the IPv6 switch from user, if any */
  if (argc > 2)
  {
    if (argv[2][0] == '1')
      ipv6 = 1;
    else if (argv[2][0] != '0')
    {
```

```
      fprintf(stderr, "Usage: %s [server_port] [1 (use IPv6)]\n", argv[0]);
      return(-2);
   }
}

fprintf(stdout, "TLS/SSL server listening at portnum=%u ipv6=%u\n",
   portnum, ipv6);

/* Create the server listener socket */
if (ipv6)
   ret = new_bound_srv_endpt(&sfd, (struct sockaddr *)&srvaddr6, AF_INET6,
      portnum);
else
   ret = new_bound_srv_endpt(&sfd, (struct sockaddr *)&srvaddr, AF_INET,
      portnum);

if (ret != 0)
{
   fprintf(stderr, "Error: new_bound_srv_endpt() failed, ret=%d\n", ret);
   return(-3);
}

/* Create a TLS/SSL context -- a framework enabling TLS/SSL connections. */
ctx = SSL_CTX_new(TLS_server_method());
if (ctx == NULL)
{
   fprintf(stderr, "Error: SSL_CTX_new() failed\n");
   close(sfd);
   return(-4);
}

/* Set default locations for trusted CA certificates for verification */
/* I found whether doing this first or last does not make a difference */
if(SSL_CTX_load_verify_locations(ctx, CA_FILE, CA_DIR) < 1)
{
   fprintf(stderr, "Error: SSL_CTX_load_verify_locations() failed to set "
      "verify location\n");
   SSL_CTX_free(ctx);
   close(sfd);
   return(-5);
}

/* Load the server's certificate and private key */
ret = load_certificate(ctx, SRV_CERT_FILE, SRV_KEY_FILE);
if (ret != SUCCESS)
{
   fprintf(stderr, "Error: load_certificate() failed, ret=%d\n", ret);
   SSL_CTX_free(ctx);
   close(sfd);
   return(-6);
}

/* Require client authentication -- this function returns void.
 * Fail the client connection request if client does not send its certificate
 * or the sent client certificate fails in verification.
 */
```

```
SSL_CTX_set_verify(ctx, SSL_VERIFY_PEER|SSL_VERIFY_FAIL_IF_NO_PEER_CERT, NULL);

  /* Server's service loop. Wait for next client and service it. */
  while (1)
  {
    /* Accept the next client's connection request */
    newsock = accept(sfd, (struct sockaddr *)&clntaddr6, &clntaddr6sz);
    if (newsock < 0)
    {
      fprintf(stderr, "Error: accept() failed, errno=%d\n", errno);
      continue;
    }

    fprintf(stdout, "\nServer got a client connection\n");

    /* Service the current SSL client */
    ret = serve_ssl_client(ctx, newsock);
    if (ret != 0)
      fprintf(stderr, "Error: serve_ssl_client() failed, ret=%d\n", ret);

    close(newsock);
  }  /* while */

  SSL_CTX_free(ctx);    /* release SSL context */
  close(sfd);           /* close server socket */
  return(0);
}
```

(b) tlsclient4.c

```
/*
 * A TLS/SSL client.
 * This program communicates with a TLS/SSL server using TLS/SSL protocol.
 * The client verifies a server certificate signed by a chain of CAs.
 * The client supplies a client certificate signed by a chain of CAs to
 * participate in client authentication.
 * Authored by Mr. Jin-Jwei Chen.
 * Copyright (c) 2014-2016, 2020-2021 Mr. Jin-Jwei Chen. All rights reserved.
 */

#include <stdio.h>
#include <errno.h>
#include <sys/types.h>
#include <sys/socket.h>
#include <netinet/in.h>    /* protocols such as IPPROTO_TCP, ... */
#include <string.h>        /* memset(), strlen(), memcmp() */
#include <stdlib.h>        /* atoi() */
#include <unistd.h>
#include <resolv.h>
#include <netdb.h>
#include <openssl/ssl.h>
#include <openssl/err.h>
#include <openssl/x509.h>
#include "myopenssl.h"
#include "netlib.h"
```

1272

```
/* Free all resources */
#define  FREEALL  \
    SSL_free(ssl); \
    SSL_CTX_free(ctx); \
    close(sfd);

/* A TLS/SSL client program */
int main(int argc, char *argv[])
{
  char           *srvhost = "localhost"; /* name of server host */
  in_port_t       srvport = SRVPORT;      /* port number server listens on */
  int             srvport_in = 0;         /* port number specified by user */

  int      ret;           /* return value */
  int      sfd=0;         /* socket file descriptor */
  int      error;         /* return value of SSL_get_error() */
  long     sslret;        /* return value of some SSL calls */

  SSL_CTX  *ctx = NULL;   /* SSL/TLS context/framework */
  SSL      *ssl = NULL;   /* SSL/TLS connection */

  char        replymsg[MAXRPLYSZ];    /* reply message from server */
  size_t      reqbufsz = MAXREQSZ;    /* size of client request buffer */
  char        *reqmsg=NULL;           /* pointer to request message buffer */
  size_t      reqmsgsz;               /* size of client request message */
  int         bytes;                  /* number of bytes received */
  int         done=0;                 /* done communicating with server */

  unsigned char  errstrbuf[ERR_STRING_LEN];  /* error string */

  /* Print Usage if requested by user */
  if (argc > 1 && argv[1][0] == '?' )
  {
    fprintf(stdout, "Usage: %s [srvportnum] [srvhostname]\n", argv[0]);
    return(0);
  }

  /* Get the port number of the target server host specified by user */
  if (argc > 1)
  {
    srvport_in = atoi(argv[1]);
    if (srvport_in <= 0)
    {
      fprintf(stderr, "Error: port number %s invalid\n", argv[1]);
      return(-1);
    }
    else
      srvport = srvport_in;
  }

  /* Get the name of the target server host specified by user */
  if (argc > 2)
    srvhost = argv[2];

  /* Connect to the server */
  ret = connect_to_server(&sfd, srvhost, srvport);
```

```
if (ret != 0)
{
    fprintf(stderr, "Error: connect_to_server() failed, ret=%d\n", ret);
    if (sfd) close(sfd);
    return(-2);
}

/* Create a TLS/SSL context -- a framework enabling TLS/SSL connections. */
ctx = SSL_CTX_new(TLS_client_method());
if (ctx == NULL)
{
    fprintf(stderr, "Error: SSL_CTX_new() failed\n");
    close(sfd);
    return(-3);
}

/* Load the client's own certificate in case client authentication needed.
 * Note that this loading client certificate step MUST be done BEFORE the
 * SSL object is created. Or the client certificate won't be sent! */
ret = load_certificate(ctx, CLNT_CERT_FILE, CLNT_KEY_FILE);
if (ret != SUCCESS)
{
    fprintf(stderr, "Error: load_certificate() failed, ret=%d\n", ret);
    SSL_CTX_free(ctx);
    close(sfd);
    return(-4);
}

/* Allocate a new SSL structure to hold SSL connection data.
 * Note: If you do this step before load_certificate(), client certificate
 * won't be sent even if the server requires it. */
ssl = SSL_new(ctx);
if (ssl == NULL)
{
    fprintf(stderr, "Error: SSL_new() failed\n");
    SSL_CTX_free(ctx);
    close(sfd);
    return(-5);
}

/* Set default locations for trusted CA certificates for verification */
if(SSL_CTX_load_verify_locations(ctx, CA_FILE, CA_DIR) < 1)
{
    fprintf(stderr, "Error: SSL_CTX_load_verify_locations() failed to set "
        "verify location\n");
    return(-6);
}

/* Set to do server certificate verification */
SSL_CTX_set_verify(ctx, SSL_VERIFY_PEER, NULL);

/* Associate the SSL object with the socket file descriptor */
ret = SSL_set_fd(ssl, sfd);
if (ret != OPENSSL_SUCCESS)
{
    fprintf(stderr, "Error: SSL_set_fd() failed, ret=%d\n", ret);
```

```
   FREEALL
   return(-7);
}


/* Initiate the TLS/SSL handshake with the TLS/SSL server */
ERR_clear_error();
ret = SSL_connect(ssl);
if (ret != OPENSSL_SUCCESS)
{
   error = SSL_get_error(ssl, ret);
   fprintf(stderr, "Error: SSL_connect() failed, error=%d\n", error);
   print_ssl_io_error(error);
   fprintf(stderr, "%s\n", ERR_error_string((unsigned long)error, (char *)NULL));
   FREEALL
   return(-8);
}


/* Connected with TLS/SSL server. Display server certificate info. */
fprintf(stdout, "Connected with TLS/SSL server, cipher algorithm is %s\n",
   SSL_get_cipher(ssl));
fprintf(stdout, "Information in the server certificate:\n");
display_ssl_certificate_info(ssl);


/* Verify the peer's certificate and get the result */
ERR_clear_error();
if ((sslret = SSL_get_verify_result(ssl)) == X509_V_OK)
{
   /* The server sent a certificate which verified OK. */
   fprintf(stdout, "Verifying server's certificate succeeded.\n");
}
else
{
   fprintf(stderr, "SSL_get_verify_result() failed, ret=%ld\n", sslret);
   fprintf(stderr, "%s\n", ERR_error_string((unsigned long)sslret, (char *)NULL));
   FREEALL
   return(-9);
}


/* Allocate input buffer */
reqmsg = malloc(MAXREQSZ);
if (reqmsg == NULL)
{
   fprintf(stderr, "Error: malloc() failed\n");
   FREEALL
   return(-10);
}


/* Send a message and get a response until done */
do
{
   /* Get next message the user wants to send */
   fprintf(stdout, "Enter a message to send ('bye' to end): ");
   reqmsgsz = getline(&reqmsg, &reqbufsz, stdin);
   if (reqmsgsz == -1)
   {
      fprintf(stderr, "Error: getline() failed, ret=%lu\n", reqmsgsz);
```

```
        break;
    }

    /* Remove the newline character at end of input */
    reqmsg[--reqmsgsz] = '\0';

    /* Send a message using SSL -- message automatically encrypted */
    bytes = SSL_write(ssl, reqmsg, reqmsgsz);
    if (bytes != reqmsgsz)
    {
      error = SSL_get_error(ssl, bytes);
      fprintf(stderr, "Error: SSL_write() failed, error=%d\n", error);
      free(reqmsg);
      FREEALL
      return(-11);
    }

    /* Receive a reply using SSL -- reply automatically decrypted */
    bytes = SSL_read(ssl, replymsg, sizeof(replymsg));
    if (bytes <= 0)
    {
      error = SSL_get_error(ssl, bytes);
      fprintf(stderr, "Error: SSL_read() failed, error=%d\n", error);
      free(reqmsg);
      FREEALL
      return(-12);
    }
    else
    {
      replymsg[bytes] = 0;
      fprintf(stdout, "Received: %s\n", replymsg);
    }

    if (!strcmp(replymsg, reqmsg))
      done = 1;

  } while (!done);

  /* release all resources */
  free(reqmsg);
  SSL_free(ssl);        /* release the SSL structure/connection */
  SSL_CTX_free(ctx);    /* release the SSL context */
  close(sfd);           /* close socket */
  return (0);
}
```

Figure 15-35 SSL/TLS server with a different implementation of
  required client authentication -- tlsserver5.c

```
/*
 * A TLS/SSL server.
 * This server program communicates with clients using TLS/SSL protocol.
 * The server verifies a client certificate signed by a chain of CAs.
 * Requiring client authentication without using the
 * SSL_VERIFY_FAIL_IF_NO_PEER_CERT flag but using SSL_get_verify_result().
 * Authored by Mr. Jin-Jwei Chen.
```

```
#include <stdio.h>
#include <errno.h>
#include <sys/types.h>
#include <sys/socket.h>
#include <netinet/in.h>        /* protocols such as IPPROTO_TCP, ... */
#include <string.h>            /* memset(), strlen(), memcmp() */
#include <stdlib.h>            /* atoi() */
#include <unistd.h>
#include <resolv.h>
#include <netdb.h>
#include <arpa/inet.h>
#include <resolv.h>
#include <openssl/ssl.h>
#include <openssl/err.h>
#include <openssl/x509.h>
#include "myopenssl.h"
#include "netlib.h"


/*
 * This function serves a newly connected SSL client.
 * Parameters:
 *   ctx (input) - SSL context.
 *   clntsock (input) - the child socket to communicate with the client.
 * Function output: return 0 on success, non-zero on failure.
 * Note that Openssl provides different functions to retrieve the actual
 * error. Unfortunately, they return different data types, some 'int'
 * (SSL_get_error()) and some 'unsigned long' (ERR_get_error()).
 * It makes it hard to return both types of errors from a function.
 * Note: If SSL_CTX_set_verify() is called in this function, it must be
 * placed before SSL_new().
 */
int serve_ssl_client(SSL_CTX *ctx, int clntsock)
{
  SSL             *ssl = NULL;        /* SSL structure/connection */
  char            reqmsg[MAXREQSZ];   /* buffer for incoming request message */
  char            reply[MAXRPLYSZ];   /* buffer for outgoing server reply */
  unsigned char   replysz;            /* length in bytes of reply message */
  int             insize;             /* actual number of bytes read */
  int             outsz;              /* actual number of bytes written */
  int             error = 0;          /* error from certain SSL_xxx calls */
  unsigned char   msgcnt;             /* count of reply messages to client */
  int             done = 0;           /* done with current client */
  int             ret;
  X509            *clnt_cert = NULL;  /* pointer to peer's certificate */

  if (ctx == NULL)
    return(EINVAL);
  ERR_clear_error();

  /* Create a new SSL structure to hold the connection data.
   * Note that to require client authentication, the call to
   * SSL_CTX_set_verify() must be done BEFORE SSL_new(). Or it has no effect.
   */
```

1277

```
ssl = SSL_new(ctx);
if (ssl == NULL)
{
   fprintf(stderr, "Error: SSL_new() failed:\n");
   ERR_print_errors_fp(stderr);
   return(OPENSSL_ERR_SSLNEW_FAIL);
}

/* Associate the SSL structure with the socket */
ret = SSL_set_fd(ssl, clntsock);
if (ret != OPENSSL_SUCCESS)
{
   fprintf(stderr, "Error: SSL_set_fd() failed:\n");
   ERR_print_errors_fp(stderr);
   SSL_free(ssl);
   return(OPENSSL_ERR_SSLSETFD_FAIL);
}

/* Wait for the TLS/SSL client to initiate the TLS/SSL handshake */
ret = SSL_accept(ssl);
if (ret != OPENSSL_SUCCESS)
{
   error = SSL_get_error(ssl, ret);
   fprintf(stderr, "Error: SSL_accept() failed, error=%d\n", error);
   ERR_print_errors_fp(stderr);
   SSL_free(ssl);
   return(error);
}

/* Display information about the peer/client certificate */
display_ssl_certificate_info(ssl);

/* Retrieve client's certificate and verify it */
clnt_cert = SSL_get_peer_certificate(ssl);
if (clnt_cert == NULL)
{
   fprintf(stderr, "Error: Client did not send its certificate.\n");
   /* Return error so that the socket connection can be closed */
   SSL_free(ssl);
   return(OPENSSL_ERR_NO_CLIENT_CERT);
}
else
{
   if ((ret = SSL_get_verify_result(ssl)) == X509_V_OK)
   {
      /* The client sent a certificate which verified OK */
      fprintf(stdout, "Verifying client's certificate succeeded\n");
   }
   else
   {
      fprintf(stderr, "SSL_get_verify_result() failed to verify client's"
        " certificate, ret=%d\n", ret);
      SSL_free(ssl);
      return(OPENSSL_ERR_CLIENT_CERT_VERIFY_FAIL);
   }
}
```

```c
  /* The service loop */
  done = 0;
  msgcnt = 1;
  do
  {
    /* Read the next request message from the TLS/SSL client */
    insize = SSL_read(ssl, reqmsg, MAXREQSZ);
    if (insize <= 0)
    {
      error = SSL_get_error(ssl, insize);
      fprintf(stderr, "Error: SSL_read() failed, error=%d\n", error);
      break;
    }

    reqmsg[insize] = '\0';
    fprintf(stdout, "Server received: %s\n", reqmsg);

    /* Process the request here ... */

    /* Construct a reply message */
    if ( !strcmp(reqmsg, BYE_MSG) )
    {
      done = 1;
      strcpy(reply, reqmsg);
    }
    else
      sprintf(reply, SRVREPLY2, msgcnt++);

    replysz = strlen(reply);

    /* Send back a reply */
    outsz = SSL_write(ssl, reply, replysz);
    if (outsz != replysz)
    {
      error = SSL_get_error(ssl, outsz);
      fprintf(stderr, "Error: SSL_write() failed, error=%d\n", error);
      break;
    }
  } while (!done);

  /* Free up resources and return */
  SSL_free(ssl);
  return(error);
}

/* TLS/SSL server program */
int main(int argc, char *argv[])
{
  int      sfd;                        /* file descriptor of the listener socket */
  struct sockaddr_in    srvaddr;       /* IPv4 socket address structure */
  struct sockaddr_in6   srvaddr6;      /* IPv6 socket address structure */
  in_port_t portnum = SRVPORT;         /* port number this server listens on */
  int       portnum_in = 0;            /* port number specified by user */
  struct sockaddr_in6   clntaddr;      /* client socket address */
  socklen_t             clntaddr6sz = sizeof(clntaddr6);
```

```
int      newsock = 0;                      /* file descriptor of client data socket */
int      ipv6 = 0;                         /* IPv6 mode or not */
int      ret;                              /* return value */
SSL_CTX      *ctx;                         /* SSL context */

/* Print Usage if requested by user */
if (argc > 1 && argv[1][0] == '?' )
{
  fprintf(stderr, "Usage: %s [server_port] [1 (use IPv6)]\n", argv[0]);
  return(0);
}

/* Get the server port number from user, if any */
if (argc > 1)
{
  portnum_in = atoi(argv[1]);
  if (portnum_in <= 0)
  {
    fprintf(stderr, "Error: port number %s invalid\n", argv[1]);
    fprintf(stderr, "Usage: %s [server_port] [1 (use IPv6)]\n", argv[0]);
    return(-1);
  }
  else
    portnum = portnum_in;
}

/* Get the IPv6 switch from user, if any */
if (argc > 2)
{
  if (argv[2][0] == '1')
    ipv6 = 1;
  else if (argv[2][0] != '0')
  {
    fprintf(stderr, "Usage: %s [server_port] [1 (use IPv6)]\n", argv[0]);
    return(-2);
  }
}

fprintf(stdout, "TLS/SSL server listening at portnum=%u ipv6=%u\n",
  portnum, ipv6);

/* Create the server listener socket */
if (ipv6)
  ret = new_bound_srv_endpt(&sfd, (struct sockaddr *)&srvaddr6, AF_INET6,
    portnum);
else
  ret = new_bound_srv_endpt(&sfd, (struct sockaddr *)&srvaddr, AF_INET,
    portnum);

if (ret != 0)
{
  fprintf(stderr, "Error: new_bound_srv_endpt() failed, ret=%d\n", ret);
  return(-3);
}

/* Create a TLS/SSL context -- a framework enabling TLS/SSL connections. */
```

```
ctx = SSL_CTX_new(TLS_server_method());
if (ctx == NULL)
{
  fprintf(stderr, "Error: SSL_CTX_new() failed\n");
  close(sfd);
  return(-4);
}

/* Set default locations for trusted CA certificates for verification */
/* I found whether doing this first or last does not make a difference */
if(SSL_CTX_load_verify_locations(ctx, CA_FILE, CA_DIR) < 1)
{
  fprintf(stderr, "Error: SSL_CTX_load_verify_locations() failed to set "
    "verify location\n");
  SSL_CTX_free(ctx);
  close(sfd);
  return(-5);
}

/* Load the server's certificate and private key */
ret = load_certificate(ctx, SRV_CERT_FILE, SRV_KEY_FILE);
if (ret != SUCCESS)
{
  fprintf(stderr, "Error: load_certificate() failed, ret=%d\n", ret);
  SSL_CTX_free(ctx);
  close(sfd);
  return(-6);
}

/* Require client authentication but do not fail the connect request.
   This function returns void. */
SSL_CTX_set_verify(ctx, SSL_VERIFY_PEER, NULL);

/* Server's service loop. Wait for next client and service it. */
while (1)
{
  /* Accept the next client's connection request */
  newsock = accept(sfd, (struct sockaddr *)&clntaddr6, &clntaddr6sz);
  if (newsock < 0)
  {
    fprintf(stderr, "Error: accept() failed, errno=%d\n", errno);
    continue;
  }

  fprintf(stdout, "\nServer got a client connection\n");

  /* Service the current SSL client */
  ret = serve_ssl_client(ctx, newsock);
  if (ret != 0)
    fprintf(stderr, "Error: serve_ssl_client() failed, ret=%d\n", ret);

  close(newsock);
}  /* while */

SSL_CTX_free(ctx);    /* release SSL context */
close(sfd);           /* close server socket */
```

```
 return(0);
}
```

15-11-5-5 Verifying Certificates Signed by Multiple CA Chains

In a real commercial deployment environment, it's very common that a server communicates with many different clients which use certificates signed by different chains of CAs. In that case, how does the server do client certificate verifications of so many different clients?

Well, as it turns out, OpenSSL has made this simple and easy again. All you need to do is put all of the CAs in the second chain in order and append them to the existing CA certificate file. If you have a third chain of CAs, you do the same. The server will load a single CA certificate file which contains all of the possible CAs of the client certificates.

Figure 15-37 shows a different SSL/TLS client, named xyzclnt, which uses a client certificate signed by a second chain of CAs and a new SSL/TLS server that is also able to communicate with the new client. What the server does differently this time is to load a CA certificate file that also contains all of the CA certificates from the second chain which has issued this new client's certificate. Notice that in the code the server now loads a different CA file containing all CA certificates from both certificate chains when it invokes the SSL_CTX_load_verify_locations() function:

```
  SSL_CTX_load_verify_locations(ctx, CAALL_FILE, CA_DIR)
```

where CAALL_FILE is the single file containing certificates of all chains of CAs.

The internal certificate store of OpenSSL can hold several pairs of private key and certificate at a time.

Notice that this new SSL/TLS server, tlsserver6, can communicate with the previous client named myclient as well as the new client named xyzclnt. Certificates of these two clients are signed by two different chains of CAs, as shown below:

```
    Client 1        Client 2
    -----------     -----------
    Jim Chen        xyzroot        root CA
       |               |
    IntermediateCA  xyzdept        intermediate CA
       |               |
    myclient        xyzclnt        client
```

   Figure 15-36 Chains of CAs

In summary, regardless of it's a server or client, to verify certificates signed by different chains of CAs, a program has to load the certificates of all possible CAs. This is why almost all computer systems have a certificate store and the administrators need to install all the well-known CAs' certificates into it so that the certificate verifications can all work automatically behind the scene when web browsers running on a system connect to all kinds of web servers around the world, and/or the web server running on a system can communicate with all sorts of web clients from around the world.

Below is a sample output from running tlsclient4 and tlsclient6 with the same server tlsserver6. Note that the client certificates of tlsclient4 and tlsclient6 are signed by two different CA chains.

```
$ tlsserver6
TLS/SSL server listening at portnum=7878 ipv6=0

   Server got a client connection
     Subject of the X509 certificate:
       C=US, ST=New Hampshire, O=Chen Systems, Inc., OU=Engineering, CN=myclient
     Issuer of the X509 certificate:
       C=US, ST=New Hampshire, O=Chen Systems, Inc., OU=Engineering,
CN=IntermediateCA

   Server received: Hello, this is tlsclient4.
   Server received: bye

   Server got a client connection
     Subject of the X509 certificate:
       C=US, ST=New Hampshire, O=XYZ Inc., OU=Engineering, CN=xyzclnt
     Issuer of the X509 certificate:
       C=US, ST=New Hampshire, O=XYZ Inc., OU=Engineering, CN=xyzdept

   Server received: Hi, this is tlsclient6.
   Server received: bye

$ tlsclient4
   Connected with TLS/SSL server, cipher algorithm is ECDHE-RSA-AES256-GCM-SHA384
   Information in the server certificate:
     Subject of the X509 certificate:
       C=US, ST=New Hampshire, O=Chen Systems, Inc., OU=Engineering, CN=myserver
     Issuer of the X509 certificate:
       C=US, ST=New Hampshire, O=Chen Systems, Inc., OU=Engineering,
CN=IntermediateCA

   Verifying server's certificate succeeded.
   Enter a message to send ('bye' to end): Hello, this is tlsclient4.
   Received: This is reply message # 1 from the server.
   Enter a message to send ('bye' to end): bye
   Received: bye

$ tlsclient6
   Connected with TLS/SSL server, cipher algorithm is ECDHE-RSA-AES256-GCM-SHA384
   Information in the server certificate:
     Subject of the X509 certificate:
       C=US, ST=New Hampshire, O=Chen Systems, Inc., OU=Engineering, CN=myserver
     Issuer of the X509 certificate:
       C=US, ST=New Hampshire, O=Chen Systems, Inc., OU=Engineering,
CN=IntermediateCA

   Verifying server's certificate succeeded.
   Enter a message to send ('bye' to end): Hi, this is tlsclient6.
```

```
   Received: This is reply message # 1 from the server.
   Enter a message to send ('bye' to end): bye
   Received: bye
```

Figure 15-37 tlsclient6.c and tlsserver6.c - verifying certificates signed by
multiple CA chains

(a) tlsserver6.c

```
/*
 * A TLS/SSL server.
 * This server program communicates with clients using TLS/SSL protocol.
 * The server verifies a client certificate signed by a chain of CAs.
 * Requiring client authentication using the SSL_VERIFY_FAIL_IF_NO_PEER_CERT
 * flag.
 * Client certificates are signed by multiple different CA chains.
 * Authored by Mr. Jin-Jwei Chen.
 * Copyright (c) 2014-2016, 2020-2021 Mr. Jin-Jwei Chen. All rights reserved.
 */

#include <stdio.h>
#include <errno.h>
#include <sys/types.h>
#include <sys/socket.h>
#include <netinet/in.h>      /* protocols such as IPPROTO_TCP, ... */
#include <string.h>          /* memset(), strlen(), memcmp() */
#include <stdlib.h>          /* atoi() */
#include <unistd.h>
#include <resolv.h>
#include <netdb.h>
#include <arpa/inet.h>
#include <resolv.h>
#include <openssl/ssl.h>
#include <openssl/err.h>
#include <openssl/x509.h>
#include "myopenssl.h"
#include "netlib.h"

/*
 * This function serves a newly connected SSL client.
 * Parameters:
 *   ctx (input) - SSL context.
 *   clntsock (input) - the child socket to communicate with the client.
 * Function output: return 0 on success, non-zero on failure.
 * Note that Openssl provides different functions to retrieve the actual
 * error. Unfortunately, they return different data types, some 'int'
 * (SSL_get_error()) and some 'unsigned long' (ERR_get_error()).
 * It makes it hard to return both types of errors from a function.
 * Note: If SSL_CTX_set_verify() is called in this function, it must be
 * placed before SSL_new().
 */
int serve_ssl_client(SSL_CTX *ctx, int clntsock)
{
  SSL            *ssl = NULL;       /* SSL structure/connection */
  char           reqmsg[MAXREQSZ];  /* buffer for incoming request message */
  char           reply[MAXRPLYSZ];  /* buffer for outgoing server reply */
```

1284

```
unsigned char   replysz;              /* length in bytes of reply message */
int             insize;               /* actual number of bytes read */
int             outsz;                /* actual number of bytes written */
int             error = 0;            /* error from certain SSL_xxx calls */
unsigned char   msgcnt;               /* count of reply messages to client */
int             done = 0;             /* done with current client */
int             ret;
X509            *clnt_cert = NULL;    /* pointer to peer's certificate */

if (ctx == NULL)
  return(EINVAL);
ERR_clear_error();

/* Create a new SSL structure to hold the connection data.
 * Note that to require client authentication, the call to
 * SSL_CTX_set_verify() must be done BEFORE SSL_new(). Or it has no effect.
 */
ssl = SSL_new(ctx);
if (ssl == NULL)
{
  fprintf(stderr, "Error: SSL_new() failed:\n");
  ERR_print_errors_fp(stderr);
  return(OPENSSL_ERR_SSLNEW_FAIL);
}

/* Associate the SSL structure with the socket */
ret = SSL_set_fd(ssl, clntsock);
if (ret != OPENSSL_SUCCESS)
{
  fprintf(stderr, "Error: SSL_set_fd() failed:\n");
  ERR_print_errors_fp(stderr);
  SSL_free(ssl);
  return(OPENSSL_ERR_SSLSETFD_FAIL);
}

/* Wait for the TLS/SSL client to initiate the TLS/SSL handshake */
ret = SSL_accept(ssl);
if (ret != OPENSSL_SUCCESS)
{
  error = SSL_get_error(ssl, ret);
  fprintf(stderr, "Error: SSL_accept() failed, error=%d\n", error);
  ERR_print_errors_fp(stderr);
  SSL_free(ssl);
  return(error);
}

/* Display information about the peer/client certificate */
display_ssl_certificate_info(ssl);

/* The service loop */
done = 0;
msgcnt = 1;
do
{
  /* Read the next request message from the TLS/SSL client */
  insize = SSL_read(ssl, reqmsg, MAXREQSZ);
```

```c
    if (insize <= 0)
    {
      error = SSL_get_error(ssl, insize);
      fprintf(stderr, "Error: SSL_read() failed, error=%d\n", error);
      break;
    }

    reqmsg[insize] = '\0';
    fprintf(stdout, "Server received: %s\n", reqmsg);

    /* Process the request here ... */

    /* Construct a reply message */
    if ( !strcmp(reqmsg, BYE_MSG) )
    {
      done = 1;
      strcpy(reply, reqmsg);
    }
    else
      sprintf(reply, SRVREPLY2, msgcnt++);

    replysz = strlen(reply);

    /* Send back a reply */
    outsz = SSL_write(ssl, reply, replysz);
    if (outsz != replysz)
    {
      error = SSL_get_error(ssl, outsz);
      fprintf(stderr, "Error: SSL_write() failed, error=%d\n", error);
      break;
    }
  } while (!done);

  /* Free up resources and return */
  SSL_free(ssl);
  return(error);
}

/* TLS/SSL server program */
int main(int argc, char *argv[])
{
  int      sfd;                          /* file descriptor of the listener socket */
  struct sockaddr_in     srvaddr;        /* IPv4 socket address structure */
  struct sockaddr_in6    srvaddr6;       /* IPv6 socket address structure */
  in_port_t  portnum = SRVPORT;          /* port number this server listens on */
  int          portnum_in = 0;           /* port number specified by user */
  struct sockaddr_in6    clntaddr6;      /* client socket address */
  socklen_t              clntaddr6sz = sizeof(clntaddr6);
  int      newsock = 0;                  /* file descriptor of client data socket */
  int      ipv6 = 0;                     /* IPv6 mode or not */
  int      ret;                          /* return value */
  SSL_CTX      *ctx;                     /* SSL context */

  /* Print Usage if requested by user */
  if (argc > 1 && argv[1][0] == '?' )
  {
```

```
      fprintf(stderr, "Usage: %s [server_port] [1 (use IPv6)]\n", argv[0]);
      return(0);
}

   /* Get the server port number from user, if any */
   if (argc > 1)
   {
      portnum_in = atoi(argv[1]);
      if (portnum_in <= 0)
      {
         fprintf(stderr, "Error: port number %s invalid\n", argv[1]);
         fprintf(stderr, "Usage: %s [server_port] [1 (use IPv6)]\n", argv[0]);
         return(-1);
      }
      else
         portnum = portnum_in;
   }

   /* Get the IPv6 switch from user, if any */
   if (argc > 2)
   {
      if (argv[2][0] == '1')
         ipv6 = 1;
      else if (argv[2][0] != '0')
      {
         fprintf(stderr, "Usage: %s [server_port] [1 (use IPv6)]\n", argv[0]);
         return(-2);
      }
   }

   fprintf(stdout, "TLS/SSL server listening at portnum=%u ipv6=%u\n",
      portnum, ipv6);

   /* Create the server listener socket */
   if (ipv6)
      ret = new_bound_srv_endpt(&sfd, (struct sockaddr *)&srvaddr6, AF_INET6,
         portnum);
   else
      ret = new_bound_srv_endpt(&sfd, (struct sockaddr *)&srvaddr, AF_INET,
         portnum);

   if (ret != 0)
   {
      fprintf(stderr, "Error: new_bound_srv_endpt() failed, ret=%d\n", ret);
      return(-3);
   }

   /* Create a TLS/SSL context -- a framework enabling TLS/SSL connections. */
   ctx = SSL_CTX_new(TLS_server_method());
   if (ctx == NULL)
   {
      fprintf(stderr, "Error: SSL_CTX_new() failed\n");
      close(sfd);
      return(-4);
   }
```

```c
    /* Set default locations for trusted CA certificates for verification */
    /* I found whether doing this first or last does not make a difference */
    if(SSL_CTX_load_verify_locations(ctx, CAALL_FILE, CA_DIR) < 1)
    {
      fprintf(stderr, "Error: SSL_CTX_load_verify_locations() failed to set "
        "verify location\n");
      SSL_CTX_free(ctx);
      close(sfd);
      return(-5);
    }

    /* Load the server's certificate and private key */
    ret = load_certificate(ctx, SRV_CERT_FILE, SRV_KEY_FILE);
    if (ret != SUCCESS)
    {
      fprintf(stderr, "Error: load_certificate() failed, ret=%d\n", ret);
      SSL_CTX_free(ctx);
      close(sfd);
      return(-6);
    }

    /* Require client authentication -- this function returns void.
     * Fail the client connection request if client does not send its certificate
     * or the sent client certificate fails in verification.
     */
    SSL_CTX_set_verify(ctx, SSL_VERIFY_PEER|SSL_VERIFY_FAIL_IF_NO_PEER_CERT, NULL);

    /* Server's service loop. Wait for next client and service it. */
    while (1)
    {
      /* Accept the next client's connection request */
      newsock = accept(sfd, (struct sockaddr *)&clntaddr6, &clntaddr6sz);
      if (newsock < 0)
      {
        fprintf(stderr, "Error: accept() failed, errno=%d\n", errno);
        continue;
      }

      fprintf(stdout, "\nServer got a client connection\n");

      /* Service the current SSL client */
      ret = serve_ssl_client(ctx, newsock);
      if (ret != 0)
        fprintf(stderr, "Error: serve_ssl_client() failed, ret=%d\n", ret);

      close(newsock);
    }  /* while */

    SSL_CTX_free(ctx);    /* release SSL context */
    close(sfd);           /* close server socket */
    return(0);
}
```

(b) tlsclient6.c

```
/*
```

```
 * A TLS/SSL client.
 * This program communicates with a TLS/SSL server using TLS/SSL protocol.
 * The client verifies a server certificate signed by a chain of CAs.
 * The client supplies a client certificate signed by a chain of CAs to
 * participate in client authentication.
 * This client uses a certificate signed by a second, different chain of CAs.
 * Authored by Mr. Jin-Jwei Chen.
 * Copyright (c) 2014-2016, 2020-2021 Mr. Jin-Jwei Chen. All rights reserved.
 */

#include <stdio.h>
#include <errno.h>
#include <sys/types.h>
#include <sys/socket.h>
#include <netinet/in.h>      /* protocols such as IPPROTO_TCP, ... */
#include <string.h>          /* memset(), strlen(), memcmp() */
#include <stdlib.h>          /* atoi() */
#include <unistd.h>
#include <resolv.h>
#include <netdb.h>
#include <openssl/ssl.h>
#include <openssl/err.h>
#include <openssl/x509.h>
#include "myopenssl.h"
#include "netlib.h"

/* Free all resources */
#define  FREEALL  \
    SSL_free(ssl); \
    SSL_CTX_free(ctx); \
    close(sfd);

/* A TLS/SSL client program */
int main(int argc, char *argv[])
{
  char          *srvhost = "localhost"; /* name of server host */
  in_port_t     srvport = SRVPORT;      /* port number server listens on */
  int           srvport_in = 0;         /* port number specified by user */

  int       ret;           /* return value */
  int       sfd=0;         /* socket file descriptor */
  int       error;         /* return value of SSL_get_error() */
  long      sslret;        /* return value of some SSL calls */

  SSL_CTX   *ctx = NULL;   /* SSL/TLS context/framework */
  SSL       *ssl = NULL;   /* SSL/TLS connection */

  char          replymsg[MAXRPLYSZ];    /* reply message from server */
  size_t        reqbufsz = MAXREQSZ;    /* size of client request buffer */
  char          *reqmsg=NULL;           /* pointer to request message buffer */
  size_t        reqmsgsz;               /* size of client request message */
  int           bytes;                  /* number of bytes received */
  int           done=0;                 /* done communicating with server */

  unsigned char errstrbuf[ERR_STRING_LEN];  /* error string */
```

```
/* Print Usage if requested by user */
if (argc > 1 && argv[1][0] == '?' )
{
  fprintf(stdout, "Usage: %s [srvportnum] [srvhostname]\n", argv[0]);
  return(0);
}
```

```
/* Get the port number of the target server host specified by user */
if (argc > 1)
{
  srvport_in = atoi(argv[1]);
  if (srvport_in <= 0)
  {
    fprintf(stderr, "Error: port number %s invalid\n", argv[1]);
    return(-1);
  }
  else
    srvport = srvport_in;
}
```

```
/* Get the name of the target server host specified by user */
if (argc > 2)
  srvhost = argv[2];
```

```
/* Connect to the server */
ret = connect_to_server(&sfd, srvhost, srvport);
if (ret != 0)
{
  fprintf(stderr, "Error: connect_to_server() failed, ret=%d\n", ret);
  if (sfd) close(sfd);
  return(-2);
}
```

```
/* Create a TLS/SSL context -- a framework enabling TLS/SSL connections. */
ctx = SSL_CTX_new(TLS_client_method());
if (ctx == NULL)
{
  fprintf(stderr, "Error: SSL_CTX_new() failed\n");
  close(sfd);
  return(-3);
}
```

```
/* Load the client's own certificate in case client authentication needed.
 * Note that this loading client certificate step MUST be done BEFORE the
 * SSL object is created. Or the client certificate won't be sent! */
ret = load_certificate(ctx, CLNT2_CERT_FILE, CLNT2_KEY_FILE);
if (ret != SUCCESS)
{
  fprintf(stderr, "Error: load_certificate() failed, ret=%d\n", ret);
  SSL_CTX_free(ctx);
  close(sfd);
  return(-4);
}
```

```
/* Allocate a new SSL structure to hold SSL connection data.
 * Note: If you do this step before load_certificate(), client certificate
```

```c
 * won't be sent even if the server requires it. */
ssl = SSL_new(ctx);
if (ssl == NULL)
{
  fprintf(stderr, "Error: SSL_new() failed\n");
  SSL_CTX_free(ctx);
  close(sfd);
  return(-5);
}

/* Set default locations for trusted CA certificates for verification */
if(SSL_CTX_load_verify_locations(ctx, CA_FILE, CA_DIR) < 1)
{
  fprintf(stderr, "Error: SSL_CTX_load_verify_locations() failed to set "
    "verify location\n");
  return(-6);
}

/* Set to do server certificate verification */
SSL_CTX_set_verify(ctx, SSL_VERIFY_PEER, NULL);

/* Associate the SSL object with the socket file descriptor */
ret = SSL_set_fd(ssl, sfd);
if (ret != OPENSSL_SUCCESS)
{
  fprintf(stderr, "Error: SSL_set_fd() failed, ret=%d\n", ret);
  FREEALL
  return(-7);
}

/* Initiate the TLS/SSL handshake with the TLS/SSL server */
ERR_clear_error();
ret = SSL_connect(ssl);
if (ret != OPENSSL_SUCCESS)
{
  error = SSL_get_error(ssl, ret);
  fprintf(stderr, "Error: SSL_connect() failed, error=%d\n", error);
  print_ssl_io_error(error);
  fprintf(stderr, "%s\n", ERR_error_string((unsigned long)error, (char *)NULL));
  FREEALL
  return(-8);
}

/* Connected with TLS/SSL server. Display server certificate info. */
fprintf(stdout, "Connected with TLS/SSL server, cipher algorithm is %s\n",
  SSL_get_cipher(ssl));
fprintf(stdout, "Information in the server certificate:\n");
display_ssl_certificate_info(ssl);

/* Verify the peer's certificate and get the result */
ERR_clear_error();
if ((sslret = SSL_get_verify_result(ssl)) == X509_V_OK)
{
  /* The server sent a certificate which verified OK. */
  fprintf(stdout, "Verifying server's certificate succeeded.\n");
}
```

```
  else
  {
    fprintf(stderr, "SSL_get_verify_result() failed, ret=%ld\n", sslret);
    fprintf(stderr, "%s\n", ERR_error_string((unsigned long)sslret, (char *)NULL));
    FREEALL
    return(-9);
  }

  /* Allocate input buffer */
  reqmsg = malloc(MAXREQSZ);
  if (reqmsg == NULL)
  {
    fprintf(stderr, "Error: malloc() failed\n");
    FREEALL
    return(-10);
  }

  /* Send a message and get a response until done */
  do
  {
    /* Get next message the user wants to send */
    fprintf(stdout, "Enter a message to send ('bye' to end): ");
    reqmsgsz = getline(&reqmsg, &reqbufsz, stdin);
    if (reqmsgsz == -1)
    {
      fprintf(stderr, "Error: getline() failed, ret=%lu\n", reqmsgsz);
      break;
    }

    /* Remove the newline character at end of input */
    reqmsg[--reqmsgsz] = '\0';

    /* Send a message using SSL -- message automatically encrypted */
    bytes = SSL_write(ssl, reqmsg, reqmsgsz);
    if (bytes != reqmsgsz)
    {
      error = SSL_get_error(ssl, bytes);
      fprintf(stderr, "Error: SSL_write() failed, error=%d\n", error);
      free(reqmsg);
      FREEALL
      return(-11);
    }

    /* Receive a reply using SSL -- reply automatically decrypted */
    bytes = SSL_read(ssl, replymsg, sizeof(replymsg));
    if (bytes <= 0)
    {
      error = SSL_get_error(ssl, bytes);
      fprintf(stderr, "Error: SSL_read() failed, error=%d\n", error);
      free(reqmsg);
      FREEALL
      return(-12);
    }
    else
    {
      replymsg[bytes] = 0;
```

```
    fprintf(stdout, "Received: %s\n", replymsg);
  }

  if (!strcmp(replymsg, reqmsg))
    done = 1;

} while (!done);

/* release all resources */
free(reqmsg);
SSL_free(ssl);       /* release the SSL structure/connection */
SSL_CTX_free(ctx);   /* release the SSL context */
close(sfd);          /* close socket */
return (0);
}
```

15-11-6 Setting Cipher Suite

Set Cipher Suite or not?

Not every cipher suite works with the particular certificates you may have. Therefore, in general I would not try to set the cipher suite and would let the system pick unless you have a reason to set it.

Some OpenSSL documentation seems to suggest that if an anonymous cipher is used, a server certificate may not be sent. If you hit that sort of snag, then you might want to call SSL_CTX_set_cipher_list() to set a cipher suite that works for you.

How to get the list of all possible cipher suites?

You may be wondering how to get or display all cipher suites used? Indeed, it's very simple. The

```
display_cipher_suites(ssl)
```

function in mycryptolib.c (Figure 15-39b) does just that.

```
void display_cipher_suites(SSL *ssl)
{
  const char *cipher;
  int        i;

  fprintf(stdout, "Cipher suite(s) used:");
  for( i = 0; (cipher = SSL_get_cipher_list( ssl, i )); i++ )
    fprintf(stdout, "  %s", cipher );
  fprintf(stdout, "\n");
}
```

As you can see, the cipher suites that can be used are in the SSL structure. You just call the SSL_get_cipher_list() function to get it one by one.

15-12 Error Handling in OpenSSL

As errors occur, OpenSSL records them in a thread's error queue.
It's a program's responsibility to be aware of and properly manage or
clean the error queue such that error reporting works correctly.

In general, there are at least two different approaches in reporting errors
in an OpenSSL program. One is to use one of the OpenSSL error printing
functions (e.g. ERR_print_errors()) to print all of the errors that have
been recorded in a thread's error queue at once. This also removes all of
the errors that have been printed from the error queue and makes the error
queue empty.

Another approach is to call one of the get error functions to get the error
code first and then use one of the ERR_error_string() functions to translate
the error code into an error string, and then print that.

We will introduce all of these functions in this section.

Data Types of Return Codes Inconsistent

Notice that it seems that the design of error/return codes in OpenSSL could
be a little bit better.

Almost every TLS/SSL program using OpenSSL invokes certain OpenSSL I/O
functions. When there is an error with these functions, the documentation
tells you to use SSL_get_error() to get the actual error code, which returns
the error code as an 'int'.

When you invoke other OpenSSL functions (for instance, SSL_new())
and if they fail, in many cases you are supposed to call the ERR_get_error()
function to get the actual error. But ERR_get_error() returns a value
of 'unsigned long', rather than 'int'.

The two return values are of different data types. Not only they have
different sizes, but one is signed and the other is unsigned!

Very often one has a function that invokes both types of these OpenSSL
functions. What data type should it return? 'unsigned long' or 'int'?
It's a tough choice to make. This makes programming with OpenSSL a bit
difficult especially in error handling.

In cases where you just want to print out the OpenSSL error, you can
invoke the ERR_print_errors_fp(stderr) function to print the OpenSSL error
to the standard error file.

15-12-1 Printing Errors

OpenSSL provides the following error printing functions for programs to use.

```
#include <openssl/err.h>

void ERR_print_errors(BIO *bp);
void ERR_print_errors_fp(FILE *fp);
```

```
        void ERR_print_errors_cb(int (*cb)(const char *str, size_t len, void *u),
            void *u)
```

ERR_print_errors() prints the error strings for all errors that OpenSSL has currently recorded in the thread's error queue to a BIO, and then clears the thread's error queue.

ERR_print_errors_fp() prints the error strings for all errors that OpenSSL has recorded to a FILE (e.g. stderr), thus emptying the error queue.

ERR_print_errors_cb() does the same except that the callback function you provide as the first argument to the function is called for each error line with the string, length, and userdata u as the callback parameters.

Keep in mind that ERR_print_errors(), ERR_print_errors_fp() and ERR_print_errors_cb() print all errors and drain the error queue empty.

15-12-2 Clear Error Queue

(1) ERR_clear_error()

To make sure getting and/or printing errors work reliably in OpenSSL, remember to clear the current thread's error queue before starting an operation, especially TLS/SSL I/O operation.

To ensure a thread's error queue is empty, invoke the ERR_clear_error() function. This function takes no argument and has no return value.

```
    #include <openssl/err.h>
    void ERR_clear_error(void);
```

15-12-3 Getting Error Code

(1) SSL_get_error()

SSL_get_error() allows a program to obtain the result code for an TLS/SSL I/O operation. The error returned is of 'int' type.

```
    #include <openssl/ssl.h>
    int SSL_get_error(const SSL *ssl, int ret);
```

SSL_get_error() returns a result code for a call to one of a few SSL I/O operations including SSL_connect(), SSL_accept(), SSL_do_handshake(), SSL_read_ex(), SSL_read(), SSL_peek_ex(), SSL_peek(), SSL_write_ex(), SSL_write(), and SSL_shutdown(). In order to retrieve the actual error, the value returned by these TLS/SSL I/O functions must be passed to SSL_get_error() as the second argument.

Note that SSL_get_error() must be used in the same thread that performed the TLS/SSL I/O operation and no other OpenSSL function calls should appear in between because SSL_get_error() inspects the current thread's OpenSSL error queue. The current thread's error queue must be empty before the TLS/SSL I/O operation is attempted, or SSL_get_error() will not work reliably.

For the possible return values of SSL_get_error(), please refer to the
man page of SSL_get_error() in OpenSSL documentation.
https://www.openssl.org/docs/manmaster/man3/SSL_get_error.html

Shown below is an example use of the SSL_get_error() function:

```
ret = SSL_connect(ssl);
if (ret != OPENSSL_SUCCESS)
{
  error = SSL_get_error(ssl, ret);
  fprintf(stderr, "Error: SSL_connect() failed, error=%d\n", error);
  SSL_free(ssl);
  SSL_CTX_free(ctx);
  close(sfd);
  return(-7);
}
```

(2) ERR_get_error(void)

Normally, in an OpenSSL program, one uses the ERR_get_error() function
to retrieve and remove the first (earliest) error from the current thread's
error queue.

```
#include <openssl/err.h>
unsigned long ERR_get_error(void);
```

Note that given the way OpenSSL error is designed, there are a number of
things to be aware of.

First, if a thread does not always drain its errors from its error queue,
then there could be some left-over errors from previous operation(s).
Hence, calling ERR_get_error() may not get the latest error as some might
think or expect.

Second, ERR_get_error() returns and removes the earliest, not the latest,
error from the thread's error queue. Most of the time, what programmers
really want is the latest error except for the case where a single operation
results in multiple errors. In that case, getting the earliest error
might be more desirable or useful.

Third, the ERR_get_error() function returns a value of 'unsigned long'.
This data type is incompatible with most Linux/Unix and other OpenSSL APIs.
Thus, if your function has to return an error to its caller and it invokes
both other APIs and the ERR_get_error() which retrieves error from many
OpenSSL functions, this could be a real challenge. How do you consolidate
the two different types of error codes into a single return type?

OpenSSL has the following error functions in getting and peeking at errors
in the error queue.

```
#include <openssl/err.h>

unsigned long ERR_get_error(void);
unsigned long ERR_peek_error(void);
unsigned long ERR_peek_last_error(void);
```

```
unsigned long ERR_get_error_line(const char **file, int *line);
unsigned long ERR_peek_error_line(const char **file, int *line);
unsigned long ERR_peek_last_error_line(const char **file, int *line);

unsigned long ERR_get_error_line_data(const char **file, int *line,
    const char **data, int *flags);
unsigned long ERR_peek_error_line_data(const char **file, int *line,
    const char **data, int *flags);
unsigned long ERR_peek_last_error_line_data(const char **file, int *line,
    const char **data, int *flags);
```

ERR_get_error() returns the earliest error code from the thread's error
queue and removes that error entry. This function can be called repeatedly
until there are no more error codes in the error queue.

ERR_peek_error() returns the earliest error code from the thread's error
queue without changing the error queue.

ERR_peek_last_error() returns the latest error code from the thread's error
queue without changing the error queue.

ERR_get_error_line(), ERR_peek_error_line() and ERR_peek_last_error_line()
are the same as the above. However, they additionally store the file name and
line number where the error occurred in *file and *line if these input
arguments are not NULL.

If there is no error in the error queue, these functions return 0.
Otherwise, the error code is returned.

15-12-4 Translate Error Code into Error String

As we mentioned earlier, you may choose to get the error code after an
operation and then do the error printing yourself.
The following OpenSSL functions translate an error code into a human-readable
error string.

```
#include <openssl/err.h>

char *ERR_error_string(unsigned long e, char *buf);
void ERR_error_string_n(unsigned long e, char *buf, size_t len);

const char *ERR_lib_error_string(unsigned long e);
const char *ERR_func_error_string(unsigned long e);
const char *ERR_reason_error_string(unsigned long e);
```

ERR_error_string(e, buf) translates an error code e into a human-readable
string representing the error code and places it in buf. Buf must be at
least 256 bytes long.

If buf is NULL then the error string is placed in a static buffer.
Note that this function is not thread-safe and does not check on the size
of the buffer. To prevent buffer overrun, use ERR_error_string_n() instead.
ERR_error_string_n() truncates the string if necessary.
For ERR_error_string_n(), the output buffer may not be NULL.

An OpenSSL error string has the following format:

```
error:[error code]:[library name]:[function name]:[reason string]
```

where error code is an 8-digit hexadecimal number and library name, function name and reason string are ASCII text.

ERR_lib_error_string(), ERR_func_error_string() and ERR_reason_error_string() return the library name, function name and error reason string, respectively.

If there is no text string registered for the given error code, the error string will contain the numeric code.

15-13 Source Code of Library Functions

This section shows the source code of the library functions used in program examples in this chapter. Figure 15-38 lists netlib.h and netlib.c which have our own networking library functions. Figure 15-39 displays myopenssl.h and mycryptolib.c which have our own security utility functions.

Figure 15-38 Our own networking library -- netlib.h and netlib.c

(a) netlib.h

```
/*
 * Defines and declarations for networking library
 * Copyright (c) 2015, 2016, 2020 Mr. Jin-Jwei Chen. All rights reserved.
 */

#include <stdio.h>
#include <errno.h>
#include <string.h>          /* memset() */
#include <stdlib.h>          /* malloc(), atoi() */
#include <ctype.h>           /* isdigit() */
#include <sys/types.h>
#include <sys/socket.h>      /* socket() */
#include <unistd.h>          /* gethostname() */
#include <netinet/in.h>      /* protocols such as IPPROTO_TCP, ... */
#include <netdb.h>           /* HOST_NAME_MAX */
#include <arpa/inet.h>       /* inet_ntop(), inet_pton() */
#include <pthread.h>

#define   MINIPADDRSZ    64      /* minimum buffer size for IP address */
#ifndef HOST_NAME_MAX
#define   HOST_NAME_MAX  255     /* maximum length of a host name */
#endif

#define   LSNRBACKLOG    1500    /* length of listener request queue */

/*
 * =================== Get host name/IP-address functions ===================
 */

/*
```

```
 * Get the hostname of this host as a pointer to string.
 * The caller must provide the buffer to hold the returned hostname.
 * The buffer must be at least HOST_NAME_MAX bytes.
 * The function returns 0 on success or a non-zero value otherwise.
 */
int get_hostname(char *buf, size_t buflen);


/*
 * Get the hostname of this host as string -- no parameter version.
 * A pointer to the hostname string is returned on success.
 * The caller must free the memory pointed at by the returned pointer.
 * A NULL pointer is returned in case of failure.
 */
char *get_hostname2();


/*
 * Get the IP address of this host as a string.
 * The IP address is returned in the ipaddr buffer which must be provided
 * by the caller. The ipaddrlen parameters specifies the size of the
 * ipaddr buffer, which must be at least MINIPADDRSZ bytes.
 * Return value: 0 if success, non-zero if failure
 * get_ipaddr() invokes get_hostname() and get_ipaddr_host().
 */
int get_ipaddr(char *ipaddr, size_t ipaddrlen);


/*
 * Get the IP address of this host as a string -- no parameter version.
 * A pointer to the IP address string is returned on success.
 * The caller is responsible for freeing that memory.
 * The caller must free the memory pointed at by the returned pointer.
 * A NULL pointer is returned in case of failure.
 * get_ipaddr() invokes get_hostname2() and get_ipaddr_host().
 */
char *get_ipaddr2();


/*
 * Get the IP address of the specified host as a string.
 * The IP address is returned in the ipaddr buffer which must be provided
 * by the caller. The hostname is specified by the hostname input parameter.
 * The ipaddrlen parameter specifies the length of the ipaddr buffer
 * which must be at least MINIPADDRSZ bytes long.
 * If hostname is NULL, it is assumed to be the current host.
 * The function returns 0 if success, non-zero if failure
 */
int get_ipaddr_host(char *hostname, char *ipaddr, size_t ipaddrlen);


/*
 * ==================== Network connection functions ========================
 */

/* Connect to a connection-oriented server */
int connect_to_server(int *sfdp, char *host, int portnum);

/* Create a bound network communication endpoint */
int new_bound_endpt(int *sfdp, struct sockaddr *srvaddrp,
  sa_family_t protocol, int portnum);
```

```c
/* Create a bound server network communication endpoint */
int new_bound_srv_endpt(int *sfdp, struct sockaddr *srvaddrp,
  sa_family_t protocol, int portnum);

/* Create a bound client network communication endpoint */
int new_bound_clnt_endpt(int *sfdp, struct sockaddr *srvaddrp,
  sa_family_t  protocol);

/*
 * ======================= Network I/O functions ===============================
 */

/* Send a message via a socket */
int send_msg(int sfd, unsigned char *bufp, size_t msgsz, int flags);

/* Receive a message via a socket */
int receive_msg(int sfd, unsigned char *bufp, size_t msgsz, int flags);

/* Print the contents of a binary buffer */
void print_binary_buf(unsigned char *buf, unsigned int buflen);
```

  (b) netlib.c

```c
/*
 * Network utility functions
 * Authored by Mr. Jin-Jwei Chen.
 * Copyright (c) 2015, 2016, 2020 Mr. Jin-Jwei Chen. All rights reserved.
 */

#include "netlib.h"

/*
 * ============================================================================
 * Utility functions for getting the name or IP address of a host.
 */

/*
 * This function returns the name of this host (i.e. the local host).
 * The caller must provide the buffer (the buf parameter) to hold the returned
 * hostname. The size of this buffer (specified by the buflen parameter)
 * must be at least HOST_NAME_MAX bytes.
 * The function returns 0 on success or a non-zero value otherwise.
 */
int get_hostname(char *buf, size_t buflen)
{
  int   ret;

  if ((buf == NULL ) || (buflen < HOST_NAME_MAX))
    return(EINVAL);

  /* Get the hostname */
  memset((void *)buf, 0, buflen);
  errno = 0;
  ret = gethostname(buf, buflen);
  if (ret != 0)
```

```
   {
      fprintf(stderr, "get_hostname(): gethostname() failed, errno=%d\n", errno);
      return(errno);
   }

   return(0);
}

/*
 * This function returns the name of this host (i.e. the local host).
 * A NULL pointer is returned in case of error or failure.
 * The caller is responsible for freeing the memory associated with
 * the returned pointer.
 */
char *get_hostname2()
{
   int    ret;
   char   *hostnamep;

   /* Dynamically allocate the buffer holding the returned hostname string */
   hostnamep = malloc(HOST_NAME_MAX+1);
   if (hostnamep == NULL)
      return((char *)NULL);

   /* Get the hostname */
   memset((void *)hostnamep, 0, (HOST_NAME_MAX+1));
   ret = gethostname(hostnamep, HOST_NAME_MAX);
   if (ret != 0)
   {
      fprintf(stderr, "get_hostname2(): gethostname() failed, errno=%d\n", errno);
      free(hostnamep);
      return((char *)NULL);
   }

   return(hostnamep);
}

/*
 * Get the IP address of the specified host as a string.
 * If the hostname argument is null, IP address of the current host is returned.
 * Parameters:
 *   hostname - INPUT: name of host whose IP address is being looked up
 *              If NULL, the IP address of the local host will be returned.
 *   ipaddr - IN/OUT: starting address of buffer to hold returned IP address
 *            The IP address of the host will be returned in this buffer.
 *   ipaddrlen - INPUT: length (in bytes) of buffer in the second parameter
 *               The minimum size is MINIPADDRSZ bytes, just in case it's IPv6.
 * Return value: 0 if success, non-zero if failure
 */
int get_ipaddr_host(char *hostname, char *ipaddr, size_t ipaddrlen)
{
   char   hostname1[HOST_NAME_MAX+1];
   char   *hostnamep;
   struct hostent  *hp;
   char   **addrlp;
   char   *ptr;
```

```
  int    ret;

  if (ipaddr == NULL || ipaddrlen < MINIPADDRSZ)
    return(EINVAL);

  /* If host name is not given, get it here */
  if (hostname != NULL)
    hostnamep = hostname;
  else
  {
    hostnamep = hostname1;
    memset((void *)hostnamep, 0, (HOST_NAME_MAX+1));
    errno = 0;
    ret = gethostname(hostnamep, HOST_NAME_MAX);
    if (ret != 0)
    {
      fprintf(stderr, "get_ipaddr_host(): gethostname() failed, errno=%d\n",
        errno);
      return(errno);
    }
  }

  /* Get the IP address of the host */
  if ((hp = gethostbyname(hostnamep)) == NULL) {
    fprintf(stderr, "get_ipaddr_host(): gethostbyname() failed, h_errno=%d\n",
      h_errno);
    return(h_errno);
  }

  addrlp = hp->h_addr_list;
  if (addrlp == NULL) return(ENOENT);
  if (*addrlp == NULL) return(ENOENT);
  else
  {
    /* Convert IP address from number to text */
    memset((void *)ipaddr, 0, ipaddrlen);
    errno = 0;
    ptr = (char *)inet_ntop(hp->h_addrtype, *addrlp, ipaddr, ipaddrlen);
    if (ptr == NULL)
    {
      fprintf(stderr, "get_ipaddr_host(): inet_ntop() failed, errno=%d\n",
        errno);
      return(errno);
    }
  }

  return(0);
}

/*
 * Get the IP address of this host (i.e. the local host).
 * The caller needs to provide the output buffer for the IP address.
 * Parameters:
 *    ipaddr: (INPUT) - starting address of the buffer to receive the IP address
 *    ipaddrlen: (INPUT) - size in bytes of the buffer pointed to by ipaddr
 *               This buffer size must be at least MINIPADDRSZ bytes.
```

```
 */
int get_ipaddr(char *ipaddr, size_t ipaddrlen)
{
  int    ret;
  char   hostname[HOST_NAME_MAX+1];

  if (ipaddr == NULL || ipaddrlen < MINIPADDRSZ)
    return(EINVAL);

  ipaddr[0] = '\0';

  /* Get the hostname of this host */
  ret = get_hostname(hostname, HOST_NAME_MAX);
  if (ret != 0)
    {
      fprintf(stderr, "get_ipaddr(): get_hostname() failed, ret=%d\n", ret);
      return(ret);
    }
  hostname[HOST_NAME_MAX] = '\0';

  /* Get the IP address of this host */
  ret = get_ipaddr_host(hostname, ipaddr, ipaddrlen);
  if (ret != 0)
    fprintf(stderr, "get_ipaddr(): get_ipaddr_host() failed, ret=%d\n", ret);

  return(ret);
}

/*
 * Get the IP address of this host (i.e. the local host).
 * A pointer to the IP address string is returned on success.
 * The caller must free the memory pointed at by the returned pointer.
 * A NULL pointer is returned in case of failure.
 */
char *get_ipaddr2()
{
  int    ret = 0;
  char   *hostnamep = (char *)NULL;
  char   *ipaddrp = (char *)NULL;

  /* Get the hostname of this host */
  hostnamep = get_hostname2();
  if (hostnamep == (char *)NULL)
    {
      fprintf(stderr, "get_ipaddr2(): get_hostname2() failed.\n");
      return((char *)NULL);
    }

  /* Allocate the memory for the buffer holding the returned IP address */
  ipaddrp = malloc(MINIPADDRSZ+1);
  if (ipaddrp == (char *)NULL)
    {
      fprintf(stderr, "get_ipaddr2(): malloc() failed.\n");
      free(hostnamep);
      return((char *)NULL);
    }
```

```
 /* Get the IP address of this host */
 ipaddrp[0] = '\0';
 ret = get_ipaddr_host(hostnamep, ipaddrp, MINIPADDRSZ);
 if (ret != 0)
 {
   fprintf(stderr, "get_ipaddr2(): get_ipaddr_host() failed, ret=%d\n", ret);
   free(ipaddrp);
   ipaddrp = (char *)NULL;
 }

 ipaddrp[MINIPADDRSZ] = '\0';
 free(hostnamep);
 return(ipaddrp);
}


/* ======================================================================
 * Utility functions for making network connections
 */


/*
 * Connect to a connection-oriented server
 * This function supports both IPv4 and IPv6 protocols.
 * Parameters:
 *   sfdp - OUTPUT, returns socket file descriptor
 *   host - INPUT, hostname or IP address of the target server
 *   portnum - INPUT, port number of the server
 * The function returns 0 on success and a non-zero value on failure.
 */
int connect_to_server(int *sfdp, char *host, int portnum)
{
 int     sfd;                    /* socket file descriptor */
 struct sockaddr_in     server;  /* IPv4 server socket's address */
 struct sockaddr_in6    server6; /* IPv6 server socket's address */
 int     option;                 /* socket option */
 struct hostent *hp;
 struct in_addr     inaddr;      /* IPv4 address as an integer */
 struct in6_addr    inaddr6;     /* IPv6 address as an integer */
 int     protocol;
 int     ret;

 /* Check input arguments */
 if (sfdp == NULL || host == NULL)
   return(EINVAL);

 *sfdp = 0;

 /* For IPv6 this needs to be changed to have a more generic solution.
  * We need to include the case of numeric IPv6 addresses.
  */
 /* Translate the server's host name or IP address into socket address. */
 if (!strcmp(host, "::1"))
 {
   protocol = AF_INET6;
   hp = gethostbyname2(host, protocol);
 }
```

```c
else if (isdigit(host[0]))
{
  /* Convert the numeric IP address to an integer. */
  protocol = AF_INET;
  ret = inet_pton(protocol, host, (void *)&inaddr);
  if (ret <= 0)
  {
    /* ret<0 means EAFNOSUPPORT, ret=0 means net addr invalid */
    protocol = AF_INET6;
    ret = inet_pton(protocol, host, (void *)&inaddr6);
    if (ret <= 0)
    {
      fprintf(stderr, "connect_to_server(): error, inet_pton() failed for"
        " [%s]," " errno=%d\n", host, errno);
      return(errno);
    }
  }
  if (protocol == AF_INET)
    hp = gethostbyaddr((char *)&inaddr, sizeof(inaddr), protocol);
  else if (protocol == AF_INET6)
    hp = gethostbyaddr((char *)&inaddr6, sizeof(inaddr6), protocol);
}
else
{
  /* Assume a host name is given if it starts with a letter. */
  protocol = AF_INET;
  hp = gethostbyname(host);
  if (hp == NULL)
  {
    protocol = AF_INET6;
    hp = gethostbyname2(host, AF_INET6);
  }
}

if (hp == NULL )
{
  fprintf(stderr, "connect_to_server(): error, cannot get address for [%s],"
    " errno=%d\n", host, errno);
  return(errno);
}

/* Copy the resolved information into sockaddr_in/sockaddr_in6 structure. */
if (protocol == AF_INET)
{
  memset((void *)&server, 0, sizeof(struct sockaddr_in));
  server.sin_family = hp->h_addrtype;      /* protocol */
  server.sin_port = htons(portnum);
  memcpy(&(server.sin_addr), hp->h_addr, hp->h_length);
}
else if (protocol == AF_INET6)
{
  memset((void *)&server6, 0, sizeof(struct sockaddr_in6));
  server6.sin6_family = hp->h_addrtype;      /* protocol */
  server6.sin6_port  = htons(portnum);
  memcpy(&(server6.sin6_addr), hp->h_addr, hp->h_length);
}
```

```c
/* Create a Stream socket. */
sfd = socket(protocol, SOCK_STREAM, 0);
if (sfd < 0)
{
  fprintf(stderr, "connect_to_server(): error, socket() failed, errno=%d\n",
    errno);
  return (errno);
}

/* Set the SO_KEEPALIVE socket option. Do this before connect. */
option = 1;
ret = setsockopt(sfd, SOL_SOCKET, SO_KEEPALIVE, &option, sizeof(option));
if (ret < 0)
{
  fprintf(stderr, "connect_to_server(): warning, setsockopt(SO_KEEPALIVE) "
    "failed, errno=%d\n", errno);
}

/* Connect to the server. */
if (protocol == AF_INET)
  ret = connect(sfd, (struct sockaddr *)&server, sizeof(struct sockaddr_in));
else if (protocol == AF_INET6)
  ret = connect(sfd, (struct sockaddr *)&server6, sizeof(struct sockaddr_in6));
if (ret == -1)
{
  fprintf(stderr, "connect_to_server(): error, connect() failed on port %d,"
    " errno=%d\n", portnum, errno);
  close(sfd);
  return(errno);
}

*sfdp = sfd;
return(0);
}

/*
 * Create a bound network communication endpoint
 * Bind to a well-known port
 * INPUT and OUTPUT:
 *    sfdp : pointer to a file descriptor
 *    srvaddrp: pointer to a sockaddr_in or sockaddr_in6 structure
 * INPUT:
 *    protocol: specify AF_INET for IPv4 or AF_INET6 for IPv6
 *    port : specify the server's port number or 0 for a client
 * Return 0 on success or other values if failure.
 */
int new_bound_endpt(int *sfdp, struct sockaddr *srvaddrp,
  sa_family_t protocol, int portnum)
{
  int    sfd;          /* socket file descriptor */
  struct sockaddr_in   *sap;     /* pointer to IPv4 socket address */
  struct sockaddr_in6  *sa6p;    /* pointer to IPv6 socket address */
  int    option;       /* socket option */
  int    ret;
```

```
/* Check input arguments */
if (sfdp == NULL || srvaddrp == NULL)
  return(EINVAL);
if (!((protocol == AF_INET) || (protocol == AF_INET6)))
  return(EINVAL);

*sfdp = 0;

/* Create a Stream socket. */
if ((sfd = socket(protocol, SOCK_STREAM, 0)) < 0)
{
  fprintf(stderr, "new_bound_endpt(): error, socket() failed,"
    " errno=%d\n", errno);
  return(errno);
}

/* Turn on SO_KEEPALIVE socket option. */
option = 1;
ret = setsockopt(sfd, SOL_SOCKET, SO_KEEPALIVE, &option, sizeof(option));
if (ret < 0)
{
  fprintf(stderr, "new_bound_endpt(): warning, setsockopt(SO_KEEPALIVE)"
    " failed, errno=%d\n", errno);
}

/* Turn on SO_REUSEADDR option */
option = 1;
ret = setsockopt(sfd, SOL_SOCKET, SO_REUSEADDR, &option, sizeof(option));
if (ret < 0)
  fprintf(stderr, "new_bound_endpt(): error, setsockopt(SO_REUSEADDR) "
    "failed, errno=%d\n", errno);
else
  fprintf(stdout, "SO_REUSEADDR option is turned on.\n");

/* Fill in the socket address. */
if (protocol == AF_INET)
{
  sap = (struct sockaddr_in *)srvaddrp;
  memset((void *)sap, 0, sizeof(struct sockaddr_in));
  sap->sin_family = protocol;
  sap->sin_port   = htons(portnum);
  sap->sin_addr.s_addr = htonl(INADDR_ANY);
}
else if (protocol == AF_INET6)
{
  sa6p = (struct sockaddr_in6 *)srvaddrp;
  memset((void *)sa6p, 0, sizeof(struct sockaddr_in6));
  sa6p->sin6_family = protocol;
  sa6p->sin6_port   = htons(portnum);
  sa6p->sin6_addr   = in6addr_any;
}

/* Bind the server or client socket to its address. */
if (protocol == AF_INET)
  ret = bind(sfd, (struct sockaddr *)sap, sizeof(struct sockaddr_in));
else if (protocol == AF_INET6)
```

```
    ret = bind(sfd, (struct sockaddr *)sa6p, sizeof(struct sockaddr_in6));

  if (ret != 0)
  {
    fprintf(stderr, "new_bound_endpt(): error, bind() failed,"
      " errno=%d\n", errno);
    close(sfd);
    return(errno);
  }

  /* If server, set maximum connection request queue length. */
  if (portnum > 0)
  {
    if (listen(sfd, LSNRBACKLOG) == -1) {
      fprintf(stderr, "new_bound_endpt(): error, listen() failed,"
        " errno=%d\n", errno);
      close(sfd);
      return(errno);
    }
  }

  *sfdp = sfd;
  return(0);
}

/*
 * Create a bound server network communication endpoint
 * Bind to a well-known port on the local host
 * INPUT and OUTPUT:
 *    sfdp : pointer to a file descriptor
 *    srvaddrp: pointer to a sockaddr_in or sockaddr_in6 structure
 * INPUT:
 *    protocol: specify AF_INET for IPv4 and AF_INET6 for IPv6
 *    port : specify the server's port number
 * Return 0 on success or other values if failure.
 */
int new_bound_srv_endpt(int *sfdp, struct sockaddr *srvaddrp,
  sa_family_t protocol, int portnum)
{
  int     ret;

  if (sfdp == NULL || srvaddrp == NULL)
    return(EINVAL);
  if (!((protocol == AF_INET) || (protocol == AF_INET6)))
    return(EINVAL);
  /* A server must use a known port number */
  if (portnum <= 0)
    return(EINVAL);

  ret = new_bound_endpt(sfdp, srvaddrp, protocol, portnum);
  return(ret);
}

/*
 * Create a bound client network communication endpoint
 * Bind to an available port number picked by the operating system
```

```
 * INPUT and OUTPUT:
 *   sfdp : pointer to a file descriptor
 *   srvaddrp: pointer to a sockaddr_in or sockaddr_in6 structure
 * INPUT only:
 *   protocol: specify AF_INET for IPv4 and AF_INET6 for IPv6
 * Return 0 on success or other values if failure.
 */
int new_bound_clnt_endpt(int *sfdp, struct sockaddr *srvaddrp, sa_family_t  protocol)
{
  int     ret;

  if (sfdp == NULL || srvaddrp == NULL)
    return(EINVAL);
  if (!((protocol == AF_INET) || (protocol == AF_INET6)))
    return(EINVAL);

  /* A client can bind to the next available port picked by the O.S. */
  ret = new_bound_endpt(sfdp, srvaddrp, protocol, 0);
  return(ret);
}

/* ====================== Network I/O functions  ============================ */

/*
 * Send a message whose fixed size is known using a socket.
 * Parameters:
 *   sfd (INPUT): socket file descriptor to be used
 *   bufp (INPUT): starting address of the message buffer
 *   msgsz (INPUT): length in bytes of the message to be sent
 *   flags (INPUT): flags for send() call
 * Return value:
 *   0 is returned on success. errno is returned if the send() call
 *   encounters an error. -1 is returned if the peer has closed its socket.
 */
int send_msg(int sfd, unsigned char *bufp, size_t msgsz, int flags)
{
  int      ret;        /* return code */
  ssize_t  nbytes;     /* number of bytes just being sent */
  size_t   total;      /* total number of bytes that have been sent */

  if ((sfd == 0) || (bufp == NULL) || (msgsz <= 0))
    return(EINVAL);

  errno = 0;
  total = 0;
  /* Make sure the entire message is sent */
  do
  {
    nbytes = send(sfd, bufp+total, msgsz-total, flags);
    if (nbytes > 0)
      total += nbytes;
    else
      break;
  } while (total < msgsz);

  if (total != msgsz)
```

```
{
   if (nbytes < 0)
   {
     /* send() encounters an error */
     fprintf(stderr, "send_msg(): error, send() failed, errno=%d\n\", errno);
     ret = errno;
   }
   else
   {
     /* Peer might have closed its socket */
     fprintf(stderr, "send_msg(): error, send() expected to send"
       " %lu bytes but sent only %lu bytes\n", msgsz, total);
     ret = (-1);
   }
 }
 else
   ret = 0;

 return(ret);
}

/* To receive a message of up to msgsz bytes from socket sfd */
int receive_msg(int sfd, unsigned char *bufp, size_t msgsz, int flags)
{
   int      ret;           /* return code */
   ssize_t  nbytes;        /* number of bytes just received */
   size_t   total;         /* total number of bytes that have been received */

   if ((sfd == 0) || (bufp == NULL) || (msgsz <= 0))
     return(EINVAL);

   errno = 0;
   total = 0;
   /* Make sure the entire message is received */
   do
   {
     nbytes = recv(sfd, bufp+total, msgsz-total, flags);
     if (nbytes > 0)
       total += nbytes;
     else
       break;
   } while (total < msgsz);

   if (total != msgsz)
   {
     if (nbytes < 0)
     {
       /* recv() encounters an error */
       fprintf(stderr, "receive_msg(): error, recv() failed, errno=%d\n", errno);
       ret = errno;
     }
     else
     {
       /* Peer might have closed its socket */
       fprintf(stderr, "receive_msg(): error, recv() expected to receive"
         " %lu bytes but got only %lu bytes\n", msgsz, total);
```

```
            ret = (-1);
        }
    }
    else
        ret = 0;

    return(ret);
}


/* Print the contents of a binary buffer */
void print_binary_buf(unsigned char *buf, unsigned int buflen)
{
    int    i;

    if (buf == NULL) return;
    printf("0x");
    for (i = 0; i < buflen; i++)
        printf("%02x", buf[i]);
    printf("\n");
}
```

Figure 15-39 Our own collection of OpenSSL utility functions (mycryptolib.c)
and its header file (myopenssl.h)

(a) myopenssl.h

```
/*
 * #defines for Openssl programs.
 */

#define   SUCCESS             0    /* Linux/Unix functions return 0 as success */
#define   OPENSSL_SUCCESS     1    /* Openssl functions return 1 as success */
#define   OPENSSL_FAILURE     0    /* Openssl functions return 0 as failure */
#define   ERRBUFLEN         256    /* length of error string buffer */


/* Constants used in client-server communications */
#define SRVPORT   7878      /* server's port number */
#define MAXREQSZ  1024      /* maximum size of client request messages */
#define MAXRPLYSZ 256       /* maximum size of server reply messages */
#define SRVREPLY  "This is a reply message from the server."
#define SRVREPLY2 "This is reply message #%2d from the server."
#define BYE_MSG   "bye"     /* input message to end session */


/* Length of error string buffer */
#define ERR_STRING_LEN  256  /* length of buffer to hold error string */


/* Structure representing a cipher in EVP */
#define MAX_CIPHER_NAME_LEN 32
struct cipher
{
    char   name[MAX_CIPHER_NAME_LEN+4];
    unsigned char  key[EVP_MAX_KEY_LENGTH+4];
    unsigned char  iv[EVP_MAX_IV_LENGTH+4];
};
typedef struct cipher cipher;
```

```
/*
 * Default values for key and IV used in encryption/decryption.
 * Note that KEYLEN and IVLEN vary from one algorithm to another.
 * These values are shared by the encryption and decryption.
 * Algorithm "bf-cbc" works in OpenSSL 1.1.1, but not OpenSSL 3.0. (2021-12-9)
 */
#define DEFAULT_CIPHER  "aes-256-cbc"
#define DEFAULT_CIPHER2 "DES-EDE3-CBC"
#define DEFAULT_CIPHER3 "aes-128-cbc"
#define IVLEN           16        /* length of IV (number of bytes) */
#define KEYLEN          32        /* key length (number of bytes) */
#define DEFAULT_IV      "2596703183564237"
#define DEFAULT_KEY     "Axy3pzsk%3q#0)yH+sTcG6Wo27yjFFiw"

/* IV and Key used by myencrypt2() and mydecrypt2() */
#define DEFAULT_IV2     "7593215400406031"
#define DEFAULT_KEY2    "Gxy3pzek%3q#0)tH+sTcG6Wc27gjFF(*"

/* Constants used by myencrypt2() and mydecrypt2() */
#define MAXMSGSZ   1024
#define MAXOUTSZ   (MAXMSGSZ+IVLEN)

/*
 * Defines for HMAC.
 */
#define HASHFUNC_NAME    "sha512"
#define HMACKEY          "15y3pz70%8q#0)yH+sTcG6Wo27yjFF(!"
#define MAC_ALGORITHM    "hmac"

/* File I/O */
#define INSIZE                 1024   /* read this many bytes each time */

/*
 * Defines for digital signatures
 */
#define  LENGTHSZ   (sizeof(unsigned int))   /* size of signature/msg length */
#define  MAXDGSTSZ 512                        /* size of buffer for digest */
#define  DEFDGSTALGRM "sha256"                /* default digest algorithm */

/* #defines for DSA signature with SHA256 256-bit digest */
#define  DSASEEDLEN    20        /* length of seed */
#define  DSASEED       "G3fLw789Os3f8JV24dZ9"  /* seed for DSA */
#define  DSABITSLEN    2048      /* bits - length of the prime number p */
#define  DSASIGLEN     80        /* buffer length of DSA signature */
#define  DSAHASH_NAME  "sha256" /* use 256 bits hash */
#define  DSAHASHKEY    "B6h8eA39%8p#4)iM+sTcG64o1eXj(!s4"  /* hash key */
#define  DSAPUBKEYFILE "DSAPubKeyFile"  /* file holding DSA public key */

/* #defines for RSA signature */
#define  RSASEEDLEN    32        /* length of seed */
#define  RSASEED       "ksNi01E$U&35Hm9ad12)KedQ3=Pnc5+="  /* seed */
#define  RSABITSLEN    2048      /* bits - length of key */
#define  RSASIGLEN     264       /* buffer length of RSA signature */
#define  RSAHASH_NAME  "sha512" /* use 512 bits hash */
#define  RSADGSTTYPE   NID_sha512           /* type of digest algorithm */
#define  RSAPUBKEYFILE "RSAPubKeyFile"  /* file holding RSA public key */
```

```
/*
 * Different types of message digest algorithms.
 * NID_sha1 NID_sha224 NID_sha256 NID_sha384 NID_sha512 NID_md5 ...
 */

#define  DGSTNAMELEN          32  /* length of digest names */
#define  SIG_ALGRTH_LEN      256  /* length of signature algorithm */
#define  PUBKEY_ALGRTH_LEN   512  /* length of key algorithm */


/*
 * Errors in calling some OPENSSL functions.
 */
#define OPENSSL_ERR_SSLNEW_FAIL          (-1001)
#define OPENSSL_ERR_SSLSETFD_FAIL        (-1002)
#define OPENSSL_ERR_BAD_CERTFILE         (-1003)
#define OPENSSL_ERR_BAD_KEYFILE          (-1004)
#define OPENSSL_ERR_KEY_MISMATCH         (-1005)
#define OPENSSL_ERR_NO_CLIENT_CERT       (-1006)
#define OPENSSL_ERR_CLIENT_CERT_VERIFY_FAIL  (-1007)


/*
 * TLS/SSL certificates for server, client and CAs.
 * For self-signed server certificate, SRV_CERT_FILE and CA_FILE must be
 * the same.
 */
/* Self-signed server certificate */
#define  CA_DIR  "./"
#define  SS_SRV_CERT_FILE "mysrv2_cert.pem"
#define  SS_SRV_KEY_FILE  "mysrv2_privkey.pem"
#define  SS_CA_FILE       "mysrv2_cert.pem"


/* Server certificate signed by a chain of CAs */
#define  SRV_CERT_FILE      "myserver_cert.pem"
#define  SRV_KEY_FILE       "myserver_privkey.pem"
#define  CLNT_CERT_FILE     "myclient_cert.pem"
#define  CLNT_KEY_FILE      "myclient_privkey.pem"
#define  CA_FILE            "myCAchain_cert.pem"
/* A second certificate chain */
#define  CLNT2_CERT_FILE    "xyzclnt_cert.pem"
#define  CLNT2_KEY_FILE     "xyzclnt_privkey.pem"
#define  CA2_FILE           "mychain2CAs_cert.pem"
#define  CAALL_FILE         "myAllCAs_cert.pem"


/* Cipher list to be used in SSL/TLS */
#define CIPHER_LIST "AES256-SHA256 "


/* Issue of non-portable data type used for length of signature in OpenSSL 3.0+ */
#ifdef USE_SIZET
#define SIZET_BAD size_t
#else
#define SIZET_BAD unsigned int
#endif


/*
 * Function prototypes
```

```
 */
void display_certificate_names(SSL* ssl);
int display_certificate_info(X509 *cert);
void print_ssl_io_error(int error);
void display_cipher_suites(SSL *ssl);
void display_ssl_certificate_info(SSL* ssl);
/* Print the encrypted message -- the cipher text */
void print_cipher_text(unsigned char *buf, unsigned int buflen);

/* Encryption and decryption APIs */
int myencrypt1(char *inbuf, size_t inlen, unsigned char *outbuf, size_t *outlen,
cipher *cipher);
int mydecrypt1(unsigned char *inbuf, size_t inlen, char *outbuf, size_t *outlen,
struct cipher *cipher);

int myencrypt2(char *inbuf, size_t inlen, unsigned char *outbuf, size_t *outlen,
struct cipher *cipherin);
int mydecrypt2(unsigned char *inbuf, size_t inlen, char *outbuf, size_t *outlen,
struct cipher *cipherin);

/* Message digest APIs */
int get_digest(char *data, unsigned int datalen, const char *dgstName,
  unsigned char *digest, unsigned int *dgstlen);
void print_digest(unsigned char *buf, unsigned int buflen);

/* Digital signature APIs */
int generate_RSAkey(int keytype, unsigned int keylen, EVP_PKEY **keypair);
int generate_DSAkey(int keytype, unsigned int keylen, EVP_PKEY **keypair);
int get_signature(EVP_PKEY *pkey, const char *dgstName, unsigned char *digest,
  unsigned int dgstlen, unsigned char *sigbuf, SIZET_BAD *siglen, int keytype);
int verify_signature(EVP_PKEY *pkey, unsigned char *digest, size_t dgstlen,
  unsigned char *sigbuf, SIZET_BAD siglen, const char *dgstName, int keytype);

/* Compute the digest of a message using the hash algorithm specified */
int message_digest(char *hashname, char *message, unsigned int msglen,
  unsigned char *digest, unsigned int *dgstlen);
int message_digest2(const EVP_MD *hashfunc, char *message,
  unsigned int msglen, unsigned char *digest, unsigned int *dgstlen);

/* Increment the IV value by one */
int increment_iv(unsigned char *inbuf, unsigned char *outbuf);

int load_certificate(SSL_CTX *ctx, char *certfile, char *keyfile);
```

    (b) mycryptolib.c

```
/*
 * Cryptographic utility functions.
 * Authored by Mr. Jin-Jwei Chen.
 * Copyright (c) 2014-2016, 2020-2023 Mr. Jin-Jwei Chen. All rights reserved.
 */

#include <stdio.h>
#include <errno.h>
#include <sys/types.h>      /* open() */
#include <sys/stat.h>
```

```c
#include <fcntl.h>
#include <unistd.h>          /* read(), write() */
#include <string.h>          /* memset(), strlen() */
#include <strings.h>         /* bzero() */
#include <stdlib.h>
#include <limits.h>          /* LONG_MIN, LONG_MAX */

#include <openssl/evp.h>
#include <openssl/err.h>
#include <openssl/blowfish.h>
#include <openssl/rsa.h>
#include <openssl/dsa.h>
#include <openssl/ssl.h>
#include <openssl/x509.h>
#include <openssl/x509v3.h>
#include <openssl/rand.h>
#include "myopenssl.h"

/* ================= encryption/decryption utility functions ================= */
/* Print the encrypted message -- the cipher text */
void print_cipher_text(unsigned char *buf, unsigned int buflen)
{
  int    i;

  if (buf == NULL) return;
  printf("Cipher text=0x");
  for (i = 0; i < buflen; i++)
    printf("%02x", buf[i]);
  printf("\n");
}


/*
 * Encryption and decryption using EVP_EncryptXXX() and EVP_DecryptXXX() APIs.
 * Encrypt the contents of the input buffer specified by 'inbuf' and
 * write the encrypted output (i.e. the cipher text) to the output buffer
 * specified by the 'outbuf' parameter using the cipher algorithm
 * specified by the 'cipher' parameter.
 */
int myencrypt1(char *inbuf, size_t inlen, unsigned char *outbuf, size_t *outlen,
cipher *cipher)
{
  const EVP_CIPHER *algrm = NULL;     /* cipher algorithm */
  EVP_CIPHER_CTX   *ctx = NULL;       /* cipher context */
  int       outlen2;                  /* length of last part of cipher text */
  int       ret;

  if (inbuf == NULL || outbuf == NULL || outlen == NULL || cipher == NULL)
    return(EINVAL);

  /* Get the EVP_CIPHER using the string name of the cipher algorithm */
  algrm = EVP_get_cipherbyname(cipher->name);
  if (algrm == NULL)
  {
    fprintf(stderr, "Error: myencrypt1(), failed to look up cipher algorithm %s\n"
    , cipher->name);
    return(-1);
```

```
    }

    /* Creates a cipher context */
    ctx = EVP_CIPHER_CTX_new();
    if (ctx == NULL)
    {
        fprintf(stderr, "Error: myencrypt1(), EVP_CIPHER_CTX_new() failed\n");
        return(-2);
    }

    /* Set up the cipher context with a specific cipher algorithm */
    ret = EVP_EncryptInit_ex(ctx, algrm, NULL, cipher->key, cipher->iv);
    if (!ret)
    {
        fprintf(stderr, "Error: myencrypt1(), EVP_EncryptInit_ex() failed, "
            "ret=%d\n", ret);
        return(-3);
    }

    /* Encrypt the message in the input buffer */
    *outlen = 0;
    if ((ret = EVP_EncryptUpdate(ctx, outbuf, (int *)outlen,
        (unsigned char *)inbuf, (int)inlen) != OPENSSL_SUCCESS))
    {
        fprintf(stderr, "Error: myencrypt1(), EVP_EncryptUpdate() failed, "
            "ret=%d\n", ret);
        return(-4);
    }

    /* Wrap up the encryption by handling the last remaining part */
    outlen2 = 0;
    if ((ret = EVP_EncryptFinal_ex(ctx, outbuf+(*outlen), &outlen2) !=
        OPENSSL_SUCCESS))
    {
        fprintf(stderr, "Error: myencrypt1(), EVP_EncryptFinal_ex() failed, "
            "ret=%d\n", ret);
        return(-5);
    }
    *outlen = *outlen + outlen2;

    EVP_CIPHER_CTX_free(ctx);

    return(0);
}

/*
 * Encryption and decryption using EVP_EncryptXXX() and EVP_DecryptXXX() APIs.
 * Decrypt the contents of the input buffer specified by 'infbuf' and
 * write the decrypted output (i.e. the plain text) to the output buffer
 * specified by 'outbuf' parameter using the cipher algorithm
 * specified by the 'algrm' parameter.
 */
int mydecrypt1(unsigned char *inbuf, size_t inlen, char *outbuf, size_t *outlen,
struct cipher *cipher)
{
    const EVP_CIPHER *algrm = NULL;    /* cipher algorithm */
```

```c
EVP_CIPHER_CTX   *ctx = NULL;           /* cipher context */
int      outlen2;                /* length of last decrypted part */
int      ret;

if (inbuf == NULL || outbuf == NULL || outlen == NULL || cipher == NULL)
  return(EINVAL);

/* Get the EVP_CIPHER using the string name of the cipher algorithm */
algrm = EVP_get_cipherbyname(cipher->name);
if (algrm == NULL)
{
  fprintf(stderr, "Error: mydecrypt1(), failed to look up cipher algorithm %s\n"
    , cipher->name);
  return(-1);
}

/* Creates a cipher context */
ctx = EVP_CIPHER_CTX_new();
if (ctx == NULL)
{
  fprintf(stderr, "Error: mydecrypt1(), EVP_CIPHER_CTX_new() failed\n");
  return(-2);
}

/* Set up the cipher context with a specific cipher algorithm */
ret = EVP_DecryptInit_ex(ctx, algrm, NULL, cipher->key, cipher->iv);
if (!ret)
{
  fprintf(stderr, "Error: mydecrypt1(), EVP_DecryptInit_ex() failed, "
    "ret=%d\n", ret);
  return(-3);
}

/* Decrypt the contents in the input buffer */
*outlen = 0;
if ((ret = EVP_DecryptUpdate(ctx, (unsigned char *)outbuf, (int *)outlen,
    inbuf, (int)inlen) != OPENSSL_SUCCESS))
{
  fprintf(stderr, "Error: mydecrypt1(), EVP_DecryptUpdate() failed, "
    "ret=%d\n", ret);
  return(-4);
}

/* Wrap up the decryption by handling the last remaining part */
/* Note that EVP_DecryptFinal_ex() returns 1 on success for all algorithms
   except aes-nnn-gcm where it returns 0 on success in OpenSSL 1.0.2 thru 3.1.
   This seems to be a bug. Hope OpenSSL will fix this someday.
*/
outlen2 = 0;
if ((ret = EVP_DecryptFinal_ex(ctx, (unsigned char *)outbuf+(*outlen),
    &outlen2)) != OPENSSL_SUCCESS)
{
  fprintf(stderr, "Error: mydecrypt1(), EVP_DecryptFinal_ex() failed, "
    "ret=%d\n", ret);
  return(-5);
}
```

```
    *outlen = *outlen + outlen2;

    EVP_CIPHER_CTX_free(ctx);

    return(0);
}

/*
 * Encryption and decryption using EVP_CipherXXX() APIs.
 * Encrypt the contents of the input buffer specified by 'inbuf' and
 * write the encrypted output (i.e. the cipher text) to the output buffer
 * specified by the 'outbuf' parameter using the cipher algorithm
 * specified by the 'cipherin' parameter.
 */
int myencrypt2(char *inbuf, size_t inlen, unsigned char *outbuf, size_t *outlen,
struct cipher *cipherin)
{
    EVP_CIPHER_CTX      *ctx = NULL;    /* cipher context */
    int                 outlen2;        /* length of last part of cipher text */
    int                 ret;            /* return code */
    struct cipher       dfcipher;       /* default cipher */
    struct cipher       *cipher;        /* the cipher used */
    const EVP_CIPHER    *algrm = NULL;  /* cipher algorithm */

    if (inbuf == NULL || outbuf == NULL || outlen == NULL)
        return(EINVAL);

    /* Use the default cipher algorithm if none is specified */
    if (cipherin != NULL)
        cipher = cipherin;
    else
    {
        strcpy(dfcipher.name, DEFAULT_CIPHER);
        strcpy((char *)dfcipher.key, DEFAULT_KEY2);
        strcpy((char *)dfcipher.iv, DEFAULT_IV2);
        cipher = &dfcipher;
    }

    /* Get the EVP_CIPHER using the string name of the cipher algorithm */
    algrm = EVP_get_cipherbyname(cipher->name);
    if (algrm == NULL)
    {
        fprintf(stderr, "Error: myencrypt2(), failed to look up cipher algorithm"
        " %s\n", cipher->name);
        return(-1);
    }

    /* Creates a cipher context */
    ctx = EVP_CIPHER_CTX_new();
    if (ctx == NULL)
    {
        fprintf(stderr, "Error: myencrypt2(), EVP_CIPHER_CTX_new() failed\n");
        return(-2);
    }

    /* Set up the cipher context with a specific cipher algorithm */
```

```
  ret = EVP_CipherInit_ex(ctx, algrm, NULL, cipher->key, cipher->iv, 1);
  if (!ret)
  {
    fprintf(stderr, "Error: myencrypt2(), EVP_CipherInit_ex() failed, "
      "ret=%d\n", ret);
    return(-3);
  }

  /* Encrypt the message in the input buffer */
  *outlen = 0;
  if ((ret=EVP_CipherUpdate(ctx, outbuf, (int *)outlen, (unsigned char *)inbuf,
     (int)inlen)) != OPENSSL_SUCCESS)
  {
    fprintf(stderr, "Error: myencrypt2(), EVP_CipherUpdate() failed, "
      "ret=%d\n", ret);
    return(-4);
  }

  /* Wrap up the encryption by handling the last remaining part */
  outlen2 = 0;
  if ((ret = EVP_CipherFinal_ex(ctx, outbuf+(*outlen), &outlen2) !=
      OPENSSL_SUCCESS))
  {
    fprintf(stderr, "Error: myencrypt2(), EVP_CipherFinal_ex() failed, "
      "ret=%d\n", ret);
    return(-5);
  }
  *outlen = *outlen + outlen2;

  EVP_CIPHER_CTX_free(ctx);
  return(0);
}


/*
 * Encryption and decryption using EVP_CipherXXX() APIs.
 * Decrypt the contents of the input buffer specified by 'infbuf' and
 * write the decrypted output (i.e. the plain text) to the output buffer
 * specified by 'outbuf' parameter using the cipher algorithm
 * specified by the 'cipherin' parameter.
 */
int mydecrypt2(unsigned char *inbuf, size_t inlen, char *outbuf,
    size_t *outlen, struct cipher *cipherin)
{
  EVP_CIPHER_CTX    *ctx = NULL;      /* cipher context */
  int               outlen2;          /* length of last part of cipher text */
  int               ret;              /* retrun code */
  struct cipher     dfcipher;         /* default cipher */
  struct cipher     *cipher;          /* the cipher used */
  const EVP_CIPHER  *algrm = NULL;    /* cipher algorithm */

  if (inbuf == NULL || outbuf == NULL || outlen == NULL)
    return(EINVAL);

  /* Use the default cipher algorithm if none is specified */
  if (cipherin != NULL)
    cipher = cipherin;
```

1319

```
  else
  {
    strcpy(dfcipher.name, DEFAULT_CIPHER);
    strcpy((char *)dfcipher.key, DEFAULT_KEY2);
    strcpy((char *)dfcipher.iv, DEFAULT_IV2);
    cipher = &dfcipher;
  }

  /* Get the EVP_CIPHER using the string name of the cipher algorithm */
  algrm = EVP_get_cipherbyname(cipher->name);
  if (algrm == NULL)
  {
    fprintf(stderr, "Error: mydecrypt2(), failed to look up cipher algorithm"
      " %s\n", cipher->name);
    return(-1);
  }

  /* Creates a cipher context */
  ctx = EVP_CIPHER_CTX_new();
  if (ctx == NULL)
  {
    fprintf(stderr, "Error: mydecrypt2(), EVP_CIPHER_CTX_new() failed\n");
    return(-2);
  }

  /* Set up the cipher context with a specific cipher algorithm */
  ret = EVP_CipherInit_ex(ctx, algrm, NULL, cipher->key, cipher->iv, 0);
  if (!ret)
  {
    fprintf(stderr, "Error: mydecrypt2(), EVP_CipherInit_ex() failed, "
      "ret=%d\n", ret);
    return(-3);
  }

  /* Decrypt the contents in the input buffer */
  *outlen = 0;
  if ((ret = EVP_CipherUpdate(ctx, (unsigned char *)outbuf, (int *)outlen,
      inbuf, (int)inlen)) != OPENSSL_SUCCESS)
  {
    fprintf(stderr, "Error: mydecrypt2(), EVP_CipherUpdate() failed, "
      "ret=%d\n", ret);
    return(-4);
  }

  /* Wrap up the decryption by handling the last remaining part */
  /* Note that EVP_CipherFinal_ex() returns 1 on success for all algorithms
     except aes-nnn-gcm where it returns 0 on success in OpenSSL 1.1.1.
     This seems to be a bug. Hope OpenSSL will fix this someday.
  */
  outlen2 = 0;
  ret = EVP_CipherFinal_ex(ctx, (unsigned char *)outbuf+(*outlen), &outlen2);
  if (ret != OPENSSL_SUCCESS)
  {
    fprintf(stderr, "Error: mydecrypt2(), EVP_CipherFinal_ex() failed, "
      "ret=%d\n", ret);
    return(-5);
```

```c
    }
    *outlen = *outlen + outlen2;

    EVP_CIPHER_CTX_free(ctx);
    return(0);
}


/*
 * This function takes a decimal numeric string and increment its value by one.
 * The parameter inbuf holds the input string and outbuf holds the output.
 * Make sure the outbuf has enough space to hold the output value.
 */
int increment_iv(unsigned char *inbuf, unsigned char *outbuf)
{
    long int   val;              /* numeric value */
    char       *endptr = NULL;   /* end pointer */
    int        ret;

    if (inbuf == NULL || outbuf == NULL)
        return(EINVAL);

    /* Convert the value from string to integer */
    val = strtol((char *)inbuf, (char **)&endptr, 10);
    if (val == LONG_MIN)
    {
        fprintf(stderr, "increment_iv(): error, strtoll() underflow\n");
        return(ERANGE);
    }
    else if (val == LONG_MAX)
    {
        fprintf(stderr, "increment_iv(): error, strtoll() overflow\n");
        return(ERANGE);
    }

    /* We limit the length of an IV to 8 characters here. */
    if (val >= 99999999)
        val = 0;

    val = val + 1;
    ret = sprintf((char *)outbuf, "%ld", val);

    return(0);
}


/* ==================== Message digest utility functions ==================== */
/*
 * A generic message digest function -- with hashname.
 * This function computes the digest (i.e. hash) of a message using the hash
 * function provided.
 * Input parameters:
 *   hashname - name of a hash function to be used
 *   message - the message whose digest is to be computed
 *   msglen - length of the message in bytes
 * Output parameters
 *   digest - digest of the message
 *   dgstlen - length of the digest in bytes
```

```
*/
int message_digest(char *hashname, char *message, unsigned int msglen,
    unsigned char *digest, unsigned int *dgstlen)
{
  const EVP_MD   *hashfunc=NULL;   /* descriptor of message digest algorithm */
  EVP_MD_CTX     *ctx = NULL;      /* digest context */
  int            ret;

  if (hashname == NULL || message == NULL || digest == NULL || dgstlen == NULL)
    return(EINVAL);

  /* Get the structure describing the message digest algorithm by name */
  hashfunc = EVP_get_digestbyname(hashname);
  if(hashfunc == NULL)
  {
    fprintf(stderr, "Error, message_digest(): unknown message digest algorithm"
      " %s\n", hashname);
    return(-1);
  }

  /* Allocate and initialize a digest context */
  ctx = EVP_MD_CTX_new();
  if (ctx == NULL)
  {
    fprintf(stderr, "Error, message_digest(): EVP_MD_CTX_new() failed\n");
    return(-2);
  }

  /* Set up digest context ctx to use the digest type specified by hashfunc */
  ret = EVP_DigestInit_ex(ctx, hashfunc, NULL);
  if (ret == OPENSSL_FAILURE)
  {
    fprintf(stderr, "Error, message_digest(): EVP_DigestInit_ex() failed\n");
    EVP_MD_CTX_free(ctx);
    return(-3);
  }

  /* Hash the current message segment into the digest context ctx. This
     can be called several times on the same ctx to hash additional data. */
  ret = EVP_DigestUpdate(ctx, message, msglen);
  if (ret == OPENSSL_FAILURE)
  {
    fprintf(stderr, "Error, message_digest(): EVP_DigestUpdate() failed\n");
    EVP_MD_CTX_free(ctx);
    return(-4);
  }

  /* Retrieves the digest value from ctx and places it in digest argument */
  ret = EVP_DigestFinal_ex(ctx, digest, dgstlen);
  if (ret == OPENSSL_FAILURE)
  {
    fprintf(stderr, "Error, message_digest(): EVP_DigestFinal_ex() failed\n");
    EVP_MD_CTX_free(ctx);
    return(-5);
  }
```

```
  /* Free the digest context allocated */
  EVP_MD_CTX_free(ctx);

  return(0);
}


/*
 * A generic message digest function -- with hashfunc.
 * This function computes the digest (i.e. hash) of a message using the hash
 * function provided.
 * Input parameters:
 *   hashfunc - pointer to a hash function to be used
 *   message - the message whose digest is to be computed
 *   msglen - length of the message in bytes
 * Output parameters
 *   digest - digest of the message
 *   dgstlen - length of the digest in bytes
 */
int message_digest2(const EVP_MD *hashfunc, char *message,
    unsigned int msglen, unsigned char *digest, unsigned int *dgstlen)
{
  EVP_MD_CTX      *ctx = NULL;        /* digest context */
  int             ret;

  if (hashfunc == NULL || message == NULL || digest == NULL || dgstlen == NULL)
    return(EINVAL);

  /* Allocate and initialize a digest context */
  ctx = EVP_MD_CTX_new();
  if (ctx == NULL)
  {
    fprintf(stderr, "Error, message_digest(): EVP_MD_CTX_new() failed\n");
    return(-2);
  }

  /* Set up digest context ctx to use the digest type specified by hashfunc */
  ret = EVP_DigestInit_ex(ctx, hashfunc, NULL);
  if (ret == OPENSSL_FAILURE)
  {
    fprintf(stderr, "Error, message_digest(): EVP_DigestInit_ex() failed\n");
    EVP_MD_CTX_free(ctx);
    return(-3);
  }

  /* Hash the current message segment into the digest context ctx. This
     can be called several times on the same ctx to hash additional data. */
  ret = EVP_DigestUpdate(ctx, message, msglen);
  if (ret == OPENSSL_FAILURE)
  {
    fprintf(stderr, "Error, message_digest(): EVP_DigestUpdate() failed\n");
    EVP_MD_CTX_free(ctx);
    return(-4);
  }

  /* Retrieves the digest value from ctx and places it in digest argument */
  ret = EVP_DigestFinal_ex(ctx, digest, dgstlen);
```

```
  if (ret == OPENSSL_FAILURE)
  {
    fprintf(stderr, "Error, message_digest(): EVP_DigestFinal_ex() failed\n");
    EVP_MD_CTX_free(ctx);
    return(-5);
  }

  /* Free the digest context allocated */
  EVP_MD_CTX_free(ctx);

  return(0);
}

/*
 * Compute the digest of the input message stored in 'data' using the message
 * digest algorithm passed in via 'dgstName'.
 * Input parameters:
 *   data - contains the input message
 *   datalen - contains the length of the input message
 *   dgstName - string name of the message digest algorithm to be used
 * Output parameters:
 *   digest - returns the message digest computed
 *   dgstlen - returns the length of the message digest computed
 *   This function returns 0 on success.
 */
int get_digest(char *data, unsigned int datalen, const char *dgstName,
  unsigned char *digest, unsigned int *dgstlen)
{
  EVP_MD_CTX      *mdctx;          /* message digest context */
  const EVP_MD    *md;            /* message digest object */
  unsigned long   error = 0L;        /* error code */
  char            errstr[ERRBUFLEN];   /* error string */

  if (data == NULL || digest == NULL || dgstlen == NULL || dgstName == NULL)
    return(EINVAL);

  /* Get the message digest algorithm by name */
  md = EVP_get_digestbyname(dgstName);
  if (md == NULL)
  {
    error = ERR_get_error();
    ERR_error_string_n(error, errstr, ERRBUFLEN);
    fprintf(stderr, "get_digest(): EVP_get_digestbyname(%s) failed. "
      "error=%lu\n%s\n", dgstName, error, errstr);
    return(-1);
  }

  /* Create the message digest context */
  mdctx = EVP_MD_CTX_new();
  if (mdctx == NULL)
  {
    error = ERR_get_error();
    ERR_error_string_n(error, errstr, ERRBUFLEN);
    fprintf(stderr, "get_digest(): EVP_MD_CTX_new() failed. error=%lu\n%s\n",
      error, errstr);
    return(-2);
```

```
    }

    /* Initialize the message digest operation */
    if (!EVP_DigestInit_ex2(mdctx, md, NULL))
    {
        error = ERR_get_error();
        ERR_error_string_n(error, errstr, ERRBUFLEN);
        fprintf(stderr, "get_digest(): EVP_DigestInit_ex2() failed. error=%lu\n%s\n"
            , error, errstr);
        EVP_MD_CTX_free(mdctx);
        return(-3);
    }

    /* Hash the next chunk of the message into the digest context. Call this
     * repeatedly if multiple chunks, once for every chunk of the message. */
    if (!EVP_DigestUpdate(mdctx, data, datalen))
    {
        error = ERR_get_error();
        ERR_error_string_n(error, errstr, ERRBUFLEN);
        fprintf(stderr, "get_digest(): EVP_DigestUpdate() failed. error=%lu\n%s\n",
            error, errstr);
        EVP_MD_CTX_free(mdctx);
        return(-4);
    }

    /* Retrieve the digest value from mdctx and place it in digest.
     * Also return length of digest in dgstlen. */
    if (!EVP_DigestFinal_ex(mdctx, digest, dgstlen))
    {
        error = ERR_get_error();
        ERR_error_string_n(error, errstr, ERRBUFLEN);
        fprintf(stderr, "get_digest(): EVP_DigestFinal_ex() failed. error=%lu\n%s\n"
            , error, errstr);
        EVP_MD_CTX_free(mdctx);
        return(-5);
    }

    EVP_MD_CTX_free(mdctx);
    return(0);
}

/* Print the digest stored in buf. Note that data is unsigned. */
void print_digest(unsigned char *buf, unsigned int buflen)
{
    int    i;

    if (buf == NULL) return;
    fprintf(stdout, "digest=0x");
    for (i = 0; i < buflen; i++)
        fprintf(stdout, "%02x", buf[i]);
    printf("\n");
}

/* =================== Digital signature utility functions =================== */

/*
```

```
 * This function computes the digital signature of a message digest
 * using the RSA or DSA algorithm and OpenSSL EVP APIs.
 * INPUT parameters:
 *   pkey - public key cryptography keypair
 *   dgstName - name of digest algorithm ("sha256", "sha512", "md5")
 *   digest - message digest to be signed
 *   dgstlen - length of the message digest
 *   keytype - indicate RSA or DSA algorithm for signing
 * OUTPUT parameters:
 *   sigbuf - buffer for the signature to be returned
 *     Maximum size of this buffer can be obtained from EVP_PKEY_get_size(pkey)
 *   siglen - length of the digital signature
 * This function returns 0 for success.
 */
int get_signature(EVP_PKEY *pkey, const char *dgstName, unsigned char *digest,
 unsigned int dgstlen, unsigned char *sigbuf, SIZET_BAD *siglen, int keytype)
{
  EVP_PKEY_CTX    *ctx;                   /* public key cryptographic context */
  unsigned long   error = 0L;             /* error code */
  char            errstr[ERRBUFLEN];      /* error string */
  int             ret=0;

  if (pkey == NULL || dgstName == NULL || digest == NULL || sigbuf == NULL
    || siglen == NULL)
    return(EINVAL);

  /* Create EVP_PKEY_CTX context from signer's private key */
  ctx = EVP_PKEY_CTX_new(pkey, NULL /* no engine */);
  if (!ctx)
  {
    error = ERR_get_error();
    ERR_error_string_n(error, errstr, ERRBUFLEN);
    fprintf(stderr, "get_signature(): EVP_PKEY_CTX_new() failed, "
      "error=%lu\n%s\n", error, errstr);
    return(-1);
  }

  /* Initialize the public key algorithm context ctx for signing */
  if (EVP_PKEY_sign_init(ctx) <= 0)
  {
    error = ERR_get_error();
    ERR_error_string_n(error, errstr, ERRBUFLEN);
    fprintf(stderr, "get_signature(): EVP_PKEY_sign_init() failed, "
      "error=%lu\n%s\n", error, errstr);
    EVP_PKEY_CTX_free(ctx);
    return(-2);
  }

  switch (keytype)
  {
    case EVP_PKEY_RSA:
      /* Set RSA padding */
      if (EVP_PKEY_CTX_set_rsa_padding(ctx, RSA_PKCS1_PADDING) <= 0)
      {
        error = ERR_get_error();
        ERR_error_string_n(error, errstr, ERRBUFLEN);
```

```
            fprintf(stderr, "get_signature(): EVP_PKEY_CTX_set_rsa_padding()"
                " failed, error=%lu\n%s\n", error, errstr);
            EVP_PKEY_CTX_free(ctx);
            return(-3);
        }
        break;

    case EVP_PKEY_DSA:
        break;

    default:
        fprintf(stdout, "get_signature(): keytype=%lu\n", keytype);
        break;
    }

    /* Set signature's digest algorithm */
    if (EVP_PKEY_CTX_set_signature_md(ctx, EVP_get_digestbyname(dgstName)) <= 0)
    {
        error = ERR_get_error();
        ERR_error_string_n(error, errstr, ERRBUFLEN);
        fprintf(stderr, "get_signature(): EVP_PKEY_CTX_set_signature_md() "
            "failed, error=%lu\n%s\n", error, errstr);
        EVP_PKEY_CTX_free(ctx);
        return(-4);
    }

    /* Alternatively, the buffer for signature can be determined and allocated
     * here as below:
     *    if (EVP_PKEY_sign(ctx, NULL, siglen, digest, dgstlen) <= 0) goto err;
     *    sigbuf = OPENSSL_malloc(*siglen);
     * But we've taken care of the business in the caller.
     * Don't reset siglen to 0 here.
     */

    /* Sign the digest. Return signature and its length in sigbuf and siglen. */
    if ((ret=EVP_PKEY_sign(ctx, sigbuf, siglen, digest, dgstlen)) <= 0)
    {
        error = ERR_get_error();
        ERR_error_string_n(error, errstr, ERRBUFLEN);
        fprintf(stderr, "get_signature(): EVP_PKEY_sign() failed, "
            "ret=%d error=%lu\n%s\n", ret, error, errstr);
        EVP_PKEY_CTX_free(ctx);
        return(-5);
    }

    EVP_PKEY_CTX_free(ctx);
    return(0);
}

/* Verify RSA or DSA signature using EVP APIs in OpenSSL 3.0+.
 * This function verifies the digital signature of a message digest
 * using the RSA or DSA algorithm and OpenSSL EVP APIs.
 * INPUT parameters:
 *    pkey - public key cryptography keypair
 *    dgstName - name of digest algorithm ("sha256", "sha512", "md5")
 *    digest - message digest that was signed
```

```
 *    dgstlen - length of the message digest
 *    sigbuf - contains the digital signature to be verified
 *    siglen - length of the digital signature
 *    keytype - indicate RSA or DSA algorithm used for signing
 * This function returns 0 for success.
 */
int verify_signature(EVP_PKEY *pkey, unsigned char *digest, size_t dgstlen,
  unsigned char *sigbuf, SIZET_BAD siglen, const char *dgstName, int keytype)
{
  unsigned long   error = 0L;           /* error code */
  char            errstr[ERRBUFLEN];    /* error string */
  EVP_PKEY_CTX    *ctx;                 /* public key algorithm context */
  int             ret;

  if (pkey == NULL || digest == NULL || sigbuf == NULL || dgstName == NULL)
    return(EINVAL);

  /* Allocates a public key algorithm context */
  ctx = EVP_PKEY_CTX_new(pkey, NULL /* no engine */);
  if (!ctx)
  {
    error = ERR_get_error();
    ERR_error_string_n(error, errstr, ERRBUFLEN);
    fprintf(stderr, "verify_signature(): EVP_PKEY_CTX_new()"
      " failed, error=%lu\n%s\n", error, errstr);
    return(-1);
  }

  /* Initialize the public key algorithm context for verification */
  if (EVP_PKEY_verify_init(ctx) <= 0)
  {
    error = ERR_get_error();
    ERR_error_string_n(error, errstr, ERRBUFLEN);
    fprintf(stderr, "verify_signature(): EVP_PKEY_verify_init()"
      " failed, error=%lu\n%s\n", error, errstr);
    EVP_PKEY_CTX_free(ctx);
    return(-2);
  }

  /* Set RSA padding */
  if (keytype == EVP_PKEY_RSA)
  {
    if (EVP_PKEY_CTX_set_rsa_padding(ctx, RSA_PKCS1_PADDING) <= 0)
    {
      error = ERR_get_error();
      ERR_error_string_n(error, errstr, ERRBUFLEN);
      fprintf(stderr, "verify_signature(): EVP_PKEY_CTX_set_rsa_padding()"
        " failed, error=%lu\n%s\n", error, errstr);
      EVP_PKEY_CTX_free(ctx);
      return(-3);
    }
  }

  /* Set the message digest type used in the signature */
  if (EVP_PKEY_CTX_set_signature_md(ctx, EVP_get_digestbyname(dgstName)) <= 0)
  {
```

```
   error = ERR_get_error();
   ERR_error_string_n(error, errstr, ERRBUFLEN);
   fprintf(stderr, "verify_signature(): EVP_PKEY_CTX_set_signature_md()"
      " failed, error=%lu\n%s\n", error, errstr);
   EVP_PKEY_CTX_free(ctx);
   return(-4);
}

/* Verify the digital signature */
/* ret == 1 means success, 0 verify failure and < 0 for some other error. */
ret = EVP_PKEY_verify(ctx, sigbuf, siglen, digest, dgstlen);
if (ret != 1)
{
   error = ERR_get_error();
   ERR_error_string_n(error, errstr, ERRBUFLEN);
   fprintf(stderr, "verify_signature(): EVP_PKEY_verify()"
      " failed, error=%lu\n%s\n", error, errstr);
   EVP_PKEY_CTX_free(ctx);
   return(-5);
}
fprintf(stdout, "verify_signature(): signature was successfully "
   "verified!\n");

EVP_PKEY_CTX_free(ctx);
return(0);
}


/*
 * This function generates RSA parameters and a pair of RSA public and
 * private keys.
 * Input parameters:
 *    keytype - specify the key type (EVP_PKEY_RSA)
 *    keylen - specify how many bits the key has
 * Output parameters:
 *    keypair - return the new asymmetric keypair generated
 *    If *keypair is NULL on input, it will be allocated, and should be freed
 *    by the caller after use.
 */

int generate_RSAkey(int keytype, unsigned int keylen, EVP_PKEY **keypair)
{
   EVP_PKEY_CTX   *ctx_kp;                 /* context for keypair generation */
   int            ret;
   unsigned long error = 0L;               /* error code */
   char           errstr[ERRBUFLEN];    /* error string */

   if (keypair == NULL)
      return(EINVAL);

   /* Allocates the key context object using the key type */
   ctx_kp = EVP_PKEY_CTX_new_id(keytype, NULL);
   if (ctx_kp == NULL)
   {
      error = ERR_get_error();
      ERR_error_string_n(error, errstr, ERRBUFLEN);
      fprintf(stderr, "generate_RSAkey(): EVP_PKEY_CTX_new_id() failed,"
```

```
      " error=%lu\n%s\n", error, errstr);
    return(-1);
  }

  /* Initialize the public key algorithm context */
  ret = EVP_PKEY_keygen_init(ctx_kp);
  if (ret <= 0)
  {
    error = ERR_get_error();
    ERR_error_string_n(error, errstr, ERRBUFLEN);
    fprintf(stderr, "generate_RSAkey(): EVP_PKEY_keygen_init() failed,"
      " error=%lu\n%s\n", error, errstr);
    EVP_PKEY_CTX_free(ctx_kp);
    return(-2);
  }

  /* Generate RSA keypair and store the result in keypair */
  /* Alternatively, ret = EVP_PKEY_keygen(ctx_kp, keypair); */
  ret = EVP_PKEY_generate(ctx_kp, keypair);
  if (ret <= 0)
  {
    error = ERR_get_error();
    ERR_error_string_n(error, errstr, ERRBUFLEN);
    fprintf(stderr, "generate_RSAkey(): EVP_PKEY_keygen() failed,"
      " error=%lu\n%s\n", error, errstr);
    EVP_PKEY_CTX_free(ctx_kp);
    return(-3);
  }

  /* Destroy all except the keypair */
  EVP_PKEY_CTX_free(ctx_kp);

  return(0);
}


/*
 * This function generates DSA parameters and a pair of DSA public and
 * private keys. Note that two separate context objects are needed in DSA.
 * Input parameters:
 *   keytype - specify the key type (EVP_PKEY_DSA).
 *   keylen - specify how many bits the key has
 * Output parameters:
 *   keypair - return the new asymmetric keypair generated
 *   If *keypair is NULL on input, it will be allocated, and should be freed
 *   by the caller after use.
 */

/* Macro for freeing all resources */
#define FREEALL  \
  EVP_PKEY_free(params); \
  EVP_PKEY_CTX_free(ctx_params); \
  EVP_PKEY_CTX_free(ctx_kp);

int generate_DSAkey(int keytype, unsigned int keylen, EVP_PKEY **keypair)
{
  EVP_PKEY      *params = NULL;      /* parameters for key generation */
```

```
EVP_PKEY_CTX  *ctx_params = NULL;  /* context for params generation */
EVP_PKEY_CTX  *ctx_kp;             /* context for keypair generation */
int           ret;
unsigned long error = 0L;          /* error code */
char          errstr[ERRBUFLEN];   /* error string */

if (keypair == NULL)
  return(EINVAL);

/* Allocates the key parameter context using the key type */
ctx_params = EVP_PKEY_CTX_new_id(keytype, NULL);
if (ctx_params == NULL)
{
  error = ERR_get_error();
  ERR_error_string_n(error, errstr, ERRBUFLEN);
  fprintf(stderr, "generate_DSAkey(): EVP_PKEY_CTX_new_id() failed,"
    " error=%lu\n%s\n", error, errstr);
  return(-1);
}

/* Initialize key parameter generation */
ret = EVP_PKEY_paramgen_init(ctx_params);
if (ret <= 0)
{
  error = ERR_get_error();
  ERR_error_string_n(error, errstr, ERRBUFLEN);
  fprintf(stderr, "generate_DSAkey(): EVP_PKEY_paramgen_init() failed,"
    " error=%lu\n%s\n", error, errstr);
  EVP_PKEY_CTX_free(ctx_params);
  return(-2);
}

/* Set DSA key generation parameters - nbits */
ret = EVP_PKEY_CTX_set_dsa_paramgen_bits(ctx_params, keylen);
if (ret <= 0)
{
  error = ERR_get_error();
  ERR_error_string_n(error, errstr, ERRBUFLEN);
  fprintf(stderr, "generate_DSAkey(): EVP_PKEY_CTX_set_dsa_paramgen_bits()"
    " failed, error=%lu\n%s\n", error, errstr);
  EVP_PKEY_CTX_free(ctx_params);
  return(-3);
}

/* Generate key parameters and store the results in params */
ret = EVP_PKEY_paramgen(ctx_params, &params);
if (ret <= 0)
{
  error = ERR_get_error();
  ERR_error_string_n(error, errstr, ERRBUFLEN);
  fprintf(stderr, "generate_DSAkey(): EVP_PKEY_paramgen() failed,"
    " error=%lu\n%s\n", error, errstr);
  EVP_PKEY_CTX_free(ctx_params);
  return(-4);
}
```

```
/* Create the public key algorithm context using the generated parameters */
ctx_kp = EVP_PKEY_CTX_new(params, NULL);
if (!ctx_kp)
{
    error = ERR_get_error();
    ERR_error_string_n(error, errstr, ERRBUFLEN);
    fprintf(stderr, "generate_DSAkey(): EVP_PKEY_CTX_new() failed,"
        " error=%lu\n%s\n", error, errstr);
    EVP_PKEY_free(params);
    EVP_PKEY_CTX_free(ctx_params);
    return(-5);
}

/* Initialize the public key algorithm context */
ret = EVP_PKEY_keygen_init(ctx_kp);
if (ret <= 0)
{
    error = ERR_get_error();
    ERR_error_string_n(error, errstr, ERRBUFLEN);
    fprintf(stderr, "generate_DSAkey(): EVP_PKEY_keygen_init() failed,"
        " error=%lu\n%s\n", error, errstr);
    FREEALL
    return(-6);
}

/* Generate DSA keypair and store the result in keypair */
/* Alternatively, ret = EVP_PKEY_keygen(ctx_kp, keypair); */
ret = EVP_PKEY_generate(ctx_kp, keypair);
if (ret <= 0)
{
    error = ERR_get_error();
    ERR_error_string_n(error, errstr, ERRBUFLEN);
    fprintf(stderr, "generate_DSAkey(): EVP_PKEY_keygen() failed,"
        " error=%lu\n%s\n", error, errstr);
    FREEALL
    return(-7);
}

/* Destroy all except the keypair */
FREEALL

return(0);
}


/* ==================== TLS/SSL utility functions ==================== */

/*
 * This function loads certificate and private key from files.
 * Parameters:
 *    ctx (input) - SSL context
 *    certfile (input) - name of certificate file
 *    keyfile (input) - name of file containing the private key
 */
int load_certificate(SSL_CTX *ctx, char *certfile, char *keyfile)
{
    int    ret;
```

1332

```
  /* Clear the error queue */
  ERR_clear_error();

  /* Load certificate from a file into the SSL context */
  ret = SSL_CTX_use_certificate_file(ctx, certfile, SSL_FILETYPE_PEM);
  if (ret != OPENSSL_SUCCESS)
  {
    fprintf(stderr, "Error: SSL_CTX_use_certificate_file() failed\n");
    ERR_print_errors_fp(stderr);
    return(OPENSSL_ERR_BAD_CERTFILE);
  }

  /* Load the private key into SSL context */
  ret = SSL_CTX_use_PrivateKey_file(ctx, keyfile, SSL_FILETYPE_PEM);
  if (ret != OPENSSL_SUCCESS)
  {
    fprintf(stderr, "Error: SSL_CTX_use_PrivateKey_file() failed\n");
    ERR_print_errors_fp(stderr);
    return(OPENSSL_ERR_BAD_KEYFILE);
  }

  /* Verify the private key just loaded into the SSL context */
  ret = SSL_CTX_check_private_key(ctx);
  if (ret != OPENSSL_SUCCESS)
  {
    fprintf(stderr, "Error: SSL_CTX_check_private_key() failed\n");
    ERR_print_errors_fp(stderr);
    return(OPENSSL_ERR_KEY_MISMATCH);
  }

  return(0);
}

/*
 * Display information in an X509 certificate.
 * Input argument: cert -- pointer to an X.509 certificate.
 */
int display_certificate_info(X509 *cert)
{
  X509_NAME *nm = NULL;          /* X509 name */
  int    version;
  ASN1_INTEGER  *serial_num;     /* serial number of the certificate */
  BIGNUM        *bignum;
  char          *serialptr;      /* pointer to a serial number */

  const ASN1_TIME *time1;        /* start time of cert valid time period */
  const ASN1_TIME *time2;        /* end time of cert valid time period */
  BIO   *outbio = NULL;          /* BIO output stream */

  int sig_algrtm_nid;            /* nid of signature algorithm */
  const char* namebuf;           /* buffer for signature algorithm's name */

  int     isca;                  /* is a valid CA certificate */
  EVP_PKEY *pubkey = NULL;       /* public key of the certificate */
  int     ret;
```

```
if (cert == NULL)
  return(EINVAL);

/* Is this a self-signed certificate? */
if (X509_check_issued(cert, cert) == X509_V_OK)
  fprintf(stdout, "This is a self-signed certificate.\n");
else
  fprintf(stdout, "This is not a self-signed certificate.\n");

/* Extract and print the subject name from the X.509 certificate */
nm = X509_get_subject_name(cert);
if (nm != NULL)
{
  fprintf(stdout, "  Subject of the X509 certificate:\n    ");
  X509_NAME_print_ex_fp(stdout, nm, 0, 0);
}
else
  fprintf(stderr, "Error, X509_get_subject_name() failed\n");

/* Extract and print the issuer name from the X.509 certificate */
nm = X509_get_issuer_name(cert);
if (nm != NULL)
{
  fprintf(stdout, "\n  Issuer of the X509 certificate:\n    ");
  X509_NAME_print_ex_fp(stdout, nm, 0, 0);
  fprintf(stdout, "\n");
}
else
  fprintf(stderr, "Error, X509_get_issuer_name() failed\n");

/* Extract and print the certificate's serial number */
serial_num = X509_get_serialNumber(cert);
if (serial_num != NULL)
{
  bignum = ASN1_INTEGER_to_BN(serial_num, NULL);
  if (!bignum)
    fprintf(stderr, "Error, ASN1_INTEGER_to_BN() failed to convert "
      "ASN1INTEGER to BN\n");
  else
  {
    serialptr = BN_bn2dec(bignum);
    fprintf(stdout, "  Serial number of the X509 certificate: %s\n", serialptr);
    BN_free(bignum);
  }
}
else
  fprintf(stderr, "Error, X509_get_serialNumber() failed\n");

/* Extract and print the certificate's valid time period */
time1 = X509_getm_notBefore(cert);
time2 = X509_getm_notAfter(cert);
outbio = BIO_new_fp(stdout, BIO_NOCLOSE);
if (time1 != NULL && time2 != NULL)
{
  if (outbio != NULL)
```

```c
  {
    BIO_printf(outbio, "  Validity period: from ");
    ASN1_TIME_print(outbio, time1);
    BIO_printf(outbio, " to ");
    ASN1_TIME_print(outbio, time2);
    BIO_printf(outbio, "\n");
  }
  else
    fprintf(stderr, "Cannot print validity period because outbio is NULL.\n");
}
else
  fprintf(stderr, "Error, failed to get start or end valid time\n");

/* Extract and print the certificate's X509 version - zero-based */
version = ((int) X509_get_version(cert)) + 1;
  fprintf(stdout, "  Version of the X509 certificate: %u\n", version);

/* Extract and print the certificate's signature algorithm */
sig_algrtm_nid = X509_get_signature_nid(cert);
if (sig_algrtm_nid != NID_undef)
{
  namebuf = OBJ_nid2ln(sig_algrtm_nid);
  if (namebuf != NULL)
    fprintf(stdout, "  Certificate's signature algorithm: %s\n", namebuf);
  else
    fprintf(stderr, "Error, OBJ_nid2ln() failed to convert nid to name\n");
}
else
  fprintf(stderr, "Error, X509_get_signature_nid() failed to get signature"
    " algorithm's nid\n");

/* See if this is a CA certificate */
isca = X509_check_ca(cert);
if (isca >= 1)
  fprintf(stdout, "  This is a valid CA certificate (ret=%d).\n", isca);
else
  fprintf(stdout, "  This is not a valid CA certificate.\n");

/* Extract and print the public key of the certificate */
pubkey = X509_get_pubkey(cert);
if (pubkey != NULL)
{
  if (outbio != NULL)
  {
    ret = EVP_PKEY_print_public(outbio, pubkey, 0, NULL);
    if (!ret)
      fprintf(stderr, "Error, EVP_PKEY_print_public() failed to print"
        " certificate's public key\n");
    /* must free the pubkey */
    EVP_PKEY_free(pubkey);
  }
  else
    fprintf(stderr, "Cannot print public key because outbio is NULL.\n");
}
else
  fprintf(stderr, "Error, X509_get_pubkey() failed to extract public key\n");
```

```
  if (outbio) BIO_free(outbio);
  return(0);
}


/*
 * Display information about the subject and issuer of a X509 certificate
 * used in an SSL/TLS handshaking.
 * If you like to see more details of the certificate, change this
 * function to call display_certificate_info(X509 *cert) instead.
 * Input argument: ssl -- a SSL structure representing a SSL connection
 */
void display_ssl_certificate_info(SSL* ssl)
{
  X509       *cert = NULL;    /* X509 certificate */
  X509_NAME *nm = NULL;       /* X509 name */

  /* Get the X509 certificate of the peer */
  cert = SSL_get_peer_certificate(ssl); /* get the server's certificate */

  /* Here we're simply interested in subject and issuer's names.
   * For full details of a certificate, call
   * display_certificate_info(X509 *cert) instead.
   */
  if ( cert != NULL )
  {
    /* Extract and print the subject name from the X.509 certificate */
    nm = X509_get_subject_name(cert);
    if (nm != NULL)
    {
      fprintf(stdout, "  Subject of the X509 certificate:\n    ");
      X509_NAME_print_ex_fp(stdout, nm, 0, 0);
    }
    /* Extract and print the issuer name from the X.509 certificate */
    nm = X509_get_issuer_name(cert);
    if (nm != NULL)
    {
      fprintf(stdout, "\n  Issuer of the X509 certificate:\n    ");
      X509_NAME_print_ex_fp(stdout, nm, 0, 0);
      fprintf(stdout, "\n\n");
    }
  }
  else
    fprintf(stdout, "No peer certificates received.\n");
}


/*
 * Print error returned from TLS/SSL I/O functions.
 */
void print_ssl_io_error(int error)
{
  switch (error)
  {
    case SSL_ERROR_NONE:
      fprintf(stderr, "SSL_ERROR_NONE\n");
    break;
```

```
   case SSL_ERROR_ZERO_RETURN:
     fprintf(stderr, "SSL_ERROR_ZERO_RETURN\n");
   break;
   case SSL_ERROR_WANT_READ:
     fprintf(stderr, "SSL_ERROR_WANT_READ\n");
   break;
/*
   case ERROR_WANT_WRITE:
     fprintf(stderr, "ERROR_WANT_WRITE\n");
   break;
*/
   case SSL_ERROR_WANT_CONNECT:
     fprintf(stderr, "SSL_ERROR_WANT_CONNECT\n");
   break;
   case SSL_ERROR_WANT_ACCEPT:
     fprintf(stderr, "SSL_ERROR_WANT_ACCEPT\n");
   break;
   case SSL_ERROR_WANT_X509_LOOKUP:
     fprintf(stderr, "SSL_ERROR_WANT_X509_LOOKUP\n");
   break;
   case SSL_ERROR_WANT_ASYNC:
     fprintf(stderr, "SSL_ERROR_WANT_ASYNC\n");
   break;
/*
   case SSL_ERROR_WANT_ASYNC_JOB:
     fprintf(stderr, "SSL_ERROR_WANT_ASYNC_JOB\n");
   break;
*/
   case SSL_ERROR_SYSCALL:
     fprintf(stderr, "SSL_ERROR_SYSCALL\n");
   break;
   case SSL_ERROR_SSL:
     fprintf(stderr, "SSL_ERROR_SSL\n");
   break;
   other:
     fprintf(stderr, "Unknown error\n");
   }
}


/*
 * Display the cipher suites used in the SSL/TLS connection.
 */
void display_cipher_suites(SSL *ssl)
{
  const char *cipher;
  int        i;

  fprintf(stdout, "Cipher suite(s) used:");
  for( i = 0; (cipher = SSL_get_cipher_list( ssl, i )); i++ )
    fprintf(stdout, "  %s", cipher );
  fprintf(stdout, "\n");
}
```

Questions

1. List and describe different aspects of security in computer network communications.

2. What aspect(s) of security does each of the following achieve?
   (a) hash (b) HMAC (c) digital signature (d) encryption

3. What are SHA-1, SHA-2 and SHA-3?

4. What is MAC? What is HMAC? What is the difference between MAC and HMAC?

5. What is symmetric cryptography? What is asymmetric cryptography?

6. What algorithms are symmetric cryptography?
   What algorithms are asymmetric cryptography?

7. Describe how RSA and Diffie-Hellman cipher algorithms work.

8. What is block cipher? And what is stream cipher?
   List some symmetric block cipher algorithms.

9. Usually which type of cryptography is used to sign a message digest and which type of cryptography is used to sign a message itself? Why?

10. What is digital signature?

11. Explain how RSA and DSA digital signature algorithms work.
    Describe the differences between RSA and DSA signatures.

12. What is nonrepudiation? How is it achieved?

13. When messages are encrypted and signed, is it safer to encrypt first and sign second?

14. Is it more secure to sign the message itself or sign its digest?

15. Why is key establishment/exchange necessary?

16. What is the difference between 'key transport' and 'key agreement'?
    Give one algorithm as an example for each.

17. Describe how Diffie-Hellman Key Exchange/Agreement works.

18. Describe how RSA Key Exchange works.

19. Explain how 'master secret' is derived during key establishment?

20. What is PKI?

21. What is public key encryption used for? And what is private key encryption used for?

22. Explain what algorithms are used for key exchange, digital signature, encryption and message digest in the TLS_DH_RSA_WITH_3DES_EDE_CBC_SHA

cipher suite?

23. What are SSL and TLS? What are they for?

24. What security features do SSL/TLS protocols provide?

25. What are the differences between SSL and TLS?

26. What messages are exchanged between an SSL/TLS client and an SSL/TLS server during the handshake phase when client authentication is required?

27. Does the design of SSL/TLS tilt toward protecting server more?

28. Which security aspect could potentially be SSL/TLS' weakest link if the server serves sensitive data?

29. What is a digital certificate? What does a digital certificate mainly contain?

30. Describe the structure of an X.509 certificate.

31. What is a CA (certificate authority)? What is a certificate chain?

32. What are the formats of certificate files?

33. How do you convert a certificate file from DER format to PEM format?

34. What are the main applications of public key cryptography?

Exercises

1. Download OpenSSL software, build and install it on your machine.

2. Dump the SSL/TLS messages when you run some of the example programs. Identify the key exchange algorithm used and the premaster secret or D-H parameters sent by each party.

3. Do performance measurements of the programs tcpclntdsa and tcpsrvdsa and list the elapsed times of each of the major steps and function calls.

4. Do a performance measurement of RSA and DSA/DSS digital signature algorithms and compare them.

5. Create certificates for your own server, intermediate CA, and root CA where root CA certificate is self-signed, intermediate CA is signed by the root CA, and the server certificate is signed by the intermediate CA.

6. Using the certificates you created for your own server, intermediate CA, and root CA, modify the file names for these certificates, rebuild the programs, and make sure the following client-server pairs run fine:
   (a) tlsclient1 and tlsserver1
   (b) tlsclient2 and tlsserver2

(c) tlsclient3 and tlsserver3
(d) tlsclient4 and tlsserver4
(e) tlsclient4 and tlsserver5

7. Modify the tlsclient4.c and tlsserver4.c to display all cipher suites.

8. Write a pair of client-server programs demonstrating use of the SSL_CTX_use_certificate_file() and SSL_CTX_use_certificate_chain_file() OpenSSL functions.

9. Write a pair of client-server programs where the client sends a file to the server. The file contents should be encrypted during transport. In addition, it should ensure that the file is received without any error or corruption. Code it such that different encryption and hash algorithms can be used.

10. Repeat the above exercise of file transferring but use SSL/TLS protocol this time.

11. Write a pair of client-server programs communicating via SSL/TLS protocols where the client tries to set a particular cipher suite.

12. Modify the mydecrypt2() function in enc_evp2.c in Figure 15-11 so that it works with encryption/decryption algorithms in GCM mode.

References

1. SSL and TLS: Designing and Building Secure Systems, by Eric Rescorla, Addison Wesley 2001

2. Computer Security: Art and Science, by Matt Bishop, Addison-Wesley 2003

3. Implementing SSL/TLS Using Cryptography and PKI, by Joshua Davies, Wiley Publishing, Inc. 2011

4. Applied Cryptography, by B. Schneier, John Wiley and Sons, New York, NY.

5. Computer Security Basics, by Deborah Russell and G. T. Gangemi Sr. O'Reilly & Associates. Inc.

6. PKI: Implementing and Managing E-Security, by Andrew Nash, William Duane, Celia Joseph, and Derek Brink, Osborne/McGraw-Hill

7. B. Moeller (May 20, 2004), Security of CBC Ciphersuites in SSL/TLS: Problems and Countermeasures.

8. Kuo-Tsang Huang, Jung-Hui Chiu, and Sung-Shiou Shen (January 2013). "A Novel Structure with Dynamic Operation Mode for Symmetric-Key Block Ciphers". International Journal of Network Security & Its Applications (IJNSA).

9. "Stream Cipher Reuse: A Graphic Example". Cryptosmith LLC.

10. FIPS 180-4: Secure Hash Standards, NIST, August 2015

11. Wikipedia, https://en.wikipedia.org/wiki/SHA-1

12. Wikipedia, https://en.wikipedia.org/wiki/SHA-2

13. Wikipedia, https://en.wikipedia.org/wiki/SHA-3

14. Wikipedia, https://en.wikipedia.org/wiki/MD5

15. https://en.wikipedia.org/wiki/Hash-based_message_authentication_code

16. Wikipedia, https://en.wikipedia.org/wiki/Block_cipher

17. https://en.wikipedia.org/wiki/Block_cipher_mode_of_operation

18. Wikipedia, https://en.wikipedia.org/wiki/Triple_DES

19. Wikipedia, https://en.wikipedia.org/wiki/Advanced_Encryption_Standard

20. https://en.wikipedia.org/wiki/International_Data_Encryption_Algorithm

21. https://en.wikipedia.org/wiki/CAST-128

22. https://en.wikipedia.org/wiki/Galois/Counter_Mode

23. Wikipedia, https://en.wikipedia.org/wiki/Public-key_cryptography

24. https://en.wikipedia.org/wiki/Public_key_infrastructure

25. Wikipedia, https://en.wikipedia.org/wiki/Diffie-Hellman_key_exchange

26. https://en.wikipedia.org/wiki/Message_authentication_code

27. https://en.wikipedia.org/wiki/Digital_Signature_Algorithm

28. https://en.wikipedia.org/wiki/Certificate_authority

29. https://en.wikipedia.org/wiki/Certificate_revocation_list

30. https://en.wikipedia.org/wiki/Transport_Layer_Security

31. OpenSSL man pages: https://www.openssl.org/docs/manmaster/

32. Security Guidance for ICA and Network Connections,
    Tariq Bin Azad, 2008
    https://www.sciencedirect.com/topics/computer-science/diffie-hellman-key-exchange

33. Diffie-Hellman key exchange, Wikipedia
    https://en.wikipedia.org/wiki/Diffie%E2%80%93Hellman_key_exchange

16 Software Design Principles and Programming Tips

The ultimate goal of this book is to help promote architecting and developing first-class software and improve the overall quality of software. This chapter discusses many software design principles and programming tips that work toward that ultimate goal.

Note that this subject is worth perhaps multiple books by itself. Here we just like to present some of the principles and tips that I find very useful in day-to-day software development.

16-1 Art, Science and Engineering of Programming

Computer programming is a very creative and yet very thoughtful activity.

It is creative because there always exist many different ways to solve a problem. And almost every engineer will come up with a different solution. That's the art component of computer programming.

However, there is also the science and engineering component of programming. That's why the major is called computer science or computer engineering at college.

Among the many different solutions to a problem, there are good and bad. And many times there are even right and wrong! This is because the quality of a software solution can be measured using many metrics and principles.

It's not like painting that any work can be claimed as good because it's pure art; being subjective in evaluating it usually does no harm. However, quality of software products is a completely different story. Bad-quality software products can kill people when they are used in airplanes and hospital equipment. And I believe to promote software quality, this science and engineering component needs to be emphasized more and all software engineers need to be more well-prepared and trained before they start working. And I hope this book could end up making its tiny share of contribution in this regard.

Unfortunately, in the real world today, many of the basics are not done right or even practiced in many world-famous software products. Many products have too many bugs and issues. And their quality is just very low.

As software practitioners, we ought to always aim at building software that is very robust, just works by itself, has no or almost no bugs, no issues, is very easy to use, very simple, secure, high-performance and scalable, needs no babysitting, needs zero or near-zero maintenance, and gets no or almost no support calls from customers. This is the standard that I believe all of us should work toward.

16-2 Designing and Developing First-class Software

All software should be first-class software.

A **first-class software** is one that is simple, robust, high-performance, secure, scalable, user-friendly, very easy to use, sharing code, always backward compatible, doing concurrency, synchronization and IPC right, and needing near-zero maintenance. It is software designed and implemented by real experts, done in the right way, has absolutely no unnecessary complexities, thoroughly tested and has no or almost no bugs.

It's the sum of doing everything the right way in so many different aspects and over so many stages, from gathering customer requirements, investigating its feasibility, designing, writing functional and design specifications, public review of the specifications, coding, building the software, developing tests, unit testing, integration testing, performance testing, stress testing, alpha and beta tests, documentation and releasing.

A first-class software is designed with all of the following key principles:

- Data Integrity
- Robustness
- Simplicity
- Security
- Ease of Use
- Scalability
- High performance
- No single point of failure
- Code sharing
- Storing data in a single place
- Maintaining backward compatibility
- Easily extensible
- Needing minimum effort to maintain
- Needing minimum effort to support

and is coded with first-class coding practices including the following:

- Always initialize a variable.
- Always check to ensure a pointer is not null before using it.
- Design error codes correctly and appropriately handle each error

We will elaborate upon these principles and practices in this chapter.

16-3 Software Design Principles -- Tips at Design Level

16-3-1 Robustness and No Single Point of Failure

It is very important that the system you design is extremely robust
and has very high availability.

System being down is a disruption to customer's business and it is costly.
Therefore, minimizing down time is always a requirement of any system design.
Traditionally, many kinds of operating systems (including Unix) have been
able to stay up and running without a reboot for many months or more than
a year or even longer. That's the minimum standard to live up to.
Software applications must do the same too at the very least.

When you design a system, whether it's hardware or software, it's very
important to make sure there is no single point of failure.

This means failure of a single component or system should not bring down the
application or entire system. Each component/system should have a redundancy
or replicated unit such that in case one fails the other could take over
and continue to function.

For instance, for high availability an enterprise database system typically
has a standby system where the primary database is replicated to another
standby/backup system in real time so that should the primary database
system fail, a failover from the primary to the standby will occur
and the business continues to operate on the standby system with
no or little disruption. Typically, companies require no downtime or a
brown-out period of just a few seconds a year.

In a distributed or clustered system where there are multiple computers in
a system, make sure the failure of a single node does not stop the entire
system from functioning.

Sometimes the original design of a system has redundancy so that no single
point of failure exists. But later on when the system is enhanced, more
components are introduced into the system and the new addition or expansion
introduces single point of failure. A regression in high availability is
introduced into the system during expansion or enhancement. Make sure you
don't do this.

I have seen a company making this mistake in two different product lines.
One is with a primary and standby database configuration.
A third system was added to the original design which provides some new
functionalities. But that new system becomes the single point of failure
because it has no standby at all.

The other is a security information repository system was added to a
cluster system where all nodes in the cluster store their security and
authentication information on the security server. The thing is without the
security information, the cluster nodes won't be able to function. So the
security server becomes a single point of failure.

A new building block is added to the entire system and that new block itself
creates a single point of failure. Ensure this does not happen to your
design or product!

Remember that if the system you design has a single point of failure, then it has an architectural flaw.

16-3-2 Always Store Data in a Single Place

Make sure a piece of data is stored in only one place, not two or more.

Over the years I have seen many designs where the same data is stored in more than one place. This is a very bad idea and design.

When the same information is stored in more than one place, it is very likely that the multiple copies will get out of sync. When that happens the same data will have two (or even more) different values depending upon from which place one gets it from. This would be a disaster.

Some may say that I can store it at two different locations (e.g. files) and always update them at the same time and keep them in sync. This has performance and consistency issues at least. First, why taking the performance hit of always having to update two copies of the same data? Second, most importantly, it's impossible to have an atomic operation that always updates two pieces of the data at the same time and guarantees they are always consistent and correct. Especially if the data is stored in files; one can always find a window where the system might crash in-between the two updates and that the two copies will end up being out of sync. We have discussed this in the concurrency control chapter. Essentially, at the very bottom level, today's computers achieve data integrity by relying on atomic assembly language instructions. And these instructions cannot update data in two separate files or even memory locations at the same time and always keep them consistent. So it's just impossible to do with today's computers.

That is, from concurrency point of view, there is no atomic instructions in any CPU I know of that can update two pieces of data at one operation and guarantee either both are changed at the same time or none. This means there is no way to guarantee two or more copies of the same data can always stay in sync. In other words, storing the same data at two different locations is almost to guarantee that they will get out of sync at some point in time unless they never get updated.

Consequently, it is very easy for the multiple copies of the same data to get out of sync and data integrity will be lost if you store the same data in more than one place. And that would be a nightmare. Therefore, make sure you never make this kind of mistake. Data integrity and consistency is paramount!

In short, it is extremely important to always store data in a single place. This is mainly for consistency sake. But it is also for simplicity and performance as well.

16-3-3 Always Ensure Integrity of Shared Data

In addition to always storing data in a single place, it's also extremely important that you always ensure data integrity.

Whenever some data is shared and can be concurrently updated by more than one thread or process, concurrency control must be implemented to serialize the concurrent updaters and ensure the integrity of the shared data. This is a data correctness issue.

It would be a disaster to not use some concurrency control mechanism to synchronize the concurrent updaters and hence lead to update loss or data corruption. A first-class software product must never let that happen! There is a reason why this book has a complete chapter on concurrency control. This is the very fundamental basis of all databases or even broader computer data processing. If data integrity is not guaranteed, then nothing is worth while.

For updating some shared data, a mutual exclusive lock must be taken to guarantee that only one updater at a time to preserve data integrity. And all threads or processes must strictly follow the same rule.

Over the course of my career, I have seen so many software engineers develop software missing necessary synchronizations and leading to numerous bugs. This should not have happened. That's why this book has a chapter (#9) on this subject.

Therefore, always guard any concurrent updates of a shared data with mutually exclusive locks to guarantee data integrity.

One type of the so-called "race condition" bugs actually is missing synchronization or not doing it right! There is no race condition if you always do the concurrency control right!

16-3-4 Always Have Necessary Synchronization

There are multiple types of synchronization. Ensuring mutual exclusion on concurrent updates of a shared data mentioned above is just one of them.

Another type of synchronization is that some application has multiple threads or processes collaborating on something and there is inter-dependency between the different tasks or jobs. Some process or thread has to wait until some or all others to finish.

While some thread or task depends on others, synchronization must also be done to ensure a thread does not proceed until its dependent is available. This is a different type of synchronization. In this case, instead of using an exclusive lock to synchronize, a condition variable, flag or counter is needed.

The producer-consumer problem we have discussed in the pthreads chapter is one of this kind where a condition variable is used for synchronization.

As a second example, imagine an application may use multiple concurrent threads to create multiple user certificates and one root certificate where the user certificates are signed by the root certificate. Since all of the user certificates must be signed by the root certificate, there exists a dependency or ordering between the threads. In this case, all the threads that create the user certificates must wait until the thread creating the root certificate successfully completes before they can complete. A flag indicating the root certificate is available can be used to synchronize the threads.

Make sure you always implement some synchronization mechanism to ensure correctness of the computation in cases like these.

16-3-5 Simplicity - Always Make Things Simple

To be honest, **simplicity** is the single area that many think the computer software industry as a whole has done poorest. It is also the area that I personally have had most frustrations with over my career from working on so many overly complex software products designed and implemented by other engineers.

Many software products in use today have enormous unnecessary complexities in them simply because their designers were not real experts and did many things the wrong way. It's a bit of shocking that even a lot of very basic things were not done right.

It's probably fair to say that the #1 crisis of the computer software industry is that many computer software products are way too complex and too buggy.

This reflects the education and training of many computer software engineers was inadequate and still has a huge room for improvements.

I have at least dozens, if not hundreds, of real examples. It's just too many to list all of them here. Just to give a couple of examples below.

In one case, I saw code doing just a network asynchronous connect takes tens of routines and more than 1500 lines of C code making dozens of subroutine calls several levels deep while I can do the same in 25 lines of very simple straight-line code with only two system calls (defined by the POSIX standard) as the only function calls. And the 25-line code works beautifully on all five different platforms supported.

In another case, an engineer was adding cross-endian support to an existing product. He ended up changing more than 50 source modules with 15,000 lines of code changes while it can be done by changing only two source modules and adding a total of 220 lines of code.

As a third example, in 1988, when I purchased AT&T System V Release 3.2 for my home PC, the entire Unix operating system, including both kernel and user spaces, came in 19 floppy disks (20 MB) and the size of the Unix kernel was just one MB in size. If you look at the sizes of today's system software products, they are all at several hundreds of MBs or even GBs.

It is extremely important that computer software engineers do things the right way and make complicated things simple. The right way to do things almost always turns out to be the simple way. In many ways, **programming is an art of knowing how to do the minimum and achieve the maximum.**

For many, this may be easier said than done.

To be able to do things the right way and make complicated things simple, software designers need to be an expert on what they do. And this means they need to have a very good understanding of many of the basic concepts, principles, technologies and techniques and know to use them. Besides, they also need to have a broad background and experience in multiple fields of computer and be familiar with the principles and technologies in those. This will enable them to see the problem at hand from the forest level instead of trees, address all potential issues in the design, take the right approach, use the right technologies and building blocks, and do the most with the least.

In a sense, this simplicity principle is what take most to achieve. One really has to be a real expert to be able to know how to solve the problem at hand in the simplest way!

Below are some of my observations over the years:

Good engineers make complicated things simple and bad engineers make simple things complicated.

Good engineers eliminate unnecessary work for themselves and for others whereas bad engineers create unnecessary work for themselves and for others.

16-3-6 Ease of Use and User-friendly

Making the software you design and implement very easy to use for the customers and users is always a very important task and part of your job as a software engineer.

It's very important that you put yourself in the end users' shoes when you are designing and developing a piece of software or component.

Ideally, a software product should just work after being installed. There is no need to do any extra configuration, setup or tuning. And if there is a user interface involved, it should be intuitive. In other words, making users' life simple is always one of the key design principles. The less users need to do or know to use the product, the better!

I have seen software products that have hundreds of tuning knobs and configuration is extremely complicated that almost no one can fully understand it. These are examples of very poor designs.

A product designed by real experts is always very simple and easy to use!

16-3-6-1 Try Not to Change User Interface

Trying not to change the user interface is one of the very basic principles of software design. It's very bad if users have to re-learn how to use your product at each new release. Who like to re-learn how to use a product every time there is a new version?

A user interface is a contract between software developers and users. If that has to change very often or even every version, it indicates that you as developers have no idea what you are doing.

It is extremely important to design the user interface right from the beginning and keep it the same throughout.

It's a terrible experience to users if the user interface of the software product you design keeps changing and the users have to re-learn each time a newer version comes out.

There have been some examples of companies failing on this. As a user of Windows I found I usually had to re-learn many things each time when I upgraded to a newer version.

I remember when Windows 8 came out, I looked at it and immediately told my friend that I would never upgrade to that version. Soon after, the product was canceled after it had been released. It's incredible that world-class companies could grow so out-of-touched and make this type of mistakes. Some of the things people failed to realize are very obvious. A all-touch-screen user interface works great for billions of casual users around the world. However, that does not mean the serious business users around the world can get their jobs done that way.

So do it right the first time and try not to change user interfaces of your product, at least not very dramatically or too often.

16-3-6-2 Make It Self-Configured, Self-Tuned or Dynamically Reconfigurable

Always try to make it very simple to use the product designed by you.

Ideally, you should make your software product setup-free, self-configured and self-tuned. Pick some default configurations and settings that would make sense to most users and start the software with those. That is, a very well-designed software should be able to start and run reasonably well without any setup, configuration or tuning by users. That's the goal everyone should shoot for.

A software should configure itself automatically, or at least configure itself at install time, based on user's inputs or machine configurations detected at install time.

If there is something that really needs to be user configurable in order to fit different needs, then try to make it automatically configured or very easy to configure or reconfigure. Always set a default value that makes senses for most users for a configurable parameter.

Try to minimize the configurations and/or tunings users have to do. If there is any setup, configuration or tuning required, make it as simple and easy as possible. Try to reduce the number of things or steps that users have to do. The less users need to do the better. It is a bad design if the software you design requires a lot of setups, user configurations or tunings, or very complicated configurations.

I have seen a very important availability product at a world famous company. And the long list of steps and extreme complexity that users have to go through to configure that product is just disgusting. I felt I did not really want to use the product or the features.

Of course, you want your product to be configurable and tunable so that it is very flexible and fits as many different customers' needs as possible. For that you want to build in some configurable or tunable parameter(s). On the other hand, you also want to minimize the configurations and tunings users have to do for your product to be user-friendly.

Try to build more intelligence into your product by automatically detecting machine hardware configurations and reconfiguring based on that information. Also try to make it self-detecting if something goes wrong or not working well and self-remedying.

And in case the user needs to reconfigure, make it very simple. The simpler the better. Make all configurations dynamic, meaning they can be done at run-time without restarting the application or system.

Having complicated setup, configuration or even tuning not only works against user experience but also is a source of bugs, mistakes and confusion. It makes the product more difficult to use and manage, decreases user satisfaction and creates more work and bugs.

16-3-7 Always Share Code -- Build and Use Subroutines and Library Functions

I still remember that when I took my first programming course at college, one of the things I learned then was that making any piece of code that is likely to appear more than once as a subroutine. Very sadly, decades later, I see this very basic is not even done in the code of a world famous company's products developed mostly by a group of very young engineers.

Making common functionalities or specific tasks as subroutines is one of the very basic principles in computer programming. We touched upon this issue in chapter 3.

Whenever a piece of code needs to appear more than once in the entire product, or whenever you are writing some code and you think someone else is likely to use it, or simply when you are just writing some code to perform a specific task, make it a function (i.e. library routine) so that it can be shared and re-used!

This practice has many advantages.

1. Code sharing. You do not repeat the same code in multiple places. It reduces the amount of code everyone has to write. It reduces the total code size of the product.

2. All components do the same processing exactly the same way by using exactly the same function/routine, a single API. This provides consistent behavior across the entire product.

3. If there is any bug or issue in the shared routine, there is a single place to fix, instead of multiple.

4. It makes the code well-structured and organized. It also makes the code simpler, easier to understand, and easy to maintain.

When you read a component's code comprising functions A, B and C, where
function A does two things by calling function D and E,
function B does three things by calling function F, G and H, and
function C does four things by calling function I, J, K and L,
you know you are getting a real treat working on this code!

When you design and develop a function, you are essentially introducing
a new API. Keep in mind that try to think it through who are the possible
clients and how they would want to use this and make it as generic as
possible through providing appropriate function parameters.

Ideally, you should not have to change the interface of the API throughout
its lifetime. Because if you do, you will have to change all of the
invocations/uses of it each time you update that function. That would result
in more work, and potentially compatibility and stability issues.

So, think it through upfront. Design it in and design it right the very
first time!

A very well designed and implemented software should always extract the
common functionalities, build them into a library, and have all components
use it so that there is absolutely no code duplication and every utility
function needed exists in the library.

Make sure that **common functionalities are always extracted and coded into
subroutines, shared and used by all components in the product.** If there is
anything goes wrong or needs to be changed or fixed, there is a single
place to do it, instead of multiple!

This is part of the reasons that this book has a chapter (#3) on how to
build and use your own library.

16-3-8 Maintain Backward Compatibility

It is very common that software needs to go through changes over time,
due to many different reasons including adding new functionalities,
enhancements, fixing bugs, performance optimizations, security fix, etc.

It's extremely important that **when you make changes to existing shipped code,
you always maintain full backward compatibility**. That is, after your change,
whatever work before must continue to work and work exactly the same way.
This is so that existing customers and users are not affected by your change
or fix at all; they don't notice any behavior or usage change after upgrading
to the new version with your changes. This very often means you have to
introduce your change/fix with a condition such that it kicks in or is in
effect only under the situation in which the problem you try to fix occurs.
The product continues to execute the old, existing code and work the same
old way in all other cases.

Typically, this is doable. That is, you can make changes to fix a bug
without changing any of the product's existing behavior. It's just you have
to try hard enough and it may need a bit of more work. In extremely rare
cases where backward compatibility cannot be maintained, it must be
documented and customers are warned. But make sure you absolutely have no
other alternatives before you break backward compatibility.

There are a couple of situations here. In a non-networking case, you just make modification to the existing algorithm and put your change inside an if statement to condition it so that your new code gets executed only in situation when it should be executed (that is, when the situation you try to fix occurs).

For example, a product may support hostnames of up to 32 characters only in current version and you would like to add an enhancement so that it will support up to 64 characters. Typically, if it was done right in the first place, this should be just one very simple change of one constant at a single place. That is it! But I have worked on a product that was terribly designed and it required not only changing code at 12 different places (instead of one) but also altering some existing algorithms because existing code uses hostnames in forming Unix Domain socket pathnames which have a maximum limit of 108 characters. As a result, I have to introduce all of my changes under an if (length_of_hostname > 32) condition to maintain 100% backward compatibility so that if users are using hostnames of 32 characters or less, nothing would change!

In a more complicated situation, if the change involves message exchanges between two programs, then versioning is what you need to do here. Make sure you have versioning built in. And to implement your change, you bump up the application protocol version, and add code in both ends of the communication channel to handle the new version of the protocol while all of the existing old protocol versions are not changed or ripped at all.

Ensure the new protocol version you are implementing with your changes works with both lower and higher versions of the product without breaking and still delivers correct or sensible results in every version combination. We have discussed how to do versioning right in chapter 14 of this book. The chapter on Distributed Application in this book demonstrates how to develop client-server software that always maintains backward compatibility.

Maintaining backward compatibility is showing basic respect to your customers and users. It helps your product win.

One of the reasons that Intel x86 microprocessors have been so successful and popular, and arguably won the processor war, is that it always maintains backward compatibility.

When 16-bit 80286 microprocessor came out,
all existing 8-bit 8086 and 8088 applications ran without modification.

When 32-bit 80386 microprocessor came out,
all existing 8086, 8088 and 80286 applications ran without modification.

When 80486 microprocessor came out,
all existing 8086, 8088, 80286 and 80386 applications ran without modification.

When Pentium microprocessor came out,
all existing 8086, 8088, 80286, 80386 and 80486 applications ran without modification. So did the multi-core processors,

and so on ...

Backward compatibility has been maintained throughout all Intel x86 families of processors over decades until now.

The number of applications written for the processor family continues to pile up and grow because backward compatibility is always kept. And that is what ultimately helps Intel win the competition and war. This is why so many other processors have come and gone (some of them were even technically superior and more advanced) but Intel x86 has been staying. It's the applications and backward compatibility that help win the war!

This is one example of maintaining backward compatibility helps win the war in computer hardware. It applies to computer software as well.

16-3-9 Always Design Security In

With network and Internet ubiquitous, security is becoming increasingly important each day. Make sure you always design security in. Indeed, each functional and/or design specification should always include a security section in it.

Security issues exist at multiple fronts: user authentication, data access, eavesdropping attack, spoofing attack, virus, denial-of-service attacks, etc. Recent attacks can even lock down a company's computer systems and cut off gas and food supply! We have touched upon some of these issues in the network security chapter (15) and also talked about how fend off some of the denial-of-service attacks in chapter 14 (14-2-1-2).

At the same time, remember to not overdo security. You want your software to be secure. But you want it to be user-friendly too. That is, you don't want to make it almost un-usable because of security. In addition, security measures often slow things down too. So be aware of its impact on performance. Sometimes tradeoff needs to be made and a delicate balance needs to be struck. **Remember don't go extreme on security and make your product almost unusable.**

16-3-10 Make It Very High-performance

It is very important that you have high-performance in mind when you design software. Making your software run faster gives it an advantage and it should always be one of your goals.

Be conscious about how long each task takes and ensure your software does not have performance bottlenecks. Understand what slows down your software and try to optimize it.

For examples, reading from disk is much slower than reading from memory. Hence, for some frequently used data residing on disk, you might want to cache it in memory. That is, reading it from disk only the first time and keeping it in memory for the rest of references, rather than reading it from disk every single time.

As a second example, as we have introduced in this book, there exist so many different interprocess communication mechanisms. Some of the tasks can be performed using more than one IPC mechanism. So you might want to do some performance measurements and comparisons and choose the best performing one. If it's interprocess communications between multiple processes on the same system, then System V shared memory can be a very good choice in terms of performance.

Another example is if some task takes long to perform, it may help to try to divide and conquer by dividing it into smaller pieces and having multiple threads or processes working on each small piece in parallel.

A fourth example is disk or network I/O is often slow compared to normal computation. It may help to perform asynchronous I/O instead of blocked I/O if the program can get some other things done while waiting for the disk or network I/O to complete. Separating the tasks into multiple threads is also an alternative.

Fifth, optimizing operations that get executed multiple times helps speed up too. For instance, we introduced multiple mutual exclusion technologies in chapter 9. Use a faster alternative to improve performance if it exists.

Sometimes a performance issue may be due to resource constraint and the limit on the resource is tunable. Examples include maximum number of processes allowed per user, maximum number of threads allowed per process, maximum stack size, maximum memory usage allowed for each process (e.g. this is tunable from command-line for a Java process), and so on. When it needs performance tuning (including networking applications), we've shown readers how in chapter 13 and section 9-9.

It is always a very good idea to include a performance section in each functional and/or design specification and do some measurements of performance of your product. Isolate the performance bottleneck spots and try to eliminate them.

16-3-11 Make It Scalable

Scalability is always important too because you want your software to be able to handle as many users or clients as possible. And you want to scale better in both cases where hardware resources remain the same and with more hardware resources available.

Make your software be able to do things in parallel or concurrently. It's very common to make your product multithreaded to scale well by taking advantage of multiple-core CPUs or multiprocessors, or even just avoiding wasting time in waiting for I/O to complete.

Remember the number of CPUs or cores available is not the only hardware resources that determine scalability. Make your software scale with the amount of memory, number of network cards, network bandwidth and so on too.

High performance helps scalability in some way too. Make your software run the fastest it can so that it's able to handle higher load given the same hardware resources.

Identify and eliminate scalability bottlenecks, if any. Develop or change your algorithms to take advantage of more resources available on the system. To improve scalability, use multithreads (chapter 8) and automatically detect hardware configurations (e.g. number of CPUs and amount of memory) and make your applications auto-scale to those.

16-3-12 Error Code Design and Error Handling

When it comes to error code design and error handling, unfortunately many engineers and architects tend to either ignore it or do it wrong. And the consequence of that is robustness and maintainability of the product are impacted.

Error codes may not seem important to many, or at least in the beginning of a project. But they are. If they are done right, it simplifies coding and makes maintaining, troubleshooting and supporting the product much easier. Life becomes much simpler and easier if you do error codes right.

Besides, correct and proper error handling is necessary for robustness of a software product.

16-3-12-1 Design the Error Codes Right

I had an opportunity to work on a product where each component defines its own enum data type for the error codes in that component. If the product has 30 components, this results in 30 different error code enum data types. You have to do type casting and error code conversion or mapping in so many places each time when the program control crosses component boundaries. It's an absolute nightmare to define one separate error data type for each component. It is not only unnecessary but also creating so much extra work and bugs. Make sure you don't do this!

The fact is that components don't stand alone. They call one another. Because components call one another, errors generated in one component must bubble up the calling stack and get passed through other components. Because errors originated in a component typically travel through many other components while bubbling up the calling stack, it's an absolute disaster to have each component defines its own error code data type! All the resulting error code mappings and error type castings when the control travels through component boundaries are all man-made overheads, unnecessary complexity and unnecessary extra work.

In the end, all of these different error codes are just numbers, integers. Why bother making them so many different data types and calling them in so many different names and then do the extra work of converting and casting them in so many different places? People did it in the name of type safety. But these are all just integers. What type unsafety there is? People just misuse the object-oriented 'type safety' concept!

Hence, **make sure you do the error codes right and make it simple!**

Each error code needs to have at least a couple of attributes. (1) It must be unique. (2) It is best if it tells what component it belongs to.

Therefore, the best way to design error codes for all components in a product written in C is to use only one error code data type, which traditionally is an integer in many Unix and Linux operating systems.

The right way to do it is to divide the value space of an integer into multiple disjoint segments and assign one separate segment to each component. That way, all of the error codes generated by all components in the product are all of the same data type and can be passed around through all components without doing any mapping or type casting.

Since the error codes from all components are all of the same data type, there is absolutely no need for any type casting anywhere. And because they never overlap or collide with each other, there is absolutely no error code mapping anywhere when the control travels across component boundaries! Every error code is unique. It tells you exactly which component it comes from.

Below is an example of how to divide up the entire error code space into different segments or ranges for use by different components.

```
#define ERROR_MIN        10000    /* minimum self-defined error code */
#define ERROR_MAX        500000   /* maximum self-defined error code */

#define ERR_COMP_A_MIN   10000    /* minimum error code from component A */
#define ERR_COMP_A_MAX   19999    /* maximum error code from component A */

#define ERR_COMP_B_MIN   20000    /* minimum error code from component B */
#define ERR_COMP_B_MAX   29999    /* maximum error code from component B */

#define ERR_COMP_C_MIN   30000    /* minimum error code from component C */
#define ERR_COMP_C_MAX   39999    /* maximum error code from component C */
    :

/* defined error codes for component A */
#define ERR_COMP_A_NODATA          10001
#define ERR_COMP_A_BAD_SIZE        10002
#define ERR_COMP_A_BAD_HOST        10003
#define ERR_COMP_A_CANNOT_CONNECT  10004
#define ERR_COMP_A_SEND_FAIL       10005
#define ERR_COMP_A_RECV_FAIL       10006
    :

/* defined error codes for component B */
#define ERR_COMP_B_BAD_INPUT       20001
#define ERR_COMP_B_USER_QUIT       20002
#define ERR_COMP_B_TIMEOUT         20003
    :

/* defined error codes for component C */
#define ERR_COMP_C_VAL_TOO_LONG    30001
#define ERR_COMP_C_NO_MEMORY       30002
#define ERR_COMP_C_TOO_MANY_FILES  30003
    :
```

This may be a bit mechanical, but that's the beauty of it!
I think you get the idea.

We start from the number 10000 because the first hundreds of integers are often reserved as operating system defined errors. We also allocate 10000 error numbers for each component. That should be enough.

To avoid overlapping with system defined errors, some prefer using negative integers. But that's not really necessary.

As you can see, there is absolutely no extra work at all if you do it right! It's extremely simple, neat and clean! This is how error codes should be done!

By the way, error messages corresponding to the error codes are typically translated into different languages for users in different countries. Besides, to help users know what to do with it, error messages typically also come with recommended actions telling users what to do to remedy the errors.

16-3-12-2 Handle Every Error Correctly

Error checking and handlings make a very crucial part of the robustness of a product.

To build a very robust product, there are at least two things must be done in this area.

One is every function, except for some very rare ones, should always return a status code. In other words, a typical function or subroutine should look like this:

```
int myfunc(...)
```

instead of

```
void myfunc(...)
```

Normally, the computation in a function can succeed or fail, except for some extremely simple ones which may never fail and in that case it's OK to have the function returning nothing (void). And the status of a function should always be returned to its caller such that the caller knows whether the task has been completed successfully or not. And if not, what the error is.

Second, once an error occurs, it is the calling function(s)'s responsibility to ensure that every error condition is checked and correctly or at least properly handled. This really in part decides how robust a product is.

Of course, in some cases, a calling function may not have the required information or be able to handle certain errors. And all it can do is to continue to pass the error up the calling stack. Therefore, deciding which function should actually handle a particular error is another factor affecting the robustness of a product.

In summary, returning, checking and correctly handling every error case is absolutely required to develop a very robust software product, besides what we will talk about in the Programming Tips section in 16-4.

16-3-13 Make It Generic

I thought this is very obvious, but we would like to point it out just in case.

Whenever you design something, a function, subroutine or even a feature, make it work for general cases, instead of a special one.

In general, try to make the software you develop as generic as possible. Don't make it work just for one particular case or two. Make it work for all (or at least most) cases.

If the different cases need to have different behaviors or processing, you can write a function for all while it takes an input parameter to distinguish the different cases. The actual value of this input parameter can come from the caller, user input, or even reading it in from a data file. This is much better than just making it work for one particular case.

As an example, if you develop a socket program, make sure it works for any host or any IP address. Do not hardwire the host name or IP address in your code. Make your program works for any computer host instead of just one particular host. In addition, it should work for both IPv4 and IPv6 protocols.

In short, make the code a function or subroutine and make it generic so that it handles all cases. Take each specific case from the caller as an input parameter.

16-3-14 Make It Agnostic

Try to make the software you design agnostic whenever you can. For instance, when you write networking socket software, try to make it agnostic to IP protocols. That is, make it work regardless of whether the system uses IPv4 or IPv6 protocol.

Another example is, if you are writing something that has to do with users (e.g. creating and reading files), make it user agnostic whenever you can. In other words, make it not specific to or only work with a particular user. The best solution is user-agnostic. That is, no matter which user creates the file and which user tries to use the file, it should always work except for any security reason, which can be controlled through the file's permission. Specifically, in general, a file created by user A should be able to be used by user B.

If there is any security concern that a certain group of users must be excluded, use the file and/or directory permissions to control it. Except for some special cases where you like to restrict access, in general a piece of code creating and reading/writing a file should work regardless what user creates the file and what user tries to read/write it.

While working at a very big and famous company, I have seen engineers creating APIs which end up being if user A creates a file and user B tries to read the file, the file cannot be found even if user B is given all read/write/execute permissions to it. It's because when the file is created, it is hidden in a subdirectory named after its creator. No wonder user B cannot access files created by user A. That is not how software should work. This type of bugs should never happen.

16-3-15 Make It Idempotent When It Makes Sense

Being idempotent means when you perform an operation one or multiple times, they all end up with exactly the same result.

The most common example is that assigning a value to a variable is idempotent. If you try to set the value of a variable x to be 5, no matter how many times you do it, the result is all the same -- its value is 5.

Another example, closing a file once, twice or three times should get the same result. So this operation should be idempotent. Releasing a lock should be idempotent, too.

Yet another example, take the example of "shutting down a software". When a user issues the command to shutdown a software, if the user issues the same command twice in a row, the end result should stay the same as the user just issues the same command once.

In other words, repeating the same operation should not cause any harm and should produce the same result as if the operation is done only once.

In computer programming, not everything should be idempotent but certain things should. For instance, increment the value of a variable by one. This operation is not and should not be idempotent.

It's a correctness and reliability issue. Therefore, make sure you correctly identify the operations that should be idempotent and make them so via your design and implementation! It's a bug if something should be idempotent but it's actually not.

16-3-16 Don't Introduce Regression

It is very important that you always make sure when a new version of the software product comes out, it does not have any regression.

Regression means going backward in quality; something used to work no longer works.

You always want to go forward rather than backward in software development. That is, every newer version must be better than, or at least as good as, its previous one. In shipping a new version, you want everything used to work continues to work plus the new features and enhancements also work. It's not good to get new features and/or enhancements with some existing functionality broken.

To avoid regression, you rely on regression test suites. Each time when you develop a new feature, fix a bug, or make a change, you write tests for it. Hence, regression tests grow and accumulate over time.

When you make changes or bug fixes or add new enhancements, make sure you always run all regression suites of the entire product and make sure there is no regression. It's very bad to ship a new version of a product with regression. Besides, to prevent anyone from accidentally breaking your code changes, you should also add a new test or test case to existing regression test suites for it.

This is part of quality control. It depends on having complete and robust test suites and you always run them. The richer and more complete your test suites are the better because it will be more likely to catch any regressions and give you higher confidence of the quality of the product.

16-3-17 Don't Break Upgrade or Downgrade

Typically, customers move to a newer version of a product by doing an upgrade rather than doing a full fresh install of the newer version. First-class software always allows customers to upgrade from one existing version to the next, instead of requiring a full reinstallation of the new version.

Each time when you make code changes, whether it's adding new functionalities or enhancements, or fixing bugs, make sure your changes don't break the upgrade process. It's very important to support upgrade and make sure the product upgrade process continues to work all the time. So have a upgrade regression test suite and run that to make sure your changes do not break the product upgrade.

All is said here applies equally to downgrade as well!

16-3-18 Do It Right the First Time and Do It Once for All

It's very important that when you design software, you do it right in the first place. This is because if you do not do things the right way in the first place, then after the product is shipped, it's often almost impossible to redo it because customers are already using the product and you are not allowed to change the design and behavior.

Besides, in many cases, if you don't do things right in the beginning, then the enhancements and/or bug fixes that come later would often have to be done in a more complex or awkward way. Complexities then multiply and may eventually explode. It's often one unnecessary complexity piles up on another, and yet another, and so on that eventually leads to complexity explosion. It all starts with things not done right in the first place.

The consequence is extremely costly when engineers do not do things the right way in the first place. It leads to over-bloated software which does not really work and is buggy. It generates too many bugs, which creates unnecessary service calls from customers. Every bug reported uses up a lot of company's resources. It takes time for service people, support engineers, engineering managers to deal with the bug reports. Then it takes engineers maintaining the code extra time to understand the code and to fix bugs. And then it takes QA engineers time to verify the fix. The extra unnecessary complexities not only take extra time for engineers to come up with a fix but also more likely for the fix to cause more bugs.

When things were not done right in the first place, bug fixes often can only be done by applying band-aid over band-aid. Complexities explore and could quickly get out-of-hand.

Every bug requires so many people to involve and the total cost of trying to resolve a bug is just huge. And this extra cost all originates from engineers did not do things right and/or did not make things simple. I have seen this dramatically lowers the productivity of an entire big group in a big company. It slows the release cycles and significantly impacts the quality of the product. Besides, customer dissatisfaction of the product and the disruption to their business operations are additional cost. Therefore, it is invaluable to do things right in the first place.

When you are designing a software solution to a problem, make sure you **do it once for all**. Please make sure you really understand the problem at hand, devise a right solution, and solve the problem once for all. The right solution almost always is a simple one. When a solution gets very complicated, one needs to start asking himself or herself, "Am I doing this right?"

Do a thorough job, get to the bottom of the problem or issue the very first time. Make sure you do enough research, study and investigation into the problem such that you fully understand the nature and scope of the problem.

Then make sure you use the right technologies and building blocks and design a solution that solves it once forever. The goal is such that no one will ever have to re-visit the same issue again in the future. Do it once for all!

Of course, the reality is that how successful one can be depends on how knowledgeable and experienced he or she is.

I have seen too many software engineers did a very poor job in this regard. They never really finish with what they do. They keep working on the same issues or components over and over again. They never finish because they never really do it right. Hence, not doing things right in the first place creates enormous amount of unnecessary extra work, for yourself and for others.

I see so many engineers create unnecessary work for themselves and others. It just lowers everyone's productivity. The overall productivity of the team, group and company suffers. Excellent software engineers have no or almost no bugs to fix for years and they are always developing new functionalities. Poor software engineers always have bugs and issues in their space and components and seem never done with them. There are always some issues. There seem always customer escalations and fires to put out. I have never experienced anything like that throughout my entire career for the software I designed and implemented. That is, I have got zero customer escalations or calls in my entire career.

I have also seen a very senior principal software engineer who fixed a bug and created another. And when he fixed the second bug he created, he introduced a third bug. Hence, a bug becomes three bugs. Therefore, many engineering managers rate engineers' performance by the number of bugs

they fix or the amount of work they have done, which is not really a true
indicator of productivity.

Below are my observations:

   Good engineers develop software with no design issues and almost no bugs,
   needing little maintenance, and the software just works by itself.
   Bad engineers develop software with many issues and bugs and the
   software only sort of works and may need a lot of baby-sittings.

   Good engineers have very few issues or bugs with the software they design
   and are often done with it after it ships while bad engineers always have
   issues and bugs with their components and can't seem to ever finish it or
   get it right.

In summary, when you design software, make sure you do it right the first time
and do it once for all. That way, you eliminate work for yourself and for
others, rather than create a lot of unnecessary work for yourself and others.
Boost, rather than lower, overall productivity of the team and company!

16-4 Programming Tips

This section presents a number of programming tips that help build a very
robust, high quality software product. These practices result in more
robust software.

16-4-1 Always Initialize a Variable

When your code declares a variable, always make sure the variable is
initialized before it is first used.

Not initializing a variable is a very common programming error which
may cause the program to crash or produce incorrect results.

I have fixed a bug by just initializing a variable in a library, a very
simple one-line change, which got rid of crashes of six different
programs in a product.

Without initializing a variable, the value of a variable will be random.
It's any value that happens to be in the memory location the variable
occupies at that time.

If the variable is a pointer, then your program will be using a pointer
with a random garbage value. This will result in a Segmentation Fault or
Access Violation error which typically leads to core dump of the program
because it attempts to access an invalid memory address. Consequently,
the program crashes.

If the variable is not a pointer but a scalar variable, then not initializing
it means it starts as a random garbage value, which will likely cause
your code to produce incorrect results.

So please always remember to initialize every variable your program
declares and uses so that your code always starts from a known, correct

state. So, remember to always initialize every variable at its declaration.

16-4-1-1 Basics of Initializing a Variable

When you declare a variable, whether it's a simple variable, an array or a structure, unless you have explicitly initialized it, its value IS garbage! Remember that computer does not automatically initialize the memory of any variable for you!

Initializing every variable before using (that is, reading or using its value) is to make sure you have an absolutely known and clean start state. It's essentially making sure both of your feet stand firmly on the ground before you set out.

Below is a simplest example of initializing a simple variable:

```
int count = 0;  /* initialize a simple variable */
```

Here is an example of initializing a buffer for a character array:

```
/* Always clear the entire memory of an allocated buffer */
#define BUFSIZE 2048
char *buf=NULL;
buf = malloc(BUFSIZE);
if (buf != NULL)
  memset(buf, 0, BUFSIZE);  /* clear the entire buffer before use */
```

Note that I have worked with software engineers having 15+ years of experience and did not know how to correctly initialize a character array. That is, they do not understand the difference between the following two ways of initializing a character array variable:

Doing the following:

```
if (buf != NULL)
  buf[0] = '\0';
```

is very different from doing this:

```
if (buf != NULL)
  memset(buf, 0, BUFSIZE);
```

The former case initializes only the very first byte of the buffer, leaving the rest of the buffer un-initialized!

The latter clears every byte of the entire buffer, leaving no chance of getting garbage values in any part of the buffer.

If all the program does is to always use the entire buffer to store a single string value, then just zeroing the first byte of the buffer may be OK. But zeroing the entire buffer is always the right thing to do.

There are very simple uses of a buffer and there are very complicated uses. In some complicated cases, the character array buffer allocated above may be used to store multiple strings or many data items, or part of the

buffer contents is used to store pointers. In these complicated uses of
buffers, without zeroing out the entire buffer is almost guaranteed to
incur bugs and crashes.

Remember that many program crashes come from uninitialized variables or
memory buffers. Make sure the programs you write never have this type of
bugs!

To be safe in all cases please always zero out every byte of an entire
buffer before even using it!

16-4-2 Always Check a Pointer Before Using It

This is another required element to develop a very robust software product.

The most common mistake many software engineers make is to use a passed-in
pointer without first making sure it is not NULL. This almost always
results in crashing the program. A good software engineer writes code
free of this type of bugs. It's something very easy that disciplined
software engineers always do.

In theory, as a programmer, one cannot tell whether a pointer value is
valid or not except making sure it is not null. But if you always
initialize every pointer variable your code declares and uses to NULL (i.e.
0), and always check to make sure a pointer is not null before using it,
then you are covered. At least you have done the best you can.

If you always do these two things, then your program becomes a lot more
robust because it is essentially free from dying due to crash on NULL or
uninitialized garbage pointers. So many bugs are simply a result of
forgetting to initialize a pointer variable or not checking to ensure
a pointer is not NULL before using it. These types of bugs should NEVER
exist in your programs! They never did in mine.

And yes, this is the standard you should hold yourself to. In my opinion,
people should waste no time in fixing this type of bugs because it is
totally preventable. It's very basic.

16-4-3 Always Check Every Input Function Argument Before Using Them

When you write a function, make sure you always check each input argument at
the very beginning of the function before it proceeds to its computation.
Return an error (for instance, EINVAL) right away if any of the arguments
fails to pass your checks.

This catches mistakes the callers make in calling the function.
It ensures that the function always computes on correct data.
It also prevents bad input data from corrupting the result or other data.
This can also prevent malicious callers from crashing your application.

16-4-4 A Function Should Always Return Status

Except for some extremely rare cases where it's just impossible for the

computation of the function to fail, every function should always return a
status code indicating whether it succeeds or fails, and if it fails what
the error is. This is in addition to whatever data the function may need
to return to its caller.

It's a poor or bad programming practice to write many functions with a void
return type. I saw many engineers did that and I am always scared.

By default, each function you write should return a status/error code,
with 0 meaning success and failure otherwise.

This is part of how to build a very robust software.
Every function returns a status or error and every invocation of it should
check the return status and handle each error correctly or at least
appropriately!

16-4-5 Ensure No Memory Leak

Always make sure the program you develop is free of memory leaks.
Memory leaks are coding bugs.

Note that memory that programs allocate at run-time by calling the malloc()
or its sibling functions is called **dynamic memory**. It resides in a memory
area called **heap**. The memory is globally available to the entire program and
lives as long as the program or until it is explicitly freed.
If your program does not free it, memory leak occurs.

Whenever your code allocates some dynamic memory, make sure you always
remember to free it. Whoever uses the memory last is responsible for
freeing it.

If you create a function which allocates dynamic memory and it needs the
caller to free that memory afterwards, please clearly say so in a comment
at the beginning of the function and in the function's specification.
Whoever calling this function must make sure it always frees that memory in
all cases. In other words, clearly documenting that a dynamic memory must
be freed by a caller is the very first step to avoid memory leaks.

However, it is not so simple in many cases. Complex programs often consist
of many different components and/or layers. Very often a dynamic memory
allocated in one component or layer needs to be passed a long way over to
another component or layer which is many layers away. In that case, the
memory allocator cannot free it itself because the data contained will be
used by some other components or layers much later in time.
It's extremely important that all components involved in passing this
allocated memory around must clearly indicate that the memory must be
eventually freed by the last user. The component that uses it last must
do that. Should anyone involved drop the ball, memory leak will occur.

When you get a memory leak bug and try to debug, you need to find out
answers to three questions:

1. Which dynamic memory causes the leak?
2. Where is the dynamic memory allocated that is not freed?
3. Where is it supposed to be freed? That is, who uses that piece of

memory last?

To answer the first question, either you could do it by hand or there are tools (e.g. parfait and many others) to run to analyze the code and get a report of all possible code paths potentially having memory leaks.

To answer the second question, you trace it down, look at function arguments. A function argument of pointer-to-pointer type usually expects the lower layer to allocate some memory and pass that address back up. Follow it down to the bottom, you should see the malloc() call and that's where the memory is allocated. Therefore, you track it downward first to find the origination of the dynamic memory.

To identify where it should be freed, you go back up. Again follow that same pointer upward and see if that pointer gets passed back up and try to locate which function uses that pointer last. If it doesn't get passed up, then the top layer function having that pointer should be responsible for freeing it.

16-4-6 Keep the Logging and Tracing Simple

Logging/Tracing

Logging/tracing helps troubleshooting and pinpointing the actual problems.

Most system software is written in C language because its simplicity, efficiency, power and portability of the language. All C compilers today support the ANSI C Standard. In the C language, logging/tracing is very easy and simple -- just use the printf() function and perhaps the application might want to redirect the output and errors (both stdout and stderr) to a file so that the messages are captured in a log file.

On top of that, it's very common that people use multiple logging/tracing levels. This divides messages into different severity levels.
For instance, error, warning, informational, etc.

Different messages are logged at different levels depending on their severities. Normally, there is a default logging level set by the product. The user can choose to change or reset the logging level. When code executes and messages are logged, only those messages with a logging level equal to or greater than the logging level set are actually written and appear in the log.

Some small software products use a single logging level which applies across the entire product. Bigger and more complex products let each component use its own logging level. That is, each component has a separate logging level parameter that users can set.
If you do this, make sure the parameters are named consistently.

For logging/tracing to be effective, the basic requirement is that developers must identify the information that is critically needed in diagnosing and code it to always log that information. It's useless or ineffective to log tons of information but miss the one that is really needed. Developers must do the necessary research and code analysis to figure out what information is really needed and critical for diagnosis and make sure it always gets logged. That's the key to the success of doing logging and tracing.

It's also very important that the code always logs the critical
information at the default logging level. It is disruptive to customers
and time-consuming if a bug is reported and the trace information logged
is insufficient to determine what was going on and one has to go back
to the customer, ask them to bump up the logging level and try to
reproduce the bug again. In addition, the bug may not reproduce again.

Therefore, make sure you always capture the critical information needed
in the log file under the default logging level and there is no need to
go back to customers and ask them to bump up the logging level and re-run
it again. This is the homework developers must do for the logging/tracing
to be effective. Make sure critical information is always logged at the
default logging level. This will save a lot of time in diagnosing and
troubleshooting.

What is the Best Default Logging Level Setting?

The logging level setting is something that is sometimes difficult to
get a one-size-fits-all value. It's also a balance point that could be
hard to strike.

Ideally, it would be best to set the logging level such that all
logging/tracing messages are captured all the time. Assuming developers
code it to log all information needed, this setting will ensure all
information needed to diagnose a problem is available without having
to increase the logging level and try to re-run and reproduce it one
more time.

However, this approach of always running the product in the most verbose
mode also has some disadvantages. First, it incurs more overhead and
makes the product run slower because message logging takes time.
Second, it takes lot of disk space too, assuming logging/tracing messages
are saved in files. And there is a potential of running out of disk space
at times.

On the other hand, the other extreme is to log as least as possible.
This saves disk space and time. However, if something goes wrong, often
developers won't get the information needed to figure out what was
really going on. This often ends up with asking customers to bump up
the logging level and run it again and try to reproduce it again in order
to collect the information needed. This is disruptive to customers.
It slows down the bug resolution. Plus, the problem may not always
reproduce. This level suits a very stable product that rarely has issues.

That's why the default logging level setting is very important and is
such a balance point that is often hard to strike.

The bottom line is the most effective and economic practice relies on
developers to first write bug-free code or/and second do a thorough
analysis of the code, identify the critical information needed and always
log the most critical information. Find out the minimum amount of critical
information needed for diagnosis and always log that at the default
logging level.

The better job developers have done in designing and implementing the product, identifying critical information and logging it at default level, the less the need to go back to customers and ask them to up the logging level and re-run to reproduce a bug or issue, and the less the need to rely on logging/tracing. And as the product becomes more stable, the default logging level can also be adjusted over time.

Don't Go Too Excessive on Logging/Tracing

Try not to become too excessive in logging/tracing. Make it simple!

I have worked for a company whose engineers went excess on logging and tracing. There are so many different ways to do logging and tracing in the same product. So many tracing APIs and hundreds of macros are defined. It takes lot of time to just learn the logging macros.
And the biggest surprise is that there are many bugs in the logging macros and logging code! Apparently, people have gone too far. These are really self-inflicted wounds.

Make sure there is a single unified way of doing logging and tracing and it is consistent across the entire product.
Don't go too excessive in defining too many new tracing APIs and macros on top of printf().

Remember there is only one extremely simple statement -- printf() -- that is ultimately needed in logging and tracing! Adding logging levels on top of that is OK and not uncommon. And that's about it. Don't create so much extra stuff above that. Some engineers really made a career out of logging/tracing. It's just silly that one has to constantly fix logging/tracing bugs like the one just mentioned above.

Appendix A   List of Example Programs

Example programs in this book. Please look it up in the index for the page number
where each program is on.

For information about how to get access to an online copy of the example programs,
please send email to jjchen8@comcast.net or jcnh888@gmail.com with the ISBN number(s),
the 14-character book ID number(s), and the printing date of the book(s)
on the last page inside the back cover of the book(s) you have.

Chapter 3

3-3 tripleIt.c, echoMsg.c
3-4 libtst1.exp (AIX)
3-5 uselink.c
3-6 useload.c

Chapter 4

4-8 gendataf.c
4-9 read.c
4-10 copy.c
4-11 (a) writer.c (b) reader.c
4-12 randomwr.c
4-14 readv.c
4-15 writev.c
4-16 aiowrite.c
4-17 aioread.c
4-18 directiowr.c

Chapter 5

5-2a linkat.c
5-3 symlink.c
5-4 unlink.c
5-5 remove.c
5-6 rename.c
5-8 pathconf.c
5-9 chdir.c
5-10 fstat.c
5-11 readdir_r.c
5-12 chmod.c

5-13 chown.c
5-14 dup2.c
5-15 fcntl.c
5-16 fcntl2.c
5-17 fcntl3.c
5-19 ioctl.c
5-20 ioctl2.c
5-21 umask.c
5-22a access.c
5-23 utime.c

Chapter 6

6-1 sig_numbers.c
6-2 sig_default.c
6-3 sig_ignore.c
6-4 sig_handler.c
6-5 sig_isalive.c
6-6 sig_sigset.c
6-7 sig_procmask.c
6-8 sig_sigpending.c
6-9 sig_sigsuspend.c
6-10 sig_sigwait.c
6-11 sig_sigusr.c
6-12 sig_sleep.c

Chapter 7

7-2 getpid.c
7-3 fork.c
7-4 wait.c
7-5 waitpid.c
7-6 execl.c
7-7 execlp.c
7-8 execv.c
7-9 execve.c
7-12 (a) pipe.c (b) pipedup.c
7-13 atexit.c
7-14 assert.c
7-15 getenv.c
7-16 sysconf.c
7-17 system.c
7-18 getrlimit.c

Appendix A

7-19 setrlimit.c
7-20 getlogin.c
7-21 getpwuid_r.c
7-22 getgrnam_r.c

Chapter 8

8-5 pt_create.c
8-6 pt_args_ret.c
8-7 pt_args_ret2.c
8-9 pt_prt_thrd_attr.c
8-10 pt_detached.c
8-12 pt_mutex_init.c
8-13 pt_mutex.c
8-15 pt_recursive_mutex.c
8-16 pt_mutex_cleanup.c
8-18 pt_produce_consume.c
8-20 pt_rwlock.c
8-21 pt_rwlock_attr.c
8-22 pt_tsd.c
8-23 pt_tsd_ptr.c
8-24 pt_tsd_reentrant.c
8-25 pt_tsd_destroy.c
8-26 pt_cancel.c
8-27 pt_signal_thread.c

Chapter 9

9-5 semcreate.c
9-6 (a) semcrerm.c   (b) mysemutil.h
9-7 semlock.c
9-8 semsetone.c
9-9 semsetall.c
9-10 (a) semupdf.c (b) semlib.c
9-14 Intel x86 spinlock.s
9-15 Intel x86 (a) unlock.s (b) trylock.s
9-16 semupdf_mylock.c
9-17 Apple Darwin (a) spinlock.s (b) unlock.s (c) trylock.s
9-18 IBM PowerPC spinlock.s
9-19 IBM PowerPC (a) unlock.s (b) trylock.s
9-20 Sun SPARC spinlock.s
9-21 Sun SPARC (a) unlock.s (b) trylock.s
9-22 HP PARISC (a) spinlock.s (b) unlock.s (c) trylock.s

Appendix A

9-23 HP/DEC Alpha (a) trylock.s (b) unlock.s (c) spinlock.s
9-24 (a) semupd_mylock.c (b) semupd_mylock_sun64.c
9-28 semupd_sema.c
9-29 semupd_posix_sema.c
9-30 semupdf2_posix_named_sem.c
9-34 semupd_mylock_deadlock.c
9-35 semupd_mylock_reentrant.c
9-36 semipcinfo.c

Chapter 10

10-3 (a) shmget.c (b) myshm.h (c) shmlib.c
10-4 shmapi.c
10-5 shmowner.c
10-7 shmread.c
10-8 shmstat.c
10-9 shmupd.c

Chapter 11

11-1 (a) fifowriter.c (b) fiforeader.c
11-2 msgget.c
11-3 msgsnd.c
11-4 msgrcv.c
11-6 msgstat.c
11-7 msgrm.c
11-8 (a) mmap_writer.c (b)mmap_reader.c

Chapter 12

12-6 socket.c
12-8 (a) udpsrv.c (b) udpclnt.c (c) udpsrv_all.c (d) udpclnt_all.c
12-9 udpclnt_conn_all.c
12-12 (a) tcpsrv1.c (b) tcpclnt1.c
12-13 get_all_sockopt.c
12-14 (a) tcpsrv_all.c (b) tcpclnt_all.c (c) mysocket.h
12-15 (a) tcpsrv_peeraddr_all.c (b) tcpclnt_peeraddr_all.c
12-16 (a) ip_ag_srv_all.c (b) ip_ag_clnt_all.c
12-17 (a) udssrv_all.c (b) udsclnt_all.c
12-18 (a) tcpsrv_async_io_all.c (b) tcpclnt_async_io_all.c
12-19 tcpclnt_async_conn_all.c
12-20 (a) tcpsrv_auto_reconn_all.c (b)tcpclnt_auto_reconn_all.c
12-21 (a) tcpsrv_auto_reconn2_all.c (b)tcpclnt_auto_reconn2_all.c

12-23 (a) multicast_snd_all.c (b) multicast_rcv_all.c (c) multicast_rcv2_all.c

12-24 tcpsrvp.c

12-25 tcpsrvt.c

12-26 tcpclnt_getsvc_all.c

Chapter 13

13-2 tcp_bufsz.c

13-3 (a) tcpsrv_bufsz.c (b) tcpclnt_bufsz.c

13-4 (a) tcpsrv_alive.c (b) tcpclnt_alive.c

13-5 (a) tcpsrv_alive_sun.c (b) tcpclnt_alive_sun.c

13-6 (a) tcpsrv_bufsz_linger.c (b) tcpclnt_bufsz_linger.c

13-8 (a) tcpsrv_reuseaddr_all.c (b) tcpclnt_reuse_all.c

13-9 tcpsrv_exclu_bind_all.c

13-10 tcpsrv_reuseport_all.c

13-11 (a) tcpsrv_timeo_all.c (b) tcpclnt_timeo_all.c

Chapter 14

14-2 get_my_endian.c

14-4 exchange_rec.c

14-5 (a) mystdhdr.h (b) myerrors.h (c) mydistsys.h

14-7 mydistlib.c

14-9 (a) mydistsys.h.v1 (b) tcpclnt_dist_all.c (c) tcpsrv_dist_all.c

14-10 (a) mydistsys.h.v2 (b) tcpclnt_dist_all_v2.c (c) tcpsrv_dist_all_v2.c

14-11 (a) mydistsys.h.v3 (b) tcpclnt_dist_all_v3.c (c) tcpsrv_dist_all_v3.c

Chapter 15

15-2 digest_evp.c

15-3 getdigest.c

15-8 enc_aes_256_cbc.c

15-9 enc_evp1.c

15-10 enc_des_ede3_cbc.c

15-11 enc_evp2.c

15-12 (a) tcpsrvenc1.c (b) tcpclntenc1.c

15-13 (a) tcpsrvenc2.c (b) tcpclntenc2.c

15-14 hmac_file.c

15-15 (a) tcpsrvhmac.c (b) tcpclnthmac.c

15-17 (a) rsa.c   (b) dsa.c

15-18 (a) tcpsrvrsa.c (b) tcpclntrsa.c

15-19 (a) tcpsrvdsa.c (b) tcpclntdsa.c

15-24 get_cert_info.c

15-30 (a) tlsserver1.c (b) tlsclient1.c
15-31 (a) tlsserver2.c (b) tlsclient2.c
15-32 (a) tlsserver3.c (b) tlsclient3.c
15-34 (a) tlsserver4.c (b) tlsclient4.c
15-35 tlsserver5.c
15-37 (a) tlsserver6.c (b) tlsclient6.c
15-38 (a) netlib.h   (b) netlib.c
15-39 (a) myopenssl.h   (b) mycryptolib.c

(240606)

INDEX

–

_exit, 244, 245, 294, 315, 316, 317, 318, 319, 344
_Exit, 315, 316, 317, 318, 319, 344

3

3DES, 1090, 1095, 1100, 1216, 1225

4

4GL, 18

A

abort (, 233, 315, 319, 320
accept (, 245, 462, 692, 719, 720, 725, 726, 728, 744, 758, 761,
    772, 783, 793, 812, 818, 838, 842, 846, 874, 892, 893, 900, 908,
    916, 918, 930, 944, 955, 959, 962, 971, 1024, 1038, 1051, 1122,
    1128, 1143, 1173, 1182, 1230, 1232, 1239, 1240, 1244, 1246,
    1249, 1253, 1256, 1258, 1265, 1266, 1267, 1269, 1272, 1278,
    1281, 1285, 1288, 1295
access, 4, 6, 23, 25, 26, 101, 102, 116, 120, 121, 122, 124, 134,
    165, 171, 179, 189, 190, 192, 199, 200, 203, 207, 214, 215, 223,
    224, 225, 226, 227, 228, 229, 231, 233, 234, 235, 245, 278, 286,
    288, 289, 308, 358, 359, 370, 371, 381, 402, 415, 416, 425, 426,
    440, 464, 467, 473, 475, 477, 478, 479, 481, 482, 483, 488, 514,
    519, 522, 570, 571, 593, 598, 599, 600, 601, 604, 617, 626, 636,
    641, 643, 649, 662, 667, 673, 677, 678, 680, 737, 738, 857, 952,
    979, 980, 1009, 1010, 1061, 1063, 1064, 1065, 1133, 1135, 1152,
    1199, 1200, 1201, 1227, 1228, 1264, 1354, 1359, 1360, 1363
access.c, 225
Accumulator, 6, 7
Address already in use, 777, 787, 833, 846, 847, 940, 941,
    948, 949, 950, 966, 967, 978, 982
address bus, 10, 11, 12, 36
address translation, 21, 598, 599, 849
AES, 324, 1090, 1091, 1097, 1100, 1103
AF_INET, 683, 684, 685, 686, 687, 692, 698, 700, 702, 703, 705,
    706, 708, 711, 712, 717, 718, 720, 722, 726, 728, 730, 731, 734,
    750, 752, 756, 758, 765, 769, 770, 771, 773, 775, 776, 792, 795,
    796, 803, 817, 818, 821, 827, 829, 831, 837, 841, 846, 869, 873,
    876,898, 899, 902, 903, 907, 908, 911, 929, 930, 933, 959, 1122,
    1128, 1143, 1232, 1248, 1258, 1271, 1280, 1287, 1305, 1306,
    1307, 1308, 1309
AF_INET6, 683, 684, 692, 717, 718, 720, 750, 756, 758, 761, 765,
    769, 770, 771, 773, 775, 776, 811, 812, 846, 942, 943, 954, 955,
    959, 960, 961, 1023, 1024, 1037, 1050, 1051, 1122, 1128, 1143,
    1232, 1248, 1258, 1271, 1280, 1287, 1304, 1305, 1306, 1307,
    1308, 1309
AF_UNIX, 683, 684, 686, 687, 692, 723, 780, 781, 782, 785, 887
aio_cancel, 148
aio_error, 148, 149, 150, 152, 154, 155
aio_return, 148, 149, 150, 152, 154, 155
aio_suspend, 148, 462
aio_write, 149
aioread.c, 152, 153
aiowrite.c, 150
AIX, v, 29, 47, 65, 77, 78, 79, 83, 84, 89, 92, 93, 96, 97, 98, 101, 103,
    105, 118, 155, 157, 158, 160, 161, 162, 164, 176, 245, 323, 324,
    325, 336, 338, 362, 365, 378, 455, 531, 532, 533, 541, 550, 589,
    592, 596, 610, 629, 632, 652, 654, 671, 742, 745, 747, 748, 754,
    759, 762, 764, 768, 774, 775, 781, 784, 791, 794, 801, 803, 807,
    808, 810, 813, 814, 816, 819, 826, 830, 832, 833, 834, 850, 851,
    864, 870, 871, 883, 890, 894, 897, 901, 905, 906, 915, 916, 918,
    919, 925, 936, 937, 940, 941, 945, 946, 958, 959, 963, 969, 973,
    974, 981, 986, 996, 997, 999, 1001, 1016, 1017, 1019, 1022, 1029,
    1031, 1032, 1036, 1043, 1044, 1046, 1049, 1057, 1058, 1059
alignment, 161, 162, 691, 999, 1009, 1011, 1017, 1030, 1044,
    1061
Alpha, 520, 530, 538, 539, 596, 984
ALU, 2, 3, 8, 30, 31, 32, 33
always check each input argument, 1365
Always check to ensure a pointer is not null,
    1344
always design security in, 1354
Always initialize a variable, 1344
Apple, v, 29, 65, 79, 84, 85, 92, 94, 96, 98, 101, 102, 103, 107, 118,
    155, 161, 162, 190, 336, 338, 365, 378, 392, 486, 487, 530, 550,
    602, 629, 634, 671, 742, 745, 759, 762, 768, 774, 781, 784, 791,
    794, 801, 808, 810, 813, 816, 819, 826, 828, 830, 833, 834, 850,
    865, 887, 891, 894, 897, 899, 901, 903, 916, 917, 922, 923, 925,
    941, 958, 963, 964, 996, 997, 999
archive library, 92
assembler, 53, 67, 68
assembly language, 3, 4, 5, 6, 7, 17, 23, 36, 67, 68, 165, 370,
    371, 472, 518, 519, 520, 521, 522, 526, 530, 534, 536, 539, 541,
    542, 545, 550, 551, 578, 582, 594, 595, 596, 625, 629, 1346
Assembly language, 17, 520
assert (, 320, 321
assert.c, 320
asymmetric ciphers, 1086
asymmetric cryptography, 1084, 1100
asynchronous connect, 672, 801, 807, 1348

Index

asynchronous I/O, 27, 111, 117, 147, 148, 150, 153, 155, 156, 166, 169, 788, 799, 1355
asynchronous signals, 232, 245
atexit, 316, 317, 318, 319, 345
atexit.c, 318
authority revocation list, 1199
auto_reconnect, 809, 813, 814, 819, 820

B

backward compatibility, v, 1009, 1011, 1067, 1215, 1352, 1353, 1354
bdynamic, 89, 90, 96, 105, 106
Bdynamic, 79, 84, 89, 97, 104, 105
bf-cbc, 1103, 1108, 1109, 1117
big-endian, 983, 984, 1011
binary semaphore, 482
bind(, 698, 700, 706, 717, 718, 719, 728, 733, 744, 753, 761, 772, 777, 778, 781, 782, 787, 792, 812, 818, 825, 829, 831, 833, 837, 841, 846, 848, 873, 900, 908, 930, 940, 941, 944, 949, 952, 955, 957, 961, 966, 967, 968, 971, 978, 1024, 1037, 1051, 1308
block cipher, 1088, 1089, 1090, 1091, 1092, 1093, 1094, 1095, 1096
Block device special files, 171
blocked signals, 259, 263, 264
Blowfish, 1091, 1092, 1097, 1100
browser, 1, 16, 34, 672, 857, 858, 1065, 1190, 1202, 1215, 1226
bstatic, 89, 96, 105, 106
Bstatic, 79, 89, 96, 104
btr, 520, 524, 531
bts, 520, 523, 525, 530, 531, 534
buffered I/O, 111, 162, 163
byte-ordering, 985

C

CA chains, 1283, 1284
cache, 3, 8, 125, 134, 156, 157, 158, 162, 163, 164, 537, 538, 602, 636, 662, 667, 1238, 1354
cancellation point, 405, 450, 451, 463
cas, 520, 534, 535, 536
CAST, 1092, 1097, 1100, 1341
catcs, 43, 44
CBC mode, 1093, 1096
certificate authority, 1191, 1196, 1198, 1203, 1209, 1226
certificate chain, 1200, 1203, 1208, 1254, 1263
certificate request, 1196, 1201, 1202, 1204, 1206, 1210
certificate revocation, 1191, 1198, 1199
certificate revocation list, 1199
certificate signing request, 1196, 1201, 1203, 1207, 1209
CertificateRequest, 1219

CertificateVerify, 1220
CFB, 1088, 1093, 1094, 1095, 1096
CFB mode, 1094, 1095
ChangeCipherSpec message, 1218
Character device special files, 170
chdev, 592
chdir.c, 187
checkin, 43
checkout, 43, 44
checksum, 1071, 1072, 1073, 1156, 1221
child process, 88, 222, 238, 253, 254, 273, 274, 276, 277, 281, 282, 289, 290, 291, 292, 293, 294, 295, 296, 297, 298, 299, 302, 303, 304, 305, 306, 307, 308, 309, 310, 311, 312, 314, 315, 344, 345, 346, 349, 500, 503, 642, 666, 668, 835, 838, 839, 840
chmod, 198, 199, 200, 229, 245, 464
chmod.c, 199, 229
chown, 184, 200, 201, 202, 203, 229, 245, 464, 1066
chown.c, 201, 229
ci, 43, 44
Cipher suite makeup, 1225
ciphertext, 1083, 1087, 1089, 1093, 1094, 1095, 1096, 1099, 1104, 1107
ClassLoader, 87
Clearcase, 42, 43
client authentication, v, 1199, 1219, 1220, 1226, 1227, 1228, 1264, 1265, 1266, 1267, 1268, 1271, 1272, 1274, 1276, 1277, 1281, 1284, 1285, 1288, 1289, 1290
client close the connection, 724
ClientHello message, 1217
ClientKeyExchange message, 1218, 1220, 1224, 1225
client-server model, 693
clock frequency, 9
close_notify, 1219, 1220
closedir, 193, 197, 464
closing a TCP socket connection, 937
CMPIB, 520, 536, 537, 538
code re-use, 73
code review, 39, 40
Code sharing, 1344, 1351
compiled language, 18, 36, 67
compiled languages, 18, 66, 67
compiler, 4, 5, 7, 18, 52, 53, 67, 68, 77, 78, 88, 92, 94, 269, 284, 286, 756, 774, 845, 956, 958, 1010, 1011, 1061, 1068
compiler padding, 1010, 1011, 1061
computer network communication security, 1069, 1070
concurrency control, v, 22, 165, 370, 373, 398, 467, 471, 474, 475, 476, 500, 514, 518, 530, 569, 599, 601, 602, 614, 637, 1346, 1347
concurrent update, 472, 473, 516, 517

Index

concurrent updates, 370, 473, 474, 475, 500, 540, 541, 548, 549, 602, 609, 624, 629, 1347

condition signal, 405, 406, 413

condition variable, 399, 400, 401, 402, 403, 404, 405, 406, 408, 409, 413, 467, 468, 1347

condition variable attribute, 401, 402

confidential, 1221

confidentiality, 1070, 1085, 1100, 1190, 1191, 1216, 1221

connect (, 462, 692, 709, 710, 712, 719, 720, 721, 722, 723, 725, 731, 747, 751, 753, 765, 776, 778, 779, 785, 796, 801, 803, 804, 805, 807, 808, 809, 815, 822, 835, 852, 859, 877, 892, 904, 913, 935, 947, 975, 1020, 1033, 1047, 1235, 1237, 1239, 1244, 1251, 1253, 1261, 1265, 1266, 1267, 1275, 1291, 1295, 1296, 1306

connect_to_server, 1120, 1125, 1131, 1147, 1177, 1186, 1234, 1250, 1260, 1273, 1274, 1290, 1299, 1304, 1305, 1306

Connection refused, 779, 807

Connection timed out, 779

connectionless communication, 704, 716, 717, 718, 857

connection-oriented communication, 704, 716, 717, 718, 719, 721, 848, 857

control bus, 10, 11, 12

control unit, 3, 30, 31, 33

copy.c, 132

cosmetic, 41

counting semaphore, 482

CPU, 2, 3, 4, 5, 6, 7, 8, 11, 12, 13, 15, 16, 17, 20, 26, 30, 32, 34, 68, 69, 157, 326, 327, 329, 330, 332, 352, 362, 372, 399, 473, 516, 522, 531, 534, 538, 539, 540, 599, 637, 667, 798, 800, 840, 845, 861, 867, 983, 985, 986, 987, 991, 993, 999, 1002, 1004, 1009, 1346, 1355

creat, 123, 126, 451, 463

CreateMutex, 570

CreateSemaphore, 571

createview, 42

CRL, 1199

cross-version interoperability, 1011

CSR. *certificate signing request*

CTR mode, 1096

CTX_check_private_key, 1240, 1243, 1333

CTX_use_certificate_file, 1240, 1241, 1333, 1340

CTX_use_PrivateKey_file, 1240, 1242, 1333

D

Darwin, v, 29, 65, 79, 84, 85, 92, 94, 96, 98, 101, 102, 103, 107, 118, 155, 161, 162, 190, 336, 338, 365, 378, 392, 486, 487, 530, 550, 602, 629, 634, 671, 742, 745, 759, 762, 768, 774, 781, 784, 791, 794, 801, 808, 810, 813, 816, 819, 826, 828, 830, 833, 834, 850, 865, 887, 891, 894, 897, 899, 901, 903, 916, 917, 922, 923, 925, 941, 958, 963, 964, 996, 997

data bus, 10, 11, 12, 36

data header structure, 1007, 1008, 1010

data integrity, 8, 370, 415, 473, 474, 514, 593, 599, 600, 629, 636, 1063, 1070, 1071, 1073, 1133, 1134, 1135, 1346, 1347

Data Integrity, 599, 1344

Datagram sockets, 682, 695, 698, 699, 701, 704, 709, 780

deadlock, 81, 82, 212, 375, 377, 386, 387, 390, 391, 398, 434, 435, 452, 468, 572, 573, 574, 575, 576, 577, 580, 581, 585, 587, 594

Deadlock avoidance, 574, 575

Deadlock detection, 573

Deadlock prevention, 573, 574

deadlock recovery, 574

deciphering, 1221

default action, 237, 238, 241, 242, 243, 245, 246, 247, 248, 251, 268, 280, 307

default actions, 242

default logging level, 1367, 1368, 1369

demand paging, 20

Denial of Service, 1005, 1006, 1070, 1071

deptca_csr.pem, 1207, 1208, 1210

DER, 1194, 1195, 1213, 1263

DES, 1064, 1088, 1090, 1091, 1095, 1096, 1097, 1100, 1201, 1216, 1224, 1225, 1341

Design error codes correctly, 1344

design specification, 37, 38, 39, 70, 1354, 1355

destructor function, 440, 441, 443, 444, 445

detached thread, 368, 369, 370, 467

device driver, 21, 22, 216, 217

Diffie-Hellman, 1097, 1099, 1220, 1221, 1222, 1223, 1224, 1225, 1341

digest_evp, 1078, 1079, 1080, 1375

digital certificate, 1190, 1192, 1194, 1195, 1196, 1197, 1203

digital commerce, 1190

digital signature, v, 1064, 1085, 1149, 1150, 1151, 1152, 1154, 1155, 1156, 1157, 1158, 1160, 1161, 1162, 1163, 1165, 1166, 1167, 1168, 1169, 1170, 1171, 1174, 1178, 1180, 1181, 1184, 1188, 1190, 1191, 1199, 1326, 1327, 1328, 1329, 1338, 1339

Digital Signature Algorithm, 1152

Digital Signature Standard, 1152

direct I/O, 13, 111, 117, 119, 157, 158, 159, 161, 162, 163, 166, 167, 169

DirectIO, 162

directiowr.c, 158, 161

directory file, 170

disk sectors, 115, 140

display_certificate_info, 1212, 1239, 1333, 1336

display_cipher_suites, 1293, 1337

display_ssl_certificate_subject, 1239

dlcose, 87, 101

DLL, 80, 81, 82, 109, 705, 707, 711, 739, 743, 746, 760, 782, 784, 850, 942, 954, 960, 970, 974, 1019, 1023, 1032, 1036, 1046, 1050

Index

DLL Hell, 80, 81, 109
DllMain, 81
dlopen, 87, 88, 100, 101, 464
dlsym, 87, 101
DMA controller, 13
DMA I/O, 13
Do it once for all, 1362
Don't Break Upgrade, 1361
DSA, 1064, 1150, 1152, 1153, 1154, 1194, 1201, 1339
DSA signature, 1152, 1153, 1154
DSABITSLEN, 1167, 1186, 1312
DSS, 1150, 1152, 1153, 1154, 1215, 1216, 1224, 1225, 1339
dup, 203, 204, 205, 206, 245, 308, 311, 312, 313, 642, 644
dup2, 203, 204, 205, 207, 245
dup2.c, 204
DYLD_LIBRARY_PATH, 85, 107
dynamic linking, 79, 80, 86, 87, 90, 94, 96, 97, 98, 109, 1064, 1068
dynamic loading, 86, 87, 88, 90, 98, 101, 102, 103, 109
dynamic port number, 854

E

Ease of Use, 1344, 1349
Easily extensible, 1344
echoMsg.c, 90, 91, 92, 93, 94, 103, 104, 105, 106, 107, 108
EDE mode, 1096
enc_aes_256_cbc.c, 1103
enc_bf_cbc.c, 1110
enc_evp1.c, 1107
enc_evp2.c, 1117
enciphering, 1221
encryption key, 1083, 1084, 1087, 1094, 1190, 1201
endian, 676, 677, 983, 984, 985, 986, 987, 988, 989, 991, 992, 993, 994, 997, 998, 999, 1000, 1001, 1002, 1003, 1004, 1011, 1016, 1017, 1029, 1030, 1043, 1044, 1057, 1061, 1348
endpwent, 340
Ensure No Memory Leak, 1366
Ephemeral Diffie-Hellman, 1224
EPROM, 10
ERR_clear_error, 1229, 1246, 1251, 1252, 1255, 1261, 1268, 1275, 1277, 1285, 1291, 1295, 1333
ERR_error_string, 1251, 1252, 1261, 1275, 1291, 1292, 1294, 1297
ERR_func_error_string, 1297, 1298
ERR_get_error, 1229, 1245, 1255, 1268, 1277, 1284, 1294, 1296, 1297
ERR_lib_error_string, 1297, 1298
ERR_peek_error, 1296, 1297
ERR_peek_last_error, 1296, 1297
ERR_print_errors, 1230, 1246, 1255, 1256, 1268, 1269, 1278, 1285, 1294, 1295, 1333

ERR_print_errors_cb, 1295
ERR_print_errors_fp, 1230, 1246, 1255, 1256, 1268, 1269, 1278, 1285, 1294, 1295, 1333
ERR_reason_error_string, 1297, 1298
EVP_bf_cbc, 1103
EVP_CIPHER_CTX_free, 1102, 1103, 1105, 1106, 1119, 1316, 1318, 1319, 1321
EVP_CIPHER_CTX_new, 1101, 1104, 1105, 1106, 1119, 1316, 1317, 1318, 1320
EVP_CIPHER_CTX_reset, 1103, 1119
EVP_DecryptFinal, 1101, 1106, 1109, 1119, 1317
EVP_DecryptFinal_ex, 1101, 1106, 1109, 1119, 1317
EVP_DecryptInit, 1101, 1106, 1119, 1317
EVP_DecryptInit_ex, 1101, 1106, 1119, 1317
EVP_DecryptUpdate, 1101, 1103, 1106, 1109, 1119, 1317
EVP_DigestFinal_ex, 1078, 1079, 1081, 1322, 1323, 1324, 1325
EVP_DigestUpdate, 1078, 1079, 1081, 1322, 1323, 1325
EVP_EncryptFinal, 1101, 1102, 1105, 1109, 1119, 1316
EVP_EncryptFinal_ex, 1101, 1102, 1105, 1109, 1119, 1316
EVP_EncryptInit, 1101, 1102, 1103, 1105, 1119, 1316
EVP_EncryptInit_ex, 1101, 1102, 1103, 1105, 1119, 1316
EVP_EncryptUpdate, 1101, 1102, 1103, 1105, 1109, 1119, 1316
EVP_get_digestbyname, 1078, 1079, 1080, 1081, 1143, 1147, 1157, 1160, 1322, 1324, 1327, 1328
EVP_MD_CTX_free, 1078, 1079, 1081, 1322, 1323, 1324, 1325
EVP_MD_CTX_new, 1078, 1079, 1081, 1322, 1323, 1324
EVP_PKEY_CTX_free, 1157, 1159, 1160, 1161, 1162, 1163, 1164, 1326, 1327, 1328, 1329, 1330, 1331, 1332
EVP_PKEY_CTX_new, 1157, 1158, 1160, 1162, 1164, 1326, 1328, 1329, 1331, 1332
EVP_PKEY_CTX_set_dsa_paramgen_bits, 1164, 1331
EVP_PKEY_CTX_set_rsa_padding, 1157, 1159, 1160, 1326, 1327, 1328
EVP_PKEY_CTX_set_signature_md, 1157, 1159, 1160, 1327, 1328, 1329
EVP_PKEY_generate, 1162, 1163, 1164, 1330, 1332
EVP_PKEY_get_size, 1157, 1166, 1168, 1326
EVP_PKEY_keygen_init, 1162, 1164, 1330, 1332
EVP_PKEY_paramgen, 1164, 1331
EVP_PKEY_paramgen_init, 1164, 1331
EVP_PKEY_sign, 1157, 1158, 1159, 1166, 1167, 1177, 1187, 1326, 1327
EVP_PKEY_sign_init, 1157, 1158, 1159, 1326
EVP_PKEY_verify, 1160, 1161, 1328, 1329
EVP_PKEY_verify_init, 1160, 1328
exchange_rec.c, 989, 1061
exclusive lock, 209, 373, 386, 434, 482, 515, 1347
execl, 299, 300, 301, 302, 303, 305
execl.c, 302
execle, 245, 299, 301, 306

Index

execlp, 299, 300, 303, 304, 305, 346

execlp.c, 303

execv, 299, 300, 305, 306

execv.c, 305

execve, 245, 299, 301, 306, 307

execve.c, 306

execvp, 299, 300, 305, 345

exit(, 244, 245, 250, 266, 272, 275, 294, 315, 316, 317, 318, 319, 344, 353, 355, 356, 357, 358, 359, 360, 361, 369, 370, 380, 381, 383, 384, 385, 388, 389, 390, 393, 394, 396, 397, 398, 407, 408, 409, 410, 411, 412, 417, 418, 419, 420, 421, 422, 423, 424, 427, 428, 429, 432, 433, 434, 437, 438, 439, 440, 442, 443, 444, 447, 448, 449, 450, 455, 456, 457, 458, 527, 542, 543, 545, 546, 551, 552, 579, 584, 698, 844, 845

F

faccessat, 224, 225, 464

fchmod, 198, 229, 464

fchmodat, 198, 199, 464

fchown, 200, 203, 229, 464

fchownat, 200, 203, 464

fcntl, 119, 126, 127, 130, 132, 136, 138, 144, 146, 151, 153, 158, 160, 161, 165, 176, 180, 191, 195, 199, 204, 205, 206, 207, 208, 209, 210, 211, 212, 213, 214, 215, 217, 222, 227, 229, 230, 245, 451, 463, 464, 486, 645, 647, 663, 665, 741, 749, 796, 801, 804, 805, 806, 990, 996, 1108, 1117, 1315

fcntl.c, 209, 229

fcntl2.c, 212

fcntl3.c, 214

fdatasync, 163, 164, 463

fdopendir, 193

fflush, 119, 164, 319, 395, 417, 418, 421, 422, 449, 464, 797, 798, 799

FIFO, 124, 125, 169, 170, 184, 195, 308, 364, 365, 367, 376, 642, 644, 645, 646, 647, 648, 649, 668, 669

fiforeader.c, 645, 647

fifowriter.c, 645, 669

file descriptor table, 121, 122, 123, 203

file handle, 118, 121, 166

file offset, 116, 117, 121, 123, 137, 138, 139, 140, 141, 144, 149, 161, 166, 203, 204, 208, 210

file system, 13, 19, 21, 22, 23, 25, 34, 112, 113, 114, 115, 116, 120, 121, 123, 125, 134, 140, 142, 156, 157, 158, 162, 163, 164, 165, 172, 180, 189, 198, 199, 200, 201, 224, 225, 226, 229, 308, 478, 606, 644, 662, 667, 677, 682, 780, 787, 863

file_exists, 645, 646, 647

file_range, 164

filesystemio_options, 162

first-class software, 1343, 1344, 1347

fixed port numbers, 855, 856

fopen, 118, 119, 451, 464, 1212

forcedirectio, 157

fork, 88, 194, 235, 245, 253, 273, 276, 291, 292, 293, 295, 297, 298, 299, 302, 303, 305, 306, 307, 309, 310, 311, 312, 325, 326, 328, 344, 500, 503, 836, 838, 839, 840

fork.c, 291

fpathconf, 184, 185, 464

fread, 118, 119, 167, 451, 464

freeaddrinfo, 748, 753, 766, 773, 777, 853, 948, 976, 1021, 1035, 1049

fstat, 189, 190, 191, 192, 195, 199, 201, 227, 245, 451, 464

fstat.c, 190

fsync, 119, 148, 150, 163, 164, 451, 463

ftok, 477, 478, 481, 482, 483, 485, 491, 496, 498, 505, 589, 590, 605, 606, 610, 616, 641, 650, 651, 653, 654, 658, 660

function specification, 38

fwrite, 118, 119, 167, 451, 464

G

GCM mode, 1096

gendataf.c, 127

generate_DSAkey, 1156, 1163, 1164, 1168, 1187, 1314, 1330, 1331, 1332

generate_RSAkey, 1156, 1162, 1166, 1177, 1178, 1314, 1329, 1330

generic rule, 52

get_all_sockopt.c, 733

get_cert_info.c, 1211

get_digest, 1081, 1082, 1083, 1156, 1157, 1162, 1163, 1166, 1167, 1168, 1173, 1177, 1183, 1187, 1314, 1324, 1325

get_my_endian.c, 987

get_signature, 1156, 1157, 1158, 1162, 1163, 1166, 1168, 1169, 1178, 1188, 1314, 1326, 1327, 1335

getaddrinfo, 464, 699, 747, 748, 752, 753, 754, 755, 764, 766, 767, 768, 770, 773, 774, 775, 776, 777, 809, 810, 813, 814, 851, 853, 946, 948, 974, 976, 1019, 1021, 1032, 1035, 1046, 1049

getcwd, 186, 187, 188, 465

getdigest, 1081, 1082, 1375

getegid, 202, 245, 287, 344

getenv, 321, 322

getenv.c, 322

geteuid, 245, 286, 287, 338, 339

getgid, 245, 287, 344

getgrgid, 197, 341, 342, 465

getgrgid_r, 341, 342, 465

getgrnam, 341, 342, 343, 465

getgrnam_r, 341, 342, 343, 465

getgrnam_r.c, 342

getgroups, 201, 202, 245, 343

gethostbyaddr, 749, 752, 754, 795, 803, 809, 810, 819, 821, 876, 902, 911, 933, 996, 1305

gethostbyname, 752, 795, 803, 809, 810, 819, 821, 875, 876, 901, 902, 910, 911, 932, 933, 1302, 1305
getlogin, 334, 335, 336, 339, 343, 346, 465
getlogin.c, 335
getlogin_r, 335, 336, 465
getnameinfo, 465, 754, 755, 768, 770, 772, 774, 775
getpeername, 757, 758, 761, 765, 772, 785
getpgid, 289, 290
getpgrp, 245, 289, 290
getpid, 245, 252, 255, 261, 265, 267, 270, 286, 290, 292, 295, 298, 646
getpid.c, 290
getppid, 245, 286, 290, 292, 295, 298
getpwent, 337, 340
getpwnam, 337, 338, 339, 346, 465
getpwnam_r, 337, 338, 339, 346, 465
getpwuid, 197, 337, 338, 339, 340, 465
getpwuid_r, 337, 338, 339, 340, 465
getpwuid_r.c, 339
getrlimit, 326, 327, 328, 330, 331, 332, 333
getrlimit.c, 328
getservbyname, 750, 849, 851, 855, 856
getservbyport, 754
getsockopt, 692, 733, 734, 735, 736, 737, 738, 801, 804, 805, 809, 825, 867, 868, 869, 870, 871, 873, 877, 903, 911, 912, 913, 915, 927, 929, 934, 943, 954, 961, 975
getuid, 245, 255, 286, 287
group file, 196, 341, 343

H

hard link, 174, 180, 181, 182, 183, 229
has_lock, 516, 517, 581, 582, 583, 584, 585, 586, 587
hash algorithms, 1072, 1073, 1075
hash functions, 1072, 1073, 1077, 1078, 1134, 1135
HMAC, v, 1064, 1096, 1134, 1135, 1136, 1137, 1141, 1142, 1144, 1145, 1147, 1148, 1149, 1155, 1156
hmac_file.c, 1137
How to Tune Kernel Parameters, 862, 864, 865
How to Tune Kernel Parameters in HPUX, 864
HP PARISC, 520, 530, 536, 984
HP-UX, 29, 76, 83, 84, 85, 92, 94, 96, 98, 103, 161, 162, 176, 536, 589, 592, 748, 759, 826, 830, 832, 833, 834, 845, 886, 890, 894, 897, 901, 914, 915, 916, 920, 921, 925, 940, 941, 958, 977, 981, 996, 997, 1016, 1029, 1043
htonl, 698, 699, 700, 703, 706, 708, 712, 718, 722, 726, 728, 731, 743, 751, 760, 792, 818, 837, 841, 858, 873, 899, 908, 930, 971, 1001, 1020, 1022, 1028, 1034, 1035, 1042, 1047, 1049, 1056, 1307
htonll, 998, 1001, 1016, 1020, 1028, 1029, 1034, 1042, 1043, 1047, 1056

htons, 698, 700, 703, 706, 708, 712, 718, 722, 726, 728, 731, 743, 760, 771, 792, 796, 803, 812, 818, 821, 827, 829, 831, 837, 841, 873, 876, 899, 903, 908, 911, 930, 933, 943, 955, 961, 971, 1001, 1024, 1037, 1051, 1305, 1307
HTTPS, 671, 677, 678, 680, 694, 716, 1135, 1214, 1215, 1226

I

IBM PowePC, 520
IDEA, 47, 1092, 1097, 1100, 1201, 1224
IEEE, 28, 29, 167, 230, 282, 347, 349, 350, 451, 469, 596, 638, 669, 673, 679, 752, 860
ifdef, 59, 60, 158, 159, 160, 323, 324, 325, 336, 339, 343, 356, 357, 383, 384, 385, 388, 389, 390, 393, 394, 395, 396, 397, 407, 408, 409, 410, 412, 427, 428, 429, 432, 433, 434, 437, 438, 439, 442, 443, 444, 447, 448, 449, 450, 455, 456, 457, 458, 486, 487, 542, 543, 544, 584, 586, 749, 899, 902, 903, 990, 995
ifeq, 59, 60
ifndef, 59, 100, 101, 158, 239, 324, 379, 381, 385, 390, 395, 396, 412, 424, 436, 437, 440, 458, 487, 1298
ifneq, 59, 60
implicit rule, 53, 54, 55
include directive, 58
inet_ntop, 758, 761, 765, 875, 932, 1298, 1302
inheritsched attribute, 362, 365
init.ora, 162
initialization vector, 1087, 1088, 1094, 1095, 1096
inode, 113, 114, 115, 120, 121, 122, 123, 166, 189, 192, 308
inode table, 120, 121, 122, 123, 166
integration testing, 40, 1344
Intel x86, 520, 522, 523, 524, 525, 530, 531, 534, 541, 625, 631, 984, 999, 1353, 1354
interleaving, 20, 471, 472, 473, 594, 1092
Internet sockets, 681, 682, 683, 684, 780, 781
interoperability, 983, 1009, 1011
interpretative languages, 66, 67
interpreted language, 18
interprocess communication, 22, 474, 600, 643, 681, 684, 856, 1354
interprocess communications, v, 600, 1355
ioctl, 119, 215, 216, 217, 218, 219, 230, 238, 451, 465
ioctl.c, 217, 230
ioctl2.c, 218
ioctlsocket, 741, 796, 801, 804, 805
IP address, 678, 689, 690, 691, 692, 697, 698, 699, 700, 702, 706, 707, 708, 711, 718, 719, 722, 723, 726, 728, 730, 731, 743, 745, 746, 750, 751, 752, 753, 754, 755, 756, 757, 758, 759, 760, 761, 762, 763, 764, 765, 766, 767, 768, 769, 770, 774, 775, 778, 779, 780,781, 792, 795, 802, 803, 809, 812, 813, 814, 818, 819, 820, 821, 824, 825, 826, 827, 829, 831, 833, 837, 841, 846, 847, 848, 849, 850, 851, 873, 876, 899, 902, 908, 910, 911, 930, 932, 933, 943, 946, 955, 961, 965, 971, 972, 973, 974, 1006, 1017,

1018, 1019, 1024, 1031, 1032, 1037, 1044, 1045, 1046, 1051, 1070, 1298, 1299, 1300, 1301, 1302, 1303, 1304, 1305, 1359

IP_ADD_MEMBERSHIP, 824, 826, 830, 832

ip_ag_clnt_all.c, 767, 773

ip_ag_srv_all.c, 767

IP_DROP_MEMBERSHIP, 824

IP_MULTICAST_IF, 778, 824, 825, 828

IP_MULTICAST_LOOP, 824, 825, 827

IP_MULTICAST_TTL, 824, 825

ipadm, 864, 884, 885, 886

IP-agnostic, 767, 773

ipcrm, 480, 484, 617

IPPROTO_TCP, 685, 687, 699, 701, 727, 729, 734, 738, 747, 749, 836, 840, 851, 869, 872, 875, 897, 898, 899, 901, 903, 904, 906, 907, 908, 910, 912, 913, 914, 917, 924, 925, 927, 932, 974, 996, 1019, 1032, 1046, 1120, 1123, 1126, 1130, 1142, 1145, 1229, 1233, 1245, 1249, 1255, 1259, 1267, 1272, 1277, 1284, 1289, 1298

IPv4, 672, 674, 678, 679, 683, 688, 690, 691, 692, 698, 702, 717, 718, 720, 722, 730, 741, 742, 744, 745, 750, 751, 752, 755, 756, 757, 758, 759, 760, 762, 765, 767, 768, 769, 770, 772, 773, 774, 775, 776, 809, 810, 823, 824, 846, 850, 918, 968, 969, 971, 973,1017, 1031, 1044, 1120, 1127, 1142, 1231, 1247, 1257, 1270, 1279, 1286, 1304, 1306, 1308, 1309, 1359

IPv6, 672, 678, 679, 683, 684, 688, 690, 692, 717, 718, 720, 722, 741, 742, 744, 745, 749, 750, 751, 752, 755, 756, 757, 758, 759, 760, 762, 765, 767, 768, 769, 770, 771, 772, 773, 774, 775, 776, 809, 810, 823, 824, 846, 850, 858, 918, 968, 969, 971, 973, 996,1017, 1031, 1044, 1120, 1121, 1127, 1128, 1142, 1143, 1231, 1232, 1247, 1248, 1257, 1270, 1271, 1279, 1280, 1286, 1287, 1301, 1304, 1306, 1308, 1309, 1359

IPV6_ADD_MEMBERSHIP, 824

IPV6_DROP_MEMBERSHIP, 824

IPV6_JOIN_GROUP, 824

IPV6_LEAVE_GROUP, 824

IPV6_MULTICAST_HOPS, 824, 825

IPV6_MULTICAST_IF, 824

IPV6_MULTICAST_LOOP, 824, 825

ISO model, 22

J

Java, 4, 5, 47, 66, 67, 69, 77, 85, 86, 87, 517

K

Keep the Logging and Tracing Simple, 1367

KeepAliveInterval, 894, 924, 925

KeepAliveTime, 893, 894, 924, 925

kernel mode, 23, 24, 25, 26, 254

key establishment, 1151, 1220, 1221, 1222

key exchange, 1100, 1151, 1216, 1218, 1220, 1221, 1222, 1223, 1224, 1225, 1339, 1341

key sizes, 1087, 1097

keyed-Hash Message Authentication Code, 1134

kill(, 237, 238, 240, 245, 251, 252, 253, 254, 263, 272, 279, 295, 297, 453, 454, 640

L

layer, 17, 21, 22, 25, 30, 32, 606, 671, 673, 674, 675, 676, 677, 678, 680, 681, 682, 688, 689, 694, 717, 780, 857, 858, 893, 894, 895, 918, 937, 938, 1214, 1215, 1366, 1367

lchown, 200, 203

LD_LIBRARY_PATH, 84, 85, 86, 97, 102, 103, 104, 105, 107, 1066, 1068, 1069

LDCW, 520, 536, 537, 538

ldd, 83

ldl_l, 520, 538

ldq_l, 520, 538, 539, 540

LIB, 84, 96, 108

libcrypto, 1064, 1068, 1135

LIBPATH, 83, 84, 85, 98, 103, 106, 108

library, 23, 24, 26, 27, 30, 49, 56, 60, 62, 67, 68, 69, 73, 74, 76, 77, 78, 79, 80, 81, 82, 83, 84, 85, 86, 87, 88, 89, 90, 91, 92, 93, 94, 95, 96, 97, 98, 99, 100, 101, 102, 103, 105, 107, 108, 109, 117, 118, 119, 121, 148, 157, 163, 272, 284, 285, 350, 371, 451, 517, 607, 625, 628, 840, 845, 977, 981, 1002, 1064, 1067, 1068, 1120, 1137, 1237, 1239, 1240, 1264, 1298, 1351, 1352, 1363

libssl, 1064, 1068, 1135

libtst1, 83, 84, 89, 90, 92, 93, 94, 95, 96, 97, 98, 99, 102, 103, 104, 105, 106, 107, 108

linkat.c, 175, 176

linker, 52, 55, 67, 68, 69, 77, 78, 79, 80, 82, 83, 84, 85, 88, 89, 93, 95, 96, 97, 101, 104, 105, 106, 109, 845

Linux, v, 25, 29, 47, 59, 64, 65, 74, 79, 83, 84, 85, 86, 87, 90, 92, 93, 95, 97, 98, 101, 102, 103, 114, 118, 119, 148, 155, 157, 158, 159, 160, 161, 162, 163, 164, 169, 171, 176, 177, 190, 220, 231, 235, 237, 241, 247, 255, 263, 275, 283, 300, 311, 313, 314, 315, 317, 334, 336, 337, 338, 345, 350, 362, 365, 378, 459, 476, 487, 490, 493, 494, 495, 496, 499, 517, 519, 522, 530, 541, 550, 587, 588, 589, 591, 592, 593, 602, 603, 604, 617, 618, 623, 629, 631, 642, 643, 644, 652, 654, 671, 683, 684, 689, 692, 693, 704, 725, 738, 739, 740, 741, 742, 745, 748, 749, 754, 759, 762, 768, 774, 777, 778, 779, 781, 784, 787, 791, 794, 801, 807, 808, 810, 813, 816, 819, 825, 826, 827, 828, 830, 832, 833, 834, 846, 847, 848, 849, 850, 855, 862, 870, 871, 879, 880, 881, 882, 883, 890, 894, 895, 897, 901, 905, 906, 915, 916, 917, 918, 923, 925, 926, 936, 940, 941, 945, 949, 950, 951, 952, 957, 958, 959, 963, 964, 965, 966, 967, 968, 969, 973, 975, 980, 996, 997, 999, 1001, 1016, 1017, 1022, 1029, 1031, 1036, 1043, 1044, 1049, 1058, 1059, 1065, 1066, 1067, 1296, 1356

Index

listen(, 692, 720, 721, 725, 728, 744, 761, 772, 783, 792, 812, 818, 837, 841, 874, 900, 908, 930, 944, 955, 958, 961, 971, 1024, 1037, 1051, 1308

little-endian, 987

load_certificate, 1232, 1240, 1248, 1258, 1264, 1271, 1274, 1281, 1288, 1290, 1332

loader, 67, 68, 69, 81, 84, 88, 89, 97, 109, 284, 1068

LoadLibrary, 81, 87, 100, 102

lock_var, 593

locking, 27, 165, 169, 208, 212, 371, 373, 378, 398, 399, 459, 473, 474, 475, 489, 490, 515, 516, 517, 518, 519, 520, 521, 522, 526, 530, 531, 532, 534, 535, 536, 538, 541, 542, 543, 545, 546, 548, 549, 550, 551, 552, 578, 580, 581, 582, 584, 587, 592, 593, 594, 595, 599, 601, 615, 628, 629, 630, 631, 632, 633, 634

lockXYZ, 578, 579, 582, 583, 586, 587

logical block, 114, 165

logical block size, 114

lseek, 119, 138, 139, 141, 149, 155, 211, 245, 465, 509, 510, 511, 512, 663, 665

lshistory, 43, 44

lstat, 189, 190, 229, 465

lwarx, 520, 531, 532, 533

M

MAC, 673, 678, 1133, 1134, 1135, 1149, 1155, 1156, 1214

machine instruction, 17

MAIN branch, 45

Maintaining backward compatibility, 1344, 1353

make command, 47, 48, 49, 50, 53, 54, 55, 58, 60, 61, 70

Make It Agnostic, 1359

Make It Idempotent, 1360

makefile, 47, 48, 49, 50, 51, 52, 53, 54, 55, 56, 58, 59, 60, 62, 65, 71

Makefile, 49, 51, 54, 55, 56, 57, 58, 59, 60, 62, 63, 65

malloc, 187, 188, 201, 202, 284, 285, 327, 328, 338, 339, 342, 358, 360, 393, 430, 432, 440, 441, 442, 447, 448, 505, 506, 751, 842, 929, 933, 1020, 1021, 1027, 1028, 1033, 1034, 1040, 1041, 1042, 1047, 1048, 1054, 1056, 1123, 1125, 1130, 1131, 1145, 1147, 1235,1252, 1262, 1275, 1292, 1298, 1301, 1303, 1364, 1366, 1367

MAP_PRIVATE, 662

MAP_SHARED, 661, 662, 664, 666

master-slave model, 694

max_buf, 864, 884, 885, 886, 890

MD2, 1064, 1074

MD4, 1064, 1074, 1075, 1077, 1078

MD5, 1064, 1074, 1075, 1077, 1078, 1135, 1154, 1225, 1341

memory layout, 285

memory leak, 284, 339, 358, 359, 440, 452, 753, 1366

memory management unit, 8, 21

memory-mapped file, 643, 660, 662, 666, 667, 668, 669

memset(, 127, 130, 132, 136, 138, 144, 146, 151, 152, 153, 154, 158, 187, 188, 191, 192, 195, 196, 201, 202, 210, 211, 212, 227, 339, 342, 343, 360, 367, 441, 442, 504, 505, 622, 698, 700, 701, 703, 706, 708, 712, 718, 722, 726, 727, 728, 730, 731, 734, 735, 736,743, 747, 749, 758, 760, 761, 764, 765, 769, 771, 775, 782, 792, 796, 803, 811, 814, 818, 821, 827, 829, 831, 836, 837, 840, 841, 851, 872, 873, 875, 876, 898, 899, 901, 902, 906, 908, 910, 911, 927, 930, 932, 933, 943, 946, 955, 961, 970, 974, 975, 995, 1019, 1022, 1024, 1025, 1032, 1035, 1037, 1038, 1046, 1049, 1051, 1052, 1104, 1108, 1117, 1120, 1123, 1125, 1126, 1127, 1130, 1132, 1142, 1145, 1148, 1212, 1229, 1233, 1245, 1249, 1255, 1259, 1268, 1272, 1277, 1284, 1289, 1298, 1300, 1301, 1302, 1305, 1307, 1315

message authentication, 1069, 1133, 1134, 1142, 1145, 1149, 1150

message authentication code, 1133, 1134

message digest, v, 1064, 1072, 1073, 1074, 1075, 1076, 1085, 1086, 1134, 1150, 1151, 1154, 1216, 1218, 1224, 1226, 1321, 1322, 1323

message digest algorithms, 1072

message integrity, 1070, 1071, 1072, 1073, 1133, 1134, 1141, 1142, 1145, 1149, 1150, 1151, 1155, 1216, 1221, 1227

message queue, 476, 605, 643, 649, 650, 651, 652, 653, 654, 655, 656, 657, 658, 659, 660, 668

mixed mode linking, 89

mkdir, 173, 222, 245, 465, 1066, 1067

mkdirat, 173, 465

mkelem, 42, 44

mkfifo, 245, 465, 644, 645, 646, 648, 649

mkfifoat, 465, 649, 668

mksandbox, 42

mkview, 42, 44

mmap, 162, 328, 660, 661, 662, 663, 664, 665, 666, 669

modulo, 1074, 1092, 1097, 1098, 1222

modulus, 1097, 1099, 1100, 1152, 1153, 1202, 1204, 1209, 1222

msgctl, 649, 656, 658, 659, 660

msgget, 649, 650, 651, 653, 654, 656, 657, 658, 659, 660

msgget.c, 650

msgrcv, 451, 463, 651, 652, 653, 655, 656, 657, 659

msgrcv.c, 653

msgrm.c, 659

msgsnd, 451, 463, 651, 652, 653, 655, 656, 657, 659

msgsnd.c, 652

msgstat.c, 658

multi-byte binary integer, 987

multi-byte integer, 983, 986, 988, 1004

multicast group, 750, 823, 824, 825, 826, 827, 828, 830, 832

multicast_rcv_all.c, 828

multicast_snd_all.c, 826

multicasting, 672, 750, 823, 824, 826, 828, 830, 941

multiprocess server, 836, 839

multiprocessor, vi, 20, 35, 539, 594

multitasking, 30, 471, 694, 835, 836
multithread, 859
multithreaded server, 352, 840, 845, 859
munmap, 660, 661, 662, 663, 664, 665, 666
mutex, 371, 372, 373, 374, 375, 376, 377, 378, 379, 380, 381, 382,
  383, 384, 385, 386, 387, 388, 389, 390, 391, 392, 393, 394, 395,
  396, 397, 398, 399, 400, 401, 402, 403, 404, 405, 406, 407, 408,
  409, 410, 411, 412, 413, 414, 415, 426, 435, 436, 437, 438,
  439, 440, 451, 454, 455, 456, 457, 458, 459, 461, 462, 467, 468,
  474, 569, 570, 571, 592, 593
mutex attribute, 373, 374, 375, 376, 381, 391, 459
mutual exclusion, 165, 370, 371, 373, 434, 474, 569, 593, 594,
  599, 624, 1347
mutual exclusion lock, 370, 371
mycryptolib.c, 1107, 1117, 1293, 1298, 1311, 1314
mydecrypt1, 1107, 1109, 1120, 1122, 1123, 1126, 1314, 1316,
  1317
mydecrypt2, 1117, 1119, 1126, 1129, 1132, 1144, 1148, 1173,
  1179, 1183, 1189, 1312, 1314, 1319, 1320, 1340
mydistlib.c, 1002
mydistsys.h.v1, 1015
mydistsys.h.v2, 1029
mydistsys.h.v3, 1042
myencrypt1, 1107, 1109, 1120, 1123, 1125, 1314, 1315, 1316
myencrypt2, 1117, 1118, 1126, 1129, 1131, 1132, 1145, 1147,
  1148, 1174, 1178, 1184, 1188, 1312, 1314, 1318, 1319
myhtonll, 997, 998, 1001, 1002, 1016, 1029, 1043
myntohll, 997, 998, 1001, 1003, 1016, 1029, 1043
myopenssl.h, 1108, 1118, 1120, 1123, 1127, 1130, 1142, 1146,
  1212, 1229, 1233, 1245, 1249, 1255, 1259, 1268, 1272, 1277,
  1284, 1289, 1298, 1311, 1315
myprog, 46, 64, 67, 68, 78, 79, 88, 89, 104, 105, 106, 107, 108, 171,
  172, 300, 302, 303, 304, 305, 742, 834, 854, 956, 957, 1068
mysemutil.h, 485, 486, 491, 496, 498, 501, 504, 526, 541, 545,
  551, 578, 581, 589
myshm.h, 607, 608, 610, 620, 622, 625, 627, 629
mysocket.h, 705, 707, 710, 742, 745, 748, 759, 763, 768, 774,
  781, 784, 791, 794, 802, 810, 813, 816, 819, 826, 828, 830, 850,
  941, 945, 953, 959, 969, 973, 1017, 1022, 1031, 1036, 1045, 1049
mysrv_privkey.pem, 1201, 1202

N

named pipe, 642, 643
named semaphore, 557, 562, 563, 564, 566, 567, 569, 595
natural language, 18, 19
ndd, 864, 865, 884, 885, 886, 887, 920, 921
Needing minimum effort to maintain, 1344
Needing minimum effort to support, 1344
net.inet.tcp.always_keepalive, 922
net.inet.tcp.keepinit, 916, 922, 923
net.inet.tcp.recvspace, 887, 888, 891

net.inet.tcp.sendspace, 887, 888, 891
net.ipv4.tcp_fin_timeout, 964, 965, 967
net.ipv4.tcp_rmem, 870, 880, 882, 883, 890
net.ipv4.tcp_tw_recycle, 964, 965, 967, 968
net.ipv4.tcp_tw_reuse, 964, 965, 966, 967, 968
net.ipv4.tcp_wmem, 870, 871, 880, 882, 883, 890
net.ipv4.udp_mem, 871, 881, 883, 890
netlib.c, 1120, 1137, 1298, 1300
netlib.h, 1120, 1123, 1127, 1130, 1142, 1146, 1229, 1233, 1245,
  1249, 1255, 1259, 1268, 1272, 1277, 1284, 1289, 1298, 1300
netstat, 23, 778, 865, 886, 887, 896
network adapter, 12, 15
Network is unreachable, 779
network layer, 680, 780
new_bound_srv_endpt, 1122, 1128, 1143, 1172, 1182, 1232,
  1248, 1258, 1271, 1280, 1287, 1300, 1308
nightly build, 39
No route to host, 779
No single point of failure, 1344
nonrepudiation, 1149, 1150, 1151, 1155, 1156, 1170, 1171,
  1175, 1180, 1181, 1185, 1190, 1191, 1338
ntohl, 858, 1001, 1021, 1025, 1027, 1034, 1035, 1038, 1040, 1041,
  1048, 1052, 1054, 1055
ntohll, 998, 1001, 1016, 1021, 1027, 1029, 1035, 1040, 1043,
  1048, 1054
ntohs, 758, 761, 765, 851, 1001

O

OCSP, 1199
OFB, 1088, 1093, 1094, 1095, 1096
OFB mode, 1095, 1096
open, 16, 25, 27, 39, 41, 66, 77, 87, 111, 116, 118, 119, 121, 122,
  123, 124, 125, 126, 128, 129, 131, 133, 134, 136, 138, 139, 141,
  143, 145, 146, 151, 153, 157, 158, 159, 160, 162, 164, 166, 169,
  173, 174, 176, 180, 189, 190, 191, 192, 193, 198, 203, 204, 205,
  206, 207, 210, 212, 213, 214, 222, 227, 229, 245, 272, 274, 293,
  307, 309, 316, 326, 327, 328, 334, 451, 452, 463, 465, 466, 482,
  483, 504, 508, 511, 513, 529, 570, 642, 644, 646, 648, 649, 661,
  662, 663, 665, 666, 669, 695, 698, 737, 839, 840, 843, 845, 857,
  865, 991, 993, 1010, 1064, 1068, 1071, 1108, 1117, 1133, 1212,
  1227, 1314
open file table, 121, 122, 123, 166
opendir, 193, 194, 196, 465
OpenMutex, 570
OpenSemaphore, 571
OpenSSL, 1063, 1064, 1065, 1066, 1067, 1068, 1071, 1077, 1100,
  1101, 1103, 1116, 1119, 1120, 1135, 1195, 1200, 1205, 1208,
  1217, 1228, 1254, 1282, 1293, 1294, 1295, 1296, 1297, 1298,
  1311, 1317, 1320, 1339, 1340, 1341
openssl ca, 1208, 1209, 1210, 1211
openssl genrsa, 1201, 1202, 1204, 1207, 1209, 1210

Index

openssl pkcs12, 1213, 1214
openssl req, 1201, 1202, 1204, 1207, 1209, 1211
openssl verify, 1202, 1208, 1211, 1263
openssl x509, 1213
optional signal, 251, 281
optional signals, 239, 275
origin integrity, 1069, 1070
orphaned process, 240, 314, 317, 345

P

padding, 690, 691, 999, 1010, 1017, 1030, 1044, 1074, 1088, 1102, 1152, 1154, 1224
parent process, 88, 238, 240, 243, 244, 253, 254, 273, 274, 276, 277, 283, 286, 288, 290, 291, 292, 293, 302, 303, 304, 306, 307, 308, 309, 310, 311, 312, 313, 314, 315, 316, 317, 344, 345, 500, 503, 642, 666, 668, 839, 840
partial block, 1088, 1102
partition, 113, 114, 165, 171
passwd file, 220, 341
PATH, 84, 85, 94, 102, 103, 104, 105, 107, 108, 184, 185, 186, 187, 188, 220, 300, 302, 303, 304, 305, 306, 307, 645, 646, 647, 648, 669, 750, 782, 785, 1066, 1067, 1069
pathconf, 184, 185, 186, 187, 188, 245, 311, 465, 649
pathconf.c, 185
Peer-to-peer model, 694
PEM, 1064, 1194, 1195, 1201, 1208, 1212, 1213, 1214, 1240, 1241, 1242, 1263, 1333
performance, v, 8, 13, 18, 19, 25, 26, 39, 41, 69, 70, 112, 114, 117, 125, 131, 140, 141, 147, 156, 157, 162, 163, 165, 167, 224, 349, 350, 353, 399, 413, 416, 514, 518, 539, 550, 575, 577, 588, 594, 595, 600, 601, 602, 629, 636, 637, 643, 667, 674, 721, 799, 800, 846, 861, 866, 867, 868, 878, 978, 980, 1009, 1010, 1089, 1091, 1096, 1154, 1224, 1339, 1344, 1346, 1352, 1354, 1355, 1362
Perl, 18, 66, 67, 69, 70, 1065, 1066, 1067
permission bits, 171, 172, 195, 643
Permission denied, 224, 478, 778, 848
PF_INET, 683, 684, 692, 717
PF_INET6, 683, 684, 692, 717
PF_UNIX, 683, 684, 692
physical blocks, 112, 114, 165
physical layer, 673
pipe, 184, 233, 234, 245, 308, 309, 310, 311, 312, 313, 334, 344, 642, 643, 644, 645, 648, 668, 857
pipe.c, 309, 311
pipedup.c, 312, 314, 346
pipes, 27, 308, 309, 344, 345, 639, 642, 643, 668, 669, 683
PKCS, 1194, 1195, 1196, 1213, 1214
PKE, 1085, 1190, 1191
PKI, v, 1063, 1153, 1155, 1190, 1191, 1192, 1338, 1340

plaintext, 1083, 1087, 1088, 1089, 1090, 1093, 1094, 1095, 1096, 1107, 1108, 1109, 1118, 1119
port number reservation, 849, 855
POSIX, v, 26, 27, 28, 29, 30, 47, 65, 111, 117, 118, 121, 123, 142, 150, 162, 167, 169, 171, 184, 185, 186, 224, 225, 229, 231, 232, 233, 235, 236, 238, 239, 241, 242, 243, 244, 246, 251, 252, 254, 255, 256, 262, 263, 268, 269, 271, 272, 275, 279, 280, 286, 287, 288, 291, 308, 322, 326, 327, 328, 334, 336, 337, 338, 341, 349, 350, 364, 365, 371, 373, 375, 376, 377, 386, 399, 400, 440, 445, 451, 459, 468, 474, 476, 483, 487, 493, 596, 602, 603, 605, 619, 635, 640, 642, 656, 660, 671, 681, 682, 684, 692, 704, 732, 733, 737, 738, 752, 754, 757, 790, 799, 836, 860, 868, 878, 879, 890, 924, 927, 937, 1001, 1004, 1348
POSIX semaphore, 480, 554, 557, 558, 559, 560, 561, 562, 564, 565, 566, 567, 568, 569
posix_memalign, 158, 159, 161
pre_master_secret, 1218
predefined macros, 52
preemption, 573, 576, 577
prime number, 1097, 1100, 1222
print_cipher_text, 1109, 1118, 1125, 1132, 1148, 1179, 1188, 1314, 1315
print_digest, 1079, 1081, 1083, 1314, 1325
prioceiling attribute, 376, 379, 468
private key, 650, 1084, 1085, 1086, 1098, 1099, 1100, 1149, 1150, 1151, 1152, 1153, 1155, 1191, 1192, 1193, 1194, 1195, 1198, 1201, 1202, 1204, 1205, 1207, 1208, 1209, 1213, 1214, 1218, 1223, 1224, 1225, 1232, 1239, 1240, 1242, 1243, 1248, 1258, 1263, 1264, 1271, 1281, 1282, 1288, 1332, 1333
private key encryption, 1085, 1150
privileged port numbers, 848
process group, 208, 214, 235, 238, 240, 252, 283, 288, 289, 290, 291, 293, 296, 317, 344, 346
process isolation, 598
Processor, 2, 7, 520
process-shared attribute, 375, 376, 400, 424, 425, 468
producer-consumer problem, 371, 372, 399, 400, 402, 406, 415, 1347
Program Counter, 5, 6, 7
programming language, 17, 70, 475
programming tips, v, 1343, 1363
protocol attribute, 376, 377, 379, 380
pselect, 463, 723, 799
pt_args_ret.c, 355, 358
pt_args_ret2.c, 359
pt_cancel.c, 446, 450
pt_create.c, 353
pt_detached.c, 368
pt_mutex.c, 383, 468
pt_mutex_cleanup.c, 392
pt_mutex_init.c, 378
pt_produce_consume.c, 406, 469

Index

`pt_prt_thrd_attr.c`, 366

`pt_recursive_mutex.c`, 387

`pt_rwlock.c`, 416, 420

`pt_rwlock_attr.c`, 420

`pt_signal_thread.c`, 454

`pt_tsd.c`, 426

`pt_tsd_destroy.c`, 441

`pt_tsd_ptr.c`, 430

`pt_tsd_reentrant.c`, 435, 468

`pthread_attr_getdetachstate`, 362, 363, 366, 460

`pthread_attr_getinheritsched`, 365, 366, 367, 460

`pthread_attr_getschedparam`, 364, 367, 460

`pthread_attr_getschedpolicy`, 364, 367, 460

`pthread_attr_getscope`, 362, 366, 460

`pthread_attr_getstackaddr`, 363

`pthread_attr_getstacksize`, 363, 460

`pthread_attr_setdetachstate`, 362, 363, 368, 369, 460, 843

`pthread_attr_setinheritsched`, 365, 366, 460

`pthread_attr_setschedparam`, 364, 365, 460

`pthread_attr_setschedpolicy`, 364, 460

`pthread_attr_setscope`, 362, 460

`pthread_attr_setstackaddr`, 363

`pthread_attr_setstacksize`, 363, 460, 843

`pthread_cancel`, 395, 444, 445, 449, 452, 458, 460

`pthread_cleanup_pop`, 394, 448, 452, 460

`pthread_cleanup_push`, 393, 448, 452, 460

`pthread_cond_broadcast`, 405, 406, 413, 461

`pthread_cond_destroy`, 401, 402, 461

`pthread_cond_init`, 401, 402, 461, 469

`pthread_cond_signal`, 405, 406, 408, 409, 413, 461

`pthread_cond_timedwait`, 381, 401, 404, 405, 406, 451, 461, 463

`pthread_cond_wait`, 381, 404, 405, 406, 407, 409, 413, 451, 461, 463

`pthread_condattr_destroy`, 400, 401, 460

`pthread_condattr_getclock`, 401, 460

`pthread_condattr_getpshared`, 400, 460

`pthread_condattr_init`, 400, 401, 402, 460, 469

`pthread_condattr_setclock`, 401, 460

`pthread_condattr_setpshared`, 400, 401, 460

`pthread_create`, 353, 354, 357, 361, 365, 368, 369, 385, 390, 397, 411, 412, 419, 423, 429, 433, 439, 443, 450, 457, 459, 461, 528, 544, 547, 553, 581, 586, 843

`pthread_exit`, 250, 266, 275, 353, 355, 356, 357, 358, 359, 360, 361, 369, 370, 380, 381, 383, 384, 385, 388, 389, 390, 393, 394, 396, 397, 398, 407, 408, 409, 410, 411, 412, 417, 418, 419, 420, 421, 422, 423, 424, 427, 428, 429, 432, 433, 434, 437, 438, 439, 440, 442, 443, 444, 447, 448, 449, 450, 455, 456, 457, 458, 461, 527, 542, 543, 545, 546, 551, 552, 579, 584, 844, 845

`PTHREAD_EXPLICIT_SCHED`, 365, 367

`pthread_getspecific`, 426, 427, 428, 431, 436, 440, 442, 461, 582, 583, 587

`PTHREAD_INHERIT_SCHED`, 365, 367

`pthread_join`, 354, 357, 358, 359, 361, 368, 385, 390, 397, 412, 420, 424, 429, 434, 439, 444, 450, 451, 458, 461, 463, 529, 541, 544, 547, 554, 581, 586

`pthread_kill`, 453, 454, 457, 461

`pthread_mutex`, 373, 374, 378, 381, 382, 386, 391, 392, 398, 461, 462, 468

`pthread_mutex_consistent`, 378, 391, 392, 395, 398, 461, 468

`pthread_mutex_destroy`, 378, 380, 381, 385, 390, 397, 412, 440, 458, 461

`pthread_mutex_init`, 373, 374, 375, 380, 385, 389, 397, 411, 439, 457, 461

`pthread_mutex_lock`, 377, 378, 382, 384, 386, 387, 391, 393, 395, 398, 404, 407, 409, 435, 436, 451, 456, 462, 468

`pthread_mutex_timedlock`, 382, 386, 462, 468

`pthread_mutex_trylock`, 382, 386, 462, 468

`pthread_mutex_unlock`, 378, 382, 384, 386, 388, 391, 392, 394, 395, 398, 408, 409, 413, 435, 436, 456, 462

`pthread_mutexattr_destroy`, 380, 381, 385, 390, 397, 412, 440, 458, 461

`pthread_mutexattr_getprioceiling`, 376, 379, 461

`pthread_mutexattr_getprotocol`, 377, 379, 461

`pthread_mutexattr_getpshared`, 376, 379, 461

`pthread_mutexattr_getrobust`, 378, 379, 461

`pthread_mutexattr_gettype`, 375, 379, 461

`pthread_mutexattr_init`, 373, 374, 378, 380, 384, 389, 396, 411, 438, 457, 461

`pthread_mutexattr_setprioceiling`, 376, 461

`pthread_mutexattr_setprotocol`, 377, 380, 461

`pthread_mutexattr_setpshared`, 376, 380, 461

`pthread_mutexattr_setrobust`, 378, 391, 396, 461

`pthread_mutexattr_settype`, 375, 387, 389, 461

`pthread_rwlock_rdlock`, 416, 417, 421, 462, 466

`pthread_rwlock_tryrdlock`, 416, 462

`pthread_rwlock_trywrlock`, 416, 462

`pthread_rwlock_unlock`, 416, 418, 419, 421, 422, 462

`pthread_rwlock_wrlock`, 416, 418, 422, 462, 466

`pthread_setcancelstate`, 393, 394, 445, 447, 448, 462

`pthread_setcanceltype`, 393, 446, 447, 462

`pthread_setspecific`, 426, 427, 428, 430, 432, 436, 437, 440, 442, 444, 461, 582, 583, 584, 587

`pthread_sigmask`, 258, 453, 454, 455, 457, 462

`pthread_testcancel`, 451, 462, 463, 468

`pthreads`, 28, 30, 56, 279, 349, 350, 353, 354, 361, 362, 364, 365, 366, 368, 370, 371, 373, 383, 399, 404, 416, 425, 426, 440, 441, 444, 445, 451, 452, 453, 459, 467, 517, 592, 593, 836, 845, 1347

`pthreads APIs`, 459

`pthreads cancellation`, **445**

public key, 1084, 1085, 1086, 1097, 1098, 1099, 1100, 1135, 1149, 1150, 1151, 1152, 1153, 1154, 1155, 1190, 1191, 1192, 1194, 1198, 1206, 1217, 1218, 1220, 1221, 1224, 1225, 1239, 1242, 1333, 1335

public key cryptography, 1084, 1085, 1086, 1149, 1150, 1190, 1191, 1192

public key encryption, 1085, 1149, 1191

public key infrastructure, 1190, 1191

public-key cryptography, 1097, 1099, 1222

putc, 163, 466

putchar, 163, 466

pwrite, 119, 463

Python, 18, 66, 69, 70

R

raise(, 263

RAM, 9, 10, 20, 36

random I/O, 111, 137, 138, 141, 155, 166, 169

randomwr.c, 138

RC2, 1091, 1097, 1100, 1224

RC4, 1089, 1091, 1097, 1224, 1225

RC5, 1091, 1097, 1100

RDBMS, 24, 25, 32, 34, 162, 479, 600, 602, 623, 636

read, vii, 10, 11, 14, 16, 19, 21, 24, 25, 44, 58, 78, 87, 111, 112, 113, 114, 115, 116, 117, 118, 119, 120, 121, 123, 124, 125, 126, 129, 130, 131, 132, 133, 134, 136, 137, 138, 140, 141, 142, 143, 144, 145, 146, 147, 148, 149, 150, 152, 153, 154, 155, 156, 157, 163, 166, 167, 169, 170, 171, 172, 189, 193, 194, 195, 204, 205, 206, 208, 209, 215, 217, 218, 219, 224, 225, 235, 237, 245, 255, 284, 288, 289, 308, 309, 310, 311, 312, 313, 314, 346, 415, 416, 417, 420, 421, 423, 424, 425, 451, 463, 468, 482, 494, 495, 503, 509, 510, 511, 512, 513, 515, 529, 531, 533, 538, 539, 541, 575, 594, 596, 601, 603, 604, 609, 613, 614, 617, 618, 619, 621, 625, 626, 627, 628, 631, 636, 642, 643, 644, 648, 651, 657, 660, 661, 666, 667, 669, 680, 684, 710, 717, 725, 787, 788, 789, 790, 794, 797, 798, 800, 801, 834, 859, 865, 937, 985, 989, 990, 992, 993, 994, 995, 999, 1000, 1008, 1009, 1026, 1027, 1039, 1040, 1053, 1054, 1057, 1061, 1070, 1085, 1087, 1092, 1108, 1117, 1212, 1229, 1230, 1236, 1237, 1239, 1240, 1245, 1246, 1252,1253, 1255, 1256, 1262, 1268, 1269, 1276, 1277, 1279, 1285, 1286, 1292, 1295, 1315, 1352, 1359, 1360

read lock, 416, 417, 421, 515

read.c, 130

readdir, 193, 194, 195, 196, 197, 198, 466

readdir_r, 193, 194, 196, 197, 466

readdir_r.c, 194

reader.c, 134, 662, 665, 669

readv, 119, 143, 144, 145, 146, 167, 245, 463

readv.c, 144

receive buffer size, 868, 871, 872, 879, 880, 881, 882, 885, 886, 887, 888, 928

recipient authentication, 1069, 1190, 1191

recv(, 245, 451, 463, 692, 710, 717, 723, 724, 725, 729, 732, 745, 748, 762, 766, 772, 773, 777, 779, 783, 786, 791, 794, 798, 806, 808, 815, 816, 822, 839, 844, 852, 859, 874, 878, 891, 901, 905, 909, 914, 925, 931, 935, 936, 945, 948, 956, 962, 969, 972, 976,977, 1021, 1025, 1026, 1034, 1038, 1040, 1048, 1052, 1053, 1054, 1057, 1122, 1126, 1128, 1132, 1144, 1148, 1310

recv_buf, 885, 886, 890

recvfrom, 245, 451, 463, 692, 696, 697, 701, 703, 706, 709, 710, 712, 713, 724, 725, 766, 767, 830, 832, 834

reentrant, 244, 245, 435, 468, 577, 581, 585, 587

reentrantable, 434, 435, 586

regression, 37, 39, 40, 65, 66, 1345, 1360, 1361

regression suites, 40, 66, 1361

regression test suites, 37, 40, 1360

regular file, 125, 170, 171, 175, 177, 184, 195, 224

ReleaseMutex, 570, 571

ReleaseSemaphore, 571, 572

remove, 50, 180, 181, 182, 229, 258, 409, 413, 452, 466, 484, 485, 486, 490, 492, 494, 497, 499, 500, 503, 554, 590, 603, 606, 615, 616, 617, 619, 620, 625, 787, 1088, 1208, 1296

rename, 182, 183, 245, 466

rename.c, 183

renameat, 182, 183, 466

RFC, 679, 680, 889, 937, 981, 982, 1199

RIPEMD-160, 1074, 1078

rmdir, 173, 180, 181, 245

robust attribute, 377, 378, 379

robust mutex, 378, 386, 391

Robustness, 386, 1344

ROM, 9, 10, 11, 13, 20, 23, 36

root CA, 1196, 1197, 1198, 1203, 1204, 1207, 1208, 1211, 1218, 1254, 1282, 1339

RSA, 1089, 1097, 1099, 1100, 1150, 1151, 1152, 1153, 1154, 1193, 1194, 1195, 1201, 1202, 1204, 1209, 1218, 1220, 1221, 1224, 1225, 1237, 1242, 1283, 1339

RSA signature, 1154

RSABITSLEN, 1166, 1176, 1312

S

SAM, 589, 592

Scalability, 840, 845, 1344, 1355

scatter/gather I/O, 142

sccsdiff, 43, 44

sched_get_priority_max, 365, 468

sched_get_priority_min, 365, 468

scheduling policy, 362, 363, 364, 365, 367, 382, 406

scripting languages, 19, 67, 69

secrecy, 1070, 1085, 1087, 1120, 1123, 1126, 1129, 1141, 1145, 1149, 1151, 1191, 1223, 1227, 1228

Index

secret key cryptography, 1084, 1085, 1098, 1134, 1135, 1155, 1221

Security, 21, 34, 676, 981, 1063, 1064, 1069, 1075, 1089, 1133, 1135, 1152, 1156, 1215, 1222, 1340, 1341, 1344, 1354

select, 10, 119, 245, 279, 463, 491, 492, 509, 511, 717, 723, 749, 768, 788, 789, 790, 797, 799, 800, 801, 804, 805, 807, 808, 809, 823, 826, 889, 996, 1217

self-signed, v, 1198, 1200, 1203, 1204, 1206, 1211, 1213, 1218, 1228, 1236, 1243, 1245, 1249, 1253, 1254, 1334, 1339

self-signed server certificate, 1198, 1200, 1236, 1245, 1249, 1254

sem_close, 562, 563, 564, 568

sem_destroy, 555, 557, 561, 562

sem_init, 555, 556, 557, 560, 561, 568

sem_open, 556, 562, 563, 564, 567

sem_post, 555, 556, 557, 558, 562, 563, 565

sem_timedwait, 463, 556

sem_trywait, 556

sem_unlink, 562, 563, 564

sem_wait, 463, 554, 555, 556, 558, 562, 563, 565

semaem, 487, 495, 588, 590, 591

semaphore, 474, 476, 477, 479, 480, 481, 482, 483, 484, 485, 486, 487, 488, 489, 490, 491, 492, 493, 494, 495, 496, 497, 498, 499, 500, 501, 502, 503, 504, 505, 506, 507, 518, 526, 530, 550, 551, 552, 553, 554, 569, 571, 587, 588, 589, 590, 592, 593, 594, 595, 596, 605, 640, 641

semcreate.c, 483

semcrerm.c, 485

semctl, 484, 485, 486, 487, 490, 491, 492, 493, 494, 495, 496, 497, 498, 499, 500, 503, 506, 554, 588, 589, 590

semget, 482, 483, 484, 485, 490, 491, 497, 498, 505, 587, 588, 590

semipcinfo.c, 589

semlib.c, 500, 501, 504

semlock.c, 490

semmap, 486, 588, 590, 591

semmni, 486, 495, 588, 589, 590, 591, 592

semmns, 486, 495, 588, 590, 591

semmnu, 486, 588, 590, 591

semmsl, 486, 495, 588, 590, 591

semop, 466, 481, 484, 486, 489, 490, 491, 492, 494, 495, 499, 507, 552, 588, 595

semopm, 486, 588, 590, 591

semsetall.c, 498

semsetone.c, 496

semume, 486, 588, 590, 591

semupd_mylock.c, 541

semupd_mylock_reentrant.c, 581

semupd_mylock_sun64.c, 545

semupd_posix_sema.c, 557, 595

semupd_sema.c, 550

semupdf.c, 501, 526

semupdf_mylock.c, 526

semupdf2_posix_named_sem.c, 564

semusz, 487, 495, 588, 590, 591

semvmx, 487, 495, 588, 590, 591

send buffer size, 868, 871, 879, 880, 881, 882, 885, 886, 888, 936

send(, 245, 451, 463, 688, 692, 710, 717, 723, 724, 725, 729, 732, 745, 748, 762, 766, 773, 776, 783, 786, 793, 806, 807, 808, 839, 844, 853, 859, 874, 878, 900, 905, 909, 914, 931, 936, 944, 948, 956, 962, 972, 976, 1020, 1021, 1022, 1028, 1034, 1035, 1042, 1048, 1049, 1056, 1123, 1129, 1145, 1309, 1310

send_buf, 885, 886, 890

sender authentication, 1069, 1085, 1134, 1149, 1150, 1151, 1190, 1191

sendto, 245, 451, 463, 688, 692, 695, 696, 701, 703, 704, 706, 708, 709, 710, 712, 713, 724, 725, 825, 828

sequential I/O, 111, 138, 141, 155, 166, 169

ServerHello message, 1217

ServerHelloDone, 1218, 1219, 1220

ServerKeyExchange, 1218

service_client, 836, 838, 839, 840, 841, 842, 845, 1022, 1024, 1025, 1026, 1027, 1036, 1038, 1039, 1040, 1049, 1052, 1053, 1054, 1061

services file, 689, 699, 851, 853, 855

Set Cipher Suite, 1293

SetAll, 162

setgid, 245, 287, 288

setpgid, 245, 289, 290

setpgrp, 289, 290

setpwent, 340

setrlimit, 326, 327, 331, 332, 333

setrlimit.c, 331

setsid, 245, 289, 290, 291

setsockopt, 692, 737, 738, 741, 744, 760, 771, 778, 792, 811, 818, 824, 825, 827, 828, 829, 830, 831, 832, 833, 867, 868, 869, 870, 871, 873, 877, 878, 879, 880, 881, 882, 885, 887, 890, 896, 897, 898, 899, 903, 904, 906, 907, 908, 911, 912, 913, 920, 924, 925, 926, 927, 929, 930, 934, 943, 954, 955, 960, 961, 964, 965, 968, 971, 975, 977, 1024, 1037, 1051, 1306, 1307

setuid, 245, 287, 288, 308

setview, 44

SHA, 1064, 1073, 1074, 1075, 1076, 1077, 1135, 1152, 1154, 1216, 1224, 1225, 1341

SHA-1, 1075, 1077, 1135, 1152, 1154, 1341

SHA-2, 1075, 1077, 1341

SHA-256, 1075, 1076, 1077, 1152, 1154

SHA-512, 1075, 1076, 1077

shared library, 76, 93, 284

shared lock, 209, 515, 550

shared memory, v, 8, 189, 400, 425, 476, 522, 550, 592, 593, 597, 598, 599, 600, 601, 602, 603, 604, 605, 606, 607, 608, 609, 610, 611, 612, 613, 614, 615, 616, 617, 618, 619, 620, 621, 622, 623,

1389

Index

624, 625, 626, 627, 628, 629, 630, 631, 632, 633, 634, 635, 636, 637, 639, 641, 643, 659, 1355
shared secret key, 1084, 1098, 1134, 1136, 1149, 1191, 1221, 1222, 1223
Shell scripts, 67
SHLIB_PATH, 85, 103, 107
shmall, 623
shmapi.c, 620
shmat, 605, 606, 617, 618, 620, 621, 626, 627, 630, 635
shmctl, 606, 611, 619, 620, 621, 622, 623, 635, 636
shmdt, 605, 606, 618, 619, 621, 626, 628, 631, 635
shmget, 603, 604, 606, 607, 608, 609, 610, 611, 616, 617, 620, 622, 623, 625, 627, 630, 635, 637
shmget.c, 617
shmmax, 623
shmmin, 623
shmmni, 588, 623
shmowner.c, 622
shmread.c, 625
shmseg, 623, 624
shmstat.c, 627
shmupd.c, 629
shutdown (, 466, 740
sig_default.c, 247
SIG_DFL, 238, 243, 246, 247, 248, 278, 307, 319, 328, 453
sig_handler.c, 249
SIG_IGN, 243, 246, 247, 249, 262, 277, 278, 281, 307, 315, 316, 317, 319, 345, 837
sig_ignore.c, 248
sig_isalive.c, 252
sig_numbers.c, 239
sig_procmask.c, 259, 281
sig_sigpending.c, 264
sig_sigset.c, 256
sig_sigsuspend.c, 266
sig_sigusr.c, 272
sig_sigwait.c, 269
sig_sleep.c, 275
SIGABRT signal, 233, 319
sigaction, 243, 245, 246, 247, 248, 249, 250, 251, 254, 255, 262, 267, 268, 273, 275, 276, 278, 282, 317, 345, 453, 836, 837, 840
sigaddset, 245, 255, 256, 258, 260, 265, 267, 270
SIGALRM signal, 233, 277, 281
SIGBUS, 239, 263
SIGCHLD, 236, 237, 238, 239, 243, 247, 281, 282, 315, 316, 317, 345, 837, 839
SIGCONT, 236, 237, 238, 239, 240, 242, 243, 317
sigdelset, 245, 255, 256, 257, 258, 261, 268, 455
sigemptyset, 245, 255, 256, 258, 260, 262, 265, 267, 268, 270
sigfillset, 245, 248, 249, 250, 255, 256, 257, 268, 273, 276, 455, 457, 837

SIGFPE, 233, 239, 242, 243, 263, 280
SIGHUP signal, 233, 240, 317
SIGILL signal, 234
SIGINT signal, 234, 259, 261, 281
sigismember, 245, 256, 257, 260, 264, 266, 269
SIGKILL signal, 234, 235, 240, 241, 295, 453
signal handler, 233, 238, 241, 242, 243, 244, 245, 246, 247, 248, 249, 250, 251, 254, 262, 265, 268, 269, 273, 274, 275, 276, 277, 278, 279, 280, 281, 282, 319, 386, 452, 453, 454, 459
signal mask, 246, 247, 251, 254, 255, 258, 259, 260, 261, 262, 265, 266, 267, 270, 279, 280, 307, 453, 458, 799
signals, v, 3, 11, 12, 14, 27, 28, 208, 214, 231, 232, 233, 235, 236, 237, 238, 239, 240, 241, 242, 243, 244, 245, 246, 247, 248, 249, 250, 251, 254, 255, 256, 257, 258, 259, 262, 263, 264, 266, 268, 269, 270, 271, 272, 274, 275, 276, 278, 279, 280, 281, 288, 291, 293, 334, 345, 352, 399, 452, 453, 454, 455, 457, 458, 459, 467, 639, 640, 673, 1222
signals for job control, 236
sigpending, 245, 263, 264, 265, 266, 269
sigprocmask, 245, 255, 258, 259, 260, 261, 262, 265, 267, 270, 278, 279, 453, 462
SIGQUIT signal, 234, 247, 248, 249, 250, 261, 264, 265, 267, 268, 270, 276, 277
SIGSEGV, 233, 234, 239, 242, 243, 263, 328
SIGSTOP, 236, 237, 238, 239, 241, 243, 244, 246, 255, 259, 262, 263, 297, 298, 455
sigsuspend, 245, 265, 266, 268, 279, 463
SIGTERM signal, 234, 235, 240, 254
sigtimedwait, 271, 458, 463
SIGTSTP, 236, 237, 238, 239, 243
SIGTTIN, 236, 237, 238, 239, 243
SIGTTOU, 236, 237, 238, 239, 243
SIGUSR1, 233, 235, 239, 242, 254, 272, 273, 274, 280, 281
SIGUSR2, 233, 235, 239, 243, 254, 272, 274, 280
sigwait, 268, 269, 270, 271, 279, 451, 454, 455, 458, 463
sigwaitinfo, 271, 458, 463
Simplicity, 1344, 1348
single-byte binary integer, 985
single-threaded, 30, 352, 453, 454, 695, 835, 859
SO_EXCLBIND, 953, 957, 958
SO_EXCLUSIVEADDRUSE, 951, 952, 953, 956, 957, 958, 980
SO_KEEPALIVE, 733, 735, 873, 891, 892, 893, 894, 895, 896, 897, 898, 899, 901, 903, 905, 906, 907, 909, 911, 912, 914, 915, 916, 918, 919, 921, 923, 924, 925, 926, 927, 929, 978, 979, 980, 1306, 1307
SO_LINGER, 733, 735, 738, 926, 927, 928, 929, 930, 931, 932, 934, 936, 937, 939, 978, 979, 980
SO_RCVBUF, 733, 735, 867, 868, 871, 872, 873, 875, 878, 880, 882, 886, 887, 890, 927, 929, 931
SO_RCVLOWAT, 733, 735, 736, 977, 978
SO_RCVTIMEO, 733, 736, 738, 968, 969, 972, 975, 977

Index

SO_REUSEADDR, 733, 736, 771, 778, 792, 811, 818, 826, 828, 829, 832, 833, 834, 940, 941, 942, 943, 945, 949, 950, 951, 952, 957, 958, 963, 964, 965, 966, 967, 968, 978, 979, 980, 1023, 1024, 1037, 1051, 1058, 1059, 1307

SO_REUSEPORT, 736, 826, 830, 831, 832, 833, 834, 846, 847, 940, 957, 958, 959, 960, 961, 963, 964, 968, 979, 980

SO_SNDBUF, 733, 736, 867, 868, 869, 870, 871, 872, 875, 877, 878, 880, 882, 886, 890, 927, 931, 934, 943, 961

SO_SNDTIMEO, 733, 736, 737, 738, 968, 977

SOCK_STREAM socket, 880, 893

socket, v, 79, 171, 208, 214, 600, 642, 671, 672, 680, 681, 682, 683, 684, 685, 686, 687, 688, 689, 690, 691, 692, 693, 695, 696, 697, 698, 699, 700, 701, 702, 703, 704, 705, 706, 707, 708, 709, 710, 711, 712, 717, 718, 719, 720, 721, 722, 723, 724, 725, 726, 727, 728, 729, 730, 731, 732, 733, 734, 735, 736, 737, 738, 739, 740, 741, 742, 743, 744, 745, 746, 747, 748, 749, 750, 751, 752, 753, 754, 755, 756, 757, 758, 759, 760, 761, 762, 763, 764, 766, 767, 768, 769, 770, 771, 773, 774, 776, 777, 778, 780, 781, 782, 784, 785, 787, 788, 789, 790, 791, 792, 794, 795, 796, 797, 800, 801, 802, 803, 804, 805, 806, 807, 808, 809, 810, 811, 812, 813, 814, 815, 816, 817, 818, 819, 820, 821, 822, 823, 824, 825, 826, 827, 828, 829, 830, 831, 832, 833, 834, 835, 836, 837, 839, 840, 841, 842, 843, 845, 846, 847, 848, 849, 850, 851, 856, 857, 858, 861, 863, 864, 865, 866, 867, 868, 869, 870, 871, 872, 873, 875, 876, 877, 878, 879, 880, 881, 882, 883, 884, 885, 886, 887, 888, 889, 890, 891, 892, 893, 894, 895, 896, 897, 898, 899, 901, 902, 903, 904, 905, 906, 907, 908, 909, 910, 911, 912, 913, 914, 915, 916, 917, 918, 919, 920, 921, 922, 924, 925, 926, 927, 928, 929, 930, 931, 932, 933, 934, 936, 937, 938, 939, 940, 941, 942, 943, 945, 946, 947, 948, 949, 950, 951, 952, 953, 954, 955, 956, 957, 958, 959, 960, 961, 963, 964, 965, 966, 967, 968, 969, 970, 971, 972, 973, 974, 975, 977, 978, 979, 980, 982, 996, 1001, 1017, 1018, 1019, 1022, 1023, 1024, 1031, 1032, 1033, 1035, 1036, 1037, 1044, 1045, 1046, 1047, 1049, 1050, 1051, 1057, 1058, 1059, 1071, 1120, 1121, 1123, 1124, 1126, 1127, 1128, 1129, 1130, 1142, 1143, 1145, 1146, 1229, 1230, 1231, 1232, 1233, 1235, 1236, 1237, 1238, 1239, 1240, 1245, 1246, 1247, 1248, 1249, 1250, 1251, 1253, 1255, 1257, 1258, 1259, 1261, 1263, 1267, 1268, 1269, 1270, 1271, 1272, 1273, 1274, 1276, 1277, 1278, 1279, 1280, 1281, 1284, 1285, 1286, 1287, 1288, 1289, 1291, 1293, 1298, 1300, 1304, 1306, 1307, 1309, 1310, 1353, 1359

socket address, 689, 690, 691, 692, 695, 696, 698, 699, 700, 706, 709, 710, 718, 719, 722, 723, 725, 726, 728, 743, 746, 751, 753, 754, 756, 757, 758, 760, 764, 766, 774, 782, 787, 792, 795, 803, 809, 811, 814, 818, 821, 837, 841, 846, 847, 848, 851, 873, 876, 899, 902, 908, 911, 930, 933, 940, 943, 946, 950, 952, 955, 957, 959, 961, 963, 970, 974, 1019, 1024, 1032, 1037, 1046, 1051, 1120, 1127, 1142, 1231, 1247, 1257, 1270, 1279, 1286, 1304, 1306, 1307

socket file, 171, 723, 740, 745, 763, 768, 774, 784, 788, 789, 790, 794, 797, 800, 801, 827, 828, 830, 850, 945, 973, 1018, 1031, 1045, 1124, 1130, 1146, 1233, 1235, 1237, 1238, 1239, 1250, 1251, 1259, 1261, 1273, 1274, 1289, 1291, 1304, 1306, 1309

socket option, 733, 734, 735, 736, 737, 741, 742, 744, 759, 760, 768, 771, 778, 792, 810, 811, 818, 824, 825, 826, 827, 828, 829, 830, 831, 832, 833, 834, 846, 869, 870, 873, 886, 891, 892, 893, 894, 895, 896, 897, 898, 899, 901, 903, 904, 905, 906, 907, 908, 909, 911, 912, 913, 914, 915, 916, 918, 919, 924, 925, 927, 929, 930, 931, 934, 936, 937, 940, 941, 942, 943, 945, 949, 950, 951, 952, 953, 954, 955, 956, 957, 959, 960, 961, 963, 964, 965, 966, 967, 968, 969, 970, 971, 972, 978, 979, 980, 1023, 1024, 1036, 1037, 1050, 1051, 1058, 1059, 1304, 1306, 1307

socket types, 684, 685, 687, 689, 721

socket.c, 685

software design principles, 1343

software development process, 37, 40, 70

Solaris, v, 29, 47, 79, 83, 84, 85, 89, 92, 93, 96, 97, 98, 101, 102, 104, 118, 155, 157, 160, 162, 269, 336, 338, 350, 362, 364, 365, 378, 533, 541, 550, 588, 589, 591, 629, 633, 652, 654, 671, 742, 745, 747, 748, 754, 759, 762, 764, 768, 774, 775, 781, 784, 791, 794, 801, 803, 806, 807, 808, 810, 813, 814, 816, 819, 826, 828, 832, 833, 834, 850, 851, 864, 870, 871, 884, 885, 890, 894, 905, 906, 907, 909, 912, 914, 916, 919, 920, 921, 925, 936, 940, 941, 945, 946, 952, 957, 958, 959, 963, 969, 973, 974, 981, 986, 996, 997, 999, 1001, 1016, 1017, 1019, 1022, 1029, 1031, 1032, 1036, 1043, 1044, 1046, 1049, 1057, 1058, 1059

source control software, 41, 42, 44

source control system, 39, 41, 42, 43, 70

special characters, 53, 54

Special-Purpose Registers, 4

speed. In the foreseeable future, IPv4 and IPv6 will, 679

spinlock, 462, 517, 519, 523, 526, 529, 530, 532, 534, 536, 537, 539, 540, 542, 545, 546, 551, 578, 582, 595, 609, 613, 615, 616

SSL, v, 676, 678, 680, 1063, 1064, 1068, 1071, 1075, 1089, 1091, 1135, 1153, 1190, 1191, 1192, 1195, 1197, 1199, 1200, 1202, 1204, 1208, 1209, 1214, 1215, 1216, 1217, 1219, 1220, 1221, 1222, 1223, 1224, 1225, 1226, 1227, 1228, 1229, 1230, 1231, 1232, 1233, 1234, 1235, 1236, 1237, 1238, 1239, 1240, 1241, 1242, 1243, 1244, 1245, 1246, 1247, 1248, 1249, 1250, 1251, 1252, 1253, 1254, 1255, 1256, 1257, 1258, 1259, 1260, 1261, 1262, 1263, 1264, 1265, 1266, 1267, 1268, 1269, 1270, 1271, 1272, 1273, 1274, 1275, 1276, 1277, 1278, 1279, 1280, 1281, 1282, 1283, 1284, 1285, 1286, 1287, 1288, 1289, 1290, 1291, 1292, 1293, 1294, 1295, 1296, 1332, 1333, 1336, 1337, 1339, 1340

SSL_accept, 1230, 1239, 1240, 1244, 1246, 1253, 1256, 1265, 1266, 1267, 1269, 1278, 1285, 1295

SSL_check_private_key, 1243

SSL_connect, 1235, 1237, 1239, 1244, 1251, 1253, 1261, 1265, 1266, 1267, 1275, 1291, 1295, 1296

SSL_CTX_load_verify_locations, 1243, 1244, 1251, 1253, 1254, 1261, 1265, 1271, 1274, 1281, 1282, 1288, 1291

Index

SSL_CTX_new, 1232, 1234, 1237, 1238, 1239, 1248, 1251, 1258, 1260, 1271, 1274, 1281, 1287, 1290

SSL_CTX_set_cipher_list, 1293

SSL_CTX_set_verify, 1243, 1244, 1251, 1253, 1261, 1265, 1266, 1268, 1272, 1274, 1277, 1281, 1284, 1285, 1288, 1291

SSL_CTX_use_certificate, 1240, 1241, 1263, 1333, 1340

SSL_CTX_use_PrivateKey, 1240, 1242, 1333

SSL_CTX_use_PrivateKey_ASN1, 1242

SSL_CTX_use_RSAPrivateKey, 1242

SSL_CTX_use_RSAPrivateKey_ASN1, 1242

SSL_CTX_use_RSAPrivateKey_file, 1242

SSL_get_cipher_list, 1293, 1337

SSL_get_error, 1229, 1230, 1231, 1234, 1235, 1236, 1245, 1246, 1247, 1250, 1251, 1252, 1253, 1255, 1256, 1259, 1261, 1262, 1268, 1269, 1270, 1273, 1275, 1276, 1277, 1278, 1279, 1284, 1285, 1286, 1289, 1291, 1292, 1294, 1295, 1296

SSL_get_peer_certificate, 1244, 1265, 1266, 1267, 1278, 1336

SSL_get_verify_result, 1208, 1243, 1244, 1252, 1253, 1254, 1261, 1266, 1267, 1275, 1276, 1278, 1291, 1292

SSL_library_init, 1237, 1239

SSL_new, 1230, 1234, 1235, 1237, 1238, 1239, 1241, 1246, 1251, 1255, 1260, 1264, 1265, 1266, 1268, 1274, 1277, 1278, 1284, 1285, 1291, 1294

SSL_set_fd, 1230, 1235, 1237, 1239, 1246, 1251, 1255, 1256, 1261, 1269, 1274, 1278, 1285, 1291

SSL_set_verify, 1244, 1253

SSL_use_certificate, 1241, 1263

SSL_use_certificate_chain_file, 1263

SSL_use_PrivateKey, 1242

SSL_use_PrivateKey_ASN1, 1242

SSL_use_PrivateKey_file, 1242

SSL_use_RSAPrivateKey, 1242

SSL_use_RSAPrivateKey_ASN1, 1242

SSL_use_RSAPrivateKey_file, 1242

SSLv3, 1135, 1215, 1217, 1218, 1238

stack, 4, 5, 14, 22, 30, 112, 247, 284, 285, 291, 326, 328, 334, 350, 351, 358, 359, 361, 363, 366, 367, 452, 522, 523, 524, 525, 531, 780, 840, 843, 845, 889, 1214, 1215, 1241, 1242, 1355, 1356, 1358

stack pointer, 4, 5, 523, 524, 525

stat, 126, 127, 130, 132, 136, 138, 144, 146, 151, 153, 158, 169, 173, 176, 189, 190, 191, 192, 194, 195, 196, 198, 199, 200, 201, 205, 210, 212, 214, 221, 222, 223, 227, 228, 229, 245, 253, 273, 274, 276, 277, 295, 296, 297, 298, 466, 486, 501, 503, 644, 645, 646, 647, 663, 665, 990, 996, 1108, 1117, 1314

static library, 76, 92

static linking, 79, 80, 85, 90, 109

status register, 4, 7, 522

stdout, 58, 122, 128, 131, 137, 139, 145, 146, 147, 151, 152, 154, 159, 163, 176, 181, 182, 183, 185, 186, 187, 188, 192, 193, 197, 199, 200, 205, 206, 211, 214, 215, 218, 219, 222, 226, 228, 229,

250, 253, 254, 256, 257, 258, 260, 261, 264, 265, 266, 267, 268, 269, 270, 271, 272, 273, 274, 275, 276, 277, 290, 292, 295, 296, 297, 298, 302, 303, 304, 306, 307, 310, 311, 313, 318, 319, 322, 323, 324, 325, 326, 329, 332, 333, 336, 339, 340, 342, 343, 346, 353, 354, 356, 357, 360, 361, 366, 367, 369, 370, 379, 380, 383, 385, 387, 388, 390, 392, 393, 394, 395, 397, 407, 408, 409, 410, 411, 412, 417, 418, 420, 421, 422, 424, 427, 428, 429, 431, 432, 434, 436, 437, 439, 441, 442, 444, 447, 448, 449, 450, 455, 456, 458, 484, 485, 486, 491, 492, 497, 498, 499, 501, 502, 503, 506, 514, 527, 528, 529, 542, 543, 544, 545, 546, 547, 551, 552, 553, 554, 578, 579, 580, 581, 582, 583, 584, 585, 586, 590, 608, 611, 612, 613, 614, 615, 620, 621, 622, 623, 626, 627, 628, 630, 631, 646, 648, 651, 653, 654, 655, 659, 660, 664, 665, 666, 685, 686, 687, 700, 701, 702, 703, 705, 706, 707, 708, 709, 711, 712, 713, 727, 728, 729, 730, 731, 732, 734, 735, 736, 737, 743, 744, 745, 746, 747, 748, 758, 760, 761, 762, 763, 765, 766, 769, 770, 772, 773, 775, 776, 777, 782, 783, 784, 785, 786, 791, 793, 794, 796, 797, 798, 802, 804, 805, 806, 811, 812, 813, 815, 816, 817, 818, 819, 822, 828, 829, 830, 831, 832, 836, 838, 839, 841, 842, 843, 844, 845, 850, 852, 869, 870, 872, 873, 874, 875, 876, 877, 878, 898, 899, 900, 901, 902, 903, 904, 905, 907, 908, 909, 910, 911, 912, 913, 914, 928, 929, 930, 931, 932, 934, 935, 942, 943, 944, 945, 946, 947, 948, 953, 954, 955, 956, 960, 961, 962, 970, 971, 972, 973, 975, 976, 992, 993, 994, 995, 1018, 1020, 1021, 1023, 1024, 1027, 1028, 1031, 1033, 1034, 1035, 1036, 1037, 1038, 1040, 1041, 1042, 1045, 1047, 1048, 1050, 1051, 1052, 1054, 1055, 1056, 1104, 1107, 1108, 1109, 1118, 1119, 1121, 1122, 1125, 1126, 1128, 1129, 1131, 1132, 1143, 1144, 1147, 1148, 1230, 1232, 1233, 1234, 1235, 1236, 1246, 1248, 1249, 1250, 1251, 1252, 1253, 1256, 1257, 1258, 1260, 1261, 1262, 1269, 1271, 1272, 1273, 1275, 1276, 1278, 1279, 1280, 1281, 1286, 1287, 1288, 1290, 1291, 1292, 1293, 1307, 1334, 1335, 1336, 1337, 1367

sticky bit, 172, 224

stl_c, 520, 538, 539

Storing data in a single place, 1344

stq_c, 520, 538, 539, 540

stream cipher, 1089, 1094, 1095, 1096, 1097

Stream socket, 723

Stream sockets, 681, 682, 688, 695, 698, 704, 780

strerror, 466, 700, 701, 703, 704, 728, 729, 731, 732, 740, 741, 747, 749, 750, 754, 764, 770, 775, 805, 814, 815, 837, 838, 839, 841, 842, 844, 851, 946, 974, 995, 1019, 1032, 1033, 1046

struct msqid_ds, 650, 656, 657, 658, 660

struct shmid_ds, 605, 609, 611, 622

stwcx, 520, 531, 532, 533

Sun SPARC, 155, 362, 364, 520, 530, 533, 534, 535, 541, 550, 629, 633, 936, 999, 1057, 1058, 1059

super block, 114, 115

symbolic link, 170, 175, 176, 178, 179, 189, 190, 195, 199, 203, 229

Index

symlink, 175, 176, 177, 178, 179, 180, 181, 182, 183, 198, 229, 466

symlinkat, 178, 179, 180, 229, 466

symmetric cryptography, 1084, 1103, 1135, 1151

symmetric encryption algorithms, 1086

sync, 28, 148, 163, 164, 466, 510, 533, 1346

synchronous I/O, 111, 125, 148, 150, 156, 166, 169

synchronous signals, 231

sysconf, 245, 321, 322, 323, 324, 325, 338, 339, 342

sysconf.c, 322

sysctl, 588, 591, 862, 863, 864, 865, 870, 871, 880, 881, 882, 883, 888, 889, 917, 918, 922, 923, 964, 965, 967, 982

sysctl.conf, 591, 862, 863, 864, 865, 889, 917, 918, 923

System V IPC, 28, 476, 477, 478, 479, 480, 481, 484, 587, 594, 602, 604, 605, 610, 616, 641, 659, 681

system(, 201, 202, 325, 326, 346, 451

system.c, 326

System.loadLibrary, 87

T

TCP FIN, 1219, 1220

tcp.keepcnt, 894, 916, 922, 923, 925

tcp.keepidle, 894, 916, 922, 923, 925

tcp.keepintvl, 894, 916, 922, 923, 925

tcp_bufsz.c, 868

tcp_ip_abort_interval, 894, 915, 920, 921, 925

TCP_KEEPALIVE, 899, 903, 904, 906, 907, 908, 912, 913, 916, 919, 920, 925

tcp_keepalive_abort_interval, 894, 905, 919, 920, 925

TCP_KEEPALIVE_ABORT_THRESHOLD, 906, 908, 912, 913, 920

tcp_keepalive_interval, 894, 905, 907, 912, 915, 919, 920, 921, 925

tcp_keepalive_intvl, 894, 895, 917, 918, 925, 926

tcp_keepalive_probes, 894, 895, 917, 918, 925, 926

TCP_KEEPALIVE_THRESHOLD, 906, 907, 908, 912, 919

tcp_keepalive_time, 894, 895, 917, 918, 925, 926

tcp_keepcnt, 894, 918, 919, 925

TCP_KEEPCNT, 897, 898, 899, 901, 904, 906, 910, 914, 915, 916, 925, 926

tcp_keepidle, 894, 918, 919, 925

TCP_KEEPIDLE, 897, 898, 899, 901, 903, 904, 906, 910, 914, 915, 916, 925, 926

TCP_KEEPINIT, 914, 915, 916

tcp_keepintvl, 894, 918, 919, 925

TCP_KEEPINTVL, 897, 898, 899, 901, 904, 906, 910, 914, 915, 916, 925, 926

tcp_recv_hiwater_def, 886, 891

tcp_recvspace, 883, 884, 890

tcp_sendspace, 883, 884, 890

tcp_xmit_hiwater_def, 886, 890

tcpclnt_alive.c, 897, 901

tcpclnt_alive_sun.c, 906, 909

tcpclnt_all.c, 741, 745, 849

tcpclnt_async_io_all.c, 790, 794

tcpclnt_auto_reconn_all.c, 809, 810, 813

tcpclnt_auto_reconn2_all.c, 809, 816, 819

tcpclnt_bufsz.c, 872, 875, 980

tcpclnt_bufsz_linger.c, 927, 931

tcpclnt_dist_all.c, 1015, 1017

tcpclnt_dist_all_v2.c, 1029, 1031

tcpclnt_dist_all_v3.c, 1042, 1044, 1061

tcpclnt_getsvc_all.c, 849

tcpclnt_peeraddr_all.c, 759, 762

tcpclnt_reuse_all.c, 941, 945, 959, 978

tcpclnt_timeo_all.c, 969, 972

tcpclnt1.c, 729, 859

tcpclntenc1.c, 1120, 1123

tcpclntenc2.c, 1126, 1129

tcpclnthmac.c, 1145

TcpMaxDataRetransmission, 894, 925

TcpMaxDataRetransmissions, 924

tcpsrv_alive.c, 897

tcpsrv_alive_sun.c, 906

tcpsrv_all.c, 741, 742, 756, 849

tcpsrv_async_io_all.c, 790

tcpsrv_auto_reconn_all.c, 809, 810

tcpsrv_auto_reconn2_all.c, 810, 816

tcpsrv_bufsz.c, 872, 980

tcpsrv_bufsz_linger.c, 927

tcpsrv_dist_all.c, 1015, 1022, 1061

tcpsrv_dist_all_v2.c, 1029, 1035

tcpsrv_dist_all_v3.c, 1042, 1049, 1061

tcpsrv_exclu_bind_all.c, 952

tcpsrv_peeraddr_all.c, 759

tcpsrv_reuseaddr_all.c, 941

tcpsrv_reuseport_all.c, 959

tcpsrv_timeo_all.c, 969

tcpsrv1.c, 727, 859

tcpsrvenc1.c, 1119, 1120

tcpsrvenc2.c, 1126

tcpsrvhmac.c, 1141

tcpsrvp.c, 836, 859

tcpsrvt.c, 840, 859

TcpWindowSize, 889

thread contention scope, 361, 362

thread specific data, 425, 426, 430, 432, 434, 435, 437, 586, 587

TIME_WAIT state, 778, 846, 847, 921, 938, 939, 940, 941, 948, 950, 957, 958, 963, 964, 968, 982

time-sharing, 20, 364

TLS, v, 676, 678, 680, 1063, 1064, 1068, 1071, 1074, 1075, 1089, 1096, 1135, 1153, 1190, 1191, 1192, 1195, 1197, 1199, 1200,

Index

1204, 1209, 1214, 1215, 1216, 1217, 1218, 1219, 1220, 1221,
1222, 1223, 1224, 1225, 1226, 1227, 1228, 1229, 1230, 1231,
1232, 1233, 1234, 1235, 1236, 1237, 1238, 1239, 1240, 1243,
1244, 1245, 1246, 1247, 1248, 1249, 1250, 1251, 1253, 1254,
1256, 1257, 1258, 1259, 1260, 1261, 1264, 1265, 1267, 1269,
1270, 1271, 1272, 1273, 1274, 1275, 1276, 1278, 1279, 1280,
1281, 1282, 1283, 1284, 1285, 1286, 1287, 1289, 1290, 1291,
1294, 1295, 1332, 1336, 1337, 1339, 1340
TLS_client_method, 1234, 1238, 1251, 1260, 1274, 1290
TLS_method, 1238
tls_process_client_certificate, 1267
TLS_server_method, 1232, 1238, 1239, 1248, 1258, 1271, 1281,
1287
tlsclient1.c, 1228, 1233
tlsclient2.c, 1245, 1249
tlsclient3.c, 1254, 1259
tlsclient4.c, 1267, 1272, 1340
tlsclient6.c, 1284, 1288
tlsserver1.c, 1228, 1229
tlsserver2.c, 1245
tlsserver3.c, 1254
tlsserver4.c, 1267, 1340
tlsserver5.c, 1276
tlsserver6.c, 1284
transistor, 17, 30, 31, 33
transport layer, 675, 678
tripleIt.c, 90, 92, 93, 94, 103, 104, 105, 106, 107, 108
trusted CAs, 1196, 1198, 1243, 1253, 1254, 1265
trylock, 462, 519, 523, 525, 531, 532, 533, 535, 536, 537, 538,
539, 540, 609
Twofish, 1092, 1097, 1100

U

udp_rcvbuf_default, 865, 886, 887, 891
udp_recvspace, 883, 890
udp_sendspace, 883, 890
udp_sndbuf_default, 886, 891
udpclnt.c, 701, 704, 710
udpclnt_all.c, 707
udpclnt_conn_all.c, 710, 859
udpsrv.c, 699, 704, 710
udpsrv_all.c, 704
udsclnt_all.c, 781, 784
udssrv_all.c, 781
umask, 220, 221, 222, 223, 245
umask.c, 222
unaligned, 1009, 1010
uncheckout, 43
unco, 43, 44
unit testing, 39, 40, 1344

Unix, vi, 19, 25, 27, 41, 47, 68, 74, 77, 85, 86, 87, 88, 101, 114, 118,
119, 157, 162, 163, 176, 231, 235, 237, 238, 283, 286, 300, 313,
314, 315, 317, 321, 337, 350, 459, 476, 499, 517, 519, 522, 538,
575, 587, 588, 592, 593, 602, 603, 604, 617, 618, 623, 641, 642,
643, 644, 671, 672, 680, 681, 682, 683, 684, 689, 691, 692, 704,
725, 738, 739, 740, 741, 742, 748, 749, 750, 754, 780, 781, 782,
784, 787, 801, 848, 849, 855, 891, 916, 922, 923, 951, 952, 957,
975, 996, 997, 1016, 1029, 1043, 1065, 1067, 1119, 1296, 1345,
1348, 1353, 1356
Unix domain sockets, 681, 682, 684, 780, 781, 787
unlink, 180, 181, 245, 467, 646, 782, 785, 787
unlink.c, 180
unlinkat, 180, 229, 467
unlock, 209, 211, 372, 375, 378, 381, 383, 384, 386, 388, 394, 395,
408, 410, 437, 456, 462, 474, 475, 488, 489, 490, 491, 492, 504,
507, 515, 516, 517, 519, 521, 523, 524, 526, 530, 531, 532, 533,
535, 536, 537, 539, 540, 542, 543, 545, 546, 551, 552, 570,
578,581, 582, 587, 595, 609, 613, 616
unnamed pipes, 642
unnamed semaphore, 555, 557, 568, 569
update loss problem, 370, 371, 472, 473, 540, 541, 593, 594
uselink, 83, 84, 90, 94, 95, 96, 97, 98, 101, 104, 105, 106, 107,
108
uselink.c, 90, 94, 95, 96, 97, 98, 101, 104, 105, 106, 107, 108
useload, 98, 102, 103, 104, 105, 106, 107, 108
useload.c, 98, 102, 103, 105, 106, 108
user authentication, 1133, 1354
user mode, 24, 25, 26, 865
utime, 226, 227, 228, 245, 293, 467
utime.c, 227

V

vectored I/O, 117, 142, 143, 144, 145, 146, 147, 166
verify a certificate, 1211, 1243, 1254
verify_signature, 1156, 1159, 1160, 1162, 1163, 1165, 1166,
1168, 1169, 1170, 1174, 1180, 1184, 1314, 1328, 1329
version numbers, 998, 1016, 1029, 1043
versioning, 983, 1009, 1011, 1012, 1015, 1027, 1041, 1054,
1057, 1353
virtual memory, 8, 15, 20, 21, 34, 283, 291, 334, 597, 598, 599,
660
VxFS, 162, 167

W

wait (, 245, 253, 255, 274, 277, 281, 282, 293, 294, 295, 296, 311,
313, 314, 315, 316, 317, 319, 325, 381, 404, 405, 406, 407, 409,
413, 451, 463, 503
wait.c, 295
WaitForSingleObject, 570, 571, 572

waitpid, 245, 254, 293, 294, 296, 297, 298, 316, 317, 319, 325, 345, 451, 463

waitpid.c, 297

web server, 33, 349, 467, 857, 858, 1070, 1135, 1190, 1196, 1226, 1227, 1283

Windows, v, 47, 59, 68, 69, 76, 77, 79, 81, 82, 84, 85, 87, 92, 93, 94, 96, 98, 102, 103, 108, 114, 350, 569, 571, 592, 593, 643, 671, 676, 677, 693, 704, 705, 707, 711, 739, 740, 741, 742, 743, 744, 745, 746, 747, 748, 749, 750, 754, 759, 760, 762, 763, 764, 767, 768, 769, 771, 773, 774, 775, 781, 782, 784, 787, 791, 794, 801, 802, 804, 808, 810, 811, 813, 814, 816, 817, 819, 820, 826, 827, 828, 829, 830, 831, 832, 833, 834, 848, 849, 850, 851, 853, 865, 866, 889, 894, 917, 923, 925, 940, 941, 942, 943, 945, 946, 951, 952, 953, 955, 956, 957, 958, 959, 960, 961, 969, 970, 971, 973, 974, 975, 981, 986, 996, 997, 1001, 1016, 1017, 1018, 1019, 1022, 1023, 1024, 1029, 1031, 1032, 1036, 1037, 1043, 1044, 1045, 1046, 1049, 1050, 1051, 1195, 1198, 1350

word size, 9, 11, 1009

write, vi, vii, 6, 11, 16, 18, 21, 24, 25, 26, 27, 38, 39, 48, 52, 55, 73, 74, 79, 94, 111, 112, 115, 116, 117, 118, 119, 121, 123, 124, 125, 126, 127, 128, 129, 131, 132, 133, 134, 137, 138, 139, 140, 141, 142, 143, 144, 146, 147, 148, 149, 150, 151, 152, 155, 157, 158, 159, 161, 163, 164, 166, 167, 169, 171, 172, 195, 199, 208, 209, 210, 211, 212, 213, 215, 216, 221, 224, 225, 230, 234, 235, 237, 238, 245, 251, 255, 289, 308, 309, 310, 311, 312, 313, 320, 321, 327, 342, 345, 346, 350, 416, 417, 418, 420, 422, 423, 424, 425, 451, 459, 463, 468, 482, 494, 495, 503, 508, 509, 510, 511, 512, 513, 515, 519, 520, 529, 538, 539, 540, 594, 595, 596, 598, 600, 601, 603, 604, 606, 609, 615, 617, 618, 619, 621, 636, 642, 643, 644, 646, 648, 657, 660, 661, 662, 663, 665, 666, 667, 669, 672, 693, 695, 710, 717, 725, 732, 751, 752, 755, 767, 787, 788, 789, 790, 801, 804, 805, 807, 808, 809, 835, 856, 857, 859, 878, 886, 988, 990, 991, 992, 995, 999, 1006, 1009, 1061, 1064, 1108, 1117, 1228, 1231, 1236, 1237, 1239, 1240, 1247, 1252, 1256, 1262, 1269, 1270, 1276, 1279, 1286, 1292, 1295, 1315, 1316, 1318, 1319, 1351, 1359, 1360, 1365, 1366, 1368

write lock, 209, 210, 416, 417, 418, 420, 422, 423, 424, 468, 515, 601

writer.c, 134, 662, 669

writev, 119, 142, 143, 144, 146, 147, 167, 463

writev.c, 146

WSACleanup, 705, 708, 711, 712, 739, 743, 747, 750, 760, 764, 773, 777, 782, 785, 792, 796, 799, 803, 811, 813, 815, 816, 818, 819, 821, 823, 827, 829, 831, 851, 943, 947, 954, 960, 970, 974, 1019, 1023, 1033, 1037, 1046, 1047, 1050

WSAGetLastError, 740, 750, 764, 804, 808, 851

WSAStartup, 705, 707, 708, 711, 739, 743, 746, 754, 760, 764, 769, 774, 775, 782, 784, 792, 795, 803, 811, 814, 817, 820, 827, 829, 831, 850, 942, 946, 954, 960, 970, 974, 1019, 1023, 1032, 1036, 1046, 1050

X

X.509 certificate, 1192, 1193, 1195, 1211, 1212, 1242, 1333, 1334, 1336

Y

your own locking routines, 521, 530, 592, 595

Z

zombie process, 314, 315, 317, 345